HANDBOOK OF VIOLENCE

HANDBOOK OF VIOLENCE

Lisa A. Rapp-Paglicci
Albert R. Roberts
John S. Wodarski

John Wiley & Sons, Inc.

This book is printed on acid-free paper. ∞

Copyright © 2002 by John Wiley & Sons, Inc., New York. All rights reserved.
Published simultaneously in Canada.

DSM-IV™ is a trademark of the American Psychiatric Association.

Library of Congress Cataloging-in-Publication Data:

Handbook of violence / edited by Lisa A. Rapp-Paglicci, Albert R. Roberts, John S. Wodarski.
    p. cm.
  Includes bibliographical references and index.
  ISBN 0-471-41467-0 (cloth : alk. paper)
  1. Violence. 2. Violence—Prevention. I. Rapp-Paglicci, Lisa A. II. Roberts, Albert R.
III. Wodarski, John S.
  HM1116.H36 2002
  303.6—dc21

            2001046679

*This book is dedicated to
the thousands of people killed
at the World Trade Center, the Pentagon,
and the four commercial airplanes
that crashed on September 11, 2001,
to their families and relatives, and
to the professionals who dedicate their lives
to intervening with and facilitating the recovery
of the survivors of violent crime.*

Contents

Section II   Community Violence

Section III   School Violence

Section IV   Workplace Violence

Preface

It is apparent that violent crime rates are at their lowest in years. Yet, despite this decrease, violence continues to be a devastating social and public health problem. For example, according to the FBI's Uniform Crime Reports, an aggravated assault occurs every 34.6 seconds; a forcible rape, every 5.8 minutes; and a murder every 33.9 minutes. The media present skewed information regarding "super predators" and "crime waves," resulting in an increased desire, by politicians and the public, for simple answers and quick fixes for all types of violence.

There are no quick fixes. Instead we present the latest empirically based research on the comprehensive topic of violence and violence prevention. A multidisciplinary, expert group of authors have prepared original and up-to-date chapters describing family, community, school, and workplace violence from a resilience viewpoint. No other book has attempted to inclusively cover the field of violence; most volumes provide a limited view of one form or type of violence (e.g., child abuse, domestic violence, school violence). The reality of violence suggests an opposite approach: Violence is interrelated and compounded. For example, children who witness a parent being battered often become violent in young adulthood, children who witness community violence are often violent in school, family violence often spills over into the workplace, and school and family violence have been repeatedly linked.

Those who work in the area of violence must increase their awareness of the breadth and depth of the problem of violence. This book expresses the enormity of violence through its comprehensiveness and its biopsychosocial perspective. Because of the prevalence of violence throughout American society, professionals have begun to systematically examine violence and violence prevention strategies in terms of: scope of the problem, classification and risk assessment, effective prevention programs, empirically based intervention, strengths perspective, and future research. Each chapter follows this framework and includes the latest evidence-based assessment and program development practices. How professionals, legislators, and society will intervene regarding the costly, life-threatening, and appalling problem of violence throughout our society is still unknown.

LISA A. RAPP-PAGLICCI
ALBERT R. ROBERTS
JOHN S. WODARSKI

Acknowledgments

We would like to thank all of the expert contributors for giving their undivided attention to this project and providing us with their superb chapters.

We would also like to thank our spouses and families for their patience and understanding of the many hours required to produce this important professional contribution. Thank you, David, Emily Ann, Beverly, Herb, and Lois Ann.

Finally, special acknowledgment goes to Deborah DeBlasi and the staff at Publications Development Company for their diligence, care for detail, and technical assistance in all aspects of the production of this volume.

L.A.R-P.
A.R.R.
J.S.W.

About the Editors ———————————

Lisa A. Rapp-Paglicci, PhD, LCSW, is an Assistant Professor at the University of Nevada, Las Vegas, School of Social Work. Dr. Rapp-Paglicci serves on the editorial board of the *Journal of Human Behavior in the Social Environment.* During the 1999–2000 academic year, Dr. Rapp-Paglicci received an award for Excellence in Teaching.

Albert R. Roberts, PhD, DACFE, is a Professor of Social Work and Criminal Justice at Rutgers-The State University of New Jersey, Piscataway. Dr. Roberts is the founding Editor-in-Chief of the journal *Brief Treatment and Crisis Intervention* (Oxford University Press), and is also the editor of the Springer Series on Social Work and on Family Violence. He has authored, edited, or co-edited 23 previous books, and has more than 130 published articles and book chapters. Three of his recent books include: *Crisis Intervention Handbook* (2000), *Visions for Change: Crime and Justice in the Twenty-First Century* (1999), and *Battered Women and Their Families: Intervention Strategies and Treatment Programs* (1998).

John S. Wodarski, PhD, MSSW, is the Director of Research at the University of Tennessee College of Social Work. Dr. Wodarski is the founding co-editor of the *Journal of Human Behavior in the Social Environment.* He has written over 400 published articles; authored, edited, or co-edited over 38 books; and has made over 300 professional presentations.

Contributor List

Sibylle Artz, PhD
University of Victoria
Victoria, BC, Canada

Ron Avi Astor, PhD
University of Michigan
School of Social Work
Ann Arbor, Michigan

Juan J. Barthelemy, MSW, Doctoral
    Student
University of Tennessee
Knoxville, Tennessee

Rami Benbenishty, PhD
University of Michigan
School of Social Work
Ann Arbor, Michigan

Gary L. Bowen, PhD
University of North Carolina at
    Chapel Hill
Chapel Hill, North Carolina

Natasha K. Bowen, PhD
University of North Carolina at
    Chapel Hill
Chapel Hill, North Carolina

Patricia Brownell, PhD
Fordham University
New York, New York

Ann W. Burgess, DNSc
Boston College
Boston, Massachusetts

Meda Chesney-Lind, PhD
University of Hawaii at Manoa
Honolulu, Hawaii

Catherine N. Dulmus, PhD
University of Tennessee, College of
    Social Work
Knoxville, Tennessee

Rodney A. Ellis, PhD
University of Tennessee, College of
    Social Work
Nashville, Tennessee

Gretchen Ely, MSW, Doctorate
    Candidate
University of Tennessee
College of Social Work
Knoxville, Tennessee

Diana Valle Ferrer, PhD
University of Puerto Rico
School of Social Work
San Juan, Puerto Rico

Carolyn Hilarski, PhD
Rochester Institute of Technology
Rochester, New York

Karin Jordan, PhD
George Fox University
Portland, Oregon

Robert I. Lynn, PhD
Fairleigh Dickinson University
Madison, New Jersey

Gordon MacNeil, PhD
University of Alabama
School of Social Work
Tuscaloosa, Alabama

Samuel A. MacMaster, PhD
University of Tennessee
Nashville, Tennessee

Heather A. Meyer, PhD
University of Michigan
School of Social Work
Ann Arbor, Michigan

Keith J. Morgan, PhD
Lehigh University
Bethlehem, Pennsylvania

Diana Nicholson, MSW
University of Victoria
Victoria, BC, Canada

William Oliver, PhD
Indiana University
Bloomington, Indiana

Ronald O. Pitner, PhD
University of Michigan
School of Social Work
Ann Arbor, Michigan

Lisa A. Rapp-Paglicci, PhD
University of Nevada, Las Vegas
Las Vegas, Nevada

Jack M. Richman, PhD
University of North Carolina at
    Chapel Hill
Chapel Hill, North Carolina

Albert R. Roberts, PhD
Rutgers-The State University of
    New Jersey
Piscataway, New Jersey

Letha A. (Lee) See, PhD
University of Georgia
Athens, Georgia

Edgar H. Tyson, MSW, Doctoral Student
University of Tennessee
Knoxville, Tennessee

Judith A. Waters, PhD
Fairleigh Dickinson University
Madison, New Jersey

Oliver Williams, PhD
University of Georgia
Athens, Georgia

Mona M. Williams, MSSW, Doctoral
    Student
University of Tennessee
Knoxville, Tennessee

John S. Wodarski, PhD
University of Tennessee
College of Social Work
Memphis, Tennessee

Michael E. Woolley, MSW, Doctoral
    Student
University of North Carolina at
    Chapel Hill
Chapel Hill, North Carolina

SECTION I

Family Violence

Chapter 1

VIOLENCE WITHIN FAMILIES THROUGH THE LIFE SPAN

ANN W. BURGESS AND ALBERT R. ROBERTS

INTRODUCTION

Case Examples

Sixteen-year-old Susan awakens in a room unaware of her surroundings. During a senior post-prom party, Susan had consumed a large amount of alcohol and was high from smoking marijuana, leaving her incoherent and in a daze. This physical state of mind left Susan unaware of Howard's aggressiveness. Eighteen-year-old Howard, Susan's new boyfriend and captain of the football team, had been taking "ecstasy" which intensified his physical and sexual feelings when he sexually abused her. Susan had gotten a ride home from her girlfriend and during the ride, tried to explain what had happened. She was not able to provide a detailed statement of what had occurred due to her semi-consciousness during the course of the events. Her parents wanted her to sign a criminal complaint against Howard, but she vehemently refused. Susan felt guilty about her own excessive alcohol and marijuana use and did not remember if she said no to Howard when he undressed her and proceeded to have sexual intercourse with her. She noticed bruises on her arms, breasts, and thighs the next day, and had no recollection of how she got bruised. However, she did agree with her father that she would never date Howard again.

Naomi is a 34-year-old single parent who was chronically abused by her husband for seven years. During her childhood, her father abused her mother. Naomi is a high school graduate and has worked for the same company for the past 14 years as a customer service representative. She described her injuries as a "broken nose, he's tried to choke me so many times I feel that when I get older I will have cancer of the throat. I have bruises all over my body. I have a bad back, and on

Case Examples *(Continued)*

three different occasions my eye has been swollen from punches. He likes to punch me in the mouth. He does it without warning. The last time he strangled me in the kitchen, I faked passing out, and he left. He might have killed me if I didn't fake passing out." ... Naomi finally left her husband after attending a support group for battered women ... She went to court and got a restraining order (Roberts, 2002; p. 74).

Complainant was a 76-year-old female victim who was interviewed in the hospital. She had suffered multiple injuries to her head and a broken hip. Complainant stated that her son, daughter, and friends had held her prisoner for several days. They stated they would kill her if she left and beat her for no reason. (Brownell, 1996; p. 44).

These three cases illustrate the fact that family violence (also known as interpersonal violence) occurs throughout the lifecycle. Although domestic violence seems to be decreasing, physical and sexual assault remains prevalent among children, adolescents, adults, and the elderly. When violence against women occurs in the family context of a shared residence, it is usually more frequent and more severe than stranger-perpetrated violence. There is rarely any warning for when the next slap, punch, kick, or series of brutal assaults may intensify. But, the research has consistently demonstrated that women who stay in battering relationships for many years, eventually sustain numerous battering incidents and injuries. In sharp contrast, there is a group of young women in dating relationships who leave the batterer permanently after the first or second incident. They leave before the abuse becomes chronic. These women in short-term abusive relationships usually leave with the help of a restraining order, the support of a parent or older sibling, or a close friend who allows them to temporarily live in their house (Roberts, 2002).

Awareness of familial violence has come a long way in the past four decades. As a result of groundbreaking research, journal articles, books, and media attention, there are now, throughout the United States, over 15,000 programs for prevention and treatment of child abuse, rape crisis, domestic violence, and elder abuse. In 1962, C. Henry Kempe (Kempe, Silverman, Steele, Droegemueller, & Silver) developed the term "The Battered Child Syndrome." By 1971, Richard Gelles, under the guidance of Professor Murray Straus, had completed his doctoral dissertation at the University of New Hampshire. His was the first study to document police, hospital, court, and social service responses to the battering of women in a small town in New Hampshire. Almost three decades ago, two esteemed psychiatric/mental health nursing professors, Ann Wolbert Burgess and

Lydia Holmstrom (1974), completed and published their classic research study at Boston City Hospital and coined the term "Rape Trauma Syndrome." At the same time, psychologists Morton Bard and Katherine Ellison were training nurses, social workers, and police officers in New York City in crisis intervention. Also, during the 1970s, several large medical centers developed rape crisis programs. By 1980, Albert R. Roberts, a prominent social worker and criminologist, had completed the first national survey of the organizational structure and functions of 89 shelters for battered women and their children. Roberts's book, *Sheltering Battered Women: A National Survey and Service Guide* (1981), focuses on staffing patterns, funding sources, crisis intervention techniques, agency and decision-making boards, positive and negative perceptions of police encounters, attempts to obtain protective orders, self-reported strengths, and limitations of shelters for battered women. Noted sociologists Murray Straus, Richard Gelles, and Suzanne Steinmetz had completed the first national prevalence study of family violence by 1980 as well.

The 1980s seemed to be the decade in which awareness of domestic violence and an aid-for-crime-victims movement flourished. Within the women's movement, local NOW chapters, statewide domestic violence coalitions, and legislative advocates all united in a call for specific domestic violence legislation, major federal funding initiatives, increased research and demonstration projects, and legal remedies. In 1984, the Victims of Crime Act (VOCA) was passed—the first major legislation that aided crime victims throughout the United States. In 1985, a child psychologist, Jane Nady Burnley, became the first Director of the new federal Office for Victims of Crime, in Washington, DC. She and her staff were responsible for distributing the VOCA funding to the states, and for monitoring and evaluating programs nationwide. By 1990, Albert Roberts, in his national survey of 184 victim/service and victim/witness assistance programs, indicated that more than 3,000 rape crisis intervention, sexual assault prevention, domestic violence intervention, and victim/witness assistance programs had been funded through the VOCA initiative.

The possibility that people might be injured or have their homes invaded by strangers is a frightening thought. But hundreds of thousands of Americans face an even more devastating reality when they are harmed, not by strangers, but by someone they trusted. Vicious crimes of violence are committed by or against children, parents, grandparents, spouses, and other close relatives. The family is still viewed as the center of society. To be abused by a partner, a parent, a trusted adult, or one's own child, or to witness such abuse, leaves deeply ingrained fears and other serious consequences. Victims of domestic violence must wrestle with feelings of fear, loyalty, love, self-blame, guilt, and shame—all at the same time. These emotions are not experienced by victims of strangers. Adults become torn between their desire to shield and help a loved one and their responsibility toward their own safety and the safety of others in the household. Children face the reality that those who should protect them are, in fact, sources of harm. For most people, home represents security. To domestic violence victims, home is a place of danger.

The problem of family violence is not new. Women have been battered by their partners in almost every society in history. In the United States, the beginning of services for battered women and children dates back to 1885, when the Chicago Protective Agency for Women, established to help women who were victims of physical abuse, provided legal aid, court advocacy, and personal assistance. An abused woman could receive up to four weeks of shelter at a refuge operated by the Women's Club of Chicago. The agency helped women to secure legal separations, divorces, and equitable property distributions. Between 1915 and 1920, 25 cities followed Chicago's lead in developing protective agencies for women; by the 1940s, few shelters remained, due, in part, to casualties and marital separations during World War II (Pleck, 1987; Roberts, 1996).

Throughout history, records of childhood are replete with suffering that was well documented from biblical times to the present. The landmark *Wilson* case, in 1874, pricked the national social conscience and opened America's eyes to the plight of many children. Eight-year-old Mary Ellen Wilson lived with her adoptive parents in New York City. She was held there in chains, starved and beaten. The police responded but could do nothing because it was a "family matter," and parents held the "rights" (Zigler & Hall, 1989). A man named Henry Berg was contacted. He had founded a protective group the preceding year: The Society for the Protection of Cruelty to Animals. Berg was able to extricate Mary Ellen from her family torture chamber.

This chapter presents definitions and current statistical trends from a developmental perspective of family violence. It covers bullying behavior as a precursor to abusive dating relationships; courtship abuse; partner threat and violence; domestic violence and pregnancy; batterers' stalking patterns; domestic homicide; child abuse, neglect, and sexual assault; and elder abuse. The chapter also discusses key concepts of family violence: socialization into violence; learned socialized violence; the psychodynamics of violent behavior, including altered attachment, jealousy, guilt, and revenge; and the biology of trauma.

BULLYING BEHAVIOR

Bullying is the abuse of power by one child over another through repeated aggressive behaviors (Connolly, Pepler, Craig, & Taradash, 2000). For bullies, power may arise from physical strength and maturity; higher status within a peer group; knowledge of another child's weakness; or recruitment of support from other children (O'Connell, Pepler, & Craig, 1999; Salmivalli, Lagerspetz, Bjorkqvist, Osterman, & Kaukiainen, 1996). As bullies age, they rely less on physical means to intimidate their victims and turn, instead, to indirect forms that entail verbal abuse and social exclusion (Olweus, 1991).

Like aggressive and antisocial children, children who bully often come from homes that are neglectful, and their parents often use harsh punishment (Olweus, 1993). Children who become bullies are at risk for continuing difficulties into adulthood, in the form of criminality, domestic violence, child abuse, and sexual harassment.

In a study of 1,758 students in grades 5 through 8, 196 young adolescents who self-reported they bullied their peers were compared to a control group of nonbullying youth. The results indicated that bullies started dating earlier and engaged in more advanced dyadic dating than comparison adolescents. Bullies were highly relationship-oriented, yet their views of their friends and boyfriends or girlfriends were less positive and less equitable than those of the comparison adolescents. Finally, bullies were more likely to report physical and social aggression with their boyfriends and girlfriends. The results suggest the hypothesis that adolescents whose peer relationships are characterized by bullying are at risk in their development of healthy romantic relationships (Connolly et al., 2000).

THE FAMILY

Because violence within families has only recently surfaced as a legal matter, research into the causes and consequences is limited. As a first step, definitions are provided in order to begin classification for the research process.

Due to the myriad of different statutes and regulations, there is no national legal definition of a family.

FAMILY VIOLENCE

Nowhere in the criminal law and its administration is the social construction of violent crime changing more rapidly than in what constitutes family violence and society's response to it (Reiss & Roth, 1993:222).

Data on family violence are classified by current marital status (married, separated, divorced, or single), spousal status (spouse/ex-spouse), or relationships among members of a household (cohabitants, child/parent, sibling, parent). Given these categories, statistics on family structure changes can be generated over time. For example, the Bureau of the Census (1990, 1991) has reported that the proportion of all households accounted for by two-parent families declined from 40% in 1970 to 26% in 1990. The number of unmarried-couple households almost tripled between 1970 and 1980 and grew by 80% between 1980 and 1990, from 1.6 to 2.9 million. The proportion of children under 18 years of age living with two parents declined from 85% in 1970 to 73% in 1990. An estimated 15% of these children were stepchildren. And, in 1990, 19% of white, 62% of black, and 30% of Hispanic children under age 18 lived with only one parent.

Trends in family violence, according to Reiss and Roth (1993), must be interpreted against a decline in the percentage of households containing, exclusively, married couples and their biological children. Violence between growing numbers of same-sex and opposite-sex cohabiting partners is increasingly being regarded as family violence, regardless of legal marital status. Violence between divorced or separated ex-couples is also listed as family violence.

The National Research Council's Panel on Understanding and Preventing Violence (Reiss & Roth, 1993) considered all violent behavior within a household as family violence—specifically, spouse assault, physical and sexual assault of children, sibling assaults, and physical and sexual assaults of other relatives who reside in the household. Missing from this list are events such as verbal abuse, harassment, or humiliation, in which psychological trauma is the sole harm to the victim. This category is under consideration by the Panel on Research on Violence Against Women, which will also be considering threat assessment and stalking behavior.

Like the term "family," the term "violence" has no universal definition. However, the definition published in the report "Understanding and Preventing Violence," by Reiss and Roth (1993), may be useful. It states that interpersonal violence is "behavior by persons against persons that intentionally threatens, attempts, or actually inflicts physical harm."

THE DYNAMIC NATURE OF FAMILY VIOLENCE

Several characteristics distinguish family violence from stranger violence (Reiss & Roth, 1993:222–223). While the continuing relationship among family members is similar to other relationships—teacher-student, employer-employee, child-caretaker, and so on—daily interaction and shared domicile increase the opportunities for violent encounters. Because family members are bound together in a continuing relationship, repeat violations by the offender are quite likely. An unequal power relationship makes the victim more vulnerable to the aggression and violence of the offender. Moreover, the offender often threatens additional violence if the incidents of violence are disclosed. The victim, anticipating stigmatization and denigration, may refrain from disclosure. Because episodes of violence often occur in private places, they are invisible to others and are less likely to be detected or reported to police.

DEVELOPMENTAL ASPECTS OF THE FAMILY AND ITS STRUCTURE

Just as there are developmental stages and tasks for the child maturing into an adult, the family may be viewed as progressing through three developmental phases. The first phase begins with dating, courtship, and marriage; the middle phase includes partnership and work, with childbearing and parenting being an option; and the third phase continues a work focus, optional grandparenting, and retirement.

Phase 1: Courtship and Marriage

The first phase of family life includes dating, courtship, and marriage. Although dating does not necessarily lead to courtship or marriage, it is instructive to review data on early relationship problems and dating aggression (Riggs, 1993). Theories of both marital aggression (Gelles & Straus, 1979) and dating aggression (Riggs & O'Leary, 1989) identify conflict as an important causal factor that can lead to aggression between partners. Dating violence appears to begin as early as age 15 or 16 (Durst, 1987; Henton, Cate, Koval, Lloyd, & Christopher, 1983). Typical tactics include slapping, pushing, beating, and threatening or attacking with weapons. Recurring and escalating episodes of violence in a relationship are quite common if the relationship is not terminated. Research has indicated that approximately 44% of acquaintance rape victims, in comparison to less than 1% of stranger rape victims, are likely to be sexually assaulted "more than once by the same offender" (Gidycz & Layman, 1996). About 50% of the victims do terminate the relationship (Cate, Henton, Koval, Christopher, & Lloyd, 1982; Henton et al., 1983; Laner, 1983; Roscoe & Benaske, 1985). Victims of acquaintance rape may be in a state of denial in the aftermath of the rape, and they often present for treatment years after the assaultive incident (Jackson, 1996). In a national study of 3,187 female college students, 52 of the respondents reported being raped by strangers versus 416 victims of acquaintance rape. Only 1.7% of the acquaintance rape victims informed the police and sought crisis intervention services. In addition, 27.8% of the acquaintance rape victims considered suicide and progressed to the point of selecting a lethal method (Petretic-Jackson & Tobin, 1996).

Although large-scale surveys have documented the prevalence of abuse in teen dating relationships [i.e., more than 25% of male and female high school students report having experienced some form of physical abuse in a dating relationship (O'Keefe & Lebovics, 1998)], the abuse often escapes attention or concern. Research indicates that a large number of college students experience physical aggression in dating relationships. Estimates of the prevalence of dating aggression among college students range from 20% (Cate et al., 1982; Makepeace, 1981) to as high as 50% (Sigelman, Berry, & Wiles, 1984).

Violence often continues within marriage. According to some researchers, spousal assault is the single most common cause of injuries for which women seek emergency medical attention. In a study of emergency treatment of women in a metropolitan hospital, the investigators reported that battered women were 13 times more likely than other women receiving emergency care to be injured in the breast, chest, and/or abdomen, and three times as likely to be injured while pregnant (Boes, 1998).

In 1988, the National Crime Survey (NCS) (Bureau of Justice Statistics, 1990) began to report annual estimates of the extent of family violence for persons age 12 and older. The NCS, however, lacks the necessary information to determine the full extent of family violence. For example, the data collection process excludes violence among coinhabitants and does not collect information on children under age 12. Given these limitations, the 1989 victimization statistics are still useful. For example, the report states that 59% of the assaults were by a spouse (41%) or ex-spouse (18%), and 29% were by other relatives. Parents inflicted 7% of the assaults, and children inflicted 5%.

The Conflict Tactics Scale developed by Straus (1979) is the main measure of domestic violence and is used in most surveys. The scale includes verbal and aggressive acts. Violent acts range in severity from hurling objects to using a deadly weapon such as a gun or knife. Using the scale in an initial national telephone survey of couples in 1975, and in a repeat of the survey in 1985 (Straus & Gelles, 1991), Straus, Gelles, and Steinmetz (1986) reported that 16 of every 100 couples admitted that at least one incident of physical aggression had occurred during the year before the survey. The prevalence of severe violence in both surveys was 4 in 100 females, and 5 in 100 males. These statistics are believed to be low because the sample excluded unmarried couples and missed segments of the population that do not have telephones (Reiss & Roth, 1993).

National estimates of the total number of women battered by their partners (spouses and cohabitants) range from 2.1 million to over 8 million annually (Dwyer, Smokowski, Bricout, & Wodarski, 1996; Roberts, 1996).

Stalking

Kurt (1995) reminds us that stalking is part of the constellation of behaviors associated with partner violence, especially when there is a difficult breakup with an intimate partner. Stalking takes various forms and has varying definitions in some states. From a legal point of view, stalking is willful, malicious, repeated following and harassing of another person, with fear of violence resulting in the victim. Meloy (1998) describes it as abnormal social behavior.

In a pilot sample of self-reported batterers, 36 (out of 120) who stalked and were charged with domestic violence were identified as belonging to one of three stalking groups. In the first group, discrediting was the key; in the second, love turned to hate, and in the third, there was a violent confrontation with the ex-partner (Burgess et al., 1997). A second study, involving 165 batterers, suggested that stalking behaviors varied from seemingly benign acts, or efforts toward being reasonable, to hidden, threatening, frightening behaviors. Batterers were said to be contacting estranged partners for two major reasons that elicit a range of contradictory and ambivalent emotions. The *conscious* motive, for the most part, appears altruistic; the emotions range from longing and confusion to hostility and revenge. In contrast, individuals with secret and clandestine behaviors were angry and aggressive and indicated a propensity for abusive action. Clinicians need expertise in the treatment of batterers who stalk, and victims and their families should be encouraged to keep in contact with law enforcement units, for safety reasons (Burgess, Harner, Baker, Hartman, & Lole, 2001).

Violence and Pregnancy

It has been estimated that as many as one in five teenagers is a victim of domestic violence during pregnancy (Parker, McFarlane, Soeken, Torres, & Campbell, 1993). Recent research has estimated that, in as many as two-thirds of teenage pregnancies, adult males are the fathers. Teenagers partnered with adult men are more likely to become pregnant than those with peer-aged partners. Domestic violence during pregnancy is often preceded by a history of abuse, but pregnancy may act as a trigger that increases the frequency and severity of the violence. This increase may be related to financial implications of the pregnancy and birth, stress surrounding altered relational and sexual roles, and increased attention toward the growing pregnancy. Additionally, pregnancy disclosure, especially when the paternity is questionable, may potentiate an already volatile situation.

Phase 2: Assaults on Children

Various commissioned governmental studies have reported on assaults on children. The U.S. Advisory Board on Child Abuse and Neglect, created by the 1988 amendments to the Child Abuse and Prevention and Treatment Act, estimated that, in 1989, at least 1,200 and perhaps as many as 5,000 children died as a result of maltreatment, and over 160,000 children were seriously harmed (U.S. Department of Health and Human Services, 1990:15) The advisory board noted that, in 1974, about 60,000 cases of child maltreatment were reported. This figure rose to 1.1 million in 1980 and more than doubled to 2.4 million in 1988 (U.S. Department of Health and Human Services, 1988:x). The increases may, however, partially reflect the use of more inclusive definitions of abuse and neglect and an increase in professional recognition of maltreatment, rather than an increase in incidence per se (U.S. Department of Health and Human Services, 1988:xxv). It is also likely that cases of child maltreatment are reported to public health or educational agencies and not to the social services agencies that provide the "countable" case figures. Many cases of intrafamilial or third-party assaults on children are never reported to any professionals concerned with the health or welfare of children (Reiss & Roth, 1993:228).

American society has a major public health and criminal justice problem to remedy as a result of the prevalence of child abuse and neglect. In 1999 alone, state child protective service agencies received 2.97 million reports of alleged maltreated children. The youngest group, children under 6 years of age accounted for approximately 86 percent of the child abuse and neglect related fatalities (Osofsky, 2001). Violence against children is a growing concern in the field of violence prevention and delinquency prevention.

Using the expanded definitions of child abuse and neglect, the second National Incidence Survey, published in 1988 (NIS-2) and commissioned by the National Center for Child Abuse and Neglect, estimated that the majority of countable cases involved the following situations (U.S. Department of Health and Human Services, 1988:3–8):

Case Category/Percentage		Number of Children per 1,000	Total Number of Children
Child neglect	(63%)	15.9	1,003,600
Physical neglect	(57%)		157,600
Educational neglect	(29%)		292,000
Emotional neglect	(22%)		223,100
Child abuse	(43%)	10.7	675,000
Physical abuse		5.7	358,000
Emotional abuse		3.4	211,000
Sexual abuse		2.5	155,900

Source: U.S. Department of Health and Human Services, 1988: 3–8.

Family violence sometimes escalates to homicide. Assessments of the risks of intrafamily homicide are considered to be more accurate than for other forms of assault (Reiss & Roth, 1993:234). Several patterns are noteworthy: Newborns, infants, and children ages 1 to 4 years are more vulnerable to homicide than are children ages 5 to 9 years (Federal Bureau of Investigation, 1990:11); infants and small children are more likely to be killed by their mothers than their fathers, perhaps in part as a result of differential risk exposure; and the risk of homicide for children under age 5 years is greater for male than female children, according to a recent case control study (Winpisinger et al., 1991:1053–1054).

Most incidents of spouse abuse do not end in homicide. During 1991, almost 2,000 deaths were found to be homicides between intimate partners (Mechanic, 1996). Slightly over two-thirds of the victims were females killed by their male partners; the other 30% were males killed by female partners (Mechanic, 1996). Men's overall homicide risk is three times that for women, but women face a greater risk of homicide by their spouses than do men (Federal Bureau of Investigation, 1990:8); intrafamily violence accounted for 15% of all family homicides in 1989; 44% involved husbands and wives. Three different studies of battered women who kill found that 57% to 83% of the women experienced death threats, from the batterer, aimed at themselves or close relatives (Browne, 1987; Roberts, 1996). Therefore, it is important to understand the self-defensive nature of spousal homicides committed by battered women against violent batterers. In Roberts's (1996) New Jersey study of 105 homicidal battered women, the overwhelming majority of the battered women had received very specific death threats in which the batterer described the method, time, and location of the woman's demise.

Phase 3: Assaults against the Elderly

The National Research Council (NRC) (1993) recommends that priority be given to the collection of more precise information about the prevalence, incidence, and consequences of violence toward the elderly. Surprisingly little is known about its occurrence in families—for several reasons. First, most studies do not distinguish between elder abuse and elder neglect. Second, families are unlikely to report the abuse because the responsible person may be a son or daughter. Third, many elderly people are homebound and no one can see what is happening to them.

National estimates of the prevalence of elder abuse indicate that 1 out of every 20 senior citizens, or over 1.5 million older people, are victims of elder abuse (Brownell, 1996; Roberts, 1996). In a stratified random-sample study of all persons 65 and older in the Boston metropolitan area, it was estimated that between 2.5 and 3.9 persons per 1,000 had experienced physical violence, verbal aggression, or neglect. Results were similar in a national survey of elder abuse in Canada.

There is a dearth of research on elder abuse and neglect. Dr. Sidney Stahl, at the National Institute on Aging, noted that a lack of the most basic scientific research in the field prevents service providers and others from knowing the real scope of the problem and ascertaining whether their interventions are working. His suggested seven-point agenda focuses on: (1) prevalence and risk factors; (2) accurate measurements; (3) natural history of abuse and neglect; (4) lack of diagnostic specificity; (5) lack of scientifically verified prevention interventions; (6) issue of self-neglect; and (7) institutional abuse and neglect (Stahl, 2000). The fact that 13% of the nation's population is over the age of 65—a figure that will rise to almost 20% in the next two decades—emphasizes the need for more research in this area.

EXPLANATIONS OF FAMILY VIOLENCE

Most theories about the causes of family violence are only partial explanations. Either they attempt to explain a single type or a few types of family violence, such as partner assault, or they seek to identify a particular factor or set of factors that can account for some of the observed variations in behavior between violent and nonviolent persons or acts (NRC, 1993). The leading explanations of family violence are derived from social, cultural, and biopsychosocial perspectives.

The Social and Cultural Perspectives

Gelles (1983) attempted to develop an integrated theory of several cultural and structural determinants and social learning. For example, feminist theory asserts that the unequal power distribution between men and women subjects women to male dominance in all spheres of life (work, family, and community life). Male power extends to the sexual relationship as well as to work and social relationships. The various ways in which coercion is used depend on men's use of their physical and social power to maintain that dominant position (Finkelhor, 1983).

The unequal distribution of power is also the basis for explaining parental physical and sexual abuse of children. The exercise of parental power over a child victim leads to disempowerment of the child and renders him or her helpless (Finkelhor & Browne, 1986:183).

Growing up within the framework of a patriarchal society that emphasizes male dominance and aggression and female victimization, children are socialized into their respective sex roles (Dobash & Dobash, 1979). In addition, they *learn* through their experience in the family or their exposure to the media. This learning becomes reinforced in the larger community, where male and female roles similarly rest on elements of macho culture.

Recent changes in family organization and structure may account for some family aggression. Changes that affect social and moral bonding among family members are probably most significant. One such change, since the 1970s, has been the deinstitutionalization of children without families, the mentally ill, the homeless, and the disabled. Temporary placement of children in foster homes, adoption, and informal placement of children with relatives may expose the children to violence from caretakers for whom the minimal moral constraints of the parenting role are less salient (Reiss & Roth, 1993:241).

A second major change is the increase in the number of children who are not living with their natural parents. These numbers are substantial, owing to serial cohabitation, divorce, and desertion (Reiss & Roth, 1993), as well as the incarceration, substance abuse, or death of the caretakers.

Social Isolation

Social isolation has been identified as a characteristic of some families that are at high risk of physical and sexual abuse of a spouse or children (Dwyer et al., 1996; Garbarino & Crouter, 1978; Pike, 1990). The isolation may be forced on the partner by the abuser. On the other hand, shame may prompt a visibly battered spouse to seek even further withdrawal. Victims often become isolated from their friends, their family of origin, their neighbors, or anyone who could become acquainted with the ongoing events. Some families isolate themselves by having an unlisted telephone number or no telephone. Their lack of a means of transportation is offered as a reason for not visiting others, and their homes may be physically shuttered against the gaze of outsiders. They often lack community ties of any kind (Garbarino & Sherman, 1980). Resick and Reese (1986) suggest that violent families rarely invite visitors to their homes, so as not to engage in social and recreational activities. They place little emphasis on personal growth and development.

Generational Transmission of Violence

The transmission of violence from one generation to the next is as much a component of subculture as any other learned behavior. Straus and colleagues (1980) reported that among adults who were abused as children, more than one-fifth will later abuse their own children. Although Widom (1989:161) cautions that the methodological limitations in these studies, especially those with retrospective design, restrict the validity of conclusions about the long-term consequences of abuse in childhood, most professionals are concerned about the potential dangers.

The Biopsychosocial Perspective

A child's perceptions of family members, and of their interactions with him or her and with each other, are important factors in a child's development. Essentially, early life attachments (sometimes called bonding) translate into a blueprint of how the child will perceive situations outside the family. A positive attachment based on warmth, affection, caring, protective behaviors, and accountability leads to basic trust, and trust is at the core of building a social human being. Through attachment, the child gets feedback for the emerging of self. Around 18 months of age, there is consolidation of a sense of self. Early development of the ability to self-soothe provides an inner core of calmness and an ability to avoid being overwhelmed by stimuli, and this ability results in an integrated sense of self.

Social bonding can fail or become narrow and selective. Caretakers might ignore, rationalize, or normalize various behaviors in the developing child or, through their own problems (such as violent behavior), they might support the child's developing distortions and projections. An ineffective social environment can result from ignoring aggressive or sexual behavior or failing to intervene to correct such behavior.

A child who lacks a caretaker's protection experiences tremendous anxiety, is overwhelmed, and may survive through dissociating himself or herself from the trauma. Such dissociation inhibits a sense of feeling connected to the outside world. In the earliest manifestations of this numbing, children are cruel to animals, siblings, friends, and even parents or grandparents. These children lack sensitivity to the pain of others and may develop a distorted association of pain with various events. Some children become isolated and disconnected from others. In a Massachusetts case, a 14-year-old youth took a 7-year-old retarded boy into a wooded area and beat him to death. He had told people he was going to do this, but no one intervened.

Similar cruel and detached behavior can be noted in date abuse that may occur in junior and senior high schools. In a high school in Glen Ridge, New Jersey, there was a gang rape of a developmentally disabled girl. Several male students inserted objects into the girl's vagina while other male students watched. They had no sense of their impact on the victim.

Attachment theory was intended as a revision of psychoanalytic theory, but it has been infused with biological principles, control systems theory, and cognitive psychology (Crittenden & Ainsworth, 1989). It began as an attempt to understand the disturbed functioning of individuals who had suffered early separations or traumatic losses, but it evolved as a theory of normal development that suggests explanations for some types of atypical development (Bowlby, 1969, 1973, 1980). Since Bowlby's preliminary formulations (1958), attachment theory has stimulated research into socioemotional development and the growth of interpersonal relationships. For example, it suggests a causal relationship between the anomalies of attachment in the parent and abuse of the child (Ainsworth, 1980).

Family violence has been linked to mental illness and personality disorders, but the links have been established for clinical populations rather than by using case control methods or general population surveys. Studies of populations in women's shelters (Cascardi & O'Leary, 1992; Frieze & Browne, 1989:197) report that depression is quite common among women who are chronic victims of domestic violence. Clinical studies have consistently found high incidences of bipolar depression, anxiety disorders, posttraumatic stress disorder (PTSD), panic disorder, and suicide ideation among chronically abused women (Housekamp & Foy, 1991; Petretic-Jackson & Jackson, 1996; Walker, 1985). A large group of batterers was diagnosed to have borderline personalities along with a constellation of behavioral shifts: angry outbursts, rage, intense jealousy, blaming, recurring moods, trauma symptoms, haunting fear of isolation and loss, binge drinking, and repetitive self-destructive thoughts.

People prone to depression may be more prone to violence. A number of studies report that abusive mothers, as well as males who physically abuse their partners, show signs of depression (Zuravin, 1989) but the causal direction is not clear. Some sources of depression (e.g., repressed anger toward others) may cause the abuse; however, the depression may result from being labeled abusive, or from other consequences of the violent act (Reiss & Roth, 1993:238).

Assaultive and Homicidal Behavior

How do we explain interpersonal violence, especially partner violence and homicide? Explanations are difficult because violence is a transgression of a basic sense of connectedness between people, and we wonder how this kind of behavior can exist. We know that early attachment disturbance and the impairment of self-regulation are major diagnostic issues with traumatized children (Van der Kolk & Fisler, 1994). In courtship violence, the aggressor may not want the relationship to end. Terrorizing death threats, stalking behavior, monitoring a house by parking outside it, and making harassing phone calls are among the tactics used. Harassers cannot tolerate separation. They feel abandoned, angry, and depressed, and they may become suicidal. Rage is often behind their depression. Rejection is an attack on their ego. Frequently, they feel that they cannot manage on their own. Their limbic system is actually affected. They may lack impulse control. Fantasy calms them temporarily, but it is filled with rage directed at the partner. The distorted thought is: "I killed her because I love her."

In a study of murderers (Ressler, Burgess, & Douglas, 1988), three negative factors were identified as contributing to the development of the hostility. The first factor is early childhood trauma, in the form of physical or sexual abuse. The developing child encounters a variety of life events, some normative and others unusual and extraordinarily negative. Within the context of the child's dysfunctional social environment, the distress caused by the trauma is probably neglected or mishandled. The child is neither protected nor assisted in recovery from the trauma; his or her external environment does not address the negative consequences of the events.

The second important factor contributing to the formative events component is developmental failure. For some reason, the child does not readily attach to his or her adult caretaker. As a result of this negative social attachment, the caretaker has no influence over the child—and later, over the adolescent.

The third factor, interpersonal failure, is the inability of the caretaking adult to serve as a role model for the developing child. Among the various reasons for this failure is the caretaker's being absent or serving as an inadequate role model (e.g., an abusive parent). The child may witness a violent home environment in which aggression during drunken fights becomes associated with the sexual behavior of adult caretakers.

In domestic murders, the killing may be spontaneous. For example, in June 1995, two young boys died of hyperthermia after being buckled into car-seat belts and abandoned for 8 or 10 hours while their 20-year-old mother partied and fell asleep at a Tennessee motel. This case did not involve intentional killing. However, some domestic murders are staged and involve careful planning, as in the case of Diane. In 1983, in Springfield, Oregon, at about 10:30 P.M., Diane pulled into a hospital emergency area and screamed for help for her three children, who had been shot. Her 7-year-old daughter Cheryl was dead on arrival; her 8-year-old daughter Christie had two small-caliber bullet wounds in her left chest and a third bullet wound through the base of her left thumb; and her 3-year-old son had a bullet entry to his spinal column. Diane had a gunshot wound in her arm. She said she had been driving in her car when she noticed a man standing in the middle of the road. She stopped and got out, and the man pulled out a gun, reached through the window, and shot the children and herself. She said she then pushed him and kicked him in the leg, jumped in her car, and sped off for the hospital. The story fell apart when her daughter Christie proved to be an eyewitness to the crime. She saw her mother go to the trunk of the car, where a gun was stored, come around the car, and shoot Cheryl, then her brother, and then herself. Another witness testified to seeing Diane's car creeping along the road at about 10:15 P.M., apparently waiting for the children to die before she drove to the hospital. Her diaries, and unmailed letters to a married letter carrier with whom she was having an affair, contained incriminating statements, such as: "You know I don't want a daddy for my kids . . . you would never be left alone with them." Her motive was to eliminate the obstacle (her children) to her fantasized relationship with her lover.

A history of Diane's background revealed child abuse, neglect, and incest. Little, if any, attachment occurred with protective caretakers. The result was clearly a flaw in human development and attachment.

We do not deny that other environmental stressors play a role in shaping moral development, but case after case will address the issue of failure of attachment and how it excludes the welfare of others. The abuser imitates the behavior of others. Such behavior is not drawn out of true individuation and appreciation of the uniqueness of others.

Elder Abuse

Aggression toward the elderly is multifaceted. Abuse may be inflicted on parents who had been abusive and exploitative. One needs to distinguish between elder spousal abuse and abuse by elder persons' children. The dynamics are different, despite many common antecedents.

Child and spousal abuse have received increasing attention in family violence research, but very little is known about the nature of elder abuse. The characteristics of individuals and families associated with abuse of the elderly need to be researched, as do the features of interventions designed for other forms of family violence. They may be adaptable to this problem.

INTERVENTIONS

There are no easy answers to problems of family violence. A comprehensive set of family support programs, or a continuum of services for families within each of the developmental phases of family life, does not exist. Although services are needed for ongoing abuse cases, it is critical to identify families at risk for potential violence. Rather than waiting for incidents of violence, counseling and education services need to build on an integration of existing interventions, and to design proactive approaches that are responsive to community needs and are feasible with community resources. Other suggestions follow.

COURTSHIP VIOLENCE

Recent research has provided a better understanding of relationship problems that lead to dating violence. In Riggs's study (1993), although aggressors generally reported more problems than did nonaggressive individuals, the difference appeared to result from specific problem areas. These included jealousy, interference of people outside the relationship (such as friends and parents), and more fighting and conflict between the couple. If one conceptualizes jealousy as a reaction to the threat of loss, writes Riggs (1993), it is possible that such a threat will also result in anger, which could lead to aggression. Other issues that may be related to jealousy, such as possessiveness and control, may also lead to aggression.

ASSAULTS ON SPOUSES

Police Response

Most research has focused on testing police arrests of the abuser in preventing recurrences of domestic violence. Arrest, in replication studies, has been shown to *not* be an effective deterrent; indeed, it may well increase the incidence of domestic violence of unemployed males with low socioeconomic status (Sherman, 1992). Research is recommended on police responses as well as police referrals to social service and substance abuse treatment agencies, and to battered women's shelters.

Shelters and Other Services

In the past few decades, programmatic efforts have focused on providing shelters for battered women—residences where abused women and their children can stay safe and receive emotional support. Approximately 1,200 shelters offer temporary emergency housing (a typical stay is from two days to three months) to more than 300,000 women and children each year (Reiss & Roth, 1993). A national survey of 622 shelters indicated that their average annual operating budget was between $135,000 and $160,000. The average staffing pattern at each shelter consisted of six full-time and four part-time paid staff and 25 volunteers (Roche & Sadoski, 1996).

The primary goal of shelters is to provide a safe and secure haven for battered women and their children. Other services are designed to help the women become self-sufficient. They include relocation assistance, day care for children, and welfare advocacy. Services directed at increasing self-esteem include support groups and courses on parenting, job readiness, and budgeting. Services for children who have witnessed family violence are often incorporated into shelter programs.

The Duluth Minnesota Domestic Abuse Intervention Project (DMIP) conducted a 12-month follow-up study in which battered women were asked their opinion of the intervention that the Project had used in an effort to have the batterer change his violent habits. Of the women studied, 60% said they felt there was improvement when the batterer took part in education and group counseling, whereas 80% of the women stated that the improvement had resulted from a combination of involvement from police, courts, group counseling, and the shelter (Pence & Paymor, 1993).

Programs to reduce partner assault include public education and awareness campaigns for batterers. Educational programs help children to develop nonviolent ways of coping with anger and frustration. Public awareness programs emphasize that family violence is a crime, and help is available. Courts also mandate that batterers attend programs that will teach them alternative ways to behave. Alcohol and drug abuse programs are required for batterers whose chemical abuse is an issue.

Pharmacological interventions may be useful. Based on the understanding that depression may affect the severity of maltreatment of children as well as lead to their neglect, medical treatment of depression may be indicated. If a significant subgroup of abusive parents or caretakers suffers from affective disorders, especially major depression, then chemical and other forms of treating depression may be a means of controlling family violence. This approach assumes that reasonably effective means are available for controlling affective disorders, particularly any volatile mood swings associated with them (Reiss & Roth, 1993:239).

CHILD ABUSE

Foster care placement is a major intervention in child abuse cases. An estimated 15% of victims of child maltreatment are placed in unrelated foster homes (American Humane Association, 1979). Several studies have noted that the more changes in placement a child experiences, the greater the likelihood of his or her adult criminality and violent criminal behavior (Hensey, Williams, & Rosenbloom, 1983; Lynch & Roberts, 1983; Widom, 1990).

Home nurse visitation is one proactive means of detecting maltreatment of infants and preschoolers. Olds (1988) and Olds and Henderson (1989) studied this intervention in high-risk groups—poor, unmarried, teenage mothers having their first child—and found that it decreased but did not totally eliminate the incidence of child abuse when compared with groups not receiving the intervention. In this study, there was a 5% rate of child abuse or neglect, suggesting a need for additional preventive or ameliorative interventions. However, there were additional positive effects of the home nursing intervention. At 12 and 24 months, infants of mothers in the high-risk group showed improved intellectual functioning on development tests. Improved family functioning was noted, along with less evidence of conflict and scolding, and less punishment of infants. Olds and Henderson also concluded that although the nurse can link families to community and social services—to ameliorate the effects of poverty, violence, and drug use—a lack of employment opportunities in the neighborhoods where these families live poses severe constraints on their continued improvement, especially when the intervention stops.

FAMILY VIOLENCE CASES BY TYPE OF CRISIS: A NEW TYPOLOGY

Clinical typologies and classificatory schemas help to define, group, organize, and structure persons by a set of rules or patterns. Types or categories are often organized around "prototypes" or "typical examples," but they often have somewhat vague end points or boundaries. The "ideal" or prototype of each crisis is easy to visualize (e.g., a traumatic crisis or a psychiatric crisis), but the boundary between the two types is fuzzy. Nevertheless, clinicians learn best about classificatory schemas or typologies through typical case illustrations and applications. This concluding section focuses on a summary description of each of the seven types of crisis and presents a clinical case vignette.

The stress-crisis continuum classification devised by Burgess and Roberts (1995) is an adaptation and expansion of Baldwin's (1978) crisis typology. Seven types are identified: (1) somatic distress, (2) transitional stress, (3) traumatic stress-crises, (4) family crises, (5) serious mental illness, (6) psychiatric emergencies, and (7) catastrophic crises. When there is advancement from type 1 to type 7, the internal biopsychosocial conflicts of the client become more serious, chronic, and lethal in nature. This continuum focuses on violence within families in crisis.

Most crisis-intervention and time-limited treatment models fail to take into account the different levels and types of acute crisis episodes. The following descriptions of the different types of acute crisis episodes among victims of family violence are based on Burgess and Roberts's (1995) seven-level stress-crisis continuum. The discussions include the nature and extent of violence, the nature of injuries, types of emotional abuse, alcohol or substance abuse, suicide attempts, and psychiatric diagnosis.

1. SOMATIC DISTRESS

Somatic distress is associated with a medical presentation of symptoms. The abuse issue is usually not disclosed. Examples of this type of crisis precipitant in domestic violence cases include bruises, fractures, and bleeding. Generally, the patient responds to this type of stress-crisis with fear, anxiety, and/or masked depressive symptoms. The etiology of the crisis is physical injury and psychological abuse. Primary care providers or emergency department staff generally diagnose and treat somatic stress-crisis. Intervention typically involves treatment of the injury, identification and confirmation of the abuse, and referral for crisis intervention and shelter. The police or family court may be contacted if the victim wishes to file for a restraining/protective order.

Case Example

Doris was a 23-year-old divorced mother of two children, ages two and four years. Her husband's abusive behavior caused multiple visits to an emergency room. While Doris was pregnant, her husband repeatedly would punch her in the stomach, throw her to the ground, and tell her how she repulsed him. Her terror of him increased because he would periodically strangle her and she noted that "his eyes were popping out." After the divorce and during a visitation, his abuse occurred in the presence of the couple's children. Doris sought medical assistance, but she never reported that she was being abused; instead, she provided a reason for each injury. She reported the following during her most recent emergency room visit. "He knocked the front teeth out of my mouth. I was in a bar and I never went to a bar while we were married. But, he started rejecting me and telling me I was ugly and stuff. He found me there and said, 'What are you doing here with all these guys looking at you?' I wasn't even looking at them. He called me a slut and punched me in the mouth with a glass and broke my teeth and bashed my head in front of everyone in the bar. I went to the emergency room but they really couldn't do anything for me but stop the bleeding. They told me to go to a dentist. I had to get two false teeth. The doctors were helpful but I lied to them because he was standing over me. I told them I fell and did it to myself."

---

2. TRANSITIONAL STRESS

Transitional stress is precipitated by life transitions over which the patient may or may not have substantial control. Abuse related to family violence may occur during pregnancy or after the delivery of the baby. In a frequent example, family members visit maternity, pediatric, and nursery units, and arguments about paternity, infidelity, or custody ensue. Sometimes, prior child protective services contacts and/or family court orders of "No contact" are not communicated to staff. These arguments, directed initially at spouses, frequently escalate into physical violence and may endanger nursing staff members who intervene. Critical-incident planning is needed to provide prior guidance and define roles for staff. Instantaneous communications (panic button, cell phones, electronic pendants, portable radio, dedicated phone line) and closed-circuit TV (taped and monitored) should be ongoing so that security staff can be summoned and may observe incidents.

Case Examples

"I was pregnant, had my daughter. He couldn't be found till I was released. The doctor told him to his face that I had eight stitches and we couldn't have sex for four to six weeks. He said he was going out drinking with the boys. He came back drunk and wanted to have sex. I fought him off for about one hour, but I was so weak. I was all bloody 'cause the stitches popped; he just pulled all my clothes off and raped me. I went to his parents' house and they told me to go to the police. So I did, but they said there is no such thing as a marital rape law. They wouldn't let me press charges."

A two-day-old infant was abducted from his hospital bassinet while his mother was in the shower. Hospital security was notified immediately and a search was initiated. Local police were called into the investigation within an hour of the abduction. A search of the apartment of the mother's ex-boyfriend revealed the infant. He was returned, unharmed, after a 14-hour search. The abductor told police that his girlfriend had acknowledged that he was the baby's father, but said she would not give him visitation rights. The case was referred to family court for resolution.

---

3. TRAUMATIC STRESS-CRISES

Traumatic crises are precipitated by externally imposed stress that overwhelms the individual. Examples include stranger rape, acquaintance/date rape, spouse assault, marital rape, and battering among cohabiting partners. The individual's response includes intense fear, helplessness, and behavior disorganization.

Case Example

A college sophomore and her roommate took the campus bus to study at the school library. After studying for three hours, two male students invited the young women back to their dorm to play cards. The game required the loser to drink a glass of beer. Over the next few hours, the four became intoxicated and the women missed the bus back to their dormitory. The young men said they would sleep on the couch and offered their beds to the women. Nancy fell asleep immediately but was awakened to the presence of one of the young men who removed her clothes and proceeded to force sex on her, despite her protests. The next morning, the women returned to the dorm and attended classes. Nancy became increasingly anxious and distressed. She could not get the thought of the

Case Example *(Continued)*

rape out of her mind. She was unable to concentrate in class, do homework assignments, continue her part-time job, or attend social functions. By the end of the semester, she had failed two courses and was on academic probation. Her roommate encouraged her to report the rape to the Women's Health Center, which she did. She also reported the rape to local police, but criminal charges were not filed. A civil suit was filed against the university and later settled out of court. Nancy received short-term counseling and attended group sessions at the local rape crisis center (Burgess & Roberts, 2000).

4. FAMILY CRISES

Family crises reflect serious disruption in partner or caregiver relationships. These crises involve failure to master developmental issues such as dependency, value conflicts, emotional intimacy, power and control issues, or attainment of self-discipline. The problem is especially noted through relationship difficulties. Examples of events that precipitate family crises include child abuse, the use of children in pornography, parental abductions, adolescent runaways, battering and rape, and domestic homicide.

Case Example

Emily died on March 13, 1995, at the age of nine months. She was the youngest in a family known to the Department of Children and Families for over three years. Emily suffered a broken leg, with no reasonable explanation, only three weeks before the injuries that led to her death.

A review of the case revealed several points at which the extreme danger to children in this family might have been recognized. First, the multiple injuries to a sibling, during the sibling's first year of life, were never recognized as suggestive of abuse by medical staff at a local hospital, during sporadic clinic appointments. When severe medical neglect of another child was reported to the Department of Children's Services, the serious consequences of that neglect were not sufficiently understood, medical information concerning the siblings was not sought (which would have revealed a pattern of possible abuse), and the case was closed. In October 1991, the police arrested the mother for risk of injury. The arrest record states that the officers found two children hanging out of an open third-story window. There were no adults in the unheated (52 degrees F) apartment, there was animal excrement on the beds, and no food was available. The responding police officers placed the children with a relative, arrested the mother, and did not call the Department of Children's Services until the next day. The last opportunity to avert tragedy came in February and March of 1995, when Emily presented at a local hospital emergency room with a spiral fracture of her leg. This injury was reported by the hospital to the Department of Children's Services six days after the child was initially treated by an emergency care physician and an orthopedist. This referral was handled by a social worker who believed the inconsistent explanation ("accidental injury") given by the mother. Emily remained in the home and was fatally raped and abused at the age of nine months (Burgess & Roberts, 2000).

5. SERIOUS MENTAL ILLNESS

Serious mental illness reflects preexisting psychiatric problems. Examples include diagnoses of psychosis, dementia, bipolar depression, and schizophrenia. The patient's response will be disorganized thinking and behavior. The etiology is neurobiological in nature. Persons with long-term and recurring severe mental illness require a mix of traditional medical and long-term treatments that are helpful in sustaining their function and role. Roberts's (1991, 1995) crisis intervention model may be used to reduce symptoms in an acute crisis. Case monitoring and management are indicated, as well as an assessment for in-patient hospitalization or sheltered care. Medication will be needed to counteract psychotic thinking. Continuity of care is critical with this level of crisis and is generally accomplished through the case manager. Other services should include referral for vocational training and group therapy.

Case Example

An editor of the *Congressional Quarterly* magazine was shot and killed on June 4, 1995, in Arlington, Virginia, because he happened to arrive home at the wrong time, according to police. The 34-year-old editor and two of his roommates were killed by an emotionally disturbed man who was a cousin of one of the roommates. According to reports, the man arrested in the triple slaying went to the house intending to kill two of the victims—his cousin and her boyfriend, with whom the killer was believed to have had ongoing problems. The killings were triggered by an argument over a bicycle, living arrangements, and other problems (Burgess & Roberts, 2000).

6. PSYCHIATRIC EMERGENCIES

Psychiatric emergencies involve situations in which general functioning has been severely impaired. The result is threat or actual harm to oneself and/or others. Examples include drug overdose, suicide attempts, stalking, aggravated assault, death threats, rape, and homicide. The clinician needs to be confident in his or her skills to manage out-of-control behavior of the client and/or to have adequate assistance available.

Dangerous and volatile situations should be handled by police and local rescue squads; these units can provide rapid transportation to a hospital emergency room. The basic intervention strategy involves: (a) rapid assessment of the patient's psychological and medical condition; (b) clarifying the situation that produced or led to the patient's condition; (c) mobilizing all mental health and/or medical resources necessary to effectively treat the patient; and (d) arranging for follow-up or coordination of services to ensure continuity of treatment as appropriate. In this type of psychiatric emergency, the skills of the crisis therapist are tested to the limit. He or she must have a capacity to work effectively and quickly in highly charged situations, and to intervene where there may be life-threatening implications of the patient's condition (Baldwin, 1978; Burgess & Baldwin, 1981).

Case Example

Mindy, age 22, a visiting nurse with a five-year-old son, described vivid scenes of violent assaults wherein her boyfriend would hit her with a lead pipe and with empty beer bottles. In an attempt to cope with the abuse, she took drugs and attempted suicide. In the words of Mindy: "I O-D'ed on cocaine intravenously. Purposely. I couldn't take it anymore. I was real depressed and upset and afraid that he was going to beat our son. I went to the hospital. They pumped my stomach and then told me I was a drug addict. They put me in a 90-day inpatient drug program which I didn't complete. The psychiatrist put me on an antidepressant and she completed short-term counseling" (Burgess & Roberts, 2000).

---

7. CATASTROPHIC CRISES

Catastrophic crisis combines a type 3 traumatic crisis with type 4, 5, or 6 stressors. Often, the victim is a battered wife and actual or threatened escalation includes the partner as well as the children. The victim has a history of unresolved traumatic or family crises during childhood or early adolescence. For example, Lila was the second oldest child in a family of 10. Her father was stabbed to death when she was 13. She moved out of the home at age 16, when she was pregnant with her first child. She missed out on high school and social activities because she had to work to support her child. She married at age 20 and had four more children. Her husband was physically abusive; he punched and kicked her, and burned her with a lit cigarette. He threatened, during a year when they were separated, that he would burn the house down when she and the children were inside. In a 1995 Maryland case, an estranged husband lured his wife and three children into his car under the pretense of driving them to a local mall to buy school clothes and supplies. He detonated a car bomb while parked in the mall parking lot, killing all five and injuring others in the vicinity.

Case Example

Police received an emergency call that a pregnant woman and her husband, driving home from a childbirth class, had been shot by an unknown assailant. The couple was located and rushed to a local hospital. Surgeons were unable to save the young woman. Her baby was born by caesarean section but died 10 days later. Following a lengthy investigation, the police identified the husband as their prime suspect. Prior to his arrest, the husband jumped off a bridge and drowned. The husband's brother was arrested and charged with aiding in a felony; he had disposed of two bags containing jewelry and the murder weapon. Police divers later located the evidence. This case qualifies as a catastrophic crisis because of the deaths of the mother and her infant, the disclosure of the wife as a silent battered woman during the marriage and pregnancy, and the suicide of the abuser.

CONCLUSION

This chapter has suggested that health care and mental health professionals need to be cautious and innovative in their initial assessment of a client's type of crisis. Many clients in a crisis state will fit one of the seven types of crisis; others will not fit at all. The seven types of acute crisis appear to be "ideal types"; they are not. A person may have two crises simultaneously—traumatic and family crises. The primary diagnostic task of the crisis clinician is to determine whether—based on the client's symptoms, characteristics, and behavior—she or he fits one of the seven types. There will always be diagnostic and classificatory uncertainty. This chapter has provided a structured and organized typology that can yield partial resolution of diagnostic uncertainty of acute crisis episodes. Identification of seven types of crisis provides clinicians with a classificatory schema and concrete intervention strategies. The case illustrations indicate the complexity of clients' presenting problems and other biopsychosocial variables.

REFERENCES

Ainsworth, M. D. S. (1980). Attachment and child abuse. In G. Gerber, C. J. Ross, & E. Zigler (Eds.), *Child abuse reconsidered: An agenda for action.* New York: Oxford University Press.

Baldwin, B. A. (1978). A paradigm for the classification of emotional crises: Implications for crisis intervention. *American Journal of Orthopsychiatry, 48,* 538–551.

Boes, M. (1998). Battered women in the emergency room. In A. R. Roberts (Ed.), *Battered women and their families: Intervention strategies and treatment approaches* (2nd ed., pp. 205–228). New York: Springer.

Bowlby, J. (1969). *Attachment and loss. Volume I: Attachment.* New York: Basic Books.

Bowlby, J. (1973). *Attachment and loss. Volume II: Separation: Anxiety and anger.* New York: Basic Books.

Bowlby, J. (1980). *Attachment and loss. Volume III: Loss: Sadness and depression.* New York: Basic Books.

Browne, A. (1987). *When battered women kill.* New York: Free Press.

Brownell, P. (1996). Social work and criminal justice responses to elder abuse in New York City. In A. R. Roberts (Ed.), *Helping battered women: New perspectives and remedies* (pp. 44–66). New York: Oxford University Press.

Bureau of Justice Statistics, U.S. Department of Justice. (1990, December). *Criminal victimization in the United States, 1988* (A national crime survey report, Report No. NCJ-122024). Washington, DC: U.S. Government Printing Office.

Burgess, A., & Roberts, A. R. (2000). Crisis intervention for persons diagnosed with clinical disorders based on the stress-crisis continuum. In A. R. Roberts (Ed.), *Crisis intervention handbook: Assessment, treatment and research* (2nd ed., pp. 56–75). New York: Oxford University Press.

Burgess, A. W., Baker, T., Greening, D., Hartman, C., Burgess, A. G., Douglas, J. E., et al. (1997). Stalking behaviors within domestic violence. *Journal of Family Violence, 12*(4), 389–403.

Burgess, A. W., & Baldwin, B. (1981). *Crisis intervention theory and practice.* Englewood Cliffs, NJ: Prentice-Hall.

Burgess, A. W., Harner, H., Baker, T., Hartman, C., & Lole, C. (2001). Batterers stalking patterns. *Journal of Family Violence, 16,* 4.

Burgess, A. W., & Roberts, A. L. (1995). Levels of stress and crisis precipitants: A stress-crisis continuum. *Crisis Intervention and Time-Limited Treatment, 2*(1), 31–47.

Cascardi, M., & O'Leary, K. D. (1992). Depressive symptomatology, self-esteem, and self-blame in battered women. *Journal of Family Violence, 7,* 249–259.

Cate, C. A., Henton, J. M., Koval, J., Christopher, F. S., & Lloyd, S. (1982). Premarital abuse: A social psychological perspective. *Journal of Family Issues, 3,* 79–90.

Connolly, J., Pepler, D., Craig, W., & Taradash, A. (2000). Dating experiences of bullies in early adolescence. *Child Maltreatment, 5*(4), 299–310.

Crittenden, P. M., & Ainsworth, M. D. S. (1989). Child maltreatment and attachment theory. In D. Cicchetti & V. Carlson (Eds.), *Child maltreatment* (pp. 432–463). Cambridge, MA: Cambridge University Press.

Dobash, R. E., & Dobash, R. (1979). *Violence against wives.* New York: Free Press.

Durst, M. (1987). Perceived peer abuse among college students: A research note. *National Association of Student Personnel Administration Journal, 24,* 42–47.

Dwyer, D. C., Smokowski, P. R., Bricout, J., & Wodarski, J. S. (1996). Domestic violence and woman battering: Theories and practice implications. In A. R. Roberts (Ed.), *Helping battered women: New perspectives and remedies* (pp. 67–82). New York: Oxford University Press.

Federal Bureau of Investigation. (1990). *Uniform Crime Reports for the United States: 1990.* Washington, DC: U.S. Government Printing Office.

Finkelhor, D. (1983). Common features of family abuse. In D. Finklehor, R. J. Gelles, G. T. Hotaling, & M. A. Straus (Eds.), *The dark side of families* (pp. 17–28). Newbury Park, CA: Sage.

Finkelhor, D., & Browne, A. (1984). The traumatic impact of child sexual abuse: A conceptualization. *American Journal of Orthopsychiatry, 55,* 530–541.

Frieze, I. H., & Browne, A. (1989). Violence in marriage. In L. Ohlin & M. Tonry (Eds.), *Family violence* (pp. 163–218). Chicago: University of Chicago Press.

Garbarino, J., & Crouter, K. (1978). Defining the community context of parent-child relations: The correlates of child maltreatment. *Child Development, 43,* 604–616.

Garbarino, J., & Sherman, D. (1980). High-risk families and high-risk neighborhoods. *Child Development, 51,* 188–198.

Gelles, R. J. (1983). An exchange social control theory. In D. Finklehor, R. J. Gelles, G. T. Hotaling, & M. A. Straus (Eds.), *The dark side of families* (pp. 151–165). Newbury Park, CA: Sage.

Gelles, R. J., & Straus, M. A. (1979). Determinant of violence in the family: Toward a theoretical integration. In R. B. Hill, F. I. Nye, & I. L. Reiss (Eds.), *Contemporary theories about the family* (pp. 549–581). New York: Free Press.

Gidycz, C. A., & Layman, M. J. (1996). The crime of acquaintance rape. In T. L. Jackson (Ed.), *Acquaintance rape: Assessment, treatment and prevention* (pp. 23–61). Sarasota, FL: Professional Resource Press.

Hensey, O. J., Williams, J. K., & Rosenbloom, L. (1983). Experiences in Liverpool. *Developmental Medicine and Child Neurology, 25,* 606–611.

Henton, J., Cate, R., Koval, J., Lloyd, D., & Christopher, D. (1983). Romance and violence in dating relationships. *Journal of Family Issues, 4,* 467–482.

Housekamp, B. M., & Foy, D. W. (1991). The assessment of post-traumatic stress disorder in battered women. *Journal of Interpersonal Violence, 6,* 367–375.

Jackson, T. L. (Ed.). (1996). *Acquaintance rape: Assessment, treatment, and prevention*. Sarasota, FL: Professional Resource Exchange.

Kempe, C., Silverman, F., Steele, B., Droegemueller, W., & Silver, H. (1962). The battered child syndrome. *Journal of the American Medical Association, 181*(1), 17–24.

Kurt, J. L. (1995). Stalking as a variant of domestic violence. *Bulletin of the American Academy of Psychiatry and the Law, 23,* 219–223.

Laner, M. R. (1983). Courtship abuse and aggression: Contextual aspects. *Sociological Spectrum, 3,* 69–83.

Lynch, M. A., & Roberts, J. (1983). *Consequences of child abuse*. London, England: Academic Press.

Makepeace, J. M. (1981). Courtship violence among college students. *Family Relations, 30,* 97–102.

Mechanic, M. B. (1996). Battered women, homicide, and the legal system. In A. R. Roberts (Ed.), *Helping battered women: New perspectives and remedies* (pp. 132–156). New York: Oxford University Press.

Meloy, J. R. (Ed.). (1998). *Psychology of stalking*. San Diego: Academic Press.

National Research Council. (1983). *Understanding child abuse and neglect.* Panel on research on child abuse and neglect. Washington, DC: Author.

O'Connell, P., Pepler, D., & Craig, W. (1999). Peer involvement in bullying: Issues and challenges for intervention. *Journal of Adolescence, 22,* 437–452.

O'Keefe, M., & Lebovics, S. (1998). Intervention and treatment strategies with adolescents from maritally violent homes. In A. R. Roberts (Ed.), *Battered women and their families: Intervention strategies and treatment approaches* (2nd ed., pp. 174–202). New York: Springer.

Olds, D. L. (1988). The prenatal/early infancy project. In R. H. Price, E. E. Cowen, R. P. Lorion, & M. Ramos (Eds.), *Fourteen ounces of prevention: A casebook for practitioners* (pp. 9–32). Washington, DC: American Psychological Association.

Olds, D. L., & Henderson, C. R. (1989). The prevention of maltreatment. In D. Cicchetti & V. Carlson (Eds.), *Child maltreatment: Theory and research on the causes and consequences of child abuse and neglect.* Cambridge, England: Cambridge University Press.

Olweus, D. (1991). Bully/victim problems among school children: Basic facts and effects of a school based intervention program. In D. Pepler & K. Rubin (Eds.), *The development and treatment of childhood aggression* (pp. 411–448). Hillsdale, NJ: Erlbaum.

Olweus, D. (1993). *Bullying at school: What we know and what we can do*. Oxford, England: Blackwell.

Osofsky, J. (2001, October). *Action plan update*. Washington, DC: U.S. Department of Justice.

Parker, B., McFarlane, J., Soeken, K., Torres, S., & Campbell, J. (1993). Physical and emotional abuse in pregnancy: A comparison of adult and teenage women. *Nursing Research, 42,* 1783–1788.

Pence, E., & Paymor, M. (1993). *Education groups for men who batter: The Duluth model*. New York: Springer.

Petretic-Jackson, P. A., & Tobin, S. (1996). The Rape Trauma Syndrome: Symptoms, stages, and hidden victims. In T. L. Jackson (Ed.), *Acquaintance rape: Assessment, treatment, and prevention* (pp. 103–153). Sarasota, FL: Professional Resource Press.

Pike, K. M. (1990). *Intrafamilial sexual abuse of children.* Paper prepared for the National Research Council Panel on the Understanding and Control of Violent Behavior. Washington, DC: National Research Council.

Pleck, E. (1987). *Domestic tyranny.* New York: Oxford University Press.

Reiss, A. J., Jr., & Roth, J. A. (Eds.). (1993). *Understanding and preventing violence. Vol. 3: Social influences.* Washington, DC: National Academy Press.

Resick, P. A., & Reese, D. (1986). Perception of family social climate and physical aggression in the home. *Journal of Family Violence, 1,* 71–83.

Ressler, R. K., Burgess, A. W., & Douglas, J. E. (1988). *Sexual homicide.* Lexington, MA: Lexington Books.

Riggs, D. S. (1993). Relationship problems and dating aggression. *Journal of Interpersonal Violence, 8,* 18–35.

Riggs, D. S., & O'Leary, D. K. (1989). A theoretical model of courtship aggression. In M. A. Pirog-Good & J. E. Stets (Eds.), *Violence in dating relationships: Emerging social issues* (pp. 53–71). New York: Praeger.

Roberts, A. R. (1981). *Sheltering battered women: A national survey and service guide.* New York: Springer.

Roberts, A. R. (Ed.). (1991). *Contemporary perspectives on crisis intervention and prevention.* Englewood Cliffs, NJ: Prentice Hall.

Roberts, A. R. (Ed.). (1995). *Crisis intervention and time-limited cognitive treatment.* Thousand Oaks, CA: Sage.

Roberts, A. R. (Ed.). (1996). *Helping battered women: New perspectives and remedies.* New York: Oxford University Press.

Roberts, A. R. (2002). The Duration and Severity of Woman Battering: A 5-level Continuum. In A. R. Roberts (Ed.), *Handbook of Domestic Violence Intervention Strategies: Policies, Programs, and Legal Remedies.* New York: Oxford University Press, pp. 64–80.

Roche, S. E., & Sadoski, P. J. (1996). Social action for battered women. In A. R. Roberts (Ed.), *Helping battered women: New perspectives and remedies* (pp. 13–30). New York: Oxford University Press.

Roscoe, B., & Benaske, N. (1985). Courtship violence experienced by abused wives: Similarities in patterns of abuse. *Family Relations, 34,* 419–424.

Salmivalli, C., Lagerspetz, K., Bjorkqvist, K., Osterman, K., & Kaukiainen, A. (1996). Bullying as a group process: Participant roles and their relations to social status within the group. *Aggressive Behavior, 22,* 1–15.

Sherman, L. W. (1992). *Policing domestic violence: Experiments and dilemmas.* New York: Free Press.

Sigelman, C., Berry, C., & Wiles, K. A. (1984). Violence in college students' dating relationships. *Journal of Applied Social Psychology, 5*(6), 530–548.

Stahl, S. (2000). *Elder justice roundtable: Medical forensic issues concerning abuse.* Washington, DC: U.S. Department of Justice.

Straus, M. A. (1979). Measuring intrafamily conflict and violence: The conflict tactics (CT) scales. *Journal of Marriage and the Family, 41,* 75–88.

Straus, M. A., & Gelles, R. (1991). *Physical violence in American families.* New Brunswick, NJ: Transaction.

Straus, M. A., Gelles, R. J., & Steinmetz, S. K. (1980). *Behind closed doors: Violence in the American family.* Garden City, NY: Doubleday.

U.S. Bureau of the Census. (1990). *Household and family characteristics* (Current population reports: Population characteristics. Series P-20, No. 47). Washington, DC: U.S. Government Printing Office.

U.S. Bureau of the Census. (1991). *Marital status and living arrangements* (Current population reports. Series P-20, No. 450). Washington, DC: U.S. Government Printing Office.

Van der Kolk, B. A., & Fisler, R. (1994). Childhood abuse and neglect and loss of self-regulation. *Bulletin of the Menninger Clinic, 58,* 145–168.

Walker, L. A. (1985). Psychological impact of the criminalization of domestic violence on victims. *Victimology: An International Journal, 10,* 281–300.

Widom, C. S. (1989). The cycle of violence. *Science, 244,* 160–166.

Widom, C. S. (1990, March 8). *Research, clinical and policy issues: Childhood victimization, parent alcohol problems and long-term consequences.* Workshop presented at the National Forum on the Future of Children. National Research Council: Institute of Medicine.

Winpisinger, K. A., Hopkins, R. A., Indian, R. W., & Hosteler, J. R. (1991, August). Risk factors for childhood homicides in Ohio: A birth certificate-based case-control study. *American Journal of Public Health, 81,* 1052–1054.

Zigler, E., & Hall, N. W. (1989). Physical child abuse in America: Past, present and future. In D. C. Cicchetti & V. Carlson (Eds.), *Child maltreatment* (pp. 38–75). Cambridge, England: Cambridge University Press.

Zuravin, S. J. (1989). The ecology of child abuse and neglect. *Violence and Victims, 4,* 101–120.

Chapter 2

ADOLESCENT DATING VIOLENCE

GRETCHEN ELY, CATHERINE N. DULMUS, AND JOHN S. WODARSKI

INTRODUCTION

This chapter focuses on the serious societal problem of adolescent dating violence. Steiner (Steiner & Feldman, 1996) defines adolescence as the second decade of life and distinguishes early (10–13 years), middle (14–17 years) and late (18–21 years) stages within that decade (p. 3). Dating violence can be defined as physical assault or acts of bodily harm, including psychological and emotional abuse, verbal or implied, that take place in private or in social situations. This definition is based partly on the earlier works of Sugarman and Hotling (1989), who stated that dating violence is "the perpetration or threat of an act of physical violence by at least one member of an unmarried dyad on the other within the context of the dating process" (p. 5). Some researchers use "courtship violence" as an interchangeable term to describe adolescent dating violence.

CURRENT TRENDS AND ISSUES

A thorough examination of the adolescent dating violence literature reveals several important current issues of concern:

- Significant gender differences are reported by many researchers and are of concern to social workers.
- Prevalence rates of current adolescent involvement in dating violence are extremely varied and inconsistent, and therefore are undetermined.
- Many methodological issues may provide an explanation for inconsistent prevalence rates.

Gender Differences

Gender differences are shown to be present in prevalence rates, perpetration rates, victimization rates, and attitudes related to involvement in adolescent dating violence. For example, girls reported higher rates of abuse in activities such as coercive sexuality and unwanted kissing of sexual body parts, and boys have consistently underreported the perpetration of such abusive acts (Koss, Gidyez, & Wisnieweski, 1987; So-Kum Tang, Critelli, & Porter, 1995). Compared to females in late adolescence, males view restrictive and coercive behavior as less controlling than it actually is (Ehrensaft & Vivian, 1999).

Research indicates that girls and boys are equally likely to report reciprocal participation in dating violence, but girls are at much greater risk of sustaining injuries from such encounters (Arias, Samios, & O'Leary, 1987; Bookwala, Frieze, Smith, & Ryan, 1992; Giordano, Millhollin, Cernovich, Pugh, & Rudolph, 1999; Molidor & Tolman, 1998; Riggs & O'Leary, 1989; Simons, Lin, & Gordon, 1998; Wekerle & Wolfe, 1999). Females report using a wider array of violent tactics; males report using more extreme forms of violence, including sexual violence, multiple times with multiple partners (Lane & Gwartney-Gibbs, 1985). One study reported that females were much more likely to report the use of physical force than were males (Shook, Gerrity, Jurich, & Segrist, 2000). Earlier data collected from victims of domestic abuse support such notions of female self-defense strategies (Saunders, 1986).

Roscoe and Callahan (1985) reported that the girls they studied were much more likely to experience dating violence than the boys were (65% versus 35%). Molidor (1995) studied gender differences in dating violence victimization and found that boys reported experiencing higher rates of psychological abuse in these areas: (a) being ordered to steal money from others; (b) being sworn at; (c) being given "the silent treatment"; (d) having affection withheld; (e) having a partner who was insensitive to sexual needs; and (f) being blamed for the partner's problems. Foshee (1996) examined gender differences in detail and found that: (a) girls perpetrate more mild violence when controlling for self-defense; (b) girls perpetrate more violence out of self-defense; (c) boys perpetrate almost all sexual violence; (d) girls sustain more sexual violence and psychological abuse than boys; and (e) girls sustain more injuries from dating violence than boys. Molidor and Tolman (1998) supported Foshee's findings. Girls in their sample were much more likely to be punched and forced into sexual activity, and boys were more likely to be pinched, slapped, scratched, or kicked. They also found that boys report being not hurt at all or hurt only a little in their most severe experience with victimization, whereas girls report being hurt 48% of the time and seriously physically injured (i.e., bruises and/or injuries needing medical attention) 34% of the time. Of the boys in their study, 17% reported that girls used violence against them only in response to sexual advances made by them. These authors further indicated that boys usually respond to violence perpetrated by girls by laughing at it or ignoring it, while girls reported having to defend themselves against violence in 36% of cases. This suggests that many of the acts reported by boys as perpetrated by girls may in fact be self-defense. Girls reported that boys initiate violence 70% of the time, as compared to boys' reports of girls' initiation of violence 27% of the time (Molidor & Tolman, 1998). Other experts found that, compared to girls, boys were significantly more likely to admit beating up their partners (Giordano et al., 1999; Makepeace, 1986).

Perpetration of violence by both genders is a characteristic unique to the problem of adolescent dating violence. The literature on domestic violence does not report the same equality of perpetration that has been identified in the adolescent dating violence literature, perhaps because the period of adolescence, a special developmental stage, is accompanied by sexual characteristics that are distinctly different from the characteristics of adults (Downs & Hillje, 1993). Wekerle and Wolfe (1999) assert that a developmental perspective may explain why perpetration rates of dating violence are more equal, by gender, than perpetration rates of domestic violence. They suggest that a mutually coercive and violent dynamic may form during adolescence, a time when males and females are more equal on a physical level. This physical equality allows girls to assert more power through physical violence than is possible for an adult female attacked by a fully physically mature man.

Prevalence

Inconsistent findings in the literature make it difficult to identify current trends in prevalence rates. Medical doctors estimate that 10% of intentional injuries to adolescents are the result of dating violence (Sege, Stigol, Perry, Goldstein, & Spivak, 1996). The Center for Disease Control (1998), in a review of a 1997 Youth Risk Behavior Survey, revealed that students in grades 9 through 12 engaged in 115 physical fights per 100 adolescents during the 12 months preceding the survey. In a recent follow-up study of this population, 1.8% of the males and 4.2% of the females reported that their most recent physical altercation was with a dating partner (Krieter et al., 1999). Bergman (1992), in her sample of ninth- through twelfth-grade students from three Midwestern high schools, found that 25% of adolescent females self-reported physical and/or sexual violence, and 32% reported experiencing some type of violence in their current dating relationships. Further, 45% of the females and 40% of the males incurred repeated physical violence. Foshee (1996) noted that 38% of the adolescents in her study reported being victimized by dating violence, and 21% reported perpetrating it. Jezl, Molidor, and Wright (1996) surveyed a group of 232 racially diverse high school students by administering a self-report questionnaire designed specifically for measuring dating violence in teenagers. Around 60% of the students reported being victims of dating violence, either in the past or currently. Molidor and Tolman (1998) reported that, among boys and girls who had ever dated, 36.5% had experienced physical violence in their relationships. Around half of "at risk" adolescents sampled in a recent study by O'Keefe (1998) reported being both victims and perpetrators of violence in their dating relationships.

Prevalence rates infrequently distinguish percentages for various races. Researchers who reported their results by race have indicated the following: Non-Caucasian adolescents have reported greater involvement in perpetration of and victimization by dating violence than Caucasian adolescents; a greater proportion of black adolescents was involved as the aggressors in all categories of violence related to serious relationships; for black and white females, there was a significant relationship between dating a high number of partners and being a dating violence victim; and, for black and white males, there was a significant relationship between number of sexual partners, physical fighting, and weapon carrying, and being a date violence victim or perpetrator (Foshee et al., 1996; Valois, Oeltemann, Waller, & Hussey, 1999). An adolescent dating violence study conducted in another culture revealed that Xhosa-speaking women in South Africa reported that male violence and coercion dominate the sexual relationships of teen girls (Wood, Maforah, & Jewkes, 1998).

Methodological Issues and Patterns

Patterns present in the methodologies of the dating violence studies examined for this chapter may explain inconsistent prevalence rates. Most of the researchers used samples of high school or middle school students, collected in classrooms within the school day. Two research teams collected data from a healthcare setting (Culross, 1999; Sege et al., 1996), and one research team implemented a community intervention in conjunction with the school system (Foshee et al., 1996, 1998). Collection of data from students during the school day may have had some impact on research results; school settings may not be the best place for collecting, from adolescents, data regarding dating violence. Researchers should consider conducting studies of adolescents in settings where they may answer personal questions more comfortably: doctors' offices, hospitals, their own homes, after-school and youth-group clubhouses, gym classes, soccer and softball practice locations, and community centers.

Many scales used to measure conflict in adolescents' relationships were originally designed to measure marital conflict in adult relationships. Few studies mention the reliability and validity of scores collected from the teen populations because the instruments used were not designed for teens' responses. Few assessment instruments have been developed and designed for specific use with adolescents who were subjected to dating violence (Riggs, 1993). Experts admit that researchers of adolescent dating violence often conduct their studies with instruments that have questionable metric qualities and can yield only small study samples (LaVoie, Vezina, Piche, & Boivin, 1995). However, some experts have developed and validated scales specifically to measure intimate violence in adolescent interpersonal relationships (i.e., Wolfe, Wekerle, Reitzel-Jaffe, & Lefebvre, 1998).

IDENTIFICATION, CLASSIFICATION, AND PREDICTION OF ADOLESCENT DATING VIOLENCE

As social workers, we are concerned with determining how to identify, classify, and predict social problems. So far, we have been unsuccessful at identifying consistent rates of adolescent involvement in dating violence. Perhaps this is due, in part, to the different definitions that are used to measure involvement in violence. Or, such rates may be hidden because incidents of adolescent dating violence are typically underreported (Bergman, 1992; Molidor & Tolman, 1998; Wekerle & Wolfe, 1999), and, because of a lack of counseling and of medical care for emotional and physical injuries, may lead to adverse effects.

Adolescents who are involved in dating violence may be classified as perpetrators or victims. Perpetrators are defined as adolescents who commit acts of violence toward a dating partner. Victims are defined as adolescents who have an act of violence inflicted upon them by a dating partner. Both boys and girls may report that they are perpetrators and/or victims of adolescent dating violence.

The violence can be classified as physical, emotional, and/or psychological. Physical violence can be defined as aggressive, tactile, bodily contact, between dating or intimate adolescents, that may result in physical and/or emotional injury. Emotional or psychological violence can be defined as improper behavior by adolescents that results in harm to the mental, emotional, and/or psychosocial functioning of a dating partner. These definitions are based on Barker's (1995) definition of violence. It is helpful to classify dating violence in these ways because it allows researchers to determine the severity of the problem and the extent of injury that results from dating violence.

The following section reviews several studies that have determined the risk and protective factors that can be used for identification, classification, and prediction of dating violence within personal, familial, and societal domains.

Personal Risk Factors Associated with Adolescent Dating Violence

Perceived beneficial outcomes have been associated with the use of dating violence among boys (O'Keefe, 1998; Williams & Martinez, 1999). Experts have reported that boys' efforts to gain control in a dating relationship, and their dissatisfaction with relationship power, predict physical and psychological dating abuse (Ronfeldt, Kimerling, & Arias, 1998). O'Keefe (1997) found that girls were more likely to be violent toward a dating partner when they believed that female-to-male violence was acceptable and male-to-female violence was not acceptable. Bethke and DeJoy (1993) reported that relationship status affected the acceptability of violence and the actions (such as ending the relationship), following a violent episode, that are viewed as being acceptable. Another study demonstrated that reactions to receipt of violence were most strongly correlated with the expressed use of dating violence. High levels of an attitude of romantic jealousy, which was also highly correlated with verbal aggression, followed (Bookwala et al., 1992). Foshee, Bauman, and Fletcher (1999) found that adolescents who were perpetrators of dating violence were more accepting of the use of dating violence than adolescents who were not perpetrators.

The length of the dating relationship and the number of dating experiences may affect the likelihood of adolescents' involvement in violence. Some studies (Bergman, 1992; Roscoe & Callahan, 1985) reported that up to 35% of violence occurred in short-term relationships (less than six months), and 6% of violence occurred in relationships of 2 years or longer (Roscoe & Callahan, 1985). Another expert suggested that longer relationships have an increased likelihood of violence (O'Keefe, 1997). Reuterman and Burcky (1989) found that adolescents who experienced dating violence reported a higher number of dating experiences. To an alarming degree, teens tend to minimize or rationalize severe abuse in more serious relationships (Becky & Farren, 1997).

Low self-esteem has been found to be a predictor of involvement in dating violence (Burke, Stets, & Pirog-Good, 1988; O'Keefe, 1998; Sharpe & Taylor, 1999; Stets & Pirog-Good, 1987). It is also reported that involvement in dating violence causes diminishment in self-esteem (Kasian & Painter, 1992); however, other researchers suggest that self-esteem is not related to involvement in dating violence (Bird, Stith, & Schladale, 1991; Makepeace, 1981).

Some evidence suggests that mental health disorders, such as antisocial personality disorder, may play a role in adolescents' involvement in dating violence, although this has not been explored at length (Williams & Martinez, 1999). Criminology researchers suggest that delinquent behavior as a child increases the likelihood of involvement in other delinquent behavior, including dating violence, as an adolescent (Giordano et al., 1999).

Success in school has been associated with the likelihood of involvement in dating violence. Bergman (1992) found a relationship between lower high school grade-point averages and involvement in dating violence. Reuterman and Burcky (1989) found that high school students involved in date fighting were more likely (a) to have been suspended or expelled from school and (b) to be following a general high school academic program, rather than a college preparatory academic program.

The following situational risk factors have also been correlated with adolescent involvement in dating violence: (a) jealousy, (b) need for power, (c) need for control, (d) disagreements about sex and sexual activity, (e) higher number of suicide attempts, (f) greater number of sexual partners, (g) riding in a car with someone consuming alcohol, (h) injection of illegal drugs, (i) alcohol use before last sexual encounter, (j) alcohol use in general, (k) unplanned pregnancies, (l) forced sexual contact, (m) inhalant use, (n) general sexual activity, (o) number of times getting someone pregnant, (p) frequency of dating experiences, (q) thoughts that one is watching out for the other's well-being, and (r) number of times threatened with physical violence in the past 12 months (Bergman, 1992; Burcky, Reuterman, & Kopsky, 1988; Carlson, 1987; Krieter et al., 1999; Molidor & Tolman, 1998; Williams & Martinez, 1999).

Violence to induce sexual activity is reported most frequently. The violence results, in most instances, from sexual advances, jealousy, or alcohol use, according to the literature examined for this chapter.

Family Factors

For some adolescents, dating violence may be a continuation of violence they have been reared with. Adolescents who grow up exposed to violence in the home may be desensitized to it (Williams & Martinez, 1999). Their experience with violence in their family of origin may increase their involvement in violent dating relationships and/or model how to interact violently in intimate relationships (Carlson, 1987; Foshee et al., 1999; Gwartney-Gibbs, Stockard, & Bohmer, 1987; O'Keefe, Brockopp, & Chew, 1986; Simons, Lin, & Gordon, 1998; Smith & Williams, 1992). O'Keefe (1998) found evidence that high school students who witnessed violence in their family of origin were more likely to be involved in dating violence either as victims or perpetrators, although not all of the students in her sample were violent with dating partners. Riggs and O'Leary (1996) found that dating aggression was associated with exposure to violence in the family of origin for female but not for male college students. Some studies have failed to find that parental violence is a factor in teen dating violence (Riggs & O'Leary, 1996; Sigelman, Berry, & Wiles, 1984; Simons et al., 1998).

Harsh corporal punishment in the family of origin has also been associated with dating violence in adolescents (Foshee et al., 1999; O'Leary et al., 1989; Simons et al., 1998). Reuterman and Burcky (1989) found that adolescents who had experienced dating violence were more likely than others to report that their parents had used various forms of violence as means of disciplining them. Harsh discipline from a father was particularly predictive of involvement in dating violence, and those involved in dating violence were less likely than others to report close relationships with their fathers. Also, being hit by a mother was not associated with the perpetration of dating violence for females, but was associated for males. In another study, being hit by a father was positively associated with dating violence for either gender (Foshee et al., 1999).

Some authors suggest that previous experience of child abuse/maltreatment may contribute to adolescent involvement in dating violence (O'Keefe, 1998; Wekerle & Wolfe, 1999). Parent-child violence has been shown as one predictor of the use of courtship violence with females but not with males (Tontodonato & Crew, 1992). Wolfe et al. (1998), using a sample of over 300 15-year-olds, reported that youths who are maltreated prior to age 12 have significantly more verbal and physical conflicts with dating partners than nonmaltreated youths. Other researchers have discovered consistent findings (Marshall & Rose, 1988; Riggs, O'Leary, & Breslin, 1990).

Simons et al. (1998) examined criminology literature and suggested that adolescent dating violence may be a manifestation of antisocial tendencies that develop in childhood, often as a result of antisocial parents who have ineffective parenting strategies. The results of their 3-year longitudinal survey of parents and adolescents in 3 counties provided strong evidence in support of their hypothesis. Experts have found evidence that unskilled parenting and family instability mediate the development of antisocial behavior, which plays an important role in dating violence with an intimate partner in adolescence (Capaldi & Clark, 1998; Wekerle & Wolfe, 1999).

Research suggests that divorce in the family of origin may contribute to dating violence in adolescence. Billingham and Notebaert (1993) reported that students who came from a divorced family reported higher involvement in violent behavior.

Societal Factors

Adolescents are often exposed to violence in their schools and communities (Krieter et al., 1999), and this exposure appears to play a role in dating violence involvement (Bergman, 1992; O'Keefe, 1998; Williams & Martinez, 1999), particularly when coupled with the stressor of violence within the family of origin (O'Keefe, 1998). Malik, Sorenson, and Aneshensel (1997) found, in their study of over 700 high school students, that weapon ownership, coupled with injuries resulting from community violence, were associated with higher rates of student involvement in dating violence. They concluded that high school students who are exposed to violence in one context, such as their community of origin, appear to have crossover effects related to victimization and perpetration in another context, such as involvement in dating violence. Another study suggested that girls who grow up in neighborhoods where more female-female fighting takes place may be more prone to commit other delinquent acts, such as participation in and acceptance of dating violence (Giordano et al., 1999). In other words, teen violence in one context may result in violence in other contexts.

O'Keefe (1998) found that male adolescents' involvement in dating violence was mediated by lower socioeconomic status. This supported the findings of a later study, which suggested that women reared in economically depressed areas might be more prone to engage in dating violence (Giordano et al., 1999). Other experts found that subjects who experienced dating violence were more likely to live in rural areas (Reuterman & Burcky, 1989). Perhaps the economic stressors often associated with rural living are somehow associated with higher rates of dating violence in rural areas.

Pop culture may encourage dating violence in adolescents (Bergman, 1992). Teens are often exposed to music and media that perpetuate the use of violence against women as acceptable and sometimes expected. Results reported from 60 African American boys and girls ranging in age from 11 to 16 years suggested significant acceptance of violence against women among adolescents who were exposed to rap music videos depicting male and female violence (Johnson, Adams, Ashburn, & Reed, 1995).

EFFECTIVE PREVENTION PROGRAMS AND EMPIRICALLY BASED INTERVENTIONS

A search of the adolescent dating violence literature revealed 7 published program evaluations of 6 empirically based adolescent dating violence intervention programs. Of two of these programs conducted in Canada, one was led by a social worker (Avery-Leaf, Cascardi, O'Leary, & Cano, 1997; Foshee et al., 1996; Foshee et al., 1998; Hilton, Harris, Rice, Krans, & Varigne, 1998; Jaffe, Sudermann, Reitzel, & Killop, 1992; LaVoie, Vezina, Piche, & Boivin, 1995; MacGowan, 1997).

An examination of these studies revealed that the results of the evaluations of the dating violence intervention programs suggest that all programs produced positive changes.

The first evaluation published about an empirically based adolescent dating violence program was the Ontario primary prevention program (Jaffe et al., 1992). This program was empirically designed to increase knowledge of violence against women, to address sexist attitudes, to promote knowledge of the warning signs of abuse, to expand the definition of abuse, to provide information to be used as a tool by helpers in the community, and to develop antiviolence commitments in the community.

Evaluators reported that, posttest statistically significant positive changes in adolescents' attitudes, knowledge, and behavior were found on 22 of 48 self-report questionnaire items. Boys experienced significantly fewer changes in attitudes than girls—an indication that this particular intervention was designed in a way that was somehow more effective for girls.

The second program that we examined was the short-term and long-term Quebec dating violence program (LaVoie et al., 1995). The goals of the short-term program were: to show students that they have control over their dating environments, and to teach them to identify and denounce forms of control in their relationships. The goals of the long program were: to establish dating partners' rights, to teach students how to apply those rights to their dating environments, and to make students aware that each partner is responsible for respecting the rights of the other partner.

The evaluation results yielded significant differences in pretest and posttest scores. Results were more positive for girls than for boys. Both the long- and the short-term program contributed toward improving attitudes. Participants in the short-term program demonstrated the greatest improvement.

The next program we examined was the *Safe Dates* project (Foshee et al., 1996; Foshee et al., 1998), which seeks to prevent dating violence by challenging dating norms, addressing gender stereotyping, and improving conflict-management and help-seeking skills, as well as cognitive factors associated with seeking help.

Treatment and control groups were compared at baseline and follow-up, in the full sample and the subsamples. The analyses were conducted with schools as one unit of analysis, and matched pairs as a parallel unit of analysis.

Evaluation results suggested that, among the students in the full sample, treatment students were found to be more positive than control students. Treatment students: (a) were less supportive of prescribed dating violence norms; (b) were more supportive of proscribed dating violence norms; (c) perceived fewer positive consequences from use of dating violence; (d) used more constructive communication skills and responses to anger; (e) were less likely to engage in gender stereotyping; and (f) were more aware of victim and perpetrator services. The following positive traits were found among the treatment students (as compared to control students in the primary prevention subsample): (a) more supportive of proscribed dating violence norms; (b) more likely to perceive negative dating violence consequences; and (c) less engaged in gender stereotyping. The following traits were more positive for victim subsample treatment students: (a) less accepting of prescribed dating norms and gender stereotyping; and (b) more aware of victim services. The perpetrator subsample was more positive in perceiving more negative consequences resulting from dating violence, and being more aware of perpetrator services.

The next intervention evaluated was the aggression intervention in Long Island, New York (Avery-Leaf et al., 1997). The goals of the Long Island dating aggression project included delivering an intervention that: treats courtship aggression as a multidetermined phenomenon; is sensitive to gender inequities, while providing a didactic, skills-based approach focused on changing attitudes and enhancing skills; and recognizes that males and females may be both perpetrators and victims. To achieve these goals, the program had the following objectives: (a) promote equity in dating relationships by demonstrating how gender inequity fosters violence; (b) challenge attitudes toward violence as a means of resolving conflict; (c) identify constructive communication skills; (d) increase support resources for victims seeking help; (e) encourage all those involved in aggressive relationships to seek help; and (f) describe alternatives to violent dating relationships.

The evaluation results of this program supported the effectiveness of the five-session program for dating violence prevention. Rates of aggression, victimization, and injury did not significantly differ between treatment and control groups. More girls than boys reported being aggressive in a dating relationship in the previous year. There were no significant gender differences in reported rates of victimization or injury. There were significant pre- to post-program changes in treatment group attitudes that had justified male-to-female aggression and dating aggression. Students in the control group showed no change.

The next intervention that was examined was the teen dating violence program of Dade County, Florida (MacGowan, 1997). The goal of the Dade County intervention was to help students recognize dating violence, understand its causes, and make decisions to avoid/end abusive relationships.

The evaluators reported that, posttest, the treatment group scored significantly higher on a self-report dating-violence measure than the control group. There was also a significant main effect: academically advanced students scored significantly higher than regular students. The male advanced students achieved the highest and most significant gains in the treatment group. Overall, treatment group students significantly improved on 6 (out of 22) items. Males improved equally on the same amount of items but not the same specific items. Boys' attitudes related to forced sex improved, but they were significantly lower than girls' responses, both pretest and posttest, on issues of physical and sexual violence. The evaluators reported that, overall, there were significant differences in mean scores between those who received the intervention and those who did not.

The last dating violence intervention that was examined was the dating violence program in Ontario (Hilton et al., 1998). The goal of the program was to provide, in one school region, a controlled and consistent dating violence intervention designed to: increase students' knowledge of practical information about risk factors for violence; provide information about the laws regarding assault and sexual assault; and how to get help for interpersonal violence. The authors also noted that they would look for backlash effects.

The evaluators indicated that a half-day antiviolence seminar conducted as part of this study showed promising results related to violence prevention—without the expected backlash effect. There was some evidence that small workshops produced more desired changes than large assemblies. The evaluators asserted that the reported improvements in knowledge were not simply the result of taking the tests three times.

Trends emerged when the results of these available adolescent dating violence program evaluations were compared. All dating violence interventions were conducted within the school setting, and self-report scales were used to determine results for the study. All evaluators reported that the programs produced positive results via attitude change. However, no evaluation team conducted a long-term study, and teams that conducted follow-up studies suggested that the reported positive attitudes were diminishing over time.

Evaluators found differing rates of reports of victimization and perpetration. Study results revealed that more victimization than perpetration was reported (Foshee, 1996). They explained this by offering that 75% of the students reported dating partners who were either older or younger than themselves and were not exposed to the intervention (Foshee, 1996).

All of the interventions took place too late for primary prevention to occur. By definition, primary prevention is an action that keeps a social problem from occurring (Barker, 1995). However, dating violence interventions administered in middle school and high school take place too late for primary prevention to take place. Early romantic involvement has been associated with higher rates of early intercourse and involvement in dating violence (Makepeace, 1987; Miller, Christopherson, & King, 1993). Burcky, Reuterman, and Kopsky (1988) reported that 28.5% of female dating violence victims were between the ages of 12 and 13 years; 40% were between the ages of 14 and 15 years; 28.5% were between the ages of 16 and 17 years; and 2.3% were age 18 or over. Of the partners of these girls, 35% were over age 18 years.

It is clear that dating behavior may begin before students are exposed to a dating violence program. To achieve primary prevention of this problem, it is necessary to begin dating violence programs as early as kindergarten. Experts have suggested that adolescent dating violence may be a manifestation of dysfunctional conflict approaches that develop during childhood (Billingham & Sack, 1986). Based on this evidence, it may be necessary to include conflict resolution training in any early dating violence interventions.

Evaluation trends indicate that girls tend to respond more positively to dating violence interventions than boys do (Avery-Leaf et al., 1997; Foshee, 1996; Jaffe et al., 1992; LaVoie et al., 1995). Although boys' attitudes have been shown to improve in some areas, adolescent boys exposed to dating violence interventions still report negative attitudes about sexual violence and coercion (Foshee, 1996; LaVoie et al., 1995; MacGowan, 1997). Researchers have suggested that interventions may cause backlash in boys—an increased use of dating violence as a result of their own increased knowledge about dating violence (Hilton et al., 1998; Winkel & De Kleuver, 1997).

CASE MANAGEMENT AND THE
STRENGTHS PERSPECTIVE

Two approaches must be taken when working with teens. First and foremost, all teens should be screened for dating violence. If dating violence is identified, a referral to a case manager would be beneficial for the victim or perpetrator alike. Case managers working with these teens need to help them determine and draw on their strengths in order to eliminate violent relationships from their lives. Case managers could be the link between adolescents who are involved in dating violence and the services they need to break free from the violent relationships. It is important to connect victims to support groups and counseling services, and to be sensitive to transportation needs to and from such support services.

Case managers could also provide vital educational links between adolescents involved in dating violence, and significant adults. Case managers could help bridge the gap between adolescents and their parents. They could also provide educational support groups for parents, teachers, and other significant adults, to increase knowledge and understanding of the problem.

FUTURE RESEARCH EFFORTS

Patterns that emerge in the adolescent dating violence literature point to several areas where future research efforts are needed. Researchers suggest that dating violence may be a precursor to marital violence later in life (Bergman, 1992; Carlson, 1987; Simons et al., 1998). More research is needed to determine the extent of the link between dating violence and domestic violence. If it is found that dating violence is truly a precursor to adult domestic violence, then the problem of dating violence has lifetime risk implications for the future well-being of families in our society. Social-work research efforts must focus on generating information that can help to stop the development of patterns of violence in intimate relationships that are established in adolescence and may continue into adulthood. Carlson (1987) found that many students who reported involvement in dating violence remained in such relationships and had been involved in multiple violent relationships.

Study results often suggest that boys have a greater tendency to believe that sexual coercion is an acceptable way to gain sexual favors. Boys in long-term relationships are more likely to believe that dating partners owe them sexual favors if they have spent money on the girl, or if the girl has given the boy sexual favors in the past. Social-work researchers need to develop projects to examine how gender-specific dating violence interventions for boys can teach them acceptable dating behaviors and attitudes. Most efforts to change battering behavior focus on men who are in later years in the life cycle and are already batterers. Research indicates that males begin to exhibit controlling and abusive behavior early in life (Molidor & Tolman, 1998).

Dating violence interventions should begin as early as kindergarten. Such interventions must be developmentally appropriate for each grade level, so it is important for social workers and researchers to concentrate their efforts on developing age-appropriate interventions.

According to the literature, both genders tend to be at higher risk for involvement in dating violence when they are abusing drugs and alcohol. This repeated finding points to the need for dating violence interventions to include a substance-abuse component. Adolescents need to know that they are still expected to respect boundaries even if they become intoxicated. They must understand that, legally, a date who is intoxicated is not able to give consent to participate in sexual activity, and they are always responsible for their behavior and can be criminally prosecuted for violent behavior, even when intoxicated. Although much research has centered on how to provide effective substance abuse interventions, there is still no agreement on which methods are most appropriate for effectively addressing this subject with adolescents. Social workers' research efforts need to generate information about how best to combine dating violence and substance abuse interventions that will move us closer to the goal of prevention of intimate violence.

Patterns in the literature indicate that the reported rates of victimization do not match the rates of reported perpetration. Reasons for this may include: (a) perpetrators do not consider their behavior unacceptable or violent; (b) victims are dating older/younger perpetrators not included in the study results; and (c) perpetrators do not honestly report their acts of dating violence. One way to address this issue might be to conduct dating violence studies on matched couples. This has been previously suggested, but, to this point, no research project has been designed with this goal in mind.

CONCLUSION

Although not all areas have been explored, the literature makes a case for the tremendous prevalence of adolescent dating violence and its proposed causes and damaging effects. It is apparent from the existing research that there is a need for programs and interventions that can address dating violence at every level. However, to establish their effectiveness, dating violence interventions must be evaluated through stringent scientific methods. Unfortunately, an extensive search of the literature revealed only seven published empirical evaluations of adolescent dating violence prevention programs. Only one appeared in the social work literature and was conducted by a social worker, and two of the published evaluations were written about the same project. This absence of empirical information generated by the social work field is alarming, considering the serious nature of the problem and the fact that many dating violence interventions are developed and administered by social workers. It is essential that social work researchers assist in developing empirically based prevention programs that social work practitioners can implement to address the serious societal problem of adolescent dating violence. We must also unite to eliminate the use of programs deemed harmful. If we focus on the research suggestions derived from this extensive literature review, we can gain insight into dating violence that may result in eliminating dating violence and other types of violence that are infecting the lives of our adolescents.

REFERENCES

Arias, I., Samios, M., & O'Leary, K. D. (1987). Prevalence and correlates of physical aggression during courtship. *Journal of Interpersonal Violence, 2,* 82–90.

Avery-Leaf, S., Cascardi, M., O'Leary, K. D., & Cano, A. (1997). Efficacy of a dating violence prevention program on attitudes justifying aggression. *Journal of Adolescent Health, 21,* 11–17.

Barker, R. L. (1995). *The social work dictionary* (3rd ed.). Washington, DC: National Association of Social Workers.

Becky, D., & Farren, P. M. (1997). Teaching students how to understand and avoid abusive relationships. *School Counselor, 44,* 303–308.

Bergman, L. (1992). Dating violence among high school students. *Social Work, 37,* 21–27.

Bethke, T., & DeJoy, D. (1993). An experimental study of factors influencing the acceptability of dating violence. *Journal of Interpersonal Violence, 8,* 36–51.

Billingham, R. E., & Notebaert, N. L. (1993). Divorce and dating violence revisited: Multivariate analyses using Straus's conflict tactics subscores. *Psychological Reports, 73,* 679–684.

Billingham, R. E., & Sack, A. R. (1986). Courtship violence and the interractive status of the relationship. *Journal of Adolescent Research, 1,* 305–325.

Bird, G. W., Stith, S. M., & Schladale, J. (1991). Psychological resources, coping strategies, and negotiation styles as discriminators of violence in dating relationships. *Family Relations, 40,* 45–50.

Bookwala, J., Frieze, L. H., Smith, C., & Ryan, K. (1992). Predictors of dating violence: A multivariate analysis. *Violence and Victims, 7,* 297–311.

Burcky, W., Reuterman, N., & Kopsky, S. (1988). Dating violence among high school students. *The School Counselor, 35,* 353–358.

Burke, P. J., Stets, J. E., & Pirog-Good, M. A. (1988). Gender identity, self-esteem, and physical and sexual abuse in dating relationships. *Social Psychology Quarterly, 15,* 272–285.

Carlson, B. E. (1987). Dating violence: A research review and comparison with spouse abuse. *Social Casework, 68,* 16–23.

Capaldi, D. M., & Clark, S. (1998). Prospective family predictors of aggression toward female partners for at-risk young men. *Developmental Psychology, 34,* 1175–1188.

Centers for Disease Control and Prevention. (1998). Youth Risk Behavior Surveillance, United States, 1997. *MMWR CDC Surveillance Summary, 47,* 31998.

Culross, P. L. (1999). Health care system responses to children exposed to domestic violence. *Future of Children, 9,* 111–121.

Downs, A. C., & Hillje, L. S. (1993). Historical and theoretical perspectives on adolescent sexuality: An overview. In T. P. Gullotta, G. R. Adams, & R. Montemayor (Eds.), *Adolescent sexuality* (pp. 1–33). Newbury Park, CA: Sage.

Ehrensaft, M. K., & Vivian, D. (1999). Is partner violence related to appraisals of coercive control by a partner? *Journal of Family Violence, 14,* 251–266.

Foshee, V. A. (1996). Gender differences in adolescent dating abuse prevalence, types and injuries. *Health Education Research, 11,* 275–286.

Foshee, V. A., Bauman, K. E., Arriaga, X. B., Helms, R. W., Koch, G. G., & Linder, G. F. (1998). An evaluation of Safe Dates, an adolescent dating violence prevention program. *Journal of Public Health, 88,* 45–50.

Foshee, V. A., Bauman, K. E., & Fletcher, L. G. (1999). Family violence and the perpetration of adolescent dating violence: Examining social learning and social control processes. *Journal of Marriage and the Family, 61,* 331–342.

Foshee, V. A., Linder, G. F., Bauman, K. E., Langwick, S. A., Arriaga, X. B., Heath, J. L., et al. (1996). The Safe Dates project: Theoretical basis, evaluation design, and selected baseline findings. *The American Journal of Preventive Medicine, 12,* 39–47.

Giordano, P. C., Millhollin, T. J., Cernovich, S. A., Pugh, M. D., & Rudolph, J. L. (1999). Delinquency, identity and women's involvement in relationship violence. *Criminology, 37,* 17–29.

Gwartney-Gibbs, P. A., Stockard, J., & Bohmer, S. (1987). Learning courtship aggression: The influence of parents, peers and personal experiences. *Family Relations, 36,* 276–282.

Hilton, N. Z., Harris, G. T., Rice, M. E., Krans, T. S., & Varigne, S. E. (1998). Antiviolence education in high schools: Implementation and evaluation. *Journal of Interpersonal Violence, 13,* 726–742.

Jaffe, P. G., Sudermann, M., Reitzel, D., & Killop, S. M. (1992). An evaluation of a secondary school prevention program on violence in intimate relationships. *Violence and Victims, 7,* 129–146.

Jezl, D. R., Molidor, C. E., & Wright, T. L. (1996). Physical, sexual and psychological abuse in high school dating relationships: Prevalence rates and self-esteem issues. *Child and Adolescent Social Work Journal, 13,* 69–87.

Johnson, J. D., Adams, M. S., Ashburn, L., & Reed, W. (1995). Differential gender effects of exposure to rap music on African American adolescents' acceptance of teen dating violence. *Sex Roles, 33,* 597–605.

Kasian, M., & Painter, S. L. (1992). Frequency and severity of psychological abuse in a dating population. *Journal of Interpersonal Violence, 7,* 350–364.

Koss, M. P., Gidyez, C. A., & Wisnieweski, N. (1987). The scope of rape: Incidence and prevalence of sexual aggression and victimization in a national sample of higher education students. *Journal of Consulting and Clinical Psychology, 55,* 162–170.

Krieter, S. R., Krowchuk, D. P., Woods, C. R., Sinal, S. H., Lawless, M. R., & DuRant, R. H. (1999). Gender differences in risk behaviors among adolescents who experience date fighting. *Pediatrics, 104,* 1286–1298.

Lane, K. E., & Gwartney-Gibbs, P. A. (1985). Violence in the context of dating and sex. *Journal of Family Issues, 6,* 45–59.

LaVoie, F., Vezina, L., Piche, C., & Boivin, M. (1995). Evaluation of a prevention program for violence in teen dating relationships. *Journal of Interpersonal Violence, 10,* 516–524.

Makepeace, J. M. (1981). Courtship violence among college students. *Family Relations, 30,* 97–102.

Makepeace, J. M. (1986). Gender differences in courtship violence victimization. *Family Relations, 35,* 383–388.

Makepeace, J. M. (1987). Social factors and victim-offender differences in courtship violence. *Family Relations, 36,* 87–91.

MacGowan, M. J. (1997). An evaluation of a dating violence program for middle school students. *Violence and Victims, 12,* 223–235.

Malik, S., Sorenson, S. B., & Aneshensel, C. S. (1997). Community and dating violence among adolescents: Perpetration and victimization. *Journal of Adolescent Health, 21,* 291–302.

Marshall, L. L., & Rose, P. (1988). Family of origin and courtship violence. *Journal of Counseling and Development, 66,* 414–418.

Miller, B. C., Christopherson, C. R., & King, P. K. (1993). Sexual behavior in adolescents. In T. P. Gullotta, G. R. Adams, & R. Montemayor (Eds.), *Adolescent sexuality* (pp. 55–76). Newbury Park, CA: Sage.

Molidor, C. E. (1995). Gender differences of psychological abuse in high school dating relationships. *Child and Adolescent Social Work Journal, 12,* 119–134.

Molidor, C., & Tolman, R. M. (1998). Gender and contextual factors in adolescent dating violence. *Violence against Women, 4,* 180–194.

O'Keefe, M. (1997). Predictors of dating violence among high school students. *Journal of Interpersonal Violence, 12,* 546–569.

O'Keefe, M. (1998). Factors mediating the link between witnessing interparental violence and dating violence. *Journal of Family Violence, 13,* 39–57.

O'Keefe, N. K., Brockopp, K., & Chew, E. (1986). Teen dating violence. *Social Work, 46,* 3–8.

O'Leary, K. D. (1988). Physical aggression between spouses: A social learning theory perspective. In V. B. Van Hasselt, R. L. Morrison, A. S. Bellack, & M. Hersen (Eds.), *Handbook of family violence* (pp. 31–55). New York: Plenum Press.

O'Leary, K. D., Barling, J., Arias, I., Rosenbaum, A., Malone, J., & Tyree, A. (1989). Prevalence and stability of physical aggression between spouses: A longitudinal analysis. *Journal of Consulting and Clinical Psychology, 57,* 263–268.

Reuterman, N. A., & Burcky, W. D. (1989). Dating violence in high schools: A profile of the victim. *Psychology, 26,* 1–9.

Riggs, D. R. (1993). Relationship problems and dating aggression. *Journal of Interpersonal Violence, 8,* 18–35.

Riggs, D. S., & O'Leary, K. D. (1989). Theoretical model of courtship aggression. In M. Pirog-Good & J. Stets (Eds.), *Violence in dating relationships: Emerging social issues* (pp. 53–71). New York: Praeger.

Riggs, D. S., & O'Leary, K. D. (1996). Aggression between heterosexual dating partners: An examination of a causal model of courtship aggression. *Journal of Interpersonal Violence, 11,* 519–540.

Riggs, D. S., O'Leary, K. D., & Breslin, F. C. (1990). Multiple correlates of physical aggression in dating couples. *Journal of Interpersonal Violence, 5,* 61–73.

Roscoe, B., & Callahan, J. (1985). Adolescents' self-reports of violence in families and dating relationships. *Adolescence, 20,* 545–553.

Ronfeldt, H. M., Kimerling, R., & Arias, I. (1998). Satisfaction with relationship power and the perpetration of dating violence. *Journal of Marriage and the Family, 60,* 70–79.

Saunders, D. G. (1986). When battered women use violence: Husband abuse or self-defense? *Violence and Victims, 1,* 47–60.

Sege, R., Stigol, L. C., Perry, C., Goldstein, R., & Spivak, H. (1996). Intentional injury surveillance in a primary care pediatric setting. *Archives of Pediatric and Adolescent Medicine, 150,* 277–283.

Sharpe, D., & Taylor, J. K. (1999). An examination of variables from a social-developmental model to explain physical and psychological dating violence. *Canadian Journal of Behavioural Science, 31,* 165–175.

Shook, N. J., Gerrity, D. A., Jurich, J., & Segrist, A. E. (2000). Courtship violence among college students: A comparison of verbally and physically abusive couples. *Journal of Family Violence, 15,* 1–23.

Sigelman, C. K., Berry, C. J., & Wiles, K. A. (1984). Violence in college students' dating relationships. *Journal of Applied Social Psychology, 5,* 530–548.

Simons, R. L., Lin, K. H., & Gordon, L. C. (1998). Socialization in the family of origin and male dating violence: A prospective study. *Journal of Marriage and the Family, 60,* 467–478.

Smith, J. P., & Williams, J. G. (1992). From abusive household to dating violence. *Journal of Family Violence, 7,* 153–165.

So-Kum Tang, C., Critelli, J. W., & Porter, J. F. (1995). Sexual aggression and victimization in dating relationships among Chinese college students. *Archives of Sexual Behavior, 24,* 47–54.

Steiner, H., & Feldman, S. S. (1996). General principles and special problems. In H. Steiner (Ed.), *Treating adolescents* (pp. 1–42). San Francisco: Jossey-Bass.

Stets, J. E., & Pirog-Good, M. A. (1987). Violence in dating relationships. *Social Psychology Quarterly, 50,* 237–246.

Sugarman, D. B., & Hotling, G. T. (1989). Violent men in intimate relationships: An analysis of risk markers. *Journal of Applied and Social Psychology, 19,* 1034–1048.

Tontodonato, P., & Crew, B. K. (1992). Dating violence, social learning theory and gender: A multivariate analysis. *Violence and Victims, 7,* 3–14.

Valois, R. F., Oeltemann, J. E., Waller, J., & Hussey, J. R. (1999). Relationship between number of sexual intercourse partners and selected health risk behaviors among public high school adolescents. *Journal of Adolescent Health, 25,* 328–335.

Wekerle, C., & Wolfe, D. A. (1999). Dating violence in mid-adolescence: Theory, significance and emerging prevention issues. *Clinical Psychology Review, 19,* 435–456.

Williams, S. E., & Martinez, E. (1999). Psychiatric assessment of victims of adolescent dating violence in a primary care clinic. *Clinical Child Psychology and Psychiatry, 4,* 427–439.

Winkel, F. W., & DeKleuver, E. (1997). Communication aimed at changing cognitions about sexual intimidation: Comparing the impact of a perpetrator-focused versus a victim-focused persuasive strategy. *Journal of Interpersonal Violence, 12,* 513–529.

Wolfe, D. A., Wekerle, C., Reitzel-Jaffe, D., & Lefebvre, L. (1998). Factors associated with abusive relationships among maltreated and nonmaltreated youth. *Development and Psychopathology, 10,* 61–85.

Wood, K., Maforah, F., & Jewkes, R. (1998). "He forced me to love him": Putting violence on adolescent sexual health agendas. *Social Science and Medicine, 47,* 233–242.

Chapter 3 ————————————————————————————

CHILDREN AND ADOLESCENTS FROM VIOLENT HOMES

LISA A. RAPP-PAGLICCI

INTRODUCTION

The home, a safe refuge for most, remains the single most dangerous place for children and adolescents. It is estimated that 3.3 to 10 million children are exposed to partner abuse each year (Straus, 1991), and this violence occurs much more frequently in homes with children under 5 years of age (Office of Juvenile Justice and Delinquency Prevention [OJJDP], 2000). Until recently, children and adolescents who were living in violent homes were simply ignored or were viewed as unfortunate bystanders to violence. However, research studies have suggested that these youths are seriously affected by, and become unwitting victims of, the partner abuse that they witness. Immediate traumatization after violent events, short- and long-term psychological effects, and increased risk of physical abuse and death are frequently indicated for children who live in violent homes.

The belief that most violence in the home occurs outside of youths' view or knowledge is a common misconception. Children witness or are aware of a majority of violent incidents within the home (Suderman & Jaffe, 1999). In addition, direct child abuse is more likely to occur in households where partner abuse is present than in households without partner abuse (American Humane Association, 1994). This exposure places children and adolescents at significant immediate bodily risk, and risk for later problems; however, lack of information about children exposed to partner abuse, and disjointed services from child protective and domestic violence programs have resulted in poor service delivery and few effective prevention and intervention protocols.

CURRENT TRENDS AND ISSUES

Approximately 1.8 to 4 million women in the United States are physically abused by their partners annually (Straus & Gelles, 1986). Other forms of violent victimization have decreased by 27% in recent years, but the statistics on the problem of family violence in the United States remain unchanged (Office of Justice Programs [OJP], 2000). The number of women *killed* by intimates actually increased by 10% between 1997 and 1998 (OJP, 2000).

Fantuzzo, Boruch, Beriama, Atkins, and Marcus (1997) found that, in households where there was a substantial incidence of female assault, youths and young children under age 5 were disproportionately represented. As many as 500,000 children are encountered by police officers during domestic violence arrests each year (OJJDP, 2000). These children and adolescents are exposed to repeated partner violence and are involved in this violence in multiple ways. Harway (2000) defines exposure to violence as directly witnessing violence or being aware of the existence of violence without directly seeing it. Although many parents believe their children are unaware of the recurring domestic violence, these same children can describe the violent incidents in detail (Harway, 2000; Jaffe, Wolfe, & Wilson, 1990). Children, and especially adolescents, sometimes try to intervene between the violent couple. They may attempt to harm the abuser but become accidentally centered in the violence instead. Many times children try to call for assistance have been the precipitant cause of the dispute that led to violence or attempt to avoid harm, but are unsuccessful and seriously injured in the process (Fantuzzo et al., 1997; Suderman & Jaffe, 1999). These findings indicate that children and adolescents are not mere witnesses to violence; they are directly maltreated as a result of it. Children and adolescents in homes where partner violence occurs are physically abused or seriously neglected at a rate of 1,500% higher than the national average (OJP, 2000). They are also at an increased risk of being murdered (OJJDP, 2000).

The United States Advisory Board on Child Abuse and Neglect (1995) found that domestic violence is the single precursor to child deaths in the United States, and families that had open Child Protective Services (CPS) cases were 1.5 times more likely to have a recurrence of child maltreatment when partner abuse was present (DePanfilis & Zuravin, 1999).

It has become apparent that violence is not discrete; families enduring partner abuse are also enduring other forms of family violence. Child abuse and partner abuse are linked in several ways. First, batterers often abuse their children as well as their adult partners. As males become more aggressive toward their spouses, they also become more violent toward their children (Mills et al., 2000). Batterers who are commonly diagnosed with Antisocial Personality Disorder are often threatening, aggressive, and violent to people and animals. Bowen (2000) found that 54% of her sample of sexually abused children came from violent homes.

As males become more aggressive toward their partners, they become more violent toward their children (Ross, 1996). This same relationship is found among women (Mills et al., 2000). Unfortunately, battered women may also be abusing their children. Women who have been abused by their partners are more likely to physically abuse their children than women who have not been beaten (American Humane Society, 1994; Walker, 1984). Sometimes, abused women abuse their children to vent the frustration and anger created by their own abuse. However, at other times, children may be abused by their mothers to quiet them and reduce the stress and escalating anger in the house. In other words, abuse may be used to diminish the likelihood that the batterer will seriously abuse the woman and the children (Mills, 1998).

McGuigan, Vuchinich, and Pratt (2000) documented negative cognitions as mediating the relationship between domestic violence and child abuse. They found that the domestic violence promotes a negative view of the child for both parents and therefore places the child at considerable risk for abuse by both the perpetrator and the victim. Furthermore, families in which partner abuse occurs have fewer social supports, formal or informal. This can isolate the family and may place the children at risk for maltreatment (DePanfilis & Zuravin, 1999). Whatever the exact relationship between domestic violence and child abuse, the final result is clear. Partner violence has spillover effects on other family relationships (Brody, Arias, & Fincham, 1996) and therefore increases the risk of minor and severe maltreatment of children.

IDENTIFICATION, CLASSIFICATION, AND PREDICTION

Short- and Long-Term Effects

There is no doubt that children exposed to violence in the home suffer consequences (Harway, 2000). Richters and Martinez (1993) reported that chronic exposure to violence, especially when occurring in settings expected to provide safety and security (i.e., home), may negatively impact children's development. Other research has found that exposure to partner abuse is similar to exposure to an alcoholic parent or to witnessing a homicide (Rutter, 1979).

Jouriles, Murphy, and O'Leary (1989) found that children living in violent homes were four times more likely to suffer from psychological problems than children living in nonviolent homes. These psychological problems included internalizing disorders (e.g., anxiety) as well as externalizing disorders (e.g., aggression). Grych, Jouriles, Swank, McDonald, and Norwood (2000) found that close to one-third of children who were exposed to partner violence developed both internalizing and externalizing problems. Other studies indicated that children who were exposed to, as well as victimized by, violence exhibited more severe problems than children who were exposed only to violent events (McCloskey & Walker, 2000; O'Keefe, 1996; Raviv et al., 2001). In addition, Pelcovitz, Kaplan, DeRosa, Mandel, and Salzinger (2000) found that adolescents who were exposed to and victimized by domestic violence were at greater risk for depression, separation anxiety disorder, post-traumatic stress disorder, and oppositional-defiant disorder than adolescents living in homes without violence. Johnson and Ferraro (2000) have begun to identify various types of partner violence as well as different types of batterers; these differences may result in different short- and long-term effects for the children and adolescents who are exposed to them.

Overall effects of exposure to partner violence can include: anxiety, depression, low self-esteem, suicide, self-blame, withdrawal, somatization, anger, aggression, acting out, and substance abuse (Henning, Leitenberg, Coffey, Turner, & Bennett, 1996; Johnson & Ferraro, 2000). Children and adolescents may also exhibit problems with loneliness, social skills, peer friendships (Gleason, 1995; McCloskey & Stuewig, 2001), motor skills, problem solving (Gleason, 1995), learning, conflict resolution, and anger control (Pepler, Moore, Mae, & Kates, 1989).

Partner abuse also affects children's beliefs about gender roles and family interactions. For example, Graham-Bermann and Brescoll (2000) found that the amount of physical and emotional abuse sustained by the mother was significantly related to how much the children believed in the inherent superiority and privilege of men and accepted violence as an acceptable and necessary part of family interactions.

Research with adults has indicated that there may be long lasting effects to witnessing partner abuse (Moon, 2000). Retrospective studies have found that these adults had problems with intimate relationships and relationships with their parents (McNeal & Amato, 1998). Downs and Miller (1998) also found that adult females who witnessed partner abuse during their youth were more likely to develop adulthood psychiatric symptomatology, low self-esteem, and alcohol problems. Bowen (2000) found that 65% of females who had been in violent homes as children were later abused by their partners. Her study also suggests that the long-term effects of witnessing partner abuse are just as damaging as being victimized by sexual abuse.

The effects on children and adolescents exposed to partner abuse can range from mild emotional and behavioral disturbances to clinical-level psychiatric disorders and long lasting disturbances throughout adulthood (Rosenberg,

Giberson, Rossman, & Acker, 2000). Those who witness more severe abuse, or who are abused themselves during violent events, appear to suffer more severe consequences.

Assessment

The assessment of family violence can take many forms. For children and adolescents exposed to partner abuse, assessing the degree of abuse witnessed, or perpetrated on the youth, is very important for identifying the appropriate intervention (Kashani & Allen, 1998). The use of diagnostic tools can also be helpful for clinicians who need to assess youths' psychological status and behavioral problems. The most common assessments emerge from structured and semistructured interviews and questionnaires (Kashani & Allen, 1998). The following instruments are helpful for assessing the degree of exposure to violence, the level of traumatization experienced by the child, and specific psychological problems:

- *The O'Leary-Porter Scale* is a 20-item instrument that assesses the frequency of conflict between parents that occurs in front of the child. The child is asked to report how frequently he or she witnesses sarcasm, verbal arguments, and/or violence by the adults in the home (Porter & O'Leary, 1980).

- *The Child Witness to Violence Interview* is an inventory that uses 42 items to assess children's exposure to partner abuse. The inventory evaluates children's attitudes and beliefs about violence, their skills for keeping themselves safe, and their tendency to ascribe blame for the partner abuse to themselves (Jaffe, Wilson, & Wolfe, 1989).

- *Physical Aggression Scale of the Conflict Tactics Scale (CTS)* has a physical aggression subscale that can be used by children to rate the frequency of physical violence between their parents. Eight acts of violence are included in the scale, and the instrument can be used by both parents and children to identify differing perspectives on the violence in the home (Straus, 1979).

- *The Children's Perception of Interparental Conflict Scale (CPIC)* is a 51-item instrument developed to measure interparental conflict from the children's viewpoint. A child rates: the frequency, intensity, and resolution of parental conflict; how much the child feels threatened by parental conflict; and the degree to which the child harbors self-blame for the parents' conflict (Grych, Seid, & Fincham, 1992; Grych et al., 2000).

- *Violence Exposure Scale for Children (VEX-R)* was constructed to assess children's reports of their exposure to violence across several settings (home, school, neighborhood, and television) (Raviv et al., 2001). The child is asked to look at cartoon drawings and rate how often he or she has observed or been a victim of particular types of violence. Although a fairly new scale, beginning research has suggested that this scale is reliable for assessing violence exposure in children as young as 8 years of age (Fox & Leavitt, 1995).

- *The Levonn Scale* is a cartoon-based scale used for assessing distress symptoms in elementary school children. There are 39 items. Children are asked to rate their level of distress, using thermometers. It has been widely used with inner city children and the instrument has good test-retest reliability (r = .81) (Richters, Martinez, & Valla, 1990).

- *Trauma Symptom Checklist for Children (TSCC)* is a self-report instrument for children 8 to 16 years of age. The instrument is appropriate for detecting post-traumatic symptoms and can also be used for identifying sexual abuse. The instrument measures anxiety, depression, dissociation, and under- and over-arousal, and has been standardized with over 3,000 children who have witnessed partner abuse (Briere, 1996; Suderman & Jaffe, 1999).

- *Child Behavior Checklist (CBCL)* is a broadband measure to assess internalizing and externalizing problems. This scale has shown good reliability and validity, and is one of the most widely used measures for children. Separate forms exist for teachers, parents, and youth (Achenbach, 1991).

- *The Youth Self-Report (YSR)* is a child self-report measure that serves as a compliment to the CBCL (see above). This is a broadband measure (includes internalizing and externalizing problems) that focuses on social competencies (17 items) and behavioral problems (103 items) (Achenbach, 1987).

- *The Eyberg Child Behavior Inventory (ECBI)* is a commonly used measure for identifying conduct and behavioral problems in children from 2 to 16 years of age. The instrument includes 36 items that can be administered in only 15 minutes (Eyberg, 1980).

- *The Conners' Rating Scale* is a frequently utilized instrument for children ages 3 to 17 years. The instrument measures conduct, learning, anxiety, psychosomatic, obsession, and antisocial problems. The scale items range from 28 through 93 items, depending on the specific form used (Goyette, Conners, & Ulrich, 1978).

- *The Diagnostic Interview for Children and Adolescents—Revised (DICA-R)* is a diagnostic interview for children and adolescents from 6 to 17 years of age. This structured interview provides for most DSM diagnoses for both children and adolescents (Wellner, Reich, Herjanic, Jung, & Amado, 1987). This may be useful for clinicians who are unsure of the diagnoses or problems the child or adolescent may be manifesting.

- *The Anxiety Disorders Interview Schedule for Children (ADIS-C)* is a structured interview schedule that has both parent and child versions. The ADIS-C has good inter-rater reliability and is particularly helpful when the clinician presumes that an anxiety disorder is present (Silverman & Nelles, 1988).

- *The Children's Depression Inventory (CDI)* is a rating scale consisting of 27 items to measure depression in children. Children rate statements based on their feelings during the past two weeks, and items are added to obtain a final score (Kovacs, 1992).

PREVENTION/INTERVENTION

Because there are so many detrimental short- and long-term effects for children and adolescents who are exposed to violence, prevention is crucial. Unfortunately, these youth have been neglected by practitioners and researchers alike. A few primary prevention programs have been developed to prevent dating violence in high school students; however, although these programs increased knowledge about violence in relationships, they had little effect on students' attitudes and/or behaviors regarding dating violence (Hilton, Harris, & Rice, 1994; Jones, 1987; Macgowan, 1997). A program evaluated by Jaffe, Suderman, Reitzel, and Killip (1992) identified some positive changes in females' knowledge and attitudes, but there were also unintended negative results from some males. Prevention programs have been virtually ineffective, for several reasons. Protocols are too brief, too shallow, and too vague. A one-day intervention with youth is clearly not enough to avert dating or partner abuse. Many youths who will later become involved in partner abuse have already witnessed it or have been abused themselves. Furthermore, providing knowledge only increases knowledge; it does not change gender or violence attitudes or behaviors.

Children exposed to partner abuse were also found to have high levels of other major risk factors, including poverty, a low educational level in the primary care provider, and a female as head of the household (Fantuzzo et al., 1997). Unfortunately, none of these risk factors is addressed in prevention protocols.

Children exposed to community violence can benefit from prevention programs that target specific components at specific developmental stages. For example, adolescents will probably benefit from prevention programs focused on dating relationships, and children ages 2 to 5 years may benefit from learning appropriate gender roles. (They are in the developmental phase that focuses on this issue.)

Because most of the interventions for children and adolescents exposed to violence originated in shelters for battered women and children, they are group-focused. This was the only means by which overwhelmed shelter workers could intervene with children from violent homes. As with preventive protocols, very few interventions have been developed for children. In addition, most reports that the intervention is effective are based solely on anecdotal information. Few rigorous research studies have yet to be conducted.

Jaffe et al. (1990) have developed a group intervention that has shown promise for 8-to-10 and 11-to-13-year-old children. The protocol has 10 sessions of 90 minutes' duration. The group sessions address: labeling feelings, dealing with anger, safety skills, social support, social competence, responsibility for violence, and understanding family violence. An evaluation concluded that there were significant differences between the randomly assigned wait-list control group and the treatment group, on attitudes, responses to anger, and responsibility for violence. These results continued after the 6-month follow-up period.

Peled & Davis (1995) have also developed a group treatment protocol for children exposed to family violence. They suggest having a male and female co-therapist team to model appropriate male-female relations during group sessions. In addition, the treatment goals are: develop new and more adaptive responses to past experiences, learn problem solving, examine responsibility for behavior, evaluate the effectiveness of aggression as a means of conflict resolution, and boost self-esteem. The protocol focuses on education and prevention, within a cognitive-behavioral framework. A qualitative study, including interviews and observations, found that most of the treatment goals were reached, upon completion of the group. However, the program has had one unintended effect: an increase in familial stress following discussions of the past traumatic events.

Among the several interventions that have been developed, two group interventions have been singled out as effective. More protocols need to be developed to assist children exposed to differing levels and types of violence. Treatment protocols for adolescents are even more uncommon, and research studies evaluating the effectiveness of any type of treatment program are extremely limited.

CASE MANAGEMENT AND STRENGTHS

Despite the deleterious results of being exposed to violence, children and adolescents always have strengths and resiliency that can be used as a foundation for treatment and case management. An ecological systems perspective can be extremely helpful in viewing problems from a multiple-system framework and assessing potential strengths of children and adolescents. After identifying the strengths in the multiple systems levels (individual, family, environment, culture), case managers can begin to develop goals and a treatment plan for the child and family. Referrals need to be comprehensive; however, as always when working with youth, they should be carefully timed so as not to overwhelm family members who are already in crisis. Multiple problem areas should be evaluated because these youth often have more than one developmental risk factor (i.e., poverty, community violence, discrimination, abuse, academic difficulties).

FUTURE RESEARCH

Despite the explicit and deadly implications for children and adolescents witnessing partner abuse, there remains a paucity of information and research regarding this problem. The lack of intervention protocols for youth exposed to family violence is especially patent. Service providers, such as CPS and domestic violence programs, usually fail to assist youths who have witnessed violence. Each agency simply assists its narrow target population and leaves other youths unassisted. Future research needs to (a) identify effective programs for children and adolescents and (b) differentiate which type of program is most beneficial for exposure to which type of violence. For example, children who have witnessed abuse *and* have been physically abused by the batterer may require differential interventions, compared to adolescents who have seen only minor violence within their household. Children who have lived a lifetime of witnessing their mother being abused by multiple men surely require distinct treatment approaches that are not needed by other children who have witnessed their father's verbal abuse of their mother. Likewise, female versus male youth, toddlers versus adolescents, and a majority versus oppressed youth often manifest varying effects from exposure to violence. Consequently, these youths need assistance that is specific to their situation, gender, age, and issues. Although domestic violence shelters have provided groups for these youths, they have been unstructured, or too brief, or unevaluated.

Prevention programs for youth witnessing violence are almost obsolete. Few programs have been introduced, and even fewer have been adequately evaluated. Those that have been developed seem to be based on the "too little too late" adage. Programs are often designed as one eight-hour schoolday for high school students. These programs are not evaluated because most prevention programs of such short duration are, by their very nature, ineffective. Schools have been the main sites for most of these programs, yet many schools have not allowed these programs because they continuously meet with resistance from male students and teachers, and from other persons who do not believe that deterring social problems should be the function of the school system.

CONCLUSION

Youth who witness partner abuse are detrimentally affected in multiple ways. Most youth who have been exposed to violence have short- and long-term consequences that seriously impair their psychological, social, educational, and physical development. Studies have verified that many children and adolescents are not insignificant witnesses to violence; rather, they have been sexually, physically, and/or emotionally abused along with the women in their families. This group might be termed an "underserved" population, but a more accurate statement is: They have been simply forgotten. Unfortunately, preventive and treatment protocols are still incommensurate with need, and research studies that evaluate the few developed programs are deficient in sample size, methodology, and follow-up. The lack of effectiveness and of interest in prevention and intervention programs is indicative of the disjointed delivery methods among service agencies (CPS and domestic violence), the silent societal acceptance of family violence, and the lack of interest in rights for children and women at the federal level.

Unfortunately, until partner abuse is taken seriously by those controlling federal funds, policies, and laws, this problem will remain unresolved and children and women will continue to be abused.

REFERENCES

Achenbach, T. (1987). *Manual for the Youth Self-Report and Profile.* Burlington: University of Vermont, Department of Psychiatry.

Achenbach, T. (1991). *Manual for the child behavior checklist and revised child behavior profile.* Burlington, VT: University Associates in Psychiatry.

American Humane Association. (1994). *Child protection leader: Domestic violence and child abuse.* Englewood, NJ: American Humane Association.

Bowen, K. (2000). Child abuse and domestic violence in families of children seen for suspected sexual abuse. *Clinical Pediatrics, 39*(1), 33–40.

Briere, J. (1996). *Trauma symptom checklist for children.* San Antonio, TX: Psychological Corporation.

Brody, G., Arias, I., & Fincham, F. (1996). Linking marital and child attributions to family processes and parent-child relationships. *Journal of Family Psychology, 10,* 408–421.

DePanfilis, D., & Zuravin, S. (1999). Predicting child maltreatment recurrences during treatment. *Child Abuse and Neglect, 23*(8), 729–743.

Downs, W., & Miller, B. (1998). Relationships between experiences of parental violence during childhood and women's psychiatric symptomatology. *Journal of Interpersonal Violence, 13*(4), 438–455.

Eyberg, S. (1980). Eyberg Child Behavior Inventory. *Journal of Clinical Child Psychology, 9*, 29.

Fantuzzo, J., Boruch, R., Beriama, A., Atkins, M., & Marcus, S. (1997). Domestic violence and children: Prevalence and risk in five major U.S. cities. *Journal of the American Academy of Child and Adolescent Psychiatry, 36*, 116–122.

Fox, N., & Leavitt, L. (1995). *The violence exposure scale for children (VEX)*. College Park: University of Maryland.

Gleason, W. (1995). Children of battered women: Developmental delays and behavioral dysfunction. *Violence and Victims, 10*(2), 153–160.

Goyette, C., Conners, C., & Ulrich, R. (1978). Normative data on revised Conners parent and teacher rating scales. *Journal of Abnormal Child Psychology, 6*, 221–236.

Graham-Bermann, S., & Brescoll, V. (2000). Gender, power, and violence: Assessing the family stereotypes of the children of batterers. *Journal of Family Psychology, 14*(4), 600–612.

Grych, J., Jouriles, E., Swank, P., McDonald, R., & Norwood, W. (2000). Patterns of adjustment among children of battered women. *Journal of Consulting and Clinical Psychology, 68*(1), 84–94.

Grych, J., Seid, M., & Fincham, F. (1992). Assessing marital conflict from the child's perspective. *Child Development, 63*, 558–572.

Harway, M. (2000). Families experiencing violence. In W. Nichols & M. Pace-Nichols (Eds.), *Handbook of family development and intervention* (pp. 391–414). New York: Wiley.

Henning, K., Leitenberg, H., Coffey, P., Turner, D., & Bennett, T. (1996). Long-term psychological and social impact of witnessing physical conflict between parents. *Journal of Interpersonal Violence, 11*(1), 35–51.

Hilton, Z., Harris, G., & Rice, M. (1994). *Evaluation of an educational intervention on aggression in high school students' relationships: Change without backlash* (Research Reports, 11(6)). Penetanguishene, Ontario: Mental Health Center.

Jaffe, P., Suderman, M., Reitzel, D., & Killip, S. (1992). An evaluation of a secondary school primary prevention program on violence in relationships. *Violence and Victims, 7*, 129–146.

Jaffe, P., Wilson, S., & Wolfe, D. (1989). Specific assessment and intervention strategies for children exposed to wife battering: Preliminary empirical investigation. *Canadian Journal of Community Mental Health, 7*, 157–163.

Jaffe, P., Wolfe, D., & Wilson, S. (1990). *Children of battered women*. Newbury Park, CA: Sage.

Johnson, M., & Ferraro, K. (2000). Research on domestic violence in the 1990s: Making distinctions. *Journal of Marriage and Family, 62*, 948–963.

Jones, L. (1987). *Dating violence among Minnesota teenagers: A summary of survey results*. St. Paul: Minnesota Coalition for Battered Women.

Jouriles, E., Murphy, C., & O'Leary, K. (1989). Interspousal aggression, marital discord, and child problems. *Journal of Consulting and Clinical Psychology, 57*, 453–455.

Kashani, J., & Allen, W. (1998). *The impact of family violence on children and adolescents*. Thousand Oaks, CA: Sage.

Kovacs, M. (1992). *Children's Depression Inventory: CDI manual*. North Tonawanda, NY: Multi-Health Systems.

Macgowan, M. (1997). An evaluation of a dating violence prevention program for middle school students. *Violence & Victims, 12*(3), 223–235.

McCloskey, L., & Stuewig, J. (2001). The quality of peer relationships among children exposed to family violence. *Development and Psychopathology, 13,* 83–96.

McCloskey, L., & Walker, M. (2000). Post-traumatic stress in children exposed to family violence and single-event trauma. *Journal of the American Academy of Child and Adolescent Psychiatry, 39*(1), 108–115.

McGuigan, W., Vuchinich, S., & Pratt, S. (2000). Domestic violence, parents' view of their infant, and risk for child abuse. *Journal of Family Psychology, 14*(4), 613–624.

McNeal, C., & Amato, P. (1998). Parents' marital violence: Long-term consequences for children. *Journal of Family Issues, 19,* 123–139.

Mills, L. (1998). Integrating domestic violence assessment into child protective services intervention: Policy and practice implications. In A. Roberts (Ed.), *Battered women and their families* (2nd ed., pp. 129–158). New York: Springer.

Mills, L., Friend, C., Conroy, K., Fleck-Henderson, A., Krug, S., Magen, R., et al. (2000). Child protection and domestic violence: Training, practice, and policy issues. *Children and Youth Services Review, 22*(5), 315–332.

Moon, M. (2000). Retrospective reports of interparental abuse by adult children from intact families. *Journal of Interpersonal Violence, 15*(12), 1323–1331.

Office of Justice Programs. (2000). *Fiscal year 2000 program plan: Resources from the field*. Washington, DC: U.S. Department of Justice.

Office of Juvenile Justice and Delinquency Prevention. (2000). *Safe from the start: Taking action on children exposed to violence* (NCJ Report No. 182789). Washington, DC: U.S. Department of Justice.

O'Keefe, M. (1996). The differential effect of family violence on adolescent adjustment. *Child and Adolescent Social Work Journal, 13,* 51–67.

Pelcovitz, D., Kaplan, S., DeRosa, R., Mandel, F., & Salzinger, S. (2000). Psychiatric disorders in adolescents exposed to domestic violence and physical abuse. *American Journal of Orthopsychiatry, 70*(3), 360–369.

Peled, E., & Davis, D. (1995). *Groupwork with children of battered women: A practitioner's guide*. Thousand Oaks, CA: Sage.

Pepler, D., Moore, T., Mae, R., & Kates, M. (1989). The effects of exposure to family violence on children: New directions for research and intervention. In G. Cameron & M. Rothery (Eds.), *Family violence and neglect: Innovative interventions* (pp. 41–73). Hillsdale, NJ: Erlbaum.

Porter, B., & O'Leary, D. (1980). Marital discord and childhood behavior problems. *Journal of Abnormal Child Psychology, 8,* 287–295.

Raviv, A., Erel, O., Fox, N., Leavitt, L., Raviv, A., Dar, I., Shahinfar, A., & Greenbaum, C. (2001). Individual measurement of exposure to everyday violence among elementary schoolchildren across various settings. *Journal of Community Psychology, 29*(2), 117–140.

Richters, J., & Martinez, P. (1993). The NIMH community violence project. I: Children as victims and witnesses to violence. *Psychiatry: Interpersonal and Biological Processes, 56,* 7–21.

Richters, J., Martinez, P., & Valla, J. (1990). *Levonn: A cartoon-based structured interview for assessing young children's distress symptoms.* Washington, DC: National Institute for Mental Health.

Rosenberg, M., Giberson, R., Rossman, B., & Acker, M. (2000). The child witness of family violence. In R. Ammerman & M. Hersen (Eds.), *Case studies in family violence* (pp. 259–291). New York: Plenum Press.

Ross, S. (1996). Risk of physical abuse to children of spouse-abusing parents. *Child Abuse and Neglect, 20*(7), 589–598.

Rutter, M. (1979). Protective factors in children's responses to stress and disadvantage. In M. W. Kent & J. E. Rolf (Eds.), *Primary prevention in psychopathology: Volume 3. Promoting social competence and coping in children* (pp. 49–74). Hanover, NH: University of New England.

Silverman, W., & Nelles, W. (1988). The anxiety disorders interview schedule for children. *Journal of the American Academy of Child and Adolescent Psychiatry, 27,* 772–778.

Straus, M. (1979). Measuring intrafamily conflict and violence: The Conflict Tactics (CT) scales. *Journal of Marriage and Family, 41,* 75–88.

Straus, M. (1991). *Children as witnesses to marital violence: A risk factor for lifelong problems among a nationally representative sample of American men and women.* Paper presented at the Ross Roundtable on Children and Violence, Washington, DC.

Straus, M., & Gelles, R. (1986). Societal change and change in family violence from 1975 to 1985 as revealed by two surveys. *Journal of Marriage and Family, 48,* 465–479.

Suderman, M., & Jaffe, P. (1999). Child witnesses of domestic violence. In R. Ammerman & M. Hersen (Eds.), *Assessment of family violence: A clinical and legal sourcebook* (pp. 343–366). New York: Wiley.

United States Advisory Board on Child Abuse and Neglect. (1995). *A nation's shame: Fatal child abuse and neglect in the United States.* Washington, DC: U.S. Department of Health and Human Services.

Walker, L. (1984). *The battered women's syndrome.* New York: Springer.

Wellner, Z., Reich, W., Herjanic, B., Jung, K., & Amado, H. (1987). Reliability, validity, and parent-child agreement studies of the Diagnostic Interview for Children and Adolescents (DICA). *Journal of Adolescent Psychiatry, 26,* 649–653.

Chapter 4

DOMESTIC VIOLENCE IN AFRICAN AMERICAN FAMILIES

LETHA A. (LEE) SEE, WILLIAM OLIVER, AND OLIVER WILLIAMS

INTRODUCTION

In early decades of America's history, domestic violence between cohabiting black partners living in slave quarters was not considered a serious, calamitous, or persistent offense. Likewise, conflictual relationships between white plantation owners and their spouses, who lived together in "the big house," were depicted as private, not felonious, family matters, and were not to be interfered with by law enforcement or ecclesiastical authorities (Cash, 1941; Elkins, 1959; Fox-Genovese, 1988; Gutman, 1976; Meier & Rudwick, 1970; Stampp, 1956).

History suggests that the white masters' age-old patterns of sovereign, and sometimes sexual, authority over black and white women, and their enforcement of obedience and enslavement were introduced by William Blackston, and codified into English Common Law in 1768. Accordingly, the established criterion—the "rule of thumb"—allowed a man to beat his wife with an instrument or a rod no bigger or thicker than his thumb (Dobash & Dobash, 1979; Schechter, 1982).

Chronologies of events during the antebellum period show that, in America's patriarchal culture, men who dominated, controlled, and violently brutalized women showed little remorse. In fact, some reasoned that their actions were justified—that it was God's way of using them as instruments for "controlling the sinful successors of Eve" (Miller, 2001, p. 108).

During this period of white male domination over black and white families, the U.S. Supreme Court upheld a Mississippi law that gave a husband the right to chastise his wife and enforce her obedience. Not until 1871 was the universal practice of wife beating declared illegal; but only two states, Alabama and

Massachusetts, vigorously enforced the law and rectified this injustice (Fox-Genovese, 1988; Miller, 2001; Steinmetz, 1971).

Because the literature fails to detail with precision the issue of domestic violence in black families (where neither men nor women had "legal personhood"), one can only deduce that the laws of each state were equally applicable to this racial subgroup. Historical transcriptions imply that titillating conversations were exchanged between white male "planters" who, in their social circles, described the beatings they administered to white women and to slave men and women (Cash, 1941; Elkins, 1959; Fox-Genovese, 1988; Franklin, 1974, 1988; Gutman, 1976; Meier & Rudwick, 1970; Stampp, 1956; Straus, Gelles, & Steinmetz, 1980).

As late as the beginning of the twentieth century, violent and contemptuous accounts were rarely quoted in the literature. Researchers did not scientifically examine, grasp, or even theorize about the dimensions of the abuse inflicted on minority groups (Daly, Jennings, Beckett, & Leashore, 1995). Even now, many African American researchers tiptoe around the issue of domestic violence, display aloof neutrality, and neglect to make a comprehensive meta-analysis of the problem, which, for some, was a part of their own childhood experience. Domestic violence, in years past, was denied, repressed, and dismissed as inconsequential by white males who viewed black and white women as little more than sources for procreation or as their own private property.

Unfortunately, contemporary America was slow in addressing domestic violence across racial lines. It spawned debates on the issue, then wantonly dismissed it. Typically, societal interest in domestic violence waxed and waned with the fluidity of the larger social order, which is often resistant to change. But some researchers began to observe a positive statistical correlation between wife beating and child abuse. When these atrocities were disseminated to the public, the problem, which involved power, politics, race, sex, and class, captured the nation's attention, tugged at its collective consciousness, and was finally placed on the national agenda.

During the 1960s—the decade marked by a convergence of the Civil Rights Movement and characterized by inner-city blacks' rebellion; urban riots; assassinations of leaders; the Vietnam Conflict; and the Peace Movement—interest in domestic violence reached its highest peak. But, against a background of so many other unsettling trends, interest in the issue waned again. New awareness was injected when Straus, Gelles, and Steinmetz (1986) conducted the first nationwide survey on domestic violence. Using an ascending continuum (The Conflict Tactics Scale of Violent Acts, or CTS) to collect data on violent acts (see Table 4.1), these researchers completed a groundbreaking effort in which 2,143 American couples participated. As reported on the CTS scale, 24% of the wives in the sample had experienced some physical abuse, and 11% of black women, compared to 3% of white women, were victims of husband-to-wife violence. Earlier, Steinmetz (1977a, 1977b) had concluded that female abuse was 400% greater among black couples than among white couples.

Between 1975 and 1985, other researchers and national surveys revealed that:

- Between 10% and 20% of all couples reported that some type of physical abuse was experienced by women (Straus & Gelles, 1986).

- A woman is physically abused every 12 seconds (Stark, Flitcraft, & Frazier, 1979); a woman is raped every 46 seconds; and a woman is murdered by a partner every six hours (American College of Obstetricians and Gynecologists [ACOG], 1989).

- Domestic violence is the leading cause of female injury and, nationally, the major cause of death among black women younger than 44 years (Stark, 1990).

- Among respondents, 16% indicated that some type of violence had occurred between spouses in the past year, and 28% reported some violence at a prior point in their marriage (Gelles & Cornell, 1990).

In sum, domestic violence has become an epidemic that reaches across every racial, socioeconomic, and class boundary in this nation. A representative number of African Americans were included in the Straus and Gelles (1986) national surveys; and the demographic profile of all groups studied matched the nation's demographic pattern as a whole, in regard to age, race, and socioeconomic status.

Following the First National Survey of Family Violence, women's groups were organized and the convergence of the "battered women's syndrome" was under way (Walker, 1979). Battered women's shelters were erected (McNeely & Jones, 1980), and the batterers' treatment movement was initiated (Walker, 1979, 1984).

In the 1980s, public tolerance for individuals who violated the law and destabilized American society was reduced. Thus, heightened interest in domestic violence led to a second national violence survey conducted by Straus and his colleagues. This investigation was comprised of a national probability sample of 2,143 married and unmarried couples (the same number of respondents as had participated in the first study). In this research, male-female relationships were more thoroughly investigated.

The intellectual turning point in collecting, compiling, and publishing research on domestic violence in African American communities came with the publication of Robert Hampton's (1987, 1991) seminal works, which laid the groundwork for research into violence perpetrated in black families. Perhaps the most controversial development from the Straus, Gelles, and Steinmetz studies was these authors' conclusion that relationship violence is being perpetrated by women who abuse their partners (McNeely & Mann, 1990; McNeely & Robinson, 1987; McNeely, Torres, & Cook, 2001; Saunders, 1988; Steinmetz, 1980; Stordeur & Stille, 1989). Although an important issue, the propensity of women to initiate, engage, and perpetuate violence is not addressed in this writing—nor is sibling violence, which is the most common form of aggression in all families (Gelles, 1997). Instead, the primary focus is on domestic partner abuse, with emphasis on black male perpetrators or family heads. Research on violence by women toward their intimate partners cannot be dismissed. At some point, this issue must be addressed if a holistic or solution framework of domestic violence in black families is to be fully understood.

In the 1990s and early 2000s, domestic violence became one of the most vibrant areas of research in the social sciences. Since the 1970s, popular accounts have contributed to a resurgence of responsible theoretical and empirical attention to domestic violence in African American families. Also, an impressive body of rigorous knowledge has brought about a better intellectual understanding of the problem across racial and ethnic groups (Edleson & Tolman, 1992; Hampton, 1987; Lockhart, 1985; Richie, 1994; Walker, 1984; West, 1999). This scholarship represents progress; for the years 1967 to 1987, only four entries on African American battered women were cited from a search of psychological, sociological, and social work literature (Coley & Beckett, 1988a, 1988b).

But, despite remarkable progress in intellectually examining violence in African American families, the Family Violence Prevention Fund and human rights outlets are reporting that battering remains the leading cause of injury to individuals from every socioeconomic and demographic status in America. Straus and Gelles (1986) estimated that between 1.8 and 3.6 million women in the United States are severely assaulted by their husbands or dating partners each year, and the American Medical Association has concluded that one in every three women in the United States can expect to be beaten by a male partner at some time during her adult life. Statistics are unclear regarding the number of males who are battered.

This chapter explores issues related to the occurrences of domestic violence in African American families. It presents an array of theoretical formulations that may prove useful to practitioners who must service both victims and perpetrators of domestic violence. A portion of the discussion stresses the use of a strengths perspective as a means of addressing the problem of domestic violence prevention. Intervention techniques that make use of empirically based group efforts in assisting black men at risk to redirect their battering behavior are presented. Finally, limitations of research associated with domestic violence in black families are addressed.

DOMESTIC VIOLENCE: A WORKING DEFINITION

Domestic violence has a plethora of definitions derived from a multiplicity of contexts. Some have been applied to negative emotions such as anger, and to motives such as the desire to harm or injure others. In any writing, the problem of semantics offers an intellectual challenge to scholars when the concept can be subjected to multiple nuances. Yet, a definition gives value and has an explicit role in distinguishing one interpretation of an issue from another. Principally, what is considered domestic violence in an African American family may well be a complex matrix of practices or an acceptable phenomenon in another culture. Confounding this problem are the many indicators of "domestic violence," as seen on Table 4.1, and each indicator falls under the rubric of partner abuse. Without a doubt, therefore, operationalization of terms is helpful in providing boundaries, clarity, and content to imprecise terms often couched or cloaked in a complex maze of verbiage. A discussion of the term "domestic violence" is virtually endless, but in this chapter it refers to a broad range of acts of interpersonal conflict involving victims and offenders who are in some way related. In sum, domestic violence may include child abuse, sibling violence, partner abuse, or elder abuse (Gelles, 1997).

One other point of clarity is in order. The terms "African American" and "black" are used interchangeably. Both represent descendants of tribes that lived along the west coast of Africa. These tribes were captured and sold as chattel to the highest bidder. Many were expatriated to "the New World"—the land areas of the eastern and southern regions of today's United States, and several island colonies in the Caribbean Sea—and sold in the slave trade. Even after 400 years of helping to build this nation, there are still culturally grounded messages and an axiom that all persons "are not" created equal. The "four horsemen"— power, pollution, population, and prejudice—still reign supreme in the United States. Vestiges of anguish, despair, hopelessness, and depersonalization (as we will later see) may well explain some of the violence exhibited by African American men and women, who continue to be marginalized in our society. Table 4.2 lists the multiple synonyms used to describe domestic violent acts.

Table 4.1 Indicators of Domestic Abuse in African American and Other Families

Physical Abuse	Emotional Abuse	Sexual Abuse	Economic Abuse
Beating	Alienating	Being forced to per-	Canceling allowance
Biting	Belittling	form:	Canceling charge
Branding	Berating	Anal sex acts	cards
Choking	Blaming	Fondling in public	Canceling insurance
Grabbing	Bullying	Forcing spouse to	Cutting allowance
Harnessing	Coercing	mimic pornography	Failing to pay for
Head banging	Cursing	Forcing wife to	children's school
Hitting	Cutting off friend-	have sex w/friends	lunches
Jobbing	ships	Genital sex acts	Hiding keys
Kicking	Falsely accusing	Oral sex acts	Hiding purse
Killing	Firearms	Rape	Threatening to make
Mutilating	Frightening	Sex with children	spouse/children
Pinching	Harassing		homeless
Preventing sleep	Humiliating		Threatening to
Pulling hair	Ignoring		repossess car
Punching	Insulating		
Pushing	Interrupting sleep		
Shoving	Intimidating		
Slapping	Isolating		
Smashing object	Leaving home for		
Stabbing	days		
Stomping	Minimizing		
Striking w/objects	Name calling		
Throwing/floor	Ostracizing		
Torturing	Ridiculing		
Tying-up	Spitting on spouse		
	Stalking		
	Stomping out of		
	room		
	Swearing		
	Terrorizing		
	Threatening		
	Vilifying		
	Withholding infor-		
	mation		

Table 4.2 Descriptions of Domestic Violence in African American Families

Domestic Violence May Be Referred to as:	
Interpersonal violence	Spousal violence
Marital violence	Wife beating
Male battering	Violent intimate relations
Female battering	Partner violence
Domestic assault	Intimate partner violence
Female-on-male violence	Wife assault
Spousal battering	Chronic abuse
Male bashing	Male assault
Cohabitant violence	Female-initiated violence
Husband battering	

USEFUL THEORIES FOR EXPLAINING DOMESTIC VIOLENCE IN AFRICAN AMERICAN FAMILIES

Sociosituational Stress and Coping Theory

Social situational stress and coping are domestic violence theories that contribute significantly to an understanding of how social conditions precipitated by the organization of American society may lead to racial disparities in the rates of intimate partner violence. Gelles (1997) has suggested that family violence is a product of the combined effects of two main factors:

1. The structural stress brought on by living conditions characterized by poverty, low income, lack of adequate education, and chronic unemployment.

2. Exposure to and acceptance of cultural norms that approve of violence as a means of resolving disputes among intimates.

Advocates of these perspectives offer the explanation that domestic violence emerges because of an interrelationship between structural pressures and cultural adaptation.

Sociosituational stress and coping theory offers another important insight into the disproportionate rates of domestic violence among African Americans. For example, a major source of the stress affecting these individuals is linked, as we will later see, to the high rates of unemployment and underemployment among black males. In a society that places considerable emphasis on construct-ing manhood identities in which men provide for their wives and children, those who are unable to adequately assume the provider/protector aspects of the tradi-tional male role are likely to experience significant stress. Psychologist Nathan Hare (1985) has suggested that many low-class African American men suffer from a "frustrated masculinity syndrome." Likewise, a host of scholars have de-scribed how adverse social conditions have contributed to deviant, dysfunc-tional, and criminal behavior among African American males. Resentment of these conditions is therefore clearly exhibited in the form of violence (Gibbs, 1988; Madhubuti, 1990; Staples, 1982).

A Social Learning/Behavioral Perspective

Another popular explanation of what causes domestic violence in black fami-lies is based on social learning theory. One of the tenets of this theory is that people learn to be violent when they grow up in violent homes and environ-ments (Bandura, 1969; Gelles, 1997). Proponents of this theory believe that the family is the central source that transmits coping strategies. Within their families, individuals learn to deal with stress and frustration. Their home is also the first place individuals experience or witness battering incidents and violent episodes—or are themselves physically victimized. Within their fam-ily, they are exposed to the techniques of how tension building is often fol-lowed by remorse and moral justification of violence as a means of settling disputes.

Social learning theory was not originally constructed to explain intimate part-ner violence among racial or ethnic groups. Nevertheless, it is a useful approach that aids our understanding of the contextual factors that contribute to the oc-currence of intimate partner violence among African Americans.

Another issue, black child development, has, for years, been a subject of in-quiry by African American social scientists and researchers (Kunjufu, 1984; Straus, 1994; Wilson, 1991). Although controversial, research on child abuse suggests that lower-class African American families appear to have higher levels of officially reported child abuse than whites and other racial groups of similar socioeconomic backgrounds. Thus, increased exposure to violence as a means of resolving disputes occurs as a consequence of residence in areas experiencing chronic rates of community violence (e.g., assault, aggravated assault, rape, robbery, and murder) within the immediate neighborhood (Jenkins & Bell, 1997). At an early age, many African American youths learn that violence is a routine feature of everyday life either within their family of origin or within their local community. This observation is supported by the evolving research that examines inner-city youths' exposure to community violence. In a study of 1,035 African American middle and high school students residing in inner-city Chicago, Uehara, Chalmers, Jenkins, and Shakoor (1996) found that 74% of their respondents had witnessed a robbery, a shooting, a stabbing, or a killing. These findings were supported by a number of other studies that examined this problem with similar respondents (e.g., Jenkins & Bell, 1997). What is significant about early exposure to intimate partner violence, or other forms of family or community violence? Individuals who have such histories are at increased risk of becoming male and female perpetrators of domestic violence (Greenfeld & Snell, 1999).

Resource Theory

The third cogent perspective that is instructive to our understanding of domestic violence is resource theory. Some researchers and practitioners have relied on this theory to explain the causes of black domestic turmoil. A fundamental assumption of this perspective is that all social systems (including families, civic organizations, governments, businesses, and so on) are to some degree dependent on force, or a threat of force, to achieve their goals. According to Gooden (1980), one of the major tenets of resource theory is that the more resources (including social, personal, and economic) a person can acquire, the less he or she will actually need to use force in an overt manner. Gooden's later (1980) position, therefore, suggests that men who lack resources (e.g., education, marketable vocational skills, income sufficient to maintain a family, and social status) are more likely to resort to violence, as a means of securing deference from their wives or girlfriends, than are men who possess wealth and power.

Resource theory has explanatory implications relative to uncovering factors that contribute to intimate partner violence among African Americans. Resource theorists have not generally sought to describe what factors contribute appreciably to the lack of resources, but they draw a link between a man's perception of his lack of resources—his lack of power to dominate and gain compliance through nonviolent means—and his subsequent reliance on violence as a means of gaining compliance. Implicit in this theory is the notion that many black men seek to dominate their romantic partners, and utilization of their greatest access to material resources facilitates domination. Moreover, when men lack legitimate resources, they generally resort to violence as a way of gaining compliance. Given their high rates of unemployment and underemployment, the disparity between the mean incomes of African American men and women is less than the mean income disparity that exists between white men and women (U.S. Bureau of the Census, 1999). Consequently, resource theorists would argue that one possible reason for the higher rates of intimate partner violence among African Americans is their access to fewer resources that are associated with nonviolent means of achieving compliance from wives and girlfriends (Lockhart & White, 1989).

Feminist Theory

Feminist theory has added another significant dimension to the professional literature on domestic violence. Although there is no single feminist position concerning domestic violence, certain commonalities are found in the literature. The basic assumption of feminist theory is that the economic and social institutions that constitute the foundation of American society are constructed to promote and support patriarchy in the social order and in the family. Partner abuse is one means used by men to maintain the subordination of women and to impose the men's will upon them. More specifically, proponents of feminist or gender-specific theories argue that the patriarchal organization of American society involves the sexualization of women as objects, restricts their access to opportunities involving decision making, denies them control over their bodies, and is the essence of the political, social, and cultural context in which men are socialized to believe they are entitled to use violence against women (Adams, 1989).

Feminist theory has recently been employed to explain a "laundry list" of "-isms" (sources of oppression in our society). For example, this theory presents an indisputable fact: Sexism is not unique to any specific group of men. Instead, it is common among men of all races, ethnicities, and class levels; that is, the gender-specific socialization of all males, regardless of their "life station," encourages them to internalize, and accept as legitimate, attitudes and behaviors that condone female domination as a male entitlement or birthright (Adams, 1989; Dobash & Dobash, 1979). Accordingly, African American men may lack the institutional and economic resources to dominate women in the same manner that is possible among majority men, but they still have been socialized to accept the belief that men should dominate women physically, emotionally, sexually, and economically (Gooden, 1980; Liebow, 1967; Ucko, 1994) (see Table 4.1). Consequently, they reinforce their ideology of male dominance by resorting to anger and frustration, which ultimately lead them to engage in acts of intimate partner violence (Gooden, 1980; Hannerz, 1969; Liebow, 1967; Oliver, 1989).

THE STRENGTHS PERSPECTIVE: A USEFUL PARADIGM IN ADDRESSING DOMESTIC VIOLENCE IN AFRICAN AMERICAN FAMILIES

So far, several theoretical propositions have been suggested that may prove useful in explaining patterns of behavior referred to by Walker (1979) as a "cycle of violence." At this juncture, it is essential to make a conceptual shift so that the strengths perspective, a potent prescriptive intervention strategy, can be presented. In the literature, there is a tendency to introduce theory that has a proclivity to create a social construction of reality that is often culturally laden with misinformation and with factual and methodological flaws. One thrust of this misinformation and these factual and methodological flaws is that African Americans—and, by extension, African American families—are dysfunctional and pathological (Herrnstein & Murray, 1994; Murray, 1984). The strengths perspective attenuates the efficacy of these assertions. Contrarily, it suggests that if progress and accomplishments were to be weighted equally, it would be seen that, despite the multiple atrocities visited upon them, African American families have exhibited great strength and made noteworthy accomplishments.

Because the strength perspective does not carry the heavy burden of scattering misinformation, it is useful in stimulating thought regarding the strength and resilience of African American families, including those adversely affected by intimate partner violence (Hill, 1999; Martin & Martin, 1985).

Because the strengths perspective posits that the inner resources of people and their environments, as well as their problems and pathologies, should be the central focus of the helping process, it rises to the level of a powerful formulation (Saleebey, 1992; Weick, 1992; Weick, Rapp, Sullivan, & Kisthardt, 1989). This perspective is rooted in the belief that people can continue to grow and change and should have equal access to resources that will assist them in developing to their finest potential. In that sense, this perspective embodies the recurring philosophical and theoretical constructs on which the helping professions rest (Cowger, 1992).

Chapin (1995) examined the life model of practice, which speaks of the incredible strength of human beings when they are thrust into an inhospitable environment and can survive only by tapping into their creative talents (Germain & Gitterman, 1996).

According to Hill (1999), the major adaptive strengths of African Americans are: (a) strong achievement orientation; (b) strong work orientation; (c) flexible family roles; (d) strong kinship bonds; and (e) strong religious orientation. These strengths have been central to how African Americans have coped with the adverse social conditions precipitated by their exposure to both historical and contemporary patterns of racial oppression. Given the documented existence of cultural strengths, how is the strength perspective useful to persons who are victims of domestic violence? The usefulness, of course, rests with the fact that this perspective calls attention to the complexity of any human condition. Suppose, momentarily, that African American families are under intense stress imposed by institutional forces and processes that have little commitment to helping poor families improve their social conditions. The strengths perspective chides these persons to recall how African American family heads, during the slavery era, reached down into their own untapped creativity and made use of family and community supports.

For practitioners utilizing the strengths perspective, however, a word of caution is in order. It may be too easily concluded that "all" African Americans have, or should have, the same degree of strength. This is a grossly erroneous assertion. It could cause services to be withheld or discontinued from women who are stereotypically perceived as abnormally strong, but who, in reality, may have little strength and resilience (West, 1999). But, beyond that caution, there is little doubt that the strengths perspective can help practitioners better focus and assist clients who resort to domestic violence. They can rechannel their behavior by making use of their inner strengths and resources.

CHRONOLOGY OF PROBLEMS FACING VIOLENT AFRICAN AMERICAN MEN

In an effort to advance an understanding of domestic violence, particularly as it is perpetrated by African American men, it is important to examine forces that have propelled these men into displaying high levels of aggression. To accomplish this task, slavery and institutional racism are among the contextual issues that must be reviewed.

In his early work, Staples (1982) argued that intimate partner violence is a reflection of the internal colonization of African Americans—more specifically, that historical and contemporary patterns of racial oppression and domination of black males produce stress and frustration, which then give rise to aggression against African American women.

The research of Gibbs (1988) and Williams (1999) has extended Staples's (1982) argument by asserting that within the past two decades, the levels of structural violence (e.g., racial oppression; police violence; differential patterns of arrest, conviction, and incarceration) against African Americans have eroded many of the formal and informal sources of social control in black communities

(Aldridge, 1991; See, 2001). Correspondingly, the disruption of the territoriality and controls in poor urban communities have been significantly affected by the exodus of advantaged middle-class blacks who left the ghetto and sought increased educational, employment, and housing opportunities in the suburbs (Wilson, 1996). Their avalanche of migration to the suburbs drained poor black communities of role models who might have displayed conventional values and behaviors. Sadly, the defection of the middle class has led to the dismantling of black institutions and has permitted racism and resentment of the poor to become entrenched. The results have been: a transformation of public concern about poverty, which has escalated into criticism regarding the behavior of the poor; racist stereotyping; misrepresentation of statistics; and media manipulation.

Along this same line, Wilson (1996) contends that with the exodus of middle-class African Americans to the suburbs, the ghetto has been left to deteriorate. Its decaying condition has resulted in a high rate of unemployment and under-employment among African American men who no longer can find low-skill, high-wage industrial manufacturing jobs. A result has been the expansion of the crack cocaine economy, which has rendered the black urban poor vulnerable to a host of adverse social behaviors, including battering their wives and misusing their families.

Oliver (1989, 2001) has suggested that intimate partner violence among high-, low-, and middle-class African Americans may be explained by the combined effects of adverse structural and cultural factors. More specifically, he argues that violence in all these groups is the result of their chronic exposure to structural violence and dysfunctional adaptations to societal pressures. The most significant dysfunctional cultural adaptation is a socialization process in which far too many young black males internalize manhood as a passage from boyhood that is accomplished by equating toughness to manhood. Hare and Hare (1984) describe this as "a matter of muscles and martial arts and the tools and trappings of machismo."

Other researchers have argued that the devaluing of African Americans within the context of the larger society has contributed to intimate partner violence. According to Hawkins (1987), violence among and between African Americans has been allowed, and even extended. This argument, therefore, attempts to describe how stereotyped beliefs of African American women have increased their vulnerability to violence within the context of their intimate partnerships. For example, some professionals argue that inherent in the racial stereotype labels of "Jezebel" and "Sapphire" is a belief that black women are promiscuous, immoral, and always desiring sex. Further, a pervasive belief among white men and women, and some black men, is that black women are strong, dominant, and aggressive "ball-bursting matriarchs." Unfortunately, this theme is emphasized in literary, cinematic, and pornographic productions (See, 1989). Consequently, acceptance of these stereotypes may shape the attitudes of African American men and justify behaviors that precipitate conflict and/or intimate partner violence (Aldridge, 1991).

RISK FACTORS OF INTIMATE PARTNER VIOLENCE IN AFRICAN AMERICAN RELATIONSHIPS AND FAMILIES

In discussing domestic violence between African American partners, several variables must be considered. First and foremost is the variable of race.

Race

The variable of race is one of the most profound and sensitive issues in American society. It does not occur in a vacuum. It is found within a complex matrix of interpersonal, social, and intergroup relations, and other eco-psychological forces. Social scientists skip around it and refuse to discuss it unless there is an urgent need to do so. During the 1990s, three national surveys were conducted: The National Family Violence Survey, The National Crime Victims Survey, and the National Violence Against Women Survey. The respondents were asked to self-report exposure to intimate partner violence. Findings in these studies showed that race is a significant risk factor for intimate partner violence victimization. What these studies consistently revealed, and what has become extremely controversial (and beyond the scope of this writing), is that African American men and women tend to have a higher rate of intimate partner victimization than white Americans and most other racial minorities. However, one criticism of the studies was that class and other culturally significant variables were not factored into the equation (Lockhart, 1985). Suffice it to say that few scholars attribute racial variations in rates of intimate partner violence to the biology of race (Greenfeld & Snell, 1999; Rennison & Welchans, 2000). Given the racial disparities in poverty levels—that is, the fact that 1 in 4 (26.5%) African Americans are classified as poor, compared to 1 in 10 (11%) white Americans (U.S. Bureau of Census, 1999)—the correlated behavior and the dynamically interacting socioeconomic problem that encompasses poverty, race, and intimate partner violence are likely to contribute to higher rates of partner abuse among African Americans.

The association between poverty and intimate partner violence is likewise aggravated by the fact that poor African American families, because of their race, are more likely to reside in areas in which the majority of their neighbors are poor. Contrarily, poor whites are more likely to reside in neighborhoods in which the majority of their neighbors earn income above the official poverty level (Wilson, 1996). This is a significant finding because it suggests that poor African American families are more likely than poor whites to reside in communities in which poverty and other social ills are concentrated. In such environments, there are fewer formal and informal resources for victims of intimate partner violence. Arguably, unlike poor white Americans, poor blacks, because of their race, are more likely to reside in neighborhoods in which the routine activities and the culture of their neighbors are organized around unemployment, underemployment, dependence on public assistance, and a more overt display of deviance and criminality within the public sphere (Wilson, 1996).

Unemployment

One of the most severe risk factors in black families is associated with employment. Intimate partner violence has been found to be positively associated with high rates of unemployment; overall, African Americans tend to have unemployment rates that are double those of white Americans (Aldridge, 1991; Aldridge & Hemmons, 2001). Consider for a moment the 1998 statistics. African Americans had an unemployment rate of 9%, whereas that of white Americans was 4% (U.S. Bureau of the Census, 1999). It is still being debated whether unemployment and low income are factors that contribute to the occurrence of stress and give rise to conflict within the context of family relations. Thus, chronic rates of unemployment among African American men may serve as a catalyst for seeking status and comfort in manhood roles that are more easily attainable in the social world of the streets (Hannerz, 1969). Roles such as "the tough guy," "the player of women," "the pimp," "the hustler," and "the gangster" are alternative manhood-role orientations that many lower-class African American males assume as a way of compensating for their inability to achieve more conventional manhood roles. These roles, which largely emerge within the context of adapting to the challenges associated with chronic unemployment, underemployment, and a generalized social impotence, are likely to condone intimate partner violence as a means of resolving disputes (Oliver, 1989).

Early Exposure to Violence

The most significant predictor of intimate partner violence is exposure to violence in the past. Research shows that experiencing, witnessing, and internalizing violence in one's family of origin tends to increase one's chance of becoming a perpetrator or victim of intimate partner violence. It has been estimated that from 3.3 million to 10 million children, ages 3 to 17 years, are exposed to marital violence and a lack of harmony in their homes (Carlson, 1984; Straus, 1994).

Early exposure to this domestic disequilibrium has been found to be associated with ineffective conflict resolutions and strategies in adulthood. Given the disproportionate levels of intimate partner violence and chronic community violence that occur in African American environs, it is understandable that an inordinate number of African American youth have histories of early exposure to violence (Attar, Guerra, & Tolan, 1994; Jenkins & Bell, 1997). Moreover, early exposure to family turmoil and chronic domestic violence may lead to increased vulnerability to victimization and to acceptance of violence as a legitimate means of resolving interpersonal conflict.

A survey conducted in 1996 found that nearly 6 out of 10 women in state prisons had experienced physical or sexual abuse in the past; just over one-third of imprisoned women had been abused by an intimate in the past, and just under one-fourth reported prior abuse. It has been concluded, therefore, that most (but not all) individuals raised in abusive homes or violent communities do not become abusive or violent in adulthood (Barnett, Miller-Perrin, & Perrin, 1997). However, many do experience dissonant relationships.

Heavy Drinking and Drug Use

Alcohol, illegal drugs, and other mood-altering substances have been found to be associated with the occurrence of domestic violence in American families (Goodman, Lovejoy, & Sherratt, 1995). Evidence supporting this finding has been reported by Coleman and Straus (1983), and by Leonard and Jacob (1988), who estimated that violence precipitated by alcohol ranged from 20% to 80%. Kaufman-Kantor (1990) found that a husband's heavy drinking was positively associated with intimate partner violence. In a recent survey of 62 incidents of domestic violence that took place in Memphis, Tennessee, during 23 consecutive seven-hour shifts of the Memphis Police Department, researchers from Methodist Hospital and the University of Memphis found that 92% of the assailants and 42% of the victims used alcohol or drugs on the day of the assault (Brookoff, O'Brien, Cook, Thompson, & Williams, 1997). According to Garske (1996), few reliable risk factors more adequately predict the likelihood of intimate partner violence in black and other families than excessive use of alcohol. This variable must be empirically examined by researchers as a key to understanding domestic violence in African American families.

Tradition

The single greatest risk factor for a man's committing intimate partner violence or domestic violence is his belief that violence toward his wife or girlfriend is an acceptable means of resolving conflict. This thinking, traceable to English Common Law, seems to be chiseled into the male psyche. It has also been noted that African American women have more economic opportunities than men, but the women are skeptical of any rationales offered toward justifying the abusiveness of their partners. Intervention strategies must be devised to assist African American men toward understanding that they, and their partners, are victims of a disempowering social system.

THE GROUP APPROACH IN WORKING WITH AFRICAN AMERICAN MALE PERPETRATORS OF DOMESTIC VIOLENCE

Our discussion, up to this point, has left a reparable crack and a somewhat clouded but interpretable picture of domestic violence in African American families, and our focus is on the male as head of the household. Correspondingly, our sociohistorical analysis of familial dynamics has been slightly porous, and thus has made intellectual leaps that may give the impression that black men assign little value to family life. As for the first assertion, clarity of the issue will develop as we move forward. Indeed, the later perception is debatable. As Martin Luther King, Jr. (1965) once voiced it: "No one in all history had to fight against so many physical and psychological horrors to have a family."

Three questions now invite attention:

1. What evaluative standards that rest on well-structured empirical foundations are available for use in practice with African American men who exhibit battering behavior?

2. What explicitly defined measuring tools are available for researching and evaluating social systems that produce batterers who abuse their partners?

3. Is there existing literature that presents empirically based reliable treatment and outcome measures that specifically address the battering behavior of African American males?

Only scant empirical data, and virtually no discrete measuring tools, are available to assist practitioners who work with black male batterers. So, in the absence of professional writings and measuring tools, but with reliability and validity, dyadic work and group work become the best intervention tools in serving African American men who become violent and weaken their family systems.

The following "nuggets of knowledge," extracted from group sessions conducted with black batterers and documented by the authors for further empirical testing, represent important observations and skills that may be useful to professionals working with African American men who have engaged in domestic violence.

The Group Process

Group treatment is a powerful approach for working with African American men who batter their partners, cause disruption in their families, and wreak havoc in their respective communities. There is no denying or repudiating the fact that African American males are responsible for assaultive violence in the African American family milieu. But, regrettably, there is equally no doubt that anemic research efforts have failed to rigorously examine why these men have the feelings of frustration and the sense of alienation that lead them to lash out at their partners with unbridled fury and aggression.

Rasheed and Rasheed (1999) have identified many kinds of groups that are designed to develop a culturally synchronic sense of masculine identity. They contend:

> [T]here is no substitute for the group process in confronting racism in the workplace, establishing working relationships with spouses and other significant women, managing anger, negotiating personal value conflicts, gaining job readiness skills, developing more effective parenting skills, managing more healthy lifestyles, gaining overall self-improvement, managing stress, and developing conflict resolution skills. (p. 109)

A nonexhaustive, classification of the kinds of groups that are recommended for working with African American men includes: (a) self-help and support groups; (b) psychoeducational and life-skills development groups; (c) counseling and psychotherapy groups; and (d) development groups. In the following discussion, attention is directed to treatment groups designed to assist African American male batterers in the development of a constructive sense of self—a way of negating the need to control others by resorting to violence.

The Purpose of Groups

For black males who engage in heinous acts of violence, groups provide an opportunity to employ personal introspection and to dispel the notion that only flawed personal inadequacies (and no structural factors) helped trigger the rage and aggressive behavior. Groups composed of young "urban dwellers" can provide a sense of collective kinship and extrafamilial support. These groups emit an atmosphere of togetherness, which is part of the black experience (i.e., referring to each other as "brother," "homeboy," "soul brother," "my man," and so on).

Groups made up of African American men who batter their partners can help black men work toward assuming greater responsibility as dependable caretakers, fathers, husbands, and citizens. The group can provide batterers a support system, and help them negotiate alternative ways of resolving conflict other than striking their partners. The group effort can help violent black men maximize their human potential, improve their psychological and interpersonal functioning (specifically, the social roles) and develop a positive self-identity. One of the authors attended the Million Man March in 1995 and was able to use that experience to exemplify how change in attitudes is often precipitated by a giant group effort. Groups can help batterers to discover their own positive potentials and to make use of their inner strength.

Planning a group activity with the expressed purpose of helping African American men cease the violence is no light undertaking. This task requires considerable preparation and a culturally competent group leader.

The Culturally Competent Group Leader

Green (1995, p. 89) defines the culturally competent group leader as one who can "provide professional services in a way that is congruent with behaviors and expectations that are normative for a given community." Leigh (1998) notes that competence in cross-cultural service requires a leader who is aware of his or her self-limitations, has a high interest in cultural contrasts, projects a systematic learning style, can use cultural resources such as the "strengths perspective" (Hill, 1999), and has basic knowledge about cultural groups.

In a national survey of batterers' programs, Williams and Becker (1994) found that most of the programs surveyed did not consider race or culture. Group treatment methods are more effective with African American batterers if the leader is familiar with the experiences and culture of the population served, and this knowledge is folded into the group treatment design.

A competent group leader—even one with multiple talents—faces challenging responsibilities, especially when the group is composed of batterers from various social classes (Franklin, 1999; Williams, 1998; Williams & Becker, 1994). Rasheed and Rasheed (1999) suggest an important prerequisite for a competent group leader: knowledge of the social sciences and the clinical practice literature on social class and social groups, with emphasis on group processes and dynamics. Some black scholars, however, have cautioned that the social sciences literature must be carefully analyzed. Many researchers, and all too many social scientists who write about battering as a form of domestic violence, have not always been objective when African American men were the targets (Hare, 1985).

The challenge faced by culturally competent group leaders has another level of complexity: All group participants (batterers) may not be low-income substance abusers or men facing prison. High-income white executives may be among the men referred to social services by the courts. Thus, class and race present a duet of variables that may present a "catastrophe ready for explosion" in a mixed group session, unless the leader can assume full charge and control of the group. In anticipation of a mix of participants from different socioeconomic classes, the culturally competent group leader must establish intervention protocols designed to reduce the isolation and resentment that poor African American men sometimes experience in the presence of high-class whites who, they feel, are responsible for their plight by denying them a decent education and good jobs with good pay.

An emerging body of literature emphasizes the sex and race of a group leader. In groups conducted by the authors, black male participants have often expressed their preference with regard to the sex and race of a group leader. Surprisingly, white women were the last choice of middle-class black abusers, and black men were registered as the group's overall preference (See, 1989). In calling attention to these responses regarding preferred leadership, one African American group member explained:

> White women are taking all the jobs away from black men, so we have no way to feed our children and care for our families, and be he-men.

This type of response is congruent with the findings of Hare and Hare (1984, p. 22), who were severely critical of the role often played by white feminists entering the labor market. They noted that:

> [I]n the process of their sexual liberation they have taken jobs from black men who were heads of families . . . middle-aged affluent housewives, who have smugly occupied the pedestal all their lives, will now saunter out and seize a job that could have gone to someone who needs it in order to focus in on finding my own identity.

Like it or not, if these attitudes are surfacing in group work with batterers, then service agency administrators and feminists must take note and determine how to address this issue in a constructive manner.

USING THE STRENGTHS PERSPECTIVE WHEN WORKING WITH AFRICAN AMERICAN MEN WHO BATTER THEIR WIVES

As stated earlier, culturally competent group leaders have very different experiences when they work with African American men who batter. This section represents accumulated knowledge that the authors have acquired and recorded in their years of working as private practitioners, university educators, and agency professionals. It is interesting to note that when observations were compared with reference to battering, group responses to specific situations were similar, although clients came from different parts of the country. Group leaders who used the strengths perspective when working with black batterers reported positive results. This led us to conclude that the strengths perspective has utility for working with black men who impose violence on their intimate partners and on their families.

As shown in Figure 4.1, African American men who are involved in a group activity for batterers must go through several stages of treatment:

1. Clients are referred to an agency, or they seek consultation from private practitioners in order to enhance their inner strength.
2. Information provided at Intake serves as baseline data for teasing out psychological, sociological, and cultural factors in the client's life that may be strengths.

    A contractual agreement is negotiated between the worker and the client delineating the obligation of each during the period of service delivery.
3. The worker invites the client to participate in a group which is a strength-enhancing activity.

    The worker conferences with each client to determine if religious intervention is appropriate. If so, pastoral counseling may be made availed as an additional source of gaining support and strength.
4. The libation ritual is designed to release the client's sense of alienation and anomie after he discloses intimate family problems. A culminating activity at this session involves the worker preparing food and soft drinks as a means of further "bonding" the group.

    The circularity ritual permits the clients to engage in open dialogue about taboos, and painful and neglected areas. Clients exhibit strength by self-disclosing their problems (Ceechin, 1987).
5. Group members re-assess, and evaluate the progress that has been made by themselves and their peers.

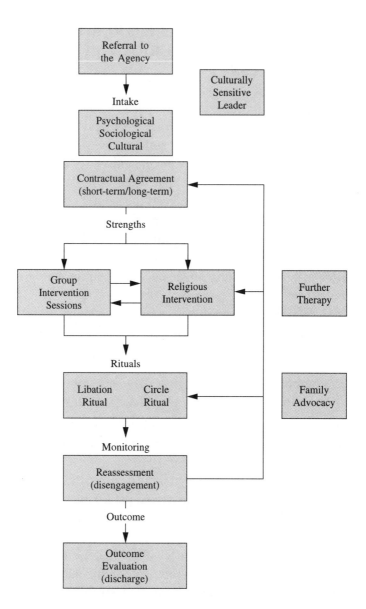

Figure 4.1   A Strengths Diagram of Group Intervention for African American Male Batterers

6. The painful process of disengagement now affects the group, and they admit to having drawn strength from each other.
7. The group work effort ends generally (but not always) on a high level of enthusiasm with each member having gained new strength. The members orally evaluate the activity.

8. The group worker evaluates his or her intervention in helping clients maximize their strengths. The worker then evaluates his or her practice by employing the Evidence-Based Practice (EBP) model (Gambrill, 1999; see, McNeely, Choi, & Torres, 2002).

The strengths diagram is flexible and can be adjusted by the leader in accordance with a specific time frame and other factors that are unique to a particular group.

ISSUES RECORDED IN WORKING WITH GROUPS OF AFRICAN AMERICAN MALE BATTERERS

Issue 1

Professionals throughout the United States agree that more effective group treatment methods must be developed if professionals are to help rehabilitate African American men who batter their families and intimate partners. First, men who engage in violence must be held accountable for their behavior, especially their victimization of black women. The most effective group treatment method is to help these members realize that, even though, from psychological, sociological, and cultural perspectives their cultural history differs from that of their white counterparts because of the black experience, that history must not be offered as a crutch during the life of the group (Williams, 1995).

The group leader has an obligation to call attention to the fact that, traditionally, black men drop out of treatment sooner and complete their tasks at a lower rate of acceptability than whites (Gondolf, 1997). In the group, they will be assisted but must complete their tasks and honor their contractual agreement.

It has been observed that many treatment programs for batterers employ a "one size fits all" model that characteristically focuses on the violent behavior and gender of the perpetrator, and resorts to cognitive approaches to induce behavioral change (Gondolf, 1997; Williams, 1995). However, in the treatment group, African American male batterers must be encouraged to defy the *deficit perspective* and embrace the *strengths perspective,* which encourages these men to use their own creativity in solving their own problems.

Issue 2

Although African American men abuse women for many reasons that are common among all men—power and control issues—sexism, as applied to African

Americans, is currently a controversial issue. Without doubt, the violence displayed by black men may result from displaced anger related to institutional experiences with racial oppression (Gibbs, 1988; Staples, 1982; Williams, 1995, 1998). It is imperative, therefore, that group leaders assist African American male batterers in making a connection between oppression and violent behavior by using the strengths perspective. For example, in a batterers' treatment group facilitated by one of the authors, one member had this to say:

> I was one of the hardest working men in our company. I was the target of ridicule by a group of white coworkers who did not spend the same amount of time on the job as I spent. One of the men was a good friend to my supervisor. When I complained about my treatment, indicating that the communication flow was cut off from me (my mail was held back, etc.), the supervisor was not responsive. Another example is one in which one of my coworkers took my car keys out of my jacket and moved my car without my permission. An ongoing truck came along and smashed my car. I felt this incident was "beyond the pale" and was a classic example of racism. I was very angry and wanted to "go off on somebody." . . . I got home and beat my wife.

The challenge here is: How should such a problem be addressed in the group? Some leaders would feel that this problem was not relevant to a domestic violence discussion. Others may feel that the situation had merit, but would deny it was associated with racial discrimination. A culturally competent leader who is fully aware of the strengths perspective would know when to acknowledge racism as a factor, and when to make a subjective call and explain what racism is not (Gary, 1995). The leader must know when to emphasize that many black men have a strong work ethic and a desire to succeed, which is indeed a strength.

In cases like the one described above, the group leader may wish to call on the group's indigenous leader (if one happens to emerge) to spearhead the group in crafting an appropriate strategy for confronting the problem presented. The group leader may then frame these thoughtful, specific questions and direct them to the complainant and the group: What were your interactions with your partner when you arrived home? Did you displace your anger onto your partner? If so, how? If not, how did you manage to avoid it? If you directed your anger at your partner, what other feelings did you have? Did you feel a sense of powerlessness and frustration? Were you aware that your feelings were escalating? Did you hit your partner?

The group can then explore appropriate nonviolent methods of interacting with one's partner when one feels powerless and frustrated. The group's responses to the questions will likely contribute significantly to improving the members' insight during these teachable moments. By comparing the group members' feelings of powerlessness, helplessness, and frustration to those of his partner, the batterer gains some understanding of the victim's feelings when she is the target of his abuse. The lesson here is: Giving thought to another person's feelings is indeed a strength.

Issue 3

African American men are uniquely affected by community environments when they are at high risk for encountering physical harm (Darling & Blake 1994; Oliver, 1998). Black-on-black crime is the leading cause of death among many African American young men, and they observe violence on a daily basis. It is important to recognize that many black men in these environments are operating on the same set of cognitive and behavioral imperatives—and violence toward women may be one of the maladaptive behaviors (Gibbs, 1988; Oliver, 1998; Rich & Stone, 1996). Consequently, when such themes are discussed in treatment, group leaders must be prepared to use the strengths perspective to make connections to the clients' behavior toward their partners. Consider, for a moment, a group session in which a client described an encounter in which he felt he had been "fronted off" (disrespected) by a male acquaintance. He explained:

> I live in a violent community where young male acquaintances were trying to force me to join them in robbing people in the community. The gang said if I did not participate, they would use violence toward me—disfigure my face and put my "water works" out of commission. I tried to find a way out of this situation and struggled with my choices. I asked myself: "Do I join with these guys in violence against others? Do I use violence against them in defense of myself? Do I run away? Can I run away? What about my manhood? Am I really a man if I don't confront this group?" I went to a store-front church and told the preacher my story, and he protected me.

In this situation, group members explained to the victim that violence was not his best choice. One member of the treatment group remembered a comment made to him by a preacher many years ago. According to his statement, the preacher said, "Sometimes people are caught in a circumstance with two bad choices—both can get you into trouble." The group complimented the member for evading violence because either choice could have landed him in jail. However, the group was not uncritical and accepting of this member when he confessed that he went home and beat his girlfriend after his ordeal. The group acknowledged his reality and helped him examine the options he had at the time of the beating.

One message of substance that the strengths perspective emphasizes is a strong religious orientation. Thus, the attitudinal transformation that the member seemed to internalize was that it was not unmanly to flee from danger. Another practical lesson was that he could tap into religious teaching and those connected with the black experience. The group harshly criticized this member for beating his girlfriend, but some members helped him to understand that by beating his girlfriend he was actually ambushing the gang members who were trying to entice him to participate in violence. The strength of a strong religious orientation played a major role in his survival, but the leader and the group posed some hard questions: "Did you displace your frustration, fear, and anger onto your girlfriend?" "When you are faced with situations caused by high tension and stressful choices, do you always abuse your intimate partner in this manner?" Finally, the group and the leader assisted the member in making a connection between the oppression he experienced and the oppression he imposed on his girlfriend. The leader, although assuming a neutral role regarding religion, explained that the power of the member's religious orientation was, in this instance, perhaps a source of strength.

Issue 4

Frequently, African American clients who live in stressful and violent community environments also live in poverty (Dennis & Key, 1995). Several urban court-mandated programs have anecdotal reports showing that a disproportionately high number of poor African American men who are charged with domestic abuse are referred to treatment (Gondolf, 1997). Group workers may wish to distribute culturally sensitive information and resources among these groups. If group workers are to be successful with African American men, particularly low-income and working-class men, information associated with poverty, substance abuse, unemployment, incarceration, homelessness, parenting, nutrition, education, and child abuse/neglect are among the issues that must be addressed in the treatment milieu (Davis, 1999; Franklin, 1999; Williams, 1998). The strength of these gestures is that the abusers will realize that community kinship bonds (an element of the black experience and the strengths perspective) are still present, and the community supports the batterer in his effort to reconstitute his family.

RITUALS

Cultural rituals that have emerged out of the African American experience have a potential for enhancing prescribed treatment to African American men who batter. Rituals are cultural expressions that dramatize change—or successful transitions from one stage in the human experience to another (Rasheed & Rasheed, 1999). "Rites of passage" impose responsibility and remind young black males that manhood is at hand and they must prepare for the transition.

One purpose of rituals is to help black men gain an understanding of the pain their violence has inflicted upon their partners and their families. Some African American men ritualistically engage in community and cultural bonding—actions that help these men assume responsibility for effecting change.

In some racially homogenous groups, not only bonding but also codes of conduct and standards of behavior become rituals. These rituals necessitate group rules, which are often adopted from the strengths, values, and principles of traditional African societies. Inclusion of this type of material in the group activities enhances the members' respect for themselves, their partners, and others. Respect for one's culture may serve as a strong deterrent against intimate partner and family violence.

It has been clearly documented that most African American men who batter have low self-esteem, self-definition, self-denigration, and mastery (Poussaint, 1993; Williams, 1995). Hooks (1992) describes this unconscious behavior as "internalized oppression." One consequence of low self-esteem is that the perpetrator devalues and dehumanizes members of his own racial group (Akbar, 1984, 1991; Wilson, 1991). For example, "Niggas ain't shit" is a common remark among men in treatment groups. The utterance projects some of the internalized oppression onto others and provides the perpetrator with a false sense of mastery. Materials and rituals may be used to explore how African American men who batter justify the victimization of their wives and girlfriends (West, 2000).

LIBATION AS A RITUAL

Libation is another powerful ritual that may be helpful in empowering African American batterers. Pioneers in the delivery of culturally relevant treatment interventions have developed it as a creative method of service delivery. For example, Antonia Vann, at ASHA Family Services in Milwaukee, and Raven Mason, at the Harriet Tubman Battered Women program in Minneapolis, have used libation in African American treatment groups to assist in helping black men get in touch with the history and culture of their ancestors. Libation is a ritual in which people of African descent drink liquid (tea, soda, coffee, and so on) as they acknowledge and reflect on important persons (usually relatives or significant elders) who have been sources of support and inspiration to them (Mbiti, 1969; Roberts, 1994). This reflection serves as a kind of catharsis and

Table 4.3   Rites of Passage and Mentoring as Cultural Strengths for African American Male Batterers

Reflective Development as a Strength Perspective

Activity	African American men in the group are asked to close their eyes and reflect on the history of black people in the United States—especially those who have struggled to achieve racial equality in a social system that has refused to drop all barriers that would lead to an egalitarian society.
Purpose	Reflection helps African American batterers get in touch with the strength of their heritage. It helps give shape, form, and understanding to their aberrant behavior, and it challenges these men to sue their heritage as a potent source of strength. Reflection reminds perpetrators of the importance of commonalty and of the old African adage: "I am, because we are. Because we are, I am."

The Whipping Ritual as a Strength

Activity	This ritual is used by African American men in a group at the Wilder Community Action Program (CAP) in St. Paul, Minnesota. It is called the "whipping ritual" and was developed by Dion Crushon. In this exercise, at the beginning of each group session, black male batterers pass a whip around the room. A modified proposed Georgia version of this ritual suggests that batterers strike themselves with the whip and experience the pain and discomfort they have imposed on others. The strength of this exercise rests with the fact that violent men are determined to achieve their goal of learning alternative ways of resolving family conflict.
Purpose	Men who batter are minded how it feels to be struck, even by oneself. The group is reminded that they have a responsibility to protect rather than impose pain and suffering on women and children. Therefore, they now know that imposing excruciating pain on a partner can destroy intimacy in male-female relationships—sometimes beyond repair.

Vicarious Mentoring

Activity	Leo Hayden, of the Treatment Alternatives for Safe Communities (TASC) program in Chicago, Illinois, uses "libation" to assist group members in reflecting on persons who have come before them. In group sessions, each man is expected to identify a person who is alive today and who he feels will build a more peaceful world. The strength in this activity is that participants generally think of family members or people within their own life space as mentors. These strong kinship bonds are important in helping young black men establish an identity.
Purpose	This activity amplifies the necessity for connecting with persons who are within reach of the batterers' present life space. It encourages the batterer to select productive black men with character as role models and mentors. This exercise will force the participant to make an unavoidable link with high achievers.

Table 4.3   Continued

Louis Armstrong Manhood Development Program (LAMPD)

Activity   The Louis Armstrong Development (LAMDP) in New Orleans, Louisiana, is a manhood development initiative designed to facilitate the development of masculine identities for African American youth. Young black men are taught skills to enhance their functioning in several areas of life: culture, economics, education, politics, recreation, religion, and sex. Achievement as a strength will help these young men form an attitudinal transformation that will aid them in making original contributions to society.

Purpose   Group sessions focus on providing antidrug education, antiviolence skills, educational development skills, group counseling mentorship, self-esteem, recreation, rites of passage, teen parenting skills, and vocational education training for young people who will eventually develop positive intimate partner relationships and assume parental roles.

Responsible African American Men United in Spirit (RAAMUS)
Academy And Young Warriors

Activity   These groups are organized to prepare young men for responsible adulthood. This involved teaching them to assume obligations as family heads in the same cultural tradition that produced strong males and fathers in earlier years. Attention is directed to school attainment and manhood development. The strength inherent in these goals embraces the idea of strong participation in the community, and the desire to model their manhood after respected elders in the community.

Purpose   The purposes of the two development groups, RAAMUS and The Young Warriors, are: (1) to provide, to young black men, knowledge that affirms the contributions of black men who helped build this country; (2) to provide in-depth knowledge about the characteristics that constitute strong black manhood; (3) to help young black men to understand that black manhood demands that black men respect black women and assume responsibility for black children; and (4) to stress the value of education as a passport to success in the future.

helps channel negative energy into positive expression. Libation then, as a strength modality, is among the rituals that give self-definition and an intellectual challenge to violent men who are seriously seeking to resolve their problems. (See Table 4.3.)

THE CIRCLE

Another example of a ritual that emits cultural strength comes from Wisconsin, where Jim Smith moderates a prison group of African American men called

"The Circle." Each week, group members are expected to recite a poem focused on the purpose of the group and to delineate the types of behavioral changes they hope to achieve through participation in the group process. Each member must recite his responsibility, as an African American man, to behave in adaptive ways and to remain strong for the other members and their families and communities.

The Louis Armstrong Manhood Development Program (LAMDP), developed in New Orleans, is a successful development program with a strengths underpinning and is receiving wide visibility (Jeff, 1994). Its rites-of-passage approach provides structure for African American youth, and several of its components are designed to reconstruct and internalize a definition of manhood and strength (Table 4.3). The strength of each innovative effort is to effect manhood training and to eradicate battering in all socioeconomic classes in our society.

SAFETY AND PROTECTION OF BATTERED AFRICAN AMERICAN WOMEN

In our discussion of domestic violence in African American families, the focus has primarily centered on black males as perpetrators of intimate partner abuse. The good, the bad, and the ugly facts of black male battering behavior have been examined, and the authors' corroborated clinical observations have presented an analysis of why black males are often filled with intransigent despair. But what are the concerns of black women regarding their personal safety and protection against these perpetrators of violence? A full exploration of these concerns is not presented here, but a few remarks regarding this issue are in order. Basically, African American women understand that black men's oppression is real. In counseling sessions, these women are pained by the demoralization, immobilization, marginalization, and sheer abuse that are essentially imposed upon black men in our society. Asbury (1987) described the "double-bind" or painful dilemma faced by African American women who attempt to protect black men at all cost and at great personal sacrifice. Asbury (1987) noted that, like their ancestors, black women today are concerned about the inequality and injustice heaped upon black men. These women are concerned about the inhumane and unjust treatment and the exploitation (sexual and economic) that black men would receive if the women reported their violent transgressions and the abusers were then committed to the criminal justice system. So, at the risk of feuding with white feminists who feel black male batterers should be imprisoned, black women refuse to hand over their intimate partners to what they view as a racist and corrupt system of American justice (Hare & Hare, 1984; See, 2001).

At the same time, African American women resent being victimized and tormented by hostile, aggressive black men whose feelings of marginality and frustration are taken out on them. In light of these dilemmas, and in view of their efforts "to keep the family together," African American women stand as "silent sufferers" and endure hostile and violent relationships to support their intimate partner or family member. In counseling sessions, black women articulate a belief that, with their support, an intimate partner can be "healed" and ultimately will change his battering behavior (Asbury, 1987). Richie (1994), in her gender entrapment theory, encourages practitioners to observe the length to which African American women will go in order to protect male perpetrators. Richie's position is that, for the sake of their own safety, African American battered women must not accept an enabler role and remain in a relationship with someone who is clearly out of control. In group therapy with black battered women, one author suggested that, for their own safety, black women may wish to reevaluate their present rationale for remaining with black male batterers who threaten extraordinary violence to them and their families (See, 1998; Williams, 1998). In like manner, women victims are helped to realize that they cannot "heal" their batterer's pain through loyalty; healing is time-consuming and must originate from within one's own persona. Battered women are also helped to understand the limits of treatment—specifically, group intervention does not ensure guaranteed change in participants. Finally, predictions of who will or will not succeed in treatment have not been determined from the present body of empirical evidence (Gondolf, 1997). Whether an intimate partner or battered woman chooses to remain in a relationship with an abuser is her choice. However, it is the responsibility of agencies to establish treatment programs that facilitate the safety of any victim. This must be a priority of a men's treatment program as well.

Intervention is offered by determining whether a battered woman has a safety plan: a planned course of action in the event she must leave the relationship because of the abuse meted out by her partner. Among the specifics included in this plan are: places to go, people to inform, clothing, and financial resources. If no safety plan has been devised, agency personnel should collaborate with battered women's services programs and help the client develop a plan. Also included should be a clear articulation of policy regarding a victim's responsibility to inform the agency if her partner is determined to be a threat to her or to himself.

All in all, service providers must be warned that, in working with female victims of violence, they must not lose sight of the fact that the primary client system is still black male batterers, and the objective is not to shift attention to female victims, but to assist these men in improving their behavior so that they will never again pose a threat to their intimate partners and their families (Davis, 1998; Hooks, 1995; Richie, 1994).

RESEARCH IMPLICATIONS

There are many areas in which empirical research is needed to enhance our understanding of the unique contextual dynamics associated with the occurrence of domestic violence in African American families. First, research that attempts to uncover the situational context of domestic violence is needed. For example, the practice and research community needs a more in-depth understanding of factors that tend to precipitate acts of intimate partner violence among African American couples. Specifically, what roles do alcohol and illegal drugs play in perpetrating acts of violence? Is there a difference in the likelihood that an African American man who batters will be under the influence of alcohol or illegal drugs, or will resort to the use of firearms or other weapons during these incidents? How do socioeconomic differences among African Americans influence the contextual dynamics of intimate partner violence?

Second, research is needed to identify the factors that are most predictive of an African American woman's risk of intimate partner violence victimization. Such research would enhance understanding of the social and cultural contexts in which African American women experience intimate partner violence.

Third, we need more evaluation studies to determine what types of interventions are most effective with African Americans who batter and with those persons who are victimized by intimate partner violence. In addition, research is needed to assess the long-term effectiveness of Afrocentric and faith-based interventions. To date, only antidotal indications of their effectiveness are available.

Fourth, there is a need for research that examines the occurrence of intimate partner violence across the life cycle of African Americans. What factors are predictive at various stages of the life cycle?

Fifth, there is a need for research that explores how community violence is related to intimate partner violence among African Americans.

CONCLUSION

There is no singular cause of intimate partner or other patterns of domestic violence. Indeed, violence is often the result of multiple causes. Consequently, what are needed are prevention and intervention strategies that include differential strategies and approaches. Effective prevention and intervention of intimate partner violence must be addressed by culturally competent professionals. Such interventions must recognize the unique structural and cultural contexts in which intimate partner violence occurs among African Americans. Moreover, it is critically important that those who work with African American men who batter, and with battered African American women and their families, be trained to utilize the strengths of African American families to facilitate their interventions. The strengths perspective is a powerful modality for fulfilling that purpose.

REFERENCES

American College of Obstetricians and Gynecologists. (1989). *The battered woman.* Technical Bulletin Number 124. Washington, DC: Author.

Adams, D. (1989). Feminist-based interventions for battering men. In L. Caesar & L. K. Hamberger (Eds.), *Treating men who batter: Theory, practice, and programs.* New York: Springer.

Akbar, N. (1984). *Chains and images of psychological slavery.* Jersey City, NJ: New Mind Productions.

Akbar, N. (1991). *Visions for black men.* Nashville, TN: Winston-Derek.

Aldridge, D. (1991). *Focusing: Black male/female relationships.* Chicago: Third World Press.

Aldridge, D., & Hemmons, W. (2001). The structural components of violence in black male/female relationships. In L. See (Ed.), *Violence as seen through a prism of color* (pp. 209–226). New York: Haworth Press.

Asbury, J. (1987). African American women in violent relationships: An exploration of cultural differences. In R. L. Hampton (Ed.), *Violence in the black family: Correlates and consequences* (pp. 89–105). Lexington, MA: Lexington Books.

Attar, B. K., Guerra, N. G., & Tolan, P. H. (1994). Neighborhood disadvantage, stressful life events, and adjustment in urban elementary school children. *Journal of Clinical Child Psychology, 23,* 391–400.

Bandura, A. (1969). *Principles of behavior modification.* New York: Holt, Rinehart and Winston.

Barnett, O. W., Miller-Perrin, C. L., & Perrin, R. D. (1997). *Family violence across the lifespan—An introduction.* Thousand Oaks, CA: Sage.

Brookoff, D., O'Brien, K. K., Cook, C. S., Thompson, T. D., & Williams, C. (1997). Characteristics of participants in domestic violence assessment at the scene of domestic assault. *Journal of the American Medical Association, 277,* 1369–1373.

Caesar, P. L., & Hamberger, L. K. (1989). Introduction: Brief historical overview of interventions for wife abuse in the United States. In L. Caesar & L. K. Hamberger (Eds.), *Treating men who batter: Theory, practice, and programs.* New York: Springer.

Carlson, B. E. (1984). Children's observations of interpersonal violence. In A. R. Roberts (Ed.), *Battered women and their families* (pp. 147–167). New York: Springer.

Cash, W. J. (1941). *The mind of the south.* Toronto, Ontario, Canada: Vintage.

Ceechin, G. (1987). Hypothesizing, circularity and neutrality revisited: An invitation to curiosity. *Family Process, 26*(4), 405–413.

Chapin, R. (1995). Social policy development: The strengths perspective. *Social Work, 10,* 20–31.

Coleman, P.M., & Straus, M. A. (1983). Alcohol abuse and family violence. In E. Gottheil, A. Durley, I. F. Skolada, & H. M. Waxman (Eds.), *Alcohol, drug abuse, and aggression* (pp. 104–123). Springfield, IL: Charles C Thomas.

Coley, S. M., & Beckett, J. O. (1988a). Black battered women: A review of empirical literature. *Journal of Counseling and Development, 66,* 266–270.

Coley, S. M., & Beckett, J. O. (1988b). Black battered women: Practice issues. *Journal of Contemporary Social Work, 69,* 483–490.

Cowger, C. D. (1992). Assessment of client strengths. In D. Saleebey (Ed.), *The strengths perspective in social work practice* (pp. 139–147). New York: Longman.

Daly, A., Jennings, J., Beckett, J. O., & Leashore, B. R. (1995). Effective coping strategies of African Americans. *Social Work, 40,* 240–255.

Darling, C. A., & Blake, W. M. (1994). The dilemmas of the African American male. *Journal of Black Studies, 24,* 402–415.

Davis, L. (1997). *Working with African American males: A guide to practice.* Thousand Oaks, CA: Sage.

Dennis, R. E., & Key, J. L. (1995). Addressing domestic violence in the African American community. *Journal of Health Care for the Poor and Undeserved, 6,* 28–299.

Dobash, R. E., & Dobash, R. P. (1979). *Violence against wives: A case against the patriarchy.* New York: Free Press.

Edleson, J. L., & Tolman, R. M. (1992). *Interventions for men who batter.* Newbury Park, CA: Sage.

Elkins, S. M. (1959). *Slavery.* New York: Grosset & Dunlap.

Fox-Genovese, E. (1988). *Within the plantation household: Black and white women of the old south.* Chapel Hill: University of North Carolina Press.

Franklin, A. J. (1999). Therapeutic support groups for African American men. In L. Davis (Ed.), *Working with African American males: A guide to practice* (pp. 5–14). Thousand Oaks, CA: Sage.

Franklin, J. H. (1974). *From slavery to freedom: A history of Negro Americans.* New York: Alfred A. Knopf.

Franklin, J. H. (1988). *From slavery to freedom: A history of Negro Americans* (2nd ed.). New York: Alfred A. Knopf.

Gambrill, E. (1999). Evidence-based practice: An alternative to authority-based practice. *Families in Society, 80,* 341–350.

Garske, D. (1996). Transforming the culture: Creating safety, equality, and justice for women and girls. In R. L. Hampton, P. Jenkins, & T. P. Gullotta (Eds.), *Preventing violence in America* (pp. 263–285). Thousand Oaks, CA: Sage.

Gary, L. E. (1995). African American men's perceptions of discrimination: A socio-culturalanalysis. *Social Work Research, 19,* 207–217.

Gelles, R. J. (1997). *Intimate violence in families.* Thousand Oaks, CA: Sage.

Gelles, R. J., & Cornell, C. P. (1990). *Intimate violence in families.* Newbury Park, CA: Sage.

Germain, C. B., & Gitterman, A. (1996). *The life model of social work practice.* New York: Columbia University Press.

Gibbs, J. T. (1988). *Young, Black, and male in America: An endangered species.* Westport, CT: Aubury House.

Gondolf, E. W. (1997). Batter programs—what we know and need to know. *Journal of Interpersonal Violence, 12,* 83–98.

Gooden, W. E. (1980). *The adult development of black men* (Vols. 1/2). Ann Arbor, MI: University Microfilms.

Goodman, J., Lovejoy, P. E., & Sherratt, A. (1995). *Consuming habits: Drugs in history and anthropology.* New York: Routledge.

Green, J. (1985). *Cultural awareness in the human services.* Boston: Allyn & Bacon.

Greenfeld, L. A., & Snell, T. L. (1999). *Women offenders.* Washington, DC: U.S. Department of Justice.

Gutman, H. G. (1976). *The black family in slavery and freedom, 1750–1925.* New York: Vintage.

Hampton, R. L. (1987). *Violence in the black family: Correlates and consequences.* Lexington, MA: Lexington Books.

Hampton, R. L. (1991). *Black family violence: Current research and theory.* Lexington, MA: Lexington Books.

Hampton, R. L., & Gelles, R. J. (1994). Violence toward black women in a nationality representative sample of black families. *Journal of Comparative Family Studies, 51,* 105–119.

Hannerz, U. (1969). *Soulside: Inquiries into a ghetto culture.* New York: Columbia University Press.

Hare, N. (1985). *Bringing the black boy to manhood: The passage.* San Francisco: Black Think Tank.

Hare, N., & Hare, J. (1984) *The endangered black family.* San Francisco: Black Think Tank.

Hawkins, D. F. (1987). Devalued lives and racial stereotypes: Ideological barriers to the prevention of family violence among Blacks. In R. L. Hampton (Ed.), *Violence in the Black family: Correlates and consequences* (pp. 189–205). Lexington, MA: Lexington Books.

Herrnstein, R. J., & Murray, C. (1994). *The bell curve: Intelligence and class structure in American life.* New York: Free Press.

Hill, R. B. (1999). *The strengths of African American families: Twenty-five years later.*Lanham, MD: University Press of America.

Hooks, B. (1992). *Black looks: Race and representation.* Boston: South End Press.

Hooks, B. (1995). *Killing rage: Ending racism.* New York: Holt.

Jeff, M. F. X. (1994). Afrocentrism and African-American male youths. In R. B. Mincy (Ed.), *Nurturing young black males* (pp. 99–118). Washington, DC: The Urban Institute Press.

Jenkins, E. J., & Bell, C. C. (1997). Exposures and responses to community violence among children and adolescents. In J. D. Osofsky (Ed.), *Children in a violent society* (pp. 9–31). New York: Guilford Press.

Kaufman-Kantor, G. (1990). Paper presented at the forty-second annual meeting of the American Society of Criminology, Baltimore, MD.

King, M. L. (1965). Address delivered at Abbott House, Westchester County, New York.

Kunjufu, J. (1984). *Developing positive self-images and discipline in black children.* Chicago: African-American Images.

Leigh, J. W. (1998). *Communicating for cultural competencies.* Boston: Allyn & Bacon.

Leonard, K. E., & Jacob, T. (1988). Alcohol, alcoholism, and family violence. In V. B. Van Hasselt, R. L. Morrison, A. S. Bellack, & M. Hersen (Eds.), *Handbook of family violence* (pp. 383–406). New York: Plenum Press.

Liebow, E. (1967).*Tally's corner.* Boston: Little, Brown.

Lockhart, L. (1985). Methodological issues in comparative racial analyses: The case of wife abuse. *Social Work Research and Abstracts, 21,* 35–41.

Lockhart, L., & White, B. W. (1989). Understanding marital violence in the Black community. *Journal of Interpersonal Violence, 4,* 421–436.

Madhubuti, H. R. (1990). *Black men—single, dangerous, and obsolete.* Chicago: Third World Press.

Martin, M. J., & Martin, E. P. (1985). *The helping tradition of the black family.* Silver Spring, MD: National Association of Black Social Workers.

Mbiti, J. S. (1969). *Introduction to African religion* (2nd ed.). Oxford, England: Heineman.

McNeely, R. L., & Jones, M. (1980). Refuge from violence: Establishing shelter services for battered women. *Administration in Social Work, 4*(4), 71–82.

McNeely, R. L., & Mann, C. R. (1990). Domestic violence is a human issue. *Journal of Interpersonal Relations, 5*(1), 129–132.

McNeely, R. L., & Robinson, G. (1987). The truth about domestic violence: A falsely framed issue. *Social Work, 32*(6), 485–490.

McNeely, T. L., Torres, J. B., & Cook, P. (2001). Is domestic violence a gender issue or a human issue? In L. See (Ed.), *Violence as seen through a prism of color* (pp. 227–251). New York: Haworth Press.

Meier, A., & Rudwick, E. (1970). *From plantation to ghetto.* New York: American Century Series. Hill & Wang.

Miller, M. L. (2001). Spousal abuse/domestic violence. In D. Peck & N. A. Dolch (Eds.), *Extraordinary behavior* (p. 108). London: Praeger.

Murray, C. (1984). *Losing ground: American social policy: 1950–1980.* New York: Basic Books.

Oliver, W. (1989). Sexual conquest and patterns of black-on-black violence: A structural-cultural perspective. *Violence and Victims, 4,* 257–273.

Oliver, W. (1998). *The violent social world of black men.* San Francisco: Jossey-Bass.

Oliver, W. (2001). Cultural racism and structural violence: Implications for African Americans. In L. See (Ed.), *Violence as seen through a prism of color* (pp. 1–26). New York: Haworth Press.

Poussaint, A. (1983). Black-on-black homicide: A psycho-political perspective. *Victimology, 8,*161–169.

Rasheed, J., & Rasheed, M. (1999). *Social work practice with African American men* (p. 109). Newbury Park, CA: Sage.

Rennison, C. M., & Welchans, S. (2000). *Intimate partner violence.* Washington, DC: U.S. Department of Justice.

Rich, J. A., & Stone, D. A. (1996). The experience of violent injury for young African American men: The meaning of being a sucker. *Journal of General Medicine, 11,* 77–82.

Richie, B. E. (1994). *Compelled to crime: The gender entrapment of black battered women.* New York: Routledge.

Roberts, G. W. (1994). Brother to brother: African American modes of relating among men.*Journal of Black Studies, 24*(1), 379–390.

Saleebey, D. (1992). Power in the people. In D. Saleebey (Ed.), *The strengths perspective in social work practice* (pp. 3–17). New York: Longman.

Saunders, D. G. (1988). Wife abuse, husband abuse or mutual combat: A feminist perspective on the empirical findings. In M. Bograd (Ed.), *Feminist perspective on wife abuse* (pp. 99–113). Newbury Park, CA: Sage.

Schechter, S. (1982). *Women and male violence.* Boston: South End Press.

See, L. A. (Lee). (1989, summer). Tensions between black women and white women. *Journal of Women and Social Work, 4*(2), 31–45.

See, L. A. (Lee). (1998). *Group session held with batterers in private practice session.* March 28, 1990.

See, L. A. (Lee). (2001). *Violence as seen through a prism of color.* New York: Haworth Press.

See, L. A. (Lee), McNeely, R. L., Choi, N., & Torres, J. B. (2002). Social work practice with Asian Americans. In D. F. Harrison, B. A. Thyer, and J. S. Wodarski (Eds.), *Culture, diversity and social work practice* (3rd ed.). Springfield, IL: Charles C. Thomas.

Stampp, K. (1956). *The peculiar institution: Slavery in the ante-bellum south.* Toronto, Ontario, Canada: Vintage.

Staples, R. (1982). *Black masculinity: The black man's role in society.* San Francisco: Black Scholar Press.

Stark, E., Flitcraft, A., & Frazier, W. (1979). Medicine and patriarchal violence: The social construction of a "private" event. *International Journal of Health Services, 9,* 461–493.

Stark, E. (1990). Rethinking homicide: Violence, race, and the politics of gender. *International Journal of Health Services, 20*(1), 3–27.

Steinmetz, S. K. (1971). *Family violence: Past, present, future.* Newark: University of Delaware.

Steinmetz, S. K. (1977a). *The cycle of violence: Assertive, aggressive, and abusive family interaction.* New York: Praeger.

Steinmetz, S. K. (1977b). The use of force for resolving family conflict: The training ground for abuse. *The Family Coordinator, 26*(1), 19–26.

Steinmetz, S. K. (1980). The battered husband syndrome. *Victimology, 2*(3/4), 499–509.

Stordeur, R. A., & Stille, R. (1989). *Ending men's violence against their partners: One road to peace.* Newbury Park, CA: Sage.

Straus, M. A. (1994). *Beating the devil out of them: Corporal punishment in American families.* New York: Lexington Books.

Straus, M. A., & Gelles, R. J. (1986). Societal changes in family violence from 1975–1985 as revealed by two national studies. *Journal of Marriage and Family, 48,* 465–479.

Straus, M. A., Gelles, R. J., & Steinmetz, S. K. (1986). *Behind closed doors: Violence in the American family.* New York: Anchor Press/Doubleday.

Ucko, L. G. (1994). Culture and violence: The interaction of African and America. *Sex Roles, 31,* 185–204.

Uehara, E., Chalmers, D., Jenkins, E. J., & Shakoor, B. (1996). Youth encounters with violence: Results from the Chicago mental health council's violence prevention-screening project. *Journal of Black Studies, 26,* 768–781.

U.S. Census Bureau. (1999). *Statistical abstract of the United States—the national data book*(119th ed.). Washington, DC: U.S. Government Printing Office.

Walker, L. E. (1979). *The battered woman.* New York: Harper & Row.

Walker, L. E. (1984). *The battered woman syndrome.* New York: Springer.

Weick, A. (1992). Building a strengths perspective for social work. In D. Saleebey (Ed.), *The strengths perspective in social work practice* (pp. 18–26). New York: Longman.

Weick, A., Rapp, C., Sullivan, W. P., & Kisthardt, W. (1989). A strengths perspective for social work practice. *Social Work, 37,* 350–354.

West, C. M. (2000). Developing an oppositional gaze: Toward the images of black women. In J. C. Chrisler, C. Golden, & P. D. Rozee (Eds.), *Lectures on the psychology of women* (2nd ed., pp. 220–233). New York: McGraw-Hill.

West, T. C. (1999). *Wounds of the spirit—Black women, violence, and resistance ethics.* New York: New York University Press.

Williams, O. J. (1995). Treatment for African American men who batter. *Cura, 25,* 12–16.

Williams, O. J. (1998). African American men who batter: Treatment considerations and community response. In R. Staples (Ed.), *The black family: Essays and studies* (5th ed., pp. 265–279). Belmont, CA: Wadsworth.

Williams, O. J. (1999). Working in groups with African American men who batter. In L. D.Davis (Ed.), *Working with African American males—A guide to practice.* Thousand Oaks, CA: Sage.

Williams, O. J., & Becker, L. R. (1994). Domestic partner abuse treatment programs and cultural competence: The results of a national study. *Violence and Victims, 8,* 287–296.

Wilson, A. N. (1991). *Understanding black adolescent male violence: Its remediation and prevention.* New York: Afrikan Infosystems.

Wilson, W. J. (1996). *When work disappears—The world of the new urban poor.* New York: Vintage.

Chapter 5

DOMESTIC VIOLENCE IN LATINO CULTURES

DIANA VALLE FERRER

INTRODUCTION

Violence against women, or gender violence, is a global problem that has been part of family life throughout recorded history. Gender violence is a daily—and often deadly—fact of life for millions of women and girls around the world, according to the Final Statement of the Women's World Forum Against Violence (WWFAV), in 2000. Representatives of 113 nations declared that gender violence not only devastates women's lives and destroys their potential, but it also undermines the development and progress of all nations, especially in terms of equality and the possibility, for women, of exercising full citizenship (WWFAV, 2000). According to the World Health Organization (WHO) in 1997, violence against women is a major health and human rights issue. The WHO statistics reflect that at least one in five women in the world has been physically or sexually abused by a man (or men) at some time in her life, and many, including pregnant women and young girls, are subject to severe, sustained, or repeated attacks (WHO, 1997). The World Bank, in its 1993 World Development Report, stated that, worldwide, it has been estimated that violence against women is as serious a cause of death and incapacity among women of reproductive age as cancer, and is a greater cause of ill health than traffic accidents and malaria combined (World Bank, 1993).

Domestic violence—the most common form of violence against women—is particularly insidious. Research consistently demonstrates that the family is a violent institution and a woman is more likely to be injured, raped, or killed by a current or a former partner than by a stranger or any other person (Koss, 1990; Straus & Gelles, 1986). The place where women and children should be—or expect to be—safe and protected is the place where they most probably face fear, anger, and humiliation from physical, psychological, and sexual abuse. Even though more incidence and prevalence studies are needed to compare statistics from different countries and across cultures, some studies estimate that between 25% and over 50% of women worldwide report having been physically or psychologically abused by a partner or former partner (Heise, Pitauguy, & Germain, 1994).

These statistics reveal that violence against women in general, and domestic violence in particular, is not an exclusive problem of developing countries or of any culture in particular. No country or society can claim to be free of domestic violence; it cuts across boundaries of culture, class, education, income, ethnicity, and age (WWFAV, 2000).

DOMESTIC VIOLENCE IN LATIN AMERICA

There is a high incidence of domestic violence in Latin America and the Caribbean area. Recent prevalence studies indicate that, every year, between 30% and 50% of adult women are victims of psychological abuse, and between 10% and 35% of women are victims of physical abuse. Prevalence statistics of physical violence, compiled from existing studies by the World Health Organization (2000), wherein the aggressor is a current or former intimate partner, are presented in Table 5.1.

Soledad Larraín (1999) reports the conclusions drawn from a review of quantitative and qualitative descriptive studies carried out in Latin America with women victims who survived domestic violence. The main conclusions from these studies are:

- Women are more likely to be victimized in their own homes than any other place. Physical and sexual abuse, as well as murder, is perpetrated by the husbands or partners of the battered women in the context of an intimate relationship.

- Reports of domestic violence incidents have increased in recent years, probably as a result of domestic violence legislation, educational campaigns implemented by feminist and women's organizations, and the establishment of programs and services for battered women.

- Studies carried out in service institutions that do not offer specialized services for battered women revealed that if specific questions about abuse were asked, a high percentage of battered women were identified. However, many institutions and service programs (like hospital emergency rooms) do not ask specific questions in relation to domestic violence.

Table 5.1   Prevalence of Physical Violence against Women

Country	Coverage	Year of Study	Sample Size	Percentage of Adult Women Who Have Been Physically Assaulted by an Intimate Partner		
				In Past 12 Months	In Current Relationship	Ever (in Any Relationship)
Chile	Metro Santiago and Santiago province	1993[a]	1,000		26.0	
Chile	Santiago	1997	310	22.5		
Colombia	National	1995	6,097[b]			19.3
México	Durango City	1996	384			40.0
México	Metropolitan Guadalajara	1996	650	15.0		27.0
Nicaragua	León	1993	360	27.0[c]		52.2[c]
Nicaragua	Managua	1997	378	30.2		
Perú	Metropolitan Lima (middle and low income)	1997[a]	359	30.9		
Puerto Rico	National	1993–1996	7,079[b]			12.8[d]

[a] The year of publication is listed because the research paper did not state field work dates.
[b] Sample group included women who had never been in a relationship and therefore were not in exposed group.
[c] Definition of physical violence includes throwing and/or breaking objects while arguing.
[d] Statistic was recalculated by WHO from raw data.

- The highest rate for domestic violence is for women between the ages of 24 and 45 years, especially during pregnancy and immediately after birth.

- The most frequent manifestations of domestic violence are psychological abuse and mild physical abuse. In general, the studies found that when there is severe physical and sexual violence, psychological abuse is also present. Another kind of abuse identified was economic abuse.

- The majority of the participants in the studies reviewed stated that the principal cause of violence was related to the control women's partners exerted over them.

The conclusions drawn by Larraín (1999) in her review of studies in Latin America are similar to the ones drown by the U.S. National Research Council in its 1996 report. The Panel on Research on Violence Against Women (Crowell & Burgess, 1996) identified a number of consistent patterns found in its more than 20 years of survey research on violence against women in the United States:

- The most common assailant is a man known to the woman—often, it is her male intimate.

- The highest rate of violence is experienced by young women.

- Rape and battering are frequently accompanied by psychological abuse and are associated with a host of both short- and long-term problems.

Even though domestic violence has been present throughout the history of Latin America and the Caribbean, the recognition of domestic violence as a problem—especially a major social, health, and women rights issue—is due mainly to the efforts of the women's and feminist movement during the past 20 years. Feminist organizations in Latin America brought the problem of domestic violence to the forefront of the political and public policy agendas in various countries of the region. Moreover, the recognition of the magnitude of the problem, as well as the interest of human rights, health, and development organizations, has made domestic violence a priority in many governmental agendas of Latin America (Morrison & Biehl, 1999).

What are the causes and consequences of domestic violence in Latin America and the Caribbean? Are they embedded in the "Latin" culture, or is domestic violence a universal problem? In Latin America, as well as in other countries, there is no consensus as to the causes or the definition of what constitutes "domestic violence." According to Larraín (1999), responses, tolerance, and acceptance of domestic violence vary from one country to another and from one sociocultural context to another. Because Latin America is not a homogeneous region—it includes countries as different from one another as Mexico, Costa Rica, Chile, and Puerto Rico—we cannot generalize from one country to another. Even though the countries are generally united by language, religion, and history, each country has its unique sociocultural and historical factors that determine the understanding of and response to domestic violence.

Definitions of domestic violence differ as a result of different theoretical frameworks (Valle, 1999) as well as with regard to behavior and expressions that are considered violent (Larraín, 1999). Larraín (1999) asserts that definitions used to describe domestic violence either emphasize its impact, the cultural values that influence the violent behavior, or describe the different types of domestic violence.

Valle (1999) asserts that three theoretical frameworks have been used in Latin America to understand and explain domestic violence: (a) the psychological perspective (interpersonal violence model); (b) the sociological approach (family violence model); and (c) the feminist perspective (gender model). These three perspectives have been used, together or separately, to try to understand, explain, and predict violence against women in families (Ferreira, 1991; Ramírez, 2000).

Psychological, sociological, and feminist theories try to provide ways in which to understand, explain, and predict violence against women, as well as to formulate ways in which the violence can be ended. The difference among them consists in the various means or forms they suggest for ending the violence. Psychological theories suggest that the route to solving the problem of abuse of women is through psychotherapy directed at changing the persons who either perpetrate the violence or are its victims. Among the therapies they recommend are: anger control and impulse control for aggressors, and assertiveness and self-esteem therapy for women "victims." Sociological theories that see the family as the problem would take the route of changing the structure of the violence-prone family institution. Feminist theories call for an end to sexist discrimination and oppression and a transformation of society so that political, sociocultural, and economic structures benefit women and men equally (Valle, 1999).

Larraín (1999) affirms that, in Latin America, the concept of domestic violence has evolved to gender violence, and this fact implies a change in the conceptualization of violence against women and the understanding of the risk factors associated with it. Moreover, the feminist or gender perspective provides a broad framework in which to understand and explain violence against women in families. It offers the big picture that violence against women is not just an individual problem, but a sociocultural and political one. Violence, abuse, and battering are forms of social control of women; they impact on women's personal, individual, psychic, physical, and social selves, as well as on their responses to violence. They also have an impact on social institutions such as marriage and the family.

M. Soledad Weinstein (1991), a feminist sociologist, argues that violence against women can be understood as a pattern of oppressive interpersonal relationships. The referent of the pattern is located in the social structure, but it extends and reproduces itself at the interior of the family and of other social subsystems. Feminist research has focused on finding the relationship between the degree of institutional violence in a given society and the presence of a patriarchal structure that imposes hierarchical and oppressive relationships on the society and on the family (Duque & Weinstein, 1990; Eisler & Loye, 1986). In this feminist model, violence is viewed simultaneously as a result and as a condition that maintains women in a subordinate position. In other words, the different manifestations of violence against women in a patriarchal society are explained as being rooted in the hierarchical structure of power relations. In this set of social relations, women are seen as being inferior and dependent on men, who are viewed as having legitimate authority. We could say that the legitimacy of this scheme rests on the construction of dichotomous parameters of what constitutes masculinity and femininity. Superiority and legitimate power or authority are associated with masculinity, and a need for protection and weakness is associated with femininity. In Puerto Rico, wife battering has been explained from a social/structural/theoretical framework, informed by socialist feminist theory (Silva Bonilla, 1985; Silva Bonilla, Rodríguez, Cáceres, Martínez, & Torres,

1990). Violence against women in the family is understood as being rooted in the hierarchical social/economic structure of inequality, where women are subordinated to men.

According to Silva Bonilla (1985), violence against women in the family has been supported historically in Puerto Rico by two main ideas: (a) women are the property of men, and (b) the home is a private domestic sphere where strangers should not interfere. Socioeconomic constraints, derived from the sexual hierarchy through which women are made economically dependent on men, place women in a subordinate position within society. Silva Bonilla (1985) explains that social and economic factors are mediated in each person by his or her personal history (e.g., socioeconomic class), the ideology the person supports or questions, and the accumulation of concrete social experiences. In a more recent publication on wife abuse, Silva Bonilla and others (1990) elaborated on the notion that women have been ideologically conditioned to feel and think of themselves as property of men (father, husband, boyfriend, lover) and to be "responsible," by their "nature," for producing and maintaining "good," loving, marital and family relationships. Women assume the responsibility of maintaining the integrity of the family and the marriage. When the marriage "fails," the woman feels guilty for its "failure." She feels that she might be responsible for the abuse. Furthermore, Silva Bonilla (1990) argues that even though many women subscribe to these ideological premises, they actually participate in a historical questioning of them. Women in their praxis, in their daily lives, actively question and resist the ideas that, many times, are kept intact in their affective and emotional sphere.

Valle (1998), in a study about the ways Puerto Rican women cope with spousal abuse, explains that women participants used more problem-focused coping strategies to "save" the marriage and family because, traditionally, the role of wife and mother has been very important in Puerto Rican as well as in other Latin American cultures. She explains that, in Puerto Rican culture, marriage and family life have a central position. Marriage not only legitimizes the bearing of children and the formation of a family, it is also related to women's self-esteem and respectability. Traditionally, women who do not marry are seen as suspect. It is suspected that something is wrong with them. Young women are pressured to get married so that they can become "real" and "good" women. Women are also seen as responsible for the well-being of both the marriage and the family. They are in charge of nurturing and maintaining the family. If a marriage fails, the woman fails as a woman, a wife, and a mother. After all, what good mother would do so much harm to her children as to leave them without a father? Divorced women are also seen as suspect, not only by society, but by other women, who feel that they might be possible rivals.

An article in a Puerto Rican newspaper (*The San Juan Star,* Wednesday, January 3, 1996) portrayed how the ideology of domesticity (family/household/motherhood) is transmitted and perpetuated in Puerto Rican culture and in social institutions such as the family and the school. A teacher in an After-School Supervised Study and Tutoring Center, which caters to elementary and junior high school students, was interviewed and quoted as saying: "Mothers today, especially in Puerto Rico, have gotten themselves loaded with work. . . . They are responsible for the solidarity of the whole family unit; for raising the children; for social relations in the community; for bringing extra income into the house; for helping with the children's homework. Not to mention their own personal health and beauty." The article goes on to say that mothers "are overloaded with responsibilities. This is a technical area that can be transferred to another mother figure, in a homelike atmosphere. It gives them time to breathe and have some space for themselves."

This quotation is representative of family ideological hegemony in Puerto Rico and Latin America. The teacher of the Study Center (and the media) perpetuates three basic points in the ideology of domesticity (Barret, 1988):

1. Women/Mothers are responsible for "everything" that goes on in the family/household, including serving the men, taking care of themselves as well as of emotional relationships, and child caring and rearing.

2. Women's work outside the home is "extra" income, perpetuating the ideology of men as the primary breadwinners.

3. The school is a prolongation of the family/home. "Mother figures," in a "homelike atmosphere" cater to children and adolescents. In addition, women are responsible (guilty, perhaps?) for having "gotten themselves" loaded with all this work, and they deserve (maybe?) to breathe a bit.

In this context of a hegemonic cultural ideology of familialism, and in the "concrete" marriage and familial personal interrelationship, women are coping, surviving, and resisting. The irony of this predicament is that women must survive (continue to exist, remain alive) in the "concrete" family to be able to "save" the ideology of familialism.

Women have been taught, through the processes of socialization and ideological formation, what is their place, what is important, and what has (or should have) meaning for them. The family/marriage/household is their context of oppression, but it is also their context of resistance and power. Through the processes of ideological formation, which Barret (1988) defines as "those processes which have to do with consciousness, motivation and emotionality and through which meaning is produced, challenged, reproduced, and transformed," women defend and subscribe to this hegemonic ideology at the same time that they question and contest it. Through the processes of ideology, women internalize "the oppressor" and they subscribe, apparently of their own free will, to a necessity resulting from a family-marriage relationship of dominance and from the hegemonic culture.

The woman/wife/mother must not only battle the man/husband/father and the dominant culture; she must also struggle with her own dicta. She must resist and confront the internalized structures of oppression—"that piece of the oppressor which is implanted deep within each of us" (Freire, 1971). The women victims/survivors of violence must confront their own values, commitments, and beliefs, which were so deeply ingrained and so tenderly and hopefully nurtured throughout their lives. They must confront their own "subjective" commitment and beliefs as well as cultural, social, and structural "objective" dicta and practices.

The women victims'/survivors' homes, their family households, their marriages, and their daily lives are the sites of oppression and, simultaneously, of resistance. They use resistance and coping strategies to defend and support their commitment to their marriages and families when they perceive that they are threatened. They were promised "protection," "love," and economic stability in exchange for being primarily responsible for servicing the male/husband, and for doing all the tasks connected with housework and children. To defend and support their commitment to their families and their marriage relationships while defending themselves and their children, they cry, argue, lie, listen, shout, strike back, go to sleep, fantasize, go to another room, or leave the abusive situation. They use different strategies to regulate their emotions and any responses that would alter their behavior and their environment. Rico (1996), a well-known researcher, states that, in Latin America and the Caribbean, women are vulnerable independently of social class or occupation. One of the factors that makes women similar to one another is the possibility that each is a victim of some type of abuse. She affirms that discussion of domestic violence is taboo. The topic is condemned to social invisibility and justified by cultural traditions.

The influence of cultural traditions and patterns has been used as another way to explain violence against women in families and societies. Ramírez Hernández (2000), using a gender perspective, explains that men in Latin America, from an early age, learn two basic social principles: (a) there are people who give orders and are served, and (b) there are inferior people who serve and obey orders. Each man is trained, from boyhood, to learn the role of man/owner/head/father that he will assume when he is an adult. Ramírez Hernández (2000) asserts that the majority of cultures accept that women are inferior to men, and men create cultural forms (myths and traditions) that define and reinforce this alleged inferiority. Violence against women by men is explained as a way for men to impose their superiority, their exertion of control through violence. To maintain their position of superiority, men feel that it is necessary to be violent. Women do not want to be placed in a position of inferiority, so they rebel against this alleged condition. When women rebel and resist, men feel justified in their use of violence. Ramírez Hernández (2000) explains this situation in the context of a patriarchal social structure. Feminist theory and research (Hooks, 1984, 1990; Levinson, 1989; Morrison & Biehl, 1999) stress that the patriarchal structure of the family legitimizes violence by men, and male authority within the family is supported by social arrangements outside the family. Feminist theory and activism have been integral to combating domestic violence in Latin America. Scholars, researchers, and activists have analyzed how the abuse of women is endemic in patriarchal societies and how societal institutions tend to support men's violence. These efforts have offered many women in Latin America new hope and strength to continue on a path of transforming themselves, their families, and their social and cultural context.

DOMESTIC VIOLENCE AND LATINO WOMEN IN THE UNITED STATES: CURRENT TRENDS AND ISSUES

It is estimated that one in six American women is abused by the man with whom she lives (Straus & Gelles, 1995), and that 22% of adult women in the United States have been physically assaulted by an intimate partner in any relationship (WHO, 2000). Violence against women, by their partners or former partners, is a major problem in the United States. However, although violence against women is considered a universal problem, legislation, policy, research, intervention, and prevention efforts in the United States have failed to focus on the experience of minority women—specifically, of Latinas.

The Second National Family Violence Survey (Straus & Gelles, 1986) provided data that compared the rates of intimate violence for African Americans, non-Hispanic whites, and Hispanics. These results revealed that black and Hispanic families had comparable rates of husband-to-wife violence, and, in both groups, the rate of severe assaults on wives was more than double the rate in non-Hispanic white families (Straus & Gelles, 1986).

In the National Crime Victimization Survey Report, in contrast to the National Family Violence Surveys, Bachman (1994) found no significant differences among Anglo-American, African American, and Hispanic groups in rates of serious violence. Earlier, Sorenson and Telles (1991) had reported that spousal violence rates for Mexican Americans born in Mexico and non-Hispanic whites born in the United States were nearly equivalent (20% and 22%, respectively); rates were highest for Mexican Americans born in the United States (31%).

Findings from the National Violence Against Women Survey, conducted by the National Institute of Justice, revealed that Hispanic women reported slightly fewer incidents of domestic violence than non-Hispanic women—54.9% and 55.9%, respectively (Tjanden & Thoennes, 1998). The studies mentioned above show contradictory conclusions for Hispanics. Apparently, Hispanics were reported to be higher (Straus & Gelles, 1995) similar (Sorenson & Telles, 1991), or lower (Tjanden & Thoennes, 1998) than non-Hispanic whites for domestic violence in marriage. However, it is possible that these differences result from sample differences, study contexts, different data collection methods, and the use of different domestic violence definitions in the various studies (Crowell & Burgess, 1996). Future research studies need to identify how structural and cultural factors such as poverty, lack of or limited education, unemployment, language, religion ethnicity, family structure, and gender interact to determine domestic violence prevalence and incidence within and across ethnic groups.

Several issues of concern are discussed in the Latino domestic violence literature and the Latino community. Among the most pressing concerns are the scarcity, fragmentation, and underfunding of domestic violence programs for Latinos in general and Latinas in particular. Negotiating multiple and fragmented programs and services is an overwhelming barrier for Latinos.

Other barriers include inaccessibility of services; discrimination; institutional racism and sexism; and lack of bilingual and bicultural personnel, written and audiovisual educational materials in Spanish, and understanding of cultural patterns and traditions.

Additional obstacles that immigrant Latinas might face include a fear of deportation, economic and emotional dependence on their abusive partner, and limited knowledge of ways to get assistance from federal, state, and community resources. Immigrant women may also be vulnerable to domestic violence because many of them depend on their husbands for information regarding their legal status. Crenshaw (1994) asserts that many women who are now permanent residents continue to suffer abuse under threats of deportation by their husbands, even if the threats are unfounded. Women who depend on their husband, or his family, for information and support may feel intimidated by such threats. Immigrant women in the United States are often without a network of friends and family who can help and support them in their efforts to confront and survive violence.

The language barrier is one of the most salient problems for some Latino victim/survivors of domestic violence. This is a structural problem that limits not only access to information about services but the actual services that women have a right to receive. Many shelters in the United States limit services to English-speaking women and deny Spanish-speaking women the security they need for themselves and their children (Crenshaw, 1994).

A woman's inability or limited ability to speak English may also keep her from seeking help. A woman may have some ability to speak English, but because domestic violence is an extremely personal and often embarrassing subject to discuss, it becomes more difficult to express in a language that is not her own. The process of disclosing and sharing domestic violence experiences is emotionally draining for both the counselor and the woman victim/survivor of violence. The experience of having someone who empathetically listens and then validates the woman's emotions, thoughts, and actions should be therapeutic. If a common language is not shared between the woman and the listener, the experience might add to the woman's traumatic and humiliating experiences of violence, oppression, and exclusion.

These examples illustrate another issue of concern within the Latino community. The National Latino Alliance for the Elimination of Domestic Violence (1997) has identified the legacy of multiple oppressions as one of the most difficult obstacles the Latino community has confronted in its efforts to respond adequately to domestic violence. The Alliance recognizes that domestic violence is a crime and the victims are largely women and children, but it asserts that the violence occurs in a context of a community suffering from a legacy of multiple oppressions that go back for centuries: poverty, both in the United States and in the Latino countries of origin; long-term discrimination; racism; and colonization. Because of this legacy, the Alliance explains, Latinos in the United States have not been able to promote their interests effectively in the legislative, legal, and program development arenas.

On the other hand, in the women-of-color literature, feminists of color (Anzaldua, 1990; Crenshaw, 1994; Hooks, 1990; Lorde, 1984; Moraga & Anzaldua, 1983; Rivera, 1994) theorize about the intersection of race, ethnicity, class, and gender hierarchies, and the multiple kinds of oppression that the powerless suffer at the hands of the powerful. Crenshaw (1994) argues that while the intersection of race, gender, and class constitutes the primary structural element of the experience of many black and Latino women in shelters for battered women, there are other sites where structures of power intersect and may threaten the women because of their immigration status and/or language barriers. Focusing on two dimensions of male violence against women—battering and rape—Crenshaw considers how the experiences of women of color are frequently the product of intersecting patterns of racism and sexism, and how these experiences tend to be unrepresented within the discourse of either feminism or antiracism. A woman's sense of her ethnicity—and, in some cases, her feminist intervention—can contribute her not reporting that she is experiencing domestic violence. Antiracist and feminist strategies may reproduce the subordination, as well as the marginalization and exclusion, of women of color with regard to domestic violence services (Crenshaw, 1994). For example, black and Latino women may often be reluctant to call the police for fear that their husbands will be mistreated in the hands of law enforcement officers, and their communities may be targeted for intrusive interventions. Many Latin women are also afraid of family and community members' ostracism for "betrayal" of their family's race or ethnic group. In many cases, a desire to protect their families from assaults from the environment may make it more difficult for Latinas to seek protection against assaults from within their own family. In Latino communities, the authority of the family is respected, and individual needs often defer to family unit and strength. For many battered Latinas, this often means hiding and minimizing abuse for the sake of family preservation.

The need for inclusion of and attention to Latinos in research has been identified as an issue of concern in the Latino domestic violence literature. Aldorondo, Josinsky, and Kaufman-Kantor, (1999) have recommended that research on wife assault should focus on the individual, relationship, social, and cultural determinants within specific ethnic groups such as Mexicans, Mexican Americans, and Puerto Ricans. Also addressed in the literature (Carrillo & Tello, 1998) is the need for more culturally sensitive research that results in more effective prevention and intervention efforts in the Latino community. In addition, research has not focused on clarification of how structural factors relating to race, ethnicity, poverty, and immigration status interact with gender to create the specific content in which violence is experienced by women (Crenshaw, 1994).

PREVENTION OF AND INTERVENTION IN DOMESTIC VIOLENCE

If domestic violence, including violence against women, is a sociocultural, political, global problem and not just an individual or family problem, how do we eradicate it? How do we intervene and prevent it? How do individuals, families, and cultural patterns change? How can policies and politics help? How can *we* help?

Domestic violence continues to exist because it is part of our social fabric; it is intertwined in the patriarchal and hierarchical structure of the power in our institutions. In pervasive and insidious ways, our society implicitly accepts and condones violence against women, supported by a belief that domestic violence is a private matter and not a public concern (Ghez, 1995). The intersection of race, ethnicity, class and gender hierarchies, and multiple kinds of oppression makes the situation of Latino women different from that of white and black women in the United States. Efforts aimed at the intervention and prevention of domestic violence have not responded effectively to Latinas' needs.

Few programs in the United States focus directly on prevention and intervention with domestic violence in the Latino community. Few shelters in the United States have attempted to deliver services to Latinas in battering relationships that are culturally specific (Campbell, Masaki, & Torres, 1997). Despite the efforts of a small number of Latino and Latino-run providers and community-based organizations to provide services to Latinas who are victims/survivors of domestic violence, these efforts are insufficient to meet the demand (Rivera, 1997). For example, there are only three Latino bilingual and bicultural domestic violence programs in New York State (two of them in Manhattan), even though according to Census 2000 (U.S. Census Bureau, 2001),15% of the state's population is Latino. For example, in a telephone interview with Evelyn García, Director for Statewide Services of the New York State Spanish Domestic Violence Hotline, she explained that in Suffolk County in Long Island, where there is a high number of Latinos, there are no domestic violence services for Latinas. Moreover, in the programs they do have for survivors of domestic violence, they lack bilingual staff workers. Based on the experience of Latinas who are survivors of domestic violence, Rivera (1997) reports that as a result of a shelter shortage and staffing deficiencies, Latinas in New York must endure long waiting periods to secure residential placement. In addition, Latinas report feeling isolated, and sometimes discriminated against, in residential programs that lack linguistic and culturally appropriate services.

If we take into account the multiple factors that cause and perpetuate domestic violence, the strategies and interventions developed to respond to it should be developed within an integrated ecosystemic framework that considers the person interacting with the environment, responding to it, and transforming it. The response to domestic violence in the United States should consider interventions at the individual, family, community, societal, and cultural levels. According to Campbell et al. (1997), structural factors such as discrimination, poverty, substance abuse, and violence all interact in complex ways; each reinforces the other and places ethnic minority groups at increased risk for domestic violence even when ethnicity is not necessarily a risk factor in and of itself. Moreover, these researchers argue that structural realities are at least as important as cultural patterns. In addition, sexism and gender violence against women in America could be viewed both as structural and cultural realities.

Responding to domestic violence from a broad perspective is essential, given the complexity and the multiplicity of variables involved in domestic violence. The only strategies that can guarantee the elimination of domestic violence are those that are implemented at different levels—individual, community, society—and confront structural and cultural variables at the same time, so that appropriate programs and services are provided for *all* women victims/survivors of violence.

In the planning, designing, implementing, and evaluating of preventive and interventionist strategies, all stakeholders—program and service participants, community-based organizations, public and private agencies, the media, and so on—should be taken into consideration. The collaboration among these stakeholders should be carried out in the context of the different levels of intervention.

WOMEN AND FAMILIES

As mentioned earlier, the family unit is central in Latinas' lives, and maintaining this unit, even at their own expense, is primary (Valle, 1999). However, in their daily lives, Latinas question and resist the cultural, religious, and dominant group views imposed on them. They resist and confront their own "subjective" commitment and beliefs, as well as cultural and social structural "objective" dicta and practices. Because their dignity, their pride, and their very lives are at stake, women are the principal agents of change in the struggle against domestic violence. Even though the feminist and battered women's movements have been crucial in identifying and confronting violence against them, women in their homes, in the context of their daily lives, and in their families and communities, have contributed to the process of creating a better political, economic, social, and cultural life for themselves and their families. Women in the Latino communities should be heard and consulted in the process of planning, implementing, and evaluating domestic violence prevention and intervention programs. To see Latinas both influenced by and influencing the social structure and culture is imperative in designing programs that effectively respond to their needs and concerns. These women survivors of domestic violence must be viewed as individual, active agents who are firmly embedded within the social, cultural, political, and economic context in which they live. Cultural and social structural variables interact with the commitments and beliefs that shape women's perception of their situation, as well as with the demands, constraints, and resources of the immediate battering situation. Latinas' personal histories of abuse, their demands regarding their present abusive situation, and their perception of the battering and of sociocultural variables, should guide the delivery of services.

Women and children exposed to abuse are thought always to be victims who are damaged in ways that obscure or override any strengths or possibilities for redemption or rebound (Saleebey, 1997). However, recognizing and building on women's history, experiences, coping strategies, and strengths are essential for the healing process. Assessment of and intervention with Latina survivors of domestic violence are more effective if the abuse is analyzed in the context of the dynamics of multiple oppressions based on gender, race, ethnicity, and class (among other variables), and within an ecosystemic framework that includes gender and strengths perspectives. In this way, women's strengths and ways of coping with abuse can be viewed as a process and contextualized in the battering situation and the society in which it occurs.

Efforts directed at the prevention of domestic violence must address the educational, employment, and child-care needs of Latinas. Legal and human rights education should be part of an integrated prevention, support, and intervention effort. Housing needs must also be a priority in any integrated effort at prevention of and intervention with domestic violence. Transitional housing programs, as well as programs giving preference to domestic violence survivors, are essential in an integrated services approach.

In the United States, few programs concentrate or prioritize directly on prevention of and intervention in domestic violence in the Latino community. However, Campbell et al. (1997) inform that successful community-based programs tend to be designed using intimate knowledge of and respect for the cultural heritage of the participants. They recommend continued preventive efforts aimed at developing community institutions and support systems, raising consciousness, and offering education in domestic violence. Community groups and public institutions should be trained to identify women, adolescents, and children who are at risk of domestic violence.

Children who are witnesses of domestic violence have been found to exhibit high levels of aggressive and antisocial, as well as fearful and inhibited behaviors (Hester, Pearson, & Harwen, 2000). Researchers have also found that children exposed to domestic violence see violence as an acceptable and useful means of resolving conflict. In a study with Puerto Rican children between the ages 8 to 11 years, who were witnesses of domestic violence, Caro Morales et al. (2000) found that these children exhibited depression and aggressive behaviors. However, one of the most significant findings of this study is that the child's abused mother was the most significant person in the child's support network. This finding illustrates the importance of working with Latinas and their children, in an effort to intervene and prevent domestic violence in the Latino community.

THE COMMUNITY AND THE SOCIETY

In the Latino community, the family and the community are central in the mediation of conflict. Therefore, any social change effort must mobilize the local community in opposing domestic violence. Community members could get involved in developing services for survivors of domestic violence and eradicating violent behavior of men against women in the family. Community education and information efforts should arise from the local communities, supported by and in collaboration with the government and the private sector.

In the area of prevention, community efforts should focus on massive education campaigns that raise the issue of domestic violence and how to prevent it. Findings of surveys and focus groups (Campbell et al., 1997), which included telephone interviews of 300 Latinos, suggest that public messages should not stress any particular causal factor of domestic violence, but should emphasize the sentiment that domestic violence is wrong and cannot be tolerated. This message would be effective with any ethnic minority only if delivered in a manner that clearly indicated that members of a particular group were not exceptions to the message (Campbell et al., 1997). It is necessary to realize that ethnicity and culture are not static, and local communities have to develop new cultural norms that respect women and view domestic violence, and all forms of violence against women and children, as unacceptable and intolerable.

Following are other responses or interventions, at community and social levels, that should respond to the diversity among cultural groups:

Community Level
- Recognize and validate the differences and diversity among Latino families.
- Work conjointly to eradicate the patriarchal ideology of the family, characterized by the domination of men and the subordination of women and children.
- Revise school curricula at all levels—elementary, secondary, and university—to eliminate gender stereotypes and promote equality and equity among individuals, without regard to racial or ethnic background.
- Evaluate the effectiveness and efficiency of the criminal justice response to domestic violence in Latino communities.
- Provide, in Latino communities, child care services to all women and families that need them.
- Evaluate traditional approaches to wife abuse to incorporate the analyses of domestic violence within a multiple oppression perspective.
- Recognize the goals, tasks, and responsibilities of collaboration among governmental, nongovernmental, and community organizations.

Sociocultural Level
- Promote sociocultural and social policy changes that demand and guarantee equality among all ethnic or racial groups, and eradicate gender inequality.

- Create employment and housing that respond to the needs of the working classes in the Latino communities.
- Promote massive educational and culture-specific campaigns for the elimination of domestic violence and violence in general.

FUTURE RESEARCH

Until recently, research on domestic violence omitted the experiences of minority women. Campbell et al. (1997) argue that omission of information about the race and ethnicity of the women studied, inclusion of nonrepresentative proportions or representative proportions of minority women in an overall sample size too small for appropriate comparisons, and failure to analyze the results according to ethnicity are typical occurrences in mainstream domestic violence research.

Other problematic issues for Latinas participating in domestic violence research are language, defective translations of research instruments, and lack of sensitivity to ethnic differences among Latinos. As mentioned earlier in this chapter, language is a barrier not only to receiving services, but also to participating in research, program planning, and evaluation of services.

Faulty translation of instruments often hinders or affects negatively the reliability and validity of research. The Latino population in the United States consists of many immigrants (and their descendants) from North, Central, and South America as well as from the Caribbean area. When translating research instruments, a variety of regionalisms have to be a taken into consideration. Another problem often encountered is the translator's faulty knowledge of the Spanish language. Important instruments should be translated by professional translators.

Lack of sensitivity for the ethnic, religious, and cultural background or immigration status of the women who are respondents also hinders the research interviewing process.

In general terms, this author agrees with the improvements in research methods recommended by the Panel on Research on Violence Against Women, established by the National Research Council in 1995 (Crowell & Burgess, 1996). Among the key topics that the panel recommends for improving research on violence against women are the following:

- Clear definition, by researchers and practitioners, of the terms used in their work;
- Development and testing of scales and other tools of measurement, to make operational the key and most used definitions;

- Improvement in the reliability and validity of research instruments through guidance from subpopulations with whom the instruments will be used— for example, people of color or specific ethnic groups;
- Clarification of theory and the outcomes expected from the intervention in evaluation research;
- The use of randomized, controlled outcome studies to identify the program and community features that account for effectiveness (or lack thereof) of legal and social service treatment interventions with various groups of offenders;
- Qualitative and quantitative research to recognize the confluence of the broad social and cultural contexts in which women experience violence, as well as the individual factors, such as race, ethnicity, socioeconomic status, age, and sexual orientation, that shape the context and experience of violence in women's lives.

In summary, future research should seek to recognize and clarify the complexity of culture and cultural influences and steer away from stereotypical and essentialist interpretations of ethnicity and cultural values and beliefs (Falicov, 1998; Hampton et al. 1998). Latino groups in the United States show the same ethnicity, but they belong to different generations, social classes, genders, educational levels, and degrees of acculturation. Future research should also address and recognize the multiple oppressions that Latinos in general, and Latino women in particular, confront in the United States. Finally, future research should seek not only to understand and explain domestic violence in Latino cultures but should result in more effective prevention and intervention efforts with the goal of eliminating domestic violence in the Latino community.

REFERENCES

Aldorondo, E., Josinsky, J. L., & Kaufman-Kantor, G. (1999). *Risk marker analyses of wife assault in Latino families.* Manuscript submitted for publication.

Anzaldua, G. (1990). *Making faces, making soul/haciendo caras: Creative and critical perspectives by feminists of color.* San Francisco: Aunt Late Books.

Bachman, R. (1994). *Violence against women: A national crime victimization survey report.* Washington, DC: U.S. Department of Justice.

Barret, M. (1988). *Women's opresión today: The marxist/feminist encounter.* London: Verso.

Campbell, D. W., Masaki, B., & Torres, S. (1997). Water on rock: Changing domestic violence perceptions in the African American, Asian American, and Latino communities.

In E. Klein, J. Campbell, E. Soler, & M. Ghez (Eds.), *Ending domestic violence: Changing public perceptions/halting the epidemic.* Thousand Oaks, CA: Sage.

Caro Morales, E., Mattei, M., Medina, G., & Ortiz, M. (2000). *Cuando a mami la maltratan: Aspectos psicológicos, conductuales, interpersonales y sociales en preadolescentes testigos de violencia doméstica en sus hogares en Puerto Rico* [When my mother is battered: Psychological behavioral, interpersonal and social aspects of preadolescents who witness domestic violence]. Unpublished thesis, University of Puerto Rico.

Carrillo, R. A., & Tello, J. (Eds.). (1998). *Family violence and men of color: Healing the wounded male spirit.* New York: Springer.

Crenshaw, K. W. (1994). Mapping the margins: Intersectionality, identity politics, and violence against women of color. In M. A. Fineman & R. Mykitiuk (Eds.), *The public nature of private violence.* New York: Routledge.

Crowell, N., & Burgess, A. (1996). *Understanding violence against women.* Washington, DC: National Research Council.

Duque, I., Rodríguez, T., & Weinstein, M. S. (1990). *Violence against women: Definitions and strategies.* Santiago, Chile: Isis International.

Eisler, R., & Loye, D. (1986). Peace and feminist theory: New directions. *Bulletin of Peace Proposals, 17,* 1–17.

Falicov, C. J. (1998). *Latino families in therapy: A guide to multicultural practice.* New York: Guilford Press.

Freire, P. (1971). *Pedagogy of the oppressed.* New York: Seabury Press.

Ferreira, G. B. (1991). *La mujer maltratada* [The abused woman]. Buenos Aires: Editorial Sudamericana, S.A.

Ghez, M. (1995). *Communications and public education: Effective tools to promote a cultural change on domestic violence.* Paper presented at the Violence against Women Strategic Planning Meeting, National Institute of Justice, Washington, DC.

Hampton, R., Carrillo, R. A., & Kim, J. (1998). Violence in communities of color. In R. Carrillo & J. Tello (Eds.), *Family violence and men of color: Healing the wounded male spirit.* New York: Springer.

Heise, L., Pitauguy, J., & Germain, A. (1994). *Violence against women: The hidden health burden.* World Bank Discussion Paper, No 255. Washington, DC: The World Bank.

Hester, M., Pearson, C., & Harwen, N. (2000). *Making an impact: Children and domestic violence.* London: Jessica Kingsley.

Hooks, B. (1984). *Feminist theory: From margin to center.* Boston: South End Press.

Hooks, B. (1990). *Yearning: Race, gender and cultural politics.* Boston: South End Press.

Koss, M. P. (1990). The women's mental health research agenda: Violence against women. *American Psychologist, 45*(3), 374–380.

Larraín, S. (1999). "Dos décadas de acción para frenar la violencia doméstica. In A. R. Morrison & M. J. Biehl (Eds.), *El Costo del Silencio: Violencia Doméstica en las Américas* [Too close to home: Domestic violence in the Americas]. Washington, DC: Inter-American Development Bank.

Levinson, D. (1989). *Family violence in cross-cultural perspective.* Newbury Park, CA: Sage.

Lorde, A. (1984). *Siter outsider.* Trumansburg, NY: Crossing Press.

Moraga, C., & Anzaldua, G. (1983). *This bridge called my back: Writings by radical women of color.* New York: Kitchen Table, Women of Color Press.

Morrison, A. R., & Biehl, M. T. (1999). *El Costo del Silencio: Violencia Doméstica en las Américas* [Too close to home: Domestic violence in the Americas]. Washington, DC: Inter-American Development Bank.

National Latino Alliance for Elimination of Domestic Violence. (1997). Available from: www.dvalianza.org.

Ramírez Hernández, F. A. (2000). *Violencia masculina del hogar* [Masculine violence in the home]. México DF: Editorial Pax México.

Rico, N. (1996). "Violencia de género: Un problema de derechos humanos" [Gender violence: A human rights problem]. *Serie Mujer y Desarrollo,* No. 16, ECLAC.

Rivera, J. (1994). Domestic violence against Latinos and Latino males: An analysis of race, national origin, and gender differentials. *Boston College Third World Journal, 14,* 231.

Rivera, J. (1995). The politics of invisibility. *Georgetown Journal on Fighting Poverty, 3*(1), 61–65.

Rivera, J. (1997). Preliminary report: Availability of domestic violence services for Latino survivors in New York State. *Public Interest, 16,* 1–32.

Saleebey, D. (1997). *The strengths perspective in social work practice.* New York: Longman.

Silva Bonilla, R. (1985). *El marco social de la violencia contra las mujeres en la vida conyugal* [Violence against women in conjugal relationships: A social theoretical framework]. Río Piedras, Puerto Rico: Publicaciones Centro de Investigaciones Sociales, Universidad de Puerto Rico.

Silva Bonilla, R. M., Rodríguez, J., Cáceres, V., Martínez, L., & Torres, N. (1990). *Hay amores que matan: La violencia contra las mujeres en la vida conyugal* [Love kills: Violence against women in the family]. Río Piedras, Puerto Rico: Ediciones Huracán.

Sorenson, S., & Telles, C. (1991). Self-reports of spousal violence in a Mexican-American and non-Hispanic white population. *Violence and Victims, 6,* 3–16.

Straus, M., & Gelles, R. (1986). Societal change and change in family violence from 1975–1985 as revealed by two national studies. *Journal of Marriage and the Family, 48,* 465–479.

Straus, M., & Gelles, R. (1995). *Physical violence in American families: Risk factors and adaptations to violence in 8,145 families.* New Brunswick, NJ: Transaction Books.

Tjanden, P., & Thoennes, N. (1998, November, 1–5). *Prevalence, incidence, and consequences of violence against women: Findings from the national violence against women survey, National Institute of Justice.* Atlanta, GA: Centers for Disease Control and Prevention.

U.S. Census Bureau. (2001). Census 2000 Redistricting Data (Public Law 94-171) Summary file (Online). Available from: www.census.gov.

Valle, D. (1998). Validating coping strategies and empowering Latino battered women in Puerto Rico. In A. R. Roberts (Ed.), *Battered women and their families.* New York: Springer.

Valle, D. (1999). Estrategias de enfrentamiento de las mujeres contra la violencia. In D. Valle, L. Albite, & I. Rosado (Ed.), *Violencia en la familia: Una perspectiva crítica* [Violence in the family: A critical perspective]. San Juan, Puerto Rico: Ediciones Familia y Comunidad.

Weinstein, M. S. (1991). "Apuntes sobre la violencia cotidiana" [The absent woman: Human rights in the world]. In X. Brinster & R. Rodríguez (Eds.), *La mujer ausente: Drechos humanos en el mundo* (pp. 109–117). Santiago, Chile: Isis International.

Women's World Forum Against Violence. (2000). *Final statement, Queen Sofía, center for the study of violence on domestic violence.* Valencia, Spain. [Online]. Available from: www.gva.es/violencia/activid/mujeres/foro_e.htm

World Bank. (1993). *World development report* [Online]. Available from: www .worldbank.org

World Health Organization. (1997). *Violence and injury prevention: Violence against women: A priority health issue.* [Online]. Available from: www.who.int /violence_injury_prevention/vaw/infopack.htm

World Health Organization. (2000). *Violence and injury prevention: Prevalence of violence against women by an intimate male partner.* [Online]. Available from: www.who.int/violence_injury_prevention/vaw/prevalence.htm

SECTION II

Community Violence

Chapter 6

CHILDREN AND ADOLESCENTS EXPOSED TO COMMUNITY VIOLENCE

CATHERINE N. DULMUS and CAROLYN HILARSKI

CURRENT TRENDS AND ISSUES

Community Violence

The United States currently has the distinction of being the most violent country in the industrialized world (Rand, 1999). Unfortunately, this "distinction" may have grave consequences for the many American children whose daily lives include exposure to chronic community violence. Each day, in the United States, 9 children are murdered and 30 children are wounded with guns (Children's Defense Fund, 1993). Manning and Baruth (1995) reported that approximately 28,200 students are physically attacked in American schools each month. Overall, annually in the United States, approximately 1.4 million assaults occur that require a hospital emergency room visit (Rand, 1999). Acts of violence that do not necessitate an emergency room visit are incalculable.

Though crime rates have been decreasing in recent years (Rand, 1999), violence continues to be a public health problem in the United States. Many urban children continue to be victims of, and eyewitnesses to, episodes of violence in their communities and schools (Richters, 1993). Some of these children have described their experiences as "living in a battle zone" (Lorion & Saltzman, 1990).

Community violence is experienced as shootings, stabbings, burglaries, hate crimes, gang and drug activities, and verbal disputes. Because of their level of violence, some urban areas are considered "war zones." For example, Dubrow and Garbarino (1989) interviewed mothers with young children, who were living in public housing. Their greatest fear was that their children might be shot. In such circumstances, children may be required by their parent(s) to sleep under their beds at night and/or play within the confines of their home during the day. Parental attempts to keep children safe while living in a violent community may actually impede the children's developmental progress. Children learn about themselves and about how to negotiate their environments through social exchanges. This essential developmental experience is often denied or severely reduced for children living in unsafe neighborhoods. In addition, parental fear, helplessness, and apprehension can be passed to the child and may be especially pronounced if the parent is a primary victim of violence (Dulmus & Wodarski, 2000).

As with children, adolescents exposed to community violence may also experience grave consequences. Unfortunately, youths and young adults under age 25 comprise the majority of serious violent-crime victims (49%), and African Americans and Hispanics are disproportionately represented in this group (Perkins, 1997; Rand, 1999). In 1991, blacks were between six and seven times more likely than whites to become victims of homicide (Lauritsen & Tonry, 1998). Likewise, Hispanics experience higher rates of violent victimization (43.1%) than non-Hispanics (38.3%) (Lauritsen & Tonry, 1998; Rand, 1999). Victims of community violence also tend to be impoverished. Rand (1999) found that 24% of victims came from homes with annual household incomes of less than $15,000.

Prevalence of Community Violence

Exposure to community violence is a very real occurrence for children and adolescents living in urban America (Richters, 1993). Indeed, estimates project that 10 million youth are exposed to one or more traumatic events each year.

Male adolescents report particularly high levels of community victimization; 3% to 22% reported physical assault in an anonymous survey (Singer, Anglin, Song, & Lunghofer, 1995). Males (37%) report being beaten up at a much greater rate than females (16%) (Farrell & Bruce, 1997).

Young children are not exempt from exposure to violence. For example, a Boston survey indicated that 10% of children under the age of 6 years had witnessed a stabbing or shooting (Groves, Zuckerman, Marans, & Cohen, 1993).

The danger for children lurks not only in the larger community but in the schools as well. A national survey of public school principals reported these statistics for school incidents: 4,000 sexual attacks, 7,000 robberies, and 200,000 physical attacks with and without weapons (U.S. Department of Education, 1997).

IDENTIFICATION, CLASSIFICATION, AND PREDICTION OF VIOLENCE

Trauma

Trauma consists of emotional and physical injuries that can occur as a consequence of exposure to community violence. Emotional damage, a normal response to an extreme event, involves the creation of emotional (frozen) memories. The stress response (cortisol) precipitated by the trauma will shift energy away from the brain cortex and toward the limbic system. This reduces a child's ability to analyze rationally, to problem solve, and to store memory appropriately (nondeclarative memory). It can also cause confusion and attention problems, which may be the foundation of learning difficulties for students (Saigh, Mroueh, & Bremner, 1997).

Secondary Trauma

Community violence, unlike child abuse, is very often discussed openly. A child may repeatedly hear of a violent event and form an image of it that can precipitate emotional and physiological responses. The focus of research attention, when attempting to understand the ramifications of exposure to violence, has generally been on the primary victim. However, of late, it has been shown that being a witness to and even having knowledge of violence can clearly be traumatic (Dulmus & Wodarski, 2000; Vig, 1996).

Emotional Consequences of Community Violence

Children exposed to violence, when compared to those not exposed, are more likely to develop a wide range of social and emotional problems. In support of this, Garbarino, Kostelny, and Dubrow (1991) found that children exposed to community violence will adapt in ways that "produce developmental impairment, physical damage, emotional trauma, and will possibly be mis-socialized into a model of fear, violence, and hatred" (p. 377).

Studies of the psychological effects of children's exposure to violence have found these distress symptoms: intrusive thoughts, fear of recurrence of violence, anxieties, difficulty concentrating, depression, sleep disturbances, psychosomatic disturbances, withdrawal, behavioral difficulties, aggression, and dissociative reactions (Nader, Pynoos, Fairbanks, & Frederick, 1990; Pynoos, Goenjian, & Steinberg, 1998; Pynoos, Nader, Frederick, Gonda, & Stuber, 1987). A child's proximity to the violent event is related to the severity of the resulting symptoms and includes developmental problems that impact interpersonal, cognitive, behavioral, and psychological processes (Figley, 1993). Garbarino, Kostelny, and Dubrow (1991) reported that "adjustments and accommodations in development are likely to include persistent post traumatic stress (PTS) symptoms, alterations of personality, major changes in patterns of behavior or articulation of ideological interpretations of the world that are politicized and that provide a framework for making sense of ongoing danger" (p. 378). In other words, the influence of community violence exposure on the young goes beyond emotional and behavioral disorders. It affects the child's world and self view, life scheme, expectations for future happiness, and moral development (Ney, Fung, & Wickett, 1994).

Aggression and Acting-Out Behaviors

Social learning theory helps to explain how a child exposed to violence at a young age might later present with aggressive or violent behavior; the learned behavior is considered "normal" (Dodge, Pettit, & Bates, 1997). Recent studies support this model. For example, Miller, Wasserman, Neugebauer, Gorman-Smith, and Kamboukos (1999) found a significant correlation between parent-rated antisocial behavior and community violence exposure, in a sample of 6-to-10-year-old males (N = 97). Affect regulation is an important developmental task with respect to learning how to regulate aggressive impulses, differentiating between various emotional states of others, and learning prosocial behavior and competence (Osofsky, 1995).

Depression

Research suggests that youths' exposure to community violence increases the likelihood that anxious and depressive symptomatology will occur (Gorman-Smith & Tolan, 1998), especially when the violence was perpetrated against the self or close "others" (Martinez & Richters, 1993).

Young children exposed to community violence may have difficulty achieving bowel and bladder control, or experience delays in language acquisition that may affect their growing sense of independence, efficacy, and mastery of their environment (Drell, Siegel, & Gaensbauer, 1993). Children and adolescents exposed to chronic violence may develop a sense of learned helplessness. This can seriously affect their mood, their development of a sense of self-control, and their future orientation and hopefulness (Eron, Gentry, & Schlegel, 1994).

Psychobiological Effects

There are several ways that violence may affect children neurobiologically. First, the brain is very sensitive to environmental information during early childhood (Cicchetti, Rogosch, Toth, & Spagnola, 1997). Research has shown that children's central nervous system is influenced by interactive experiences (Cicchetti & Toth, 1998). Children exposed to violence may experience neurological anomalies due to the over- or understimulation of certain brain structures at specific developmental periods. Second, environmental violence can affect a child's ability to modulate attention and arousal. For example, parents suffering with mental health, economic, and/or safety issues may be so overwhelmed with their own life issues that they have a difficult time bonding with their child. This dysfunctional "attachment" does not give the child an opportunity to develop appropriate schema around issues of problem solving and social interactions. The child is then deficient in language and self-regulatory skills. The results are: difficulty in getting needs met, and increased "acting out" behaviors, which perpetuate the child's rejection by others. Without intervention, these early antisocial behaviors may increase the risk of later, more devastating issues.

Post-Traumatic Stress Disorder and Symptoms

An additional serious and potentially long-lasting problem for children exposed to community violence is post-traumatic stress disorder (PTSD). According to the most current *Diagnostic and Statistical Manual of Mental Disorders* (*DSM-IV*) (APA, 1994), a diagnosis of PTSD may be made only if:

> Symptoms are present following an exposure to a traumatic event, in which both of the following were true: (a) the person experienced, witnessed, or was confronted with an event or events that involved actual or threatened death or serious injury, or a threat to the physical integrity of self or others: and (b) the person's response involved intense fear, helplessness, or horror. (APA, 1994, pp. 427–428)

The *DSM-IV* (APA, 1994) requires three criteria to be met to warrant a diagnosis of PTSD. The first criterion involves re-experiencing the trauma in at least one of several ways:

> Recurrent and intrusive recollections; recurrent distressing dreams of the event; acting or feeling as if the trauma were recurring (e.g., illusions, hallucinations, dissociative flashbacks); intense psychological distress at exposure to internal or external cues that symbolize or resemble an aspect of the trauma; or physiological

reactivity when exposed to such cues. The second criterion is persistent avoidance of stimuli associated with the trauma and numbing of general responsiveness that was not present before the trauma. Diagnosis requires that these avoidance symptoms are expressed in at least three of the following ways: efforts to avoid thoughts, feelings or conversations associated with the event; efforts to avoid activities, places or people that arouse recollections of the event; markedly diminished interest or participation in significant activities; feelings of detachment or estrangement from others; restricted range of affect; or a sense of a foreshortened future. The third symptom criterion requires the presence of at least two persistent symptoms of increased arousal: difficulty falling or staying asleep; irritability or outbursts of anger; difficulty concentrating; hypervigilance; or an exaggerated startle response (in adolescents, PTSD may be expressed by disorganized or agitated behavior). (p. 428)

The *DSM-IV* (APA, 1994) requires that all three criteria be present for at least one month to warrant a diagnosis. Finally, the symptoms must be sufficiently strong to cause clinically significant distress or impairment in social, occupational, or other important areas of functioning. A differentiation is also made between symptoms that are acute (lasting less than three months) and those that are chronic (lasting more than three months) (pp. 427–429).

Theoretical Foundation for PTSD Symptoms

There are several explanations for a resulting PTSD symptomatology. For example, from a behavioral viewpoint, PTSD symptoms (e.g., hyperarousal and intrusive recollections) are the results of classically conditioned linkages between unconditioned stimuli (e.g., gunfire) and the original traumatic event (e.g., being shot, or witnessing a shooting). The avoidance symptoms are explained in terms of operant conditioning—avoidance of stimuli suggestive of the traumatic event (e.g., gunfire) is reinforced by its consequence of protecting the patient from the symptoms of anxiety.

Biological theorists explain that trauma activates certain physical and psychological reactions. Sensory information is introduced to the child and these data are shared with the limbic system (amygdala, thalamus, and hippocampus), where basic emotions and narrative coherence are attached (Bremner, 1999). To use the previous example, the limbic system concluded (e.g., from witnessing a shooting) that there was a threat; it then stimulated the production of noradrenaline. The "fight/flight" response caused the stressor memory to freeze, with the emotion still attached. This left the child's memory (an emotional picture—nondeclarative) of the original trauma "locked," stored subcortically at the point of release of the noradrenaline, and feeling as if the initial stressor was still continuing. As a result, the child experiences anxiety and re-experiences avoidance and nightmare be-havior. This process tends to perpetuate the negative cycle of PTSD.

Violence is on the public health agenda (Glodich, 1998). The mission is to ex-plore the problem of community violence and find ways to reduce the number of deaths and injuries that result. Yet, research on the psychological effects of chronic exposure to community violence is in its infancy. Violence in the homes, schools, churches, and communities of urban poor children has created a devas-tating legacy in our nation. However, some youths are able to withstand the con-sequences of violence.

CHILDHOOD VULNERABILITY AND RESILIENCE

Until recently, children's reactions to violence were ignored. The children were presumed to be too young to understand or even remember a traumatic event (Os-ofsky, 1995). The children's inability to describe a post-trauma event with any measure of clarity further supported this hypothesis. However, research is now finding that children are deeply affected by trauma (Pynoos et al., 1998). A child's inability to describe a traumatic event is now understood as a defense mechanism called denial, which allows the child to escape from the negative emo-tions elicited by the violent event(s).

However, it is not enough to appreciate that children suffer from stressful cir-cumstances. Researchers must understand what factors protect a child from the devastating and often long-term consequences of chronic stress. This shift in at-tention from risk to resilience factors supports the search for those variables that deter rather than strengthen negative consequences. They offer much-needed prevention effort information.

Stress has been defined as an imbalance between demands and an individual's ability to cope with those demands (Garmezy, 1988). Youths under stress may seek and find helpful resources, or may withdraw from family members, peers, teachers, and other community members because they feel unsafe and/or per-ceive environmental input as inadequate. The latter situation adds to the youths' already traumatic circumstance.

Childhood Vulnerability as Related to Development

The primary effects (e.g., post-traumatic symptoms) of exposure to community violence can ultimately affect the child's developmental progress (Boney-McCoy & Finkelhor, 1995). For example, regressive behavior (e.g., bedwetting) is often a result of trauma exposure in young children (Osofsky, 1995). This behavior can affect the child's social interactions or academic achievement (e.g., because of reduced concentration in school).

Age is not a mechanism that protects against the negative consequences of exposure to violence. Consequently, infants are vulnerable; they perceive circumstances from their caregiver's interpretations (Osofsky, 1995). If the caregiver is distressed, this will be translated to the infant, who may then present with sleep disturbances, fear of being alone, and irritability (Osofsky, 1998).

Children must struggle with the developmental task of establishing relationships. This requires a child to acquire the ability to show empathy, problem solve, and regulate emotions. However, a child exposed to community violence and suffering with hypervigilance to aggressive external stimuli may misinterpret environmental cues (Dodge, Lochman, Harnish, Bates, & Pettit, 1997). This behavior has social and academic consequences; the child has a limited—and more often negative—repertoire of interactional responses.

Social Support and Resilience in Children Exposed to Violence

Research shows that positive and stable social support is a vital resource for defending against the stressful effects of exposure to community violence (Garmezy, 1988). The perception that others (e.g., teachers, clergy, family members, and peers) are available to provide emotional as well as practical support contributes to youths' adjustment and personal development, which buffers the negative effects of stress (Hawkins, Farrington, & Catalano, 1998). This happens because the youths feel secure and cared for. Secure relationships offer opportunities to obtain needed resources, advice, self-disclosure, and emotional release. Consequently, youths are less likely to withdraw and further increase the negative effects of the stressful circumstance.

Positive school environments provide further protection from the negative effects of community violence. Individuals in the school environment can be vital resources when a child needs someone to turn to for help (Noddings, 1996).

Children may respond differently to trauma, depending on their age (Wilson, 1995). Young children may present with few post-trauma symptoms because most of the PTSD indicators involve verbal description of feelings and experiences. Instead, young children who feel helpless may generalize their distress to people and events that are not related to the trauma. They may have great difficulty with communication (e.g., mutism), experience nightmares, and fear going to sleep. Young children may repeat certain words or themes and developmentally regress. Children ages 7 to 12 years may experience panic as a result of flashbacks. This can precipitate health and emotional concerns about such intense feelings and may interfere with concentration and normal sleep patterns. Children often have difficulty remembering the sequence of events of a trauma and may form beliefs that there were warning signs (not heeded) that predicted the traumatic event. Additionally, they may engage in compulsively repeating some specific aspect of the trauma (which does not relieve anxiety) and/or recreate portions of the trauma event in play.

Adolescents present with more of the *DSM-IV* symptom criteria. However, instead of post-traumatic play, they may actually "play out" portions of the trauma in their daily lives. This age group is more likely to engage in impulsive and/or aggressive behaviors.

This symptom description corresponds with the *DSM-IV* typology, although children may present with additional symptoms, such as amnesia, regression, repetitive play, flat affect, hypervigilance, and irritability. A child does not need to present with all of these symptoms to be diagnosed with PTSD.

EMPIRICALLY BASED PREVENTION/INTERVENTIONS

Individual Interventions

PTSD Interventions

Children suffering from PTSD or post-traumatic symptoms have great difficulty trusting; yet, a trusting relationship is imperative if an intervention is to be effective. Techniques for encouraging trust include empathy, active listening, and active support and encouragement, and these must be central to the therapeutic relationship. Interventions for PTSD should include three goals: (a) the child should be helped to develop strategies to control intrusive thoughts and images; (b) the child needs to be taught techniques that help to reduce the physical symptoms (e.g., tense muscles) of anxiety and/or the panic from flashbacks; (c) the child will need to develop a sense of safety and adequacy. However, in spite of the need for them, there are no empirically proven methods for achieving these goals.

Children with PTSD or related symptoms are effectively treated with cognitive/behavioral therapy (CBT), either alone or in combination with medications. However, research has not fully investigated the effectiveness of medications with children. CBT therapy generally involves 12 sessions with occasional follow-up and includes teaching the child alternative thinking that offsets "catastrophizing." CBT challenges children's false beliefs, such as a belief that the world is unsafe. Play and art therapy are exposure methods that can help children to remember the traumatic event safely and to express their feelings about it. Anxiety management techniques such as relaxation and assertiveness training are also essential intervention components (Finch, Nelson, & Ott, 1993).

Exposure-Based Exercises

Systematic exposure to the traumatic trigger is deemed essential in reducing symptoms associated with post-traumatic stress (Fairbank, Schlenger, Caddell, & Woods, 1993). These techniques are most helpful for a child who is distressed by trauma-related memories or reminders. The goal is to modify behavioral, cognitive, or affective processes, or a combination thereof. It is believed that, through direct experience of the traumatic event, children's mastery expectations are raised (Bandura, 1977). Exposure can be done gradually and can be paired with relaxation so that the children can learn to relax while recalling their experiences. Through this procedure, they learn that they do not have to be scared of their memories.

Coping Skills

Coping is critical in competency and vulnerability models of child and adolescent psychopathology (Rutter, 1990). In this interpretation, coping is a process that may serve as a protective factor that helps to buffer individual responses to stressful life events. Thus, exposure to violence challenges the victim's and/or the witness's capacity to generate adaptive coping responses, and promotes the use of maladaptive coping responses. These might include self-blame, anger, withdrawal, blaming others, and so on (Scheppele & Bart, 1983). These maladaptive coping responses, if sufficiently intense, may facilitate the intrusive memories and avoidance reactions associated with post-traumatic stress (Resick & Schnicke, 1992) and interfere with successful emotional processing during the exposure-based exercise. In group cognitive behavioral therapy, coping skills enhancement provides youths with corrective information as it relates to a particular maladaptive coping response. Thus, coping skills enhancement improves the coping responses of the youths and moderates post-traumatic stress symptoms.

Coping skills training is presented in a variety of forms. As noted above, the process of exposure, in and of itself, may serve to enhance children's coping as children's mastery expectations are raised via successful exposure experience. Similarly, drawing, writing, and reading exercises are media that enhance coping skills. Children might be asked to draw pictures or write stories not only about their experiences but also about various ways to handle situations. Discussion about the advantages of these various ways can then follow.

Social Support

Peers serve as a major source of social support for youths (Levitt, 1991), and traumatic events deplete social support (Kaniasty & Norris, 1992). Existing evidence suggests that the broader and deeper the network of social support, the greater the chance of ameliorating the negative effects of stressful life events (Kaniasty & Norris, 1992). In group cognitive behavioral therapy (GCBT), the social support enhancement comes from the group itself. To enhance other sources of social support, youths are taught, through role play, modeling, feedback, and contingency contracting, to elicit support from siblings and friends.

Community Interventions

Mentoring

Mentoring is an inexpensive program in which adult (same-sex) volunteers spend time with children or adolescents (generally from single-parent homes), usually engaging them in sports or educational activities. However, there is little research regarding the benefits of this intervention. A study by Turner and Cooper (1996) found that mentored boys scored significantly higher on self-concept measures than boys without mentors. However, the behavioral scores completed by their mothers did not yield a difference in the two groups.

Tierney, Grossman, and Resch (1995) examined the Big Brother/Big Sister mentoring program and found that the mentored youths described less fighting in comparison to wait-list controls, and gained a perception of positive family relations. Between the groups, there were no significant differences in delinquent behavior.

A significant problem with mentoring interventions is retaining mentors long enough to sustain a meaningful relationship that will allow significant change to occur. Morrow and Styles (1995) looked at approaches to mentoring and found that mentors who were flexible and relationship-focused in their approach to mentoring retained their relationships longer than mentors who were more directive and tended to prescribe activities and topics of discussion. Dreman, Aldor, and Katz (1995) found that mentors were expected to fill a substitute parent role by mentored children's mothers. Further research needs to measure, across several milieus—perhaps by comparing mentoring styles and roles—children's interactive and academic behavior as a result of mentoring interactions.

Supervised Recreational Programs

Juvenile crime (as a result of trauma-related history) occurs most often after school. Many children are unsupervised at this time because their parents are working (Farrell & Bruce, 1997). This void in child supervision is a structural problem for reducing juvenile crime. Thus, after-school programs are potentially of great value and need serious consideration in communities' prevention planning. However, there is a great lack of empirical outcome research for the prudence of this intervention, although two promising studies have demonstrated positive results. Farrell and Bruce (1997) showed that, among 96 youths who participated in a Milwaukee midnight basketball league, delinquent behavior was reduced 30%. Kaltreider and St. Pierre (1995) found that community-based youth organizations are very helpful supplements to school-based efforts against crime and drugs.

This type of program would be helpful if incorporated into a multisystemic treatment plan. One of the important protective factors for youths is a positive connection to the community via appropriate role models and circumstances that provide the practice of newly learned skills. Further research is needed to explore these possibilities.

Child-Focused and School-Based Interventions

Child-school bonding encourages active, age-appropriate involvement in the educational process, in addition to development and use of behavioral, cognitive, emotional, and interpersonal skills and competencies, and reinforcement of prosocial and academic efforts through teachers' praise and approval (Hawkins et al., 1998). As mentioned previously, social support (e.g., school) is a resiliency factor, whereas community violence is a variable. Children suffering with PTSD may present with disruptive behaviors as their symptomatology. Thus, offering universal programs that arm children with skills to deal with intense emotions and/or difficult social interactions increases resiliency factors.

Effective preventive/interventive programs for increasing resiliency factors against aggressive behavior include: teaching social competence and providing a positive and calm (safe) environment that has behavioral standards and rules (safety issues) (Slaby, 1998). The following programs are suggested.

The Brainpower Program

Hudley et al. (1998) examined the Brain Power Program, which is designed to counteract attributional biases and reactive aggression in aggressive children. It was implemented in four elementary schools in southern California: 384 African American and Latino males (aged 10 to 12 years) were paired with nonaggressive peers and exposed to a 12-lesson, school-based intervention focused on improving the accuracy of their perceptions and interpretations of others' actions. Teachers' ratings indicated that the Brainpower Program was successful in improving the identified group's behavior. A 12-month follow-up showed diminished effects.

PATHS

The curriculum, Promoting Alternative Thinking Strategies (PATHS), develops emotional and social competencies and helps to reduce aggressive behavior by increasing self-control, emotional awareness, and interpersonal problem-solving skills in elementary school children. The curriculum includes a 6-volume manual and research book (Greenberg, Kusche, Cook, & Quamma, 1995).

Problem-Solving Skills Training

The Problem-Solving Skills Training model has been well researched (Kazdin, Siegel, & Bass, 1992). It is based on literature that demonstrates how youths with disruptive behaviors often show cognitive deficits and distortions that can lead to aggression. By altering the way these youths perceive environmental events and interpret the intent of the behavior of others, aggression is reduced. A youth works individually with a therapist to learn appropriate self-statements for interpersonal situations that lead to effective solutions to a problem. Prosocial solutions are fostered through the therapist's active role in treatment, which may include modeling, role playing, coaching and practice, direct reinforcement, and mild punishment (e.g., loss of points). Over the course of treatment, the youth increasingly uses the new skills in real-life situations.

Family-Focused Interventions

A resilient child maintains competence and recovers from trauma in spite of high-risk factors in his or her life (Werner, 1994). Earls (1994) stated that resilient children possess easy temperaments, have high IQ scores, are more autonomous, have at least one supportive adult, and are attached to school. Similarly, Werner (1994) found that resilient children possessed temperaments that elicit positive responses from caring "others," sought supportive environments, and had involved parents and/or extended family. Thus, encouraging family participation in the process of prevention is imperative.

Family-focused interventions have demonstrated their ability to affect the behavior of a youth with aggressive behavior. These interventions require ongoing involvement of a parent or family member, and the parent must complete tasks or practice skills outside the treatment session. The immediate goal of the intervention is to develop, in the parents, specific skills that will alter the interactional patterns maintaining aggressive and antisocial behavior. The parent training approach teaches parents the benefits of refocusing their attention away from their child's negative activities and centering more on positive behaviors. Parents also learn different behavioral techniques and practice them through structured role-playing.

There is some evidence to support the use of parent training techniques based on social and behavioral learning theory for children with conduct disorder (Larson, 1998). However, parent training more effectively reduces behavior problems in younger children than in older children. Optimal effects are achieved before the fourth grade. Problematic behaviors then appear to become firmly entrenched through association with deviant peers.

Policy Interventions

Community violence is a social problem that must be addressed on a macro level. The results of this review further support the need for policy change, at the federal, state, and local levels, to address the problem of community violence and its negative consequences for children and families. At a minimum, policies addressing gun control, drugs, gangs, unemployment, a lack of access to mental health and substance abuse services, and poverty must be improved if we are to make neighborhoods safe.

A sense of community may be hard to achieve among individuals living in violent neighborhoods. When most of a community's collective energy is absorbed by ongoing stressors related to violence (such as constant threats to personal safety and property), little may be left to invest in the community itself. African American communities are further burdened with the consequences of discrimination and societal oppression.

To reduce violence in impoverished African American communities—and thus improve the mental health of African American children living therein—the identification of problems and their subsequent solutions must come from within the communities themselves (McMillan, 1996). Federal, state, and local funds should be provided directly to communities so that they can develop their own preventive interventions to reduce community violence. With this assistance, communities can organize, empower themselves, and provide internal resources to tackle the problems of violence in their neighborhoods. They can serve as extended families, providing programs, mentors, and role models for children.

Case Management and the Strengths Perspective

Ecological theory (Bronfenbrenner, 1979) provides a multisystem perspective based on recognition that children's behavior is shaped by individual, family, and environmental factors. Because community violence impacts multiple systems, it requires intervention on multiple levels. Implications for practice suggest that social workers doing case management take an ecological approach to their work with children and adolescents from violent communities, and provide assessment and intervention from a multisystem perspective.

Social workers encounter victims of violence in various settings. The literature clearly indicates that children exposed to chronic community violence may suffer grave consequences as a result of that exposure. Further, parents' victimization as a result of community violence may constitute a risk factor—in development of distress symptoms—for some children. For these reasons, social workers must be educated about these potential risk factors for children and remain aware of them when they provide assessment and intervention.

Furthermore, social workers working with children in inpatient and outpatient clinic settings should expand their psychosocial assessment to include questions about previous exposure to violence. In addition, they should ask whether the children's parents have ever been victims of violence. In particular, children from urban communities may have presenting symptoms that could be attributed, in full or in part, to exposure to community violence and/or parents' victimization, warranting a full assessment of these potential stressors.

Along with addressing distress symptoms, social workers should emphasize any strengths and/or protective factors the children possess, especially when these children live in urban communities. This is especially important because children from violent neighborhoods generally *return* to their violent neighborhoods.

FUTURE RESEARCH

Research on children's exposure to chronic community violence is in its infancy. Limited research to date has documented that indeed many children living in urban American cities are exposed to chronic community violence, and some children are negatively affected by this exposure. Systematic future research into this social problem must be conducted, to build on the inadequate knowledge base that currently exists.

Researchers must continue toward developing a full understanding of children's responses to community violence. Future research must examine the effects of chronic community violence on children, including any effects due to their parents' victimization, and must develop empirically tested interventions as indicated. Researchers should not limit their inquiries to individuals. They must also direct them toward communities as a whole, where interventions are desperately needed to combat violence.

REFERENCES

American Psychiatric Association. (1994). *Diagnostic and statistical manual of mental disorders* (4th ed.). Washington, DC: Author.

Bandura, A. (1977). Self-efficacy: Toward a unifying theory of behavioral change. *Psychological Review, 84*(2), 191–215.

Boney-McCoy, S., & Finkelhor, D. (1995). Prior victimization: A risk factor for child sexual abuse and for PTSD-related symptomatology among sexually abused youth. *Child Abuse and Neglect, 19*(12), 1401–1421.

Bremner, J. D. (1999). Alterations in brain structure and function associated with post-traumatic stress disorder. *Semin Clinical Neuropsychiatry, 4*(4), 249–255.

Bronfenbrenner, U. (1979). *The ecology of human development: Experiment by nature and design.* Cambridge, MA: Harvard University Press.

Children's Defense Fund. (1993). *Annual report: The State of America's Children.* Washington, DC: Author.

Cicchetti, D., Rogosch, F. A., Toth, S. L., & Spagnola, M. (1997). Affect, cognition, and the emergence of self-knowledge in the toddler offspring of depressed mothers. *Journal of Experiential Child Psychology, 67*(3), 338–362.

Cicchetti, D., & Toth, S. L. (1998). The development of depression in children and adolescents. *American Psychology, 53*(2), 221–241.

Dodge, K. A., Lochman, J. E., Harnish, J. D., Bates, J. E., & Pettit, G. S. (1997). Reactive and proactive aggression in school children and psychiatrically impaired chronically assaultive youth. *Journal of Abnormal Psychology, 106*(1), 37–51.

Dodge, K. A., Pettit, G. S., & Bates, J. E. (1997). How the experience of early physical abuse leads children to become chronically aggressive. In D. Cicchetti & S. L. Toth (Eds.), *Developmental perspectives on trauma: Theory, research, and intervention* (pp. 263–288). Rochester, NY: University of Rochester Press.

Drell, M. J., Siegel, C. H., & Gaensbauer, T. J. (1993). Post-traumatic stress disorder. In C. H. Zeanah, Jr. (Ed.), *Handbook of infant mental health* (pp. 291–304). New York: Guilford Press.

Dreman, S., Aldor, R., & Katz, D. (1995). The Big Brother in the Single Parent Family: Family, Friend, or Counselor. *Journal of Divorce and Remarriage, 24*(3/4), 59–70.

Dubrow, N. F., & Garbarino, J. (1989). Living in the war zone: Mothers and young children in a public housing development. *Child Welfare, 68*(1), 3–20.

Dulmus, C. N., & Wodarski, J. S. (2000). Trauma-related symptomatology among children of parents victimized by community violence. *American Journal of Orthopsychiatry, 10*(2), 272–277.

Earls, F. J. (1994). Violence and today's youth. *Future Child, 4*(3), 4–23.

Eron, L. D., Gentry, J. H., & Schlegel, P. (Eds.). (1994). *Reason to hope: A psychosocial perspective on violence and youth.* Washington, DC: American Psychological Association.

Fairbank, J. A., Schlenger, W. E., Caddell, J. M., & Woods, M. G. (1993). *Posttraumatic stress disorder.* New York: Plenum Press.

Farrell, A. D., & Bruce, S. E. (1997). Impact of exposure to community violence on violent behavior and emotional distress among urban adolescents. *Journal of Clinical Child Psychology, 26*(1), 2–14.

Figley, C. R. (1993). Coping with stressors on the home front. *Journal of Social Issues, 49*(4), 51–71.

Finch, A. J., Nelson, W. M., & Ott, E. S. (1993). *Cognitive-behavioral procedures with children and adolescents.* Boston: Allyn & Bacon.

Garbarino, J., Kostelny, K., & Dubrow, N. (1991). What children can tell us about living in danger. *American Psychologist, 46*(4), 376–383.

Garmezy, N. (1988). Stressors of childhood. In N. Garmezy & M. Rutter (Eds.), *Stress, coping, and development in children* (pp. 43–84). Baltimore: Johns Hopkins University Press.

Glodich, A. (1998). Traumatic exposure to violence: A comprehensive review of the child and adolescent literature. *Smith College Studies in Social Work, 68,* 321–345.

Gorman-Smith, D., & Tolan, P. (1998). The role of exposure to community violence and developmental problems among inner-city youth. *Development and Psychopathology, 10*(1), 101–116.

Greenberg, M. T., Kusche, C. A., Cook, E. T., & Quamma, J. P. (1995). Promoting emotional competence in school-aged children: The effects of the PATHS curriculum. *Development and Psychopathology, 7*(1), 117–136.

Groves, B. M., Zuckerman, B., Marans, S., & Cohen, D. J. (1993). Silent victims. Children who witness violence. *Journal of the American Medical Association, 269*(2), 262–264.

Hawkins, J. D., Farrington, D. P., & Catalano, R. F. (1998). Reducing violence through the schools. In D. S. Elliott & B. A. Hamburg (Eds.), *Violence in American schools: A new perspective* (pp. 188–216). New York: Cambridge University Press.

Hudley, C., Britsch, B., Wakefield, W. D., Smith, T., Demorat, M., & Cho, S.-J. (1998). An attribution retraining program to reduce aggression in elementary school students. *Psychology in the Schools, 35*(3), 271–282.

Kaltreider, D. L., & St. Pierre, T. L. (1995). Beyond the schools: Strategies for implementing successful drug prevention programs in community youth-serving organizations. *Journal of Drug Education, 25*(3), 223–237.

Kaniasty, K., & Norris, F. H. (1992). Social support and victims of crime: Matching event, support, and outcome. *American Journal of Community Psychology, 20*(2), 211–241.

Kazdin, A. E., Siegel, T. C., & Bass, D. (1992). Cognitive problem-solving skills training and parent management training in the treatment of antisocial behavior in children. *Journal of Consulting and Clinical Psychology, 60*(5), 733–747.

Larson, E. (1998). Reframing the meaning of disability to families. *Social Science and Medicine, 47*(7), 865–875.

Lauritsen, J. L., & Tonry, M. (1998). Minorities, crime, and criminal justice. In M. Tonry (Ed.), *The handbook of crime and punishment* (pp. 58–84). New York: Oxford University Press.

Levitt, M. J. (1991). Attachment and close relationships: A life-span perspective. In J. L. Gewirtz & W. M. Kurtines (Eds.), *Intersections with attachment* (pp. 183–205). Hillsdale, NJ: Erlbaum.

Lorion, R., & Saltzman, W. (1990). Children's exposure to community violence: Following a path from concern to research to action. In D. Reiss, J. E. Richters, M. Radke-Yarrow, & D. Scharff (Eds.), *Children and violence* (pp. 55–65). New York: Guilford Press.

Manning, M. L., & Baruth, L. G. (1995). *Students at risk*. Boston: Allyn & Bacon.

Martinez, P., & Richters, J. E. (1993). The NIMH Community Violence Project: II. Children's distress symptoms associated with violence exposure. *Psychiatry: Interpersonal and Biological Processes, 56*(1), 22–35.

McMillan, D. (1996). Sense of community. *Journal of Community Psychology, 24*(4), 315–325.

Miller, L. S., Wasserman, G. A., Neugebauer, R., Gorman-Smith, D., & Kamboukos, D. (1999). Witnessed community violence and antisocial behavior in high-risk, urban boys. *Journal of Clinical Child Psychology, 28*(1), 2–11.

Morrow, X. V., & Styles, M. B. (1995). *Building relationships with youth in program settings: A study of Big Brothers/Big Sisters*. Philadelphia: Public/Private Ventures.

Nader, K., Pynoos, R., Fairbanks, L., & Frederick, C. (1990). Children's PTSD reactions one year after a sniper attack at their school. *American Journal of Psychiatry, 147*(11), 1526–1530.

Ney, P. G., Fung, T., & Wickett, A. R. (1994). The worst combinations of child abuse and neglect. *Child Abuse and Neglect, 18*(9), 705–714.

Noddings, N. (1996). Learning to care and to be cared for. In A. M. Hoffman (Ed.), *Schools, violence, and society* (pp. 185–198). Westport, CT: Praeger.

Osofsky, J. D. (1995). The effect of exposure to violence on young children. *American Psychologist, 50*(9), 782–788.

Osofsky, J. D. (1998). Children as invisible victims of domestic and community violence. In G. Holden & R. Geffner (Eds.), *Children exposed to marital violence: Theory, research, and applied issues* (pp. 95–117). Washington, DC: American Psychological Association.

Perkins, C. (1997). Age patterns of victims of serious violent crime. *Bureau of Justice Statistics: Special Report* (NCJ Publication No. 16231). Washington, DC: Department of Justice.

Pynoos, R. S., Goenjian, A. K., & Steinberg, A. M. (1998). A public mental health approach to the postdisaster treatment of children and adolescents. *Child and Adolescent Psychiatric Clinics of North America, 7*(1), 195–210, x.

Pynoos, R. S., Nader, K., Frederick, C., Gonda, L., & Stuber, M. (1987). Grief reactions in school age children following a snipe attack at school. *Israel Journal of Psychiatry Relation Sciences, 24*(1/2), 53–63.

Rand, M. (1999). Violence related injuries treated in hospital emergency departments. *Bureau of Justice Statistics: Special Report* (NCJ Publication No. 156921). Washington, DC: U.S. Department of Justice.

Resick, P. A., & Schnicke, M. K. (1992). Cognitive processing therapy for sexual assault victims. *Journal of Consulting Clinical Psychology, 60*(5), 748–756.

Richters, J. E. (1993). Community violence and children's development: Toward a research agenda for the 1990s. *Psychiatry, 56*(1), 3–6.

Rutter, M. (1990). Psychosocial resilience and protective mechanisms. In J. E. Rolf & A. S. Masten (Eds.), *Risk and protective factors in the development of psychopathology* (pp. 181–214). New York: Cambridge University Press.

Saigh, P. A., Mroueh, M., & Bremner, J. D. (1997). Scholastic impairments among traumatized adolescents. *Behaviour Research and Therapy, 35*(5), 429–436.

Scheppele, K. L., & Bart, P. B. (1983). Through women's eyes: Defining danger in the wake of sexual assault. *Journal of Social Issues, 39*(2), 63–81.

Singer, M. I., Anglin, T. M., Song, L. Y., & Lunghofer, L. (1995). Adolescents' exposure to violence and associated symptoms of psychological trauma. *Journal of the American Medical Association, 273*(6), 477–482.

Slaby, R. G. (1998). Preventing youth violence through research-guided intervention. In P. K. Trickett & C. J. Schellenbach (Eds.), *Violence against children in the family and the community* (pp. 371–399). Washington, DC: American Psychological Association.

Tierney, J. P., Grossman, J. B., & Resch, N. L. (1995). *Making a difference: An impact study of Big Brothers/Big Sisters.* Philadelphia: Public/Private Ventures.

Turner, S., & Cooper, M. (1996). The dual diagnosis of obsessive-compulsive disorder and alcoholism. *Alcoholism Treatment Quarterly, 14*(3), 77–93.

U.S. Dept. of Education. (1997). *Principle/School Disciplinarian Survey on School Violence.* Washington, DC: National Center of Education Statistics. Available from: http://nces.ed.gov/pubs98/violence/98030003.html

Vig, S. (1996). Young children's exposure to community violence. *Journal of Early Intervention, 20*(4), 319–328.

Werner, E. E. (1994). Overcoming the odds. *Journal of Developmental and Behavioral Pediatrics, 15*(2), 131–136.

Wilson, J. P. (1995). The historical evolution of PTSD diagnostic criteria: From Freud to *DSM-IV.* In G. S. Everly, Jr. & J. M. Lating (Eds.), *Psychotraumatology: Key papers and core concepts in post-traumatic stress* (pp. 9–26). New York: Plenum Press.

Chapter 7

ASSESSING VIOLENT BEHAVIOR

EDGAR H. TYSON, CATHERINE N. DULMUS, AND JOHN S. WODARSKI

CURRENT ISSUES IN MEASURING VIOLENT BEHAVIOR

Interpersonal violence continues to be an epidemic problem in society. Accurate assessment can lead to treatment, and prevention of violence is critical. Ongoing research related to this societal problem has become increasingly important to practitioners and policy makers, and certainly to individuals whose lives are shattered by acts of violence. Practitioners and researchers have been concerned about the impact of violence for several decades now, but only in the past 20 years has violence been subjected to the scrutiny of empirical research (Ammerman & Hersen, 1999). Most researchers have primarily investigated the prevalence of the types of violence, risk factors associated with violence, and, in particular, the effects of family violence on its victims (see Dwyer, Smokowski, Bricout, & Wodarski, 1995, for review). An issue that has received greater attention in recent research is assessment of the risk of child maltreatment (Combs-Orme, Martin, Fox, & Faver, 2000). Improvements in violence research methodology are significant, but few empirical studies have addressed the issue of measuring individual violent behaviors of persons with a history of violence.

Researchers and practitioners use a variety of instruments that measure violence indirectly, from the perspective of victims or other observers. The reasons for this are many, not the least of which is the underreporting by perpetrators of violence, often cited in the literature (Ammerman & Hersen, 1999; Jasinski & Williams, 1998; Wekerle & Wolfe, 1999). Although this is a very sound approach to measuring and/or predicting violent behavior, assessing and reporting actual incidents of violence from the perspective of perpetrators is clearly a vital component of violence research. In light of this trend, our aim is to identify and briefly discuss the current state of research in measuring violent behavior from a variety of perspectives. Particular attention is given to instruments used by individuals who actually commit violent acts.

FUNDAMENTAL MEASUREMENT ISSUES

Researchers and practitioners in the area of family violence primarily rely on standardized measures to gauge the incidence, prevalence, and severity of violence. Fischer and Corcoran (1994) define standardized measures as "uniform procedures for administration and scoring, and . . . a series of structured questions or statements designed to elicit information from [a] respondent" (p. 34). Information regarding the psychometric properties of such instruments is frequently obtainable. Such information includes: the purpose and interpretation of the measure, its reliability and validity, scoring and administration, and comparison norms if available (Fischer & Corcoran, 1994). Social scientists, in their efforts to examine the causes, prevalence, severity, and ramifications of domestic violence, utilize a variety of these measures. Increasingly, researchers are using multivariate statistical analysis to test their theories. These techniques require accurate measures of the concepts under investigation. It is critical, in any serious discussion of their findings, to include a critique of the measures used to quantify the variables studied. The aim of this chapter is to identify and describe the psychometric properties of a variety of violent behavior measures that either have a well-documented research history or have begun to demonstrate significant promise for research and practice. Before we begin reviewing specific instruments, we will briefly clarify two vital concepts in measurement: reliability and validity.

Reliability

Rubin and Babbie (2001) define reliability as the ability of a measure to produce the same data each time, in repeated observations. The most commonly used approach for assessing reliability is internal consistency, which examines the homogeneity of a measure by dividing the instrument into two individual halves and calculating the (Pearson's r) correlation coefficient between the scores of the two halves. Cronbach's alpha (α) coefficient, which is the mean correlation of all possible split halves, is also a commonly preferred approach because it reveals a more comprehensive estimate of reliability.

Validity

There are several approaches to assessing evidence for the validity of an instrument. Content validity is the degree to which a measure covers the range of meanings included within a particular concept. This is usually accomplished by correlating the scores obtained from two measures of the same phenomenon. Construct validity is the degree to which a measure relates to other variables, as expected within a system of theoretical relationships (Rubin & Babbie, 2001). Another type of construct validity is factorial validity, which tests whether similar items correlate well (and dissimilar items do not correlate well). A rigorous test of factorial validity is confirmatory factor analysis (CFA), which (a) compares competing models, (b) evaluates overall goodness of fit, (c) obtains parameter estimates adjusted for measurement error, and (d) tests, simultaneously, the first- and second-order structures (Hudson & McMurtry, 1997).

MEASURES OF VIOLENT BEHAVIOR IN YOUTH

Indirect Measures of Violent Behavior in Youth

Psychopathy Checklist—Revised (PCL-R)

The PCL-R (Hare, 1991) is a 20-item inventory designed to assess the clinical construct of psychopathy. It has been used in many settings, with a variety of populations, and has been particularly useful with youthful offenders from a variety of racial backgrounds and ethnic heritages (Poythress, Edens, & Lilienfeld, 1998). This scale involves practitioner or informant ratings on 20 dimensions of psychopathy, and yields a total score as well as separate scores on two factor-analytically derived dimensions of psychopathy (e.g., superficial charm, manipulative tendencies, lack of empathy). Furthermore, factor 2 represents antisocial or deviant features (e.g., juvenile delinquency, poor behavior controls, parasitic lifestyle). Ratings are based on an extensive clinical interview plus review of available clinical files. Scores of 30 or higher are considered psychopathic (Poythress et al., 1998). PCL-R has the limitation of routinely taking up to two hours to complete; with extensive file data, it may take considerably longer (Poythress et al., 1998). However, the PCL-R has been reported to have a very good reliability and validity in controlled studies (Hare, Hart, & Harpur, 1991).

Several researchers, using a sample of offenders from Sweden, have found substantial evidence for the validity of the PCL to predict the use of violence

(Grann, Langstroem, Tengstroem, & Kullgren, 1999). Salekin, Rogers, and Sewell (1996) conducted an extensive review and meta-analysis of 18 studies on the PCL and found the PCL to be a good predictor of violence and general recidivism. These authors also suggested that the PCL could be used as a component of an assessment of the dangerousness of violent offenders.

Modified-Conflict Tactics Scales (M-CTS)

The M-CTS (Neidig, 1986), a 19-item instrument that measures an individual's means of resolving conflict, is derived from the widely researched and robust Conflict Tactics Scales (CTS) (Straus, 1979). It was developed to establish the use of this well-documented measure with adolescents. This measure, which can be used to obtain data on self-reported physical aggression and victimization, is very short and easy to understand. The current discussion of this measure concerns the self-reported physical aggression items of the M-CTS, although information regarding the victimization scales is available (Neidig, 1986).

A recent study revealed significant findings regarding the psychometric properties of the M-CTS (Cascardi, Avery-Leaf, O'Leary, & Slep, 1999). These researchers tested the validity of the M-CTS with a sample of 2,320 high school students (1,140 females and 1,180 males) from seven multiethnic high schools in Long Island, New York. Students completed the survey as part of a larger study (an evaluation of a teen dating violence prevention program). Confirmatory factor analysis was used to assess the factor validity of the M-CTS. Normed and non-normed fit indices (NFI and NNFI) and comparative fit indices (CFI) with values above .90 indicate good model fit (Cascardi et al., 1999). Females' conflict tactics (current and recent daters) validity scores were NFI = .88, NNFI = .90, and CFI = .92. After modifications to the model (i.e., loading "threw, hit, or kicked something" on both the Psychological and Physical Aggression factors), fit improved significantly (NFI = .92, NNFI = .95, CFI = .96). Males' conflict tactics (current daters) validity scores were NFI = .65, NNFI = .63, and CFI = .69. After modifications to the model (loading "threatened to hit or throw something at partner" on both the Psychological and Physical Aggression factors), the model fit was significantly improved (NFI = .84, NNFI = .86, CFI = .89).

This instrument provides several advances in research on dating violence in terms of self-reported aggression, particularly as it relates to male and female differences. Although the present analysis concerns the physical aggression items on the M-CTS, similar results were reported in the study on the validity of the victimization items. Reliability information was not reported in the study. Researchers who use this tool are encouraged to assess and report reliability for the sample it was used with. A critical point must be noted here: When writing reports of a study in which an instrument was used, researchers should always report the reliability data of that instrument for the sample from which they collected the data. This is important because reliability is sample-dependent (Croker & Algina, 1986).

Multiproblem Screening Inventory (MPSI)

The MPSI (Hudson & McMurtry, 1997) is a paper-and-pencil self-report measure that has 334 items and requires 30 to 45 minutes to complete. This inventory was developed to gather a large amount of detailed information on many possible problem areas. Practitioners can obtain detailed information about client problems in 27 areas of personal and social functioning. The problems that are important for the purposes of this review are: aggression, nonphysical abuse, and physical abuse. The scale is somewhat lengthy, but it has several advantages over other lengthy scales such as the Minnesota Multiphasic Screening Inventory because it does not require a licensed psychologist to complete it. The MPSI can also be used for research and clinical purposes. The psychometric properties of the MPSI were tested on 311 students who were expected to have sufficient variability. Cronbach's alpha coefficients for 16 of the subscales were found to be .90 or greater, and 26 of the subscales had an alpha of .80 or better. The only subscale to have lower than .80 was Aggression (.71).

Hudson and McMurtry (1997) assessed the validity of the MPSI using the multiple group method (see the 1997 article for review) and reported results in terms of the percentage of factor-loading failures and successes for all 27 subscales. The Child Problems and Ideas of Reference subscales had 15% and 5% factor-loading failure rates, respectively. The remaining subscales had 100% success rates. Construct validity of the MPSI was assessed using the discriminant validity method. The subscales were correlated with unrelated variables (in this case, background variables). The correlations between the subscales and the background variables ranged between .09 and .14, with a mean correlation of .08. The MPSI appears to have good validity and reliability. As noted earlier, the major limitation of this measure is that it is somewhat lengthy.

Shortform Assessment for Children (SAC)

The SAC (Glisson, Hemmelgran, & Post, in press) is a paper-and-pencil informant-rater instrument (for parents' and teachers' use) with 48 items: 24 internalizing behavior items and 24 externalizing behavior items, randomly arranged in two columns on one page. These researchers present a good model for conducting and reporting reliability and validity procedures on an instrument.

There are three response categories. The informant is asked to describe each item as "not true," "somewhat true," or "very true" of a child. One of the major advantages of the SAC is that, while it maintains the comprehensiveness of the Child Behavior Checklist (CBCL) (Achenbach, 1991a, 1991b), it requires less than five minutes to complete (Glisson et al., in press). Also available is software for scoring responses to the SAC. Software that produces T-scores and percentiles from general population norms, as well as child welfare and juvenile justice population norms, is also available.

The reported psychometric properties of the SAC were based on data analyses of scores from a sample of 3,790 adolescents. Of these, 83% were adolescent (12 to 18 years old), 17% were preadolescent (5 to 11 years old), 41% were minority (38% African American), and 63% were male. Rigorous confirmatory factor analyses (CFA) (see Glisson et al., in press, for review) were conducted to assess the validity of the factors in this instrument, and these resulted in model fit indices for each age and gender subgroup for both teacher and parent informants. Fit indices and their respective rule-of-thumb scores used in the analyses of this instrument included standardized root mean squared residual (SRMR < .08), root mean squared error of approximation (RMSEA < .10), comparative fit index (CFI > .90), and adjusted goodness of fit (AGFI > .90). The following are the ranges of teachers' CFA model fit indices for girls and boys: SRMR = .079 to .082; RMSEA = .084 to .090; CFI = .92 to .95; and AGFI = .93 to .93. The following are the ranges of parents' CFA model fit indices for girls and boys: SRMR = .059 to .068; RMSEA = .064 to .070; CFI = .94 to .99; and AGFI = .94 to .96. The externalizing alpha reliabilities for the teacher informant, for girls and boys of both age subgroups, ranged from .95 to .96; for the parent informant, for boys and girls of both age subgroups, they ranged from .94 to .95.

The SAC appears to be a significant advancement in the assessment of child behavior problems because it has several advantages over all other children's assessment instruments. It combines brevity (one page), breadth (externalizing and internalizing dimensions), generalizability (designed for both preadolescent and adolescent boys and girls), and multiple informants (parent or teacher) in one scale. Contrast this measure with the CBCL and the Teacher Report Form (TRF; Achenbach, 1991b), which are longer (each has more than 100 items) and require two different forms to obtain parental and teacher descriptions. Furthermore, the SAC seems to assess youth across various cultures extremely well. No other one-page instrument has these qualities. The one limitation of the SAC is that it is in its infancy. Further utility of this measure remains to be tested.

Direct Measures of Violent Behavior in Youth

Adolescent Antisocial Behavior Checklist

The Adolescent Antisocial Behavior Checklist (AABC) is a 57-item, self-report, and observer-rater instrument originally designed for use with inpatient adolescents diagnosed with conduct disorder (Marohn, Offer, Curtiss, & Feczko, 1980). Several researchers have found the AABC to be a very useful tool for assessing aggressive behaviors (Kaplan, Busner, Kupietz, Wasserman, & Segal, 1990). It is divided into six scales:

1. Physical harm to self and others;
2. Physical threats of harm to self and others;
3. Verbal harm and verbal threats to self and others;
4. Damage and threats of damage to property;
5. Violations of norms or rules;
6. Responsibility difficulties.

Items are rated as to their frequency of occurrence (on a scale of 0 to 3) within a period of a week, and should be completed over a two- to three-week period. This is an excellent tool when attempting to get a specific delineation of a wide variety of aggressive behaviors.

The researchers reported reliability on four subscales: (a) Violence Toward Self, $r = .59$; (b) Violence Toward Others, $r = .81$; (c) Violence Toward Property, $r = .51$; and (d) Other Antisocial Behavior, $r = .62$. Validity was reported as convergent scores with the Manifest Aggression Scale of the Jesness Inventory (Jesness & Wedge, 1984): Violence Toward Self, $r = .47$; Violence Toward Others, $r = .44$; Violence Toward Property, $r = .46$; and Other Violent Behavior, $r = .43$. The overall validity score for the entire instrument was $r = .47$. The AABC has several limitations. The samples used to investigate its reliability and validity were small (two samples of 20 each). It was developed through work with a clinical sample and may have difficulty assessing appropriate cut-off scores within a sample from the general population. Moreover, these researchers do not provide information on its use with females, and they have not conducted cross-cultural studies with this measure.

Adolescent Violence Survey (AVS)

The AVS (Kingery, 1998), considered an improvement in the assessment of violent behavior in youth, was specifically developed to fill a need in the research for an adequate scale to directly measure violence. It is a 41-item scale, with six subscales:

1. Perceived reputation for violence at school;
2. Vengeful thoughts;
3. Respect for fighting;
4. Rationalization of violence;
5. Angry delinquency;
6. Delinquency.

The six subscales had stable factor loadings, ranging from .44 to .84. The instrument is divided into a Violence Composite and a Delinquency Composite. The author has reported that there is sufficient evidence for the validity of this instrument; it is a reliable tool for assessing violence at low to moderate levels, particularly over time; and it has shown particular salience in middle school and high school settings (Kingery, 1998). The AVS was investigated in a sample of 1,374 adolescents (eighth and ninth graders) in a central, moderate size American city. The broader violence scale had an internal consistency of .95 (Cronbach's alpha) and a test-retest reliability of .91 (Pearson r) over a one-week period. It is simple to score and can be administered over a 30-minute period.

Conflict in Relationships (CIR)

The CIR (Wolfe, Reitzel-Jaffe, Gough, & Wekerle, 1994) is an 80-item self-report scale that measures the frequency of physically, sexually, and emotionally abusive and nonabusive behaviors committed or experienced by the respondent. It was developed specifically as a measure of positive and negative communication patterns as well as verbal and physical violence and abuse in reference to social dating situations. There are separate male and female instructions for using this instrument, although, with the exception of pronoun changes, the scale itself is identical for both genders. It has the ability to assess current or past relationship conflict. The CIR has two parts. Part A reflects behaviors the respondent has shown toward a partner, and Part B reflects behaviors a partner has shown toward the respondent.

The psychometric value of this instrument was assessed in a recent study by the authors of the CIR (Wolfe, Wekerle, Reitzel-Jaffe, & Lefebvre, 1998). The reliability and validity scores were obtained from a sample of 356 youth. A principal component analysis was conducted for the entire sample. The higher level of Abuse/Coercion items had factor loadings between .94 and .96 (with the exception of "threatened partners verbally or physically to have sex with them," .58). Lower-level items of abuse/coercion had modest to low factor loadings (e.g., threaten to end relationship, .31). The Negative Communication items had factor loadings between .60 and .35 for higher-level negative communication. The Positive Communication items had even lower factor loadings (i.e., from .51 to .17). The alpha coefficients for each factor were as follows: Abuse/Coercion, .90; Negative Communication, .79; and Positive Communication, .78.

MEASURES OF VIOLENT BEHAVIORS IN ADULTS

Measures Used with Perpetrators or Victims

The Aggression Questionnaire (AQ)

The Aggression Questionnaire (AQ) (Buss & Perry, 1992) is a 29-item self-report instrument in which each respondent has to rate each item on a scale from 1 ("extremely uncharacteristic of me") to 5 ("characteristic of me"). Four factors yield factor scores: (a) the physical aggression factor; (b) verbal aggression; (c) anger; and (d) hostility (anger) factor. The AQ appears to have use in both research and practice. The questionnaire was developed to address the limitations and criticism of the original Buss-Durkee Hostility Inventory (Buss & Durkee, 1957). Although the Hostility Inventory is one of the most frequently cited questionnaires on aggression (Bushman, Cooper, & Lemke, 1991), it has increasingly become a subject of controversy (Buss & Perry, 1992). The older inventory lacked test-retest reliability and its form was in the antiquated true-false format. The authors of the new instrument maintain that it retains the major virtues of the older inventory and also successfully meets current psychometric standards.

The psychometric properties of the AQ were assessed from data obtained from 1,253 male college students, most of whom were between 18 and 21 years of age. Chi-squares were computed and then divided by the degrees of freedom in a procedure that resulted in ratio scores to test goodness of fit. (See Buss & Perry, 1992, for review.) Ratios below 2.0 suggest a reasonable fit. Three models were tested. In the first model, all items were loaded on a single factor and produced a 2.27 ratio (poor fit). The second and third models produced 1.94 and 1.95 ratios, respectively. The latter ratio includes four factors of aggression linked by a higher-order factor of general aggression. The following alphas were reported: Aggression, .85; Verbal Aggression, .72; Anger, .83; and Hostility, .77 (total score = .89). Test-retest correlations were based on a sample of 372 subjects within a nine-week interval. The Physical Aggression score = .80; the Verbal Aggression score = .76; the Anger score = .72; and the Hostility = .72 (total score = .80).

More recently, further evaluation of the AQ has yielded positive results, suggesting that it has a good degree of construct validity (Harris, 1997). However, additional investigation of its psychometric properties on cross-cultural samples is needed.

Abuse Behavior Inventory (ABI)

The ABI (Shepard & Campbell, 1992) has been used in several research studies and has been found to be a good measure of potential abusive behavior (McEllistrem & Subotnik, 1994; Mills & Malley-Morrison, 1998; Neufeld, McNamara, & Ertl, 1999). The ABI is a 30-item self-report instrument that uses a 5-point Likert-type scale to measure the frequency of abusive behaviors during a 6-month period. There are identical forms for men and women, except that different pronouns focus on the use of abusive behaviors by men only (e.g., men are asked to report how often they had "kicked her," and women are asked to report how often their male partner "kicked you"). This tool was initially developed to evaluate domestic abuse programs. Therefore, it reflects the feminist perspective, which guides most domestic abuse programs. There is an interesting contrast with the Conflict Tactics Scale (CTS; Straus, 1979). The ABI does not set the violence in the context of family disagreement or the result of attempts to deal with conflict. The authors' rationale is that violence is reported to be a set of behaviors used for the purpose of maintaining dominance and not necessarily a tool to resolve conflict.

Twenty psychological abuse items were drawn from five subcategories: (a) emotional abuse, (b) isolation, (c) intimidation, (d) use of "male privilege," and (e) economic abuse. The authors suggest that these items are considered psychologically abusive when set in the context of physically abusive relationships. Ten physical abuse items are classified as assaultive behaviors, including forcing a woman to engage in sexual activity against her will. Frequency ratings for each psychological abuse item are summed and then divided by 20 to obtain an average psychological abuse score. The scores range from 1 (no psychological abuse) to 5 (very frequent psychological abuse). Similar physical abuse scores are calculated by dividing the physical abuse ratings by 10.

The psychometric properties presented here were based on a sample of 100 males and 78 females, equally divided into groups of abusers/abused and nonabusers/nonabused. The reliability of the ABI was reported in terms of the alpha coefficients and the standard error of measurement (SEM) for the two subscales. It is particularly useful to report the SEM when interpreting individual scores (Bloom, Fischer, & Orme, 1999). The SEM gives the range in which to view a person's true score. Generally, the smaller the SEM, the more reliable the measure of a particular score. The reliabilities and their respective standard errors of measurement for the sample were as follows:

	Nonabusive Men	Abusive Men
Physical	$\alpha = .82$ SEM $= .03$	$\alpha = .82$ SEM $= .07$
Psychological	$\alpha = .79$ SEM $= .06$	$\alpha = .88$ SEM $= .08$
	Nonabused Women	Abused Women
Physical	$\alpha = .88$ SEM $= .07$	$\alpha = .70$ SEM $= .08$
Psychological	$\alpha = .92$ SEM $= .11$	$\alpha = .88$ SEM $= .12$

Validity was assessed by using three different approaches: (a) criterion, (b) construct, and (c) factor validity. All three approaches were found to reveal good validity scores for the ABI; two of those three approaches are reported here. The rigorous efforts these researchers employed to assess the validity of their scale are not often seen in the literature and are indicative of the importance these researchers placed on validating their instrument. Their attention to detail is highly commendable.

Criterion validity depends on the ability of a scale to distinguish groups from one another on some external criterion (Rubin & Babbie, 2001). An ANCOVA (analysis of covariance) was conducted using group status as the independent variable and abusive scores as the dependent variables. The differences in the men's psychological abuse, group mean ($M = .55$), and their physical abuse, group mean ($M = .42$), were found to be significant ($p = .0001$). The women's psychological abuse, group mean was $M = .80$, and their physical abuse, group mean was $M = .55$. These were also significant. For both men and women, the ABI psychological and physical abuse scores for those in abusive relationships were 25% higher than scores for those who were not in abusive relationships—another significant statistic.

Construct validity was determined by assessing the convergent and discriminant validity of the ABI. The reported results suggested that the ABI subscales demonstrated good construct validity because, for both men and women, each of the variables predicted to be highly correlated to an abusive relationship had stronger correlations to the ABI subscales than variables predicted to be less strongly related. For example, men's physical and psychological abuse scores correlated poorly with age ($r^2 = .0713$, and $r^2 = .0562$, respectively). Another example is the correlation between psychological and physical abuse scores and whether the men were arrested or not. Men's physical and psychological abuse scores had correlations of $r^2 = .3795$, and $r^2 = .2756$, respectively. A complete review of the results of the validity scores reported on this instrument can be found in the original article (Shepard & Campbell, 1992).

Revised Conflict Tactics Scale (CTS2)

The CTS (Straus, 1979, 1990) has been the most widely used scale in family violence research. More than 70,000 respondents, from a rich array of cultural backgrounds in at least 20 countries, were involved (see Straus, Hamby, Boney-McCoy, & Sugarman, 1996, for review). The CTS measures the extent to which partners in a dating, cohabiting, or marital relationship engage in psychological and physical abuse toward each other. Another feature of the CTS is that it measures a person's use of reasoning or negotiation to deal with conflicts. For example, respondents are asked how many times, in a given period, they used reasoning or argument, verbal or symbolic aggression, or physical aggression, during disagreements or fights. The most robust application of the CTS has been to assess violence perpetrated on a partner by gathering data on physical assaults on a partner (Straus et al., 1996). As a result of its widespread use, a number of revisions of the CTS have been suggested.

Straus et al. (1996) introduced a revised CTS and referred to it as the CTS2. Several improvements were made in this new version. Among the important additions to the items on the CTS were questions related to "sexual coercion" and the consequential "physical injury from assaults by partner." Moreover, awkward language presentations such as "his/her" and "him/her" were replaced with "my partner." The CTS2 is now able to identify context and explicit intent of the violent behavior by specifically stating action-intent items such as: "Threw something at my partner that could hurt." The format of the CTS2 is also different. One of the concerns about the previous matrix format was that, because it is often used as a self-administered test, it may be a confusing tool for the general population (Straus et al., 1996).

With the CTS2, each item asks what the participant does and is followed by what the partner has done, sometimes in this simple form: "My partner did this to me." Because there are now two questions for each item, the CTS2 is comprised of 78 items, in contrast to the 39 items on the previous version. However, the administration time remains relatively brief; the CTS2 can be completed within 15 minutes—a practical time span in terms of clinical and research applications. When shorter assessments are needed, the CTS2 mirrors the CTS in offering three subscales that take 7 to 10 minutes each.

The psychometric properties of the CTS2 were based on analyses data obtained at two colleges, from a sample of 317 undergraduates (minimum age 18 years) who had been in a relationship for at least one month during the previous year. Construct validity was assessed via a series of steps consistent with conventions, as determined by the author (see Straus et al., 1996, for review). Psychological aggression and sexual assault revealed r = .66 for men and r = .25 for women. Physical assault and sexual coercion revealed r = .90 for men, and r = .26 for women. Physical assault and injury demonstrated a higher correlation for men (r = .87) than for women (r = .29), as had been predicted. Internal consistency reliabilities ranged from .79 to .95. Therefore, the CTS2 appears to have strong evidence of reliability and moderate evidence of validity. The preliminary nature of the evidence presented here suggests that future research might reveal significant findings on the psychometric qualities of the CTS2.

Measures for the Victims of Abuse

Index of Spouse Abuse (ISA)

The ISA (Hudson & McIntosh, 1981) is a 30-item self-report, summated-category, partition scale that was designed to measure the severity or magnitude of physical and nonphysical violence inflicted upon women by spouses or partners. This index can be used to assist researchers in monitoring and evaluating the practice, as well as understanding the frequency and severity, of partner abuse. It takes about 5 minutes to complete and is easy to administer and score. The measure covers abusive behaviors ranging from very serious to much less serious. The degree of differences must be taken into account when interpreting the scores obtained from use of this scale. The scale allows two different scores to be produced for each respondent: (a) an ISA-Physical (ISA-P) abuse score that represents the severity of physical abuse, and (b) an ISA-Nonphysical (ISA-NP) abuse score that represents the severity of nonphysical abuse. The authors report specific scoring procedures within the original article (see Hudson & McIntosh, 1981).

The reliability data were reported from a study that had two samples of women: one relatively large sample (N = 398) and one moderate size sample (N = 107). The ISA-P and the ISA-NP alpha coefficients for the large sample were $\alpha = .90$ and $\alpha = .91$, respectively, as compared to the smaller sample: $\alpha = .94$ and $\alpha = .97$, respectively. These coefficients appear to support the claim that the ISA subscales are unidimensional measures. The researchers also reported the SEM for the subscale scores. The average SEM of the ISA-P subscale was 3.68, and the average SEM for the ISA-NP was 3.30.

Validity was assessed using the discriminant validity and construct validity methods. The instrument appears to have discriminated well from other clinical scales and from the age and education of the respondent. The alpha coefficient for the discriminant validity of the subscales was $\alpha = .73$ for the ISA-P and $\alpha = .80$ for the ISA-NP. Construct validity was assessed by determining the extent to which the measure correlated poorly with theoretically unrelated variables, and correlated well with theoretically related variables. These researchers gathered data on a group of personal and social variables that were believed to have very little to do with spouse abuse. The alpha coefficients for the comparison between the ISA-P and ISA-NP and these personal and social problems were, respectively, $\alpha = .11$ and $\alpha = .14$. These researchers also gathered additional data on a group of personal and social problems that were believed to have a more direct relationship to spouse abuse. The alpha coefficients for the correlation between the ISA-P and ISA-NP and these more closely related constructs were $\alpha = .29$ and $\alpha = .38$, respectively. The authors of the ISA reported that the correlation between the ISA-P and clinical abuse status was $\alpha = .73$, and the correlation between ISA-NP and clinical abuse status was $\alpha = .80$. Clinical cutting scores for both the ISA-P and ISA-NP successfully classified 90.7% of the total sample. The limitation of this scale is that the reliability data are somewhat low. Additional investigation is needed to determine the validity and reliability of this tool for assessment of various cultural groups.

Partner Abuse Scale: Non-Physical (PASNP) and Physical Abuse of Partner Scale (PAPS)

These instruments come in the form of two sets. One set is for self-reporting of physical and nonphysical abuse of a partner (Physical Abuse of Partner Scale, PAPS; Non-Physical Abuse of Partner Scale, NPAPS). For perceived abuse experienced by an individual in an intimate relationship, the authors developed another set (Partner Abuse Scale: Physical, PASP; Partner Abuse Scale: Non-Physical, PASNP). Both sets of scales were developed by Hudson, MacNeil, and Dierks (1992).

These instruments assess the perceptions of the abuser and the abused in a particularly unique way. Each form can be used as a check for the other, which can be of special interest to the researcher or clinician. Together, they offer an opportunity to do a good assessment of abuse in a relationship. Both are 25-item scales. They produce scores that range from 0 to 100, which, for practical purposes, can be regarded as true ratio scale values.

Fischer and Corcoran (1994) report that all four scales have alpha coefficients at or above .90, which suggests good internal consistency. Hudson et al. (1992) make the claim that these instruments have good content and factorial validity, and they report that accumulating evidence supports the construct validity. Additional research has been conducted on these scales. Attala, Hudson, and McSweeney (1994) found that the PASP and PASNP successfully discriminated between 90 women who reported they were abused, and 50 women who did not report abuse. In the same study, these scales were able to identify the physically abused women with a 87% accuracy rate (identified 76, although 66 had said they were abused). These instruments are brief, easy to administer, methodologically sound, and relatively easy to score. However, their limitation is that, at present, little is known about their use with diverse populations. More extensive validity data are needed.

Psychological Maltreatment of Women Inventory (PMWI)

The PMWI (Tolman, 1989) is a 58-item self-report scale that includes a broader range of behaviors than both the ISA (Hudson & McIntosh, 1981) and the CTS (Straus, 1979). A strong quality of the PMWI is that it has parallel forms for both men and women to complete. Much like other abuse self-report scales, the format of the PMWI requires the individual to report the relative frequency of each type of behavior. Two subscales—Dominance-Isolation and Verbal-Emotional Abuse—were factor analytically derived, and both of these subscales have high reliability ($\alpha > .90$). In a recent study (Tolman, 1999), the author of the PMWI, found that it successfully differentiated among three distinct groups, although two of the groups are theoretically similar: (a) battered women, (b) relationship-distressed but nonbattered women, and (c) women in nondistressed relationships.

The PMWI has undergone recent revisions. The result has been the introduction of a shortened scale containing 14 items that reflect both subscales found in the longer form of the PMWI (Tolman, 1999). The original scale continues to have good utility, although some researchers or practitioners may prefer the shorter version under certain circumstances. The subscales on this short form also demonstrated good reliability (dominance-isolation, $\alpha = .88$; verbal-emotional, $\alpha = .92$). Additional investigation of the psychometric properties of this new version of the PMWI should reveal further information as to its utility.

Measures Assessing Perpetrators of Child Abuse

Although all types of alleged and confirmed acts of abuse across all populations are of profound importance to researchers and practitioners, child abuse allegations and confirmed acts are of the highest concern with respect to measurement in general and predictability in particular. Child abuse is an act(s) of violence by adults against children. Generally, children have to rely on adults to protect them from harm. Unfortunately, adults sometimes fall short of that responsibility. To the extent that there are additional tools to help estimate the potential for and the actual delivery of acts of child abuse, researchers and practitioners must use these measures, as needed, in this very sensitive area.

It is vitally important to assess child maltreatment with as much accuracy as possible, given the availability of resources. Because of this issue, predictive or screening measures are routinely assessed, as a matter of convention, for their "specificity" and "sensitivity." Specificity is the ability of an instrument to identify individuals as not having a particular situation, which is often referred to as "true negative" identification. Sensitivity is the ability of an instrument to correctly identify a particular individual as having an identified situation, which is referred to as "true positive" identification. The crux of the issue with predictive or diagnostic measures is that, ideally, we want increased sensitivity because this reduces false negatives; at the same time, we want to increase sensitivity because this decreases false positives. However, the problem is that increasing sensitivity has the disdainful effect of decreasing specificity. (For a more thorough review of these issues, see Caldwell, Bogat, & Davidson, 1988.)

Child Abuse Potential (CAP) Inventory

Given the issues addressed above, this chapter will discuss and review one well-documented instrument used for the purpose of screening for child abuse, the Child Abuse Potential (CAP) Inventory (Milner, 1986). Although several other instruments have been developed, many of them have not been sufficiently investigated for their predictive utility. The CAP is a 160-item self-report instrument that is presented in an agree/disagree format. One of the qualities of this tool is that it has a very good (third grade) readability level (Milner & Wimberly, 1980). The scale has a 77-item abuse scale and an 18-item lie scale (Milner, 1986). Factors derived from the abuse scale describe various psychological difficulties (i.e., distress, rigidity, unhappiness) and interpersonal problems (i.e., problems with child and self, with family, and with others) (Milner, 1986). Scores on this measure range from 0 to 486. Sample items include: "Spanking that only bruises a child is okay," "People expect too much of me," and "A crying child will never be happy."

Milner (1986) reported extensive reliability data on the CAP abuse scale (e.g., Kuder-Richardson's 20 coefficients range from .92 to .96). These researchers have reported data that indicate the CAP has a correct classification rate for abusers ranging from 86.4% to 92.4%, depending on what cutoff scores are used (Milner, 1994). However, a more recent study of the CAP's utility with adolescent mothers (Blinn-Pike & Mingus, 2000) revealed that it is barely an acceptable tool with this population because alpha reliabilities fell below acceptable levels.

The CAP is perhaps the best validated screening and predictive instrument of child abuse potential and behavior currently available. The CAP produced scores that, to a significant degree, were positively correlated with self-report history (Miller, Handal, Gilner, & Cross, 1991) as well as repeat physical abuse in at-risk parents (Milner, Gold, Ayoub, & Jacewitz, 1984). In the latter study, 100% of the confirmed abuse cases had scores above the cutoff level. Milner, Charlesworth, Gold, and Gold (1988) conducted a study on the convergent validity of the CAP and found that a student sample and prison sample had correlations of .63 and .71, respectively, when compared with five factors on the Mental Health Index (MHI; Veit & Ware, 1983). Additionally, these researchers present an extensive review of previous validation studies on the CAP (Milner et al., 1988). (For specific discussions of the convergent and discriminant validity, readers should review Robertson and Milner, 1985.) The CAP has more recently produced extensive cross-validation data with diverse cultures in several countries, including Croatia (Pecnik & Ajdukovic, 1995), Greece (Diareme, Tsiantis, & Tsitoura, 1997), and Chile (Haz & Ramirez, 1998). One of the major criticisms of the CAP comes from its weakness as a tool with adolescent populations. Nonetheless, the CAP remains one of the most useful tools for predicting child abuse. Researchers using the CAP should continue to include, as with all measures of violent behavior, a complete assessment of its psychometric properties.

IMPLICATIONS AND FUTURE DIRECTIONS IN MEASURING VIOLENT BEHAVIOR

Violence is one of the most critical social problems facing society today. For this reason, measurement and assessment of various aspects of violent behavior are of paramount importance to researchers and practitioners. The technology of quantifying violent behavior, and family violence in general, continues to make advances. The research in this area improves our ability to deconstruct the phenomena. The proliferation of measures will undoubtedly continue, and the direction should include, for both perpetrators and victims, measures that are culture- and gender-specific, as well as developmentally appropriate. When considering perpetrators of violence, it is essential that we improve our ability to accurately identify violent behavior in such individuals to protect victims, as well as to enhance both the treatment and prevention of future violent behavior. More than the development of new instruments, we need concerted efforts, on the part of researchers, to improve upon the existing instruments in this area. Measures that are easy to administer, have good reliability and validity, and are easy to score and interrupt are beneficial for researchers and practitioners alike (Rapp-Paglicci, Dulmus, Wodarski, & Feit, 1999). As the research continues to develop in this area, so should the quality of the instruments being utilized.

As for the decision to use a particular instrument, whether for clinical or research purposes, it seems paramount that criteria for appropriately selecting a measure should be established. The following list of questions is aimed at specifying those criteria:

- Does the instrument rely on a theoretical foundation consistent with that of the researcher, the research question, or the clinical intervention?
- Given the instrument's intended use, what level of validity and reliability is necessary?
- How practical is the administration of the instrument for the research purpose under consideration?

This chapter has provided researchers and clinicians with a foundation that can be used as a source of reference when searching for a particular instrument, and has presented options for future research on measures of violent behavior.

REFERENCES

Achenbach, T. M. (1991a). *Manual for the Child Behavior Checklist/4–18 and 1991 profile.* Burlington: University of Vermont Department of Psychiatry.

Achenbach, T. M. (1991b). *Manual for the Teacher's Report Form and 1991 profile.* Burlington: University of Vermont Department of Psychiatry.

Ammerman, R. T., & Hersen, M. (1999). Current issues in the assessment of family violence. In R. T. Ammerman & M. Hersen (Eds.), *Assessment of family violence: A clinical and legal sourcebook* (pp. 3–23). New York: Wiley.

Attala, J. M., Hudson, W. W., & McSweeney, M. (1994). A partial validation of two short-form partner abuse scales. *Women and Health, 21*(2/3), 125–139.

Blinn-Pike, L., & Mingus, S. (2000). The internal consistency of the Child Abuse Potential Inventory with adolescent mothers. *Journal of Adolescence, 23,* 107–111.

Bloom, M., Fischer, J., & Orme, J. G. (1999). *Evaluating practice: Guidelines for the accountable professional* (3rd ed.). Boston: Allyn & Bacon.

Bushman, B. J., Cooper, H. M., & Lemke, K. M. (1991). Meta-analysis of factor analyses: An illustration using the Buss–Durkee Hostility Inventory. *Personality and Social Psychology Bulletin, 17*(3), 344–349.

Buss, A. H., & Durkee, A. (1957). An inventory for assessing different kinds of hostility. *Journal of Consulting Psychology, 21,* 343–349.

Buss, A. H., & Perry, M. (1992). The Aggression Questionnaire. *Journal of Personality and Social Psychology, 63*(3), 452–459.

Caldwell, B., Bogat, G. A., & Davidson, W. S. (1988). The assessment of child abuse potential and the prevention of child abuse and neglect: A policy analysis. *Journal of Community Psychology, 16,* 609–624.

Cascardi, M., Avery-Leaf, S., O'Leary, D., & Slep, A. M. (1999). Factor structure and convergent validity of the Conflict Tactic Scale in high school students. *Psychological Assessment, 11*(4), 546–555.

Combs-Orme, T., Martin, L., Fox, G. L., & Faver, C. A. (2000). Risk for child maltreatment: New mothers' concerns and screening results. *Children and Youth Services Review, 22*(7), 517–537.

Croker, L., & Algina, J. (1986). *Introduction to classical and modern test theory.* Chicago: Holt, Rinehart and Winston.

Diareme, S., Tsiantis, J., & Tsitoura, S. (1997). Cross-cultural validation of the Child Abuse Potential Inventory in Greece: A preliminary study. *Child Abuse and Neglect, 21*(11), 1067–1079.

Dwyer, D. C., Smokowski, P. R., Bricout, J. C., & Wodarski, J. S. (1995). Domestic violence research: Theoretical and practice implications for social work. *Clinical Social Work Journal, 23*(2), 185–198.

Fischer, J., & Corcoran, K. (1994). *Measures for clinical practice.* New York: Free Press.

Glisson, C., Hemmelgran, A. L., & Post, J. A. (in press). The Shortform Assessment of Children (SAC): An assessment and outcome measure for child welfare and juvenile justice. *Research on Social Work Practice, 12*(1).

Grann, M., Langstroem, N., Tengstroem, A., & Kullgren, G. (1999). Psychopathy (PCL-R) predicts violent recidivism among criminal offenders. *Law and Human Behavior, 23*(2), 205–217.

Hare, R. D. (1991). *Manual for the Psychopathy Checklist–Revised.* Toronto, Ontario, Canada: Multi-Health Systems.

Hare, R. D., Hart, S., & Harpur, T. (1991). Psychopathy and the DSM-IV criteria for antisocial personality disorder. *Journal of Abnormal Psychology, 100*(3), 391–398.

Harris, J. A. (1997). A further evaluation of the aggression questionnaire: Issues of validity and reliability. *Behaviour Research and Therapy, 35*(11), 1047–1053.

Haz, A. M., & Ramirez, V. (1998). Preliminary validation of the Child Abuse Potential Inventory in Chile. *Child Abuse and Neglect, 22*(9), 869–879.

Hudson, W. W., MacNeil, R., & Dierks, S. (1992). *Six new assessment scales: A partial validation.* Tempe: Arizona State University, School of Social Work.

Hudson, W. W., & McIntosh, S. R. (1981). The assessment of spouse abuse: Two quantifiable dimensions. *Journal of Marriage and the Family, 43,* 873–874.

Hudson, W. W., & McMurtry, S. (1997). Comprehensive assessment in social work practice: The Multi-Problem Screening Inventory. *Research on Social Work Practice, 7*(1), 79–98.

Jasinski, J. L., & Williams, L. M. (Eds.). (1998). *Partner violence: A comprehensive review of 20 years of research.* Thousand Oaks, CA: Sage.

Jesness, C., & Wedge, B. (1984). Validity of a revised Jesness Inventory I-Level classification with delinquents. *Journal of Consulting and Clinical Psychology, 52*(16), 997–1010.

Kaplan, S. L., Busner, J., Kupietz, S., Wasserman, E., & Segal, B. (1990). Effects of methylphenidate on adolescents with aggressive conduct disorder and ADDH: A preliminary report. *Journal of the American Academy of Child Adolescent Psychiatry, 29*(5), 719–723.

Kingery, P. M. (1998). The Adolescent Violence Survey: A psychometric analysis. *School Psychology International, 19*(1), 43–59.

Marohn, R. C., Offer, D., Curtiss, G., & Feczko, M. (1980). The AAB Checklist. *Clinical Psychology, 36,* 594–601.

McEllistrem, J. E., & Subotnik, L. (1994). The reduction of male abusiveness as a result of treatment: Reality of myth. *Journal of Interpersonal Violence, 9*(4), 307–316.

Miller, T. R., Handal, P. J., Gilner, F. H., & Cross, J. F. (1991). The relationship of abuse and witnessing violence on the Child Abuse Potential Inventory with black adolescents. *Journal of Family Violence, 6,* 351–346.

Mills, R. B., & Malley-Morrison, K. (1998). Emotional commitment, normative acceptability, and attributions for abusive partner behaviors. *Journal of Interpersonal Violence, 13*(6), 682–699.

Milner, J. S. (1986). *The Child Abuse Potential Inventory: Manual* (2nd ed.). Webster, NC: Psytec.

Milner, J. S. (1994). Assessing physical child abuse risk: The Child Abuse Potential Inventory. *Clinical Psychology Review, 14*(6), 547–585.

Milner, J. S., Charlesworth, J. R., Gold, R. G., & Gold, S. R. (1988). Convergent validity of the Child Abuse Potential Inventory. *Journal of Clinical Psychology, 44*(2), 281–285.

Milner, J. S., Gold, R. G., Ayoub, C., & Jacewitz, M. M. (1984). Predictive validity of the Child Abuse Potential Inventory. *Journal of Consulting and Clinical Psychology, 52*(5), 879–884.

Milner, J. S., & Wimberly, R. C. (1980). Prediction and explanation of child abuse. *Journal of Clinical Psychology, 36,* 875–884.

Neufeld, J., McNamara, J. R., & Ertl, M. (1999). Incidence and prevalence of dating partner abuse and its relationship to dating practices. *Journal of Interpersonal Violence, 14*(2), 125–137.

Neidig, P. M. (1986). *The Modified Conflict Tactics Scale.* Beaufort, SC: Behavioral Sciences Associates.

Pecnik, N., & Ajdukovic, M. (1995). The Child Abuse Potential Inventory: Cross-validation in Croatia. *Psychological Reports, 76,* 979–985.

Poythress, N. G., Edens, J. F., & Lilienfeld, O. (1998). Criterion-related validity of the Psychopathic Personality Inventory in a prison sample. *Psychological Assessments, 10*(4), 426–430.

Rapp-Paglicci, L., Dulmus, C. N., Wodarski, J. S., & Feit, M. (1999). Screening of substance abuse in public welfare and child protective service clients: A comparative study of rapid assessment instruments vs. the SASSI. *Journal of Addictive Disease, 18*(2), 83–88.

Robertson, K. R., & Milner, J. S. (1985). Convergent and discriminant validity of the Child Abuse Potential Inventory. *Journal of Personality Assessment, 49*(1), 86–88.

Rubin, A., & Babbie, E. (2001). *Research methods for social work* (4th ed.). Stamford, CT: Wadsworth, Brooks/Cole.

Salekin, R. T., Rogers, R., & Sewell, K. W. (1996). A review and meta-analysis of the Psychopathy Checklist and Psychopathy Checklist-Revised: Predictive validity of dangerousness. *Clinical Psychology: Science and Practice, 3*(3), 203–215.

Shepard, M. F., & Campbell, J. A. (1992). The Abusive Behavior Inventory: A measure of psychological and physical abuse. *Journal of Interpersonal Violence, 7*(3), 291–305.

Straus, M. A. (1979). Measuring intra-family conflict and violence: The Conflict Tactics Scale. *Journal of Marriage and the Family, 41,* 75–88.

Straus, M. A. (1990). The Conflict Tactics Scale and its critics: An evaluation and new data on validity and reliability. In M. A. Straus & R. J. Gelles (Eds.), *Physical violence in American families: Risk factors and adaptations to violence in 8,145 families* (pp. 49–73). New Brunswick, NJ: Transaction.

Straus, M. A., Hamby, S. L., Boney-McCoy, S., & Sugarman, D. B. (1996). The revised Conflict Tactics Scales (CTS2). *Journal of Family Issues, 17*(3), 283–303.

Tolman, R. M. (1989). The development of a measure of psychological maltreatment of women by their male partners. *Violence and Victims, 4,* 159–178.

Tolman, R. M. (1999). The validation of the psychological maltreatment of women inventory: Preliminary report. *Violence and Victims, 41*(1).

Veit, C. T., & Ware, J. E. (1983). The structure of psychological well-being in general populations. *Journal of Consulting and Clinical Psychology, 51,* 730–742.

Wekerle, C., & Wolfe, D. A. (1999). Dating violence in mid-adolescence: Theory significance and emerging prevention initiatives. *Clinical Psychology Review, 19*(4), 435–456.

Wolfe, D. A., Reitzel-Jaffe, D., Gough, R., & Wekerle, C. (1994). *Conflicts in relationships: Measuring physical and sexual coercion among youth.* (Available from the Youth Relationships Project, Department of Psychology, The University of Western Ontario, London, Canada N6A 5C2.)

Wolfe, D. A., Wekerle, C., Reitzel-Jaffe, D., & Lefebvre, L. (1998). Factors associated with abusive relationships among maltreated and non-maltreated youth. *Development and Psychopathology, 10,* 61–85.

Chapter 8

CONDUCT DISORDER AND SUBSTANCE ABUSE

JUAN J. BARTHELEMY, CATHERINE N. DULMUS, AND
JOHN S. WODARSKI

INTRODUCTION

Drug abuse and mental disorder behaviors are significant pressing problems
that afflict adolescents today (Costello, Erkanli, Federman, & Angold, 1999;
Disney, Elkins, McGue, & Iacono, 1999). Currently, more than 12% of children
and adolescents suffer from a mental disorder. Often, these youths are not diagnosed until it is too late. Frequently, not until an individual begins to exhibit an
aberrant lifestyle does intervention take place. Unfortunately, acts such as drug
and alcohol use, poor school performance, violence, depression, and subsequent
suicide take place before it is realized that there is a problem. Research has
found that drug abuse and mental disorders often coexist (Grant & Dawson,
1999; Hilarski & Wodarski, in press). Children and adolescents have emotional
and behavioral symptoms of mental disorders. Cognitive behavior treatment
modifies dysfunctional behaviors and replaces them with healthier alternatives
(Smokowski & Wodarski, 1998). Comorbid psychiatric disorder and drug abuse
problems are as important in adolescent as in adult populations (Bukstein,
1995). Establishing effective treatments of adolescent drug abuse and pursuing
research on the impact of mental disorders will contribute to improving care,
especially in public-sector agencies.

Mediation of adolescent substance abuse can help reduce the occurrence of
adolescent violence because a strong correlation exists between adolescent
drug use and violent behavior (Bukstein, 1994; Marohn, 1992). Studies have
found that individuals with a propensity for aggression become more violent

under the influence of substances (Goldstein, Glick, Reiner, Zimmerman, & Coultry, 1987).

Substance abuse has extensive economic and social ramifications for persons at all levels of society. Drug-abuse-related deaths or injuries, disease, and family and emotional disturbances are consequences that cannot be measured in monetary figures (Wodarski & Wodarski, 1993). The U.S. Health and Human Services studies have reported that 40% of teenage deaths occur in traffic crashes and 50% of those crashes involve alcohol. Adolescence is the developmental stage in which experimentation with mood-altering substances is most active (Kagan, 1991; Novacek, Raskin, & Hogan, 1991). Short-term consequences of adolescent substance abuse include premature death due to traffic and other accidents, antisocial behaviors and their related consequences, suicide, increased risk for HIV infection, and school-related difficulties (Oetting & Beauvais, 1990). More long-term consequences of teenage substance abuse include later-life health problems, failure to adequately prepare for adult life, and problems resulting from arrests while under the influence of drugs or alcohol (Kagan, 1991; Oetting & Beauvais, 1990; Vander & Damirjian, 1990). Stark (1993) has asserted that black youths are killing their race by engaging in the self-abusive behaviors of violence, drug addiction, and suicide.

Adolescents are faced with daily decisions about the role that alcohol and drugs will play in their lives. There is a crucial need for teenagers to have an accurate, broad, well-rounded foundation of knowledge to draw upon when they make decisions about alcohol and drug use (Wodarski & Wodarski, 1993).

This chapter focuses on conduct disorder and substance abuse. In addition to providing an overview of each diagnosis and its related trends and issues, the chapter discusses this comorbid disorder in relation to gender differences, preventive interventions, and recommendations for case management of troubled youths who are diagnosed with both conduct disorder and substance abuse.

CURRENT TRENDS AND ISSUES

Drug and alcohol use has been found to be strongly related with delinquent and antisocial behavior (Leukefeld, 1998), though the use of substances can, in and of itself, be defined as an antisocial behavior. Drug and alcohol use shares with antisocial behavior many of the same correlates: family discord, family structure, previous antisocial behavior, and low academic achievement (Sanford et al., 1999). Elliott, Huizinga, and Menard (1989) found that certain types of drug use precede certain types of delinquent behavior.

Gender Differences

As in the general adolescent population, male psychoactive substance abusers engage in more conduct disorder behaviors than female abusers; however, the relative occurrence of conduct disorder behaviors in both sexes is similar (Brown, 1996). The rates of conduct disorder and disruptive behavior are, in general, much higher in boys than in girls. Approximately two-thirds of children diagnosed with conduct disorder are boys (Dadds, 1997). The research has also indicated that more boys are diagnosed with early-onset conduct disorder than girls (Sanford et al., 1999). Males with a diagnosis of conduct disorder exhibit more aggressive behavior than females. Fighting, stealing, vandalism, and discipline problems are more common for males, whereas females are more likely to exhibit lying and truancy behaviors, and to run away (American Psychiatric Association, 1994).

Mezzich, Moss, Tarter, and Wolfenstein (1994) studied gender differences in the patterns and progression of substance use in conduct disorder adolescents. They found that females were more likely to have experimented with nonprescriptive diet pills and caffeine, and males were more likely to have experimented with snuff or chewing tobacco. Females started drinking alcohol at a later age than did males, although the age at which they qualified for a diagnosis of alcohol abuse/dependence did not differ. The study also found that the interval between alcohol use and diagnosis of alcohol abuse/dependence was shorter for females than for males, and that females exhibited a shorter interval between cannabis use and a diagnosis of a cannabis abuse/dependence.

Riggs, Mikulich, Whitmore, and Crowley (1999) researched gender differences in substance-dependent juvenile delinquents. They found that males' progression to illicit drug use was dependent on prior use of alcohol, whereas, for females, either cigarette use or alcohol use was sufficient to predict a progression to marijuana. For both males and females, severity of nicotine dependence contributed to a severity of nonnicotine substance use disorder. For males only, a younger onset of regular smoking was related to later nicotine and nonnicotine substance use disorders. The severity may be partially explained by males' having more severe conduct disorder. A diagnosis of more severe conduct disorder has been related to an earlier onset of conduct symptoms and of substance involvement (Riggs, 1999).

A study conducted by Kessler, Berglund, and Foster (1997) stated that teenagers with psychiatric disorders are at a higher risk of becoming teenage parents. Conduct disorder and substance abuse were among the disabilities that were significantly correlated with teen pregnancy. For a multitude of reasons, teen pregnancy is an important issue. About 16% of mothers receive welfare benefits; however, families started by teen mothers account for about 50% of the total welfare budget (Kessler et al., 1997).

Types of Conduct Disorder Behaviors Associated with Substance Use

Youths with comorbid conduct disorder and substance use disorders may report different types of conduct disorder symptoms than do conduct disorder youths who do not meet the criteria for substance use disorder.

A study by Reebye, Moretti, and Lessard (1995) found that conduct-disordered youths with a comorbid substance disorder were more likely to endorse skipping school, cutting class, running away, breaking and entering, and causing harm or cruelty to others. Among teens with substance use disorder, the most common preadolescent conduct disorder behaviors are: lying, stealing without confrontation, repeated truancy, fighting, property destruction, and cruelty to animals. The average age at which the behaviors are first exhibited is 7 years (Myers, Brown, & Mott, 1995).

A study of the relation between drug abuse and delinquency among adolescents found that all types of delinquency (especially rule breaking) were quite strongly associated with the use of alcohol and cannabis. Other illegal drugs were associated more with rule breaking than with other forms of delinquency. However, heroin was most associated with vandalism, and inhalants were more linked with theft (Otero-Lopez, 1994).

Among individuals with comorbid conduct disorder and substance use disorder, the most commonly used drugs are alcohol, cannabis, and tobacco (Crowley, 1998)—perhaps because these substances are more accessible to adolescents than cocaine or heroin.

IDENTIFICATION, CLASSIFICATION, AND PREDICTION

Overview of Conduct Disorder

The term *conduct disorder* (CD) refers to a persistent cluster of antisocial behaviors occurring in approximately 5% of school-age children and adolescents. The most common behaviors include antisocial behavior, aggression against others, opposition behavior to caregivers, theft, vandalism, fire setting, truancy, and lying (Dadds, 1997). Conduct disorder is a formal diagnosis specified by the

Diagnostic and Statistical Manual of Mental Disorders (*DSM-IV*) of the American Psychiatric Association (APA, 1994).

Conduct disorder is one of the most common forms of psychopathology in children and adolescents. Its occurrence among youths seems to have increased over the past few decades (Steiner, 1997). This increase is of particular concern when one considers that childhood conduct disorder is one of the necessary antecedents of anti-social personality disorder (ASPD), although not all youths with conduct disorder will develop ASPD (APA, 1994). General-population studies of youths show very sharp drops in delinquent acts around ages 17 and 18 years. Maturation may account for much of the reduction in conduct symptoms (Crowley, 1998).

Overview of Substance Use Disorders

The prevalence and persistence of adolescent alcohol use and other drug problems are national health concerns (Brown, 1996). In *DSM-IV* (APA, 1994), abuse and dependence are diagnoses for pathologic substance use. *Dependence* implies use, which is more problematic, compulsive, and difficult to stop despite adverse consequences. Substance dependence criteria include increased tolerance; withdrawal symptoms; quantity of use exceeding intentions; unsuccessful efforts to cut down; excessive time spent obtaining, using or recovering from the substance; interference with other important activities; and continued use despite knowledge of a program related to the substance (APA, 1994). *Abuse,* another maladaptive pattern of substance use, is of less serious magnitude. Substance abuse is recurrent use of one or more substances, resulting in a failure to fulfill major role obligations at work, school, or home; use in physically hazardous situations; use related to legal problems; or use that combines or exacerbates persistent social or interpersonal problems (APA, 1994).

Currently, in the United States, over 80% of high school seniors have consumed alcohol (Hawkins, 1997). Drug use by high school students has risen steadily since 1992, and it is estimated that 9% of adolescent girls and up to 20% of adolescent boys meet adult diagnostic criteria for an alcohol use disorder (Winters, 1999).

A number of psychoactive substances have potential for use with different pharmacological properties. There is evidence that adolescents initiate use of these substances in a sequence that typically begins with alcohol or tobacco and proceeds through a period of alcohol use before beginning the use of marijuana.

Marijuana use typically progresses to the use of other illegal drugs (Hawkins, 1997).

Comorbidity of Conduct Disorder and Substance Use Disorder

A comorbid diagnosis is defined as two distinct diagnoses that are present in an individual at the same time. Conduct disorder has been found to co-occur with several other diagnoses, especially substance use disorders (Loeber & Keenan, 1994; Weinberg, Rahdert, Colliver, & Glantz, 1998). Conduct disorder and substance use disorders in adolescence represent two serious, prevalent, and costly public health problems (Grilo & Becker, 1995; Rounds-Bryant, Kristiansen, & Hubbard, 1999). Conduct disorder (a) tends to occur concurrently with alcohol and other drug abuse in the general adolescent population, and (b) is a common comorbid psychiatric diagnosis among teens in treatment for alcohol and drug abuse (Brown, 1996). Estimates and actual incidence of conduct disorder among clinical samples of adolescent alcohol abusers and other drug abusers range from 40% to 60% (Brown, 1996). Early behavioral problems, hyperactivity, impulsivity, inattention, and aggressivity have all been implicated as etiological factors in the development of substance abuse (Riggs, 1999). Several longitudinal studies have documented an association between child and adolescent aggression and increased risk for alcohol abuse, as well as other psychoactive substance use disorders (Moss & Kirisci, 1995). There is substantial evidence that antecedents of these disorders may be seen in children as early as first grade (Ialongo et al., 1999).

Considerable research on adolescents has documented that conduct disorder frequently co-occurs with substance abuse (Grilo & Becker, 1996; Weinberg et al., 1998). Research consistently reveals a high co-occurrence between psychiatric disorders and substance abuse (Myers et al., 1995). For example, a study of 226 adolescents on an inpatient alcohol and drug abuse unit found that 54% of teens met the criteria for conduct disorder, a greater prevalence than for any other disorder (Myers et al., 1995). In an examination of affective comorbidity among 156 teens hospitalized on a dual-diagnosis unit for teen alcohol and drug abusers, it was reported that 70% of the teens met the criteria for conduct disorder (Myers et al., 1995). Thus, investigations to date have consistently found that conduct disorder is the prevalent comorbid diagnosis in clinical samples of alcohol- and drug-abusing teens. When youths with mental or behavioral disorders begin to use substances, the problems can worsen (Riggs, 1999). In a study linking conduct disorder to substance abuse, it was noted that if a diagnosis of conduct disorder persists after age 15, there is a greater likelihood of substance use. After age 15, the diagnosis of antisocial personality disorder is used to describe conduct disorder (Disney et al., 1999). In a study of 626 pairs of 17-year-old twins in Minnesota, Disney et al. (1999) found that 64.8% of the boys and 93.9% of the girls diagnosed with antisocial personality disorder also had a diagnosis of substance use/abuse. Myers, Stewart, and Brown (1998) reported that the findings of behavior that occurs prior to and independent of substance abuse may serve to identify individuals at risk for persisting antisocial behavior. The earlier the onset of conduct disorder, especially when combined with a greater diversity of problem behaviors and a recent use of drugs, the greater the chances that this condition will develop into adolescent and adult antisocial personality disorder (Myers et al., 1998).

It has been unclear whether conduct disorder precedes alcohol and other drug involvement or whether alcohol and other drug involvement creates conduct disorder behaviors. A number of studies of severely disturbed adolescents, utilizing a variety of assessment methods, have found that conduct disorder precedes substance use disorders (Boyle, 1992; Grilo & Becker, 1996; Moss & Kirisci, 1995; Myers et al., 1998). Similarly, findings from two major longitudinal studies suggested that conduct disorder symptoms and antisocial behaviors in early adolescents predict substance abuse in later adolescence (Robins & Price, 1991; Windle, 1990). A study by Reebye, Moretti, and Lessard (1995) showed that 97.1% of youths with comorbid conduct and substance use disorders manifested conduct disorder prior to the development of a substance use disorder.

Assessment

Accurate assessment of comorbid disorders is critical. Standardized assessment instruments should be used whenever possible, to assist the practitioner with diagnosis and evaluation of the youth and his or her family. A complete assessment should include evaluation of the youth's behavior at home, in school, and in the community. Multiple sources should be used to compile a complete profile of the youth's functioning. Parents, siblings, relatives, teachers, and community contacts (such as a coach, church leader, or probation officer), as well as the youth, should be interviewed and given assessment measurements to complete (Dulmus & Wodarski, 1996).

Many youths present for treatment of substance use disorders, and their psychiatric disorders may go unnoticed. However, research has shown that a high prevalence of people who abuse alcohol also experience psychiatric disorders.

Assessment is important because alcoholics with antisocial personality disorder start drinking at a younger age and develop dependence sooner (Modesto-Lowe & Kranzler, 1999).

EFFECTIVE PREVENTION PROGRAMS

The problems encountered with assessment and the heterogeneous characteristics of youths continue to pose difficulties when it becomes necessary to intervene to prevent conduct disorder and substance abuse. Of particular importance is the accurate identification of conduct disorder and substance abuse. Myers et al. (1998) states that a careful assessment of the extent to which conduct disorder occurs independently of substance use is critical in determining an appropriate approach to treatment. Adolescents whose conduct disorder occurs primarily while using substances, or whose onset occurred after the use of substances, may not require as much intervention beyond substance treatment. However, youths who have more severe conduct disorder will require more intensive treatment to achieve and maintain positive results.

It is also necessary to accurately identify comorbidity, because treatment of psychiatric disorders is more effective when the person is able to maintain sobriety. However, some persons use the substances as a way of coping with the psychiatric disorder. Early treatment and prevention seem to be more effective than later interventions, but no single intervention can be used for every youth who has a comorbid conduct and substance use disorder, these youths are too diverse for that approach (Hawkins, 1997). If children can be diagnosed between ages 5 and 10 years as being at risk for substance abuse—if they show early signs of aggression, poor impulse control, and other conduct disorder behaviors—then prevention interventions can be targeted specifically to those children (Leukefeld, 1998).

Interventions designed to prevent the development of substance abuse and dependence in high-risk youths may be less effective if delivered in mid- to late childhood or before adolescence. If interventions do not occur prior to adolescence, it is quite likely that these youths may have already established entrenched substance use patterns that are extremely difficult to alter (Reebye et al., 1995). Interventions that focus on dealing with the underlying causes of psychological distress and assist in the development of effective coping strategies are more likely to be successful in preventing the development of chronic drug use (Reebye et al., 1995). At the level of specific techniques (rather than the more generic classes of treatment), the number of procedures would be large. Well over 200 different techniques in use in clinical practice can be identified (Kazdin, 1995,

1997), but some may lack empirical evidence. Structural-strategic family therapy (SSFT) has been shown to be efficacious in reducing adolescent substance use and improving adolescent-parent relationships. SSFT focuses on all family members because drug and alcohol abuse are related to dysfunctional family patterns (e.g., over- or underinvolvement) and interactional patterns between family members (e.g., problem solving) (Weinberg et al., 1998).

Medication has also been shown to be useful in treating delinquent boys who have conduct disorder and substance use disorders (Riggs et al., 1999; Weinberg et al., 1998). Medications have limited effectiveness against antisocial personality disorder in people with alcohol use disorders. Medications should be selected based on targeted behaviors, and medications with potential for abuse should be avoided. Pharmacological interventions for comorbid disorders should be monitored closely (Modesto-Lowe & Kranzler, 1999).

EMPIRICALLY BASED INTERVENTIONS

To date, 10 empirically based prevention and intervention programs have been identified as being effective in reducing adolescents' violent crime, aggression, and substance abuse (Muller & Mihalic, 1999). These model programs are referred to as the Blueprints for Violence Prevention. They include: (a) Prenatal and Infancy Nurse Home Visitation, (b) The Bullying Prevention Program, (c) Promoting Alternative Thinking Strategies, (d) Big Brothers/Big Sisters of America, (e) Quantum Opportunities, (f) Multisystemic Therapy (MST), (g) Functional Family Therapy (FFT), (h) The Midwestern Prevention Project, (i) Life Skills Training, and (j) Multidimensional Treatment Foster Care. However, assessment knowledge—specific empirical guidelines to assign youth to appropriate interventions—is lacking. Other empirically based programs have been deemed promising but will require further investigation to determine their effectiveness.

The Prenatal and Infancy Nurse Home Visitation program has been cost-effective; the government now saves money during the first four years of a child's life. The program has successfully reduced complications in pregnancy by not allowing health-related behaviors such as prenatal cigarette smoking and improper diet. The program has also reduced the number of incidents of child abuse and neglect. The low-income mothers and children participating in the program have benefited from lifestyle changes that have improved their quality of life—for example, reductions in repeat pregnancies and in substance use and abuse. The program has also helped its participants to stay out of trouble, as indicated by a reduction in the number of reported arrests, convictions, and probation violations (Olds, Hill, Mihalic, & O'Brien, 1998).

The Bullying Prevention Program has reduced the number of student-reported bullying incidents in the schools using the program. This program has been studied in elementary, middle, and junior high schools in Bergen, Norway; the southeastern region of the United States; Sheffield, England; and the state of Schleswig-Holstein, Germany. In a study conducted in Bergen, Norway, between 1983 and 1985, 2,500 students participated in the program. Teachers and students reported that bullying/victim problems were reduced by as much as 50%. Other studies have produced similar results. It was also noted that results varied when different components of the program were used independently. The authors reported that the program seemed to produce results that lasted long after the program had ended, and it appears to have reduced antisocial behaviors in later adolescence (Olweus & Limber, 1999).

Greenberg, Kusche, and Mihalic (1998) conducted three controlled studies on the effectiveness of Promoting Alternative Thinking Strategies (PATHS). They used randomized versus experimental groups (during one year of PATHS implementation with pre-, post-, and follow-up data) in examining three different populations, including children with impaired hearing who were in regular education and special education classifications. Results from the experiments included increases in interpersonal social skills, improved prosocial skills, and improved cognitive skills and academic performance on standardized tests. The results of the study also indicated that students who participated in the program demonstrated a reduction in maladaptive behaviors. For example, at the one-year follow-up point, students reported fewer symptoms of sadness and depression and fewer conduct problems. At the same time, teachers reported decreases in internalizing behaviors, such as withdrawal and sadness, and a reduction in disruptive and aggressive behaviors in special-needs classrooms.

An 18-month study of the Big Brothers/Big Sisters (BBBS) of America by Public/Private Ventures (P/PV) indicated that wide ranges of benefits can be gained from an adult/younger person partnership in a mentoring program. P/PV conducted, at eight BBBS agencies, a study of nearly 1,000 youngsters 10 to 16 years old. The study randomly assigned them to either a treatment group or a control group's waiting list (waiting time: 18 months). The results showed that the students who participated in the program were less likely to start using drugs or alcohol, reported better attendance and school outcomes, and improved their interpersonal social skills with peers and family members (McGill, Mihalic, & Grotpeter, 1999).

Reports on the Quantum Opportunities program indicated that, in 11 academic and functional skill areas, the average scores of students who participated in the program were higher than the scores of the control group and indicated notable gains. Students who participated in the Quantum Opportunities Program had higher educational goals and generally expected to further their education after high school. They were less likely to have children than the control group, and they reported less than half the number of the control group's arrests. In a one-year follow-up after the program, students were asked whether they had received any awards in the previous 12 months. There were large differences between the number of awards or honors reported by students in the program and students in the control group (Lattimore, Mihalic, Grotpeter, & Taggart, 1998).

Multisystemic Therapy (MST) has been demonstrated to reduce criminal activity, drug-related arrests, violent offenses, and incarceration. The first study on MST was published in 1986. Three randomized clinical experiments with violent and chronic juvenile offenders have been conducted since then. Further, students have been designated to generalize MST to juveniles who have other types of clinical and family problems (Henggeler, Mihalic, Rone, Thomas, & Timmons-Mitchell, 1998).

Alexander et al. (1998) reports that Functional Family Therapy (FFT) was designed to be used with at-risk youth between the ages of 11 and 18. The outcome driven prevention program addresses issues such as Conduct Disorder, delinquency, violence, substance use, Oppositional Defiant Disorder and Disruptive Behavior Disorder. FFT has been shown to reduce the need for social services by at-risk adolescents and prevent them from entering the criminal system. Other benefits include the reduction of presenting problem behaviors and the ease of intervention use across different settings, which include in-home, clinic, juvenile court, and at time of re-entry from institutional placement.

The Midwestern Prevention Project has been shown to effectively reduce tobacco, marijuana, alcohol, and cocaine/crack use. The program has produced reductions (up to 40%) of smoking among some of the participants. In the Kansas City Intervention Schools, lower cocaine and crack use is reported for the ninth and tenth graders who participated in the program. Adults who have recently graduated from schools that have used this program have demonstrated a reduction in the need for alcohol and substance abuse treatment (Pentz, Mihalic, & Grotpeter, 1997).

Studies conducted over the past 15 years have shown that the Life Skills Training Program (LSTP) has been successful in reducing drug use for adolescents. Drug use has been cut in half for juveniles who have participated in the program. The primary focus has been on the use of tobacco, alcohol, and marijuana, but reductions in the use of more serious drugs have been demonstrated as well. The studies indicate that results have been long-term and clinically significant. The program has been evaluated using seventh- and eighth-grade students ranging from middle-class white youths to poor inner-city African American and Hispanic/Latino youths (Botvin, Mihalic, & Grotpeter, 1998).

Chamberlain and Mihalic (1998) reported positive outcomes for Multidimensional Treatment Foster Care (MTFC). They conducted a study of juveniles between the ages of 12 and 17 years, with an average age of 14.3 years. These youths were all on probation or parole and had been labeled as chronic offenders by the Department of Youth Services. Collectively, they averaged 13 previous arrests and 4.6 felonies. The 79 juveniles who participated in the study were mandated by the juvenile court to go into or out of home care. They were randomly placed in MTFC or group care and tracked for a two-year period. The children placed in MTFC had fewer subsequent arrests and a lower number of runaways than the group placed in group care.

Overall, interventions that (a) help to reduce multiple risk factors, (b) enhance protective factors in family, school, peer, and community environments, and (c) are maintained over the course of infant, child, and adolescent development hold the greatest promise for preventing many adolescent health and behavior problems (Hawkins, 1997). It is also important to realize that interventions should target and be focused on individual needs while incorporating the idea that "one size does not fit all."

Approaches to Prevention

Primary interventions are targeted to the general population. There is a connection between low academic achievement and antisocial behavior; therefore, early intervention programs such as Head Start may appear to serve as viable options (Ialongo et al., 1999; Larson, 1994). Larson identified two "Second Step" programs designed specifically for the prevention of violence in the elementary grades. They are titled "A Violence Prevention Curriculum" and "The Violence Prevention Curriculum for Adolescents."

"The Second Step: A Violence Prevention Curriculum" (SSVPC) was developed as a "curriculum designed to reduce impulsive and aggressive behavior in young children and increase their level of social competence. SSVPC approaches these objectives through direct classroom instruction in a series of skill areas labeled empathy, impulse control, and anger management" (Larson, 1994).

Research supporting the SSVPC program's effectiveness is very limited. Larson (1994) cited a pilot study using a pre- and posttest design that suggested differences between the experimental and the control groups. The study favored the experimental group. A total of 306 students in grades 3 through 8 were taught via the curriculum for one semester. Teachers and administrators were then surveyed on their perceptions of the program. Teacher and administrator questionnaires collected at the end of the pilot study yielded a high regard for the potential of the curriculum.

"Second Step: The Violence Prevention Curriculum for Adolescents" (SSVPCA) was designed as a school-based health education curriculum for high school students. The curriculum was designed to: (a) educate students about the prevalence of violence and homicide; (b) provide students with alternatives to fighting; (c) help students to use anger positively; (d) teach students to recognize situations in which a fight could occur; and (e) help students create a non-violent atmosphere in the classroom (Larson, 1994).

The curriculum was implemented with 106 tenth-grade students using instruments that measured knowledge and attitudes about anger, violence, and homicide. Significant differences were yielded from pre- and posttest designs. The effects of the curriculum were measured on a subject pool of 347 students in four major urban areas in the United States. The students using the curriculum reported fewer fights than the control group students in all four major urban areas (Larson, 1994).

Ialongo et al. (1999) assessed the effects of two first-grade early prevention programs that were designed to address poor achievement, concentration problems, aggression, and shy behaviors. (These behaviors are associated with early identification of conduct disorder and substance use.) The first program, the Good Behavior Game (GBG), significantly reduced (a) aggressive behaviors in children (especially boys) in the second to sixth grades, and (b) experimentation with tobacco among students who participated in the program. The second program, the Mastery Learning (ML) program, significantly improved the stability and reduction of depressive symptoms, especially in the first-grade girls (Ialongo et al., 1999).

Secondary prevention efforts seek to identify children who are at high risk for later, more serious problems while providing them with the social skills necessary to reduce their risk status, if possible. Children at high risk for later adolescent conduct problems, including aggressive behavior, can be reliably predicted from early characteristics such as high rates of aggressive responses to social problems. Secondary prevention includes programs such as Parent Management Training; Anger Coping Intervention with Aggressive Children; and Dealing with Anger: A Violence Prevention Program for African American Youth (Larson, 1994).

Parent Management Training (PMT) has the most accumulated evidence regarding the therapeutic value and efficacy of the treatment of conduct disorder (Dadds, 1997). According to a study conducted by Kazdin (1997), early intervention for behavioral problems through parent training has been suggested to be preventive of conduct disorder and to reduce the risk of substance use disorder. Parent Management Training focuses on developing effective parenting techniques. Parents learn how to identify problem behaviors, code these behaviors, and intervene effectively. They are also taught social learning skills, such as reinforcement, planned ignoring, mild punishment, negotiation, and contingency contracting (Kazdin, 1995). When they are trying to provide effective, nonadverse discipline and communication to their children, parents become empowered to deal constructively with other stresses that may compromise family stability, discipline, and communication (Dadds, 1997).

Parent Management Training is designed for preschool and kindergarten children who arrive at school with patterns of aggressive behavior. The program is designed to help parents change the socialization process used when interacting with their children, in order to decrease the children's aggressive behaviors and conduct disorders. Parents are taught how to: teach their children reasonable levels of compliance; monitor the children's behavior in and out of school; and recognize, reinforce, and model prosocial behavior that will reduce aggressive behavior.

The Anger Coping Intervention with Aggressive Children program was designed as a group program for fourth- to sixth-grade boys. The program's 18 sessions are designed to be presented in sequence; each session lasts about an hour. The sessions are designed to address both the cognitive and the affective processes associated with aggression. Emphasis is on the remediation of the social skills that the children lack in conflict situations that involve affective arousal. School psychologists in the Milwaukee Public Schools have made extensive use of this program. A study by Lochman, Dunn, and Klimes-Dougan (1993) compared the effects of the anger coping program on 20 aggressive boys. The program produced higher levels of on-task behavior and less parent-rated aggression, and it increased the boys' levels of general self-worth by the end of the program. Long-term effects for the program are inconclusive.

Another secondary intervention program is titled Dealing with Anger: A Violence Prevention Program for African American Youth. This program, which was implemented to address the intensity and frequency of violence among this minority youth group, is comprised of three videotapes: (a) "Givin' It" (expressing anger), (b) "Takin' It" (accepting criticism), and (c) "Workin' It Out" (learning negotiation). All of the parts are played by African American adolescents using reality-based conflicts. The program is to the point and uses culturally sensitive advice. The treatment effects are not supported by research. This program shows great promise, but further research is necessary.

Tertiary prevention is a reactive method used to reduce the occurrence of future aggressive behavior (Larson, 1994). Examples of tertiary prevention programs are: (a) Adolescent Anger Control: Cognitive-Behavioral Techniques; (b) Aggression Replacement Training: A Comprehensive Intervention for

Aggressive Youth; and (c) Think First: Anger and Aggression Management for Secondary Level Students.

Adolescent Anger Control: Cognitive-Behavioral Techniques is an adaptive skills training program for adolescents. The program, a 12-session group intervention aid, is designed to reduce the intensity, frequency, and duration of aggression that is a result of poor anger-expression skills. The program is divided into three phases that collectively teach acceptable adaptive social skills. Phase one is the educational/cognitive preparation phase; phase two, the skill acquisition phase, includes cognitive skills training and behavioral component skills training; and phase three is the skills application phase. The program has clear guidelines and can be modified for individual clients (Larson, 1994). Further research is necessary to show the effects of this program.

According to Larson (1994), the Aggression Replacement Training: A Comprehensive Intervention for Aggressive Youth combines components from three programs that had been primarily developed: (a) the anger-control work of Feindler, Marriott, and Iwata (1984); (b) a moral education program adapted from Arbuthnot, Sparling, Faust, and Kee (1983); and (c) a structured skills program adapted from Goldstein, Sprafkin, Gershaw, and Klein (1983). The program was developed to teach adolescents more advanced reasoning skills and to help them develop a more advanced moral reasoning stage (Larson, 1994). The research on this program is limited. The program was evaluated at two juvenile corrections facilities, and the results were favorable. Significant increases in prosocial skills and a decrease in acting-out behaviors were reported (Goldstein, Glick, Reiner, Zimmerman, & Coultry, 1987).

Think First: Anger and Aggression Management for Secondary Level Students is a 14-session program developed specifically for work with aggressive student behaviors at the middle and high school levels. In a prerecorded videotape, white and African American students model anger-control skills in a series of vignettes. The last part of the videotape, and an accompanying manual, provide training in a cognitive-behavioral problem-solving model. The program mainly focuses on the role of anger and aggression in school-related situations (Larson, 1994).

CASE MANAGEMENT AND THE STRENGTHS PERSPECTIVE

In case management, an integrative and comprehensive approach that builds on the adolescents' strengths is essential. Integrative approaches to addressing conduct disorder and substance abuse are more effective. Several approaches have been designed to intervene or to take into account the youth's broader social network. For example, some approaches have included teachers, police, and peers, all of whom have an influence on the youth's drug use and problem behaviors (Weinberg et al., 1998).

When planning services, case management professionals should take into account the higher rates of teen pregnancy among youths with psychiatric disorders. Females in this population may be extremely vulnerable, for a multitude of reasons—for example, the low self-esteem and insecurities associated with their disabilities, and their easy attachment to people who show them positive affection. They may also be at risk when their substance use lowers their inhibitions (Kessler et al., 1997). Along with teen pregnancy, this population may be at great risk for contracting sexual diseases as a result of having multiple partners and unprotected sex.

Additionally, the case manager must work toward ensuring that the adolescent receives educational services. It is imperative that all youth today have an adequate education, to ensure their employability as adults.

FUTURE RESEARCH

Conduct disorder is a powerful factor that can influence substance-related outcomes. The majority of the research suggests that children who tend to have conduct problems are at a significantly increased risk of alcohol, tobacco, and illicit drug use. Early identification and treatment of conduct disorder and substance use/abuse appear to be more effective. The earlier the onset of conduct disorder combined with substance abuse, the more a person is likely to develop more severe forms of antisocial personality disorder. More severe forms of the disorder are still treatable, but improvement may be limited when compared with the recovery of youths who do not exhibit conduct problems (Myers et al., 1998). In the treatment of conduct disorder and substance abuse, prevention efforts are the best form of intervention. Later interventions are best if they are designed and tailored specifically to the individual.

A review of current literature indicates a need for assessment tools that are specifically developed to address conduct and substance abuse disorders in minority youth. Little has been done in this area, and the literature suggests that current assessment instruments may not do a good job of detecting substance use when the client is defensive or in denial. Development of assessment tools specifically designed for females is also necessary to address some of the unique needs of females and the different behavioral profiles of females who have conduct disorder and substance use/abuse problems. Adequate assessment is necessary to identify and develop appropriate treatment approaches for youth experiencing problems associated with comorbidity.

Additionally, further research is needed in the area of racial differences among the population of comorbid conduct-disordered substance abusers. The majority of research on conduct disorder and substance use disorder focuses on alcohol, tobacco, and marijuana. Further research should explore the relationship of conduct disorder to other forms of illegal drugs, such as cocaine, heroin, hallucinogens, and inhalants. More research is also needed on treatment programs that are designed specifically to address the needs of teenagers who meet the criteria for co-morbid disorders (Rounds-Bryant et al., 1999).

REFERENCES

Alexander, J., Barton, C., Gordon, D., Grotpeter, J., Hansson, K., Harrison, R., et al. (1998). *Blueprints for violence prevention, Volume 3: Functional family therapy.* Denver, CO: C&M Press.

American Psychiatric Association. (1994). *Diagnostic and statistical manual of mental disorders* (4th ed.). Washington, DC: Author.

Arbuthnot, J., Sparling, Y, Faust, D., & Kee, W. (1983). Logical and moral development in pre-adolescent children. *Psychological Reports, 52*(1), 209–210.

Botvin, G. J., Mihalic, S. F., & Grotpeter, J. K. (1998). *Blueprints for violence prevention: Life skills training.* Boulder, CO: Center for the Study and Prevention of Violence.

Boyle, M. H. (1992). Predicting substance use in late adolescence: Results from the Ontario Child Health Study follow-up. *American Journal of Psychiatry, 149,* 761–767.

Brown, S. A. (1996). Conduct disorder among adolescent alcohol and drug abusers. *Journal of Studies on Alcohol, 57*(3), 314–324.

Bukstein, O. (1994). Treatment of adolescent alcoholism abuse and dependence. *Alcohol Health and Research World, 18*(4), 296–302.

Bukstein, O. (1995). Influences on the risk and course of substance use and abuse in adolescents. *Current Opinion in Psychiatry, 8,* 218–221.

Chamberlain, P., & Mihalic, S. F. (1998). *Blueprints for violence prevention: Multidimensional treatment foster care.* Boulder, CO: Venture.

Costello, E. J., Erkanli, A., Federman, E., & Angold, A. (1999). Development of psychiatric comorbidity with substance abuse in adolescents: Effects of timing and sex. *Journal of Clinical Child Psychology, 28*(3), 298–311.

Crowley, T. J. (1998). Substance-dependent, conduct-disordered adolescent males: Severity of diagnosis predicts 2-year outcome. *Drug and Alcohol Dependence, 49,* 225–237.

Dadds, M. R. (1997). Conduct disorder. In R. T. Ammerman & M. Hersen (Eds.), *Handbook of prevention and treatment with children and adolescents* (pp. 521–550). Toronto, Canada: Wiley.

Disney, E. R., Elkins, I. J., McGue, M., & Iacono, W. G. (1999). Effects of ADHD, conduct disorder, and gender on substance use and abuse in adolescence. *American Journal of Psychiatry, 156*(10), 1515–1521.

Dulmus, C. N., & Wodarski, J. S. (1996). Assessment and effective treatments of childhood psychopathology: Responsibilities and implications for practice. *Journal of Child and Adolescent Group Therapy, 6*(2), 75–99.

Elliott, D. S., Huizinga, D., & Menard, S. (1989). *Multiple problem youth: Delinquency, substance abuse, and mental health problems.* New York: Springer-Verlag.

Feindler, E., Marriott, S., & Iwata, M. (1984). Group anger control training for junior high school delinquents. *Cognitive Therapy and Research, 8*(3), 299–311.

Goldstein, A., Glick, B., Reiner, S., Zimmerman, D., & Coultry, T. (1987). *Aggression replacement training: A comprehensive intervention for aggressive youth.* Champaign, IL: Research Press.

Goldstein, A., Sprafkin, R., Gershaw, J., & Klein, P. (1983). Structured learning: A psychoeducational approach for teaching social competencies. *Behavioral Disorders, 8*(3), 161–170.

Grant, B. F., & Dawson, D. A. (1999). Alcohol and drug use, abuse, and dependence: Classification, prevalence, and comorbidity. In B. S. McCrady & E. E. Epstein (Eds.), *Addictions: A comprehensive guidebook* (pp. 9–29). New York: Oxford University Press.

Greenberg, M. T., Kusche, C., & Mihalic, S. F. (1998). *Blueprints for violence prevention: Promoting Alternative Thinking Strategies (PATHS).* Boulder, CO: Venture.

Grilo, C. M., & Becker, D. F. (1995). Psychiatric comorbidity in adolescent inpatients with substance use and disorders. *Journal of the American Academy of Child and Adolescent Psychiatry, 34*(8), 1085–1097.

Grilo, C. M., & Becker, D. F. (1996). Conduct disorder, substance use disorders, and coexisting conduct and substance use disorders in adolescent inpatients. *American Journal of Psychiatry, 153*(7), 914–920.

Hawkins, D. J. (1997). Substance use and abuse. In R. T. Ammerman & M. Hersen (Eds.), *Handbook of prevention and treatment with children and adolescents* (pp. 203–237). Toronto, Canada: Wiley.

Henggeler, S. W., Mihalic, S. F., Rone, L., Thomas, C., & Timmons-Mitchell, J. (1998). *Blueprints for violence prevention: Multisystemic Therapy.* Boulder, CO: Venture.

Hilarski, C., & Wodarski, J. S. (in press). Comorbid substance abuse and mental illness: Diagnosis and treatment. *Journal of Social Work Practice in the Addictions.*

Ialongo, N. S., Werthamer, L., Kellam, S. G., Hendricks-Brown, C., Wang, S., & Lin, Y. (1999). Proximal impact of two first-grade preventive interventions on the early risk behaviors for later substance abuse, depression, and antisocial behavior. *American Journal of Community Psychology, 27*(5), 599–641.

Kagan, J. (1991). Etiologies of adolescents at risk. *Journal of Adolescent Health, 12*(8), 591–596.

Kazdin, A. E. (1995). *Conduct disorders in childhood and adolescence* (2nd ed.). Thousand Oaks, CA: Sage.

Kazdin, A. E. (1997). Parent management training: Evidence, outcomes, issues. *Journal of the American Academy of Child and Adolescent Psychiatry, 36*(10), 1349–1356.

Kessler, R. C., Berglund, P. A., & Foster, C. L. (1997). Social consequences of psychiatric disorders. II: Teenage pregnancy. *American Journal of Psychiatry, 154,* 1405–1411.

Larson, J. (1994). Violence prevention in the schools: A review of selected programs and procedures. *School Psychology Review, 23*(2), 151–164.

Lattimore, C. B., Mihalic, S. F., Grotpeter, J. K., & Taggart, R. (1998). *Blueprints for violence prevention: The Quantum Opportunities Program.* Boulder, CO: Venture.

Leukefeld, C. G. (1998). Adolescent drug use, delinquency and other behaviors. In T. P. Gullotta, G. R. Adams, & R. Montemayer (Eds.), *Delinquent violent youth: Theory and interventions* (pp. 98–128). Thousand Oaks, CA: Sage.

Lochman, J. E., Dunn, S. E., & Klimes-Dougan, B. (1993). An intervention and consultation model from a social cognitive perspective: A description of the anger coping program. *School Psychology Review, 22*(3), 458–471.

Loeber, R., & Keenan, K. (1994). Interaction between conduct disorder and its comorbid conditions: Effects of age and gender. *Clinical Psychology Review, 14*(6), 497–523.

Marohn, R. C. (1992). Management of the assaultive adolescent. *Hospital and Community Psychiatry, 43*(5), 522–524.

McGill, D. E., Mihalic, S. F., & Grotpeter, J. K. (1999). *Blueprints for violence prevention: Big Brothers Big Sisters of America.* Denver, CO: C&M Press.

Mezzich, A. C., Moss, H., Tarter, R. E., & Wolfenstein, M. (1994). Gender differences in the pattern and progression of substance use in conduct-disordered adolescents. *American Journal on Addictions, 3*(4), 289–295.

Modesto-Lowe, V., & Kranzler, H. R. (1999). Diagnosis and treatment of alcohol dependent patients with comorbid psychiatric disorders. *Alcohol Research and Health, 23*(2), 144–149.

Moss, H. B., & Kirisci, L. (1995). Aggressivity in adolescent alcohol abusers: Relationship with conduct disorder. *Alcoholism and Clinical Experimental Research, 19*(3), 642–646.

Muller, J., & Mihalic, S. F. (1999). *Blueprints: A violence prevention initiative.* Washington, DC: U.S. Justice Office of Juvenile Justice and Delinquency Prevention.

Myers, M. G., Brown, S. A., & Mott, M. A. (1995). Preadolescent conduct disorder behaviors predict relapse and progression of addiction for adolescent alcohol and drug abusers. *Alcoholism and Clinical Experimental Research, 19*(6), 1528–1536.

Myers, M. G., Stewart, D. G., & Brown, S. A. (1998). Progression from conduct disorder to antisocial personality disorder following treatment for adolescent substance abuse. *American Journal of Psychiatry, 155*(4), 479–485.

Novacek, J., Raskin, R., & Hogan, R. (1991). Why do adolescents use drugs? Age, sex, and user differences. *Journal of Youth and Adolescence, 20*(5), 475–492.

Oetting, E. R., & Beauvais, F. (1990). Adolescent drug use: Findings of national and local surveys. *Journal of Consulting and Clinical Psychology, 58*(4), 385–394.

Olds, D. L., Hill, P. L., Mihalic, S. F., & O'Brien, R. A. (1998). *Blueprints for violence prevention: Prenatal and infancy home visitation by nurses.* Denver, CO: C&M Press.

Olweus, D., & Limber, S. (1999). *Blueprints for violence prevention: Bullying Prevention Program.* Denver, CO: C&M Press.

Otero-Lopez, J. M. (1994). An empirical study of the relations between drug abuse and delinquency among adolescence. *British Journal of Criminology, 34*(4), 459–478.

Pentz, M. A., Mihalic, S. F., & Grotpeter, J. K. (1997). *Blueprints for violence prevention: The Midwestern Prevention Project.* Denver, CO: C&M Press.

Reebye, P., Moretti, M. M., & Lessard, J. C. (1995). Conduct disorder and substance use disorder: Comorbidity in a clinical sample of preadolescents and adolescents. *Canadian Journal of Psychiatry, 40,* 313–319.

Riggs, P. D. (1999). Relationship of ADHD, depression, and non-tobacco substance use disorders to nicotine dependence in substance-dependent delinquents. *Drug and Alcohol Dependence, 54,* 195–205.

Riggs, P. D., Mikulich, S. K., Whitmore, E. A., & Crowley, T. J. (1999). Relationship of ADHD, depression, and non-tobacco substance use disorders to nicotine dependence in substance-dependent delinquents. *Drug and Alcohol Dependence, 54*(3), 195–205.

Robins, L. N., & Price, R. K. (1991). Adult disorders predicted by childhood conduct problems: Results form the NIMH Epidemiologic Catchment Area Project. *Psychiatry, 54,* 116–132.

Rounds-Bryant, J. L., Kristiansen, P. L., & Hubbard, R. L. (1999). Drug abuse treatment outcome study of adolescents: A comparison of client characteristics and pretreatment behaviors in three treatment modalities. *American Journal of Drug and Alcohol Abuse, 25*(4), 573–591.

Sanford, M., Boyle, M. H., Szatmari, P., Offord, D. R., Jamieson, E., & Spinner, M. (1999). Age-of-onset classification of conduct disorder: Reliability and validity in a prospective cohort study. *Journal of the American Academy of Child and Adolescent Psychiatry, 38*(8), 992–1000.

Smokowski, P., & Wodarski, J. (1998). Cognitive-behavioral treatment for cocaine addition: Clinical effectiveness and practice guidelines. *Journal of Applied Social Sciences, 23* (1), 23–32.

Stark, E. (1993). The myth of black violence. *Social Work, 38*(4), 485–490.

Steiner, H. (1997). Practice parameters for the assessment and treatment of children and adolescents with conduct disorder. *Journal of the American Academy of Child and Adolescent Psychiatry, 36*(10), 122–168.

Vander, M., & Damirjian, A. (1990). Yes I can't: Confusion and drug use during adolescence. *New York Department of Substance Abuse Services Newsletter.* Albany, NY: Author.

Weinberg, N. Z., Rahdert, E., Colliver, J. D., & Glantz, M. D. (1998). Adolescent substance abuse: A review of the past 10 years. *Journal of the American Academy of Child and Adolescent Psychiatry, 37*(3), 252–261.

Windle, M. (1990). A longitudinal study of antisocial behaviors in early adolescence as predictors of late adolescent substance use: Gender and ethnic group differences. *Journal of Abnormal Psychology, 99,* 86–91.

Winters, K. C. (1999). *Treatment of adolescents with substance use disorders.* Treatment Improvement Protocol Series (Publication No. 32). Rockville, MD: U.S. Department of Health and Human Services.

Wodarski, J. S., & Wodarski, L. A. (1993). *Curriculums and practical aspects of implementation: Preventative health services for adolescents.* Lanham, MD: University of America Press.

Chapter 9

GIRLS' DELINQUENCY AND VIOLENCE: MAKING THE CASE FOR GENDER-RESPONSIVE PROGRAMMING

MEDA CHESNEY-LIND, SIBYLLE ARTZ, AND DIANA NICHOLSON

INTRODUCTION

Girls in the juvenile justice system were once dubbed "the forgotten few" (Bergsmann, 1989). In the United States, that construction of female delinquency has rapidly faded. Increases in girls' arrests have dramatically outstripped those of boys for most of the past decade. Girls now account for one out of four arrests, and attention is being called to the fact that their arrests for nontraditional, even violent, offenses are among those showing the greatest increases. These shifts and changes bring into sharp focus the need to (a) better understand the dynamics involved in female delinquency and (b) tailor responses to the unique circumstances of girls growing up in the new millennium.

This chapter examines the prevalence of female juvenile delinquency and reviews the literature from a sociological and practice perspective. Specifically, we focus attention on girls' aggression and violence, and we argue that close analysis of the data indicates that changes in arrests of girls for certain violent offenses reflect complex changes in the policing of girls' aggression (including the arrest of girls for minor forms of family violence) rather than actual changes in girls' behavior. We compare what's happening to girls in the United States with the experiences of delinquent girls in Canada. Finally, we briefly review trends in the treatment of girls by the juvenile justice system, and we discuss the emerging literature on promising interventions with girls.

Patterns in Girls' Delinquency: Are Girls Really Closing the Gender Gap in Violence?

Between 1989 and 1998, girls' arrests in the United States increased 50.3%, compared to 16.5% for boys (Federal Bureau of Investigation, 1999). Concomitant with these increased arrests are increases in girls' referrals to juvenile courts; between 1987 and 1996, the number of delinquency cases involving girls increased by 76%, compared to a 42% increase for males (Stahl, 1999). Arrests of girls for serious violent offenses increased by 64.3% between 1989 and 1998; arrests of girls for "other assaults" increased by an even more astounding 125.4% (Federal Bureau of Investigation, 1999, p. 215). The Office of Juvenile Justice and Delinquency Prevention (1999) found that the female violent crime rate for 1997 was 103% above the 1981 rate, compared to a 27% increase for males. This prompted an assertion that "increasing juvenile female arrests and the involvement of girls in at-risk and delinquent behavior has been a pervasive trend across the United States" (p. 2). Discussions of girls' gang behavior—and, more recently, girls' violence—have also been extremely prevalent in the media (see Chesney-Lind, 1999a, for a review).

Because of different legal considerations in juvenile justice and differences in statistical reporting, it is not easy to directly compare events in the United States with those north of the border. However, it is noteworthy that in Canada, between 1991 and 1995, the number of girls placed in secure custody increased by 55%. DeKeseredy (2000, p. iv) describes the situation as one of sweeping up young women "in an imprisonment binge" similar to that in the United States. The Canadian Centre for Justice Statistics (1999) and the Police Services Division of the British Columbia Ministry of the Attorney General (BC Crime Trends, 1998) reported that the violent crime rate, for both male and female youths, increased steadily during the 1980s and mid-1990s. For male youths, the rate rose from a level of 8.5 per 1,000 in 1988 to a peak of 16.2 per 1,000 in 1994, and then began, in 1995, to decline. The rate for females rose from a level of 2.2 per 1,000 in 1988 to a peak, in 1996, of 5.6 per 1,000. It remained at approximately 5.3 per 1,000 over the next two years, and began to decline only in 1999.

What Do We Really Know about the Capacity of Girls to Be Aggressive and Violent?

In attempting to determine whether girls are engaging in "nontraditional" delinquency, one must first recognize that girls' capacity for aggression and violence has historically been ignored, trivialized, or denied. For this reason, self-report data, particularly from the 1970s and 1980s, have always shown higher involvement of girls in assaultive behavior than official statistics would indicate. As an example, Canter (1982) reported a male-versus-female self-reported delinquency ratio of 3.4:1 for minor assault and 3.5:1 for serious assault. At that time, arrest statistics showed much greater male participation in aggravated assault (5.6:1; Federal Bureau of Investigation, 1980) and simple assault (3.8:1; Canter, 1982). Currently, arrest statistics show a 3.54:1 ratio for "aggravated assault" and a 2.25:1 ratio for "other assaults" (Federal Bureau of Investigation, 1999). Taken together, these numbers suggest that instead of a course change in girls' participation in serious violence, the gap is closing between what girls have always done (and reported, when asked anonymously) and the arrest statistics.

In Canada, 20.9% of 703 adolescent girls and 51.9% of 763 adolescent boys surveyed in schools reported having "beaten up another kid" at least once or twice in the year in which the survey was conducted (Artz, 1998). This suggests a ratio of 2.5:1 for males over females and supports the notion that the gender gap is growing smaller.

Detailed comparisons drawn from supplemental homicide reports from unpublished FBI data also hint at a central, rather than a peripheral, way in which gender has colored and differentiated girls' and boys' violence. In a study of FBI data on the characteristics of girls' and boys' homicides between 1984 and 1993, Loper and Cornell (1996) found that girls accounted for "proportionately fewer homicides in 1993 (6%) than in 1984 (14%)" (p. 324). In comparison to boys' homicides, girls who killed were more likely to use a knife than a gun and to murder someone as a result of conflict (rather than in the commission of a crime). Girls were also more likely than boys to murder family members (32%) and very young victims (24% of their victims were under the age of 3 years, compared to 1% of the boys' victims). When involved in a peer homicide, girls were more likely to kill alone and to kill as a result of an interpersonal conflict. Boys were more likely to kill with an accomplice. Loper and Cornell concluded that "the stereotype of girls becoming gun-toting robbers was not supported. The dramatic increase in gun-related homicides . . . applies to boys but not girls" (p. 332).

Reitsma-Street (1999) noted that although the number of overall charges against girls in Canada in 1995 and 1996 was at an all-time high, the absolute numbers for serious charges like arson, breaking and entering, fraud, robbery, major theft, and trafficking or possession of drugs were low and have remained constant.

To further support this notion, other research on trends in self-report data of youthful involvement in violent offenses also fails to show the dramatic changes found in official statistics. Specifically, a matched sample of "high-risk" youth (ages 13 to 17 years) surveyed in the 1977 National Youth Study and in the more recent 1989 Denver Youth Survey revealed significant *decreases* in girls' involvement in felony assaults, minor assaults, and hard drugs, and no change in a wide range of other delinquent behaviors—including felony theft, minor theft, and index delinquency (Huizinga, 1997). A summary of two more recent studies on self-reported aggression (see Table 9.1) also reflects that while about one-third of girls reported having been in a physical fight in the past year, this was true of over half of the boys in both samples (Girls Incorporated, 1996).

In Canada, DeKeseredy (2000) states that Canadian girls are not becoming more violent, although highly publicized freak, albeit horrific, events give the impression that violence among girls is increasing. The number of girls in Canada who commit homicide is so low that it is difficult to draw firm conclusions about differences between boys and girls. The typical female youth involved in violence is not profiled in the media, but the public is horrified by the perspective on violent youth conveyed by the media's repeated recycling of "isolated incidents of extreme violence" (Corrado, Cohen, & Odgers, 1998, pp. 13–14). Further, girls who kill their parents often do so for revenge against or escape from their abuse (DeKeseredy, 2000). Table 9.2 shows the numbers of boys and girls charged with homicide and attempted murder in Canada between 1992 and 1996. Table 9.3 shows how many boys and girls were charged with violent crimes in Canada between 1992 and 1999.

Note that, in Tables 9.2 and 9.3, actual numbers are presented, rather than rates of charges. Because of the low base rate among females who commit

Table 9.1   Actual and Potential Involvement in Physical Violence

	Females (%)	Males (%)	Source
Involved in:			
Physical Fight in Past Year	34	51	Adams et al.
	32	51	Kann et al.
Four or More Physical Fights in the Past Year	9	15	Adams et al.
Fought with:			
Stranger	7	15	
Friend	24	46	
Date/Romantic Partner	8	2	Adams et al.
Parent/Sibling	34	9	
Other	4	6	
Several of the Above	24	26	
Carried a Weapon:			
In the Past Month	7	17	Adams et al.
	9	34	Kann et al.

Source: Adams, Schoenborn, Moss, Warren, & Kann (1995: ages 14 to 17, 1992 data) and Kann et al. (1995: grades 9 to 12, 1993 data) in Girls Incorporated (1996).

Table 9.2   Canadian Boys and Girls Charged with Homicide and Attempted Murder, 1992–1996

	Actual Number Charged, by Year				
Type of Offense	1992	1993	1994	1995	1996
Homicide					
Boys	49	33	48	49	47
Girls	4	3	4	12	3
Attempted Murder					
Boys	66	61	103	81	81
Girls	12	9	9	4	6

Source: W. DeKeseredy, *Women, Crime and the Canadian Criminal Justice System.* Cincinnati, OH: Anderson, 2000.

violent crimes, it is important to view actual numbers in order to avoid presenting a distorted picture. Corrado, Cohen, and Odgers (1998, p. 12) provide a good example. In Canada in 1986, 1,728 females were charged with violent crimes, as compared to 5,096 in 1993. Charges against males during the same period rose from 7,547 to 16,735. The increase for females was 3,368 and the increase for males was 8,828. However, if reported in terms of rate increases, the percentage increase for females would be much higher (approximately 295%) than the percentage for males (approximately 221%).

The psychological literature, which considers forms of aggression other than physical aggression (or violence), is also relevant here. For example, Tremblay (2000), in Canada, states that results from a large (N = 16,038) national longitudinal survey of children and youth (ages 4 to 11 years) indicate that although boys exhibit higher levels of physical aggression at all ages, girls demonstrate higher levels of indirect aggression (defined as "behavior aimed at hurting someone without the use of physical aggression," p. 20) than do boys at each age, from

Table 9.3   Male and Female Youths Charged with Violent Crimes, 1992–1999

	Violent Crimes: Actual Number Charged, by Year							
	1992	1993	1994	1995	1996	1997	1998	1999
Boys	15,734	16,381	16,753	17,288	17,206	16,556	16,534	15,787
Girls	4,294	5,096	4,903	5,153	5,315	5,616	5,661	5,294

Source: Statistics Canada (2001), *Youths and Adults Charged in Criminal Incidents, Criminal Code, Federal and Provincial Statutes, by Sex.* Ottawa, ON: CANSIM, Matrices 2198 and 2199 and Catalog No. 85-205-XIB. www.statcan.ca/english/Pgdb/State/Justice/legal14.htm

4 to 11 years. This literature generally reflects that, although boys and men are more likely to be physically aggressive, differences begin to even out when verbal aggression is considered (yelling, insulting, teasing; Bjorkqvist & Niemela, 1992). Further, girls in adolescence may be more likely than boys to use "indirect aggression"—gossip, telling bad or false stories, telling secrets (Bjorkqvist, Osterman, & Kaukiainen, 1992). Tremblay (2000) contends that the use of indirect aggression increases with age for girls *and* boys. When this broad definition of "aggression" is utilized, only about 5% of the variance in aggression is explained by gender (Bjorkqvist & Niemela, 1992).

Some research done in Australia is noteworthy here because the researchers looked at gender differences in aggressive behavior (Owens, 1996, 1997) and distinguished between children's aggression toward same- and cross-sex targets (Russell & Owens, 1999). The results of their most recent study suggest that girls direct more physical aggression toward boys than to girls, but more verbal and indirect aggression toward girls than to boys. Thus, they indicate that "in the case of some forms of aggression, girls' aggression is directed more at other girls than to boys" (Russell & Owens, 1999, p. 374).

Those who study aggression in young children and young adults also note that girls' aggression is usually within the home or "intrafemale" and, thus, likely to be less often reported to authorities (Bjorkqvist & Niemela, 1992). The fact that these forms of aggression have been largely ignored by scholars, as well as by the general public, also means that there is substantial room for girls' aggression to be "discovered" at a time when concern about youthful violence is heightened.

The historical lack of attention to girls' aggression can largely be explained by the small numbers of girls who are represented by official statistics and the fact that violence has traditionally been viewed as a masculine fault, and girls who use it have not been deemed representative of female behavior (Artz, 1998; Chesney-Lind & Shelden, 1998).

Girls' behavior, including violence, needs to be put in its patriarchal context. In her analysis of self-reported violence in girls in Canada, Artz (1998) has done precisely that, and the results are striking. First, she noted that violent girls reported (a) significantly greater rates of victimization and abuse than their nonviolent counterparts, and (b) greater fear of sexual assault, especially from their boyfriends. Specifically, 20% of violent girls stated that they were physically abused at home, compared to 10% of violent males and 6.3% of nonviolent girls. Patterns for sexual abuse were even starker. Roughly, 1 out of 4 violent girls had been sexually abused, compared to 1 of 10 nonviolent girls (Artz, 1998). Follow-up interviews with a small group of violent girls found that they had learned at home that "might makes right," and they engaged in "horizontal violence" directed at other powerless girls (often with boys as the audience).

These findings provide little ammunition for those who would contend that the "new" violent girl is a product of any form of "emancipation."

DeKeseredy (2000, p. 46) supports the contentions of Artz (1998) in noting that the "ideology of familial patriarchy . . . supports the abuse of women who violate the ideals of male power and control over women." This ideology is acted out by those males and females who insist on women being obedient, respectful, loyal, dependent, sexually accessible, and sexually faithful to males (DeKeseredy, 2000). Artz (1998) suggests that violent girls, more often than not, "buy in" to these beliefs and "police" other girls' behaviors, thus serving to preserve the status quo, including their own continued oppression.

In their case studies of the life experiences of girls in custody in British Columbia, Canada, Artz, Blais, and Nicholson (2000, p. 31) found that the majority of girls were largely male-focused. They wanted very much to have boyfriends and always made sure that they had at least one, both in and out of jail. One girl, who strongly identified with the boys and saw herself as "one of the guys," also admitted that she had "always wanted to be a boy." Only one girl spoke little about boys; at 18 years of age, she was the oldest girl in the center. When they spoke about girls, all the girls used derogatory terms, and their words reflected views of females as "other." Many girls saw other girls as threats, particularly if they were pretty or "didn't know their place" (i.e., thought they were better than other girls). A "pretty" girl, or a girl whom boys paid attention to, was a primary target for girl-to-girl victimization because she had the potential to unseat those who occupied the top rung on the "pretty power hierarchy" (Artz et al., 2000, p. 124). An "ugly" or "dirty" girl (a girl designated as a slut) was also a primary target for girl-to-girl victimization because she "deserved" to be beaten for her unappealing looks and "unacceptable" behavior.

However, what needs to be understood about girls' delinquency, particularly from a programmatic and policy standpoint, is the clear link among victimization, trauma, and girls' delinquency. The other major theme that must be addressed is the fact that, most often, this trauma produces not violent offenses but what have long been regarded as "trivial" or unimportant offenses (e.g., running away from home).

The Relationship among Trauma, Victimization, and Serious Delinquency among Girls

Researchers studying the backgrounds of girls in custody in Canada have found a pattern of criminalizing girls' survival strategies, as reported in the United States (see Chesney-Lind & Shelden, 1999). In their examination of the lives of girls before coming into custody, Artz, Blais, and Nicholson (2000) found that only 1 of the 7 girls they interviewed had lived at home consistently throughout her childhood. All of the other girls' lives had been characterized by multiple moves and multiple caregivers. Of the 7 girls, files of 3 girls provided evidence of prior sexual abuse, and all 7 reported exposure to family violence. Five of the 7 girls were currently in custody for violent crimes, but their original offenses were less serious in nature, ranging from shoplifting and theft to fire setting and drug charges. Six of the 7 girls committed their first offense in the company of friends; 4 of the 6 were initiated into lawbreaking by older boyfriends.

Reitsma-Street (1999, p. 345) has commented on policing practices that serve to enforce expectations of "good girls." Shunning and slandering are everyday means used to punish differences in, and police the reputations of, delinquent or nondelinquent girls. More public forms of policing girls include the youth justice system, which has steadily decreased its use of the least intrusive types of sentencing for girls.

DeKeseredy (2000, p. 25) points to prostitution as another survival strategy for some adolescent females in Canada. He suggests that prostitution is often just a way for adolescent females to make a living, "a means of survival in a gender-stratified society." He notes that adolescent females are in higher demand as prostitutes than adult females, and the street culture that accompanies prostitution also provides a sense of belonging and a sense of autonomy, through financial independence, for girls who often have not experienced security or safety within their family homes.

Corrado, Odgers, and Cohen (2000) are other Canadian researchers who have provided valuable insights into the experiences of female young offenders. Recently, they completed an extensive study of incarcerated female young offenders and concluded that young women are usually more of a risk to themselves than to others. They suggested that the youth justice system in British Columbia demonstrates a clear desire to protect female youths from drugs, street life, and forms of abuse. The girls in the study reported recognizing that incarceration was meant as an opportunity for them to "get off and stay off drugs," reduce the control and authority of their pimps, and/or remove them temporarily from abusive environments (p. 17). Of the girls in their study, 27% were incarcerated for a violent offense. The majority (68.8%) were incarcerated for relatively minor offenses: 44.8% for breaches of court orders and 23.8% for property offenses. Like Artz, Blais, and Nicholson (2000), these researchers found that the majority of girls in their study had experienced very little residential stability in their lives.

Review of the girls' criminal histories revealed that the majority of prior offenses were status offenses; only 6% of previous charges against the girls in their sample were violent in nature. Corrado, Odgers, and Cohen (2000) reported that, after release from custody, 80.4% of the girls in their sample who recidivated during the one-year follow-up period committed nonviolent crimes—most commonly, a breach of probation orders. Of the 13.4% of girls who reoffended violently, 13 had charges of Level-1 assault, and 2 had been charged with robbery.

These authors also looked at drug use and responses to addiction and found no relationship between the use of marijuana, heroin, cocaine, acid, or downers, and reoffending. They did find, however, that girls who were frequent crack cocaine users were more likely to be charged with an administrative breach offense. Further, they contended that most youth custody institutions are not adequately equipped to deal with the special needs of female youths who have severe drug addictions.

Corrado, Odgers, and Cohen (2000) concluded that while the criminal justice system is proving to provide effective "short-term" protection for these girls, the "non-moralistic, paternalistic decision-making practices . . . under the justice-based Young Offenders Act" continues to incarcerate young women at high levels without long-term positive outcomes. These authors point to the need for innovative community programs in the form of noncustodial treatment and protection options to deal with the "multiproblem realities of young women's lifestyles and immediate priorities" (p. 19).

Chesney-Lind (1999a) and Chesney-Lind and Shelden (1998) also outlined a variety of risk factors that push girls to become involved with the juvenile justice system. Some of the risk factors are not different from those that affect boys (living in violent communities, poverty, academic failure, and substance abuse), but others are more specific to the experiences of girls (self-esteem, sexual abuse, enduring responsibilities for the care of others). We will look more closely at some of these in the next section.

Nonaggressive Offenses

The media have focused attention on girls' violent, nontraditional delinquency, but most of girls' delinquency is not of that sort at all. An examination of the types of offenses for which girls are actually arrested indicates that most are arrested for less serious criminal acts and status offenses (noncriminal offenses for which only youths can be taken into custody, e.g., "running away from home" or curfew violation). In 1998, roughly half of girls' arrests were for either larceny theft (21.5%)—much of which, particularly for girls, is shoplifting (Shelden & Horvath, 1986)—or status offenses (22.1%). Boys' arrests were far more dispersed.

Relabeling Status Offenses

But what about dramatic increases, particularly in arrests of girls for "other assaults"? Relabeling of behaviors that were once categorized as status offenses (noncriminal offenses like "runaway" and "person in need of supervision"), and making them violent offenses, cannot be ruled out in explanations of arrest-rate shifts, nor can changes in police practices with reference to domestic violence. A review of over 2,000 cases of girls referred to Maryland's juvenile justice system for "person-to-person" offenses revealed that virtually all of these offenses (97.9%) involved "assault." Further examination of these records revealed that about half were "family-centered" and involved such activities as "a girl hitting her mother and her mother subsequently pressing charges" (Mayer, 1994).

More recently, Acoca's study of nearly 1,000 girls' files from four California counties found that while a "high percentage" of these girls were charged with "person offenses," a majority of these involved assault. Further, "a close reading of the case files of girls charged with assault revealed that most of these charges were the result of nonserious, mutual combat situations with parents." Acoca details cases that she regards as typical, including: "Father lunged at her while she was calling the police about a domestic dispute. She (girl) hit him." Finally, she reports that some cases were quite trivial in nature. One girl was arrested "for throwing cookies at her mother" (Acoca, 1999, pp. 7–8).

In essence, when exploring the dramatic increases in the arrests of girls for "other assault," it is likely that changes in enforcement practices have dramatically narrowed the gender gap. As noted in the previous examples, a clear contribution has come from increasing arrests of girls and women for domestic violence. A recent California study found that the female share of these arrests increased from 6% in 1988 to 16.5% in 1998 (Bureau of Criminal Information and Analysis, 1999). African American girls and women had arrest rates roughly three times higher than those of white girls and women in 1998: 149.6 compared to 46.4 (Bureau of Criminal Information and Analysis, 1999).

In Canada, the Young Offenders Act (YOA), which came into force in 1984, eliminated "status offenses" and was expected to result in fewer girls ending up in custody. However, this did not happen. The percentage of girls admitted to custody or a welfare institution in 1988 and 1989 was higher than it was prior to the YOA (12.7% vs. 6.7% prior to 1984) (Reitsma-Street, 1993). Further, the situation in Canada does not appear to be improving. More girls are being sent to custody facilities, and fewer girls are receiving less serious dispositions such as fines, community service orders, restitution, or absolute discharges.

Reitsma-Street (1999) provides an updated analysis of the Canadian scenario that reflects a continuing propensity to incarcerate female young offenders on status offenses. She stresses that, up to 1996, the high increase in charges against female young offenders in Canada is well explained by replacement of old status offenses with new "statuslike" offenses that focus on girls' failure to comply with court orders. The trend to lock up girls on "failure to comply" offenses is similar to the trend in the United States. In recent years, in Canada, criminal justice officials have reclassified status offenders into categories that are available in the YOA. They include breach of probation or of the assigned undertaking; escaping from custody; failure to appear in court; and contempt of court (DeKeseredy, 2000).

In essence, it has long been known that arrests of youths for minor or "other" assaults can range from schoolyard tussles to relatively serious but not life-threatening assaults (Steffensmeier & Steffensmeier, 1980). These authors first noted an increasing tendency to arrest girls for these offenses in the 1970s, and they commented that "evidence suggests that female arrests for 'other assaults' are relatively nonserious in nature and tend to consist of being bystanders or companions to males involved in skirmishes, fights, and so on" (Steffensmeier & Steffensmeier, 1980, p. 70). Currie (1998) adds to this the fact that these "simple assaults without injury" are often "attempted" or "threatened" or "not completed." At a time when official concern about youth violence is almost unparalleled, and school principals are increasingly likely to call police onto their campuses, it should come as no surprise that youthful arrests in this area are up.

This observation is supported by recent research on the dynamics of juvenile robbery in Honolulu (another violent offense where girls' arrests showed sharp increases). In one decade, Hawaii, like the rest of the nation, had seen an increase in the arrests of youths for serious crimes of violence,* coupled with a recent decline. In Hawaii, murder, rape, robbery, and aggravated assault increased 60% from 1987 to 1996 but then had an 8.6% decline between 1996 and 1997 (Crime Prevention and Assistance Division, 1997, 1998). Most of the change can be attributed to increases in the number of youths arrested for two offenses: aggravated assault and robbery. Between 1994 and 1996, for example, the number of youths arrested for robbery doubled in Honolulu.

These increases prompted a study of the actual dimensions of juvenile robbery in Honolulu (see Chesney-Lind & Paramore, 1999). In this study of two time periods (1991 and 1997), police files that focused on robbery incidents resulting in arrest were identified. According to these data, the vast majority of those arrested for robbery in Honolulu in 1991 were male—114 (95%) versus 6 (5%). However, a shift occurred in 1997: 83.3% were males. Thus, the proportion of robbery arrests involving girls more than tripled between 1991 and 1997.

Taken alone, these numeric increases, along with anecdotal information, explain the "surge" in girls' violence. However, in this study, we were able to carefully characterize each of these "robberies" during the two time periods.

---

*In this report, "serious crimes of violence" will refer to the Federal Bureau of Investigation's index offenses, which are used to measure violent crime: murder, forcible rape, aggravated assault, and robbery.

Essentially, the data suggested that no major shift in the pattern of juvenile robbery occurred between 1991 and 1997 in Honolulu. Rather, it appeared that less serious offenses, including a number committed by girls, were swept up into the system, perhaps as a result of changes in school policy and parental attitudes. (Many of the robberies occurred as youths were going to and from school.) Consistent with this explanation are the following observable patterns in our data:

- During the two time periods under review, the age of offenders shifted downward, as did the value of the items taken. In 1991, the median value of the items stolen was $10.00; by 1997, the median value had dropped to $1.25.
- More significantly, the proportion of adult victims declined sharply and the number of juvenile victims increased.
- More of the robberies involved weapons in 1997, but those weapons were less likely to be firearms, and the incidents were less likely to result in injury to the victim.

In short, the data suggest that the problem of juvenile robbery in the city and county of Honolulu is largely characterized by slightly older youths who are bullying and "hijacking" younger youths for small amounts of cash (and, occasionally, jewelry), and that arrests of youths for these forms of robbery accounted for virtually all of the increase observed.

In Canada, Corrado, Odgers, and Cohen (1999) have distinguished between the experiences of nonviolent female delinquents and those of violent females. They reported that nonviolent females were "the most disadvantaged in terms of economic, social, and educational resources . . . and came from families with the highest level of dysfunction as measured by alcohol use, mental illness, unemployment and placement in foster care" (p. 10). Further, nonviolent females had been kicked out of their homes at an early age and with greater frequency than violent females. The profiles of violent females were not dissimilar to those of violent males. The researchers suggested that the most significant differences exist between nonviolent and violent females—an important consideration for developing programs for girls in custody.

Charging Girls with Status Offenses

Status offenses have always played a significant role among the offenses that bring girls into the juvenile justice system. In the United States, they accounted for about a quarter of all girls' arrests in 1998, but only 10% of boys' arrests, and these figures had remained relatively stable during the previous decade. In 1998, over half (58.7%) of those arrested for one status offense—running away from home—were girls (Federal Bureau of Investigation, 1999). Running away from home and prostitution remain the only two arrest categories in which more girls than boys are arrested, and, despite the intention of the Juvenile Justice and Delinquency Prevention Act of 1974—which, among other things, encouraged jurisdictions to divert and deinstitutionalize youth charged with status offenses—arrests for these offenses have remained stable or have actually been climbing in recent years. Between 1989 and 1998, for example, the number of girls arrested for running away remained about the same (a 1.2% decrease), and arrests of girls for curfew violations increased by an astonishing 238.5% (Federal Bureau of Investigation, 1999).

Why are girls more likely to be arrested than boys, for running away from home? There are no simple answers to this question. Studies of actual delinquency (not simply arrests) show that girls and boys run away from home in about equal numbers. As an example, in the United States, Canter (1982) found, in a National Youth Survey, that there was no evidence of greater female involvement, compared to males, in any category of delinquent behavior. Indeed, in this sample, males were significantly more likely than females to report status offenses. There is some evidence to suggest that parents and police may be responding differently to the same behavior. Parents may be calling the police when their daughters do not come home, and police may be more likely to arrest a female than a male runaway youth.

Research on the characteristics of girls in the California Youth Authority (CYA) system reveals that although these girls cannot be incarcerated in the Youth Authority for status offenses, nearly half (45%) had been charged with status offenses prior to their incarceration in the CYA for more serious offenses (Bloom & Campbell, 1998). Focus groups working with program staff in a variety of settings in California also indicated that these individuals felt that girls in that state were chiefly involved in the juvenile justice system for offenses such as "petty theft, shoplifting, assault and battery, drug violations, gang activity and truancy, lying to a police officer, and running away" (Bloom & Campbell, 1998).

Much the same pattern has been observed in Canada where well over a quarter of all the girls (27.3%) brought to youth courts in 1995 and 1996 were charged with "failure to comply," compared to only 5.7% in 1980 (Reitsma-Street, 1999). In fact, the situation could well be worse for Canadian girls than for their U.S. counterparts. Canadian courts are increasing the rate of incarceration of female youth at a significant and alarming rate. As an example, the number of girls placed in "secure custody" increased, in the space of just four years

(1991–1995), by an alarming 55%. This increase was virtually all explained by the incarceration of girls for "administrative" offenses (e.g., violating the conditions of probation, or being held in contempt of court) and other violations of court rules, rather than for criminal acts (DeKeseredy, 2000).

Underlying Racism

Relabeling of girls' arguments with parents—from status offenses (like "incorrigible" or "person in need of supervision") to assault—is a form of "bootstrapping" and has been particularly pronounced in the official delinquency of African American girls (Bartollas, 1993; Robinson, 1990). This practice also facilitates the incarceration of girls in detention facilities and training schools—something that would not be possible if the girl were arrested for noncriminal status offenses.

In Canada, aboriginal youth are overrepresented throughout the criminal justice system (Fisher & Jantti, 2000). In 1996 and 1997 in British Columbia (B.C.), aboriginal people constituted just 3.8% of the province's population and 20% of the province's youth custody population. Aboriginal females are incarcerated at much greater rates than nonaboriginal females. Local data gathered by a provincial government office in B.C. documents the gender and racial bias in incarcerating young offenders (Ministry for Children and Families Justice Services, 2000). Rates of custody admissions to a center in western Canada for breach of probation offenses in 1999 and 2000 were at 16.5% for all young offenders, 31% for female young offenders, and 47.8% for aboriginal female young offenders. In regional reports of the number of girls processed through the courts in Canada, a distinct racial bias emerges that reinforces the high rate of custodial admissions for aboriginal girls on breach charges (noted previously). DeKeseredy (2000) outlines the differences among regions across Canada. They point to a higher rate of girls processed in youth court in the region having the highest aboriginal population, thus reflecting an unfair degree of legal scrutiny for aboriginal girls. Reitsma-Street (1999) acknowledges that the systemic racism and pervasive injustice in the youth justice system has only recently begun to be uncovered. She states that it is even more difficult to see "how white ideas of justice are themselves rooted in contradictory values, including on one hand impartial fairness to all, and on the other hand an oppressive notion that there is but one just approach to justice" (p. 353). Alternative forms of justice, like "restorative justice, are premised on individual guilt, accountability, the protection of society, and the administration of a 'just' punishment, but rather, seek to restore harmony in the lives of the offenders, victims, and society at large through healing, teaching, respect, honesty, and resources for self-determination" (p. 355).

It would seem that youth justice officials involved in charging and incarcerating African American youth in the United States and aboriginal youth in Canada reflect the tendencies documented by Corrado, Odgers, and Cohen (2000) in which paternalistic decisions are made regarding who requires the most protection.

Sexual and Physical Abuse

Research illustrates the differences in the reasons boys and girls have for running away. Girls, for example, are much more likely than boys to be the victims of child sexual abuse. Some experts estimate that roughly 70% of the victims of child sexual abuse are girls (Finkelhor & Baron, 1986). Not surprisingly, the evidence suggests a link between this problem and girls' delinquency—particularly their running away from home.

Studies of girls on the streets or in court populations are showing high rates of both sexual and physical abuse. A study of a runaways' shelter in Toronto, Canada, found, for example, that 73% of the females and 38% of the males had been sexually abused. This same study found that sexually abused female runaways were more likely than their nonabused counterparts to engage in delinquent or criminal activities such as substance abuse, petty theft, and prostitution. No such pattern was found among the male runaways (McCormack, Janus, & Burgess, 1986).

Detailed studies of youths entering the juvenile justice system in Florida have compared the "constellations of problems" presented by girls and boys entering detention (Dembo, Borden, & Manning, 1995; Dembo, Williams, & Schmeidler, 1993). These researchers found that female youths were more likely than male youths to have abuse histories and contact with the juvenile justice system for status offenses; male youths had higher rates of involvement with various delinquent offenses. Further research on a larger cohort of youths (N = 2,104) admitted to an assessment center in Tampa concluded that "girls' problem behavior commonly relates to an abusive and traumatizing home life, whereas boys' law-violating behavior reflects their involvement in a delinquent lifestyle" (Dembo et al., 1995, p. 21).

More recent research confirms Dembo et al.'s insights. Cauffman, Feldman, Waterman, and Steiner (1998) studied the backgrounds of 96 girls in the custody of the California Youth Authority (CYA) and compared the results with those garnered from a comparison sample of male youth (N = 93) held by CYA. In this comparison, Cauffman et al. found that although boys were more likely to be traumatized as observers of violence, "girls were more likely to be traumatized as direct victims" (more than half the girls were victims of either sexual or physical abuse). Perhaps as a result, girls were significantly more likely than boys to be currently suffering from post-traumatic stress disorder; the level of PTSD (65%) found in this population was "significantly higher than among the general adolescent female population" (11%; Cauffman et al., 1998). Interestingly, about two-thirds of the girls in this sample were serving time for a violent offense (murder, assault, robbery), and 43% of the girls were identified as gang members (Cauffman et al., 1998).

Girls are also exposed to indirect traumatization. In Canada, for example, 37% of victims of spousal violence reported that their children (totaling 500,000 overall) had witnessed violence in their homes (Statistics Canada, 2000). Children in Canada were almost twice as likely to witness violence against their mothers than against their fathers, and, in over half the cases in which children saw a violent incident against their mother, the mother reported having feared for her life because of violence.

It is well known that children who witness violence are at risk for involvement in violence later in their lives. Findings from the most comprehensive survey about violence against women indicate that parents underestimate the effects that living in a climate of fear has on children (Sudermann & Jaffe, 1999). Children are affected by woman abuse in their homes even when they have not directly witnessed an assault. The effects of woman abuse on children can be clearly seen in symptoms that arise across all developmental levels, beginning even in infancy. If, by the time children reach their adolescent years, they have not had treatment for the trauma they have experienced, they are likely to become truant at school, drop out of school, run away from home, become involved in a negative peer group, engage in delinquent acts, develop an avoidant style of coping, have difficulty focusing on plans for the future, suffer depression, or commit suicide (Sudermann & Jaffe, 1999).

Programming for Girls

With few exceptions, girls in the juvenile justice system in the United States and Canada have not been well served by youth programming. The specific needs of girls are either shortchanged or simply ignored because attention is focused on the needs of the population of boys, who outnumber them, and there is a prevailing disbelief regarding the need for gender-specific programming (Chesney-Lind, 1999b; Corrado et al., 1999).

Programs for young women in general (and delinquents in particular) have received low funding priority. Chesney-Lind (1999b, p. 26) provides a brief review of the history of the juvenile justice system in the United States and concludes that its "paternalism and sexism make it a problematic site for gender-specific services."

Further, gender-based beliefs about aggression can interfere with the fair treatment of girls in custodial programs. Artz, Blais, and Nicholson (2000) report that staff working with young offenders in custody expected girls to engage in indirect aggression such as intimidation through body language, and would, at times, issue behavioral consequences when they assumed a girl was engaging in indirect aggression. When questioned about their lack of evidence for issuing the consequence, they justified their actions on the grounds that they expect girls to engage in indirect or verbal aggression ten times more often than staff are able to observe. Further, in interviews, youth custody workers did not report boys' engagement in indirect forms of aggression, although young male offenders, in their interviews, described frequently engaging in nonverbal forms of intimidation directed at other males.

Few descriptions of gender-specific programs exist, and even fewer are accompanied by rigorous evaluation. One exception comes from Canada. The work of Artz and Riecken (1997) showed the importance of focusing on gender *and* the desirability of crafting interventions that are gender-specific. They reviewed the outcomes of 13 individual violence-prevention initiatives in Canadian schools, employing pre- and posttests of reported violence, and concluded that "one size does not fit all" in violence prevention. Specifically, they found that boys are far less likely than girls to have participated in students' groups that promote violence prevention, and less likely than girls to adopt the antiviolence messages of their school's violence prevention programs. Girls, even when they had a history of violence, were more likely to see violence as problematic and to change as a result of interventions (particularly interventions based on skills-based programs and positive reinforcement). General consciousness raising was found to be ineffective for both sexes. Finally, young males tended to be reached only when men participated in the violence prevention efforts and when fathers (not mothers) condemned bullying (Artz & Riecken, 1997).

Insights about the essential elements of programs for girls can be gleaned from what *is* known broadly about girls' development and girls' delinquency. Careful reviews of the risk factors for boys and girls are sensitive to the fact that young people live in a gendered universe. While clearly not all girls at risk will end up in the juvenile justice system, a gendered examination of youth problems can help to set a standard for examining delinquency prevention and intervention programs.

Some promising early and continuing interventions have been developed by the Earlscourt Child and Family Centre in Toronto: The Girls Connection program is the first reported attempt to offer young Canadian girls who have behavior problems a gender-specific, multifaceted intervention committed to staying involved with girls and their families as long as necessary (Levene, 1997). Girls as young as 3 years of age are referred to the program, demonstrating an early intervention focus. Referrals continue for girls up to age 11. Supports, in the form of follow-up services that are available to girls and their families, continue until the girls turn 18. Varied services for parents, and for the family as a unit, comprise other portions of the multifaceted approach.

Based on her work and research with adolescent female delinquents in the United States, Chesney-Lind (1999b) points to some needs that girls' programs should specifically address. Many of these needs are universal and should be part of programs for all youth, but most of them are particularly important for young women. They include:

- Dealing with the physical and sexual violence in their lives (from parents, pimps, boyfriends, and others).
- Confronting the risk of AIDS.
- Dealing with pregnancy and motherhood.
- Overcoming drug and alcohol dependency.
- Facing family problems.
- Gaining employment and safe housing assistance.
- Managing stress.
- Developing a sense of efficacy and empowerment.
- Addressing learning disabilities and providing educational opportunities.

Programs should also be scrutinized to ensure that they are culturally specific as well as gender-specific, because girls' lives are colored by both their culture and their gender (Chesney-Lind, 1999b).

Artz, Blais, and Nicholson (2000) offer insights into programming that were provided by girls in their comments about living in custody.

What Girls Want

Girls, like boys, in custody stressed how much they appreciate staff spending time talking with them. For them, this is an important source of validation. They described feeling reticent to share their thoughts and feelings openly with other youth in custody, partially because they were aware of the very real possibility that in showing any signs of weakness (i.e., emotions), they would make themselves vulnerable to victimization by peers. They spoke about wanting staff to be consistent in their application of rewards and consequences tied to behaviors they exhibit. In general, however, girls' comments did not include detailed suggestions for improving their experiences in custody. This lack of suggestions may have been related to the fact that custody provided the girls with some things (regular meals, the absence of drugs, and predictable and secure housing) that they didn't always receive when they were on the "outs" (not in custody). Coupled with this, the girls pointed out that they believed the custody center could be a lot worse and, therefore, was generally quite acceptable.

Despite girls' relatively accepting comments about their experiences in custody, the overall findings of the research project by Artz, Blais, and Nicholson (2000) indicate that girls in custody would benefit greatly from programs that included efforts to dismantle gender stereotypes. Most of the girls in their study had virtually no idea of how gender socialization influenced their lives. After the implementation of a unit that enabled the custody center to segregate girls and boys within the center, girls began to express more positive attitudes toward other girls. However, what did not change was that boys were still seen as romantic interests who functioned as a means to consolidate and ensure girls' power and security, and as such, continued to perpetuate a competitive and defensive positioning among all the girls.

What Workers Think about Working with Girls

Although workers in the custody center that was the subject of the project by Artz, Blais, and Nicholson (2000) reported treating boys and girls the same, their reports of what they did with boys and girls in custody indicated that they actually treated them quite differently. A particularly clear example, mentioned earlier in this chapter, was related to workers' views of gender-specific forms of aggression. Girls' subtle victimization of others was characterized as much worse and much more manipulative than boys' subtle victimization. Another example is found in workers' references to equal gym time for boys and girls. However, when it was revealed that girls and boys were given time in the gym *together,* the researchers also learned that, most often, the boys would play sports and the girls would watch. *Real* equality occurred when, after concerted efforts to provide gender-segregated programming in the center, girls went to the gym by themselves and staff noticed that girls who wouldn't normally participate in physical activities were on the floor, engaging in active play.

Researchers in the custody center also reported believing that girls were much more difficult to work with than boys (Artz et al., 2000). Other researchers have voiced the same opinion (Bains & Alder, 1996). However, when the descriptions provided by workers are examined closely, one discovers that much of what workers suggest make girls "harder" to work with are requests that girls make to have their needs attended to. These needs are not easily responded to, given the structure and procedures of custody facilities (i.e., girls' needing to go to the bathroom more often than boys necessitates a staff person's accompanying them to the locked bathroom and being available to unlock the door and release them several minutes later). Worrall (1999) states that young women generally find it more difficult than young men to settle into life in custody. Such findings underscore the need for custody centers to rethink the practices they employ that have historically been premised on the needs of boys. As Chesney-Lind and Freitas (1999, p. 16) stress, work with girls is "different" from work with boys, and "this distinction requires different techniques and approaches." Additionally, as mentioned earlier in this chapter, Corrado, Odgers, and Cohen's (1999) findings about the differences between nonviolent and violent female delinquents are important to remember when developing appropriate programs for girls.

Finally, the gender perspectives of people who work with young female offenders are a critical component for effective programs for girls. Female staff in the youth custody study (Artz et al., 2000) reported that while some male workers would respond appropriately to girls' flirting with them, some of their male colleagues would just "eat it up." If male workers also view females as sexual objects, the custodial relationship sometimes evolves into an abusive situation. Some male staff eventually act on their beliefs; they sexually abuse even female adolescents in custody (see Chesney-Lind & Shelden, 1999).

CONCLUSION

Sensational discussions of girls' violence, particularly those found in the popular press, do little to help us understand the serious problems that girls, particularly those who are aggressive and violent, are experiencing.

This chapter has focused on the context within which girls' violence typically erupts, and on the roles that victimization and trauma play, not only in girls' conventional delinquency, but, more specifically, in girls' aggression and violence.

In our view, it is particularly important that the patriarchal context of girls' violence not be forgotten. Girls who act out violently are a far cry from being empowered. They are more likely than their nonviolent female peers to fear and experience male violence. In fact, in their violence, they often mimic that male violence, and their victims, rather than their victimizers, are similarly situated girls. Boys are often both the "cause" and the audience of girls' violence against other girls. Violence by girls tends to erupt around competition for boys' attention. Rumors about a girl's sexual reputation, as well as the well-known policing of girls' appearance that goes on in preteen and teen cliques (Adler & Adler, 1998, p. 50), tend to play major roles in girls' aggression and violence.

The role that the sex/gender system plays in traditional girls' delinquency (especially running away) is more easily understood. Girls and boys run away in roughly the same numbers, but the reasons for such behavior—and, more importantly, the societal reaction to these behaviors, based on the gender of the delinquent—are clear. Girls on the run from disturbed and/or abusive family situations find only further victimization on the streets. The juvenile justice system, which has long failed to craft effective, nonincarceratory responses to girls' noncriminal behavior, responds to minor forms of delinquency by relying on detention and incarceration in the name of "protection." In more recent years, as we have seen, the minor forms of violence (particularly family-related violence) that have also been part of girls' delinquent behavior have been criminalized, and these charges are used to justify detention and institutionalization.

As a consequence, girls who find their way into institutions typically have a different profile than their male counterparts. Despite this difference, they find themselves in an androcentric juvenile justice system—in both the United States and Canada—that is increasingly modeled after the adult criminal justice system. This characterization is particularly true of detention centers and training schools in the United States, which have long focused on security. Even when these institutions offer programs, the programs are crafted with the problems of boys and men in mind. No surprise, then, that workers in the juvenile justice system find working with girls problematic. Girls are understood to be more "emotional" and "difficult to work with" for those long used to dealing with boys.

We contend that gender *matters* in the lives of girls and boys, and any programming to address their problems must account for gender (and gender-related problems). By focusing on the ways in which gender works in the lives of girls, this chapter has sketched out some preliminary thoughts about programming that might effectively address the many important issues that girls in trouble bring to the table. Issues that might inform this work include: specific attention to gender stereotypes, the often corrosive role of the media in the lives of young women, and discussion of healthy relationships with boys and young men, to say nothing of how to find employment and safe and sober housing. As we work to craft these responses, our research, as well as the research of others, points to the wisdom of listening to the girls. We should attempt to work in partnership with them as we seek to create the bright future they so richly deserve after such a rough start in life.

REFERENCES

Acoca, L. (1999). Investing in girls: A 21st-century challenge. *Juvenile Justice, 6*(1), 3–13.

Adler, P., & Adler, P. (1998). *Peer power.* New Brunswick, NJ: Rutgers University Press.

Artz, S. (1998). *Sex, power and the violent school girl.* Toronto, Canada: Trifolium Books.

Artz, S. (2000). Considering adolescent girls' use of violence: A researcher's reflections on her inquiry. *The B.C. Counsellor, 22* (1).

Artz, S., Blais, M., & Nicholson, D. (2000). *Developing girls' custody units.* Unpublished report.

Artz, S., & Riecken, T. (1997). What, so what, then what?: The Gender Gap in School-Based Violence and Its Implications for Child and Youth Care Practice. *Child and Youth Care Forum, 26*(4), 291–303.

Bains, M., & Alder, C. (1996). Are girls more difficult to work with? Youth workers' perspectives in juvenile justice and related areas. *Crime and Delinquency, 42*(3), 467–485.

Bartollas, C. (1993). Little girls grown up: The perils of institutionalization. In C. Culliver (Ed.), *Female criminality: The state of the art* (pp. 469–482). New York: Garland Press.

BC Crime Trends. (1998, November). *Youth Crime, BC Crime Trends, 2.* Vancouver, BC: British Columbia Ministry of the Attorney General, Public Safety and Regulatory Branch, Police Services Division.

Bergsmann, I. R. (1989). The forgotten few: Juvenile female offenders. *Federal Probation, 53*(1), 73–78.

Bjorkqvist, K., & Niemela, P. (Eds.). (1992). New trends in the study of female aggression. In K. Bjorkqvist & P. Niemela (Eds.), *Of mice and women: Aspects of female aggression.* San Diego, CA: Academic Press.

Bjorkqvist, K., Osterman, K., & Kaukiainen, A. (1992) The development of direct and indirect aggressive strategies in males and females. In K. Bjorkqvist & P. Niemela (Eds.), *Of mice and women: Aspects of female aggression* (pp. 51–64). San Diego, CA: Academic Press.

Bloom, B., & Campbell, R. (1998). Literature and policy review. In B. Owen & B. Bloom (Eds.), *Modeling gender-specific services in juvenile justice: Policy and program recommendations.* Sacramento, CA: Office of Criminal Justice Planning.

Bureau of Criminal Information and Analysis. (1999). *Report on arrests for domestic violence in California, 1998.* Sacramento: State of California, Criminal Justice Statistics Center.

Canadian Centre for Justice Statistics. (1999). *The Daily.* July 21, 1999. Ottawa, ON: Statistics Canada.

Canter, R. J. (1982). Sex differences in self-report delinquency. *Criminology, 20,* 373–393.

Cauffman, E., Feldman, S. S., Waterman, J., & Steiner, H. (1998). Posttraumatic stress disorder among female juvenile offenders. *Journal of the American Academy of Child and Adolescent Psychiatry, 31*(11), 1209–1216.

Chesney-Lind, M. (1988). Girls in jail. *Crime and Delinquency, 34*(2), 150–168.

Chesney-Lind, M. (1997). *The female offender: Girls, women and crime.* Thousand Oaks, CA: Sage.

Chesney-Lind, M. (1999a). Media misogyny: Demonizing "violent" girls and women. In J. Ferrel & N. Websdale (Eds.), *Making trouble: Cultural representations of crime, deviance, and control* (pp. 115–141). New York: Aldine.

Chesney-Lind, M. (1999b, September). *What to do about girls? Thinking about programs for young women.* Paper presented at the International Community Corrections Annual Research Conference, Washington, DC.

Chesney-Lind, M., & Freitas, K. (1999). *Working with girls: Exploring practitioner issues, experiences and feelings* (Rep. No. 403). Honolulu: University of Hawaii at Mänoa, Social Science Research Institute.

Chesney-Lind, M., & Paramore, V. (1999). Are girls getting more violent? Exploring juvenile robbery trends. *Journal of Contemporary Criminal Justice.*

Chesney-Lind, M., & Shelden, R. G. (1998). *Girls, delinquency, and juvenile justice* (2nd ed.). Belmont, CA: Wadsworth.

Corrado, R., Cohen, I., & Odgers, C. (1998). Teen violence in Canada. In R. Sommers & A. Hoffman (Eds.), *Teen violence: A global perspective.* San Diego, CA: Greenwood.

Corrado, R., Odgers, C., & Cohen, I. (1999). Girls in jail: Custody or care? In R. Roesch, R. Corrado, & R. Dempster (Eds.), *Psychology in the courts: International advances in knowledge.* Amsterdam: Harwood Academic.

Corrado, R., Odgers, C., & Cohen, I. (2000, April). The incarceration of female young offenders: Protection for whom? *Canadian Journal of Criminology, 189–207.*

Crime Prevention and Assistance Division. (1997). *Crime in Hawaii 1996.* Honolulu: Department of the Attorney General, State of Hawaii.

Crime Prevention and Assistance Division. (1998). *Crime in Hawaii 1997.* Honolulu: Department of the Attorney General, State of Hawaii.

Currie, E. (1998). *Crime and punishment in America.* New York: Metropolitan Books.

DeKeseredy, W. (2000). *Women, crime and the Canadian criminal justice system.* Cincinnati, OH: Anderson.

Dembo, R. S. C., Borden, S. P., & Manning, D. (1995, August). *Gender differences in service needs among youths entering a juvenile assessment center: A replication study.* Paper presented at the annual meeting of the Society of Social Problems, Washington, DC.

Dembo, R., Williams, L., & Schmeidler, J. (1993). Gender differences in mental health service needs among youths entering a juvenile detention center. *Journal of Prison and Jail Health, 12,* 73–101.

Federal Bureau of Investigation. (1980). *Crime in the United States 1979.* Washington, DC: U.S. Government Printing Office.

Federal Bureau of Investigation. (1999). *Crime in the United States 1998.* Washington, DC: U.S. Government Printing Office.

Finkelhor, D., & Baron, L. (1986). Risk factors for child sexual abuse. *Journal of Interpersonal Violence, 1,* 43–71.

Girls Incorporated. (1996). *Prevention and parity: Girls in juvenile justice.* Indianapolis: Girls Incorporated National Resource Center.

Huizinga, D. (1997). *Over-time changes in delinquency and drug-use: The 1970s to the 1990s.* University of Colorado: Research Brief.

Fisher, L., & Jantti, H. (2000). Aboriginal youth and the youth justice system. In J. Winterdyk (Ed.), *Issues and perspectives on young offenders in Canada* (2nd ed.). Toronto, Ontario, Canada: Harcourt.

Levene, K. (1997). The Earlscourt girls connection: A model intervention. *Canada's Children, 4*(2), 14–17.

Loper, A. B., & Cornell, D. G. (1996). Homicide by girls. *Journal of Child and Family Studies, 5,* 321–333.

Mayer, J. (1994, July). *Girls in the Maryland juvenile justice system: Findings of the female population taskforce.* Presentation to the Gender Specific Services Training, Minneapolis, MN.

McCormack, A., Janus, M. D., & Burgess, A. W. (1986). Runaway youths and sexual victimization: Gender differences in an adolescent runaway population. *Child Abuse and Neglect, 10,* 387–395.

Ministry for Children and Families Justice Services. (2000). *Victoria youth custody centre profile of young offenders, 1999–2000.* Victoria, BC: unpublished report.

Office of Juvenile Justice and Delinquency Prevention. (1999, October). *Guiding principles for promising female programming* [Online]. Available from: www.ojjdp.ncjrs .org/pubs/principles/contents.html.

Owens, L. (1996). Sticks and stones and sugar and spice: Girls' and boys' aggression in schools. *Australian Journal of Guidance and Counselling, 6,* 45–55.

Owens, L. (1997, July 15–19). *Teenage girls: Voices of aggression.* Paper presented at the 20th International School Psychology Colloquium, Melbourne, Australia.

Reitsma-Street, M. (1993). Canadian youth court charges and dispositions for females before and after the implementation of The Youth Offenders Act. *Canadian Journal of Criminology, 35*(4), 437–458.

Reitsma-Street, M. (1999). Justice for Canadian girls: A 1990s update. *Canadian Journal of Criminology, 41*(4), 335–363.

Robinson, R. (1990). *Violations of girlhood: A qualitative study of female delinquents and children in need of services in Massachusetts.* Unpublished doctoral dissertation, Brandeis University.

Russell, A., & Owens, L. (1999). Peer estimates of school-aged boy's and girls' aggression to same- and cross-sex targets. *Social Development, 8*(3), 364–379.

Shelden, R., & Horvath, J. (1986). *Processing offenders in a juvenile court: A comparison of male and female offenders.* Paper presented at the annual meeting of the Western Society of Criminology, Newport Beach, CA.

Stahl, A. L. (1999). *Delinquency cases in juvenile courts, 1996* (OJJDP Publication No. 109). Washington, DC: U.S. Department of Justice.

Statistics Canada. (2000). *Criminal Justice Indicators Graphical Overview.* Ottawa, ON: Canadian Centre for Justice Statistics.

Steffensmeier, D. J., & Steffensmeier, R. H. (1980). Trends in female delinquency: An examination of arrest, juvenile court, self-report, and field data. *Criminology, 18,* 62–85.

Sudermann, M., & Jaffe, P. (1999). *A handbook for health and social service providers and educators on children exposed to woman abuse/family violence.* Ottawa, ON: Health Canada.

Tremblay, R. (2000). The Origins of Youth Violence. *Isuma, 1*(2), 19–24.

Worrall, A. (1999). Troubles or troublesome? Justice for girls and young women. In B. Goldson (Ed.), *Youth justice: Contemporary policy and practice.* Brookfield, NY: Ashgate.

Chapter 10

YOUTH GANG VIOLENCE

RODNEY A. ELLIS

INTRODUCTION

Escalating gang membership over the past two decades has demanded increasing attention from government officials, law enforcement agencies, social service agencies, and the general public. Gangs are sources of a myriad of criminal activities, including property crimes, drug-related offenses, sexual crimes, and a variety of violent activities. As the numbers of gangs and gang members have increased in the United States, the number and severity of these offenses have also increased. They are threatening community safety and stretching the resources and ingenuity of law enforcement personnel, social service professionals, and officers of the court (Office of Juvenile Justice and Delinquency Prevention [OJJDP], November 2000). One of the most significant problems has been the proliferation of violent activities by and among gang members (Covey, Menard, & Franzese, 1997).

"Youth gang" refers to a group of two or more members, between the ages of 12 and 24 years who: (1) share a common sense of identity; (2) use common attire, signs, symbols, and colors; (3) have a relatively stable membership; (4) are generally associated with a specific geographic area; and (5) are involved in various types of criminal activity (Covey et al., 1997; Curry & Decker, 1998). They are most often male members of an inner-city, low-socioeconomic-class family of ethnic origin; however, in recent years, many juveniles from European nonurban communities have also become associated with gangs (Klein, 1995).

Some increases in violent crime have been associated with or fueled by increases in gang membership. For example, although the increase has not been directly linked to gang activity, the juvenile homicide rate doubled during a period when gangs were experiencing their explosive growth (Covey et al., 1997). According to the 1998 National Youth Gang Survey, 84% of all areas surveyed reported firearms use by gang members in assault crimes, at least on occasion; 94% reported at least some involvement in aggravated assault by gang members; and 82% reported gang involvement in robberies (OJJDP, November 2000). Many cities have also noted increases in drive-by shootings. In Los Angeles, between 1989 and 1996, 33% of the gang-related homicides resulted from drive-by shootings (Hutson, Anglin, & Eckstein, 1996).

The most recent National Youth Gang Survey (OJJDP, November 2000) indicates a slight decrease in gang activity between 1996 and 1998. Even allowing for this decrease, estimates place the number of gangs operating in the United States at 28,700, composed of 780,200 members. Suburban counties and large cities reported decreases in gang membership (–21 % and –6%, respectively), but rural areas reported a 43% increase, and small cities noted a 3% increase.

Some progress may have been made in dealing with youth gangs and associated violent activity, but a great deal remains to be done. This chapter focuses on what has been done and what needs to be done in response to youth gang violence. The major sections examine: (a) current trends and issues; (b) identification, classification, and prediction, as they relate to gang violence; (c) effective prevention programs; (d) empirically based interventions; (e) case management and the strengths perspective; and (f) future research. The implications of these factors are discussed in the respective sections.

CURRENT TRENDS AND ISSUES

To understand gang violence, it is necessary to understand both the history and the culture of gangs. This chapter is based on the premise that modern gang culture is inherently violent, and effective prevention and intervention must address not only violence, but also the organizations that support it. Gangs have evolved from a complex web of historical events and societal conditions. An understanding of those events and conditions provides a foundation for identifying critical current issues and shaping future response.

Current Trends

Youth gang activity was recorded as early as the first decade of the twentieth century (Puffer, 1912). Goldstein (1993) observed that the writers of that era viewed gangs as somewhat playful and benign, despite their involvement in a variety of criminal activities. Whether this perspective was accurate or was a product of the type of denial that has historically characterized society's reaction to gang activity is uncertain. What is clear is that the gangs of early eras were predominantly ethnic and were most often headquartered in clearly defined portions of communities that had a low socioeconomic status (Thrasher, 1927). Over the years, these geographic areas came to be known as the gang members' "turf."

Gang activity persisted and grew throughout the twentieth century. Although there is some evidence that membership has fluctuated over long periods of time, careful examination reveals that an overall pattern of growth was sometimes distorted by scientific error and media bias. During the Depression era of the 1930s, youth gangs operated as subsidiaries of adult criminal organizations. In the 1940s and 1950s, the gangs emerged as increasingly autonomous organizations (Goldstein, 1993; Klein, 1971).

Reports from law enforcement organizations, social service agencies, and the media provide conflicting information about gang activity during the 1960s. Klein (1971) summarized activity in four major cities: Los Angeles, Chicago, New York, and Philadelphia. Reports conflicted; they varied by community, media report, and category of activity. Klein noted that violence may have decreased in some communities and increased in others. Alternatively, he observed that apparent fluctuations in activity may have simply been misperceptions created when the media turned attention to other events, such as civil rights demonstrations and the Viet Nam War. He noted that perceived decreases in activity might have actually been the result of shifts in category of activity. He offered Philadelphia as an example. Gang fights decreased between 1962 and 1968, and shootings, stabbings, and killings increased.

The 1970s were relatively quiet, perhaps due to media inattention (Klein & Maxson, 1989). Still, there is evidence of substantial activity during that decade. The gang membership explosion of the 1980s may have actually begun in the latter part of the 1970s (Miller, 1975).

During the 1980s and early 1990s, gang activity grew and intensified. Miller (1992) estimated that 2,000 gangs, including almost 100,000 members, existed in 1980. By 1996, estimates had risen to include 30,818 gangs, composed of 846,428 members (OJJDP, November 2000). Only since 1996 have slight decreases been identified.

The growth in gang membership has occurred in tandem with several other trends. The ready availability of automobiles has enhanced the mobility of gang members by allowing freer invasion of others' turf, and fueling waves of drive-by shootings in some communities. Easy access to firearms has turned street brawls into shootouts. Increased availability of various illicit drugs has encouraged some gangs to become distribution networks, and many such groups have been involved in violent disputes. Immigration and acculturation processes have broken the racial barriers that existed earlier. In communities where socioeconomic status was once thought to protect children from gang involvement, parents are beginning to notice the tattoos and attire that identify gang members among their own children.

Gang names, memberships, and practices have also changed. Initiatory rituals now include either "beating in" or "sexing in" an initiate. When members are beaten in, they must endure a physical beating at the hands of all other members. Girls may be sexed in by having intercourse with all male members of the gang. Names such as "Bloods," "Crips," "People," and "Folk" have replaced gang names of earlier eras. Gang culture has also evolved to include new language, identifying "tags," and a deep sense of commitment to other members. Gang culture is also infused with violence, from the "beating in" rituals to the measures members are required to take to defend the gang's territory and honor.

The commitment of gangs to violence is expressed in some of their foundational documents, often referred to as charters or constitutions. Constitutions include the rules and guidelines by which gang members are governed. The following descriptions of the constitutions of prominent gangs reflect the violent nature of the culture. The constitutions were obtained from Florida law enforcement officials while the author was working in a prevention and intervention partnership in that state.

The charter of the Manic Latin Disciples describes the violent consequences its members may experience if they choose to violate any of its policies. Death is the penalty for at least two offenses: "Any member who attempts to overthrow the leadership will be eradicated." and "Any member who implicates another in a crime will be eradicated." (*Manic Latin Disciples,* date unknown, p. 12.) Those who commit other offenses—such as drug use, or lying to or stealing from other members—are to be severely punished. (*Manic Latin Disciples,* date unknown.)

The Constitution of the Spanish Cobra (Spanish Cobra, 1979) contains eulogies for departed members who died as a result of "lack of security," reflecting the consequences of warfare with rival gangs and conflict with law enforcement units. Members are told: "If you are confronted with a situation in which you are being physically and aggressively offended, then you are to move first, fast, and effectively" (p. 18). The gang's commitment to illegal activity is also seen in the document's instructions regarding how members should act when arrested or incarcerated, and an extensive discussion about the benefits of Miranda rights. In a portion of the Constitution entitled *Seguridad* (Spanish for security), members are encouraged to take precautions when engaging in criminal activity. "If the matter demands that you use any incriminating material that can be used against you in a court of law as evidence, then be 100% sure that all the material is disposed of because the outcome can surely end in a drastic way. . . . It is strongly emphasized that you leave nothing behind that is incriminating such as masks, gloves, arms, and subjects etc. . . . " (p. 18).

The Gangster Two-Six Nation urges members to avoid "petty crimes," such as "jack-rolling" the elderly, women, and children. Such crimes are said to be below members' standard. Members should restrict themselves to more worthy crimes, consistent with their "classy image" (p. 17). Older members are required to instruct younger members regarding survival and security when dealing with the police and "opposing forces" (p. 18). Specific instructions are also given regarding appropriate conduct when incarcerated (*Gangster Two-Six Nation,* date unknown).

The Amalgamated Order of Lordism (date unknown), also known as the Vice Lords, emphasizes that its members must be willing to die for other members. Members are warned that treason may be punished "by no less than a life of misery." This life of misery is deemed appropriate only when "the most serious extreme" (presumably, death) is to be avoided "out of consideration and preservation for our most truest, and righteous representative" (p. 12).

Several researchers have documented norms supporting violence. Decker and Van Winkle (1996), in commenting on the centrality of violence, observed that it deepens bonds among members. Violence is central to proving one's manhood (Horowitz, 1983; Sanchez-Jankowski, 1991), obtaining status, settling disputes (Short & Strodtbeck, 1965), protecting turf, and defending the gang's and one's own honor (Block & Block, 1993).

These norms of today's gangs create a culture of violence that seems to have been far less prevalent in the past. This culture supports at least four varieties of violence: (a) intrapersonal, as illustrated by burning tattoos and other identifiers into one's skin; (b) intragang, as demonstrated by the initiatory practice of "beating in" and by the disciplinary measures described in the gangs' constitutions; (c) intergang, as seen in gang warfare, drive-by shootings, and turf battles; and (d) extragang, observed in assault, robbery, and other criminal activities.

Although the literature clearly acknowledges the presence of these varieties of violence among youth gangs, it also indicates that some types are more prevalent than others. The most frequent type is intergang violence, in which the members of one gang respond violently to members of another. Decker (1996) identified a seven-step process that leads to periods of escalation and de-escalation in gang violence. The steps are:

1. Membership cohesion is low. Violence is minimal.
2. Group bonding and cohesion are increased by a perceived threat from another gang.
3. In this atmosphere of perceived threat, an event (or series of events) occurs and mobilizes one of the gangs.
4. Activity escalates.

5. One gang strikes out violently at the other.

6. Violence and activity de-escalate quickly.

7. The other gang strikes back with violence.

The predominance of intergang violence might be anticipated by Miller's (1992) identification of the motives for gang violence: (a) defense of honor, (b) defense of turf, (c) control of resources and facilities, and (d) financial and material gain. The first three motives would most often produce interaction between gangs. The fourth motive might bring more frequent conflict with nongang individuals.

It is apparent that gangs also engage in nonviolent criminal activity; however, many of these activities are related to violence. One example is the drug trade that some gangs, such as the Vice Lords and the Black Gangster Disciples, have developed (Block & Block, 1993).

The overall decrease in gang membership and activity over the past three years may indicate that intensive prevention and intervention efforts have begun to bear fruit. On the other hand, it may be the result of other factors, such as changes in reporting standards, changes in definitional standards, or the unpredictable fluctuation that characterizes many criminal institutions and activities. For the present, it is perhaps best to view the overall increase in membership and violent behavior during the past two decades as being typical of the trend in gang activity.

Current Issues

Several issues are currently facing the professionals who deal with gang violence. These issues might be categorized as follows: (a) distribution of gangs, (b) composition of gangs, and (c) appropriate responses (by community leaders and professionals).

Distribution of Gangs

It is clear that the distribution of gang membership is changing. Historically, gangs have been thought of primarily as composed of inner-city residents. Recently, however, experts have identified growth trends in areas traditionally viewed as having low risk: the suburbs, small cities, and rural areas. As gangs move into these areas, the likelihood of related violence also increases. Among the various explanations offered for these changes are: migration to expand illicit activity; imitation; and family relocation.

There is evidence that some gangs have relocated some of their members to increase income-generating activities such as drug trafficking. Given the relationship between drugs and violence, as well as the internalized violence in the culture of gangs, it is easy to understand that violence would escalate in the communities to which the gangs move. Skolnick, Correl, Navarro, and Rabb (1988) found that the Bloods and the Crips had migrated across the country from Los Angeles to expand their drug distribution network. Other experts have concluded that migration is infrequently the result of the expansion of criminal enterprises. In these experts' view, gang members migrate as the result of domestic conditions, such as family relocation (Maxson, Woods, & Klein, 1996).

Composition of Gangs

Three earlier characteristics of gang composition have changed substantially, which raises questions about why the changes occurred and how they are likely to affect gang activity, including violence. These characteristics include the advent and increase of girls in gangs, an increase in the number of gangs that are composed of diverse ethnicities, and a diversity of socioeconomic status among gang members.

Many researchers have concluded that female gang membership has increased over the past several years (Curry, 1995a, 1995b; Klein, 1995). However, other studies have suggested that these trends either may not exist or may be limited to specific geographical areas (Chesney-Lind, 1993; Moore, 1991). Howell (1998) notes that it is difficult to determine the exact status of female membership because of the absence of national data. The 1998 National Youth Gang Survey (OJJDP, November 2000) found male membership to be at 92%, up 2% from 1996. The survey indicated that females were more prevalent in gangs in small cities (12%) and rural areas (11%) than in large cities (7%).

Girls may have one of three types of gang status: (a) they may be members of predominantly male gangs, (b) they may be members of all-female gangs ancillary to existing male gangs, and (c) they may be members of gangs that are free-standing (Howell, 1998). Regardless of the nature of their membership, girls who are gang members are much more likely to engage in serious delinquent behavior than are their nongang counterparts (Bjerregaard & Smith, 1993). Other researchers have found that the girls exceed nongang males in violent and other serious offenses (Fagan, 1990). Thus, although the extent and spread of female gang membership are at issue, the levels of violence and serious delinquent behavior among female gangsters are not.

Gang composition has also changed in terms of ethnicity. Although many gangs are composed of African Americans and Hispanics, increasing numbers are composed of other ethnicities, such as East Asians, Haitians, and Pacific Islanders. Predominantly Caucasian gangs have also emerged, and other groups that have been traditionally composed of a single ethnic group have begun to accept members from other backgrounds (Klein, 1995).

Ethnic diversification has been accompanied by socioeconomic diversification. Increasing numbers of juveniles from middle- and upper-class homes have become involved with gangs. Gangs were once regarded as primarily a lower-socioeconomic class phenomenon. Now, membership has penetrated some communities and schools once regarded as inviolable.

Appropriate Responses

Escalating gang membership and related violent activities have generated divergent responses from officials. These responses have included: (a) a continuum of reaction ranging between recognition and denial, (b) a debate as to the degree to which response should rely primarily on law enforcement or social services, (c) a discussion as to the effectiveness of various categories of prosecutorial response, and (d) discussion about the acceptability of policies that affect individual liberties.

As gang membership and violence have spread, local leaders, such as mayors and commissioners, have faced a difficult choice: Recognize and deal with the problem, or deny that it exists. Those who have chosen recognition have sometimes been able to prevent or retard gang proliferation. Those who have opted for denial have often seen gang activity and violence spread across their communities. With remarkable consistency, community leaders have chosen denial, and their communities have experienced the consequences.

Another issue has involved the effectiveness of law enforcement versus social service responses. Some leaders and groups have argued that a strong response from police agencies, prosecutors, and the courts provides the only effective solution. Others have contended that gang problems exist because of individual and social conditions that can be alleviated through intervention and treatment. Indeed, it appears that neither side is accurate in excluding the other. This standoff will be discussed in greater depth later in the chapter.

Related to this issue is the question of prosecutorial response. Some jurisdictions mandate or allow adult prosecution for any juvenile accused of a gang crime. Others have adopted special prosecutorial techniques, such as vertical prosecution, in which a single prosecutor is assigned to individual gang members and follows those juveniles through each prosecution.

Debate has also arisen around official responses that attempt to control gang presence at the expense of individual rights. One example is school dress codes. Recognizing the color schemes and use of symbols that typify gangs, school systems have developed rules that exclude certain attire. By preventing gang members from dressing in identifying clothing, officials hope to reduce gang activity and its associated violence. Civil libertarians object that this policy infringes on the rights of students to dress as they please and should not be a practice in the school systems.

IDENTIFICATION, CLASSIFICATION, AND PREDICTION

Identification of gang members can be difficult because of: (a) differing definitions, between jurisdictions, of gang membership and gang crime; (b) difficulties in distinguishing copycats, "wannabees," and associates from gang members; and (c) strong restrictions and consequences for "dropping dime" (informing on fellow gang members). The propensity of individual gangs or members toward violence can be difficult to predict because violent activity varies both within and between gangs.

Identification and Classification

Although experts have moved toward commonality, definitions related to gangs, membership, and activities still vary. Although gang members share modes of dress, interactive styles, tattoo types, and other physical characteristics, others who want to appear to be gang members (copycats), hope to become gang members (wannabees), or are affiliated with gangs (associates) often adopt these characteristics. Gang attire can be a warning signal for parents and professionals, but is not adequate for identifying members.

Gang members are forbidden to reveal the identities of members of their own gangs. Strong consequences associated with informing on others make it very difficult for law enforcement to gain information about membership from other members. Although it is sometimes possible to gain information from rival gangs, it is difficult to know when this information can be trusted.

To facilitate the identification of gang members, some law enforcement agencies have developed shared databases of membership, operated by specialized gang task force personnel. These databases often include sections for suspected members and verified members. When criteria for accurate identification have been met, members are moved from the suspected list to the verified list. The system provides a mechanism for tracking total gang membership, illegal activity, and prosecutorial efforts.

Gang crime is also difficult to identify. Suppose, for example, one gang member kills another in a dispute over turf. That is clearly related to gang membership. Alternatively, imagine that a gang member kills a nonaffiliated person while committing a robbery. If the robbery was to support the gang, would the crime be gang-related? If it was solely for the killer's own benefit, should that be considered gang-related? Inconsistencies between agencies and jurisdictions result in serious problems related to identification and classification.

Prediction

Prediction of gang-related behavior is also difficult, in part because of definitional problems. If there is no consistent definition of what constitutes a gang or a member, it is virtually impossible to predict trends in membership. Further, because definitional problems preclude identification of many gang members, it can be difficult to predict what a gang member is likely to do. Several things, however, are clear:

- Gang members are more likely to engage in criminal activity than are juveniles with no gang affiliation.
- Gang members are more likely to commit violent offenses and to become involved in group violence, such as fights and drive-by shootings.
- Some gangs are more prone to violence than others, but the factors distinguishing those gangs are not always easy to identify. For example, activities related to the distribution of drugs increase the violence among groups such as the Vice Lords, but other gangs may engage in violence only to protect their turf or reputation.

In the experience of the author, some gangs exist purely for self-defense and engage in violent activity very infrequently.

EFFECTIVE PREVENTION PROGRAMS

Many experts agree that the most successful interventive strategies rely on prevention technologies. Prevention strategies rely on early recognition of risk factors (characteristics that increase the risk that a juvenile will engage in problem behavior), protective factors (characteristics that decrease the probability that a juvenile will engage in problem behavior), and special needs, or need factors (characteristics that do not, in themselves, generate risk but, when combined with risk factors, enhance the probability of problem behavior). Interventions attempt to eliminate or decrease the effects of risk factors, create or enhance the effects of protective factors, and correct or eliminate deficiencies generated by the effects of special needs (Ellis, 1997; Sherman et al., 1997).

Several researchers have identified risk, need, and protective factors related specifically to gang membership (Esbensen, 2000). Most of these factors are not different from those associated with other delinquent activity. This similarity between the dimensions of problem behavior supports the argument of Ellis (1997), Hawkins, Catalano, and Miller (1992), Henggeler (1993), and others, that prevention and intervention activities should focus on multiple factors for each youth rather than target only those associated with a particular phenomenon. Ellis (1997) suggests that truly effective prevention must be multisystem (addressing every social system), multifactor (addressing every risk, need, and protective factor), and multilevel (active at every level from the family to the federal government).

Prevention can also be viewed as a continuum of intention and intensity that has "primary," "secondary," and "tertiary" levels. Within the context of gang membership, primary prevention refers to activities designed to prevent juveniles who are at risk for membership from becoming involved with gangs. Secondary prevention refers to programs that target juveniles who have already developed some level of gang involvement. Tertiary prevention is directed toward those who are gang members and are involved in criminal activity. Earlier in this chapter, we described the degree to which violence is imbedded in the culture and activities of gangs. Given this condition, this section and the one that follows are focused on preventing and treating gang membership, and on the most effective methods of preventing and treating gang violence.

Several promising programs have been developed for primary, secondary, and tertiary prevention. Esbensen (2000) cites one example of each. The Gang Resistance Education and Training Program (GREAT) is an example of primary prevention. Middle-school students receive instruction regarding the negative aspects of gang membership, and training in conflict resolution and cultural sensitivity. The nine weekly classes are taught by police officers. Evaluations have noted a small increase in the students' ability to resist peer pressure and gang membership.

The Boys and Girls Clubs of America offer Gang Prevention Through Targeted Outreach, a promising secondary prevention program composed of recreational, educational, and life skills components. Case managers are assigned to targeted youth, and detailed records of program participation, school performance, legal system involvement, and other life dimensions are maintained. These records allow the case managers to monitor youths' progress and to become aware of subtle signs (truancy, status offenses, failing grades) that may indicate behavioral problems or growing gang involvement.

Tertiary prevention activities often use law enforcement/citizen partnerships to focus on suppression of gang activities. Many police agencies have formed specialized gang units and adopted community policing strategies. These strategies equip police and citizens with essential knowledge regarding gang activities and create increased police presence in communities with a gang problem. Examples include the Chicago Police Department's Gang Crime Section and the Los Angeles Police Department's Community Resources Against Street Hoodlums (CRASH).

EMPIRICALLY BASED INTERVENTIONS

Most experts appear to agree that the most successful gang prevention and intervention programs are comprehensive in nature. Spergel et al. (1994) developed the Comprehensive Community-Wide Approach to Gang Prevention, Intervention, and Suppression Program. This model has been used in several communities with promising results. For example, the Gang Violence Reduction Program in Chicago has experienced positive results (Spergel & Grossman, 1997). Comprehensive programs should also include the recommendations of the OJJDP's Comprehensive Strategy for Serious, Violent, and Chronic Juvenile Offenders (Howell, 1995), such as priority arrest and adjudication, vertical prosecution, intensive probation, and transfer to the adult system.

CASE MANAGEMENT AND THE STRENGTHS PERSPECTIVE

Case management is used at various levels of prevention and intervention for gang members. The Gang Prevention Through Targeted Outreach program, mentioned previously, is an example of case management in a secondary prevention setting. Two intensive case management models have shown particular promise and can be adapted to any level of prevention. These models are: Multi-Systemic Therapy (MST) and the Intensive Aftercare Program (IAP).

MST, developed by Henggeler and colleagues (1992) uses an intensive case management model to provide a broad range of services to juveniles and their families. Case management teams offer and broker services for needs that are recognized in a formal process of ongoing assessment. Services are designed to meet multiple needs and enhance multiple strengths across juveniles' social systems. Although MST has not yet been tested specifically as a gang intervention, it has been used successfully with serious and chronic juvenile violent offenders.

IAP, developed by Altschuler and Armstrong (1999), is an intensive case management model recommended by the OJJDP for use with juveniles who have been incarcerated and are being returned to the community. It differs from MST in several ways—most notably in a strong law enforcement component that emphasizes surveillance, monitoring, and a system of graduated sanctions. As of this writing, IAP has not been evaluated for use with gang members, but its components are sound and are empirically supported. Its emphasis on both treatment and community safety make it inherently appealing for managing violent gang members.

FUTURE RESEARCH

Future research should include ongoing evaluation of current programs, and development of other creative alternatives. Researchers must reach common ground, with one another and with law enforcement, as to operational definitions of gang membership, gang crime, and other phenomena. Research should continue into risk, need, and protective factors and the use of those factors in successful prevention and intervention. In addition, more effective systems of collaboration among the many individuals and agencies that deal with and are affected by gang violence should be developed and evaluated. A comprehensive approach to gang prevention and intervention appears to be the most promising alternative at the current time. Given its promise, it should be refined and evaluated, and its results should be disseminated.

CONCLUSION

This chapter has examined the phenomenon of gang violence. Overall trends were noted, and the violent nature of gang culture was described. Based on this culture of violence, a discussion of identification, classification, prevention, and intervention was initiated. Identification and classification are challenging because experts cannot agree on definitions and the reports of gang members are not reliable. When gang members or those who are at risk of becoming members are identified, effective prevention and intervention programs are available.

REFERENCES

Altschuler, D. M., & Armstrong, T. L. (1999). Reintegration, supervised release and intensive aftercare. *Juvenile Justice Bulletin.* Washington, DC: Office of Juvenile Justice and Delinquency Prevention.

Amalgamated Order of Lordism. (n.d.). *Charter of the Amalgamated Order of Lordism* (for internal use). Published by the Amalgamated Order of Lordism.

Bjerregaard, B., & Smith, C. (1993). Gender differences in gang participation, delinquency and substance abuse. *Journal of Quantitative Criminology, 9,* 329–355.

Block, R., & Block, C. R. (1993). Street gang crime in Chicago. In *Research in Brief.* Washington, DC: Department of Justice Programs.

Chesney-Lind, M. (1993). Girls, gangs, and violence: Anatomy of a backlash. *Humanity and Society, 17,* 321–344.

Covey, H. C., Menard, S., & Franzese, R. J. (1997). *Juvenile gangs* (2nd ed.). Springfield, IL: Charles C. Thomas.

Curry, G. D. (1995a). *Gang community, gang involvement, gang crime.* Paper presented at the American Sociological Association annual meeting, Washington, DC.

Curry, G. D. (1995b). *Responding to female gang involvement.* Paper presented at the annual meeting of the American Society of Criminology, Boston.

Curry, G. D., & Decker, S. H. (1998). *Confronting gangs: Crime and community.* Los Angeles: Roxbury.

Decker, S. H. (1996). Collective and normative features of gang violence. *Justice Quarterly, 13,* 243–264.

Decker, S. H., & Van Winkle, B. (1996). *Life in the gang: Family, friends, and violence.* New York: Cambridge University Press.

Esbensen, F. (2000, September). *Preventing adolescent gang involvement* (Juvenile Justice Bulletin). Washington, DC: Office of Juvenile Justice and Delinquency Prevention.

Ellis, R. A. (1997). Filling the prevention gap: Multi-factor, multi-system, multi-level intervention. *Journal of Primary Prevention, 19,* 57–71.

Fagan, J. E. (1990). Social process of delinquency and drug use among urban gangs. In C. R. Huff (Ed.), *Gangs in America* (pp. 183–219). Newbury Park, CA: Sage.

Gangster Two-Six Nation. (n.d.). *The essence of the Two-Six* (for internal use). Published by the Gangster Two-Six Nation.

Goldstein, A. P. (1993). Gang intervention: A historical review. In A. P. Goldstein & C. R. Huff (Eds.), *The gang intervention handbook.* Champaign, IL: Research Press.

Hawkins, J. D., Catalano, R. F., & Miller, J. Y. (1992). Risk and protective factors for alcohol and other drug problems in adolescence and early adulthood: Implications for substance abuse prevention. *Psychological Bulletin, 112*(1), 64–105.

Henggeler, S. W. (1993). *Multisystemic treatment of serious juvenile offenders: Implications for the treatment of substance-abusing youth.* NIDA Research Monograph 137 (DHHS Publication No. ADM 88-1523). Washington, DC: U.S. Government Printing Office.

Henggeler, S. W., Melton, G. B., & Smith, L. A. (1992). Family preservation using multisystemic therapy: An effective alternative to increasing serious juvenile offenders. *Journal of Consulting and Clinical Psychology, 60*(6), 953–961.

Horowitz, R. (1983). *Honor and the American dream: Culture and identity in a Chicano community.* New Brunswick, NJ: Rutgers University Press.

Howell, J. C. (1995). *Guide for implementing the comprehensive strategy for serious, violent, and chronic juvenile offenders.* Washington, DC: Office of Juvenile Justice and Delinquency Prevention.

Howell, J. C. (1998, August). Youth gangs: An overview. *Juvenile Justice Bulletin.* Washington, DC: Office of Juvenile Justice and Delinquency Prevention.

Hutson, H. R., Anglin, D., & Eckstein, M. (1996). Drive-by shootings by violent street gangs in Los Angeles: A five-year review from 1989 to 1993. *Academic Emergency Medicine, 3,* 300–303.

Klein, M. W. (1971). *Street gangs and street workers.* Englewood Cliffs, NJ: Prentice Hall.

Klein, M. W. (1995). *The American street gang.* New York: Oxford University Press.

Klein, M. W., & Maxson, C. L. (1989). Street gang violence. In N. A. Weiner & M. E. Wolfgang (Eds.), *Violent crime, violent criminals.* Newbury Park, CA: Sage.

Manic Latin Disciples (n.d.). *Manic Latin Disciples: The past present and future.* Published by the Manic Latin Disciples as an internal document.

Maxson, C. L., Woods, K., & Klein, M. W. (1996, February). Street gang migration: How big a threat? *National Institute of Justice Journal, 230,* 26–31.

Miller, W. B. (1975). *Violence by youth gangs and youth groups as a crime problem in major American cities.* Report to the National Institute for Juvenile Justice and Delinquency Prevention, Washington, DC.

Miller, W. B. (1992). *Crime by youth gangs and youth groups as a crime problem in major American cities.* Washington, DC: Office of Juvenile Justice and Delinquency Prevention.

Moore, J. W. (1991). *Going down to the barrio: Homeboys and homegirls in change.* Philadelphia: Temple University Press.

Office of Juvenile Justice and Delinquency Prevention. (2000, November). *1998 National Youth Gang Survey: Summary.* Washington, DC: Author.

Puffer, J. A. (1912). *The boy and his gang.* Boston: Houghton Mifflin.

Sanchez-Jankowski, M. S. (1991). *Islands in the street: Gangs and American urban society.* Berkeley: University of California Press.

Sherman, L. W., Gottfredson, D., MacKenzie, D., Eck, J., Reuter, P., & Bishway, S. (1997). *Preventing crime: What works, what doesn't, what's promising* (Research Report). Washington, DC: Office of Justice Programs.

Short, J. F., & Strodtbeck, F. L. (1965). *Group process and gang delinquency.* Chicago: University of Chicago Press.

Skolnick, J. H., Correl, T., Navarro, E., & Rabb, R. (1988). *The social structure of street drug dealing* (Unpublished report to the Office of the Attorney General of the State of California). Berkeley, CA: University of California, Berkeley.

Spanish Cobra. (1979). *The constitution of the Spanish Cobra.* Published by the Spanish Cobra as an internal document. USA.

Spergel, I., Chance, R., Ehrensaft, K., Regulus, T., Kane, C., Laseter, R., et al. (1994, October). *Gang suppression and intervention: Community models.* Washington, DC: Office of Juvenile Justice and Delinquency Prevention.

Spergel, I., & Grossman, S. F. (1997). The Little Village Project: A community approach to a gang problem. *Social Work, 42,* 456–470.

Thrasher, F. M. (1927). *The gang.* Chicago: University of Chicago Press.

Chapter 11

YOUTH VIOLENCE: CHRONIC VIOLENT JUVENILE OFFENDERS

MONA M. WILLIAMS, SAMUEL A. MACMASTER, AND RODNEY A. ELLIS

INTRODUCTION

Despite apparent recent decreases in the juvenile crime rate, violence by juveniles remains a significant problem. According to the 1999 National Report of Juvenile Offenders and Victims, published by the Office of Juvenile Justice and Delinquency Prevention (OJJDP, April, 2000a), 1,400 murders committed in 1997 were known to involve juveniles. The OJJDP also indicates that, because of a number of data collection problems, this number may be an underestimate. If only the reported murders are considered, juveniles accounted for 38% of the total number of murders committed in that year. In addition to homicides, the National Crime Victimization Survey reports that juveniles participated in 27% of *all* violent victimizations. This included 30% of all robberies and 27% of all aggravated assaults.

This chapter addresses the issue of youth violence. First, it examines current trends and describes some of the more salient issues related to the problem. Next, it explores the areas of identification, classification, and prediction. Finally, it reviews current promising and empirically supported programs for prevention and intervention. One aspect of youth violence—youth gang violence—has been omitted here because it is discussed in depth in another chapter of this book.

CURRENT TRENDS

Crimes against individuals affect all members of a community. When crime is violent, families, communities, and society as a whole become concerned for their personal safety. When the crime rate rises, society demands punitive actions against the perpetrators, even when the perpetrators are children. Thus, public demands both frame and drive the trends observed by statisticians, often in ways that make the findings of researchers difficult or impossible to interpret. As an example, juvenile violent crime may appear to increase statistically because public opinion has demanded stronger and more consistent enforcement. Alternatively, juvenile crime rates may decrease because, through prosecutorial efforts, more juveniles are transferred to adult court.

Issues regarding violent offense rates are compounded by the fact that the public is often unable to differentiate between violent and nonviolent crimes. More than 80% of crimes are against property, yet many consider *all* crimes violent. Although juveniles have been portrayed as committing the majority of violent crimes, only about 20% of juvenile crime is violent (Roberts & Brownell, 1999).

Researchers have often cited the increase in violent juvenile crime during the late 1980s and early 1990s (Stone, 1998). This relatively short but dramatic rise in violent crime led some to project that a new class of "super predators" would emerge and the nation would face a surge of youth violence (OJJDP, 2000b). According to federal statistics, no such trend emerged. Violent arrest rates for juveniles dropped by 30% between 1994 and 1998 (OJJDP, 1999). However, the impact of public fear on policy and programming will be felt for years because many states, preparing for the "superpredators" who never emerged, rewrote their laws pertaining to violent juvenile offenders.

After years of focusing on prevention and treatment goals, the juvenile court system has assumed a more punitive perspective. This trend has been driven by public perception that, despite fluctuations in juvenile arrest rates, youth crime was increasing. Many states began to automatically transfer certain offenders to the adult system. This move toward punitiveness was enhanced by the brief crime rate increases of the early 1990s. Between 1992 and 1997, 47 states enacted laws that made their juvenile justice system more punitive (OJJDP, 2000c).

Although the pendulum has swung toward punishment and away from rehabilitation, there are positives in the renewed attention that juvenile justice has received. The attention that all levels of government have directed toward eliminating serious juvenile offenses has led to critical investigations of juvenile programs. This new empirical literature has given policy makers guidelines for what works and what is less effective. Programs based on prevention technologies have been found to be particularly effective.

Costs of Violent Crime

The cost of violent crime involves not only immediate losses, but also the long-term expense of treating and managing the offender (Ellis & Sowers, 2000).

Incarceration is costly and problematic: facilities are overcrowded, management is often poor, and incarceration has not demonstrated efficacy in reducing recidivism (Altschuler & Armstrong, 1999). In many cases, incarceration is counterproductive (Steffensmeier, Ulmer, & Kramer, 1998). Coates, Miller and Ohlin (1978) found that incarcerated juveniles demonstrated higher rates of reoffending and subsequent harsher sentencing. Once released, offenders may experience difficulties obtaining employment (Borduin, 1999), and the result is further costs to the community.

The costs of violent juvenile crime underscore the importance of effective intervention and further research into program efficacy. Recidivism rates for juveniles receiving traditional services range from 24% to 65% (Niemeyer & Shichor, 1996; Roy, 1993). Given the consequences of public reaction to violent crime, the cost of crime to society, and the harsh outcomes for juveniles who repeatedly commit violent offenses, it is imperative that practitioners both use and develop empirically supported interventions.

IDENTIFICATION, CLASSIFICATION, AND PREDICTION

The processes of identification, classification, and prediction present substantial challenges to professionals and researchers. Past violence is a strong predictor of future violence, but when juveniles have no history of violent behavior, it is often difficult to determine which children will behave violently in the future. Because of the difficulty in predicting individual behavior, some experts (Ellis, 1998; Henggeler, Melton, & Smith, 1992) have supported a comprehensive approach to the prevention and treatment of all delinquent activity. They argue that by considering multiple risk-related factors across each of a juvenile's social systems, practitioners can be sure that the potential for any form of delinquent behavior has been addressed.

A few instruments have been developed to facilitate classification and prediction. Many others are related to delinquency in general rather than violence specifically. One example is the Michigan Youth Services Delinquency Risk Assessment Scale (MYSS)(OJJDP, 1994). This scale includes 11 questions about various risk factors. Scores for each question reflect the severity of risk for a particular dimension. Item scores are then tallied to determine an overall score.

The Alaska Youth Services Needs Assessment Scale (AYSNAS) (OJJDP, 1994) is a similar tool. The AYSNAS contains 13 questions covering more dimensions of risk than does the MYSS. For both scales, a higher score indicates a higher degree of risk.

Neither scale has predictive power because neither has been tested scientifically. It should also be noted that both were developed to help anticipate recidivism. Despite the fact that they include many of the risk factors for primary prevention, neither was developed with that process in mind.

Among the scales that have been tested to determine their degree of predictive capacity, some have been relatively accurate; others have not. A discussion of several of these tools can be found in a literature review by Wiebush, Baird, Krisberg, and Onek (1995). There is a weakness in such instruments; regardless of their predictive capacity, most were designed for use in a treatment-related setting. This means that juveniles who are evaluated have already experienced some level of delinquent activity, so early intervention is impossible. One priority of future research should be the development of an effective instrument that can be used with younger children in non-treatment-related settings such as school and playgrounds.

EFFECTIVE PREVENTION PROGRAMS

Few studies have demonstrated effectiveness for chronically violent juveniles (OJJDP, 1999). However, by recognizing risk factors, understanding prevention technologies, knowing effective service delivery models, and diligently using and applying this information, promising results have been produced with several categories of offenders. Prevention technologies can be applied at primary, secondary, and tertiary levels (Ellis, 1998; OJJDP, 2000b). Primary prevention is intended to divert potentially violent juveniles from their first offense. Secondary prevention is designed for juveniles whose violent behavior has begun to escalate. Tertiary prevention is for previous offenders and is intended to prevent recidivism.

Standards for Determining Effectiveness

Many programs have claimed to be effective for preventing violent juvenile crime. Under scrutiny, however, few have lived up to that promise. When evaluating effectiveness, common procedures for and definitions of success are critical.

The OJJDP has identified 10 "Blueprints" programs for violence prevention. Inclusion of a program as a "Blueprint" was dependent on several criteria. The programs were required to be evaluated using experimental or quasi-experimental design, to be replicable, and to produce statistically significant positive outcomes that were persistent (University of Colorado, 2001). These standards can be useful in evaluating the effectiveness of other programs.

Another crucial factor is intervention integrity. This refers to whether the program is actually implemented as planned. Integrity is critical to successful programming and effective evaluation. When effective programs are identified and adopted, administrators must ensure that they are consistently applied (Lipsey, 1999).

Organizational culture and climate are also critical to effective intervention. The work of Glisson and Hemmelgran (1998) and Glisson (2000) underscores the importance of a positive and supportive environment in the agency that delivers an intervention. It is conceivable that an inadequate organizational environment could detract from an otherwise effective prevention program so as to render it either ineffective or less effective than it might have been in other settings.

When to Conduct Programs

Prevention programs should be in place when youths are most likely to offend. If programs are unavailable or are not in place during peak times for crime, their effectiveness may be diminished. "Prime crime" periods occur before school, at lunch, in the halls, and after school (OJJDP, 2000a; Olweus & Limber, 1999). Most violent juvenile crimes (57%) are committed on school days, between 2:00 and 6:00 P.M. (OJJDP, 1999). On nonschool days, violent juvenile crimes peak between 8:00 and 10:00 P.M. When school is out of session, prevention programs include late-night activities (OJJDP, 2000a).

Where to Conduct Programs

Knowing where juveniles can be targeted is also critical. Potter and Krider (2000) point out the importance of public health agencies in prevention. For instance, some sexual assaults might be prevented by educating males about the consequences of assault and informing both genders about techniques of effective communication. Schools are ideal places for prevention activities. The Centers for Disease Control and Prevention (CDC, 2000) report that 4% of students are absent from school as a result of fear of violence. Yet schools are places where many juveniles congregate and where they tend to be more readily accessible to prevention professionals. Because of schools' importance to juveniles and natural value as prevention sites, four types of in-school prevention programs are discussed here: bullying prevention, residential student assistance programs (REAP), family-focused services, and community-oriented police services (COPS).

Preventing Bullying

In addition to causing pain for victims, bullying can have long-term effects on offenders. Bullying is often a precursor of other antisocial behavior (Dupper & Meyer-Adams, in press; Olweus & Limber, 1999; Pellegrini, 1998). It is also fairly common. The Maine Project Against Bullying reports that 80% of adolescents were bullied during their school careers. Bullying has three characteristics. It is (a) aggressive, targeted behavior, (b) over a period of time, (c) by someone who has power over another (Olweus, Limber, & Mihalic, 1999; Pellegrini, 1998). The aggression is usually verbal but may also be physical.

Successful Bully Prevention (an OJJDP Blueprint Program) has been implemented in many schools. Teachers, counselors, principals, and students work together to produce a more nurturing environment. Teachers and staff place themselves where minimum supervision exists or at locations where bullying has taken place. School staff members make it known that bullying will not be permitted (Dupper & Meyer-Adams, in press), and bullies and victims are targeted for specific intervention. Prevention programs have resulted in reductions in bullying, reductions in antisocial behavior, and improvement in classroom climate (Dupper & Meyer-Adams, in press; Olweus & Limber, 1999).

Residential Student Assistance Programs (REAP)

Alcohol and drug use is correlated with violent offenses. Effective prevention programs that address substance use are therefore critical. The Residential Student Assistance Program (REAP) is an example of such a program. Its effectiveness was supported in a study by Morehouse and Tobler (2000), who created a quasi-experimental, pretest/posttest design to evaluate its effectiveness. REAP was effective in reducing both the frequency of drug use and the number of drugs used.

Two other Blueprint programs offer effective school-based strategies:

- The Life Skills Training program reduced tobacco, alcohol, marijuana, and polydrug use; smoking; and the use of inhalants, narcotics, and hallucinogens (Botvin, 1998).
- The Midwestern Prevention Project reduced the use of tobacco, marijuana, and alcohol, and increased parent-child substance use discussion (Pentz, Mihalic, & Grotpeter, 1997).

Functional Family Therapy

Effective family therapy programs enhance communication skills and develop problem solving for the entire family. The programs can help parents understand the importance of consistency and structured supervision—two factors known to protect against serious juvenile crime (Sherman et al., 1997).

Functional Family Therapy (FFT), another blueprint program, can be used for prevention or intervention in the home, the school, or an agency. It provides accountability, is flexible, and promotes maintaining cultural sensitivity. It can be used at any point during a youth's involvement with the juvenile justice system: diversion, alternative to incarceration, probation, and reentry into the community (OJJDP, 2000b). Generally, treatment is short-term, but it can be lengthened if necessary. FFT is also particularly attractive for its cost-effectiveness (OJJDP, 2000b).

Community-Oriented Police Services

Community-Oriented Police Services (COPS) units use police/community involvement to reduce juvenile crime. The focus is on community-related activities rather than on juveniles and families. Police officers use foot patrols, front stations, and community partnerships to increase citizen contact and involve citizens in violence prevention (Eck & Rosenbaum, 1994; Jolin & Moose, 1997).

Studies have found that greater citizen contact increases participation and satisfaction among police and decreases citizens' fear (Cordner, 1994; Sissom, 1996). Routine store checks increase satisfaction levels among community members (Sissom, 1996). Improved relationships between citizens and law enforcement officers create a positive environment for citizen involvement in crime reduction through block watches, crime watches, and similar organized efforts.

EMPIRICALLY BASED INTERVENTIONS

For the purposes of this chapter, intervention is being treated as synonymous with tertiary prevention. Despite good intentions, there is substantial evidence that many interventions of the past have harmed, rather than helped, troubled juveniles (Ellis, Klepper, & Sowers, 1999; Ellis, O'Hara, & Sowers, 2000; Posner, 1994). Fortunately, recent research has identified a number of interventions that are effective for violent juveniles (Borduin, Henggeler, Blaske, & Stein, 1990; Lipsey, 1999; OJJDP, 2000c). In addition, Lipsey (1999) identified some of the critical characteristics of these programs through a meta-analysis of the treatment outcome literature.

Noninstitutionalized Youth

Lipsey (1999) found several variables that have differential effects on outcome. The most important factor was the individual attributes of offenders. Juveniles were more likely to benefit from intervention if their offenses were person-and-property crimes (rather than only property crimes). Treatment was more beneficial to serious offenders than to less serious offenders. The second most critical factor was the type of treatment employed. Specifically, individual counseling, interpersonal skill training, and behavioral programs demonstrated the most positive effects.

Individual Counseling Using Volunteers

Moore (1987) found that, among juveniles receiving individual therapy in aftercare, volunteers were effective. Volunteer counselors were assigned to juvenile offenders when the offenders were considered high-risk or were experiencing difficulties in adjusting. The counseling was in addition to regular probation services. Excluding traffic offenses, juveniles receiving the volunteer counseling reoffended less than those not receiving counseling, and their offenses were less severe.

MST

Multisystemic therapy (MST) is another Blueprint program aimed at reducing recidivism. This program targets juveniles and all their social systems (Henggeler et al., 1992; Borduin et al., 1990). Positive effects, in addition to reduced recidivism, have been noted. Henggeler and colleagues (1999) found improved family functioning and decreases in external (peer) influence. MST has been demonstrated to be effective with violent offenders (Henggeler et al., 1992), sex offenders, and other delinquents (Borduin et al., 1990).

Interpersonal Skills Training

Interpersonal skills programs assist juveniles in developing prosocial behaviors. Some programs target aggressive behavior, but not necessarily other antisocial acts (OJJDP, 2000c). Programs that include social skills training as a component have been effective.

Aggression Replacement Training (ART) is an example of a program that utilizes social skills training as one component of a multifaceted curriculum (Goldstein & Glick, 1994). ART uses a technique known as *skillstreaming* to develop 50 related prosocial behaviors. The anger control component educates youth about the physiological symptoms of anger, the consequences of acting out, and the actions they should take when they become angry.

Victim-Offender Mediation

Victim-Offender Reconciliation Programs (VORPs) provide a service known as Victim-Offender Mediation (VOM; Umbreit, 2000). In a VOM, victims and offenders are presented with an opportunity for structured, face-to-face inter-action. Through a series of meetings, the victims and offenders are encouraged to explore and express their ideas and emotions related to the offense, and to negoti-ate a contract for restitution (Ellis & Sowers, 2000). Victims often gain a sense of control over the implementation of justice, receive restitution, and gain feelings of being safe from revictimization (Umbreit, 2000). Victims are able to ask the of-fender questions, explain how the victimization affected them or their families, and recognize that the offender is a human person, not a monster. Offenders often want to "make things right" with the victim (Umbreit & Coates, 1993).

Outcomes for VOM on recidivism rates have been positive. Compared with court-ordered restitutions, restitution contracts are completed four times as often. Some authors suggest restitution completion rates from 57% to 100% in one year (Nugent, Umbreit, Winamaki, & Paddock, in press; Roy, 1993).

Interventions for Institutionalized Juveniles

Juveniles who are or have been institutionalized are most likely to recidivate and are therefore important recipients of services. This group also includes a high number of violent offenders. Two types of programs demonstrate particular effectiveness in reducing recidivism among institutionalized juveniles: (a) in-terpersonal skill programs (Lipsey, 1999; OJJDP, 2000c) and (b) Intensive Af-tercare Program (IAP).

As discussed in an earlier section, interpersonal skill programs can often be applied, with particular effectiveness, to incarcerated juveniles because of the op-portunities to create a controlled learning environment. Special attention must be given to the transfer and generalization skills, however, because the juvenile will be released into an environment where he or she has not utilized the skills.

The Intensive Aftercare Program (IAP), a model case management program designed by the Department of Justice, specifically manages services for gradu-ates of institutional programs. Because it is by nature a case management inter-vention, it will be discussed in greater detail in the next section.

CASE MANAGEMENT AND THE STRENGTHS PERSPECTIVE

At least two model programs use an intensive case management delivery system to treat juveniles who are either potentially violent or already violent. Those two programs are multisystemic therapy (MST) and the Intensive Aftercare Pro-gram (IAP). MST, discussed earlier, may be used for any level of prevention: primary, secondary, or tertiary.

IAP is designed to help juveniles who are leaving residential treatment to be reintegrated into the community (Altschuler & Armstrong, 1999). IAP services begin before the juvenile is released. When possible, planning involves parents, community agency representatives, and employees of the institution where the juvenile has been incarcerated. IAP is based on the premise that, because incarceration does not prevent recidivism, aftercare must do so. IAP provides counseling, service brokerage, monitoring, surveillance, advocacy, and other interventive services. Interestingly, it closely resembles MST but incorporates a law enforcement perspective.

FUTURE RESEARCH

Many issues concerning chronic and/or violent juvenile offenders remain to be explored. These issues include gender differences, issues involving juveniles of color, and characteristics of effective prevention and intervention strategies.

Research has suggested that females differ from males across multiple dimensions of problem behavior and psychosocial problems (Ellis et al., 2000; Liu & Kaplan, 1999; Rapp & Wodarski, 1998). For example, females have greater empathy and exhibit more internalizing behaviors than males (Glisson, Hemmelgran, & Post, in press). Males are more prone to become delinquent (Liu & Kaplan, 1999; Rapp & Wodarski, 1998). Liu and Kaplan (1999) found that males are more likely to have delinquent friends, resist authority, and hold unconventional values; therefore, they are more probable to engage in illegal activities.

Research samples for violent juvenile offenders have been composed predominantly of males (Lipsey, 1999; Moore, 1987); however, girls are becoming increasingly violent (OJJDP, 1999). In light of growing juvenile female violence, researchers must include more female juveniles. For example, Stone (1998) found that girls who are incarcerated may be harmed more by involvement in the juvenile justice system because the system was designed to treat boys. Ellis et al. (2000) found important treatment-related differences between boys and girls, and discovered many relevant recommendations for treatment in the literature that addressed these differences. As female violent offense increases, the need to understand the phenomenon and its treatment must also increase.

Much prevention and intervention research has used predominantly Caucasian samples (Ellis et al., 1999; Moore, 1987). Yet juveniles of color are disproportionately arrested for and convicted of violent crimes. They also are given more severe sanctions and are overrepresented in residential programs and detention centers (OJJDP, 1999). Research should identify risk and protective factors that are exclusive to or particularly important for juveniles of color. Specialized prevention and intervention programs should be developed and tested. Researchers should also examine decision points in the juvenile justice system to determine what forces drive minority overrepresentation, and to devise methods of addressing those forces.

Ongoing outcome research into prevention and treatment effectiveness is needed. Researchers must learn more about why juveniles become violent, what kinds of juveniles commit violent offenses, and how potentially violent juveniles can be identified. Ultimately, they must use this information to develop and evaluate new, more effective interventions.

CONCLUSION

The phenomenon of juvenile violence is of paramount importance. Although trends are unclear because of the influence of public opinion and related policy reactions, a disturbing portion of the juvenile population is known to engage in violent behavior that inflicts a substantial burden on individuals and on society as a whole.

Many of the risk factors for violent behavior are known and can be addressed through well-conceived interventions. Successful programs have been developed and are now recognized as Blueprint programs by the OJJDP. Much work remains to be done, however, if we are to understand the phenomenon of youth violence, identify those who are likely to engage in violent activities, and determine what kinds of prevention and intervention programs will be effective in addressing chronic youth violence.

REFERENCES

Altschuler, T., & Armstrong, A. (1999). *Reintegration, supervised release and intensive aftercare* (Juvenile Justice Bulletin). Washington, DC: Office of Juvenile Justice and Delinquency Prevention.

Borduin, C. M. (1999). Multisystemic treatment of criminality and violence in adolescents. *Journal of American Academy of Child Adolescent Psychiatry, 38,* 242–249.

Borduin, C. M., Henggeler, S. W., Blaske, D. M., & Stein, L. J. (1990). Multisystemic treatment of adolescent sexual offenders. *International Journal of Offender Therapy and Comparative Criminology,* 105–113.

Botvin, G. J., Mihalic, S. F., & Grotpeter, J. K. (1998). *Blueprints for violence prevention: Life skills training.* Boulder, CO: Center for the Study and Prevention of Violence.

Centers for Disease Control and Prevention. (2000). *Facts about violence among youth and violence in schools.* Available from: www.cdc.gov

Coates, R. B., Miller, A. D., & Ohlin, L. E. (1978). *Diversity in a youth correctional system: Handling delinquents in Massachusetts.* Cambridge, MA: Ballinger.

Cordner, G. W. (1994). Foot patrol without community policing: Law and order in public housing. In D. P. Rosenbaum (Ed.), *The challenge of community policing: Testing the promises* (pp. 182–191). London: Sage.

Dupper, D. R., & Meyer-Adams, N. (in press). Low-level violence: A neglected aspect of school culture. *Urban Education.*

Eck, J. E., & Rosenbaum, D. P. (1994). The new police order: Effectiveness, equity, and efficiency in community policing. In D. P. Rosenbaum (Ed.), *The challenge of community policing* (pp. 3–23). London: Sage.

Ellis, R. A. (1998). Filling the prevention gap: Multi-factor, multi-system, multi-level intervention. *Journal of Primary Prevention, 19,* 57–71.

Ellis, R. A., Klepper, T. D., & Sowers, K. M. (1999). Similarity, diversity, and cultural sensitivity: Considerations for intervention with juveniles of African descent. *Journal for Juvenile Justice and Detention Services, 14*(2), 28–45.

Ellis, R. A., O'Hara, M., & Sowers, K. M. (2000). Profile-based intervention: Developing gender-sensitive treatment for adolescent substance abusers. *Research on Social Work Practice, 10*(3), 327–347.

Ellis, R. A., & Sowers, K. M. (2000). *Juvenile justice practice: A cross-disciplinary approach to intervention.* Pacific Grove, CA: Brooks Cole/Wadsworth.

Glisson, C. (2000). Organizational climate and culture. In R. J. Pattie (Ed.), *The handbook of social welfare management.* Thousand Oaks, CA: Sage.

Glisson, C., & Hemmelgran, A. (1998). The effects of organizational climate and interorganizational coordination on the quality and outcomes of children's service systems. *Child Abuse and Neglect, 22*(5), 401–421.

Glisson, C., Hemmelgran, A. L., & Post, J. A. (in press). The shortform assessment for children (SAC): An assessment and outcome measure for child welfare and juvenile justice. *Research on Social Work Practice.*

Goldstein, A P., & Glick, B. (1994). *The prosocial gang: Implementing aggression replacement training.* Thousand Oaks, CA: Sage.

Henggeler, S. W., Melton, G. B., & Smith, L. A. (1992). Family preservation using multisystemic therapy: An effective alternative to increasing serious juvenile offenders. *Journal of Consulting and Clinical Psychology, 60*(6), 953–961.

Henggeler, S. W., Rowland, M. E., Randall, J., Ward, D. M., Pickrel, S. G., Cunningham, P. B., et al. (1999). Home-based multisystemic therapy as an alternative to the hospitalization of youths in psychiatric crisis: Clinical outcomes. *Journal of American Academy of Child and Adolescent Psychiatry, 38*(11), 1131–1339.

Jolin, A., & Moose, C. A. (1997). Evaluating a domestic violence program in a community policing environment: Research implementation issues. *Crime and Delinquency, 43*(3), 279–297.

Lipsey, M. W. (1999). Can intervention rehabilitate serious delinquents? *Annals of the American Academy of Political and Social Science, 564,* 142–166.

Liu, X., & Kaplan, H. B. (1999). Explaining the gender difference in adolescent delinquent behavior: A longitudinal test of mediating mechanisms. *Criminology, 37*(1), 195–214.

Moore, R. H. (1987). Effectiveness of citizen volunteers functioning as counselors for high-risk young male offenders. *Psychological Reports, 61,* 823–830.

Morehouse, E., & Tobler, N. S. (2000). Preventing and reducing substance use among institutionalized adolescents. *Adolescence, 35*(137), 1–28.

Niemeyer, M., & Shichor, D. (1996). A preliminary study of a large victim/offender reconciliation program on reoffense. *Research on Social Work Practice, 6*(2), 155–178.

Nugent, W. R., Umbreit, M. S., Winamaki, L., & Paddock, J. (in press). *Participation in victim-offender mediation and the prevalence and severity of subsequent delinquent behavior.*

Office of Juvenile Justice and Delinquency Prevention. (1994). *Juvenile intensive supervision: Planning guide.* Washington, DC: Author.

Office of Juvenile Justice and Delinquency Prevention (1999). *Juvenile offenders and victims: 1997 update on violence* [Online]. Available from: www.ojjdp.ncjrs.org

Office of Juvenile Justice and Delinquency Prevention. (1999, December). *Juvenile Justice Bulletin: Juvenile arrests 1998* [Online]. Available from: www.ojjpd.ncjrs.org

Office of Juvenile Justice and Delinquency Prevention. (2000a, April). *Juvenile offenders and victims: 1999 national summery* [Online]. Available from: www.ojjpd.ncjrs.org

Office of Juvenile Justice and Delinquency Prevention. (2000b, April). *Juvenile Justice Bulletin: Prevention of serious and violent juvenile offending* [Online]. Available from: www.ojjdp.ncjrs.org

Office of Juvenile Justice and Delinquency Prevention (2000c, April). *Juvenile Justice Bulletin: Effective intervention for serious juvenile offenders* [Online]. Available from: www.ojjpd.ncjrs.org

Olweus, D., Limber, S., & Mihalic, S. F. (1999). *Blueprints for violence prevention: Bullying Prevention Program.* Boulder, CO: Center for the Study and Prevention of Violence.

Pellegrini, A. D. (1998). Bullies and victims in school: A review and call for research. *Journal of Applied Developmental Psychology, 19*(2), 165–176.

Pentz, M. A., Mihalic, S. F., & Grotpeter, J. K. (1997). *Blueprints for violence prevention: The Midwestern Prevention Project.* Boulder, CO: Center for the Study and Prevention of Violence.

Posner, M. (1994, May/June). Research raises troubling questions about violence prevention programs: There's no evidence that they reduce serious violence and growing concern that the design of many school-based programs is too simplistic. *Harvard Education Letter, 10*(3).

Potter, R. H., & Krider, J. E. (2000). Teaching about violence prevention: A bridge between public health and criminal justice educators. *Journal of Criminal Justice Education, 11*(2), 339–351.

Rapp, L., & Wodarski, J. (1998). Conduct disorder. In B. A. Thyer & J. S. Wodarski (Eds.), *Handbook of empirical social work practice* (pp. 75–90). New York: Wiley.

Roberts, A. R., & Brownell, P. (1999). A century of forensic social work: Bridging the past to the present. *Social Work, 44*(4), 359–369.

Roy, S. (1993). Two Types of juvenile restitution programs in two midwestern counties: A comparative study. *Federal Probation, 57*(4), 48–53.

Sherman, L. W., Gottfredson, D. C., MacKenzie, D. L., Eck, J., Router, P., & Bushway, S. D. (1997). Preventing crime: What works, What doesn't, What's promising. (Research Report). Washington, DC: Office of Juvenile Justice and Delinquency Prevention.

Sissom, K. (1996, December). Community-oriented policing means business. *FBI Law Enforcement Bulletin, 10*–14.

Steffensmeier, D., Ulmer, J., & Kramer, J. (1998). The interaction of race, gender, and age in criminal sentencing: The punishment cost of being young, black and male. *Criminology, 36*(4), 763–790.

Stone, S. S. (1998, May). Changing nature of juvenile offenders. *Juvenile Justice Journal* [Online]. Available from: www.ojjdp.ncjrs.org

Umbreit, M. S. (2000). *The handbook of victim offender mediation: An essential guide to practice and research.* San Francisco: Jossey-Bass.

Umbreit, M. S., & Coates, R. B. (1993). Cross-site analysis of victim-offender mediation in four states. *Crime and Delinquency, 39*(4), 565–585.

University of Colorado. (2001). *Blueprints for violence prevention: Model program selection criteria* [Online]. Available from: www.colorado.edu/cspv/blueprints/about/criteria.htm

Wiebush, R., Baird, C., Krisberg, B., & Onek, D. (1995). Risk assessment and classification for serious, violent, and chronic juvenile offenders. In J. Howell, B. Krisberg, J. D. Hawkins, & J. Wilson (Eds.), *A sourcebook: Serious, violent, and chronic juvenile offenders* (pp. 171–212). Thousand Oaks, CA: Sage.

SECTION III

School Violence

Chapter 12

SCHOOL BULLYING: AN OVERVIEW

GORDON MACNEIL

INTRODUCTION

Mark Twain commented, "Thunder is good, thunder is impressive; but it is lightning that does the work" (M. Twain, unpublished letter, August 28, 1908). Similarly, in the realm of school violence, catastrophic events such as the killings in Littleton, Colorado, garner media attention, but pernicious daily acts of abuse and violence cause the majority of harm in American schools (Fitzpatrick, 1999; Furlong & Morrison, 2000). Bullying rarely results in death, but thousands of students in this country are victims of bullying every day (Hazler, 1996). In addition to physical injury, the effects of bullying can include chronic absenteeism, low self-esteem, reduced academic performance, increased anxiety, loneliness and social isolation, a decision to drop out of school, and suicide (Hazler, 1996; Roberts & Coursol, 1996). Thus, the number of youths affected by bullying, and by the numerous adverse effects it can produce in victims, indicates that it is a substantial problem.

Bullying is typically perpetrated by stronger individuals or groups against weaker, isolated individuals—often, while other students witness the interaction. It festers in environments where students do not raise an alarm about their plight, but is drastically reduced in schools where the ethos is for zero tolerance of bullying behaviors. No single intervention is effective, but a combination of prevention programs and swift, assertive responses to incidents of victimization can drastically reduce incidents of bullying (Hazler, 1996; Rigby, 1996; Tattum & Herbert, 1997).

CURRENT TRENDS AND ISSUES

Bullying is pervasive throughout the world. It exists in nearly all schools in America (Furlong & Morrison, 2000). Rural, suburban, and city students report very similar rates of victimization from bullying. Approximately 50% of students report being bullied, and 65% admit to witnessing bullying (Gutscher, 1993; Hazler, Hoover, & Oliver, 1992); yet teachers report that only about 15% of their students are victimized by bullies (Barone, 1997).

The general population of America has become sensitized to violence in schools. However, much of the population is only now acknowledging the connection between bullying behaviors and violent events such as those that occurred in Littleton, Colorado. The past decade has shown, only too well, the relationship between those who are bullied and their potential to become violent retaliators. There is also evidence to suggest a link between name-calling and violent behavior (Greenbaum, 1987). Name-calling accounted for 4% of the gun violence in American schools from 1986 to 1990 (Glazer, 1992). The lighthearted image presented in movies such as *The Revenge of the Nerds* has given way to the macabre vengeful images of *The Basketball Diaries*. Consequently, most school systems are taking steps to address bullying behaviors as preemptive measures to reduce violence in schools (see Crews & Counts, 1997; Dorn, 2000).

Bullying behaviors result from multiple causal factors, so no simple solution for addressing the problem is likely (Dorn, 2000; Hazler, 1996; Rigby, 1996; Tolan & Guerra, 1994). The most successful efforts involve mobilizing entire school (and community) environments to create safer schools (see Barone, 1997; Olweus, 1978; Rigby, 1996; Tattum & Herbert, 1997). Establishing a positive environment that is not tolerant of bullying behaviors has longer-lasting effects than efforts that rely on identified personnel to address the problem (see Hazler, 1996; Rigby, 1996; Sullivan, 2000; Tattum & Herbert, 1993, 1997).

IDENTIFICATION, CLASSIFICATION, AND PREDICTION

Bullying is commonly defined as repeatedly harming another person or persons. This can be done by physical attack or by hurting another's feelings through words, actions, or social exclusion. Bullying may be done by one person or by a group. It is an unfair match; the bully is physically, verbally, and/or socially stronger than the victim (Hazler, 1996; Olweus, 1993). *School* bullying adds another dimension. The bullying behaviors take place on the school grounds or while the participants are en route to or from school, or they are initiated because of school-related relationships (Furlong & Morrison, 2000). The necessary condition of the behavior's being repeated is particularly trouble-some because it reinforces the vulnerability of the victim. A lack of involvement by bystanders often serves to enflame the bully's actions and increase the isolation and humiliation of the victim (Hazler, 1996).

Teasing is the most common form of bullying behavior (Hazler, Hoover, & Oliver, 1991). Although many people (including many teachers) think that teasing is harmless, or at least not hurtful, victims are equally traumatized whether the bullying behavior that victimizes them is physical or verbal (Hoover, Oliver, & Hazler, 1992).

Students of all ages are victimized, but most of the bullying occurs from sixth to ninth grades—the years of pubertal onset and social development as youths begin interacting more seriously with members of the opposite sex (Hazler et al., 1991). Some studies have found nearly equal distribution between the sexes. Females typically use social coercion, and males use physical means to victimize their targets (Hazler et al., 1992).

Characteristics of Bullies

Bullies tend to have poor self-concepts and have limited feelings of being loved or important to significant persons in their lives. Abuse—verbal, physical, and emotional—is common in the families of aggressive youths. Bullies at school are frequently victims at home (Hunt, 1993; Mendler, 1992). Aggression is transmitted from the family to the child, and flows through generations (Hunt, 1993).

A common denominator among bullies appears to be their inclination to see hostile intent in the actions of others (Dodge, Murphy, & Buchsbaum, 1984). Unlike other children, they tend to be less likely to recognize prosocial responses to problematic situations, so they see no alternatives to aggression (Dodge et al., 1984; Greenbaum, 1987).

Bullies, in general, have little empathy for their victims (Besag, 1989), so they seldom express remorse for their actions. Compared to other children, bullies are quicker to anger and quicker to use force to resolve their problems, so they are more likely to hurt others without regret (Edmondson, 1988). Bullies differ from basically aggressive children because they pick their targets more selectively (Hazler, 1996).

Male bullies tend to be physically mature, dominant males (Olweus, 1978). They are generally athletic but are not necessarily involved in organized athletics. Others assume that the bully could be an athlete if he wanted. Female bullies may be strong, but they are just as likely to be small. Their bullying, commonly done verbally, focuses on social dominance rather than physical dominance (Hazler, 1996).

Bullies may or may not have problems with academics, but they tend to have a less positive attitude toward schoolwork, despite their academic abilities (Lagerspetz, Bjoerkquist, Berts, & King, 1982). It is realistic to think that a good deal of their intellectual energy is spent planning and carrying out bullying activities rather than focusing on schoolwork. Despite this deviation, bullies place importance on remaining in school because that is where their victims are found, and victimizing others is easier in this setting.

The future prospects for bullies are problematic; they often carry their aggressive behavior patterns into adulthood. Eron, Huesmann, Dubow, Romanoff, and Yarmel (1987) found that they are more likely than their peers to abuse their spouses, and they tend to punish their children more harshly. This often results in additional generations of bullies. In fact, 8-year-old bullies have a 1-in-4 chance of having a criminal record by their thirtieth birthday, as compared with a 1-in-20 chance for their peers.

Characteristics of Victims

Victims tend to be physically weak and either overweight or underweight (Hazler, 1996). They tend to have difficulty relating to peers in general (not just bullies), and their social skills are poor or ineffective (Besag, 1989). They are frequently less popular than others (Smith, 1991), and this commonly leads to their being isolated (Greenbaum, 1989). Victims tend to have poor coordination (Olweus, 1978). They are typically smaller and weaker, and have lower energy levels and lower pain tolerances than other students (Besag, 1989). The victims of bullying are generally younger than their bullies (Besag, 1989; Jenson & Howard, 1999; Olweus, 1978).

Being victimized has painful social, emotional, and academic consequences. Victims of name-calling may experience embarrassment, rejection, and anxiety. Some may retaliate with names of their own, and some may withdraw. Others may develop a tough facade, or react with tears. Many may experience a decline in academic performance (Hazler et al., 1992).

Where Bullying Occurs

Bullying happens in all areas of a school. Bullying in classrooms is generally subtle, due to the presence of the teacher, but it occurs there nevertheless. Most bullying takes place in areas of the school where supervision is limited: the lunchroom, the playground, hallways, and restrooms (Astor, Pitner, & Duncan, 1996). Additionally, bullying takes place off-campus, when students are traveling to or from their homes. During these times, students are generally thought to be under the legal care of the school, and any bullying is, de facto, a school problem (Furlong & Morrison, 2000).

PREVENTION PROGRAMS

In recent years, minors have increasingly used weapons in their attempts to resolve interpersonal disputes (see Furlong & Morrison, 2000, for a summary of pertinent literature). Many school systems have instituted harsh measures to reduce the number of weapons in their institutions, and schools generally serve as a barrier to weapon and gun possession. Higher rates of weapon possession occur outside of schools than in schools (Kann et al., 1998). Efforts that emphasize law enforcement strategies for prevention of school violence tend to promote "us versus them" attitudes among students and authorities. Efforts that rely on having all members of the school community collectively working toward a safer environment tend to promote a joint ownership of the outcomes (Furlong & Morrison, 2000).

Two strategies of antibullying prevention warrant mention before a specific plan is presented here. The first strategy suggests that individuals who are sufficiently engaged and challenged in school have little need to victimize others. In other words, if a student feels good about his or her own educational progress, there will be little need to misbehave with others. This goal cannot be met by all students all of the time, but it does suggest that paying attention to the emotional needs of all students could lessen the likelihood of aggressive misbehavior (Furlong & Morrison, 2000; Morrison, Furlong, & Morrison, 1994; Rigby, 1996).

The second prevention strategy suggests that, in order for a crime (or aggressive act) to occur, the following elements must be present: a law or school policy, a perpetrator, a targeted victim, and a suitable *place* for the act to occur. Without a location in which all of these intersect, no crime can occur. Therefore, reducing the number of places that are potentially viable for aggressive acts serves as a prevention strategy (Quarles, 1993). Specific goals are: making access to the target too difficult or time-consuming; increasing the likelihood of detection by reducing the amount of hiding places; making successful escape difficult by reducing viable escape routes and increasing observation opportunities (O'Block, 1991). Although it is difficult to alter the architecture of a school's physical plant, it is possible to minimize the potential for bullying by increasing supervision and setting precedents for reacting to incidents in assertive and professional ways.

Although successful antibullying prevention plans have been implemented in other parts of the world for almost three decades, they have been introduced to the United States only within the past 15 years or so (Hazler, 1996; Olweus,

1978). A number of specific models have emerged, but most share the following elements:

- The planning stage includes as many stakeholders as possible.
- The work group develops an antibullying philosophy to which all constituents agree.
- The philosophy is translated into a policy to which all constituents agree. (Common elements of an antibullying policy are listed in Table 12.1.)
- The policy provides clear definitions of behavioral expectations that identify/define the culture of the school.
- Programs are developed to introduce and promote the ongoing maintenance of the policy. These should target the silent majority of students, asking them to: stand up to bullies, get adult help, and reach out in friendship to peers who are excluded. The goals of this component are: to build peer pressure against bullying, to stop copycat bullying, and to increase support for victims.
- Performance that fulfills the behavioral expectations is rewarded by an ongoing recognition system.
- Misbehavior results in corrections. Problem behaviors are not ignored or rewarded. Consequences are predictable, inevitable, immediate, and escalating, and are based on uniform expectations for all. Inconsistent enforcement makes the problem worse.
- Information concerning student behavior is collected and analyzed in an ongoing manner (Horner & Sugai, 2000; Olweus, Limber, & Mihalic, 1999; Rigby, 1996; Sullivan, 2000; Tattum & Herbert, 1993).

Table 12.1 Common Elements of an Antibullying Policy

1. The school/administration's position on bullying.
2. A definition of bullying, with examples of bullying behaviors.
3. The rights of children regarding bullying.
4. Responsibilities of students, parents, and school staff who witness bullying or receive verbal reports of bullying.
5. What the school/administration will do to address the problem of bullying.
6. What the school/administration will do to evaluate the effects of the policy.

Source: Adapted from K. Rigby, 1996. *Bullying in schools: And what to do about it.* Melbourne, Victoria, Australia: ACER.

After a policy has been established, it must be clearly communicated to the students and parents. The old truism that actions speak louder than words holds in this situation; students (bullies, victims, and bystanders) will know, from the actions of the school personnel, how cohesive they are in enforcing antibullying policies. A positive environment is created when the actions of the adults create a safe school (Hoover & Hazler, 1991; Shakeshaft et al., 1997).

How adults in positions of authority respond to reports of victimization will impact on future reports from students. If students feel unsupported or betrayed by these adults, they will be unwilling to report further incidents of bullying. If adult responses do not solve the problem, they encourage further victimization by the bullies. The victim is then violated twice: once by a bully and once by the system that is supposed to be protective (see Elliott & Tolan, 1999; Epp & Watkinson, 1997; Rigby, 1996; Roberts & Coursol, 1996; Shakeshaft et al., 1997; Tattum & Herbert, 1993).

Additional prevention measures include teaching problem-solving or conflict-resolution skills, and presenting bullying-awareness and assertiveness-training programs. These prevention programs can lessen the impact of the inevitable incidents of bullying, but only if they are ongoing rather than short-term (Hoover & Oliver, 1996; Olweus, 1993). Only when the programs are infused into the curriculum can they sustain their effectiveness (Flannery & Huff, 1999).

INTERVENTIONS

Our culture often seeks to reduce social problems to simplistic levels and then apply simplistic interventions to them. These interventions typically prove unsuccessful or inadequate. As Hoagwood indicates: "Eliminating youth violence will require stepping outside the narrowing and popularized frameworks that provide unidimensional and generally individualized explanations and, instead, thinking deeply about the transactional meaning of youth violence in a violent society" (Hoagwood, 2000). This work is in its infancy; thus, much of the literature on youth violence (and on bullying in particular) reflects the simplistic notion that individual interventions produce positive outcomes. This is simply not the case.

There is no simple or single approach to maintaining a safe school. Efforts ranging from additional security officers, metal detectors, and video cameras to threat-assessment consultants and software programs to track crime are available to address school violence problems (Dorn, 2000). However, overlooking the complexity of school violence problems and the multidimensional factors that create these problems is likely to dissatisfy those who desire successful prevention and intervention outcomes (Dorn, 2000; Hoagwood, 2000; Wasserman & Miller, 1998). For instance, weapons are tools by which violence is inflicted, but their absence does not eliminate the threat of violence.

Interventions that have met with the greatest success are multifaceted and target multiple elements of the problem (Hazler, 1996; Hoover & Oliver, 1996; Olweus, 1993). The model identified in the preceding section often serves as the basis of ongoing intervention for many schools. It provides a plan for schoolwide intervention, to which classroom-based components and individual-based components are added. These latter two intervention components should provide discipline and counseling for the perpetrator and support for the victim (Hazler, 1996; Olweus, 1993; Olweus et al., 1999).

Discipline and therapy are related to one another, but they are separate issues and should not be performed by the same people (Hazler, 1996). Three basic tasks are necessary in an intervention program: (a) recognition of the problem, (b) enforcement of school or class policies, and (c) counseling. Everyone in the school should perform the recognition task. Minor transgressions can be handled by teachers, but most problems are best resolved when the different tasks are performed by separate people. Role confusion and distrust result when a single person is charged with multiple tasks (Hazler, 1996). Fortunately, teachers, administrators, and counselors are trained to perform specific tasks in this process.

An important element of successful interventions is the elimination of "bystanding"—observing bullying behaviors without attempting to stop them. In schools where bullying is not tolerated, students who stand by as another is harmed are seen as facilitating the problem and are admonished for their inaction (Olweus, 1993; Rigby, 1996; Sullivan, 2000). It is crucial that bystanding by teachers not be permitted. By ignoring name-calling, shoving, fighting, harassment, and psychological terrorism, teachers educate students that these behaviors are tolerated by society (Epp & Watkinson, 1997; Olweus, 1993).

Interventions Targeting the Bully

For most people, a first inclination when dealing with bullies is to give them a taste of their own medicine. However, this response is sure to lead to resentments and reprisals—exactly the opposites of the desired response. Thus, although punitive measures must be introduced to the extent necessary to maintain the safety of others, the greater need is to help the perpetrator understand why these behaviors are unacceptable, and help the individual to develop alternative behaviors. Bullying is, by definition, a repetitive behavior; therefore, its pattern, rather than a specific incident, should be addressed. Responding to bullying in a nonpunitive way is contingent on the spirit of the school and the cooperation of parents of the participants (Masheder, 1998). One should attempt to avoid humiliating the perpetrator because this will likely lead to emotion-driven responses rather than thoughtful ones (Masheder, 1998). It is often useful to minimize public scrutiny and defensiveness by addressing the problem one-on-one with an appropriate adult, in a setting other than the classroom.

Bullies often come from homes where there is little nurturing and affection, and where they may be subjected to harsh physical discipline, regardless of their age. Thus, although much of bullies' behavior may be related to their home life, tact and care must be taken when informing a bully's parents about their child's behavior (Hazler, 1996; Tattum & Herbert, 1997). Attempts to address parent-child interactions should be based on the child's in-school behaviors and should be offered under the auspices of the school's social worker.

Goldstein suggests that many therapeutic failures can be attributed to a poor match of a model of intervention to a client (in this case, the bully). He contends that most youths from middle-class backgrounds are taught to be introspective about their misbehaviors. For instance, the parent might respond to hair-pulling misbehavior by asking, "Why did you do that? How do you think that makes Betty feel? You're old enough to not need to do that." Youths from low-income homes are more likely to be reared with a model that focuses on outcomes based on authority rather than self-control. Thus, in response to the hair-pulling behavior, the parent slaps the child and tells him to stop the misbehavior (Goldstein, 1999). Children raised with the latter model of parenting are more likely to benefit from prescriptive models of intervention that focus on training youth to be competent in interpersonal interactions. Goldstein's Prepare Curriculum is an example of this model (Goldstein, 1989).

The Prepare Curriculum includes components that provide social skills training (skillstreaming), anger control training, moral reasoning training, problem-solving training, empathy training, situational perception training, cooperation training, recruiting of supportive models, and an understanding and use of group process modules (Goldstein, 1989). The first three modules serve as the core for the program. Youths are taught appropriate social skills through a training program in which six groupings of skills are introduced. Through a role-playing and performance-feedback process, the skills are mastered. The youths are taught to control their anger by identifying their personal physiological and psychological triggers and developing new ways to respond to those triggers. The moral reasoning element is taught by introducing a series of moral dilemmas in group sessions during which possible responses to the dilemmas are discussed. Others have suggested that this kind of curriculum needs to be complemented by education that stresses acknowledging actions, and restitution, as consequences for the misbehavior (Olweus, 1993; Olweus et al., 1999). Lax responses such as serious talks, requests to apologize, asking why, pleading, and expressions of frustration are unlikely to help (Wheeler, 1999).

Various forms of the "No Blame Approach" have become popular in Great Britain and Australia (Rigby, 1996; Sullivan, 2000). This approach is based on the premise that arousing empathy in the bullies will cause them to stop mistreating others. The approach (which can be used with groups as well as individuals) does not excuse the misbehavior, but follows the reasoning that, in order for the change within the bully to occur, the threat of blame and punishment needs to be removed. When empathy has been established, responsible positive behaviors can be substituted for negative behaviors, and this will resolve the problem. Obviously, this process requires monitoring and follow-up!

The seven steps of the No Blame Approach are: (1) interview the victim to elicit the individual's feelings; (2) convene a group meeting of the bullies and the bystanders; (3) communicate to the group how the victim feels; (4) attribute to the group the responsibility for improving the victim's situation; (5) elicit helpful suggestions; (6) hand over, to the group, the responsibility to act; (7) hold follow-up meetings with participants (the victim and individual members of the bullying faction) (Robinson & Maines, 1997).

The No Blame Approach is dependent on the interpersonal skills of the adult leading the sessions, and it has been more effective with younger than with older students (Rigby, 1996). Similar models (the Method of Shared Concern and the Pikas model of Shared Concern) have been developed that work well with older youth (see Sullivan, 2000). A primary difference in these models is that they emphasize the importance of seeing the perpetrators prior to the victim, to minimize the possibility that the victim may be viewed as "snitching" or invoking the intervention.

Interventions Targeting the Victim

Following the basic tenets of crisis intervention to ensure the safety of the victim should be the first step toward intervention with the victim (Roberts & Coursol, 1996). In addition to determining the physical injury of the victim, notification (perhaps mandatory) of authorities may be warranted. If this is the case, the limits of confidentiality should be explained to the victim (Roberts & Coursol, 1996).

Victims of bullying need two kinds of support. The first kind, psychological support, allows the student to have his or her perceptions of the incident(s), and the emotions related to the event, heard. The second form of support includes a measure of psychological support but also seeks to facilitate skill development so that the individual can better respond to bullying behaviors he or she may encounter in the future (Rigby, 1996). To respond to bullying incidents, potential victims need to know (a) how to make realistic appraisals of situations in which they may be hurt; (b) how to respond in an assertive (but not aggressive) manner; (c) how to enlist the help of others, and (d) how to leave a dangerous situation (Rigby, 1996).

Knowledge of the aforementioned skills is necessary but not sufficient. The child must be able to perform these tasks in the heat of tense situations. One-on-one counseling can provide this training, but many think it is more effective to conduct this training in small homogeneous groups of youths who are experiencing similar difficulties or are at risk for these problems (Rigby, 1996; Roberts & Coursol, 1996; Sullivan, 2000).

Skills groups for victimized children often focus on the following skills: how to be assertive (including "how to say *no*"); how to respond unemotionally to name-calling; how to get away from dangerous situations; and how to call for help (Sharp & Cowie, 1994). It is important to have the skills taught through an experiential format in which the skills are demonstrated. The children can then replicate the skill until they are proficient and comfortable doing it (Masheder, 1998; Rigby, 1996). Social skills training models have been widely used. The basic process of these models has been elaborated elsewhere—see LeCroy, Daley, & Milligan (1999), or Goldstein (1989), for example—so the steps of the process will not be specified here. These models provide a structure and process for conducting social skills training with this population.

Some have argued that self-defense training or other physical conditioning can bolster youths' self-esteem and provide individuals with skills for more assertively responding to bullying (Sullivan, 2000). However, because most victims of school bullies are not particularly athletic, compared with their (male) counterparts, the self-defense training must be well learned if it is to be useful (Masheder, 1998). Unless youths are dedicated to learning self-defense, it is probably wise to encourage them to employ other strategies to address the problem.

Two interventions for victims of school bullies do not appear to be successful when used alone. In the first, the victim is asked to solve the problem by being assertive, ignoring the bully, or pretending to not be affected by the bully. This approach places the responsibility for stopping the misbehavior on the victim. It teaches the victim that he or she needs to resolve problems without the assistance of authorities. Given that most victims are younger and weaker than their victimizer(s), this is not a reasonable demand. The second misguided intervention is whole-population education, where sensitivity training or alternatives to aggression are taught, to build empathy. The training may raise the empathy level of the general student body, but the message is frequently missed by bullies. They become bored or deny their own behavior because they lack self-awareness (Olweus et al., 1999). Both of these interventions could contribute toward positive outcomes for both bullies and victims, but only when they are components of more comprehensive intervention packages.

CONCLUSION

School bullying is a significant problem in American schools. It encompasses both physical and psychological intimidation and may have both short- and long-term effects. Both the perpetrator and the victim are likely to be social outcasts, and both deserve the attention of adults, in order to end the bullying behaviors. Schools that institute strong, sustained prevention programs coupled with zero-tolerance ex post facto interventions have had good success in reducing bullying problems. Schools that have taken a less comprehensive approach (often focusing only on the punitive aspects of intervention) have had minimal success. When a school ethos of safety and active participation by all school citizens is created to eliminate bullying, it appears to produce the greatest impact on all members of the school environment.

REFERENCES

Astor, R. A., Pitner, R. O., & Duncan, B. E. (1996). Ecological approaches to mental health consultation with teachers on issues related to youth and school violence. *Journal of Negro Education, 65*(3), 336–355.

Barone, F. J. (1997, September). Bullying in school: It doesn't have to happen. *Phi Delta Kappan, 78*(1), 80–83.

Besag, V. (1989). *Bullies and victims in schools: A guide to understanding and management.* London: Oxford University Press.

Crews, G. A., & Counts, M. R. (1997). *The evolution of school disturbance in America: Colonial times to modern day.* Westport, CT: Praeger.

Dodge, K. A., Murphy, R. R., & Buchsbaum, K. (1984). The assessment of intention-cue detection skills in children: Implications for developmental psychopathology. *Child Development, 55,* 163–173.

Dorn, M. (2000, July). No one answer. *School Planning and Management,* 18.

Edmondson, D. (1988, April). Bullies. *Parents,* 100–106.

Elliott, D. S., & Tolan, P. H. (1999). Youth violence prevention, intervention, and social policy. In D. J. Flannery & C. R. Huff (Eds.), *Youth violence: Prevention, intervention, and social policy.* Washington DC: American Psychiatric Press.

Epp, J. R., & Watkinson, A. M. (Eds.). (1997). *Systemic violence in education: Promise broken.* Albany: State University of New York Press.

Eron, L. D., Huesmann, L. R., Dubow, E., Romanoff, R., & Yarmel, P. W. (1987). Aggression and its correlates over 22 years. In D. H. Crowell, I. M. Evans, & C. R. O'Donnell (Eds.), *Childhood aggression and violence* (pp. 249–262). New York: Plenum Press.

Fitzpatrick, K. M. (1999). Violent victimization among America's school children. *Journal of Interpersonal Violence, 14*(10), 1055–1069.

Flannery, D. J., & Huff, C. R. (1999). Implications for prevention, intervention, and social policy with violent youth. In D. J. Flannery & C. R. Huff (Eds.), *Youth violence: Prevention, intervention, and social policy* (pp. 293–306). Washington, DC: American Psychiatric Press.

Furlong, M., & Morrison, G. (2000). The school in school violence: Definitions and facts. *Journal of Emotional and Behavioral Disorders, 8*(2), 71–85.

Glazer, S. (1992, September). Violence in schools. *Congressional Quarterly Researcher, 4,* 787–803.

Goldstein, A. P. (1999). Teaching prosocial behavior to antisocial youth. In D. J. Flannery & C. R. Huff (Eds.), *Youth violence: Prevention, intervention, and social policy* (pp. 253–274). Washington, DC: American Psychiatric Press.

Goldstein, A. P. (1989). *The prepare curriculum.* Champaign, IL: Research Press.

Greenbaum, S. (1987). What can we do about schoolyard bullying? *Principal, 67,* 21–24.

Gutscher, C. (1993, Fall). Violence in schools: Death threat for reform? *America's Agenda, 10.*

Hazler, R. J. (1996). *Breaking the cycle of violence: Interventions for bullying and victimization.* Washington, DC: Accelerated Development.

Hazler, R. J., Hoover, J. H., & Oliver, R. (1991). Student perceptions of victimization by bullies in school. *Journal of Humanistic Education and Development, 29,* 143–150.

Hazler, R. J., Hoover, J. H., & Oliver, R. (1992). What kids say about bullying. *Executive Educator, 11,* 20–22.

Hoagwood, K. (2000, Summer). Research on youth violence: Progress by replacement, not addition. *Journal of Emotional and Behavioral Disorders, 8*(2), 67.

Hoover, J., & Hazler, R. J. (1991, February). Bullies and victims. *Elementary School Guidance and Counseling, 25,* 212–219.

Hoover, J. H., & Oliver, R. (1996). *The Bullying Prevention Handbook: A guide for principals, teachers, and counselors.* Bloomington, IN: National Education Service.

Hoover, J. H., Oliver, R., & Hazler, R. J. (1992). Bullying: Perceptions of adolescent victims in the Midwestern, U.S.A. *School Psychology International, 13,* 5–16.

Horner, R. H., & Sugai, G. (2000, Fall). School-wide behavior support. *Journal of Positive Behavior Interventions, 2*(4), 231.

Hunt, R. (1993). Neurobiological patterns of aggression. *Journal of Emotional and Behavioral Problems, 1,* 14–19.

Jenson, J. M., & Howard, M. O. (1999). Prevalence and patterns of youth violence. In J. M. Jenson & M. O. Howard (Eds.), *Youth violence: Current research and recent practice innovations* (pp. 3–18). Washington, DC: National Association of Social Workers.

Kann, L, Kinchen, S. A., Williams, B. I., Ross, J. G., Lowry, R., Hill, C. V., et al. (1998). Youth risk behavior surveillance–United States, 1997. *Journal of School Health, 68,* 355–369.

Lagerspetz, K. M., Bjoerkquist, K., Berts, M., & King, E. (1982). Group aggression among school children in three schools. *Scandinavian Journal of Psychology, 23*(1), 45–52.

LeCroy, C. W., Daley, J. M., & Milligan, K. B. (1999). Social skills for the twenty-first century. In R. Constable, S. McDonald, & J. P. Flynn (Eds.), *School social work: Practice, policy, and research perspectives* (pp. 376–390). Chicago: Lyceum.

Masheder, M. (1998). *Freedom from bullying.* Rendlesham, England: Green Print.

Mendler, A. N. (1992). *What do I do when—? How to achieve discipline with dignity in the classroom.* Bloomington, IN: National Educational Service.

Morrison, G. M., Furlong, M. J., & Morrison, R. L. (1994). From school violence to school safety: Reframing the issue for school psychologists. *School Psychology Review, 23,* 236–256.

O'Block, R. L. (1991). *Security and crime prevention* (2nd ed.). Boston: Butterworth.

Olweus, D. (1978). *Aggression in the schools: Bullies and whipping boys.* New York: Wiley.

Olweus, D. (1993). *Bullying at school: What we know and what we can do.* London: Blackwell.

Olweus, D., Limber, S., & Mihalic, S. F. (1999). Bullying Prevention Program. In D. S. Elliott (Series Ed.), *Blueprints for violence prevention* (Vol. 9). Boulder: University of Colorado, Center for the Study and Prevention of Violence.

Quarles, C. L. (1993). *Staying safe at school.* Thousand Oaks, CA: Sage.

Rigby, K. (1996). *Bullying in schools: And what to do about it.* Melbourne, Victoria, Australia: ACER.

Roberts, W. B., & Coursol, D. H. (1996). Strategies for intervention with childhood and adolescent victims of bullying, teasing, and intimidation in school settings. *Elementary School Guidance and Counseling, 30,* 204–212.

Robinson, G., & Maines, G. (1997). *Crying for help: The no-blame approach to bullying.* Bristol, England: Lucky Duck.

Shakeshaft, C., Mandel, L., Johnson, Y. M., Sawyer, J., Hergenrother, M. A., & Barber, E. (1997). Boys call me cow. *Educational Leadership, 55*(1), 22–23.

Sharp, S., & Cowie, H. G. (1994). Constructive conflict resolution, peer counseling and assertiveness training: Empowering pupils to respond to bullying behavior. In P. K. Smith & S. Sharp (Eds.), *School bullying and how to cope with it.* London: Routledge.

Smith, P. K. (1991). The silent nightmare: Bullying and victimization in school peer groups. *The Psychologist: Bulletin of the British Psychological Society, 4,* 243–248.

Sullivan, K. (2000). *The anti-bullying handbook.* Oxford, England: Oxford University Press.

Tattum, D., & Herbert, G. (1993). *Countering bullying: Initiatives by schools and local authorities.* Stoke-on-Trent, England: Trentham Books.

Tattum, D., & Herbert, G. (1997). *Bullying: Home, school, and community.* London: Fulton.

Tolan, P. H., & Guerra, N. (1994). *What works in reducing adolescent violence: An empirical review of the field* (Monograph prepared for the Center for the Study and Prevention of Violence). Boulder: University of Colorado.

Wasserman, G. A., & Miller, L. (1998). The prevention of serious and violent juvenile offending. In R. Loeber & D. P. Farrington (Eds.), *Serious and violent juvenile offenders: Risk factors and successful intervention* (pp. 197–247). Thousand Oaks, CA: Sage.

Wheeler, N. S. (1999, June). *Troubled students and schools.* Paper presented at the Summit on Education, Nashville, TN.

Chapter 13

PUBLIC CONCERN AND FOCUS ON SCHOOL VIOLENCE

RON AVI ASTOR, RONALD O. PITNER, RAMI BENBENISHTY, AND
HEATHER A. MEYER

INTRODUCTION

Opinion surveys continually show that the general public perceives school safety
as the top problem facing American schools (e.g., Elam & Rose, 1995; Elam,
Rose, & Gallup, 1994, 1996; Kaufman et al., 2000; Morrison, Furlong, & Morrison 1997; Rose & Gallup, 1999, 2000; Rose, Gallup, & Elam, 1997; U.S Departments of Education and Justice, 2000). The highly publicized mass homicides on
school grounds during the late 1990s have intensified the public concern over
school violence (e.g., Bragg, 1997; Gegax, Adler, & Pedersen, 1998; Hays, 1998;
Witkin, Tharp, Schrof, Toch, & Scattarella, 1998). In response to this growing
public concern, politicians, school officials, education scholars, parents, teachers, law enforcement agencies, and pupil personnel organizations created research programs/task forces and appropriated large fiscal resources in an effort
to find ways of addressing the school violence problem (e.g., American Psychological Association, 1993; Dwyer, Osher, & Warger, 1998; Kaufman et al., 1998;
National Education Goals Panel, 1995; U.S. Departments of Education and Justice, 2000; Vossekuil, Reddy, Fein, Borum, & Modzeleski, 2000). These efforts
have produced dozens of government reports, practice guides, prevention programs, and research reports aimed directly at the topic of school violence (e.g.,
Kann et al., 2000; Kaufman et al., 2000; U.S. Departments of Education and
Justice, 2000; Vossekuil et al., 2000).

Overall, this effort appears to be very positive. It has generated debate, new
empirical data, and, in many disciplines, numerous research projects on the
issue of school violence. Although the increase of school violence in recent years
has caused great concern among the general public, the recent empirical data

documenting national rates of different kinds of school violence over time present a temporal portrait of school violence in the United States that differs from the one currently portrayed in the general media. Multiple national surveys from credible government organizations (for discussions, see Kann et al., 2000; Kaufman et al., 2000; U.S. Departments of Education and Justice, 2000) indicate that many rates of school violence have decreased or remained stable over time. Although the federal government has published many recent documents detailing these trends, the national media have not reported them extensively, and the public still believes that school violence rates have increased rather than decreased or remained stable. To understand school violence as a phenomenon and to appreciate the context of current school violence prevention programs, it is important to be aware of these national trends.

School violence has become a major focus of research and practice; many new programs show empirical effectiveness. Consequently, the objectives of this article are: (a) to provide a broad overview of the trends and issues currently surrounding the school violence problem; (b) to highlight major conceptual problems pertaining to school violence research and interventions; (c) to identify a list of common components present in unsuccessful and successful school violence programs; (d) to discuss empirically based and promising school violence programs; and (e) to describe both quantitative and qualitative assessment processes that could help toward creating schoolwide awareness of the problem, identifying problems specific to the schools' setting, and developing or evaluating violence prevention programs.

SCOPE OF THE PROBLEM: MAJOR TRENDS AND ISSUES

School violence covers a wide array of intentional or reckless behaviors; they include physical harm, psychological harm, and property damage. During the past 30 years, many physically and psychologically harmful behaviors have been included within the term *school violence.* This trend parallels developments in the literatures of family violence, child abuse, youth violence, and bullying, which also have expanded the range of behaviors considered to be violent. Currently, the term *school violence* could include behaviors that vary in severity and frequency, such as murder (Bragg, 1997; Hays, 1998); the presence of weapons (Pittel, 1998); sexual harassment (Stein, 1995); school fighting (Boulton, 1993; Schafer & Smith, 1996); bullying, verbal threats, and intimidation (Batsche & Knoff, 1994; Olweus, 1993; Olweus, Limber, & Mihalic, 1999); corporal punishment (Youssef, Attia, & Kamel, 1998); gang violence (Kodluboy, 1997; Parks, 1995); rape (Page, 1997); hate crimes (Berrill, 1990); vandalism (Goldstein, 1996); and dating violence (Burcky, Reuterman, & Kopsky, 1988; Cano, Avery-Leaf, Cascardi, & O'Leary, 1998). This chapter presents an overview of the trends and prevalence rates of select types of school violence, based on recent national data. Because most surveys and studies of school violence do not address all forms of school violence, this review will not cover the full range of violent acts, but will focus on specific forms of violence that are of national interest.

Is the School Violence Problem in the United States Getting Worse?

This discussion relates to increases and decreases in school victimization *rates,* which are key to the headline question. "Getting worse" highlights a rate of change (increasing, stable, or declining) of school violence. If the problem were rephrased to "Is school violence a problem in the United States?" it would be only partly related to increases and decreases in rates. Instead, it would be more related to changes in the philosophical and social norms of what our society considers acceptable rates of school violence. In recent publications on school violence, questions like these have been used interchangeably, avoided, or dismissed (e.g., Kaufman et al., 2000; U.S. Departments of Education and Justice, 2000). We suggest that these two queries should be approached separately. Knowing the increase or decrease of violence rates is critical for understanding the scope of the problem and determining whether policy interventions are impacting rates, or norms are changing. We start with the question "Is school violence getting worse?" and then deal with the question "Is school violence a problem?" These issues interact with how assessments of school violence are conducted, how we understand programs that work and don't work, and how we generate or use data to shape our response to school violence.

The Myth of a Continual Rise in School Violence Rates

Fatal Victimization on School Grounds

When public attention is focused on school violence, that focus is most likely associated with media attention given to recent homicides on school grounds. In 2001, violent deaths on school grounds were considered tragic events that evoked national concern. The public's awareness and willingness to address violent deaths on school grounds ought to continue to be a high priority. However, federal government data indicate that violent deaths are not common occurrences on school grounds. For example, if we examine murders between students as a subset of "violent deaths," there were 2,717 murders *off* school grounds and 35 murders *on* school grounds in 1997–1998 (Kaufman et al., 2000; U.S. Departments of Education and Justice, 2000). Because of the intense media coverage of the Columbine shootings, the general public may have an impression that violent deaths in schools are a relatively new phenomenon and that fatalities are increasing on school grounds in the United States.

Government data and independent research indicate that violent deaths on school grounds occurred at comparable *or higher* rates before the intense media coverage of the late 1990s. For example, Kachur et al. (1996) reported, in the *Journal of the American Medical Association,* that there were 105 violent deaths on school grounds in 1992–1993. (This number includes suicide, manslaughter, student, and nonstudent deaths.) However, in 1997–1998 (the year of the Columbine shootings), there were 60 violent deaths on school grounds, and in 1998–1999, there were 50 violent deaths on school grounds. If we examine the number of fatal *events* (not the number of people who died), government data show a decrease in recent years (e.g., 49 events in 1995/1996 versus 34 events in 1998/1999). One could argue that we now have a greater awareness of school deaths and will not tolerate even 50 deaths. (We support such a position.) However, this should not negate the fact that we may have had more than a 50% reduction in violent deaths on school grounds since 1992/1993.

The patterns of fatal student victimization fluctuate over time and differ among ethnic groups. This is true in our society generally (Ash, Kellermann, Fuqua-Whitley, & Johnson, 1996; Gray, 1991; Hammond & Yung, 1993; Issacs, 1992; Prothrow-Stith & Weissman, 1991) and it is also true on school grounds (Astor, Pitner, & Duncan, 1996; Kachur et al., 1996; Kaufman et al., 1998). For instance, in 1998, Hispanic students were five times more likely than white students to suffer a school-related lethal event, and African American students were nine times more likely than white students (Kaufman et al., 1998). Another public myth of the post-Columbine era is that school fatalities were, for the first time, occurring in suburban areas, whereas, prior to the Columbine shootings, fatal school deaths were occurring primarily in urban settings. Another slightly contradictory media myth is that violent deaths (especially those involving shootings) did not occur in inner-city/urban schools and that violent deaths were associated with a new phenomenon of alienated, angry, white suburban males.

Nevertheless, Kachur et al. (1996) reported, prior to the Columbine shootings in 1992/1993, that 30% of the school fatalities occurred in suburbs, 62% occurred in urban areas, and 8% occurred in rural settings. Statistics like these raise serious questions as to why the media and the general public continue to perpetuate unsubstantiated and potentially harmful myths. Especially disturbing is the fact that the statistics cited are in the public domain and originated from supposedly credible research organizations such as the Centers for Disease Control (CDC), U.S. Department of Education, U.S. Department of Justice, Federal Bureau of Investigation (FBI) and various research organizations. (For a full listing of the agencies involved, see Kaufman et al., 2000; U.S Departments of Education and Justice, 2000). To sum up, it appears that high rates of fatalities occurred in schools before the late 1990s, both in the suburbs and in urban areas. It also appears that school fatalities that occurred earlier in the decade, in both urban and suburban areas, did not receive the same national media attention as those occurring in the late 1990s in the suburbs. The decline in fatalities mirrors declines in other violence-related behaviors.

Weapons on School Grounds

The potential for lethal violence in schools remains high because of the availability of weapons. However, the American public is generally not aware of the impressive declines in the presence of weapons on school grounds in recent years. This lack of awareness is particularly problematic because many federal, state, and school district policies have been focused on the reduction of weapons on school grounds (U.S. Departments of Education and Justice, 2000). For example, between 1993 and 1999, the Department of Education reported that the percentage of students in grades 9 through 12 who reported bringing a gun to school during the 30 days preceding the survey dropped from 12% to 7%. If accurate, this would be an astonishing 42% reduction in the *number* of students who brought weapons onto school grounds. There are still significant gender differences in the rates of weapons carried. Male students are more likely to carry a weapon on school property (11%) than female students (2.8%) (Kann et al., 2000; U.S. Departments of Education and Justice, 2000).

Perhaps the greatest finding underreported by the media is that, among African American students, the rate of weapons on school grounds has dropped considerably more than the national average and the rate of any other ethnic group in the United States. Between 1993 and 1999, the rate of African American students who reported carrying weapons on school campuses had dropped by two-thirds. Compared with other groups, African American students went from having the highest reported rates of weapons (in 1993) to the lowest reported rates (in 1999). This accomplishment should be tempered with the knowledge that the national percentage of students in grades 9 through 12 who reported being threatened and/or injured by someone using a weapon on school grounds remained very constant (between 7% and 8%) from 1993 through 1997. These injury rates appear slightly higher (9% to 10%) for African American and Hispanic groups (Kann et al., 2000; Kaufman et al., 2000; U.S. Departments of Education and Justice, 2000).

Expulsion for Weapons and Zero Tolerance

Some observers are crediting the zero-tolerance gun laws as the major cause for the overall decline of weapons on school campuses. Under the provisions of national and state zero-tolerance laws, many students have been expelled for bringing weapons onto school grounds in recent years. However, consistent with the other data presented in this chapter these expulsion rates have gone down. In 1996–1997, 5,724 students were expelled for carrying firearms; whereas in 1998–1999, 3,658 students were expelled for carrying firearms. These school expulsions reduced the number of students with weapons; however, there ought to be great social concern over where these expelled and potentially violent students go after they are expelled (U.S. Departments of Education and Justice, 2000).

From a public policy perspective, it does not make sense to expel, and therefore deprive an education to, potentially violent and armed youth, without providing alternative programs, tracking the success of these programs, and tracking the expelled students' whereabouts. Currently, U.S. government data suggest that 44% of expelled students were referred to alternative programs; however, we do not know how many students actually went to, or stayed in, those programs. The U.S. Department of Education is expected to release official data on this problem (U.S. Departments of Education and Justice, 2000). This problem represents a serious public health/safety gap in the current zero-tolerance laws, and it needs to be addressed. As a corollary, some advocacy groups and academicians have argued that the zero-tolerance laws should be administered more judiciously in order to create a "safe" climate rather than a punitive climate of fear (Noguera, 1995). It has been argued that what has been defined as "security" is not necessarily the same as a safe environment (Noguera, 1995). Hyman and Snook (2000) suggest that these kinds of extreme measures have created an authoritarian punitive environment that may be inconsistent with the public schools' overall goals of creating democratic citizens.

School Physical Fights

From 1993 to 1999, annual rates of fights on school grounds, among students in ninth to twelfth grades, showed a slight decline (from 16% to 14%). Overall, male students (20%, versus 9% of females) were more likely to report that they had been involved in a physical fight on school property in the past 12 months. Rates of being involved in a physical fight on school property also varied by grade level; students in lower grades reported that they had been involved in more fights on school property than students in upper grades. More specifically, approximately 21% of ninth graders reported being involved in a physical fight in the past year, compared to only 10% of twelfth graders (Kaufman et al.,

2000). Statistics from the Youth Risk Behavior Surveillance System (YRBSS; Kann et al., 2000) estimate that 14% of students reported that they had been in a physical fight on school grounds in the 12 months preceding the survey. Kann et al. (2000) also reported significant racial and ethnic differences in students' involvement in fights on school property. Overall, African American students (18.7%) were significantly more likely than white students (12.3%) to report that they had been involved in a physical fight on school grounds during the 12 months prior to the survey.

We caution readers about the interpretation of the historical school-fight statistics. The term "school grounds" was not defined in these studies, and it is unclear whether students excluded fights that occurred immediately after school, just beyond school grounds. This issue of school versus community fights is important because Department of Justice statistics indicate that the highest rates of student/youth fights and assaults occur mainly on school days between 3:00 P.M. and 4:00 P.M. (much closer to 3:00 than to 4:00) near school grounds. We believe that many of these fights emanated from school social dynamics (i.e., are potentially controllable by the schools) and should be categorized as school fights. Currently, fights occurring after 3:00 P.M. are most likely not counted as *school* fights. Hence, the number of school-related fights would probably be much higher than is indicated by the percentages above.

Given this caveat, and as a way of understanding the total amount of fights, we cite the CDC's statistics in 1997: 37% of secondary-school students were involved in serious fights (all contexts) during that year (46% of males and 26% of females). Again, the vast majority of these fights occurred just after 3:00 P.M. and only on school days. If school social dynamics were not a key component, we would see much higher rates on nonschool days and more variation in the after-school hours. In fact, the rate of fights on nonschool days is very low and does not have the afternoon spike in events that accounts for most fights (Snyder & Sickmund, 1999). These overall fight percentages have also declined slightly since 1993. The real percentage of school fights probably lies somewhere between the current school-fight questions and the overall fight percentages.

Other Nonfatal Forms of Violence

If the total number of student victimization events is examined (including nonfatal crimes such as rape, sexual assault, robbery, aggravated assault, and simple assault), there were significant declines in victimization between 1992 (144 crimes per 1,000 students) and 1998 (101 per 1,000 students). That translates into 700,000 fewer crimes committed against students in 1998 than in 1992. If we break down the total amount, some of the declines in specific crimes are notable. For example, in 1992, there were 95 thefts per 1,000 students (ages 12 to 18) whereas in 1998 there were 58 thefts per 1,000 students. In 1992, more students reported being victims of serious violent crimes and assault (48 per 1,000) than in 1998 (43 per 1,000). These data offer more evidence that we are in the midst of a profound decline in student victimization rates (Kaufman et al., 2000; U.S. Departments of Education and Justice, 2000).

Gang Activity at School

Between 1995 and 1999, there were extraordinary reductions in reported gang activity in schools. Despite all the media hyperbole of the late 1980s and early 1990s on the influence of gangs on school violence, these reductions have gone virtually unnoticed in the national media and the public's awareness. The percentage of students who reported that gangs were present in their school dropped significantly from 1995 (29%) to 1999 (17%). The reduction of gang activity in schools has been strong across all settings (urban, 16% reduction; suburban, 10% reduction; rural, 9% reduction). The reduction in gang activity on school grounds has also been strong across different ethnic groups (10% reduction for African American youths, 22% reduction for Hispanic youths, and 10% for white youths) (Kaufman et al., 2000; U.S. Departments of Education and Justice, 2000).

Students' Perceptions of Safety at School/on the Way to and from School

The report of the U.S. Departments of Education and Justice indicated that, from 1995 to 1999, there were decreases (9% to 5%, respectively) in the percentages of students who reported that they avoided places *at school* because they feared attack (Kaufman et al., 2000). The reductions of fear were greater in urban settings (12% versus 6% in 1995 and 1999, respectively) and for Hispanic students (13% vs. 6% for 1995 and 1999, respectively). In 1995, students in urban settings were more likely to be fearful at school, whereas in 1999, fear among urban students dropped so significantly that urban and suburban students were *equally likely* to be fearful of violence at schools. Students were also less likely to fear that they would be attacked while traveling to and from school (1995 to 1999, 7% to 4%, respectively). Across all years, trends suggest that younger students (grades 9 and 10) were more likely than older students (grades 11 and 12) to fear being attacked while traveling to and from school (Kann et al., 1998; Kaufman et al., 2000; U.S. Departments of Education and Justice, 2000).

Is School Violence a Problem?

Given all the statistics cited in the first section of this chapter, some readers might be tempted to ask whether school violence is currently a problem in the United States. Some might conclude that school violence is no longer a problem (or only a small problem) because, overall, occurrences of school violence have declined. We believe this conclusion, if based only on frequency of occurrence, would be a mistake. School violence rates have gone down across multiple forms of victimization, but these rate reductions do not address how society *should* define when school violence is a problem. This question pertains directly to the nation's willingness to articulate what kind of behaviors, how many behaviors, and how severe these violent behaviors need to exist in a setting before we would be willing to categorize one school's or the nation's schools as having a school violence problem. When does a specific school cross the threshold from having an average level of school violence to being a problematic school? Conversely, how do we know when a school is considered a "model" safe school? These are not solely abstract, moral, or academic issues. Several state and national politicians, organizations, and task forces have already publicly declared that punitive measures should be taken against schools that are "unsafe" (shut them down, hire new staff, and so on). During the 2000 presidential election, shutting down unsafe and problem schools (schools that "don't work") was a common mantra for both Republican and Democratic candidates. Yet no one has put forth criteria for what would constitute an unsafe school district or school. This lack of philosophical discussions is a serious problem because as a society, as practitioners, and as researchers we must have agreed-upon ways to understand what is an extremely safe school or an extremely dangerous school. Otherwise, we run the risk of behaving in an arbitrary manner in both our supportive and punitive attempts to stem violence. Finally, how are we to assess the success or failure of prevention/intervention programs, and schools' efforts/improvements, if we cannot form common criteria as to what is a safe or unsafe school?

To date, researchers and government officials have relied mainly on comparative frequencies of violence to determine the extent of the problem (e.g., see Harel, Kenny, & Rahav, 1997). However, as discussed in the first section of the chapter, even massive national reductions in school victimization may not be sufficient criteria when dealing with the question: "Is school violence a problem?" The public's growing awareness of violence may be changing and becoming less tolerant toward even minor events that have not historically been considered "violence" (behaviors such as pushing, hitting, sexual harassment, intimidations, threats, bullying, and so on). Consequently, there is a fine interplay between needed philosophical criteria and empirical data in determining whether school violence is a national problem.

This tension between data and changing norms is even more evident when trying to determine whether a school district or a school site is unsafe or problematic. To apply or interpret the meaning of the national data, school district officials, school site administrators, and teachers would need to be able to compare/contrast their school district, school, and class with the national averages or with other schools in their own district. To date, we have not seen any published study that explores how individual school sites or school districts determine when schools are problematic as compared to the national/state/or district norms. There is also a dearth of examples showing how school districts/school sites use empirical data to generate interventions. Moreover, we have not come across any studies that systematically explore how some schools are perceived by administrators, teachers, and parents as being safer, and other schools, within the same school districts, are perceived as more dangerous. Practitioners, politicians, and the general public know that these kinds of determinations are commonly made about schools and school districts. It is unclear whether schools are seen as unsafe based on data, knowledge of publicized events, rumors, racial stereotypes, socioeconomic status (SES) stereotypes, or combinations of these variables.

For example, one can ask: "How many violent events are necessary before a school is perceived to have a school violence problem?" Current research or conceptual discussions do not address this threshold issue at the site or district level. Even so, readers should be aware that severity or frequency of violence does not necessarily address how safe or dangerous the school is perceived in reality—or, even more importantly, how safety *should* be categorized. How children, teachers, and the public judge the overall safety or extent of a problem in any particular school *as a whole* is not the same as judging *a particular behavioral event.* For example, students or teachers may be reluctant to categorize their school setting (as a whole) as having a violence "problem," even though they may be aware of multiple violent events. Furthermore, a school may be safe in some respects and in some areas, but unsafe in others. Classroom spaces during class time might be considered safe, but the cafeteria during lunch time may be seen as dangerous. Some children may avoid unsafe areas entirely; others may be continually exposed to dangerous situations within the same school setting.

From the perspective of school constituents who were victims of violence, and parents whose children were victimized, it could be argued that one severe act of violence (such as a potentially lethal event) would qualify a school as having a violence problem. However, if the criteria are a combination of both severity and frequency, defining a problem school could be difficult. One could ask: "Is a school that had 6 potentially lethal events—compared with a school that had 10 potentially lethal events—during a given year a "safer school?" If frequency and severity are the chief considerations in the current definition of violence being a school problem, then how many severe events (shootings, rapes, knifings, beatings, or fights that require medical attention) does a school need to have before school staff and students perceive the school as having a *serious* violence problem? The same questions can be asked about lower-level violent events such as pushing, punching, and tripping. Do educators or researchers have a sense of what the threshold is for a "big" problem when they discuss the school climate as a whole? In our many contacts with principals and teachers, we have asked: "How many playground fights (per month or per year) would it take before you would be willing to say that your playground has a violence problem? 50? 200? 400? 1,000?" To date, we have not found administrators who are able to define frequency criteria that would qualify a school as having a school violence problem. The questions of "How many?" and "What types of violence constitute a problem?" are difficult to answer because they have not yet been addressed on a philosophical level.

Interventions

In the next section, we will discuss various types of interventions that are used to address school violence. Some of the interventions discussed are commonly used but have very little research to support their effectiveness. Other interventions have studies supporting their effectiveness. Had this chapter been written 10 years ago, we would most likely conclude that very few interventions show any kind of effectiveness. Within the past 10 years, many new programs and curricula have emerged, and multiple studies support their effectiveness.

However, these programs should be considered within the limitations of the studies showing their effectiveness. Although research has been conducted on the interventions presented as model or promising programs, not all of them have used randomization with control/experimental schools. Many of the studies are using a multiple baseline model over time, and few are using very strict controls. Given the large declines in national violence rates, multiple baseline evaluations of programs that were conducted during this historical time frame can be deceiving; they may be reflecting the national normative reductions in victimization rates, and not the effectiveness of the program itself. This would be less of a problem if school violence rates were increasing nationally and the multiple assessments showed a reduction. Even so, there is enough regional and school-district variation in victimization rates to indicate that matched or random control schools are essential in any future research aimed at determining the true effectiveness of the program.

TYPES OF INTERVENTIONS

Characteristics of Ineffective Interventions

A Singular Focus on the Source of the Problem

Most practitioners and researchers would agree that school violence is associated with a wide array of individual, family, community, and societal variables. Figure 13.1 presents select examples of correlates commonly mentioned in the

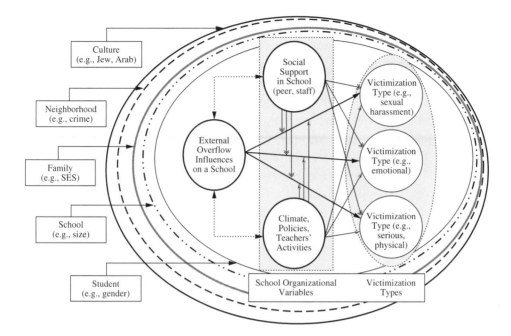

Figure 13.1   A Model of Social-Ecological Influences on Student Victimization

school violence practice and research literatures. These correlates are presented at different ecological levels.

Given the number of variables associated with school violence, one would expect school violence interventions to target *multiple* factors. Instead, most school violence interventions focus on only one or two variables or ecological levels (e.g., the child, the family, or the classroom) and tend to ignore the complex interplay of multiple variables. Consequently, it is not surprising that programs that address only one variable tend to be ineffective in reducing levels of school violence. Figure 13.1 also represents our theoretical conceptualization of how, with the help of programs or self-initiated interventions, the school could buffer or exacerbate outside influences that come from factors external to the school environment. As shown in Figure 13.1, the school policies/procedures and social supports could impact differently on various forms of student victimization. Based on our assessment of the research, we believe that successful programs are strengthening the school infrastructure and social environment to buffer students from many risk factors external to the school and, ultimately, to reduce overall rates of victimization in the schools (see Lorion, 1998, for a discussion of community/school influences). We suspect that less successful programs tend not to focus on the school social environment at the core of the interventions.

A Psychological/Behavioral Focus

The most popular school violence interventions are psychological and behavioral interventions (e.g., anger management, conflict mediation, peer counseling, curriculum-based programs). Historically, psychology has focused on identifying cognitive, emotional, and social-relational reasons why individual children become violent (American Psychological Association, 1993). Consequently, school-based psychological interventions have focused mainly on psychological variables. These types of interventions have been primarily geared toward individual children (or their families) and have given very little focus to the interplay between social dynamics of normative contexts (such as schools) and violence in the school setting (Hudley, Britsch, Wakefield, Demorat, & Cho, 1998). Unfortunately, barring a few exceptions, research suggests that narrowly focused social skills interventions, peer counseling/mediation, and other psychological interventions geared only for acting-out or aggressive children have been ineffective in reducing levels of school violence. Some programs (e.g., peer mediation groups and programs like DARE) have been shown to increase the level of aggression and violence in schools (see Gottfredson, 1997, for a detailed empirical review of these types of programs). Overall, psychological programs have been effective only when used conjointly with other interventions that target the organizational or social system of the school (Gottfredson, 1997; Olweus, 1993).

Conceptual Underdevelopment and Underuse of the School Context

Many "packaged" programs omit the normal components of the school social structure and tend to be "add on" programs (Larson, 1998). These types of programs are often unrelated to the academic curriculum and social goals of a school. This situation is due, in part, to the fact that the social variables associated with the context of schools and school violence have not been clearly conceptualized. (See Astor, 1998, for a discussion of these issues.) For example, researchers have conducted very few studies regarding the social dynamics surrounding a hallway fist fight or sexual harassment on school grounds. Moreover, until very recently, researchers or practitioners have not carefully distinguished between the concepts of *school violence* and *youth violence* (Astor, 1998; Astor & Meyer, 1998). Ironically, many youth violence studies have collected their data on school grounds using classroom peer and teacher rating scales. In essence, these "youth violence" studies may have been measuring the social dynamics/structure of violence within the school and classroom, but did not include or conceptualize the school as part of the theoretical paradigm (with the exception of grades/academic achievement as an outcome). Instead, many articles on and analyses of youth violence are presented in an acontextual manner, with a strong implicit assumption that the youth is the "carrier" of violent behavior and that dynamics within settings play a small or tangential role in violent behavior.

Focus on Deficits in Children

Many school violence interventions are based on either formal or implicit theoretical assumptions of deficits surrounding what is causing violent behavior in individual children or subpopulations of children. For example, most social skills programs are based on the theoretical assumption that aggressive children are lacking in either the social-cognitive or the behavioral skills needed to deal with conflict appropriately, due to a lack of social exposure and practice. Without these more complex skills, it is believed that children naturally gravitate toward using aggression as a solution to social conflict. Consequently, these types of programs systematically target specific deficits in cognitive and behavioral skills within specific children or entire schools.

Types of Interventions and Programs That Schools Are Using

The Scope of Programs

Nationwide, approximately 78% of principals report that they currently have programs addressing violence in their schools (Kaufman et al., 1998). Among the schools, 11% had programs that lasted only one day or less, 24% reported that they had only ongoing violence programs, and 43% indicated that they had both ongoing and one-day programs designed to address school violence. It is unclear what types of programs principals consider to be violence interventions.

Few evaluations have assessed the effectiveness of interventions normally used by schools (expulsion, suspension, referral to special education, sending a child to the principal's office, during- and after-school detention, parent conferences, and counseling). However, interventions such as expulsion, suspension, and school transfer are common responses to acts of school violence. During the 1996–1997 school year, 39% of school principals said they expelled, suspended, or transferred a student because of fighting. Of the nation's principals, 27% reported that they used suspension, expulsion, or transfer for students who had a weapon on school grounds (U.S. Department of Education, 1998). Other common interventions include contacting parents, parent/teacher meetings about aggressive behaviors, or school-based consequences such as staying after school. Better adult supervision in the school yard and better monitoring of the routes to and from the school and of violence-prone areas within the school should be further researched. Data from Europe and Australia suggest that these types of interventions are easy to implement and may be highly effective in reducing some types of school violence, such as "bullying" (Olweus, 1993; Sharp & Smith, 1994; Smith & Sharp, 1994).

Special Education and Violence

Another common response of schools to persistent and chronic aggression in individual children is special education referral, assessment, and placement. Unfortunately, the school violence literature has not closely examined the relationships between special education and violence reduction in schools. Nevertheless, many children are likely to receive services for aggressive behavior through special education. These interventions include counseling, parent training, contained classrooms, a specialized curriculum, and day treatment facilities. This area of research should be developed further because it is possible that social workers, psychologists, counselors, and teachers view the special education process as an important strategy to use with some aggressive children.

Promising Prevention and Intervention Programs

In this section, we present some examples of prevention and intervention programs available to schools and practitioners. The programs discussed in this section do not represent an exhaustive list of available programs. Table 13.1 offers a longer listing of programs that have either been evaluated or are widely used. Here, we highlight a handful of programs that either show promise or have already demonstrated their effectiveness in at least one study.

School-Based Bully-and-Victim Intervention Programs

A comprehensive nationwide antibullying program was conducted in Norway (see Olweus, 1993, for details; see Smith et al., 1999, for research conducted in other countries). During the 1970s, surveys in Norway found that bullying was a considerable problem for students in Norwegian schools. In an effort to reduce bully-and-victim problems, Dan Olweus, a Norwegian professor, developed a nationwide program for children in grades 1 through 9. The program has many simple interventions and is aimed at students, teachers, and parents in schools, classrooms, and individual settings. Findings from 42 schools that participated in the program showed a 50% reduction in rates of bullying and victimization. Furthermore, the positive effects of the program appeared to increase over time, as did students' satisfaction with school life (Olweus, 1993). Similar antibullying programs have been developed in Great Britain (see Sharp & Smith, 1994, and Smith & Sharp, 1994, for empirical evaluations and detailed practical procedures for educators) and Australia (Rigby, 1996). Evaluations of those programs show significant reductions in aggressive behaviors, and increases in

Table 13.1 Selected Empirically-Based School Violence Prevention and Intervention Programs

Program Name	Description of Intervention	Author(s)
Adolescent Anger Control: Cognitive-Behavioral Techniques	A 12-session group anger-control program for adolescents.	Feindler & Ecton, 1986
Aggression Replacement Training: A Comprehensive Intervention for Aggressive Youth	A program combining anger management, moral education, and social skills training for aggressive youth.	Goldstein, Glick, Reiner, Zimmerman, & Coultry, 1985
Anger Coping Intervention with Aggressive Children	Eighteen one-hour group sessions for boys in grades 4 to 6 who exhibit chronic patterns of aggressive behavior.	Lochman, Lampron, Gemmer, & Harris, 1986
BrainPower Program	A 12-lesson attribution retraining intervention for grades 3 to 6.	Hudley et al., 1998
Baltimore Good Behavior Game Intervention	A behavior modification program aimed at decreasing early aggressive and shy behaviors in elementary-grade children, to prevent later criminality.	Kellam, Rebok, Ialongo, & Mayer, 1994
FAST Track Program	A multistage program for high-risk youths, grades K to 5; combines family, child, and school.	Dodge, 1993; Greenberg, Lochman, & McMahon, 1996; http://www.Colorado.EDU/cspv /blueprints/promise/fastTrack .htm
I Can Problem Solve	Teaches thinking skills to help children in grades K to 6 to resolve interpersonal problems and avoid antisocial behavior.	Wahler, Fetsch, & Silliman, 1997; http://www.Colorado.EDU /cspv/blueprints/promise/ICPS .htm
Peace Builders	A schoolwide program implemented by staff and students; fosters a positive school climate for students in grades K to 6+.	Embry, Flannery, Vazsonyi, Powell, & Atha, 1996; Flannery & Vazsonyi, 1996; Flaxman, Schwartz, Weiler, & Lahey, 1998
Perry Preschool Program	Provides high-quality early childhood education to disadvantaged children in order to improve their later school and life performances.	Schweinhart, Barnes, & Weikart, 1993; http://www. Colorado.EDU/cspv /blueprints/promise/perPre.htm
Positive Adolescents Choices Training (P.A.C.T.)	Twenty one-hour weekly group sessions focusing on social skills training, violence awareness, and anger management for African American youths.	Yung & Hammond, 1998
Positive Youth Development Program	A 20-session curriculum for sixth and seventh graders; emphasizes social competence.	Caplan et al., 1992

(continued)

Table 13.1   Continued

Program Name	Description of Intervention	Author(s)
Preventive Intervention	A curriculum-based program focused on preventing juvenile delinquency, substance use, and school failure for high-risk middle and high school children.	Bry, 1982; http://www.Colorado.EDU/cspv/blueprints/promise/preventI.htm
Project PATHE	A comprehensive program that increases bonding to the school, self-concept, and educational and occupational attainment for middle and high school children.	Gottfredson, 1986; http://www.Colorado.EDU/cspv/blueprints/promise/PATHE.htm
Promoting Alternative Thinking Strategies (PATHS)	A curriculum that develops emotional and social competencies and helps to reduce aggression in children in grades K to 5.	Greenberg, Kusché, & Mihalic, 1998; http://www.Colorado.EDU/cspv/blueprints/model/ten_paths.htm
Resolving Conflict Creatively Program	A curriculum-based program that integrates conflict resolution and intergroup relationships for grades K to 12.	Aber, Brown, Chaudry, Jones, & Samples, 1996; Coben, Weiss, & Mulvey, 1994; Gregg, 1998
School-based Bully/Victim Intervention Program	A nationwide campaign integrating family, school, and community, to reduce and prevent bully/victim problems.	Olweus, 1993; Olweus et al., 1999; http://www.Colorado.EDU/cspv/blueprints/model/ten_bully.htm
School Transitional Environmental Program (STEP)	A curriculum-based program that focuses on reducing the complexity of school environments and decreasing vulnerability to academic and emotional difficulties for middle and high school students.	Larson, 1998; Yung & Hammond, 1998; http://www.Colorado.EDU/cspv/blueprints/promise/STEP.htm
Seattle Social Development Project	A program that focuses on intervening early in children's development to increase prosocial bonds, strengthen attachment and commitment to schools, and decrease delinquency; designed for grade school and middle school.	Hawkins et al., 1992; http://www.Colorado.EDU/cspv/blueprints/promise/Seattle.htm
Second Step: A Violence Prevention Curriculum	A skill-building curriculum designed to reduce impulsive and aggressive behavior; preschool to middle school.	Committee for Children, 1992; Gregg, 1998; Grossman et al., 1997
Social Competence Promotion Program for Young Adolescents (SCPP-YA)	Teaches self-control, problem solving, and communication skills to grades 5 to 8.	Wahler et al., 1997 http://www.nnfr.org/violence/yvp_litrev.html
The Parents and Children Series: A Comprehensive Course Divided into Four Programs	Uses videotaped programs to train parents of children with conduct problems.	Bierman et al., 1992

Table 13.1   Continued

Program Name	Description of Intervention	Author(s)
The Prepare Curriculum: Teaching Prosocial Competencies	Ten one-hour weekly sessions that teach a range of skills, including problem solving, anger control, and moral reasoning, to grades 6 to 12.	Wahler et al., 1997; http://www.nnfr.org/violence /yvp_litrev.html
Training and Implementation Guide for Student Mediation in Elementary Schools	A curriculum-based program focused on teaching communication and conflict resolution skills; preschool to grade 6.	Wahler et al., 1997; http://www.nnfr.org/violence /yvp_litrev.html
Viewpoints Training Program	Treatment-based program focused on altering the beliefs and attitudes of violent youths toward the legitimacy of violence; grades 6 to 12.	Guerra & Panizzon, 1986; Wahler et al., 1997; http://www.nnfr.org/violence /yvp_litrev.html
Violence Prevention Curriculum for Adolescents	A curriculum-based health education program for high school students.	Prothrow-Stith, 1987

students' satisfaction with school life (especially during lunch and recess). In a Department of Justice review, Gottfredson (1997; see also Gottfredson, Fink, Skroban, & Gottfredson, in press, for a thoughtful discussion) suggested that such a systemic and broad approach could be successful in the United States.

Although large-scale antibullying programs have not been conducted in the United States, Gottfredson (1997) cites similar positive effects from U.S.-based "capacity building programs" that focus on school improvement, staff development, and policy creation around issues of crime, violence, and discipline (e.g., Projects Pathe, Basis, and Status). These programs appear to have many of the same school, classroom, and individual components developed in the Norwegian program. Specifically, they attempt to: (a) increase the clarity of rules; (b) promote consistency of rule enforcement; (c) increase students' and staffs' sense of responsibility and involvement around discipline issues; (d) create a sense of ownership to solve the schools' violence problem; (e) focus on the entire school; (f) involve all of the school staff and students in owning their rules and consequences; (g) change the overall norms about school violence; and (h) target many levels (i.e., student, teacher, parent, administrator, classroom, individual school) of the school system for interventions.

High-Quality Early Childhood Education

From a primary prevention perspective, high-quality preschools may help in reducing violence rates. Recent data from the Perry Preschool High Scope study suggest that a high-quality preschool education can be highly effective in reducing violence throughout the life span (Schweinhart, Barnes, & Weikart, 1993). In a longitudinal study, researchers found that children who were randomly assigned to participate in a high-quality preschool environment were far less likely to have been involved in criminal and violent activity through development than those who were assigned to a lower-quality preschool program. These longitudinal data are important because they suggest that the effects carry through early development into adulthood (age 27 was the latest follow-up). By age 27, students who were assigned to low-quality preschool programs were five times more likely than the high-quality preschool students to have been arrested five or more times (many, for violent acts). In addition, children in high-quality classes were significantly more likely than children in low-quality classes to earn more money, own a house, and graduate from high school. Alternatively, they were significantly less likely to use social services. A cost-benefit analysis suggested that participation in a high-quality preschool saved the general public $57,585 per child (in 1992 dollars) on issues related to crime and victimization alone. Researchers (Schweinhart et al., 1993) believe that the preschools' focus on social responsibility, empowerment, decision making, and conflict resolution is an important contributor to the reductions in violence. Also, the Perry Preschool High Scope program emphasized parent education and involvement around parenting issues, and in-depth teacher training regarding issues of conflict and discipline. Schweinhart, Barnes, and Weikart (1993) believe that the tripartite focus on students, parents, and teachers accounts for the lower levels of violence throughout development.

Second Step

Based on the "habit of thought" model, which posits that violence can be unlearned, the Second Step program targets children in preschool through kindergarten, grades 1–3, and grades 4–5. Second Step is a curriculum-based approach that attempts to prevent aggressive behavior by increasing prosocial behavior through competence in peer interactions and in interpersonal conflict resolution skills. The curriculum, administered twice a week, has an average of 50 to 60 lessons. The specific lessons include activities to help children acquire empathy, impulse control, problem-solving, and anger management skills.

An evaluation found that the program has some level of impact on participants (Grossman et al., 1997). After completing the 30-lesson curriculum, participants illustrated that Second Step decreased the amount of physical aggression of youth and increased positive and prosocial behaviors both on the playground and in the lunchroom. Another study that trained elementary and middle school teachers in use of the curriculum suggested that teachers and administrators reported considerable respect for the capacity of the curriculum (Milwaukee Board of School Directors, 1993).

Practitioners should be aware that other similar curriculum-based conflict resolution programs have not performed well when intensively evaluated (Webster, 1993). For example, the popular Violence Prevention Curriculum for Adolescents (Prothrow-Stith, 1987) has little empirical support for its claim that it actually reduces violence (Larson, 1998; Tolan & Guerra, 1994).

Peace Builders

The Peace Builders program is a schoolwide violence prevention program for students in grades K through 5 (Embry, Flannery, Vazsonyi, Powell, & Atha, 1996). It is currently operating in almost 400 schools in Arizona, California, Ohio, and Utah. Implemented by both staff and students, the program incorporates strategies to change the school climate by promoting prosocial behavior among students and staff, enhancing social competence, and reducing aggressive behavior. Children learn five principles: (1) praise people, (2) avoid putdowns, (3) seek wise people as advisers and friends, (4) notice and correct any hurts you cause, and (5) right wrongs. Teachers, administrators, and parents reinforce and model these behaviors. Peace Builders is different from most school-based programs because it is not curriculum-based. Instead, it is described as "a way of life" (Flaxman, Schwartz, Weiler, & Lahey, 1998). Currently, the program is in the midst of a 6-year longitudinal evaluation of process and outcome data by the Centers for Disease Control. The initial evaluation results were positive and demonstrated a significant decrease in aggressive behavior and a significant increase in social competence (Flannery & Vazsonyi, 1996).

Positive Adolescents Choices Training

The Positive Adolescents Choices Training (PACT) program was "designed to teach African American youth social skills to aid in prevention of violence" (Hammond & Yung, 1991, 1993; Yung & Hammond, 1998). A unique aspect of PACT is that it is culturally relevant and aimed at reducing aggression and victimization in high-risk youth. The program's components include anger management, prosocial skills training, and violence-risk education. The sessions are built around videotapes that demonstrate culturally sensitive social situations. Participants learn the specific skills needed to solve the situations peacefully. Participants in the program increased an average of 33.5% in the areas of giving negative feedback, problem solving, and resisting peer pressure. Teachers also observed a significant improvement in the targeted skills of trained youth (30.4%) compared to untrained youth (−1.1%). In addition, students perceived their greatest improvement in their ability to provide negative feedback, but they felt they had made the least gain in problem solving. Most importantly, students demonstrated a significant reduction of physical aggression at school. Their overall aggressive behavior was improved during the training and was maintained when they graduated from the program (Yung & Hammond, 1998).

Based on our review of programs, it appears that successful schoolwide intervention programs have core implementation characteristics:

- They raise the awareness and responsibility of students, teachers, and parents regarding the types of violence in their schools (e.g., sexual harassment, fighting, weapon use) and create clear guidelines and rules for the entire school.
- They generally target the various social systems in the school and clarify, to the entire school community, what procedures should be followed before, during, and after violent events.
- They focus on getting the school staff, students, and parents involved in the program.
- The interventions often fit easily into the normal flow and mission of the school setting.
- They utilize faculty, staff, and parents in the school setting in order to plan, implement, and sustain the program.
- They increase monitoring and supervision in nonclassroom areas.

A Focus on the Entire School: Using Data to Define the Problems, Create Grass-Roots Interventions, Implement New Programs, and Assess Interventions

Lack of Data at the School Site and District Levels

Now we return to some earlier questions:

- When or how do school professionals, students, politicians, or parents decide that a particular school has a violence problem?
- Under what circumstances should a school consider programs that show empirical promise?
- How should schools select a program that will address the specifics of their own school violence issues?
- If a school selects one of the programs described earlier, how will the school constituents know whether the program was effective?
- How will the school know whether violence rates have increased or decreased?

Unfortunately, most schools lack the resources or professional expertise to conduct formal evaluations of the violence prevention programs they adopt. Earlier in this chapter, we characterized the question "Does a school have a violence problem?" as a "philosophical" area that needs to be addressed by educators. However, to set a criterion, school professionals first need to have a basic sense of the frequency of violence in their schools. Ideally, it would be very helpful for these professionals to know how their school compares with other schools, in their district and nationally.

Without reliable data on school violence at the site or district level, the implementation process used to institute model programs in schools has not been explored by school violence researchers. There is an inherent conflict between the needs of a research study used to evaluate the programs described earlier, and the needs of a school that desires to adopt and implement a model program. School violence studies that are well done (we include many of those cited in this chapter) are intensive, are conducted with large-scale funds, have detailed oversight by a large and trained university staff, and have rigid implementation controls. Thus, success in a research study does not necessarily mean that any school or school district could automatically adopt the program and get similar positive results.

The goodness of fit among the nature of the schools' specific problems, the focus of the program, and the process of implementation is rarely examined systematically, based on the schools' data. For example, one school may have a problem with sexual harassment among the younger male students; another school in the same district may have a problem with weapons brought to the school grounds by older students. These two types of problems may necessitate very different kinds of programs. Instituting a district-wide, uniform program intervention for both schools, or for schools across an entire district, is not likely to effectively address the specific problems that exist in each school. As obvious as this may seem, there is a paucity of studies that examined what happens when local school districts adopt uniform school violence programs (and many do just that!). Therefore, it is unclear whether these empirically supported programs continue to be effective outside the context of a highly monitored and controlled research study. We suspect that, in many districts, only sections or parts of the programs are implemented and there is no real detailed sense of the effectiveness of adopted programs at the school-site level. In sum, implementation of "effective programs" in a natural uncontrolled setting is a topic that deserves further attention.

Most reliable assessments related to school violence have been designed and applied toward assessing aggression in individuals. From a historical perspective, this is due to the conceptualization of youth violence in the field of youth psychopathology (rather than the context of the school) and the need to diagnose children with conduct disorders in order to design effective treatments for individuals.

Other kinds of student-focused measures have been developed; their goal is to conduct studies on childhood aggression (Macgowan, 1999). Currently, scores of excellent assessment batteries, instruments, and procedures have been designed for diagnostic and research purposes at the individual child level. For a comprehensive review of these kinds of assessments, and of ethical and conceptual issues related to the assessment of individuals, we refer readers to Macgowan (1999). However, we feel that focusing only on individuals can be stigmatizing toward those individuals and will not change the schools' approach to violence as an organizational entity that will function as depicted in Figure 13.1. We believe that focusing on the school context "as a whole," rather than on individual students or groups of students, is less stigmatizing and more effective in reducing overall rates of school violence. In the last portion of this chapter, we present two schoolwide data-based approaches to thinking about assessment that depart from an individual-student orientation and turn toward assessment.

The following sections on monitoring and school mapping are presented as possible solutions to this problem.

Setting Up a System of School Violence Monitoring at the Site, District, State, and National Level: The Use of High Technology and Computer Software as Intervention and Evaluation Tools

Monitoring is a public health concept. In practical terms, it means that uniform data are collected at regular intervals and used to track the ebbs and flows of a variety of physical illnesses and social ailments. Monitoring is used most often at the national level. However, it has been used at the agency level on a variety of issues. (See Benbenishty & Oyserman, 1995, for a model of how it was used in foster care agencies.) In medicine or public health, monitoring helps policymakers assess whether a problem is increasing or decreasing, and which policies seem to be working toward addressing a given issue. Surveillance is another word that is often used interchangeably with monitoring. Several of the national surveys reported earlier in this chapter are monitoring tools (e.g., see Kaufman et al., 2000; Kingery, Coggeshall, & Alford, 1998; U.S. Departments of Education and Justice, 2000, for discussions of these surveys).These national monitoring systems have been helpful in creating a national awareness and establishing normative parameters concerning the scope of the school violence problem. However, with a topic as broad as school violence, school districts and school sites often vary widely on their rates of school violence, as well as on the different types of reported violence.

Therefore, national statistics rarely inform a particular school regarding its own problem. As mentioned earlier, schools and school districts seldom have uniform data regarding how they compare with other schools in their district, state, or nation. Even if schools used their own funds to conduct expensive evaluations of programs they have adopted (many are currently engaged in such a process), they would still not know how their school compares with other schools on victimization outcomes. Not having site-specific and comparative data could be a significant obstacle in assessing whether a school has a problem, selecting a program, and evaluating the implementation process and outcomes of the program over time.

One conceptually practical solution to this "lack of data" problem would be to have entire school districts, and individual school sites within those districts, select a core set of questions that are also asked annually on the national monitoring surveys (e.g., questions about school fights, name calling, weapons on campus). If all the students in the district answer the survey questions once or twice a year, this could be a powerful tool for schools that must deal with particular school violence issues. Two authors of this chapter (Benbenishty and Astor) have initiated a multiyear pilot project* that examines the uses of linked-school-site, school-district, and national data for a school district consisting of 29 schools and close to 12,000 students in Israel. For this project, school violence data were collected at the grade level and the school level for all the schools in the district. Survey items were first selected by the schools (with the help of the researchers) from a nationally representative school violence monitoring study (Benbenishty, Zeira, & Astor, 1999). As a result, if the district surveyed its students, each school would have comparative data on each question by school, grade level, and specific types of victimization. Schools would have the ability to compare themselves with the school district, with grades or gender groups in their school, and/or with national normative data on any given type of victimization or item.

Keeping the data aggregated at the class and school levels avoided the potential stigmatization of specific children, teachers, or classes. From an ethical perspective, all agreed that it was important to have the data structured for constructive rather than punitive purposes. Hence, for the first year, specific school sites were shielded from district-level administrators and given only their school data. In this way, a school had a year to improve its scores and work from within (without worrying about school district politics) to understand what the data meant for the particular schools. The school district administrators were given collapsed district-wide data. They were able to use district-wide detailed data for policy planning and interventions. Moreover, these data were used to determine how to allocate resources regarding training, pupil personnel, teacher-student ratios, and programs. Although this is rarely done for school violence

*Funded by the Kellogg Foundation, the University of Michigan School of Social Work's Global Youth Initiative, Hebrew University, and the Hertzelia School District.

issues, most schools and school districts already collect similar comparative data on academic subjects such as mathematics, reading, and writing. Hence, measuring this issue was not a concept foreign to most teachers and principals.

One of the major obstacles in running a district-wide census of school violence rates is purely pragmatic. The amount of person power, funds, data entry, and analysis expertise that is needed may be beyond the capacity of most individual school districts. Furthermore, feedback data are only useful if they are given back to the school or school district quickly (within a month). The time lag in presenting the data back to the school or school district is one reason why even well done evaluations are often not immediately helpful to a school. If the turnaround is a year or more, the data are outdated and the schools cannot respond easily because the specific issues that are revealed may be qualitatively different a year later. As recently as five years ago, such a data collection process, and a linking of district, school site, and national data, was fiscally and organizationally prohibitive. Therefore, aside from showing the uses of a sociofeedback monitoring system, the goal of the project was to develop ways that schools and school districts could collect school violence data efficiently, quickly, reliably, and at low cost (compared to research studies and formal evaluations).

Very recent advances in computers, computer software, the use of scanners, and scanning and statistical software made it possible for schools and school districts to gather, enter, and interpret their own data at very manageable costs. Recent technological and software advances have also made it possible for schools to collect this kind of comparative data on their schools several times a year. These "easy to use" comparative data help school constituents decide which problems are most pressing for their school and which solutions best fit their school. Because the data collection, entry, and outputs are easily implemented (in one school, the students have assisted in the entire process), the data could help schools decide whether the programs they have adopted are effective or not. Another way of thinking about a quick, flexible, and easy-to-use monitoring system is that it is an ongoing sociofeedback system. Like a biofeedback system, this socially oriented feedback system allows schools to develop their own questions for targeting specific issues or topics (e.g., school climate, teacher morale, teacher/parent interactions), and to regulate the data themselves. Philosophically, a linked school, school district, and national monitoring system has the potential to empower school sites, school districts, and school practitioners.

Examples of Linked Monitoring Data

This section focuses on examples of comparative monitoring data. Because the computer, scanner, and software are preprogrammed, it is important to emphasize that the school district and the school need to select questions from the national survey and administer the short questionnaire to all schools in the district. The automated high-speed scanners compile all the student data into a flexible database, and the software then produces tables, graphs, and comparative data—for the principal, school district, or students—on the type of violence being examined. For example, the school district wanted to know how to allocate resources for violence programs, and at what ages students should get more intensive interventions. Figure 13.2 was extremely helpful for the district because it showed the rates of student victimization, by age and gender, for the entire school district. Note that specific schools were purposely not mentioned at the district level in order to avoid stigmatization. Figure 13.2 clearly demonstrated to the district (and the mayor's office) that boys' overall rates of victimization were higher than girls. Nevertheless, the age trends for boys and girls in the school district mirrored each other. The data in Figure 13.2 also suggested that it would be wise to allocate resources and prevention efforts before the seventh grade and definitely before the eighth grade in this particular district. Boys and girls in the eighth and ninth grades had the highest levels of overall school victimization.

During the first year of the project, the school district was given only district-wide data. To avoid punitive responses, principals requested to be shielded from

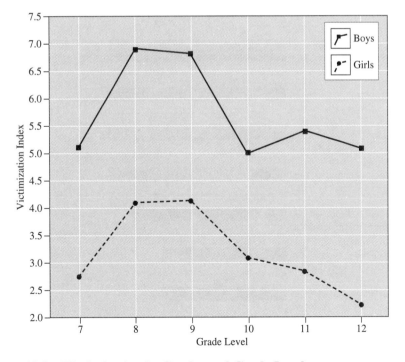

Figure 13.2   Victimization by Gender and Grade Level

the district's scrutiny during the first year. However, both the school district and the principals agreed to have school-by-school data by the second year. Even though the school district could not identify the specific schools that had the highest rates during the first year, the mayor and superintendent of schools were able to compare the entire district with the national norms on specific types of victimization. Figure 13.3 is an example of a chart used by the school district to compare its schools with national norms on 7 sexual harassment behaviors. Figure 13.3 gave administrators evidence that, on 4 sexual harassment behaviors, the school district was slightly below the national average, and on 3 behaviors, it was similar to or above the national average. Based on these results, school district officials felt that, overall, the sexual harassment problem was greater than they felt it should be (even though, in some areas, it was lower than the national data). The district-wide data were shared with school principals, students, parent groups, and pupil personnel to create dialogue on what could be done about sexual harassment from a district perspective. The school principals were asked to take the data back to their schools and initiate internal discussion there. Each school was also given its own data, indicating how it compared with the district and the national norms (again, not given at the district level) on shared data.

Principals could also use the monitoring sociofeedback system to compare their schools' rates of serious victimization with those of the school district as a

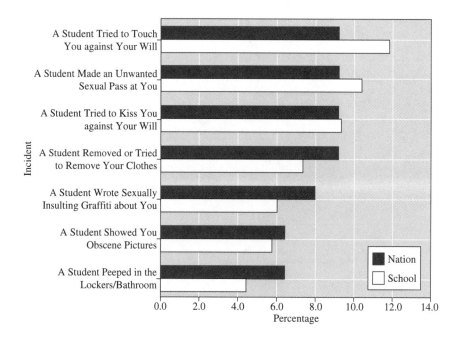

Figure 13.3   Sexual Harassment in the District and in the Nation

whole. Figure 13.4 is a chart used in one school to depict how serious victimization in that school compared with the district norms. The bar graph format showed teachers, students, parents, and administrators that, on every behavior, the school had higher rates of victimization than the district as a whole. These data were shared with the student body in their classrooms, with the teachers in scheduled meetings, and with the Parent-Teacher Organization (PTO). The data were used to create awareness and generate collaborative solutions; more importantly (at the first stage), they were used to anchor the dialogue (among staff, students, administration, and parents).

A school could also use this monitoring system to identify a particular problem. For example, if a school wanted to know where violence was occurring most, the data could be organized around that question. Table 13.2 shows the percentage of students who rated certain areas in their school as dangerous. The school gate (at the end of the school day), the locker room, and the school yard were areas that caused concern. Compared to boys, girls in the school were twice as likely to be fearful of the school gate (after school) and the locker room. Boys, on the other hand, were more likely to rate the school gate (before school) and the school yard as dangerous. The data show that the school gate (after school), the locker room, and the school yard were particular problems for the tenth and eleventh graders but were less problematic for the twelfth graders.

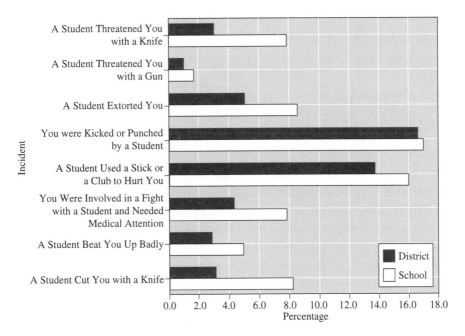

Figure 13.4   Serious Victimization in the District and in the School

Table 13.2 Examples of Actual Tables Given to Principals Regarding Dangerous Times and Places in School

(a) How Dangerous are Times and Places in School?

	Not at All	A Little	Dangerous	Quite Dangerous	Mean
	1	2	3	4	
Class	70%	20%	7%	3%	1.43
School Yard	35	30	25	10	2.10
School Gate, When School Starts	70	15	12	3	1.48
School Gate, When School Ends	30	24	26	20	2.36
Locker Room	32	22	25	21	2.35

(b) How Dangerous are Times and Places in School—by Gender?*

	Boys (%)	Girls (%)
Class	8	12
School Yard	42	28
School Gate, When School Starts	20	10
School Gate, When School Ends	30	62
Locker Room	33	59

(c) How Dangerous are Times and Places in School—by Grade?*

	Tenth Grade (%)	Eleventh Grade (%)	Twelfth Grade (%)
Class	11	11	8
School Yard	42	40	23
School Gate, When School Starts	12	17	16
School Gate When School Ends	53	58	27
Locker room	55	57	26

* Entries are percentages of students who say the place is either "quite dangerous" or "dangerous."
Note: The original figures provided to staff were translated, shortened, and modified for tabular presentation.

Reports like these, and site-specific data, were automatically generated and given to all the students, teachers, and parents. Dialogue groups were formed in classes, to talk about the problem and to generate, from students, teachers, and the principal, possible solutions to this issue. Most principals and schools have no problem interpreting these data; however, an initial orientation is helpful in familiarizing school administrators with interpretations of the data. Bar charts and line graphs are interpreted most easily, but the presentation format is chosen by each school.

Each of the school sites used these data in different ways. Currently, a district-wide qualitative study is under way, to document how schools develop their own interventions. The programs adopted by schools were quite diverse. They included: school beautification projects (introducing murals, planting grass, targeting violence-prone locations), increased student-staff ratios and oversight in key times and locations, efforts to improve staff and school morale, a bully-victim program, a review of policies and procedure surrounding sexual harassment, community interventions that targeted locations where students felt unsafe walking to and from school, and many more.

Initial reports indicated that some schools were struggling with the feedback system that evaluates their intervention efforts. For example, one school made extraordinary staff and student efforts to target violence-prone locations. The vice principal's offices were relocated near the bathrooms, and the physical structure was reorganized to improve the social interaction and staff/student monitoring of behaviors. The surveys showed great improvement in school morale/school spirit and subjective feelings about school. However, the school has not been able to reduce its high rates of specific forms of school violence (e.g., fights), even though the staff subjectively felt that "things were getting better." Although this feedback was initially disappointing to the staff, it prompted them to focus more on reducing violence rates and introducing new approaches, rather than on school climate interventions alone. This school has now worked out a system in which the students and staff are scanning and analyzing their own data. This allows the school to add its own questions and to carry out analyses to explore specific questions.

Aside from the concept of monitoring, the key elements of this data system are: It is easy to use, schools have the data almost immediately after they are scanned in, and schools are not totally dependent on external review-and-evaluation companies. Having data is essential, but we believe that the process used to discuss the data is equally important. The mapping procedure described in the next section provides a qualitative data-based method and a process (which can be used with the quantitative data as well) for discussing the shared data. Because it is process-oriented, the procedure is described in detail.

A Qualitative Data Alternative: Mapping Violence within the School

We believe the process and procedure described here could contribute to the success of grassroots strategies. The procedure is designed to aid practitioners in better understanding how violence within a school building interacts with locations, patterns of the school day, and social organizational variables (e.g., teacher and student relationships, teachers' professional roles, and the school's organizational response to violence). An important goal of this procedure is to *allow students and teachers to convey their personal theories* about why specific locations and times in their schools are more dangerous. This approach assumes that students, teachers, school staff, and administrators have important information that should be the foundation for *setting specific interventions*. These interventions should emerge from the information presented by the students, teachers, staff, and administrators in each school.

This process is designed to document (a) the locations and times within each school where violence occurred, and (b) the perspectives of students, teachers, staff, and administrators regarding the school's organizational response (or nonresponse) to violent events in these locations. This assessment process is particularly sensitive to areas that are "unowned"—times and places that are not perceived to be the responsibility of any adults in the school. Prior research indicated that these unowned spaces are the locations where most school violence occurs (Astor, Meyer, & Behre, 1999; Astor & Meyer, 1999; Astor, Meyer, & Pitner, 2001). It also should be noted that the following process could be conducted with the data generated from the sociofeedback monitoring system described in the prior section. The main idea is to use the data to generate discussion, yield more clarity about the nature of the problem, and introduce a diverse perspective on possible causes and solutions to the problem. Although we focus mainly on the mapping data, this process or procedure could be adapted to quantitative data as well.

We recommend that students, teachers, and staff (e.g., administrators, hall monitors, cafeteria workers) be interviewed (in four or five separate focus groups) about the physical spaces where violence has been committed, and the time of day the violence occurred. The students, teachers, and staff should represent various constituencies of the school organization, as well as locations within the school. For the assessment focus groups, we recommend that administrators (e.g., vice principals, principals, district-level officials), teachers, staff, and students be interviewed in separate focus groups—otherwise, students may fear repercussions from teachers, and teachers may be wary of openly discussing issues in front of administrators. It is important to ensure focus group members' anonymity, especially with regard to comments about the school's response to violence. To allow for in-depth discussion and responses to questions, we recommend that there be 6 to 8 individuals per focus group. The entire focus group process should take about one hour. Using this procedure, practitioners can conduct an ecological assessment of violence within the school in about 6 hours of interview time.

Based on prior interviews with school staff, practitioners can anticipate themes that include a sense of "being caught in the middle." Some teachers may have expressed a personal desire to prevent violence but may not possess the skills or knowledge needed to intervene. We have also found that many staff members are unclear about their professional role in nonclassroom locations. (See Astor et al., 1999, for a detailed description of the types of themes that can be anticipated from each group.)

We also recommend including the nonteaching staff in focus groups. Nonteaching staff members often suggest very specific interventions associated with their area of the school. For example, cafeteria workers in one school revealed that only two or three adults were expected to supervise more than 1,000 children during the lunch period. In several schools, secretaries had very clear suggestions for interventions regarding children who were sent to the office for fighting during less supervised periods (such as recess, lunch, or transitions between classes).

Obtaining School Maps

The first step in this assessment procedure is to obtain a map of the school. It is not necessary to obtain a detailed blueprint. Usually, the school office has a small (8″ by 11″) map of the school, as required by fire marshals. Ideally, the map should contain all internal school territory, including the areas surrounding the school, and the playground facilities. In communities where the routes to and from school are dangerous, a simple map of the surrounding neighborhood may be added to the assessment process.

The maps are an essential part of the interviewing process. They help to anchor discussions to places and times in ways that interviews about "issues" alone cannot. Two sets of the school maps should be photocopied for each participant in the focus groups (one marked "A" and the other marked "B" at the upper corner of the two sets). In addition to the maps, each interviewee should have a pencil or pen and a set of 8 circular colored stickers. The circular stickers should be used to mark violent events on the map (described in the following section).

When the focus groups are convened, the facilitator should distribute two sets of identical maps to each individual. The facilitator should then orient the group to how the different areas of the school are represented on the map. Also, participants should be encouraged not to identify, by name, any individual who may have been involved in violence. The purpose of the discussion is to identify *locations* rather than individuals.

Map A: Three Most Violent Events

The first map should be used to determine the location of the most violent events in or around the school building. Using the stickers, participants should be asked to identify, on the maps, the locations of up to three most violent events that occurred within the past academic year. In some schools, the most violent event may be a lethal shooting; in other schools, fights may be the most violent events.

The participant is free to interpret "most violent" subjectively. Our research suggests that students and school personnel take this task seriously and tend to report fairly severe events. Next to each event (marked by a circular sticker on the map), participants are asked to write, directly on the map, the following information: (a) the general time frame of the event (e.g., before school, after school, morning period, afternoon period, evening sports event, between classes); (b) the grade and gender of those involved in the violence; and (c) knowledge of any organizational response to the event (e.g., sent to the principal's office, suspended, sent to peer counselor, nothing).

Map B: Dangerous Areas in and around School

When the first set of maps has been completed, participants should be given the second map of the school. Group members should be asked to circle, using a pencil or pen, *areas* or *territories* that they perceive to be "unsafe" or potentially dangerous. We have found that asking about unsafe places reveals different information than asking for events alone. This second map provides information about areas within the school that participants avoid, even though they may not possess knowledge of a particular violent event. Participants should then be asked to explain, in a few sentences (on the second set of maps), *why* they believe this particular area or time is prone to violence or should be avoided. Completion of both sets of maps will consume approximately 10 minutes of focus group time.

Discussion of Violent Events and Areas

The first part of the group discussion should center on the specific violent events and the areas marked as "unsafe or dangerous" on their personal maps. We have asked questions such as: "Are there times when those places you've marked on the maps are less safe?" "Is there a particular group of students that is more likely to get hurt there?" "Why do you think that area has so many violent events?" The locations marked on both maps will be extremely helpful in identifying specific areas and times that are violence-prone.

The overall purpose of the group interviews is to explore *why* violence is occurring, where and when it is. Consequently, the interviews should also focus on gathering information regarding the organizational response to the event (e.g., "What happened to the two students who fought?" or "Did the hall monitors intervene when they saw the fight?"), procedures (e.g., "What happens when someone is sent to the office after a fight?"), follow-up (e.g., "Do the teachers, hall monitors, and/or administrators follow up on any consequences given to the students?" or "Did anyone check on the welfare of the victim?"), and clarity of procedures (e.g., "Does it matter who stops the fight?" e.g., a volunteer, security guard, teacher, or principal).

Interviewers should also explore participants' ideas for solutions to the specific problems (e.g., "Can you think of ways to avoid this type of violence in that place?" or "If you were the principal, what would you do to make that place safer?"). In addition, the interviewer should explore any obstacles participants foresee with implementation (e.g., "Do you think that type of plan is realistic?" "Has that been tried before? What happened?" or "Do you think that plan would work?"). Such obstacles could range from issues related to roles (e.g., "It's not my job to monitor students during lunch."), to discipline policy and issues of personal safety (e.g., "I don't want to intervene because I may get hurt.").

In schools that already have programs designed to address school violence, specific questions should be asked about the effectiveness of those interventions: why they work or do not work, and what could be done to make the current measures more effective. We recommend that the interviewer ask both subjective questions (e.g., "Do you like the conflict management program?") and specific questions related to the reduction of violence (e.g., "Do you believe the conflict management program has reduced the number of fights on the playground? Why or why not?").

Transferring all of the reported events onto one large map of the school enables students and staff to locate specific "hot spots" for violence and dangerous time periods *within each individual school*. For example, in one school, events were clustered by time, age, gender, and location. In the case of older students (eleventh and twelfth graders), events were clustered in the parking lot outside of the auxiliary gym immediately after school; among younger students (ninth and tenth graders), events were reported in the lunchroom and hallways during transition periods. For this school, the map suggested that interventions should be geared specifically toward older students, directly after school, by the main entrance and in the school parking lot. Students and teachers agreed that increasing the visible presence of school staff in and around the parking lot for 20 minutes after school had great potential for reducing the number of violent events. Younger students were experiencing violence mainly before, during, and after lunch, near the cafeteria. Many students expressed feelings of being unsafe in the hallways, between classes.

Interview Data

Compiling all the suggestions into readable themes is an important step in creating context-relevant interventions. Students, teachers, and administrators may have differing viewpoints regarding the organizational response of the school toward violence. Relaying the diversity of responses to students, teachers, and administrators can provide an opportunity for reflection and may generate ways to remedy violence in certain situations.

We believe this format also provides an interesting way to exemplify the different perspectives that may exist—among students, staff, and administrators—on how to deal with violent events. We recommend creating tables that list the comments for each important theme for a particular school. In the past, we have organized students', teachers', and principals' comments related to race, gender, poverty, community, and religious conflict when it was perceived that these variables were contributing factors toward violence within a school. Also, in schools that already have measures to prevent violence, we recommend the compilation of tables regarding those interventions (e.g., metal detectors, security guards, electronic and video monitoring, and suspension/expulsion policies).

Together, the poster-size map of violent events, the interview data organized by themes, and the information on the potential obstacles can provide concrete intervention strategies to reduce violence in school communities. At a minimum, the organized data provide a formal opportunity for various school subsystems to discuss these issues. We believe this assessment process is powerful because the organized information presented back to the school constituents has emerged from the setting. It contrasts with other assessment approaches in which outside "experts" determine what the problem and the intervention should be. With time, some schools may want to create an ongoing "hot spot" map to track unsafe places and times on a monthly basis.

CONCLUSION

The authors of this chapter have described recent drops in school violence rates and have raised questions regarding the categorization of a violence problem in schools. The review of the literature suggests that schools need to use both objective and subjective data in determining whether they are hosting a violence problem. We have argued that the entire school setting should be the focus of assessment and violence-prevention strategies. We have advocated strongly for the use of school data as the basis for interventions and their subsequent evaluations. One novel method we have endorsed is the creation of a comprehensive sociofeedback system that links school sites and school districts to national norms. Furthermore, we have suggested an alternative school violence procedure that integrates school maps (to locate violent "hot spots" in the school) and focus groups that include students, teachers, school staff, and administrators (to identify reasons why violence is occurring in certain places and potential solutions). Information obtained through either the sociofeedback monitoring or the mapping process could (a) increase the dialogue among students, teachers, and school staff on issues of school violence, (b) serve as an evaluation of school violence interventions already used in a school setting, and (c) increase school involvement in violence interventions. A long research history of failed school violence interventions points to the hard fact that implementation of programs in schools does not work if school staff, teachers, and students are not involved or invested in the intervention. Fitting the needs of the school with the violence prevention program is one way of maximizing the goodness of fit between the school and the program. The sociofeedback monitoring system and mapping/interviewing process also create opportunities to generate grassroots interventions that will help to secure the safety of children within the school community.

REFERENCES

Aber, J. L., Brown, J. L., Chaudry, N., Jones, S., & Samples, F. (1996). The evaluation of the Resolving Conflict Creatively Program: An overview. *American Journal of Preventive Medicine, 12,* 82–90.

American Psychological Association. (1993). *Violence and youth: Psychology's response* (Vol. 1). Washington, DC: Author.

Ash, P., Kellermann, A., Fuqua-Whitley, D., & Johnson, A. (1996). Gun acquisition and use by juvenile offenders. *Journal of the American Medical Association, 275,* 1754–1758.

Astor, R. (1998). Moral reasoning about school violence: Informational assumptions about harm within school subcontexts. *Educational Psychologist, 33,* 207–221.

Astor, R., & Meyer, H. (1998). *Making schools safe: A first prerequisite for learning.* Paper presented at the annual meeting of the American Educational Research Association, San Diego, CA.

Astor, R., & Meyer, H. (1999). Where girls and women won't go: Female students', teachers', and school social workers' views of school safety. *Social Work in Education, 21,* 201–219.

Astor, R., Meyer, H., & Behre, W. (1999). Unowned space and time in high schools: Mapping violence with students and teachers. *American Educational Research Journal, 36,* 3–42.

Astor, R., Meyer, H., & Pitner, R. (2001). Elementary and middle school students' perceptions of violence-prone school sub-contexts. *The Elementary School Journal, 101,* 511–528.

Astor, R., Pitner, R., & Duncan, B. (1996). Ecological approaches to mental health consultation with teachers on issues related to youth and school violence. *Journal of Negro Education, 65,* 336–355.

Batsche, G., & Knoff, A. (1994). Bullies and their victims: Understanding a pervasive problem in the schools. *School Psychology Review, 23,* 165–174.

Benbenishty, R., & Oyserman, D. (1995). Integrated information systems for human services: A conceptual framework, methodology and technology. *Computers in Human Service Organizations, 12,* 311–326.

Benbenishty, R., Zeira, A., & Astor, R. A. (1999, November). *A national study of school violence in Israel—Wave II: Fall 1999.* Jerusalem: Israeli Ministry of Education.

Berrill, K. (1990). Anti-gay violence and victimization in the U.S.: An overview [Special issue]. *Journal of Interpersonal Violence, 5,* 274–294.

Bierman, K., Cole, J., Dodge, K., Greenberg, M., Lochman, J., & McMahaon, R. (1992). A developmental and clinical model for the prevention of conduct disorder: The FAST Track Program. *Development and Psychopathology, 4,* 509–527.

Boulton, M. (1993). Aggressive fighting in British middle school children. *Educational Studies, 19,* 19–39.

Bragg, R. (1997, December 3). Forgiveness, after 3 die in Kentucky shooting: M. Carneal opens fire on fellow students at Heath High School in West Paducah. *The New York Times,* p. A16.

Bry, B. (1982). Reducing the incidence of adolescent problems through preventive intervention: One- and five-year follow-up. *American Journal of Community Psychology, 10,* 265–276.

Burcky, W., Reuterman, N., & Kopsky, S. (1988). Dating violence among high school students. *School Counselor, 35,* 353–358.

Cano, A., Avery-Leaf, S., Cascardi, M., & O'Leary, K. (1998). Dating violence in two high school samples: Discriminating variables. *Journal of Primary Prevention, 18,* 431–446.

Caplan, M., Weissburg, R. P., Grober, J. S., Sivo, P. J., Grady, K., & Jacoby, C. (1992). Social competence promotion with inner city and suburban young adolescents: Effects on social adjustment and alcohol use. *Journal of Consulting and Clinical Psychology, 60,* 56–63.

Coben, J., Weiss, H. B., & Mulvey, E. P. (1994). A primer on school violence prevention. *Journal of School Health, 64,* 309–313.

Committee for Children. (1992). *Second step: A violence prevention curriculum (preschool-kindergarten teacher's guide).* Seattle, WA: Author.

Dodge, K. (1993). *Effects of intervention on children on high risk for conduct problems.* Paper presented at the meeting of the Society for Research in Child Development, New Orleans, LA.

Dwyer, K., Osher, D., & Warger, C. (1998). Early warning, timely response: A guide to safe schools: Washington, DC: U.S. Department of Education.

Elam, S., & Rose, L. (1995). The 27th annual Phi Delta Kappa/Gallup poll of the public's attitudes toward the public schools. *Phi Delta Kappan, 77,* 41–56.

Elam, S., Rose, L., & Gallup, A. (1994). The 26th annual Phi Delta Kappa/Gallup poll of the public's attitudes toward the public schools. *Phi Delta Kappan, 76,* 41–56.

Elam, S., Rose, L., & Gallup, A. (1996). The 28th annual Phi Delta Kappa/Gallup poll of the public's attitudes toward the public schools. *Phi Delta Kappan, 78,* 41–59.

Embry, D., Flannery, D., Vazsonyi, A., Powell, K., & Atha, H. (1996). Peace Builders: A theoretically driven, school-based model for early violence prevention. *American Journal of Prevention Medicine, 12,* 91–100.

Feindler, E., & Ecton, R. (1986). *Adolescent anger control: Cognitive-behavioral techniques.* New York: Pergamon Press.

Flannery, D., & Vazsonyi, A. (1996). *Peace Builders: A school-based model for early violence prevention.* Chicago, IL: American Society of Criminology.

Flaxman, E., Schwartz, W., Weiler, J., & Lahey, M. (1998). Trends and issues in urban education, 1998. [Online]. Available from: http://eric-web.tc.columbia.edu /monographs/ti20 [1999, January 20].

Gegax, T., Adler, J., & Pedersen, D. (1998, April 6). The boys behind the ambush. *Newsweek, 131,* 21–24.

Goldstein, A. (1996). *The psychology of vandalism.* New York: Plenum Press.

Goldstein, A., Glick, B., Reiner, S., Zimmerman, D., & Coultry, T. (1985). *Aggression replacement training: A comprehensive intervention for aggressive youth.* Champaign, IL: Research Press.

Gottfredson, D. (1986). An empirical test of school-based environmental and individual interventions to reduce the risk of delinquent behavior. *Criminology, 24,* 705–731.

Gottfredson, D. (1997). School based crime prevention. In L. Sherman, D. Gottfredson, D. MacKenzie, J. Eck, P. Reuter, & S. Bushway (Eds.), *Preventing crime: What works, what doesn't, what's promising: A report to the United States Congress.* Washington, DC: Department of Justice.

Gottfredson, D., Fink, C., Skroban, S., & Gottfredson, G. (in press). Making prevention work. In R. P. Weissburg (Ed.), *Issues in children's and families' lives. Volume 4: Healthy children 2010: School- and community-based strategies to enhance social, emotional and physical wellness.*

Gray, D. (1991). *The plight of the African American male: An executive summary of a legislative hearing.* Detroit, MI: Council President Pro Tem Gil, the Detroit City Council Youth Advisory Commission.

Greenberg, M., Kusché, C., & Mihalic, S. (1998). *Blueprints for violence prevention. Volume 10: Promoting Alternative Thinking Strategies (PATHS).* Boulder, CO: Center for the Study and Prevention of Violence.

Greenberg, M., Lochman, J., & McMahon, R. (1996, May). *Abstract: An initial evaluation of the Fast Track Program.* Proceedings of the fifth national prevention conference, Tysons Corner, VA.

Gregg, S. (1998). *School-based programs to promote safety and civility* (AEL Policy Briefs). Charleston, WV: Appalachia Educational Laboratory.

Grossman, D., Neckerman, H., Koepsell, T., Liu, P., Asher, K., Beland, K., et al. (1997). Effectiveness of a violence prevention curriculum among children in elementary school. *Journal of the American Medical Association, 277,* 1605–1611.

Guerra, N., & Panizzon, A. (1986). *Viewpoints training program.* Santa Barbara, CA: Center for Law-Related Education.

Hammond, W., & Yung, B. (1991). Preventing violence in at-risk African American youth. *Journal of Heath Care for the Poor and Underserved, 2,* 358–372.

Hammond, W. R., & Yung, B. (1993). Psychology's role in the public health response to assaultive violence among young African-American men. *American Psychologist, 48,* 142–154.

Harel, Y., Kenny, D., & Rahav, G. (1997). *Youth in Israel: Social welfare, health and risk behaviors from an international perspectives.* Jerusalem: JDC.

Hawkins, D., Catalano, R., Morrison, D., O'Donnell, J., Abbott, R., & Day, E. (1992). The Seattle Social Development Project: Effects of the first four years on protective factors and problem behaviors. In J. McCord & R. E. Tremblay (Eds.), *Preventing antisocial behavior: Interventions from birth through adolescence.* New York: Guilford Press.

Hays, K. (1998, April 26). Boy held in teacher's killing. *The Detroit News and Free Press*, p. 5A.

Hudley, C., Britsch, B., Wakefield, T., Demorat, M., & Cho, S. (1998). An attribution retraining program to reduce aggression in elementary school students. *Psychology in the Schools, 35,* 271–282.

Hyman, I. A., & Snook P. A. (2000). Dangerous schools and what you can do about them. *Phi Delta Kappan, 81*(7), 488–501.

Issacs, M. (1992). *Violence: The impact of community violence on African-American children and families: Collaborative approaches to prevention and intervention.* Arlington, VA: National Center for Education in Maternal and Child Health.

Kachur, P., Stennies, G., Powell, K., Modzeleski, W., Stephens, R., Murphy, R., et al. (1996). School-associated violent deaths in the United States, 1992 to 1994. *Journal of the American Medical Association, 275,* 1729–1733.

Kann, L., Kinchen, S., Williams, B., Ross, J., Lowry, R., Hill, C., et al. (1998). Youth risk behavior surveillance—1997. *Morbidity and Mortality Weekly Report Surveillance Summary, 48*(SS-3), 1–89.

Kann, L., Kinchen, S., Williams, B., Ross, J., Lowry, R., Grunbaum, J., et al. (2000). Youth risk behavior surveillance—1999. *Morbidity and Mortality Weekly Report Surveillance Summary, 49*(SS-5), 1–32.

Kaufman, P., Chen, X., Choy, S., Chandler, K., Chapman, C., Rand, M., et al. (1998). *Indicators of school crime and safety, 1998* (NCES 98-251/NCJ-172215). Washington, DC: U.S. Departments of Education and Justice.

Kaufman, P., Chen, X., Choy, S., Ruddy, S., Miller, A., Fleury, J., et al. (2000). *Indicators of school crime and safety, 2000* (NCES 2001-017/NCJ-184176). Washington, DC: U.S. Departments of Education and Justice.

Kellam, S., Rebok, G., Ialongo, N., & Mayer, L. (1994). The course and malleability of aggressive behavior from early first grade into middle school: Results of a developmental epidemiologically-based preventive trial. *Journal of Child Psychology and Psychiatry, 35,* 259–282.

Kingery, P. M., Coggeshall, M. B., & Alford, A. A., (1998). Violence at school: Recent evidence from four national surveys. *Psychology in the Schools, 35*(3), 247–258.

Kodluboy, D. (1997). Gang-oriented interventions. In A. Goldstein (Ed.), *School violence intervention: A practical handbook* (pp. 189–214). New York: Guilford Press.

Larson, J. (1998). Managing student aggression in high schools: Implications for practice. *Psychology in the Schools, 35,* 283–295.

Lochman, J., Lampron, L., Gemmer, T., & Harris, S. (1986). Anger coping intervention with aggressive children: A guide to implementation in school settings. In P. Keller & S. Heyman (Eds.), *Innovations in clinical practice: A source book* (Vol. 6, pp. 339–356). Sarasota, FL: Professional Resources Exchange.

Lorion, R. (1998). Exposure to urban violence: Contamination of the school environment. In D. Elliott, B. Hamburg, & K. Williams (Eds.), *Violence in American schools: A new perspective* (pp. 293–311). New York: Cambridge University Press.

Macgowan, M. J. (1999). Assessment of childhood aggression and youth violence. In J. M. Jenson & M. O. Howard (Eds.), *Youth violence: Current research and recent practice innovations* (pp. 43–86). Washington, DC: NASW Press.

Milwaukee Board of School Directors. (1993). *An evaluation of the Second Step Violence Prevention Curriculum for elementary students.* Milwaukee, WI: Author.

Morrison, G., Furlong, M., & Morrison, R. (1997). The safe school: Moving beyond crime prevention to school empowerment. In A. Goldstein & J. Conoley (Eds.), *School violence intervention: A practical handbook* (pp. 236–264). New York: Guilford Press.

National Education Goals Panel. (1995). *The National Education Goals Report. Volume I: National Data. Volume II: State Data.* Washington, DC: U.S. Government Printing Office.

Noguera, P. A. (1995). Preventing and producing violence: A critical analysis of responses to school violence. *Harvard Educational Review, 51,* 546–564.

Olweus, D. (1993). *Bullying at school.* Oxford, England: Blackwell.

Olweus, D., Limber, S., & Mihalic, S. F. (1999). *Blueprints for violence prevention. Volume 9: Bullying Prevention Program.* Boulder, CO: Center for the Study and Prevention of Violence.

Page, R. (1997). Helping adolescents avoid date rape: The role of secondary education. *High School Journal, 80,* 75–80.

Parks, C. (1995). Gang behavior in the schools: Reality or myth? *Educational Psychology Review, 7,* 41–68.

Pittel, E. (1998). How to take a weapons history: Interviewing children at risk for violence at school. *Journal of the American Academy of Child and Adolescent Psychiatry, 37,* 1100–1102.

Prothrow-Stith, D. (1987). *Violence prevention curriculum for adolescents.* Newton, MA: Education Development Center.

Prothrow-Stith, D., & Weissman, M. (1991). *Deadly consequences.* New York: Harper Collins.

Rigby, K. (1996). *Bullying in schools: And what to do about it.* Melbourne, Victoria, Australia: Australian Council for Educational Research.

Rose, L., & Gallup, A. (1999). The 31st annual Phi Delta Kappa/Gallup poll of the public's attitudes toward the public schools. *Phi Delta Kappan, 81,* 41–56.

Rose, L., & Gallup, A. (2000). The 32nd annual Phi Delta Kappa/Gallup poll of the public's attitudes toward the public schools. *Phi Delta Kappan, 82,* 41–66.

Rose, L., Gallup, A., & Elam, S. (1997). The 29th annual Phi Delta Kappa/Gallup poll of the public's attitudes toward the public schools. *Phi Delta Kappan, 79,* 41–56.

Schafer, M., & Smith, P. (1996). Teacher's perceptions of play fighting and real fighting in primary school. *Educational Research, 38,* 173–181.

Schweinhart, L., Barnes, H., & Weikart, D. (1993). Significant benefits: The High/Scope Perry preschool study through age 27. *Monographs of the High/Scope Educational Research Foundation* (No. 10).

Sharp, S., & Smith, P. (1994). *Tackling bullying in your school: A practical handbook for teachers.* London, England: Routledge.

Smith, P., Morita, Y., Junger-Tas, J., Olweus, D., Catalano, R., & Slee, P. (1999). *The nature of school bullying: A cross-national perspective.* New York: Routledge.

Smith, P., & Sharp, S. (1994). *School bullying.* London, England: Routledge.

Snyder, H. N., & Sickmund, M. (1999). *Juvenile offenders and victims: 1999 national report.* Washington, DC: Office of Juvenile Justice and Delinquency Prevention.

Stein, N. (1995). Sexual harassment in the school: The public performance of gendered violence. *Harvard Educational Review, 65*(2), 145–162.

Tolan, P., & Guerra, N. (1994). Prevention of delinquency: Current status and issues. *Applied and Preventive Psychology, 3,* 251–273.

U.S. Department of Education. National Center for Educational Statistics. (1998). *Violence and discipline problems in U.S. public schools: 1996–1997* (NCES 98-030). By S. Heaviside, C. Rowand, C. Williams, & E. Farris. Project officers Shelley Burns and Edith MaArthur. Washington, DC: Author.

U.S. Departments of Education and Justice. (2000). 2000 *Annual Report on School Safety.* Washington, DC: Author.

Vossekuil, B., Reddy, M., Fein, R., Borum, R., & Modzeleski, W. (2000). *U.S.S.S. Safe School Initiative: An interim report on the prevention of targeted violence in schools.* Washington, DC: U.S. Secret Service, National Threat Assessment Center.

Wahler, J., Fetsch, R., & Silliman, B. (1997, January 8). *Research-based, empirically-effective violence prevention curricula: A review of resources.* Retrieved January 25, 2000. Available from http://www.nnfr.org/violence/yvp_litrev.html.

Webster, D. (1993). The unconvincing case for school based conflict resolution programs for adolescents. *Health Affairs, 4,* 126–141.

Witkin, G., Tharp, M., Schrof, J., Toch, T., & Scattarella, C. (1998, June 1). Again. In Springfield, a familiar school scene: Bloody kids, grieving parents, a teen accused of murder. *U.S. News and World Report, 124,* 16–21.

Youssef, R., Attia, M., & Kamel, M. (1998). Children experiencing violence. II: Prevalence and determinants of corporal punishment in schools. *Child Abuse and Neglect, 22,* 975–985.

Yung, B., & Hammond, R. (1998). Breaking the cycle: A culturally sensitive violence prevention program for African-American children. In L. Lutzker (Ed.), *Handbook of child abuse research and treatments.* New York: Plenum Press.

Chapter 14

REDUCING SCHOOL VIOLENCE: A SOCIAL CAPACITY FRAMEWORK

GARY L. BOWEN, NATASHA K. BOWEN, JACK M. RICHMAN, AND MICHAEL E. WOOLLEY

INTRODUCTION

On May 21, 1998, 15-year-old Kip Kinkel killed two students and shot 22 others at Thurston High School in Springfield, Oregon. Voted by his classmates as "Most Likely to Start World War III," Kip Kinkel had shot his parents the day before. On April 20, 1999, high school students Eric Harris, age 18, and Dylan Klebold, age 17, entered Columbine High School in Littleton, Colorado, with an arsenal of weapons. In a terrorist-like assault, they killed 12 students and a teacher and wounded 23 others before ending their own lives. This was the worst school shooting in U.S. history. These shootings had been preceded by highly publicized murders at schools in Pearl, Mississippi; West Paducah, Kentucky; Jonesboro, Arkansas; and Edinboro, Pennsylvania.

Despite the public outcry about school violence after the Columbine tragedy, the shootings did not stop. The murder of 6-year-old Kayla Rolland by her 6-year-old classmate in Mt. Morris Township, Michigan, and the shooting of a middle school teacher in Palm Beach County, Florida, in 2000 are vivid reminders of the potential consequences when kids have access to guns.

The high-profile nature of these shootings makes it appear that schools are battlefields in which only the most aggressive, protected, or lucky prevail. Yet, schools remain one of the safest locations for youths, and the number of school-associated murders and school violence rates in general have been declining (Brooks, Schiraldi, & Ziedenberg, 2000; Kaufman et al., 2000). Still, too many youths are victims of violence at school (we include physical and psychological intimidation and harassment), and many go to school fearful that they may be the next victims (Bowen, Bowen, & Richman, 1998). Such precarious environments have detrimental effects on youths, whether they are perpetrators, victims, or bystanders. Exposure to violence and personal victimization has been associated with delinquent behavior, use of violence, school failure, and precocious transitions (Barton, Coley, & Wenglinsky, 1998; Bowen & Bowen, 1999; Bowen, Richman, Brewster, & Bowen, 1998; DuRant, Getts, Cadenhead, Emans, & Woods, 1995).

This chapter directs primary attention to the identification, classification, and prediction of school violence among middle school and high school youths. School violence has eluded consistent and precise definition in the empirical literature, and may include a wide range of disruptive and illegal behaviors. The definition by Astor, Vargas, Pitner, and Meyer (1999) frames the present review: "School violence covers a wide range of intentional or reckless behaviors that include physical harm, psychological harm, and property damage" (p. 140). School violence is distinguished from the more general category of violence only by the location of the behavior. This includes student and staff victimization taking place on school campuses, or confrontations with threats and violent behavior on their way to and from school or in the course of performing school-related duties or participating in school-associated activities. Primary attention in this chapter is directed to violence where students are either victims or perpetrators.

This review of factors associated with youth violence in general and school violence in particular is framed by an ecological perspective that views students as active agents in a broader structural and dynamic context (Richman & Bowen, 1997). Efforts to identify, classify, and predict school violence inform the design of social interventions and the targeting of services and programs to those students most vulnerable to its occurrence and effects. In this context, we first review current trends and issues in school violence, including rates of school violence, subjective fears of students, and current responses.

A social capacity framework is offered as a conceptual model for informing intervention and prevention activities, which are discussed in the closing section. From a social capacity perspective, primary attention is focused on macrolevel factors distinguishing schools and the communities in which schools are embedded, rather than microlevel characteristics distinguishing victims and perpetrators. In part, this macrolevel perspective balances the emphasis in the school violence literature on victims and perpetrators, and it is consistent with social work's contextual orientation as reflected in ecological theory and the strengths perspective.

We believe school violence is a problem that schools cannot solve alone. Effective solutions require a community approach—a coalition of formal and informal community networks working together to create a safe environment supportive of youth development and student success. We agree with James

Garbarino (2001) who concludes, in a chapter entitled "Making Sense of Sense-less Youth Violence": "The eventual goal is to detoxify the social environment and provide a more supportive setting, particularly for psychologically vulner-able individuals, replacing the dark secrets of violence with the enduring truths of love and peace" (p. 94).

CURRENT TRENDS AND ISSUES

Crime and Violence in Schools

Information from administrative sources and national surveys has chronicled students' experiences with violence and crime at school and their fears and con-cerns about their personal safety. The number of school-associated violent deaths decreased from 43 in the 1997–1998 school year to 26 in the 1998–1999 school year (Brooks et al., 2000), but physical attacks and intimidation, fights, and robbery are not uncommon events in many public schools (Astor et al., 1999). More than one-quarter of middle and high school students who partici-pated in the 1996–1997 national administration of the School Success Profile reported fights among students (28%), stealing (27%), destruction of school property (27%), student use of alcohol (28%), and illegal drugs (30%) as "big problems" in their schools (Bowen et al., 1998). One in five students participat-ing in the same survey (16% of middle school students and 24% of high school students) reported that they knew someone who had carried a weapon to school in the last 30 days.

Although violent death remains a rare event in our public schools, and overall rates of serious violent crime at school declined between 1992 and 1998 (Kauf-man et al., 2000), student victimization is not uncommon. More than one in three junior high and high school students (36%) participating in the 1996 Metropoli-tan Life national survey reported that they had been the victim of a violent inci-dent in or around their school (Harris & Associates, 1996). In this same survey, one in four junior high school students (25%) and about one in three high school students (30%) felt that the level of violence at their schools had increased in the past year. In the most recent Metropolitan Life national survey, nearly one in five (18%) public school students in grades 7 through 12 reported school safety as the most important issue facing America today (Harris & Associates, 2000).

In view of students' confrontation with crime and violence in their schools, it is not surprising that many students report a lack of security and safety. Nearly one in three middle and high school respondents (30%) who participated in the national administration of the School Success Profile reported that they were sometimes or often afraid of being hurt or bothered at school, including 38% of middle school students and 24% of high school students (Bowen et al., 1998). More than one in four students (26%) who completed the same survey reported that they were sometimes or often afraid of being hurt or bothered on their way to and from school (32% of middle school students and 21% of high school students).

From their national data, Bowen et al. (1998) concluded that students may feel safer at school than is warranted by objective conditions. In their analysis, nearly two-thirds of the students who either reported some type of crime and violence as a big problem at their school or had experienced personal threats to their safety at school also reported that they felt safe. A smaller subset of students evidenced incongruity in the other direction—they felt afraid in situations in which they reported no incidents of disruption or personal threats to their well-being.

An important finding in these analyses by Bowen et al. (1998) is the positive and significant correlation between perceived danger at school and perceived danger in the neighborhood (r = .42). Events and situations at school do not only explain the fears students report at school. Consistent with an ecological perspective and with the social capacity perspective advanced in this chapter, it is important to consider students in the multiple contexts in which they are embedded. In agreement with a recent report on youth violence by the Centers for Disease Control and Prevention (cited in Brooks et al., 2000), we believe that school violence should not be examined in isolation from the general violence youths face in the broader community.

Responses to School Violence

Efforts to address school violence have tended to be reactive, narrowly targeted toward single correlates of violence, and student-focused in orientation (see Astor et al., 1999). In general, interventions have neglected conditions in the broader social environment fueling violent behavior at school. Effective strategies must also aim to change the nature of opportunities and social relationships in the school and broader community so that all students experience success, self-esteem, a sense of belonging, and attachment to adults in the school and community. These efforts augment a more student-focused approach and represent a more proactive and preventive approach to school violence.

In response to specific acts of violence, for example, youths are often singled out for punishment and/or treatment. From this perspective, individuals are viewed as the cause of violence, and practitioners select interventions aimed at changing or controlling individuals. Micro-interventions targeting cognitive and decision-making skills and anger management (e.g., Dubow, Huesmann, & Eron,

1987; Kendall & Braswell, 1982; Lange & Jakubowski, 1976; Lochman, Lampron, Gemmer, & Harris, 1987), for example, assume that violence arises from individual deficits in these cognitive-behavioral skills.

Another reactive approach, confronting violence by "target-hardening procedures" (Alexander & Curtis, 1995), also aims to control or limit the opportunities of individuals to act violently. Such approaches may include installing metal detectors; hiring security staff; requiring students to wear identification badges; and training staff on how to maintain personal safety, diffuse potentially violent situations, and respond to violent acts. On the positive side, these measures may reduce the number of weapons in schools and prevent violent acts at certain times and locations. On the negative side, these actions may merely divert crime temporally or spatially rather than prevent it.

Overly reactive interventions and those that are narrowly focused on the individual disregard the body of theory and empirical evidence showing that the behavior of children and adolescents is inextricably linked to characteristics of and events in multiple levels of the social environment. They also ignore a substantial body of evidence demonstrating that interventions targeting only one contributor to violence, such as the problem-solving skills of the small number of students most likely to commit violent acts, have limited results. For example, what Wasserman and Miller (1998) have called "single-focused" interventions are limited in terms of their short- or long-term impact on behavior, the generalizability of their effects to other negative behaviors or other settings, and/or the populations who benefit from the treatments (Kazdin, 1995; McMahon & Wells, 1989; Wasserman & Miller, 1998).

PREDICTION, IDENTIFICATION, AND CLASSIFICATION

Predictors of Youth Violence

Those who study school violence can benefit from the extensive knowledge base related to youth violence in general. According to a comprehensive review of the research (Hawkins et al., 1998), predictors of youth violence include numerous individual and environmental factors. Individual factors include biological, behavioral, and cognitive characteristics, such as birth complications, attention deficit/hyperactivity disorders, anxiety, aggression, violence, and delinquency in middle childhood and early adolescence, and antisocial attitudes. Negative attitudes toward school, poor school performance, poor attendance, dropping out, and transferring from one school to another at certain ages have also been substantiated as predictors.

Environmental predictors listed in the Hawkins et al. (1998) review include family factors, such as poverty; parental conflict, substance abuse, mental illness, and criminality; abuse or neglect; nonauthoritative parenting styles; negative parent-child relationships; family stress; and favorable attitudes toward violence on the part of parents. Youth violence is also predicted by attendance at schools with high rates of delinquency, and exposure to siblings and peers who are delinquent or antisocial or who have favorable attitudes toward delinquency.

In the broader social environment of the community, predictors of youth violence include poverty, poor housing, neighborhood disorganization, illegal drug availability, and community crime and violence. Experiences of racial discrimination and prejudice were also predictive of youth violence, according to the review by Hawkins et al. (1998). Some distinctions can be made between those who are victims of violence and those who engage in violence, but, in general, youths who live in settings characterized by the features predictive of youth violence are more likely to experience violence as perpetrators, victims, or both.

Correlates Identified in the School Violence Literature

The body of literature on violence that takes place in schools is more limited than the general youth violence literature, but it identifies characteristics of individuals and the social environment that are consistent with the factors listed above. The literature on youth violence in general specifies characteristics of adult-child relationships in the family and community; the school-specific literature also identifies variables related to the climate of schools and the nature of relationships between students and school staff. Below, we summarize findings from the literature on factors associated with school violence.

The literature identifies correlates of school violence that are characteristic of the individuals most likely to experience violence (as perpetrators or victims); characteristics of the families of youths who are most likely to engage in violent acts; demographic and geographic characteristics of the schools these youths attend and the neighborhoods they live in; and characteristics of the *relationships* and *interactions* between youths and adults and among adults in schools and communities. We contend that the last set of factors—characteristics of relationships and interactions of youths and adults at multiple levels of the social environment—are key to understanding the causes of violence and developing solutions and prevention strategies for violence. Although school violence needs to be addressed through a combination of strategies, the most effective strategies involve targeting adult-child relationships in the school and other settings.

Characteristics of Individuals

Characteristics of students that have been associated with school violence include gender, sexual orientation, race/ethnicity, age, cognitive and decision-making skills, and exposure to violence (Alexander & Curtis, 1995; Bowen & Bowen, 1999; Harris & Associates, 1999; Singer & Miller, 1999; Snyder & Sickmund, 1999; Youth Pride, 1997). Although the number of aggressive acts committed by girls in schools rose during the second half of the 1990s (Harris & Associates, 1999), boys continue to be the primary offenders and victims in school violence (Singer & Miller, 1999; Snyder & Sickmund, 1999). Males were also more likely to report carrying a weapon to school (Snyder & Sickmund, 1999). Barton et al. (1998) presented national data indicating that male eighth graders are more likely than females to feel unsafe or very unsafe at school. Because perceptions of safety are likely to be associated with actual rates of victimization and offending (Welsh, 2000), these perceptions are indicative of patterns of school violence.

Sexual orientation is also associated with school violence. According to figures presented by Youth Pride (1997), 45% of gay males and 20% of lesbians reported experiencing verbal harassment and/or physical violence as a result of their sexual orientation during high school. Victimization based on sexual orientation is best explained as a consequence of the characteristics of the school social environment. Youth Pride also presented figures indicating that virtually all (97%) public high school students report regularly hearing homophobic comments from their peers, and more than half (53%) report hearing homophobic comments made by school staff.

Some studies indicate that whites may experience less exposure to school violence, African Americans experience more school violence (Bowen & Bowen, 1999), and African Americans and Hispanics may be more likely than others to fight at school (Snyder & Sickmund, 1999). Snyder and Sickmund also found that African American and Hispanic students were more likely than white students to report that they missed school because they felt unsafe at or on the way to school. Hispanic students were more likely than whites and African Americans to report that street gangs were present in their schools, according to one report (Barton et al., 1998). This finding is relevant because students in schools with gangs were also reportedly more likely to be victimized by violent crime. Barton et al. (1998) also presented data indicating that Hispanic students in the eighth grade are more likely than white eighth graders to feel unsafe or very unsafe at school.

Several studies indicate that experiences with violence also vary by age, but the findings are inconsistent. Singer and Miller (1999) reported that among children ages 7 to 15 years, those in higher grades engaged in more violent behavior. Bowen and Bowen (1999) found that high school students reported more experiences with school violence than middle school students. Results of another study (Snyder & Sickmund, 1999), however, indicated that ninth and tenth graders were more likely to fight than older high school students. The same report found that ninth graders of both genders were more likely than twelfth graders to report missing school because they felt unsafe there.

Exposure to violence has been shown to predict violent behavior. Singer and Miller (1999) reported that experiencing or witnessing violence in the past was a significant predictor of self-reported violent behaviors in third through eighth graders. The same study found that TV viewing habits, including content and hours of viewing, contributed to the prediction of violent behavior.

Characteristics of Families

Researchers have also found associations among school violence, family demographics, and parenting behavior. Low socioeconomic status and having only one parent in the home have been associated with school violence (Barton et al., 1998; Bowen & Bowen, 1999; Orpinas & Murray, 1999). In a study by Orpinas and Murray (1999), inverse relationships were found between aggression (including fighting at school) and levels of parental monitoring, positive parent-child relationships, and parental support for avoidance of fighting. Parental attitudes toward fighting (based on students' reports) constituted the strongest predictor of aggression. Singer and Miller (1999) also identified low parental monitoring as a correlate of child violence. The more extensive explication of family processes, relationships, and demographics in the general youth violence literature described above can be used to supplement the literature focusing on school violence.

School and Community Demographics

School Demographics. Demographic features of schools—such as number of students, gang presence, and location—have been associated with levels of school violence. School size appears to affect subjective and objective levels of school violence and danger (Barton et al., 1998; Bowen, Bowen, & Richman, 2000; Welsh, 2000). In a study of middle school students in a nationally representative sample, for example, Bowen, Bowen, and Richman (2000) found that perceptions of school safety were lowest in the largest schools (1,000 to 1,399 students), and highest in the smallest schools (fewer than 400 students). Schools that have gang members among their students are more dangerous: Barton et al. (1998) reported that students in schools with gangs are more likely to be victims of violent crime.

Barton et al. (1998) presented data indicating that among eighth graders in a national study, students attending public schools were more likely than those in Catholic schools and non-Catholic private schools to feel unsafe or very unsafe. Students in schools in the southeastern United States, furthermore, were more likely to feel unsafe than those in the northeast.

Community Demographics.   Some studies have not found significant differences in perceptions of safety or violence based on urbanicity (Barton et al., 1998; Singer & Miller, 1999); others have (Bowen et al., 1998; Harris & Associates, 1999). Bowen et al. (1998) found that students in urban schools were more likely than those in suburban and rural schools to report that three or more types of crime and disruption were big problems at their school, and that they knew someone who carried a weapon to school in the previous 30 days. In this study, based on over 1,800 middle and high school students in a nationally representative sample, urban teens were *less* likely than suburban teens to have fought with another student in the previous 30 days. In the Harris and Associates study, students and teachers in urban areas were more likely than those in nonurban areas to report gang problems, and teachers were more likely to feel unsafe at school. Inadequate school resources, which reflect community resources, have been associated with school violence (Welsh, 2000).

Neighborhood characteristics have also proven to be predictive of school violence. Schools located in communities with high levels of crime, poverty, and unemployment experience more school violence and victimization (Bowen & Bowen, 1999; Welsh, 2000). In the Bowen and Bowen study, neighborhood characteristics were more predictive of school disruption than school characteristics. In a study by Gottfredson and Gottfredson, cited in Barton et al. (1998), crime and violence in the community was the strongest predictor of school crime.

Characteristics of School and Community Relationships

Community Relationships.   "Collective efficacy," defined by Sampson, Raudenbush, and Earls (1997) as "social cohesion among neighbors combined with their willingness to intervene on behalf of the common good" (p. 918), refers to relationships among adults in a neighborhood, and between adults and youth. Greater collective efficacy was associated with lower rates of neighborhood violence in the Sampson et al. study. Higher levels of collective efficacy in neighborhoods also have been shown to be related to more positive perceptions, by adolescents in single-mother households, of family integration and parental support (Bowen, Bowen, & Cook, 2000). Collective efficacy is assumed to operate as a protective factor for youths by increasing opportunities for prosocial pursuits and decreasing opportunities for deviant and illegitimate acts.

Because neighborhood violence is related to school violence, collective effi-cacy in the neighborhood is a relevant target for school violence reduction ef-forts. Efforts to promote social integration among residents and strengthen social control mechanisms in neighborhoods are likely to contribute to youth and family functioning. Related to collective efficacy, which acts as an informal social control mechanism, formal collaboration among schools and community agencies—law enforcement, juvenile justice, and social services—can reduce school violence (Vera Institute of Justice, 1999). Strengthening the operation of community networks is an important function of formal collaborations—one that is essential to the development of collective efficacy.

School Relationships.   Aspects of the school social environment that have been associated with school violence include norms for behavior and interactions, multiple components of teacher-student relationships, disciplinary strategies, and administrative leadership (Alexander & Curtis, 1995; Welsh, 2000; Yogan, 2000). Research findings substantiate the importance of multiple dimensions within a school's climate in the reduction of violent behaviors at school.

Using self-reported data from over 6,000 middle school students in Philadel-phia, Welsh (2000) examined the effects of various school climate indicators (clarity and fairness of rules, respect for students, students' influence on school affairs, and efforts to plan and implement school improvement) on five aspects of school disorder: (a) self-reported offending, (b) avoidance of certain school areas because of safety concerns, (c) misconduct, (d) victimization, and (e) safety of the school environment. The data revealed variations not only in students' percep-tions of school climate across schools, but also in the levels of disorder as they re-lated to school climate.

The indicators of school climate differed in their effects on each aspect of school disorder. For example, perceptions of the school environment's safety were predicted by respect for students, student influence, clarity of rules, and planning and action. A low rate of victimization was positively related to re-spect for students, planning and action efforts, and perceived fairness and clar-ity of rules. Offending was also predicted to be low because of respect for students, clarity and fairness of rules, and student influence. The conclusion of the study was that characteristics of and expectations about the relationships among children and staff at the school were associated with perceived levels of safety, victimization, offending, and other components of school disorder.

Related to the findings about clear and fair rules are findings from other stud-ies that underscore the importance of consistent and systematic disciplinary re-sponses to school violence (Barton et al., 1998; Welsh, 2000). Such responses usually occur in schools with clear administrative leadership and teacher-administrator agreement on disciplinary goals and methods (Welsh, 2000).

The academic treatment of students by school staff may also be a component of school climate. One author (Yogan, 2000) has argued, from a symbolic interaction perspective, that academic tracking reduces the quality of teacher-student relationships and student-student relationships in schools, and may promote violence. The placement of students into ability groupings, which often correspond to differences in race/ethnicity, socioeconomic status, behavior, and past academic performance, Yogan argues, has negative consequences for learning and social opportunities for those in the lower ability groups, as well as for the development of their self-esteem, identity, and school bonding. Because positive engagement in and attachment to school is negatively associated with delinquency and violence, tracking may contribute to violence. Related to Yogan's argument are comments by Welsh (2000), who maintains that unrewarding academic and social experiences at school impede the development of bonding and commitment to school and, therefore, commitment to conventional rules and activities.

Tolerance of prejudicial treatment of students by other students and/or staff, based on race/ethnic status, gender, economic status, or sexual orientation, is also a component of school climate that contributes to school violence (Alexander & Curtis, 1995; Welsh, 2000; Youth Pride, 1997). In the Welsh study, for example, less respect for students was an important predictor of school disorder. Administrative tolerance of homophobic attitudes and behaviors contributes to verbal and physical abuse of gay and lesbian students.

Implications of the Correlates of School Violence

The fact that variables in all of the domains described above have been associated with school violence indicates that each domain needs to be considered in efforts to reduce school violence. As with the general youth violence literature, what is more important than any specific items on the list of predictors of school violence is the notion that violence, like all human behavior, is a consequence of a wide variety of interacting individual and environmental characteristics. Violence can neither be understood by examining only one domain of contributing factors, nor successfully addressed by targeting only one of those domains (Gottfredson, 1986).

More effective approaches to curbing and preventing violence can be designed when violent behavior is viewed as a symptom of characteristics of multiple interrelated domains of the social environment in which youths exist. Such approaches target both multiple levels of the social environment and individuals, include prevention as well as intervention components, and involve the collaborative efforts of adults in the school, family, and community. Strengthening the relationships and interactions of youth and adults at multiple levels of the social environment is key to developing solutions and prevention strategies for violence. The concept of social capacity, as we explain later, captures the qualities of these relationships that are most desirable. We focus on the social environmental level not only because of its importance as a central component of effective interventions for school violence, but also because it has received far less attention in terms of intervention and prevention development, documentation, and implementation than the more micro-level components.

A SOCIAL CAPACITY FRAMEWORK

The application of a social capacity framework to the examination of school violence evolves from the work of Bowen, Martin, Mancini, and Nelson (2000) in addressing the antecedents and consequences of community capacity, as well as the work of Bowen, Richman, and Bowen (2000) in examining families in the context of communities. In schools with high social capacity, community stakeholders (human service agencies, business leaders, and leaders in the faith community; community members and parents; school administrative leaders and staff; and students themselves) demonstrate two features: (a) a sense of shared responsibility for the safety, general well-being, and successful performance of students, and (b) collective competence in taking advantage of opportunities for addressing students' needs and confronting situations that threaten the safety, general well-being, and successful performance of students. The two components, shared responsibility and collective competence, mutually reinforce each other over time.

Social capacity is about action rather than the potential for action, and it encompasses mechanisms of social care and social control in community and school settings—mechanisms that are consistent with the definitions of collective efficacy cited earlier. The first component in the definition of social capacity—a sense of shared responsibility—provides the motivational anchor for this action orientation. Without a sense of shared responsibility, stakeholders may have the competence to solve problems but lack the will or motivation to do so.

As a characteristic feature of social organization in schools and communities, the concept of social capacity has linkages to the concepts of social capital (Coleman, 1988) and collective efficacy (Bandura, 1986). In schools with high social capacity, stakeholders work together—in the context of opportunity, adversity, and positive challenge—to identify needs and assets at both macro and micro levels, define common goals and objectives, set priorities, develop strategies for collective action, implement actions consistent with agreed-upon strategies, and monitor results (cf. Denham, Quinn, & Gamble,

1998). From a school violence perspective, attention is directed to getting adults in communities and schools connected with one another and involved in the lives of youths.

Social capacity may have both a preventive and a therapeutic effect in reducing the probability of school violence. First, high social capacity may have a positive influence—a preventive effect—on community- and school-related risk and on protective factors associated with school violence. These features include geographic, social, demographic, and formal and informal networks operating inside and outside school boundaries. Although some of these features are relatively fixed, such as the size of the community in which a school is located, other features may be targeted for intervention and prevention planning, such as community crime and violence.

In the discussion above, a number of community- and school-related factors were identified as correlates of school violence. Identification of these correlates is a first-order task when one is working from a social capacity perspective. These factors serve as potential targets for collective mobilization and action because of their implications for reducing school violence.

Second, by shaping the opportunity structure available to students and the prevailing social norms that inform students' values and behavioral choices, high social capacity may influence the probability of school violence directly—a therapeutic effect. For example, as a result of leadership from several keystone parents whose children have been victims of violence at school, an active campaign may be initiated in the school to increase parents' visibility and involvement in school activities and events. The probability of school violence is expected to be lower in schools with high social capacity.

EFFECTIVE PREVENTION PROGRAMS

No magic bullet, no one-size-fits-all response, exists for the problem of school violence. The following sequence of activities is consistent with the social capacity framework and associated with effective program responses. These steps can be applied to target a variety of programmatic levels (e.g., a classroom, school, or community).

Identify Leadership and Stakeholders

A school is a system with a hierarchical leadership structure. The level of leadership support of any plan or intervention will influence its success. In most schools, this means starting with the principal. If the principal is supportive of program ideas, and the resources are available, this is the ideal level at which to intervene. An intervention may be initiated in a classroom rather than across the school; the plan can then expand after some demonstrated success. In either case, the principal is an important player and, from the beginning, should be involved in intervention planning.

In addition to working with school leadership, it is important to identify key stakeholder groups and potential intervention partners for a successful program, such as students, families, and school staff and administrators. Community-level partners may include the police department, mental health agencies, juvenile justice personnel, family service agencies, religious/faith and service organizations, and other public and private agencies that provide services to youths and families in the community. A meeting that brings together key school staff and stakeholder groups can solidify leadership and start the assessment process, which may include creating dissatisfaction with the status quo.

Assess the Problem

This step involves gathering information from stakeholders on the nature and extent of the violence and violence-related problems in the targeted student population. This can be accomplished by the use of administrative data, surveys, interviews, and/or focus groups. One survey that gathers comprehensive data about students with respect to multiple risk and protective factors in the school environment is *the School Success Profile* (SSP) (Bowen, Woolley, Richman, & Bowen, 2001). This comprehensive student survey gathers data about school-violence-related issues and examines students' experiences in the context of school, family, peers, and neighborhood.

Use of administrative data and of interviews with students, staff, and families augments survey data and is essential in the data-gathering process. For example, Astor et al. (1999) have presented school mapping as a helpful data-gathering process. Using a map of the school, students and staff identify where violence occurs. These areas often include playgrounds, parking lots, hallways, stairwells, bathrooms, and the cafeteria. Violence in these problem areas may be unknown to staff—an important reason for including students in the mapping process.

Information from various sources—including baseline estimates for violence-related problems and associated correlates of school violence—is organized and presented to stakeholder groups in the form of briefings for input and discussion. The aim is to develop and expand available information into a comprehensive picture of relevant issues for informing intervention and prevention activities. As part of this process, program result goals defined through group discussion are associated with reducing the probability of school violence. These program result goals serve as targets for intervention and prevention activities.

An important step in this process, as reported by Olweus, Limber, and Mihalic (1999), occurs when the students hear from the adults—parents and school staff—that they are aware of the problem and are committed to creating change. An assembly attended by all students may be an effective vehicle for accomplishing this and asking for students' commitment to the change process as well. The main goal is to create a school-level and community-level commitment for change.

Design and Implement Appropriate Interventions

The goal of this step is to match intervention targets identified in the assessment process with activities designed to influence them. A school should strive to develop interventions that build on school strengths. One natural outgrowth of involving various stakeholder groups early in the process is that by the time this step is reached, stakeholders, including community agencies, may be stepping forward to offer staff time and resources. As the leverage points for intervention come into clearer focus, stakeholders will be looking for ways in which they can be part of building a successful program.

Pentz, Mihalic, and Grotpeter (1997), in a demonstrated drug and alcohol prevention program, suggest staggering the components of a multifaceted program over time, so that the components support and build on each other. Planning this time line for a specific school is one of the goals of this step in the process. Again, input from stakeholders and committed community partners should be part of this time line planning.

Monitor Progress

Monitoring intervention outcomes and processes is a critical part of any successful program. Indicators and measures of results and activities must be developed and carefully monitored to help ensure that the plan is being implemented as designed, and anticipated effects are being achieved. Measurable changes in outcomes provide an opportunity to reward and recognize stakeholders' efforts, further reinforcing commitment and ownership in the process for change. Feedback to principals and administrators can help make a case for expanding an effective program, accessing more resources when needed, and providing support when ongoing modifications are sought in the program. Finally, after the original goals have been achieved, interventions designed to maintain the positive changes can be identified.

EMPIRICALLY BASED PRACTICE PRINCIPLES

A growing body of research literature describes successful programs for addressing school violence (Alexander, Pugh, & Parsons, 1998; de Anda, 1999; Henggeler, Mihalic, Rone, Thomas, & Timmons-Mitchell, 1998; Jenson & Howard, 1999; Olweus et al., 1999; Pentz et al., 1997). An inductive review strategy has yielded three practice principles for informing the design of successful school violence interventions. These practice principles, identified from the literature, are consistent with the social capacity framework, emphasize seeing school violence as part of a larger community issue, and include components of primary prevention, secondary prevention, and intensive intervention.

Establish School and Community Partnerships

School violence is a complex and multifaceted problem. Effective interventions rest on a foundation of partnerships between school and community stakeholders (Alexander & Curtis, 1995). At the school level, this means involving teachers, students, parents, specialists, and administrators in the process from the beginning.

Students are key stakeholders in efforts to reduce school violence. They are the primary victims of school violence, and changing their attitudes and behavior is an important focus of any school violence program. Unfortunately, students are often left out of schools' policy and program planning phases. Establishing an atmosphere of partnership with students is a vital initial step in creating a program that works. Students have critical information about the problems associated with school violence and can be significant partners in its prevention.

Schools can be catalysts in bringing school representatives and community members together to address the collective goal of reducing violence. Participation by parents is critical and should include not just the families of aggressive students who are the target of intensive support services, but other parents who are willing to participate in school-wide and community-based efforts.

Schools do not own school violence. As discussed earlier, many of the risk factors for school violence begin in the community. Therefore, for a school violence program to effectively utilize available resources and address relevant risk factors, partnerships with the community are necessary. Public and private organizations with a stake in the problem, including law enforcement, should be contacted early in the process.

Research has shown that when schools work with community service providers, an effective step is taken toward reducing school violence (Catalano, Loeber, & McKinney, 1999). Several important partnerships should be established between the school and the community. Partnership with mental health service providers is important. In an analysis of three school violence prevention programs, Fiester and Nathanson (1996) reported that mental health agencies providing services in schools can be effective supplements to a program aimed at reducing school violence. They stated that these agencies need to become involved during the planning stages, and will require some autonomy and flexibility in how they interface with the school. Ongoing communications are necessary to address differing missions and methods.

Promote a Supportive and Violence-Free School Climate

The second principle for building an effective school violence program is to endorse the development of a supportive school climate, a move that is consistent with research presented earlier (e.g., Welsh, 2000). A recent approach to reducing school violence, with an overall goal of impacting the climate of a school, comes from the emerging field of peacemaking criminology. Peacemaking, as an approach to crime, goes well beyond crime control and addresses the environment in ways that reduce crime and suffering and work toward peace and social justice (Caulfield, 2000). This approach to creating a school climate that reduces school violence is demonstrated in Project Peace (de Anda, 1999).

Project Peace is a 10-session group violence prevention program for high school students. It is designed to help students understand anger arousal, discriminate between thoughts and emotions, identify triggers, and identify and utilize alternative actions in conflictual situations. The program goes beyond cognitive/behavioral techniques. It seeks to change students' attitudes toward violence and to increase perceptions of safety and security at school as the result of students' increased confidence in the school's staff.

Significant results with a mainly Latino and African American group of ninth graders in a Los Angeles high school have been reported by de Anda (1999). Besides showing improvement in their attitudes toward the use of violence, students reported more favorable opinions about the school climate and more positive peer interaction; most significantly, they effected a large decrease in actual violent behavior. As de Anda concludes, programs like Project Peace afford an opportunity for partnerships between teachers and school social workers to create school climates that reduce violence.

Provide Intensive Intervention for Aggressive Students

The third principle, in the reduction of school violence, is the provision of intensive support services to students identified as aggressive or at risk for violent behavior. Although services targeted at aggressive students are an important component of any multifaceted intervention, attention to aggressive students should not be the sole, or even the primary, target of a program. Given the many demands on school social workers, outside agencies who can partner with social workers to provide these intensive services can give a tremendous boost to a successful program.

Programs to reduce violent behavior in identified aggressive youth fall roughly into two categories: intensive family-oriented programs, and group-oriented cognitive/behavioral programs. Two highly regarded intensive family intervention programs are Functional Family Therapy (Alexander et al., 1998) and Multisystemic Therapy (Henggeler & Hoyt, 2001; Henggeler et al., 1998).

Functional Family Therapy involves 8 to 12 one-hour sessions that address risk and protective factors in the child and family. Multisystemic Therapy has a somewhat longer treatment course: 50 hours of contact over a 4-month period, with a therapist available 24 hours a day, 7 days a week. The program emphasizes the interconnected systems affecting a family and focuses on empowering the family by developing indigenous resources and support systems. Multisystemic Therapy is consistent with the principle of creating partnerships by helping families to take advantage of support systems in their community.

Many cognitive/behavior-oriented group programs have been designed to reduce aggression in at-risk students; these programs can be implemented by school personnel. Two key programs are titled "Anger Coping Program" (Lochman, Whidby, & FitzGerald, 2000; Lochman & Wells, 1996) and "I Can Problem Solve" (Shure, 1992).

The "Anger Coping Program" (ACP) is a cognitive/behavioral intervention program for preadolescent to early adolescent aggressive boys. ACP has been implemented in clinic and school settings. It entails 12 to 18 group sessions, each 60 to 90 minutes in length, attended by 4 to 7 students. The students learn to identify situations that provoke strong feelings; maintain self-control; decode verbal and nonverbal cues to avoid misjudging others' intentions; understand physiological arousal; and employ new social problem-solving skills. ACP has been shown to reduce disruptive-aggressive off-task classroom behavior. A three-year follow-up study demonstrated lower levels of substance abuse and higher levels of self-esteem and social problem-solving skills (Lochman, 1992). The developers of ACP are currently working on the "Coping Power Program," an updated version of ACP that will include a parent component, consultation with teachers, a longer intervention course, and individual sessions to supplement the group process (Lochman & Wells, 1996). The program's inclusion of parent involvement and consultation with teachers is consistent with the social capacity framework presented here.

The "I Can Problem Solve" (ICPS) program has four distinct levels: (a) preschool, (b) kindergarten, (c) primary grades, and (d) intermediate elementary grades. The program was developed within a multiethnic, economically disadvantaged population. The programs for younger children are designed to be fun and to feel like games. Teachers and other school staff can easily implement the program. ICPS teaches children how to assess and deal with problems—how to figure out what to do instead of always being told what to do. The theory of change underlying ICPS is: When children develop problem-solving skills, their social adjustment improves. This leads to increased concern for others' feelings, frustration tolerance, sharing, taking turns, and independence (Shure, 1992). An important goal of this program—integration of its principles and content into the classroom and curriculum—makes ICPS fit well with the previously stated goal of including all the students in the process for change. ICPS has demonstrated effectiveness in reducing behavior problems and long-term delinquency, and increasing caring, sharing, and cooperation.

A school violence-prevention program that creates partnerships, addresses the whole school climate, and provides intensive support services to aggressive students is a formula for comprehensive success.

IMPLICATIONS FOR FUTURE RESEARCH

This chapter has attempted to outline the very complex nature of school violence. The risk factors, correlates, and predictors of school violence have been presented; they include characteristics of students, families, schools, and neighborhoods. As described previously, innovative interventions to reduce crime and violence in schools are growing in number. Evaluations of these programs have been revealing positive results and are leading to improvements.

Most of the existing violence reduction interventions target students, groups of students, or families, all of whom are important targets of intervention and prevention strategies. However, as previously discussed, research has shown that neighborhood characteristics (Bowen & Bowen, 1999), and community crime and violence (Barton et al., 1998) are strong predictors of school violence. A survey of school social workers revealed their belief that the source of school violence lies in contexts outside school (Astor, Pitner, Meyer, & Vargas, 2000). Additionally, the climate of a school has been shown to be associated with multiple measures of school disorder, including offending and safety concerns (Welsh, 2000).

Additional research that further illuminates the relationship between school violence and school, neighborhood, and community characteristics will be vital to the development of a more comprehensive understanding of school violence. How school climate impacts school violence, and how violence in the community and family crosses the threshold of the schoolhouse door will be particularly helpful. A greater understanding of the connection between school, neighborhood, and community characteristics and school violence will inform the development of prevention and intervention strategies that address the complex nature and interrelationship of social organizational patterns and processes in the social environment of students.

REFERENCES

Alexander, J., Pugh, C., & Parsons, B. (1998). *Blueprints for violence prevention: Functional family therapy* (Vol. 3). Golden, CO: Venture.

Alexander, R., & Curtis, C. M. (1995). A critical review of strategies to reduce school violence. *Social Work in Education, 17*(2), 73–82.

Astor, R. A., Pitner, R. O., Meyer, H. A., & Vargas, L. A. (2000). The most violent event at school: A ripple in the pond. *Children and Schools, 22,* 199–216.

Astor, R. A., Vargas, L. A., Pitner, R. O., & Meyer, H. A. (1999). School violence: Research, theory, and practice. In J. M. Jenson & M. O. Howard (Eds.), *Youth violence: Current research and recent practice innovations* (pp. 139–172). Springfield, VA: Sheridan Books.

Bandura, A. (1986). *Social foundations of thought and action: A social cognitive theory.* Englewood Cliffs, NJ: Prentice-Hall.

Barton, P. E., Coley, R. J., & Wenglinsky, H. (1998). *Order in the classroom: Violence, discipline, and student achievement* (Policy Information Report). Princeton, NJ: Educational Testing Service, Policy Information Center.

Bowen, G. L., Bowen, N. K., & Cook, P. (2000). Neighborhood characteristics and supportive parenting among single mothers. In G. L. Fox & M. L. Benson (Eds.), *Families, crime, and criminal justice* (pp. 183–206). New York: Elsevier.

Bowen, G. L., Bowen, N. K., & Richman, J. M. (1998). *Students in peril: Crime and violence in neighborhoods and schools.* Chapel Hill: University of North Carolina at Chapel Hill, Jordan Institute for Families, School of Social Work.

Bowen, G. L., Bowen, N. K., & Richman, J. M. (2000). School size and middle school students' perceptions of the school environment. *Social Work in Education, 22,* 69–82.

Bowen, G. L., Martin, J. A., Mancini, J. A., & Nelson, J. P. (2000). Community capacity: Antecedents and consequences. *Journal of Community Practice, 8*(2), 1–21.

Bowen, G. L., Richman, J. M., & Bowen, N. K. (2000). Families in the context of communities across time. In S. J. Price, P. C. McKenry, & M. J. Murphy (Eds.), *Families across time: A life course perspective* (pp. 117–128). Los Angeles: Roxbury.

Bowen, G. L., Richman, J. M., Brewster, A., & Bowen, N. K. (1998). Sense of school coherence, perceptions of danger at school, and teacher support among youth at risk of school failure. *Child and Adolescent Social Work Journal, 15,* 273–286.

Bowen, G. L., Woolley, M. E., Richman, J. M., & Bowen, N. K. (2001). Brief intervention in schools: The School Success Profile. *Brief Treatment and Crisis Intervention, 1,* 43–54.

Bowen, N. K., & Bowen, G. L. (1999). Effects of crime and violence in neighborhoods and schools on the school behavior and performance of adolescents. *Journal of Adolescent Research, 14,* 319–342.

Brooks, K., Schiraldi, V., & Ziedenberg, J. (2000). *School house hype: Two years later.* Washington, DC: Justice Policy Institute. Covington, KY: Children's Law Center, Inc.

Catalano, R. F., Loeber, R., & McKinney, K. C. (1999). *School and community interventions to prevent serious and violent offending.* Washington, DC: Office of Juvenile Justice and Delinquency Prevention.

Caulfield, S. (2000). Creating peaceable schools. *Annals of American Academy of Political and Social Science, 567,* 170–186.

Coleman, J. (1988). Social capital in the creation of human capital. *American Journal of Sociology, 94,* S95–S120.

de Anda, D. (1999). Project peace: The evaluation of a skills-based violence prevention program for high school adolescents. *Social Work in Education, 21*(3), 137–149.

Denham, A., Quinn, S. C., & Gamble, D. (1998). Community organizing for health promotion in the rural South: An exploration of community competence. *Family and Community Health, 21*(1), 1–21.

Dubow, E. F., Huesmann, L. R., & Eron, L. D. (1987). Mitigating aggression and promoting prosocial behavior in aggressive elementary schoolboys. *Behaviour Research and Therapy, 25*(6), 527–531.

DuRant, R. H., Getts, A., Cadenhead, C., Emans, S. J., & Woods, E. R. (1995). Exposure to violence and victimization and depression, hopelessness, and purpose in life among adolescents living in and around public housing. *Developmental and Behavioral Pediatrics, 16,* 233–237.

Fiester, L., & Nathanson, S. P. (1996). Lessons learned from three violence prevention program projects. *Journal of School Health, 66,* 344–347.

Garbarino, J. (2001). Making sense of senseless youth violence. In J. M. Richman & M. W. Fraser (Eds.), *The context of youth violence: Resilience, risk, and protection* (pp. 83–95). Westport, CT: Praeger.

Gottfredson, D. C. (1986). An empirical test of school-based environmental and individual interventions to reduce the risk of delinquent behavior. *Criminology, 24,* 705–730.

Harris & Associates, Inc. (1996). *The Metropolitan Life survey of the American teacher, 1996: Students voice their opinions on violence, social tension and equality among teens.* New York: Metropolitan Life Insurance Company.

Harris & Associates, Inc. (1999). *The Metropolitan Life survey of the American teacher, 1999: Violence in America's public schools—five years later.* New York: Metropolitan Life Insurance Company.

Harris & Associates, Inc. (2000). *The Metropolitan Life survey of the American teacher, 2000: Are we preparing students for the 21st-century?* New York: Metropolitan Life Insurance Company.

Hawkins, J. D., Herrenkohl, T., Farrington, D. P., Brewer, D., Catalano, R. F., & Harachi, T. (1998). A review of predictors of youth violence. In R. Loeber & D. P. Farrington (Eds.), *Serious and violent juvenile offenders* (pp. 106–146). Thousand Oaks, CA: Sage.

Henggeler, S. W., & Hoyt, S. W. (2001). Multisystemic therapy with serious juvenile offenders and their families. In J. M. Richman & M. W. Fraser (Eds.), *The context of youth violence: Resilience, risk, and protection* (pp. 115–131). Westport, CT: Praeger.

Henggeler, S. W., Mihalic, S. F., Rone, L., Thomas, C., & Timmons-Mitchell, J. (1998). *Blueprints for violence prevention: Multisystemic therapy* (Vol. 6). Denver, CO: C&M Press.

Jenson, J. M., & Howard, M. O. (1999). *Youth violence.* Springfield, VA: Sheridan Books.

Kaufman, P., Chen, X., Choy, S. P., Ruddy, S. A., Miller, A. K., Fleury, J. K., et al. (2000). *Indicators of school crime and safety, 2000*(NCES 2001-017/NCJ-184176). Washington, DC: U.S. Departments of Education and Justice.

Kazdin, A. E. (1995). *Conduct disorders in childhood and adolescence* (2nd ed.). Thousand Oaks, CA: Sage.

Kendall, P. C., & Braswell, L. (1982). Cognitive-behavioral self-control therapy for children: A components analysis. *Journal of Consulting and Clinical Psychology, 50,* 672–689.

Lange, A. J., & Jakubowski, P. (1976). *Responsible assertive behavior: Cognitive/behavioral procedures.* Champaign, IL: Research Press.

Lochman, J. E. (1992). Cognitive-behavioral intervention with aggressive boys: Three-year follow-up and preventive effects. *Journal of Consulting and Clinical Psychology, 60*(3), 426–432.

Lochman, J. E., Lampron, L. B., Gemmer, T. C., & Harris, S. R. (1987). Anger coping intervention with aggressive children: A guide to implementation in school settings. In P. A. Keller & S. R. Heyman (Eds.), *Innovations in clinical practice: A source book* (Vol. 6). Sarasota, FL: Professional Resource Exchange.

Lochman, J. E., & Wells, K. C. (1996). A social-cognitive intervention with aggressive children. In R. D. Peters & R. J. McMahon (Eds.), *Preventing childhood disorders, substance abuse, and delinquency.* Thousand Oaks, CA: Sage.

Lochman, J. E., Whidby, J. M., & FitzGerald, D. P. (2000). Cognitive-behavioral assessment and treatment with aggressive children. In P. C. Kendall (Ed.), *Child and adolescent therapy: Cognitive-behavioral procedures.* New York: Guilford Press.

McMahon, R. J., & Wells, K. C. (1989). Conduct disorders. In E. J. Mash & R. A. Barkley (Eds.), *Treatment of childhood disorders* (pp. 73–132). New York: Guilford Press.

Olweus, D., Limber, S., & Mihalic, S. (1999). *Blueprints for violence prevention: Bully prevention program* (Vol. 9). Golden, CO: Venture.

Orpinas, P., & Murray, N. (1999). Parental influences on students' aggressive behavior and weapon carrying. *Health and Education Behavior, 26,* 774–788.

Pentz, M. A., Mihalic, S. F., & Grotpeter, J. K. (Eds.). (1997). *Blueprints for violence prevention: The Midwestern prevention project* (Vol. 1). Denver, CO: C&M Press.

Richman, J. M., & Bowen, G. L. (1997). School failure: An ecological-interactional-developmental perspective. In M. W. Fraser (Ed.), *Risk and resilience in childhood: An ecological perspective* (pp. 95–116). Washington, DC: NASW Press.

Sampson, R. J., Raudenbush, S. W., & Earls, F. (1997). Neighborhoods and violent crime: A multilevel study of collective efficacy. *Science, 277,* 918–923.

Shure, M. B. (1992). *I can problem solve: An interpersonal cognitive problem-solving program.* Champaign, IL: Research Press.

Singer, M. I., & Miller, D. B. (1999). Contributors to violent behavior among elementary and middle school children. *Pediatrics, 104,* 878–885.

Snyder, H. N., & Sickmund, M. (1999). *Juvenile offenders and victims: 1999 national report.* Washington, DC: Office of Juvenile Justice and Delinquency Prevention.

Vera Institute of Justice. (1999). *Approaches to school safety in America's largest cities* (Prepared for Lt. Governor's Task Force on School Safety). New York: Vera Institute of Justice.

Wasserman, G. A., & Miller, L. S. (1998). The prevention of serious and violent juvenile offending. In R. Loeber & D. P. Farrington (Eds.), *Serious and violent juvenile offenders: Risk factors and successful interventions* (pp. 197–247). Thousand Oaks, CA: Sage.

Welsh, W. N. (2000). The effects of school climate on school disorder. *Annals of the American Academy of Political and Social Science, 567,* 88–108.

Yogan, L. J. (2000). School tracking and student violence. *Annals of the American Academy of Political and Social Science, 567,* 108–123.

Youth Pride. (1997). *Creating safe schools for lesbian and gay students: A resource guide for school staff* [Online]. Youth Pride. Available from: http://members.tripod.com/~twood/guide.html

Chapter 15 ──────────────────────────────────

SCHOOL VIOLENCE AMONG CULTURALLY DIVERSE POPULATIONS

KARIN JORDAN

INTRODUCTION

Many analysts believe that schools are reflections of the communities they serve, and this belief is borne out in the increasing violence in today's schools and in society in general. For example, racial tensions between African Americans and first-generation Asian immigrants in one community are mimicked in its local high school, where aggressive acts between African American students and second-generation Asian students have resulted in physical harm and psychological pain. Given the increasing cultural diversification in our society, there is a pressing need for mental health professionals to be ready for an accompanying increase in school violence.

In a chapter on intercultural communication, L.E. Sarbaugh (1988) noted that the extent of culturally diverse populations present in a given interaction depends on the degree of heterogeneity in the worldview of those interacting, as well as on their belief systems, overt behaviors, verbal and nonverbal code systems, relationships, and intentions. Additionally, cultural diversity is not limited to extreme contrasts such as language or national origin; instead, it often involves subtle differences in class, age, gender, and religion (Kavanagh & Kennedy, 1992). From their own culture, individual students have learned a system of symbols with shared values, meanings, and behaviors, but this system may not be shared by students of other cultures.

CURRENT TRENDS AND ISSUES

Given the increasing diversification within U.S. communities and educational institutions, as well as the increased student victimization at schools (U.S.

Department of Education, National Center for Education Statistics [NCES], 1998), it is not surprising that today's students, parents, and educators mandate a broader understanding of climate and cultural diversity in educational institutions and a need for safety. It is important to remember, however, that school violence is not restricted to nonmajority students.

Cultural Diversity

Cultural diversity exists in all schools where there is not a cultural homogeneity or sameness. In U.S. schools, the term *cultural diversity* tends to mean divergence or deviation from a single standard, which generally refers to underlying Anglo- or European American expectations and ideals. Cultural diversity is often viewed as an assortment of contrasts, variations, and combinations that are nearly limitless—a learned system of symbols with shared values, meanings, and behavioral norms. Cultural differences involve patterned lifeways, values, beliefs, ideas, and practices. Cultural and subcultural differences are not limited to extreme contrasts; they also involve more subtle differences (Kavanagh & Kennedy, 1992).

Varying patterns between cultural and subcultural groups reflect social organization and process. Members of particular cultures share characteristics that distinguish them from members of other cultures. Membership in cultural and subcultural groups is based primarily on the symbolic meanings of a culture, and patterned characteristics are generally used to classify, categorize, or label members of different cultural groups (Kavanagh & Kennedy, 1992). These characteristics can be found in students of various cultures who relate to their ethnic identity, which provides a sense of belonging (Phinney, 1990). According to Phinney (1990), ethnic identity formation is a three-stage developmental model of (a) unexamined identity (limited or no exposure to ethnic identity issues; preference for the dominant culture), (b) exploration (study of and involvement in one's own culture), and (c) ethnic identity (positive toward dominant culture, well adjusted). Vargas (1994) developed a four-stage model: (a) ideal self (one wants to be), (b) feared self (one wants not to be), (c) claimed self (hopes of what others believe), and (d) real self (person's beliefs). He also believes that students who struggle with their self-identity often gravitate toward a desired self, which could include a macho self, as a way to cover up their insecurities. Bernal, Saenz, and Knight (1991) hypothesized that nonmajority students who are alienated from the dominant culture might engage in cultural inversion/oppositional (from the dominant culture) social identity. For example, African American elementary students of low socioeconomic status saw peers of their own culture as lazy and dumb, and held the role expectation of being "bad," believing that "the badder they were, the greater their social status" (Elrich, 1994, p. 14). Ethnic identity of students influences their way of interacting with different cultures.

Contact and interaction among culturally diverse students who identify themselves as culturally distinct from one another present overt behaviors, verbal and nonverbal code systems, and relationships according to the degree of heterogeneity in their worldviews as well as in their belief systems (Sarbaugh, 1988). Communication and other contact among culturally diverse students can be "multicultural," "cross-cultural," or "transcultural" (Collier & Thomas, 1988; Paderson, 1988). Multicultural communication is distinguished from "cross-cultural" and "transcultural" communication, in that it denotes maintenance of several distinct cultures. For example, students of one culture or subculture may not engage in collaborative or interactive activities with students of a different culture or subculture. Cross-cultural and transcultural ways of communication imply a bridging of significant differences in cultural and subcultural communication styles, beliefs, and practices—for example, when students of one culture or subculture effectively communicate and interact with peers of a different culture or subculture.

School Violence

School violence should not be viewed as a cultural or racial issue. Its etiology should be viewed using Glasser's (1998) *choice theory*—that youths who are lonely, frightened, bored, and/or alienated tend to join gangs or destructive cliques in order to satisfy their need for belonging, power, fun, and security. The choice theory's etiology of school/youth violence can be supported by the histories of some of the recent school shooters.

- Eric Harris, 18, and Dylan Klebold, 17, were described as "outcasts." They were members of the "Trench Coat Mafia," a cult group that worshipped Adolf Hitler and were known to be involved in the Gothic scene. They killed 12 students and a teacher, and wounded many more in Littleton, Colorado, in 1999.

- Thomas Solomon, Jr., 15, turned sullen after being dumped by his girlfriend and spoke of taking his life. He injured 6 students in Conyers, Georgia, in 1999.

- Shawn Cooper, 16, lived with his grandfather, who had gained legal custody of him after he and his brother turned up at a local hospital suffering from malnutrition. He injured a student in Notus, Idaho, in 1999.

- Kip Kinkel, 16, was voted by his classmates as "Most Likely to Start World War III" and was constantly in trouble at school and, apparently, at home. He killed his parents, 2 teachers, and 2 students, and wounded 22 others in Springfield, Oregon, in 1998.

- Jacob Davis, 18, was in a dispute with another boy, over a girl both had dated. He shot that boy in Fayetteville, Tennessee, in 1998.

- Andrew Wurst, 14, was carrying small amounts of marijuana at the time of his arrest. He killed a teacher and wounded 3 students in Edinboro, Pennsylvania, in 1998.

- Mitchell Johnson, 13, was described as a troubled youth who had begun bragging about joining a gang. He killed 4 female students and a teacher, and injured 9 students and a teacher in Jonesboro, Arkansas, in 1998.

- Michael Carneal, 15, was described as a self-proclaimed atheist who would occasionally heckle an informal worship group (which he targeted during his shooting spree). He killed 3 students and wounded 5 in West Paducah, Kentucky, in 1997.

- Luke Woodham, 17, known as "Kroth," was distraught over a breakup with his girlfriend. He killed 1 student and injured 8 others (including his ex-girlfriend) in Pearl, Mississippi, in 1997.

- Evan Ramsey, 16, was described as "an outcast" and a "troublemaker"; he frequently got into fights and was suspended from school. He killed a student and a teacher in Bethel, Alaska, in 1997.

- Barry Loukaitis, 14, described as an "outsider," killed 2 students and a teacher and wounded a student in Moses Lake, Washington, in 1996 (*The Washington Post* Online, 2000).

These school shooters—often quiet, isolated, and withdrawn—appear to have been driven by a consistent feeling of being psychologically hurt and in pain; they felt rejected, abandoned, and cast aside to a place of isolation and aloneness. This feeling can be followed by a desire to hurt the world, including parents, school peers, teachers, and/or sometimes the school itself, which they most likely perceived to be responsible for their pain and hurt (Harper & Ibrahim, 2000). Violence against a particular person from a racial or ethnic group is often driven by cultural intolerance and a lack of understanding and acceptance of intergroup differences.

Juvenile crime is increasing across cultures. Firearm use and violent behavior show higher rates with increased age (Federal Bureau of Investigation, 1991) and, across cultures, occur more frequently in boys and men than in girls and women (Cotton et al., 1994). The rate of violent offending, including gun violence for boys, peaks at age 17. During this age, 36% of African American and 25% of Caucasian boys reported that they had committed a violent crime (Elliott, 1994). For girls, the age peak is between 15 and 16; violent offenses occur in 1 of 5 African American and 1 of 10 Caucasian girls (Elliott, 1994). In 1995, a national survey of 16,000 adolescents in the ninth through twelfth grades revealed that 11.8% had brought a weapon onto school grounds within the past 30 days. In 1994, 7.3% of these same students had been threatened or injured with a weapon (Orton, 1996). Students who bring weapons to school rob themselves and their peers of a safe learning environment. They create stress and fear, and they force teachers out of their school and potentially out of the profession. Coie, Dodge, Terry, and Wright (1991) found that aggressive preadolescent African American boys who were identified as socially rejected by peers, in comparison to nonaggressive peers, engaged more frequently in violent behavior, including bullying.

Bullying behavior by students, which has negative consequences for students and for the school atmosphere, occurs across and within different cultures. According to Olweus (1992), bullying is the exposure of an individual, over and over again, to negative interactions on the part of one or more dominant persons who gain in some way from the discomfort of the victim. Bullying includes intentional hurt and pain. It can involve physical contact, ostracism, and social isolation, as well as words (i.e., teasing) and insulting gestures directed at victims who have problems defending themselves. In today's technological era, it is not surprising that students use technology to attack. Today, we have to contend with "techno-bullies." Cox (2000) wrote:

> Christopher Fletcher was amazed when he came down to breakfast one morning to find his 14-year-old son Mark in a flood of tears, begging to not be sent to school that day. His amazement turned to shock and rage when he found out that some of his son's classmates had set up a Web page devoted to Mark. Posted on the site were a variety of abusive taunts. It had already been seen not only by the pupils in Mark's class, some of whom had accessed it via the computers at their school, but by other children in the area, one of whom had phoned to alert Mark. (p. EV7)

Sadly enough, when Mr. Fletcher asked for help at his son's school, where the e-mails had originated, the overall tone from the school was "Boys will be boys." Bullying, techno- and otherwise, has a negative influence on students; it creates stress and fear, and it impacts academic achievement. It may also impact school cohesiveness.

Fighting in school (e.g., in hallways, bathrooms, playgrounds, lunchrooms, and entrance or exit areas) is one of the most commonly reported incidents of school violence among and across different cultures. This fighting is believed to be the result of individual students' deficits in an array of cognitive-social skills necessary to stem conflict before it escalates into physical violence (National Education Goals Panel, 1995). School fights are influenced by multiple causes and risk factors (i.e., physical abuse, violent parental discipline, and witnessing violence between parents). It is believed that children who experience and/or witness violent acts by their parents show elevated rates of aggressive behavior. DuRant, Cadenhead, Pendergrast, Slavens, and Linder (1994) reported that past exposure to violence explained 27% of the variance in self-reported violent behavior in a sample of low-income, urban, African American adolescents. Astor (1998) asked readers to "Consider the following statement."

> You wanna see a fight, all you need to do is go to the boys' and girls' bathrooms after the bell rings [between classes]. I just saw a bad one just before you come to get me. One guy got punched while he was going [to the bathroom]. We've got it right there every day, all the time, and no one does nothing about it. I sometimes just hold it in 'til I get home, but if I gotta go—I'll just go. If anyone messes with me while I'm going [to the bathroom], I'll kill 'em, and they know that, so no one is gonna mess with me there. [pause] I still would hold it in if I can. (12-year-old boy, middle school) (p. 209)

This is a good example of a student's identification of the bathroom as a place where violence occurs; the passivity of the school staff, which allows the violence to continue; and how violent acts provoke violent responses. A recent national survey conducted by the Centers for Disease Control and Prevention (1996) revealed that 46% of high school males and 30% of high school females reported having been in at least one fight that required medical attention by a doctor or nurse, during the past year.

Identification, Classification, and Prediction

As with most complex social phenomena, determining the nature and the scope of cultural diversity and school violence in the United States is a complex task. Cultural diversity and school violence constitute a multidimensional issue that is highly related to understanding cultural diversity's correlation to the presence of violence in our society. Crews and Counts (1997) believe that the violence in our culturally diverse society leaks into the school system. "High levels of aggression in our homes, our streets, and in our mass media rapidly find parallel expression in our schools" (Goldstein & Conoley, 1997, p. 16). In 1993, a federal government report found that almost 3 million crimes in schools were annually reported, which translates to about 16,000 crimes per school day. Goldstein and Conoley (1997) also reported that violent crime for youths under the age of 18 increased to 29.1% between 1988 and 1992. The violent death rate for teens aged 15 to 19 increased by 13% between 1985 and 1990 (Vargas, 1994). These increases were particularly evident in ethnic or racial minority youth. Violent death rates per 100,000 teens were highest in states that have high concentrations of minorities, such as the District of Columbia (208.3), New Mexico (121.1), Louisiana (115.0), and Alabama (101.7) (Vargas, 1994). In 1989, the leading cause of death for male and female African Americans, ages 15 to 34, was homicide (National Center for Health Statistics, 1990). According to the U.S. Department of Health and Human Services (1991), homicide accounts for 42% of all deaths in African American male adolescents. This ethnic group is the subpopulation that is at greatest risk of death by homicide. Additionally, for boys ages 15 to 19 years, the risk of dying from homicide is nine times higher for African Americans than for Caucasians (Fingerhut, Ingram, & Feldman, 1992). Mercy et al. (1986) reported that African American young males are most frequently victimized by male friends or acquaintances. They further reported that young African American males were most often killed at home, with the weapon being a handgun, whereas young Latino men were more often killed on the street by members of other ethnic groups. We need to gain a better understanding of social behaviors in culturally diverse children and youth, and of how their home and community environments interplay with the school.

Culturally Diverse Children and Adolescents

African American children and adolescents account for 16% of all students in American schools and are believed to comprise the largest minority group in the United States (King, 1993). According to a study in which teachers were asked to compare African American students to those of other races, teachers described them as friendly, interactive, and people-oriented, but also distractible; physically active, with poor self-control; and argumentative, with poor conflict management (Feng & Cartledge, 1996). The study further indicated that African American students are liked by other-race peers and are believed to deal assertively with problem situations. Their arguing style, according to Irvine (1992), is direct and heated, does not include turn taking, is believed to be rooted in their socialization (as a means to counteraggress for survival), and is misunderstood by other-race peers. Additionally, it is believed that African American students are taught to not seek assistance from adults for working out conflict; instead, they are expected to resolve them by using physically and verbally aggressive behaviors (Feng & Cartledge, 1996). African American children are three times more frequently (than Caucasian children) suspended and expelled, and receive three times more corporal punishment (Killelea, 1980). Irvine (1992) found that African American males who are disproportionately singled out for disciplinary action in school show an increased level of aggressive behavior.

The Hispanic/Latino American population is the second fastest growing minority group in the United States and encompasses persons from Spanish and Mexican origin and descent (Mexican American, Chicano, Puerto Rican, Boricuan, Cuban, or Other Spanish/Hispanic) (Ford Foundation, 1984). Given the present growth rate of this population, some predict that Hispanics will surpass African Americans as the largest ethnic group in the near future (Atkinson, Morton, & Sue, 1993). Interpersonal difficulties of Hispanic American children and adolescents are believed to be linguistically based—rooted in inadequate English skills as well as in the need to maintain their primary language, Spanish. Hispanic students reported additional daily stressors (being in new classes, peer pressure, fear for their physical safety, poverty, and racial and ethnic intolerance) and depression more than their non-Hispanic, nonminority peers (Aguilar-Gaxiola & Gray, 1994). These elements contributed to substance abuse: alcohol, inhalants, stimulants, tranquilizers, and heroin (Ramirez, 1989); gang involvement (Soriano, 1993); and homicide (Hammond & Yung, 1993). Language and cultural differences can lead to home, student, and school conflict. Parents perceive the behavioral standards of the school to be too strict, students feel singled out for remedial instruction, and teachers have difficulty accepting these students' unorthodox productivity (Mulhern, 1995). Hispanic American students often perceive the school as an alien environment, because of their language and cultural differences.

Asian Americans originate from East Asia (China, Japan, and Korea), Southeast Asia, India, and the South Pacific Islands. They make up 2.9% of the U.S. population and had a growth rate of over 200% in 1990 (Min, 1995). Feng and Cartledge (1996) reported that Asian American students were identified by teachers as being task-oriented, self-controlled, and cooperative. Sue and Sue (1993) reported that Asian American students were more obedient, conservative, conforming, and inhibited (p. 205). Howes and Wu (1990) reported that Asian American students rated low on communication but were more likely than African American, European American, and Latino peers to enter cross-ethnic interactions. An at-risk subgroup of Asian American students contains refugees from China, Hong Kong, and Taiwan who are unaccompanied by parents and/or guardians (Chin, 1990). These students face language problems and may be placed in classes with much younger students in order to "catch up." They often respond with frustration or disciplinary and other problems (dropping out; violence toward members of their own ethnic community). Glasser (1998) noted that these youngsters often join gangs in their search for a sense of belonging, power, fun, security, respect, a common language, and a community that helps them deal with the loss of their family by war and/or immigration law.

Native Americans are the smallest (about 1.5 million) of the major ethnic and racial minorities (Atkinson et al., 1993). Thomason (1993) wrote that "a Native American is legally defined as a person who is an enrolled or registered member of a tribe or whose blood quantum is one-fourth or more, genealogically derived" (p. 172). LaFromboise and Low (1989) said "many of them speak an entirely different first language, practice an entirely different religion, perform successfully according to conventional Anglo educational criteria" (p. 119). Native American children and adolescents are perceived to have different language-based behavior and verbal assertions (avoiding eye contact with adults as a sign of respect, not initiating conversation with mixed age groups, and showing self-control) (Powless & Elliott, 1993). Research on this student group is limited but has shown that an impoverished and stressful life has resulted in at least 50% of these students struggling with school problems (one third of Native Americans are illiterate [LaFromboise & Low, 1989]), substance-abuse problems (33% of seventh- and twelfth-grade Native Americans abuse alcohol and marijuana [Oetting et al., 1983]), and suicide (Native American adolescent suicide rates are the highest for any group in the United States [Grossman, Milligan, & Deyo, 1991]).

Home and Community Environment Interplay with the School

When looking at cultural diversity and school violence, it is important to look from an ecological systems theory perspective in order to frame appropriate questions and generate effective school-based responses. Bronfenbrenner (1979) identified four inseparable and interconnected systems: (a) the microsystem, (b) the mesosystem, (c) the exosystem, and (d) the macrosystem, which, together, create the ecosystem that frames all human transactions and influences human development (see Figure 15.1).

The microsystem is "a pattern of activities, roles and interpersonal relations experienced by the developing person in a given setting with particular physical and material characteristics" (Bronfenbrenner, 1979, p. 22). For a nonmajority child or adolescent, it would include interaction within the home (which often is culturally specific and might include, for example, speaking only Spanish at home), the school (dealing not only with peers and school personnel of the same

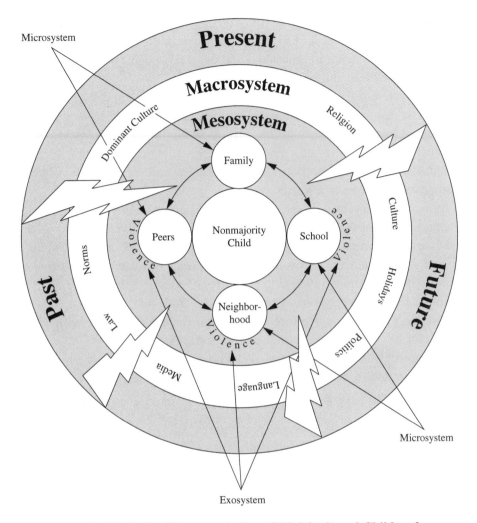

Figure 15.1   An Ecological Representation of Multicultural Child and Adolescent Development

culture, but also with those of diverse cultures and, most likely, the dominant culture), and neighborhood peer groups (of the same or different culture). Each of these interactions can be further broken down—for example, the neighborhood is composed of neighbors, peers, gangs, and so on.

The mesosystem is the interaction and relationship of two or more microsystems. According to Bronfenbrenner (1979), it consists of ". . . other persons who participate actively in both settings, intermediate links in a social network, formal and informal communications among settings, and, again clearly in the phenomenological domain, the extent and nature of knowledge and attitudes existing in one setting about the other" (p. 25). For example, the involvement of parents with their child's school might be limited if parents are first-generation immigrants and speak little or no English. This restricts the discussion of troubled children and could result in emotional and aggressive behavior, as well as academic failure in these children.

The exosystem refers to " one or more settings that do not involve the developing person as an active participant, but in which events occur that affect or are affected by what happens in the setting containing the developing person" (Bronfenbrenner, 1979, p. 25). For example, an adolescent African American male may live with his family in "the projects," where he regularly witnesses shootings and other violent acts.

The macrosystem involves overall structural patterns of the culture (i.e., the economy, laws, political events, and religious beliefs) in which a nonmajority child lives and grows. Included are similar education, customs, and behavior within a specific culture, as well as the differences between subcultures and systems. Bronfenbrenner (1979) identified it as "consistencies, in the form and content of lower-order systems (micro-, meso-, and exo-) that exist, or could exist, at the level of the subculture or the culture as a whole, along with any belief systems or ideology underlying such consistencies" (p. 26).

It is apparent that to understand nonmajority child/adolescent development and behavior, and to develop preventive school violence services, a multilevel, ecological systems theory approach should be applied.

EFFECTIVE PREVENTION PROGRAMS

Effective school violence programs are ecological in orientation and support collaborative initiatives. Rather than seeing nonmajority students as underachievers and troublemakers, they should be viewed as having interactional problems that are often perceived as appropriate within their own culture but may deviate from the dominant culture and be interpreted as problematic. Three types of effective interrelated prevention programs can help these nonmajority students to be socially and academically successful. Primary prevention programs are implemented through policies that benefit students of all cultures, after a need has been identified by school authorities. Secondary prevention programs are designed to help at-risk (not at-crisis) nonmajority students who need specialized social and academic prevention. Tertiary prevention programs focus on nonmajority students who are in a crisis that has impacted their academic and social adjustment (Cole, 1995). Effective intervention programs should be implemented in early childhood and in collaboration with the parents and the community, to avoid antisocial and aggressive behavior during preadolescence. Offord and Boyle (1993) reported that treating youth after they engage in disturbances is less successful than early childhood prevention.

Primary Prevention Programs

These programs should focus on helping nonmajority students deal with language problems in order to realize academic success and promote prosocial skills among and across cultures. These programs should include conflict resolution (such as peer mediation by peers of the same and different cultures); anger management skills and cooperative learning/problem solving for families; English as a Second Language (ESL); parenting classes and support groups; encouragement and support of parents' involvement; and regular contact with the school, through committees and informational meetings, to encourage parents' participation in their child's/adolescent's education (Cole, 1995; Larson, 1994). In primary prevention programs, teachers incorporate life skills curricula and focus on good decision making, cultural diversity, and conflict resolution. They establish behavioral guidelines that are clearly identified, consistent (independent of the child's/adolescent's culture), enforced, and fairly applied toward all students. They also manage their classroom, break up fights in other areas of the school, and keep the school a safe place.

Secondary Prevention

These programs should be designed to help behavioral, social interactional, and cognitive at-risk nonmajority children and adolescents. A multidisciplinary team for these programs can give important assistance with the consultation and problem-solving process. Anger management and problem resolution can be addressed in the context of groups of peers of the same or different cultures (race and ethnicity). Social skills are often learned by nonmajority children/adolescents from their parents, who need to model prosocial behavior to their children. Programs dealing with self-management anger techniques should be offered to these parents (Larson, 1994). Nonmajority children are often perceived as having cognitive problems, but these problems are often language-based. Teachers must work collaboratively with culturally diverse families and their children. They must believe that nonmajority students can be successful and deserve an opportunity to learn in culturally sensitive classes that offer proper accommodations. In classes consisting of nonmajority and majority students, teachers must develop disciplinary strategies and appropriate goals for each student.

Tertiary Prevention

These programs should be designed to address nonmajority children and adolescents who repeatedly engage in aggressive behavior and previously have not been identified or have not responded to interventions. Focus should be given to anger control and stress inoculation, through methods such as "I statements," relaxation techniques, and self-assessment (Meichenbaum, 1985). These programs can be used in the context of individual and family therapy, as well as in groups of culturally same (in ethnicity and race) and/or diverse peers. School administrators and teachers need to establish clear behavioral guidelines that are consistent and are fairly applied to *all* students and not only to nonmajority students.

EMPIRICALLY BASED INTERVENTIONS

Cultural Sensitivity

In recent years, cultural sensitivity and violence prevention have become popular in the literature and in colloquia. This is an important development which, hopefully, will result in significant program development in schools. Because these risk factors vary from group to group, violence prevention programs should be tailored to the risks experienced by specific ethnic groups. Young African American males, for example, face the greatest risk from violence by acquaintances and friends; therefore, they would most likely benefit from skill-building programs that deal with nonviolent peer conflict resolution. Asian Americans' risk relates to stranger-to-stranger violence, suggesting a need for prevention programs geared toward relationship skills. Because the risk for gang membership exists in most groups, interventions that provide alternatives to gang membership should be implemented (Hammond & Yung, 1993). Any intervention programs that are culturally sensitive should include: educational techniques that are accepted within the culture—e.g., folk tales (Costantino, Malgady, & Rogler, 1986); role models similar to the target population (Hammond & Yung, 1991); and indigenous outreach workers to recruit participants in community-based education (Chen, 1989).

Early Intervention

Effective school violence prevention programs, as described above, should start in early childhood, because this time frame is believed to reduce aggression and risk factors associated with antisocial behavior (American Psychological Association, 1993). Because antisocial behavior tends to increase during adolescence, early prevention programs can prepare children as they move developmentally into adolescence. Graham and Hudley (1992) reported that elementary-school-age African American boys who participated in a school-based intervention program to alter hostility bias were significantly less likely to infer harmful intention and expressed less anger in response to peer provocation. Milton (1994) used a primary-level curriculum to decrease aggressive and increase prosocial behaviors of inner-city African American kindergartners and first and second graders, and found success in getting parents more involved in their children's schools' programmed social skill instruction.

Teacher/Parent Collaboration

Another study revealed that African American parents who received a weekly form (Gain Appropriate Behavior [GAB] Sheet) that identified the skills taught at school during that week and described how they could evaluate their nonmajority child's/adolescent's performance, exhibited positive response to the project and to the child's/adolescent's improved social skills. This study is particularly important because research has shown that teachers are less likely to contact a minority parent (compared to a Caucasian middle-class parent) because they believe that minority parents are indifferent (Turnbull & Turnbull, 1986).

Social Skills Training

According to Cartledge and Milburn (1996), culturally sensitive direct social skills training involves several components, including models, stimulus material, and group composition. Cartledge and Milburn also conducted a study on social skills training with urban adolescent males. They found that these students were interested in social skills training only after they were given permission to use their own language style to develop scripts and scenarios. These students showed a marked improvement in game-related social behavior.

Academic Performance

It is believed that African American, Hispanic/Latino, and Native American students often end up in lower class levels, with inexperienced teachers. Woo (1995) reported on a study by Steel and Aronson that "'pervasive negative stereotypes about blacks' intellectual ability create a 'situation pressure' that distracts them and depresses their academic performance" (p. 6B). Steel and Aronson (1995) revealed that African American students who were told that their verbal reasoning abilities were being tested scored significantly lower than students who were not told that their reasoning was being tested. It is believed that suggestions of performance assessment result in African American students' laboring "harder, but with ill effect ... they reread questions ... work less efficiently and make more mistakes" (Woo, 1995).

Disciplinary Measures

Irvin (1990) reported on research showing that black students receive four to five more suspensions, and longer suspensions, at a younger age than Caucasian students. Several demographic studies have shown that minority students (African American and Hispanic American), when compared to Caucasian students, have been disciplined disproportionately for behavioral and learning problems (Maheady, Algozzine, & Ysseldyke, 1985). Leal (1994) found that within low-income districts, the attitude toward school safety and discipline is "Be tough," which has resulted in criminal activity and imprisonment. Additional research has shown that minority males with behavioral problems, in comparison to their Caucasian peers with behavioral problems, were more often given pathological labels and frequently ended up in juvenile court, without getting therapy (Forness, 1988).

CASE MANAGEMENT AND THE STRENGTHS PERSPECTIVE

Today, many schools have become battlegrounds where antisocial and oppositional behaviors range from bullying to assault. From an ecological point of view, an interplay among the student, the student's family, the school, and society has resulted in conflict and violence. Exposure to and perception of danger in families, schools, and neighborhoods impact school achievement and threaten the ability of nonmajority children and adolescents to fulfill their potential in the school setting and to graduate. Nonmajority students might feel singled out to receive unduly harsh punishment from the school and the legal system. Problems in communication and social interaction then result.

Early intervention programs should be implemented for nonmajority children, with the parents and the school collaborating for the well-being of the child. Schoolwide primary and secondary prevention measures are essential if nonmajority children are to feel safe at school. Students' participation and involvement in violence prevention are critical. The school is their "world," and it must be safe and secure for optimal learning.

Tyrone, a 13-year-old African American male, witnessed his mother's repeated abuse by males. He experienced street violence firsthand at age 12, when he and his brother (a gang member) were shot. His brother died that night. Tyrone has carried a gun with him ever since, even though he was told not to do so unless he wanted to die like his brother did. During the past year, Tyrone felt singled out by his teacher as a "trouble maker" and often was put on suspension when nonminority peers were given little or no consequences for the same, or worse, behavior. Tyrone's teachers and counselor had made multiple attempts over the years to involve Tyrone's mother in her son's education, but had little success. A new (African American) teacher and a change in the school administrators brought about change for Tyrone. The new teacher's curriculum was sensitive to diversity, and rules were clearly identified and consistently followed, regardless of the student's culture. For the first time in his life, Tyrone had a role model to look up to. The principal requested that peer mediation training be provided, and it was actively used to help students resolve their conflicts. Tyrone learned, through peer mediation and an anger management group for African American boys, how to express his anger and frustration in a nonviolent way. For the first time in Tyrone's life, he learned how his style of communication—avoidance of eye contact and combative/aggressive responses to his peers, both of which were necessary to survive in his neighborhood—often was perceived as hostile.

Tyrone learned new ways to communicate, and he no longer was labeled as a "problem child." He raised his grades gradually and consistently, and told his teacher that he wanted to become a teacher. His mother, after repeated and persistent requests from the teacher, started meeting monthly with her and became more interested and involved in her son's schoolwork. She often volunteered her time and talents to the school. Two years later, Tyrone was the first person in his family to graduate from high school, and he went on to college to become a teacher.

FUTURE RESEARCH

Cultural diversity and school violence are topics that have received relatively little attention in the literature (Cartledge & Johnson, 1997). Children and adolescents are increasingly witnessing and experiencing abuse and other violent acts in their families (e.g., spouse/partner abuse, substance abuse, child abuse), their community (e.g., gang activities, street crime), and their schools (e.g., bullying, fighting, homicide, suicide). They often respond with intense and profound feelings of hopelessness, frustration, isolation, irritation, and hostility, and might bring these feelings to school. Most school-based interventions are generally founded on the specific problems students bring with them, and outsiders are often recruited to provide special services that are specific to a child or a culture. However, until now, research has focused on the importance of recruiting school staff and personnel to interrupt and address violent acts (through such programs as peer mediation) among and across nonmajority students. Programs and curricula that address cultural diversity and conflict management/resolution need to be evaluated. It is this author's belief that school violence needs to be viewed from an ecological perspective, in order to understand (a) school violence between and across culturally diverse students, and (b) the influences that nonmajority children experience within their family, neighborhood, companions, role models, and so on. Research in this area is needed; thus far, little has been conducted even though national data reveal an increase in the risk that children and adolescents may become victims and perpetrators of violent acts. We have not yet identified a unified theory that explains violence among nonmajority children and adolescents. We need to develop a conceptual framework to explore contributing factors (personal, social, and cultural) and start developing preventive approaches.

REFERENCES

Aguilar-Gaxiola, S. A., & Gray, T. (1994, August). *Diagnostic concordance between computerized and paper-and-pencil.* Spanish versions of the moon disorders sections of the SCID-P in Hispanics. Paper presented at the 102nd annual convention of the American Psychological Association, Los Angeles.

American Psychological Association. (1993). *Commission on violence and youth* (Report). Washington, DC: Author.

Astor, R. A. (1998). Moral reasoning about school violence: Informational assumptions about harm within school subcontexts. *Educational Psychology, 33*(4), 207–221.

Atkinson, D. R., Morton, G., & Sue, D. W. (1993). *Counseling American minorities: A cross-cultural perspective.* Madison, WI: Brown & Benchmark.

Bernal, M. E., Saenz, D. S., & Knight, G. P. (1991). Ethnic identity and adaptation of Mexican American youth in school settings. *Hispanic Journal of Behavioral Sciences, 13,* 135–154.

Bronfenbrenner, U. (1979). *The ecology of human development.* Cambridge, MA: Harvard University Press.

Cartledge, G., & Johnson, C. T. (1997). School violence and cultural diversity. In A. P. Goldstein & J. C. Conoley (Eds.), *School violence intervention: Practical handbook* (pp. 391–425). New York: Guilford Press.

Cartledge, G., & Milburn, J. F. (1996). *Cultural diversity and social skills instruction: Understanding ethic and gender differences.* Champaign, IL: Research Press.

Center for Disease Control and Prevention. (1996). *Youth risk behavior surveillance: United States, 1995* (No. SS-4). Atlanta, GA: Author.

Chen, M. (1989). The indigenous model and its application to heart health for Southeast Asians. *Health Education, 20*(5), 48–51.

Chin, K. (1990). *Chinese subculture and criminality.* New York: Greenwood Press.

Coie, J., Dodge, K., Terry, R., & Wright, V. (1991). The role of aggression in peer relations: An analysis of aggression episodes in boys' play groups. *Child Development, 62,* 812–826.

Cole, E. (1995). *Role-playing: An avenue for building inclusive classrooms for new Canadian students.* Toronto, Ontario, Canada: Toronto Board of Education.

Collier, M. J., & Thomas, M. (1988). Cultural identity: An interactive perspective. In Y. Y. Kim & W. B. Gudykunst (Eds.), *Theories in interactive communication* (pp. 99–120). Newbury Park, CA: Sage.

Costantino, G., Malgady, R., & Rogler, L. (1986). Cuento therapy: A culturally sensitive modality for Puerto Rican children. *Journal of Counseling and Clinical Psychology, 54,* 639–645.

Cotton, N. U., Resnick, J., Browne, D. C., Martin, S. L., McCarraher, D. R., & Woods, J. (1994). Aggression and fighting behavior among African-American adolescents: Individual and family factors. *American Journal of Public Health, 84,* 618–622.

Cox, A. (2000, October 8). Techno-bullies are a new force to contend with. *St. Louis Post-Dispatch,* E.V., 7.

Crews, G. A., & Counts, M. R. (1997). *The evolution of school disturbance in America colonial times to modern day.* Westport, CT: Praeger.

DuRant, R. H., Cadenhead, C., Pendergrast, R. A., Slavens, G., & Linder, C. W. (1994). Factors associated with the use of violence among urban black adolescents. *American Journal of Public Health, 84,* 612–617.

Elliott, D. S. (1994). Serious violent offenders: Onset, developmental course and termination—The American Society of Criminology 1993 presidential address. *Criminology, 32,* 1–21.

Elrich, M. (1994). The stereotype within. *Educational Leadership, 51,* 12–15.

Federal Bureau of Investigation. (1991). *Age-specific arrest rates and race-specific arrest rates for selected offenses, 1965–1989.* Washington, DC: Unified Crime Reporting Program, 1990.

Feng, H., & Cartledge, G. (1996). Social skills assessment of inner-city Asian, African, and European American students. *School Psychology Review, 25,* 227–238.

Fingerhut, L. A., Ingram, D., & Feldman, J. (1992). Firearm and non-firearm homicide among persons 15 through 19 years of age. *Journal of the American Medical Association, 267,* 3048–3053.

Ford Foundation. (1984, June). *Hispanics: Challenges and opportunities.* New York: Author.

Forness, S. R. (1988). Planning for the needs of children with serious emotional disturbance: The National Special Education and Mental Health Coalition. *Behavioral Disorders, 13*(2), 127–139.

Glasser, W. (1998). *Choice theory: A new psychology of personal freedom.* New York: HarperCollins.

Goldstein, A. P., & Conoley, J. C. (1997). Student aggression: Current status. In A. P. Goldstein & J. C. Conoley (Eds.), *School violence intervention: A practical handbook* (pp. 3–22). New York: Guilford Press.

Graham, S., & Hudley, C. (1992). An attributional approach to aggression in African-American children. In D. Schunk & J. Meece (Eds.), *Students perceptions in the classroom* (pp. 75–94). Hillsdale, NJ: Erlbaum.

Grossman, D. C., Milligan, C., & Deyo, R. A. (1991). Risk factors for suicide attempts among Navajo adolescents. *American Journal of Public Health, 81,* 870–874.

Hammond, W., & Yung, B. (1991). Preventing violence in at-risk African American youth. *Journal of Heath Care for the Poor and Underserved, 2,* 358–372.

Hammond, W. R., & Yung, B. R. (1993). Psychology's role in the public health response to assaultive violence among young African men. *American Psychologist, 48*(2), 142–154.

Harper, F. D., & Ibrahim, F. A. (2000). Violence and schools in the USA: Implications for counseling. *International Journal for the Advancement of Counseling, 21,* 349–366.

Howes, C., & Wu, F. (1990). Peer interactions and friendships in an ethnically diverse school setting. *Child Development, 61,* 537–541.

Irvin, G. M. (1990). The social behavior of primary school children and the relationship of preschool experience versus no preschool experience on this behavior. (Doctoral dissertation, Wayne State University, 1990). *Dissertation Abstracts International, 50,* 70-A.

Irvine, J. J. (1992). Making teacher education culturally response. In M. E. Dilworth (Ed.), *Diversity in teaching education: New expectations* (pp. 79–92). San Francisco: Jossey-Bass.

Kavanagh, K. H., & Kennedy, P. H. (1992). *Promoting cultural diversity: Strategies for health care professionals.* Newbury Park, CA: Sage.

Killalea, E. (1980). *State, regional, and national summaries.* Washington, DC: Department of Health and Human Services, Office for Civil Rights.

King, S. H. (1993). The limited presence of African-American teachers. *Review of Educational Research, 63*(2), 115–149.

LaFromboise, T. D., & Low, K. G. (1989). American Indian children and adolescents. In J. T. Gibbs, L. N. Huang, & Associates (Eds.), *Children of color* (pp. 114–147). San Francisco: Jossey-Bass.

Larson, J. (1994). Violence prevention in the schools: A review of selected programs and procedures. *School Psychology Review, 23*(2), 151–164.

Leal, R. (1994). Conflicting views of discipline in San Antonio schools. *Education and Urban Society, 27,*15–23.

Maheady, L., Algozzine, B., & Ysseldyke, J. E. (1985). Minorities in special education. *Education Digest, 51,* 50–53.

Meichenbaum, D. H. (1985). *Stress inoculation training.* New York: Pergamon Press.

Mercy, J., Goodman, R., Rosenberg, M., Allen, N., Loya, F., Smith, J., et al. (1986). Pattern of homicide victimization in the city of Los Angeles, 1970–1979. *Bulletin of the New York Academy of Medicine, 62,* 427–445.

Milton, M. (1994). A response to bond. *Counseling Psychology Review, 9*(2), 5–6.

Min, P. G. (1995). *Asian Americans: Contemporary trends and issues.* Thousand Oaks, CA: Sage.

Mulhern, M. M. (1995, April). *A Mexican-American child's home life and literacy learning from kindergarten through second grade.* Paper presentation at the annual meeting of the American Educational Research Association, San Francisco.

National Center for Health Statistics. (1990). *Prevention profile: Health, United States, 1989* (DHHS Publication No. PHS 90-1232). Hyattsville, MD: U.S. Department of Health and Human Services.

National Education Goals Panel. (1995). *The National education goals report* (Vol. 1–2). Washington, DC: U.S. Government Printing Office.

Oetting, E. R., Beauvais, F., Edwards, R., Waters, M. R., Velarde, J., & Goldstein, G. (1983). *Drug use among Native American youth: Summary of findings (1975–1981).* Fort Collins: Colorado State University.

Offord, D., & Boyle, M (1993). Helping children adjust: A tri-ministry project. *ORBIT, 24,* 25.

Olweus, D. (1992). Bullying among school children: Intervention and prevention. In R. Peters, R. McMahon, & V. Quincy (Eds.), *Aggression and violence throughout the lifespan* (pp. 100–125). London: Sage.

Orton, G. L. (1996). *Strategies for counseling with children and their parents.* Pacific Grove, CA: Brooks/Cole.

Paderson, P. (1988). The three stages of multicultural development: Awareness, knowledge, and skill. In P. Pedersen (Ed.), *A handbook for developing multicultural awareness* (pp. 3–18). Alexandria, VA: American Association for Counseling and Development.

Phinney, J. S. (1990). Ethnic identity in adolescents and adults: Review of research. *Psychological Bulletin, 108,* 499–514.

Powless, D. L., & Elliott, S. N. (1993). Assessment of social skills of Native American preschoolers: Teachers' and parents' ratings. *Journal of School Psychology, 31,* 293–307.

Ramirez, O. (1989). Mexican American children and adolescents. In J. T. Gibbs, L. N. Huang, & Associates (Eds.), *Children of color* (pp. 150–224). San Francisco: Jossey-Bass.

Sarbaugh, L. E. (1988). A taxonomic approach to intercultural communication. In Y. Y. Kim & W. B. Gudykunst (Eds.), *Theories in intercultural communication* (pp. 22–38). Newbury Park, CA: Sage.

Soriano, F. (1993). Cultural sensitivity and gang intervention. In A. P. Goldstein & C. R. Huff (Eds.), *The gang intervention handbook* (pp. 141–161). Champaign, IL: Research Press.

Steel, C.M., & Aronson, J. (1995). Stereotype threat and the intellectual test performance of African-Americans. *Journal of Personality and Social Psychology, 69,* 797–811.

Sue, D., & Sue, D. W. (1993). Ethnic identity: Cultural factors in the psychological development of Asians in America. In D. R. Atkinson, G. Morton, & D. W. Sue (Eds.), *Counseling American minorities: A cross-cultural perspective* (pp. 199–210). Madison, WI: Brown & Benchmark.

The Washington Post Online. (2000, November 25). *Juvenile violence time line.* Available from: www.washingtonpost.com/wp-srv/national/longterm/juvmurders /timeline.htm

Thomason, T. C. (1993). Counseling Native Americans: An introduction for non-native American counselors. In D. R. Atkinson, G. Morton, & D. W. Sue (Eds.), *Counseling American minorities: A cross-cultural perspective* (pp. 171–191). Madison, WI: Brown & Benchmark.

Turnbull, A. P., & Turnbull, H. R. (1986). *Families, professionals, and exceptionality: A special partnership.* Columbus, OH: Merrill.

U.S. Department of Education, National Center for Educational Statistics. (1998). *Violence and discipline problems in U.S. public schools. 1996–1997* (NCES 98-030). Washington, DC: U.S. Government Printing Office.

U.S. Department of Health and Human Services. (1991). *Healthy people 2000* (Rep. No. PHS 91-50212). Washington, DC: U.S. Government Printing Office.

Vargas, A. M. (1994, August). *Culture-focused group therapy: Identity issues in gang involved youth.* Paper presented at the 102nd annual convention of the American Psychological Association, Los Angeles.

Woo, E. (1995, December 17). Stereotypes "psych out" students. *Columbus Dispatch,* p. 6B.

SECTION IV

Workplace Violence

Chapter 16

PREVENTING WORKPLACE VIOLENCE

JOHN S. WODARSKI AND CATHERINE N. DULMUS

INTRODUCTION

Workplace violence has emerged as a critical safety and health issue in America. Workplace violence is defined as any physical or psychological act against an employee, including physical or verbal assaults, threats, coercion, intimidation, or other harassment (Lenius, 1999). Three main theoretical bases address causation of violence in the workplace: (a) personality assessments and characteristics of violent types of individuals, (b) improper screening and background checks of potential employees, and (c) the setting and internal characteristics of organizations, which impact workplace violence.

This theoretical investigation first analyzes the personality profiles of potentially aggressive employees and describes how hiring smart can avoid high-risk applicants. Company culture regarding behaviors in the workplace is then discussed. Through this analysis, we hope to provide a broad understanding of the theoretical reasons why, each year, more than 2 million people become victims of violent crime at work (Lenius, 1999). Commentary is included on the various ways workplace violence can be prevented through an informed understanding of the precipitating factors of workplace violence. It is proposed that increased awareness of psychological variables in human behavior can prevent violence in the workplace. The chapter concludes with recommendations to: (a) inform employers about how certain behavioral characteristics place companies at risk; (b) be thorough in screening employees, and understand the techniques of detecting violent perpetrators; and (c) realize that organizations can prevent aggression in the workplace through more skillful personnel management.

HUMAN AGGRESSION AND PERSONALITY PROFILES

A substantial body of research indicates that individuals differ substantially in their ability or propensity to be aggressive. Neuman and Baron (1998) state that certain people respond mildly to strong provocation, while others react with strong emotions and overt aggression to mild forms of annoyance. Responses, therefore, can be conceptualized on a continuum. The authors suggest that social and situational factors play an integral role in an individual's susceptibility to aggressive behavior. Certain behavior patterns are categorized as possibly leading to aggression (Neuman & Baron, 1998).

Individuals in the "Type A" behavior pattern are referred to as one classification. These individuals are often impatient and irritable, prefer to work alone, and, when they must work with others, desire to control the situation. Individuals classified as "Type B" show the opposite pattern of behavior; they are much calmer. For example, Type A personalities lose their temper more frequently, and, compared to Type B personalities, demonstrate higher levels of aggression and report a higher frequency of conflict with subordinates at work. They are defined as being "more irritable on the job" (Baron & Neuman, 1998). The literature reveals a significant relationship between Type A behavior patterns and three forms of workplace aggression: (a) hostility, (b) obstructionism, and (c) overt aggression. These individuals are classified as high in self-monitoring and are considerably socially sensitive; they alter their words or deeds to produce favorable impressions on others. When they interpret others' behaviors as hostile, they are likely to feel aggrieved and retaliate toward those others (Baron & Neuman, 1998). Research suggests that some individuals perceive hostile intent on the part of others, even when this intent is lacking. These individuals may develop an expectancy that others will respond to them in hostile ways, prior to any interaction's taking place.

The research in the area of workplace violence says that our internal psychological state and our cognitive appraisal (how we feel and what we think) have substantial impacts on what we do. Baron and Neuman (1998) state:

> Negative affect (e.g., negative moods, unpleasant physiological arousal) may evoke unpleasant thoughts and memories. These, in turn, may lead to irritation, annoyance, and anger. Aggression-related thoughts and memories may elicit unpleasant feelings and arousal, just as personality traits may predispose individuals to particular forms of behavior. The intensity of these internal states and level of cognitive procession may influence the choice of action or perceptions of the problem. (p. 16)

No single characteristic or combination of personality characteristics will influence an individual to be aggressive. Each individual is different and will react differently to certain stimuli. The more an individual exhibits the above characteristics, however, the higher the probability of violent behavior.

PROFILE OF VIOLENT INDIVIDUALS

Research shows that workers in the lower regions of a hierarchy are perceived by others as more vulnerable targets of aggressive actions. Low-status people are viewed as having less formal power and less retributional potential (Aquino, Grover, Bradfield, & Allen, 1999). They will be less able to effectively punish those who treat them poorly.

According to the Federal Bureau of Investigation (FBI), the profile of a person most likely to commit workplace violence is: White male, between 30 and 40 years old, with a keen interest in guns. The U.S. Department of Justice has added the following warning signs to that profile:

- Someone who holds irrational ideas and beliefs.
- An employee experiencing exceptional stress outside of work, such as divorce or lack of money.
- A person who is fascinated by weapons.
- An employee who displays unwarranted anger.
- A person who can't take criticism.
- Someone who expresses a lack of concern for the safety of others.

Marino (1997) states that homicide-prone workers are narcissistic; those individuals are offended by "slights" and are convinced that "enemies" surround them. They think of themselves as "victims of injustice." They are controlling and demanding. They tend to resist counseling, admonitions, or appeals to reason. They make coworkers uncomfortable and anxious. They own multiple guns and are attracted to paramilitary groups, law enforcement, survivalist organizations, and fascist role models. In their minds, mistakes are always someone else's fault. They file grievances and collect legal documents and articles to support their claims of injustice. They are angry and express interest in reports of violent acts such as spousal abuse, bombings, shooting sprees, and the like. They belong to fringe right-wing, antigovernment, or racist groups. They are task-oriented rather than people-oriented. They are often good workers in the technical sense—they pay obsessive attention to details—but they are insensitive to people. Finally, they have minor criminal records and drug or alcohol abuse problems.

HIRING SMART TO AVOID WORKPLACE VIOLENCE

Workplace violence permeates our culture with alarming frequency. The term "disgruntled employee" has become synonymous with violence. The Occupational Safety and Health Administration (OSHA), citing statistics regarding documented trends and frequencies of workplace violence, indicates that, on average, nearly 1,000 workers are murdered, and 1.5 million are assaulted every year (U.S. Department of Labor, 1998). Personal problems of employees need to be identified and addressed to ensure a safe and productive work environment. Variables to be considered when attempting to identify a potentially problematic employee are: marital and relationship problems, domestic violence and related family problems, boss or coworker hatred and incompatibility, workplace coping problems, alcohol or drug abuse, psychological illnesses, housing or transportation problems, and legal problems (Albrecht, 1997).

A practical safeguard for reducing workplace violence consists of perfecting and elaborating the scope of the preemployment hiring process. Industrial psychologists have found that traditional interviews that rely on hypothetical questions are poor ways to determine an applicant's ability to do a job (Chartrand, 1997a). Careful screening of applicants is essential for weeding out future potential problem employees. A first impression is usually a good indicator of what is to come. If an application is sloppy, misspelled, tattered, soiled, and illegible, it is probably a safe bet that the author is suffering from chaos in his or her life. Gaps in employment that cannot be accounted for should be questioned with scrutiny.

THE ROLE OF COMPANY CULTURE IN WORKPLACE VIOLENCE

The changing face of the modern workplace is indicated as creating a greater predictor of stress and hostility at work. The violation of important social norms, such as the replacement of long-term employee-employer relationships with temporary and part-time affiliations, may be a precursor to violent behaviors. These "contingent" employee relationships are associated with higher levels of stress and frustration (Baron & Neuman, 1998).

Poor air quality, noise levels, crowding, and high humidity are environmental factors that are associated with negative affect (unpleasant internal states) and increased levels of stress and aggression. Work-shift (change in work hours) is also a source of stress and frustration, especially as it relates to rotating shifts and associated sleep deprivation.

The research indicates that "(a) setting an example (climate of honesty displayed by leadership), (b) treating employees with trust, respect, and dignity, (c) providing adequate compensation, (d) communicating a policy concerning counterproductive behavior, (e) consistently punishing unacceptable behavior, and (f) reducing job stress" (Baron & Neuman, 1998) are ways to prevent the deterioration of the organized culture.

One of the most intriguing points in the literature on organizational identity and its correlation to violence in the workplace is the concept of "persecutory organizational identity" (Diamond, 1997). In his study of workplace violence, Diamond explores how workers who feel powerless and disrespected come to feel persecuted by the executive leadership. The emotional relationship of workers and leaders is affected by managers who do not effectively represent them; managers who are poor communicators and incompetent mediators between leadership and the workforce make the organization vulnerable to workplace violence. Organizations where there is (a) a lack of mutual respect, and (b) a lack of worker participation in the organization enable a form of persecutory transference by the individual. Unilateral and "top-down" decisions within an organization may encourage feelings of being mistreated and disrespected. The company may be viewed as immoral if safeguards are not in place to create an effective forum to discuss problems and share feedback. "Problem solving is collective action that heals through the process of collaboration and mutual respect. Engaging in solving problems and resolving conflicts empowers the organizational participants" (Diamond, 1997).

ASSESSMENT OF WORKPLACE VIOLENCE

The focus of this section is to investigate methods of assessing violence in the workplace and the dynamics involved in understanding this phenomenon. Various tasks are involved when assessing workplace violence, including preemployment screening, worksite environment screening, and the social and personal aspects of screening employees for their potential to become violent in the workplace. The increasing frequency and the costs of violent incidents have led to serious attention by CEOs and company owners. Under federal and state OSHA regulations, employers are required to provide employees with a workplace that is free from recognized hazards and risks that could possibly cause death or serious injury (Guardian Security Services, 1999). It may be stated that assessing the potentiality for workplace violence is of utmost importance to workplace safety.

Preemployment Screening

Perhaps the first line of defense for workplace violence is preemployment screening. It is important for employers to hire carefully and realistically. It is much better to screen out potential problems than to have to deal with them because a wrong person was hired (Guardian Security Services, 1999). Numerous procedures are involved in the process of employee selection; the most common elements are applications, background checks, references, tests, and interviews.

A written *application* is utilized universally and is usually the initial step in the selection process. Customarily, the application requests routine biographical information, such as work experience, education, and qualifications. It also exposes unexplained gaps of time between former jobs. As stated earlier, the appearance of the completed application is a powerful indicator of the state of mind of the applicant.

When an application is completed and submitted, a *background check* is commonly required. Applicants must list the names of several references—people who can testify to the applicant's abilities or provide letters of recommendation. However, a completed application may not reveal enough information about a potential employee. Applicants are often able to choose who writes their letters of recommendation, thus drawing the recommendation's reliability into question. A check for a history of a criminal record is also important, although one must keep in mind the laws regarding privacy (National Credit Information Network, 1998). Employers have a duty to investigate the background of a potential employee in order to protect other employees from the dangers of workplace violence.

Some employers opt to utilize *additional procedures* for screening prospective employees. Often, the employment selection process requires *testing*. Tests may evaluate (but are not limited to) mental ability, aptitude, motor skills, illegal drug use, and personality profiles. Such preemployment screening can be effective in identifying problematic behaviors and practices, such as: alcohol abuse, drug abuse, impaired judgment, emotional difficulties, financial problems, legal problems, strained family relations, strained relationships with former employers or coworkers, and occupational failures. These practices and behaviors can be caused by high levels of stress or by mental illness, both of which can inherently produce personality problems within an individual. A potentially violent situation may result if that individual becomes an employee. Mattman (2000) reported the following:

> Most experts agree that social issues, especially substance abuse, layoffs and poverty are major contributors to occupational violence. The ease with which guns can be obtained, excessive graphic violence on television and in movies, language and ethnic differences among workers and the general acceptance of violence as a form of communication by a large segment of our population are other causes frequently cited by those closely associated with this problem. (p. 2)

According to the Illinois State Police (2000), a violent person's profile includes poor self-esteem, a history of substance abuse, and a history of aggression and complaints of stress. Implementing proper screening procedures during the hiring process will help to keep dangerous individuals out of the workplace. The preemployment screening procedures should include a clear warning to prospective employees that a thorough background check will be conducted. Applicants will be required to sign a release allowing the potential employer access to criminal driving records; previous employment history; and financial, military, and other appropriate records. In addition, prospective employees should be warned that they are subject to random drug and alcohol testing, and failure of such a test is grounds for immediate termination. When this type of policy is clearly stated, many would-be applicants never complete their applications. Early assessment of a prospective employee's potential is the key to keeping violent individuals out of the workplace.

The validity of personality measures for the purposes of personnel selection has been investigated for several years (Nowack, 1997). The concluding report states that personality, as a predictor of job performance, is low in validity and has been found to be not much more relevant than an unstructured interview. However, because personality conflicts are still cited as the leading cause of workplace violence (Guardian Security Services, 1999), they may be used to indicate personality flaws that may possibly lead to conflict.

An impressive amount of research has focused on accumulating evidence for a five-factor model of personality that spans several theoretical frameworks and uses different instruments. This five-factor model is often referred to as "the Big Five." Of the five factors, the second factor, Emotional Stability, is important in determining whether a potential employee is anxious, depressed, angry, worried, insecure, or emotional. Any of these conditions, if present in an individual, may result in future problematic situations in the workplace.

Two recently developed personality inventories, the Hogan Personality Inventory and the Neuroticism, Extraversion, Openness (NEO) Five Factor Inventory are based on the Big Five model. According to Nowack (1997), both inventories appear to be promising and are increasingly being utilized by organizations to assess individual personalities.

According to Section 703(h) of Title VII of the Civil Rights Act of 1964 (Jansson, 1993), an employer can lawfully give an employee a professionally developed ability test, as long as its results are not used to discriminate because of race, color, religion, or sex. Such tests should be administered by experts, in accordance with the Uniform Guidelines on Employee Selection Procedures (Arthur, 1994). Personality inventories are valuable tools for preemployment screening practices.

As previously mentioned, substance abuse screening is an important factor during preemployment screening. Because the probability of violence increases when individuals are under the influence of drugs or alcohol, substance abuse is one of the indicators of a violent personality. Drug testing can be accomplished through urine samples, blood tests, hair analysis, critical tracking tests, and papillary tests. Health officials report that between 10% and 23% of American workers use dangerous drugs on and off the job, and 85% of American companies rely on drug testing (Arthur, 1994) to screen out potentially violent individuals.

If an applicant graduates to the next phase of the hiring process, a personal interview, the interviewer must be savvy enough to utilize the face-to-face interview in filtering out difficult candidates. Chartrand (1998b) notes several questions that can be used during an interview of individuals who are potentially violence prone. The most notable question is: "When have you felt that you have been treated unfairly in your life?" Research has revealed that an employee's perception of unjust treatment has been related to nearly every commission of some type of violence on the job. Utilizing techniques such as Behavior Interviews, Stress Interviews, and Target Interviews, employers have been able to "red flag" questionable behavior. The Theory of Interview Techniques begins with an assessment of the applicant's goals and then determines the candidate's basic qualifications and evaluates specific personality traits that might predispose the individual toward violence in the workplace (Chartrand, 1997b).

Thorough background checks should be the rule, not the exception, when considering a candidate for hire. Drug testing, reference checks, employment records, driving records, credit histories, academic records, and credit checks (all within the scope of the law) are encouraged in the research as standard practices. Employers should also test for psychological fitness, using tools such as the Minnesota Multiphasic Personality Inventory (MMPI). To predict whether an applicant is qualified and will be a good fit with the company, management should evaluate every available resource. Careful hiring procedures that give thorough attention to detail can reduce workplace violence.

Preemployment screening may consist of personality inventories, substance abuse screening, criminal history checks, and interviews conducted by skilled personnel. Such screening assists employers in assessing workplace violence.

WORKSITE ASSESSMENT

The literature suggests that organizational and/or company factors may lead to increased violence in the workplace (Baron & Neuman, 1998). These variables are numerous; they include: treatment of employees by supervisors, environmental factors in the work setting, lack of employee support systems, stress emanating from the ways in which employees are dismissed (e.g., downsizing), unfair treatment, and ostracism of personnel by fellow employees (Baron & Neuman, 1998).

A study of workplace harassment found that 32% of the respondents indicated that they had observed others being "shouted at loudly or being exposed to humiliating comments, insinuating glances, negative gestures, undue criticism, and unfairly damaging performance evaluations" (Baron & Neuman, 1998). The research suggests that these types of behaviors are potentially damaging to organizations and increase the likelihood of aggressive retaliation by employees. Obstructionism is especially relevant in work settings where an immediate superior has the power to minimize employees and, as a result, a passive aggression is formed in the face of injustice.

Thus, in addition to a thorough assessment of an individual prior to hiring, the worksite environment should be assessed for any vulnerability to violent acts. This assessment should include a review of the day-to-day organizational procedures that could potentially contribute to stress-provoking situations. Also, changes in the workplace environment that could lead to increased levels of stress should be evaluated. A study conducted in 1992 by Brockner, Tyler, and Cooper-Schneider supported research indicating that when changes occurring in the workplace escalate, the potential for aggression of various forms increases. A worksite assessment should always include an examination of the physical characteristics of the workplace.

The Occupational Safety and Health Administration (OSHA) (U.S. Department of Labor, 1998) suggests a team approach to analysis of a worksite. The team should consist of top-level managers, lower-level managers, employee assistance program staff, security personnel, human resources staff, and several employee representatives. This Threat Assessment Team (TAT), as it is often called, has several tasks. Among them is a review of records of previous injuries, illnesses, absences, and incident reports regarding acts of aggression or violence. These records can be used to determine patterns (particular job duties or times of day when incidents occurred) or to identify employees who are most often involved in incidents. The records can track needs for improvements and identify possible risk factors, which may be individual, personal, or related to the organization itself. The National Safety from Violence in the Workplace Institute (as cited in Kinney, 1995) suggests having standardized incident report forms that indicate the who, when, where, and how for recording incidents at work.

Several organizational factors have been identified as precipitating or triggering events of possible workplace violence in its various forms. A TAT should assess these triggers, which may become motives for violence: coworker support, layoff worry, work schedules, public contact, and money handling (Cole, Grubb, Sauter, Swanson, & Lawless, 1997). Other internal factors that require attention include procedural aspects of hiring, termination, promotions, performance appraisals, and disciplinary actions (Barrett, Riggar, & Flowers, 1997a; Greenberg & Barling, 1999). Kenway, Fitzclarence, and Hasluck (2000) reported that a lack of power and status could be a factor in an employee's use of violence. Additionally, a corporation's encouragement of social alienation and class distinctions can create an oppressive culture that may lead to violence.

Physical factors need to be assessed as well. Factors to investigate include: location of the worksite; isolation of the worksite; where entrances and exits are located and whether they are monitored; access to the building by employees and visitors during and after hours; and security systems that may involve clearance checks, cameras, and guards (Barrett, Riggar, & Flowers, 1997b). In addition, OSHA (U.S. Department of Labor, 1998) warns that other high-risk factors may make the physical environment vulnerable: lack of communication devices and alarm systems, improper lighting, poor temperature control, objects that are easily accessible and can be used as weapons, small numbers of employees who work late at night or early in the morning, and glass windows.

The TAT's conduct of employee surveys is important because front-line employees are usually more aware of the potential risk factors. They may interact with perpetrators of violence more than managers do. An assessment of the employees' opinions about the interpersonal climatic factors—such as levels of trust, respect, and communication—should be conducted via surveys. A worksite assessment survey should include the types of stress relievers that are present, such as health and fitness centers, accessibility of Employee Assistance Programs (EAPs), and day care. The employees should also be surveyed regarding their opinions of and experiences with security and the other physical/environmental factors that could potentially make the worksite vulnerable. In addition to the inventories mentioned in the preemployment screening section, there are tools that can be used after the employee has been hired. The individuals in the working environment, the worksite environment itself, and the workplace as an organization can be assessed with these tools.

VIOLENCE ASSESSMENT MEASURES

Presently, there is no specific assessment tool for measuring aggressive behaviors in the workplace. Greenberg and Barling (1999) attempted to develop a measure specific to the workplace by modifying the Conflict Tactics Scale developed by Straus. This modified version assesses the number of times an individual has used any of 22 behaviors ranging from psychological aggression to violent acts. A limitation of this modified assessment tool is that the authors eliminated some items from the violence subscale; items regarding threats with or use of a knife or a gun have been removed. These items are important in a workplace; threats are a large part of the forms of aggression that occur. The measures described below are among those used to assess the potential for workplace violence.

- The Job Stress Inventory (JSS) (Vagg & Spielberger, 1998) was developed to assess work-related stress as measured by 30 stressor event questions. The JSS also evaluates the severity and frequency of these stress-provoking events. Included are subscales to measure stress associated with job pressure and with a lack of organizational support. As reported in the worksite assessment portion of this chapter, job pressure and lack of organizational support have been included as risk factors of the worksite itself because they could make a workplace vulnerable to violence.

- Another tool for measuring job stress is the Occupational Stress Inventory (OSI) (Osipow & Davis, 1988). The six scales of this inventory measure stress-provoking work roles, including physical environment, role overload, and role insufficiency. Four subscales measure personal strain, including psychological and interpersonal strain. Four coping resources subscales include measures of social support and rational/cognitive coping. In total, the OSI has 140 items and includes a professional manual that addresses validity and research studies using the OSI.

- The Personality Assessment Inventory (PAI) (Morey, 1999) takes only 3 to 5 minutes to administer; thus, it is often used as a triage tool. It can assess whether a full psychological evaluation is necessary. Ten areas are measured by the PAI's 22 items: (a) negative affect, (b) hostile control, (c) acting out, (d) suicidal thinking, (e) health problems, (f) alienation, (g) psychotic features, (h) alcohol problems, (i) social withdrawal, and (j) anger control. A professional manual describing reliability, validity, and internal consistency is available.

- Mehrabian (1990) developed the Risk of Eruptive Violence Scale (REV). It was designed to measure individuals who appear nonaggressive and nonviolent, withdrawn and restrained, but may have extreme anger. That anger may cause the individual to wish to hurt someone or to suddenly become violent under certain circumstances. This scale has validity findings with the Brief Anger and Aggression Scale (Maiuro, Vitaliano, & Cahn, 1987), which can be used for rapid assessment of overt anger and aggression levels of violence-prone males.

All of these instruments can be used by EAP professionals. The Job Stress Survey, Occupational Stress Inventory, and Work Environment Scale appear to measure organizational factors that could create a hostile environment and stressful working conditions. The Threat Assessment Team can use these in their worksite assessment surveys and as prevention tools to assess areas that need improvement. The Employee Assistance Program Inventory and the Personality Assessment Screener measure factors related to individual or personal issues that may highlight warning signs of potential aggression and violence.

Several other general measures of aggression that are applicable for various populations are available. Bech and Mak (1995) reported that the most frequently used aggression questionnaire is the Buss-Durkee Hostility Inventory, a self-rating scale that measures verbal and physical aggression as well as anger and hostility.

Another self-rating scale is the Feelings and Acts of Violence (FAV) Scale—shortened version. This 12-item scale estimates violent tendencies and can be used with a broad range of populations. It has high internal reliability and discriminant validity (Plutchik & van Pragg, 1990).

There are observer scales that could also be used by peers or supervisors concerned about an individual. As reported by Bech and Mak (1995), these include the Staff Observation Aggression Scale (SOAS) and the Scale for Assessment of Agitated and Aggressive Behavior (SAAB). Both scales include questions regarding verbal and/or physical aggression.

The State-Trait Anger Expression Inventory—2 (STAXI) (Spielberger, Sydeman, Owen, & Marsh, 1999) measures state and trait anger. State anger is measured to determine the intensity of anger at a given time; trait anger assesses how often a person experiences angry feelings. Other subscales include: feeling angry, feeling like expressing anger verbally and physically, anger temperament and reaction, and how anger is expressed and controlled.

The STAXI consists of 57 items and takes about 10 minutes to complete. The manual includes data on validity.

THREAT ASSESSMENT

Threat assessment is defined as a "term to describe the investigation and operational techniques used to identify, assess, and manage the risks of targeted violence and its potential perpetrators" (Fein, Vossekuil, & Holden, 1995, p. 3). Threat assessment includes awareness of the various behavioral signs and problems that lead up to the culmination of a serious violent act, and the characteristics of perpetrators. Assessing threats for workplace violence is extremely important.

Current and former employees account for 43% of workplace violence, according to Duncan (1995). As reported by Neuman and Baron (1998), workplace aggression can take many forms on a continuum: from verbal to physical, active to passive, and indirect to direct. It is important for employers to be aware of what the forms are and where they fall on the continuum, because behaviors on the low end of the scale may be warning signs leading up to higher-level behaviors such as assault and homicide. Violence in the workplace rarely occurs "out of the blue" or spontaneously; rather, it is a process that occurs over time, in various degrees. Often, there are warning signs such as inappropriate behaviors that increase in frequency and intensity.

In addition to being aware of the types of aggression, one must be knowledgeable about signs indicating that an employee is becoming stressed, frustrated, and angry. Reynolds (1999) reports that these signs include: tense body language, such as clenched jaws and fists; increased rate of breathing; avoiding eye contact, or staring; changes in rate of speech, voice level, or volume change; more statements that begin with "Yes, but . . ."; excessive complaining; and swearing or insulting language.

The typical perpetrator usually displays certain characteristics that one should be familiar with (in addition to the warning signs): white male aged 25 to 30 years; few outside interests and a lack of participation in organizational activities; a belief that he has been treated with injustice; fear of losing his job; numerous absences or tardiness; several stressors, such as financial, medical, or legal problems; isolation from family; blames others for problems; low self-esteem; impulsive; poor anger control; violates workplace rules and policies; and military training or fascination with military mandates (Mantell & Albrecht, 1994; Miller, 1999; Paul & Townsend, 1998). Additionally, a perpetrator tends to have a fascination with weapons, a history of violent or criminal behavior and of substance abuse, evidence of severe stress, impaired psychological functioning or changes in personality, changes in work productivity, poor hygiene, and social isolation or difficulties with peers (Davis, 1997).

A potential perpetrator may have several psychological impairments. Signs of Type A behaviors—impatience and irritability, and a perception that others are acting hostile—may be exhibited (Neuman & Baron, 1998). The perpetrator may have a history of mental illness in accordance with the *DSM-IV*, such as depression, clinical paranoia, schizophrenia, borderline personality disorder, antisocial personality disorder, and intermittent explosive disorder (Flannery, 1995; Mantell & Albrecht, 1994; Paul & Townsend, 1998). These warning signs and characteristics form a profile of a potentially violent employee. The National Safe Workplace Institute (1994) suggests that characteristics such as stable finances; being chemical-free; ties to community, family, religion, and friends; and outside interests could act as buffers to inhibit violent acts. A few models have been developed regarding the identification and assessment of violent perpetrators in the workplace. These models include the POSTAL formula and the Stages model. The POSTAL formula (Grimme & Grimme, 2000) stands for Profile, Observable warning signs, Shotgun, Triggering events—Always Lethal. The characteristics or factors included in each part of the POSTAL formula are similar to the factors involved in the Stages model.

Davis (1997) has divided violent behaviors into three stages, for assessment. Stage 1 behaviors are indicators of early potential for violence. These inappropriate behaviors include "objectifying and dehumanizing others, challenging authority, regularly argumentative, alienating customers, starting and spreading lies about others, verbal abuse and sexual harassment" (p. 11). Davis suggests that individuals in Stage 1 usually do not commit violent acts, but those in Stage 2 are close to violent acts. Stage 2 behaviors indicating escalated potential include: ". . . physical confrontations and altercations, displaying weapons and attempts to commit or actually committing assault" (p. 21). Davis reported that everyone would pass through all of these stages. This parallels what was mentioned earlier: violence occurs on a continuum. It is important to have the TAT or EAP complete an assessment of an individual who is exhibiting these behaviors—before they become Stage 3 behaviors or actual acts of violence.

When an employee has actually made a threat, whether the threat is direct ("I will kill Mr. Smith"), conditional ("If I get laid off, I will get even"), or valid (actual aggressive behavior) (Kinney, 1995), it is important to have the employer take that threat seriously. The TAT should evaluate the potential harm to employees and the worksite. When a threat and potential for violence must be evaluated, the TAT should decide, in advance, who will collect each part of the necessary information (U.S. Office of Personnel Management, 1998).

In threat assessment, one must be aware of the laws regarding obtaining personal information and psychological testing. Some of these laws are included in the Privacy Act and the Fair Employment Act (U.S. Office of Personnel Management, 1998). An employer should have legal counsel join the TAT, so as not to infringe on employees' rights. A consulting psychologist may also join the TAT; he or she should be knowledgeable about testing that is or is not permitted.

An evaluation of the individual who makes the threat is crucial. The tasks involved include a personal interview with the potential perpetrator. The EAP professional or a consulting psychologist should conduct this intervention. Information about stressors—such as health, family, financial and legal problems, motives, lethality and suicide attempt, and possession of weapons—is essential.

It is important to assess whether the perpetrator has a plan for, and the means to carry out, an act of violence, and whether a potential victim has been identified. Information about any history of substance abuse, psychiatric history (including medications), and past use of violence should also be gathered (Resnick & Kausch, 1995). To gain a complete history, the EAP professional or psychologist may also need to perform a complete mental status examination and interview family members, other work staff, police, and social service agencies with whom the employee is involved.

While the interview is taking place, management or the human resources staff can gather background information on the employee by researching his or her personnel file. This process may also include talking with employees who work closely with the potential perpetrator. It is important to investigate marital status, length of employment, sociability with coworkers, and any prior discipline reports (Lion, 1999) or threats that may not have been recorded.

Another piece of the threat assessment involves gathering information about the possible target, if that person has been identified. Included should be places and times that allow the potential perpetrator to have access to the target, and what their relationship with each other has been. There is another important reason for assessing the possible victim. If the target has experienced some sort of aggression or violence, she or he could possibly become a future perpetrator (Flannery, 1995).

If violence occurs in the workplace, the TAT should maintain and analyze records to track risk factors and trends for future prevention purposes. Information to be collected includes: characteristics of the perpetrator and victim, what happened prior to and after the violent act, location, time of day, and injuries (Kinney, 1995; Leather, Beale, Lawrence, Brady, & Cox, 1999; U.S. Department of Labor: OSHA, 1998).

A thorough assessment of employee/workplace violence involves investigating several factors on a case-by-case basis. The factors that have been discussed include the individual preemployment screening, worksite environment screening, and the social and personal aspects of screening employees for potential violence in the workplace.

PREVENTION OF WORKPLACE VIOLENCE

Clearly, something must be done. Workplace violence can be neither accepted nor tolerated. All employers have an ethical and legal duty to provide employees with a safe and healthy work environment. This section identifies the responsibilities of various persons and ends with a company policy statement. The major focus is on primary, secondary, and tertiary intervention measures to reduce workplace violence. The intervention measures progress according to intensity and cost.

Responsibilities

Specification of the responsibilities of the various agency members is a precautionary safety measure. The responsibilities of each role in the agency are defined; therefore, the role expectations can be assumed. The following list, adapted from the *OSHA Handbook on Workplace Violence* (U.S. Department of Labor, 1999), provides a detailed description of the responsibilities of the various persons:

Employees
- Be familiar with department/agency policy and procedures regarding workplace violence.
- Be responsible for securing your own workplace.
- Be responsible for questioning and/or reporting strangers to supervisors.
- Be aware of any threats, physical or verbal, and/or any disruptive behavior of any individual, and report such to supervisors.
- Take all threats seriously.
- Be familiar with the resources of the Employee Assistance Program.

Managers and Supervisors
- Inform employees of department/agency workplace violence policies and procedures.
- Respond to potential threats and escalating situations.

- Take all threats seriously.
- Check prospective employees' backgrounds prior to hiring.

Agency Heads

- Develop a policy statement indicating that the agency will not tolerate violent or disruptive behavior and that all reports of incidents will be taken seriously and dealt with appropriately.
- Provide adequate resources for employee training and awareness.
- Include workplace violence training in all employee orientation and supervisory training sessions.
- Provide funding for appropriate safety and security of employees.

Employee Assistance Program Counselors

- Provide short-term counseling and referral services to employees at no cost.

Security Staff

- Serve as the liaison with law enforcement.
- Work with the facility personnel to improve the security level of the buildings, grounds, parking lots, and so on.

Primary Interventions

Interventions can be developed in different stages. Primary prevention is the intervention of choice to prevent workplace violence. There are several situations that may cause employees to become angry—for example, termination can be upsetting. To avoid workplace violence during termination and layoffs, there should be proper planning. According to Smith (1994), experts agree that proper planning can avoid workplace violence. Smith also cites Peter Abeson's four emotional responses: anger, denial, depression, and hysteria.

Although these feelings have been associated with termination and layoffs, the primary preventions used for each emotion can be applied to other situations. In the event that an employee expresses anger, the manager should speak in a soft voice. According to Abeson's response, confrontation is diffused by using a soft voice if an employee is speaking loudly; this creates a one-sided argument and may cause it to come to an end (Smith, 1994). Denial is possible in certain situations, and it is important to remind employees that life exists outside the workplace. Employees may become stressed if they hear the word "termination"; they may believe that they will have nothing if they are terminated. The third emotion is depression. To intervene with depression, one must be able to notice it and then to refer the depressed employees to counseling. The fourth emotion, hysteria, can be common. Management needs to provide support, even if expressed via something as small as a glass of water. A glass of water and a box of tissues can help to defuse a confrontation because the manager would be expressing compassion (Smith, 1994).

The ability to defuse or avoid confrontation may decrease workplace homicides, which are a growing concern (Pastor, 1994). Researchers such as Moore (1997) focused their studies on preventing homicide in the workplace. Moore's study indicated that homicide is the cause of 12% of deaths in the workplace. He also indicated that preemployment screening, explicit nonharassment policies, employee counseling, physical security measures, and establishment of a method to report and assess threatening behaviors are ways to prevent workplace violence. Each of these strategies targets persons who are at risk for a potential violent act. Finding those persons early can avoid future homicides in the workplace.

Moore (1997) supports Pastor's strategies for prevention. He proposes that reporting techniques of threatening behavior is an important factor in detecting potentially violent employees. Accepting that violence exists in the workplace is also important in developing prevention strategies. Moore indicates that establishing a response and practice plan may decrease workplace violence. Determining intervention techniques that will prevent violence is important because it raises awareness in places of employment.

There are other ways to raise awareness in places of employment. Educating workers about safety tips is a primary prevention technique. Moore (1997) indicates that training all supervisors and employees to be alert and to report warning signs can decrease workplace violence. Employees likewise should be trained in conflict management as a means of primary prevention.

Provision of appropriate hardware—cellular phones and company vehicles—is another means of primary prevention in the workplace. Some of these hardware preventatives can detect or provide warning signs that a violent act may soon occur. Cell phones and company cars can provide the emergency services needed to decrease homicide rates (Moore, 1997; Pastor, 1994). According to Moore (1997), it is important to be aware of any malfunctioning equipment if it is to serve in primary prevention.

Primary prevention protects employees from potentially violent situations. It is important to note that some primary measures can also be used as secondary and tertiary interventions. Primary prevention includes guidelines to follow *before* a violent act occurs. Once a violent act has occurred in the workplace, agencies must look to secondary measures of intervention.

Secondary Interventions

There are several things companies can do to create a safer environment, even after a violent act has occurred. Secondary measures, also referred to as postincident response, and evaluations are essential to an effective violence prevention program. All workplace violence programs should provide treatment for employees who may be traumatized by having witnessed a workplace violence incident (U.S. Department of Labor, 1999). If an organization cannot afford high-tech security (e.g., swipe cards, cameras, security guards), a modest investment in locks, background checks on potential employees, and a plan for addressing potential threats in the workplace can make workers feel more secure.

If a firm has security personnel or a risk management department, administrators are urged to sit down with them and evaluate the access people have to the workplace. Interventions to workplace violence could include increases in physical security. The security could be used for keeping track of current versus former employees, establishing visitor access, and noting employee rosters. These are also very critical interventions to workplace violence; they may help to control people who are entering and exiting the firm (Keim, 1999).

Employee counseling and training are also essential interventions; they include courses on how to deal with customers' anger and with workplace arguments and fights (Plaggemars, 2000). Companies should invite rehabilitation counselors to assist in forming crisis response teams, and to make recommendations regarding the plan. A crisis response team should include representatives from security, human resources, management, public relations, and medical/psychological services. Outside authorities and emergency responders can be contacted as the situation warrants (Keim, 1999).

Following the resolution of the incident and completion of any preliminary police and security actions, those involved should be offered psychological support. The human resources department generally would be responsible for seeking psychological assistance for the survivors and for others who witnessed or were impacted by the event. When rehabilitation counselors and human resources departments have close relationships from previous cases, the human resources director may call on these counselors for assistance. Their role can take a number of forms. Rehabilitation counselors can work with the perpetrator (if not incarcerated, injured, or deceased) to determine the nature of the problem and attempt to resolve it in a psychologically healthy manner. Assistance with outplacement counseling is another service that might be provided (Keim, 1999).

Often, counseling following workplace violence is offered in the form of a debriefing, which generally consists of five phases. Initially, the debriefing is introduced as consisting of expectations, informed consent, and voluntary participation. Participants then are asked to disclose what happened—what they thought they saw and heard—as well as their role in the incident (Keim, 1999). As the debriefing continues and the level of disclosure increases, participants discuss what feelings and reactions they have experienced in relation to the event. Next, the counselors explore the signs of stress that participants are experiencing and how they are coping with their stress. Counselors utilize this opportunity to suggest various effective coping strategies and to normalize the participants' experiences. The final step consists of closure. Counselors help participants with closure by providing a summary and giving referrals for additional counseling when appropriate (Keim, 1999).

Aside from physical harm, workplace violence can lead to trauma and substance abuse. It also negatively affects workers' morale and productivity, and it increases absenteeism, turnover, and costs for security and workers' compensation. Yarborough (1994) states: "Some companies have policies in which the loss of life is cheaper than making workplaces safer for their employees" (p. 29). Yarborough says that the worst of these are fast-food chains, where posters in the windows shield the activity going on inside the restaurant, and where employers would rather advertise tacos than protect their low-wage employees. Unless managers take a proactive stance, hostile behavior in the workplace can lead to tremendous emotional and punitive damage for workers and their employers.

Tertiary Interventions

Primary and secondary means of intervention have been discussed previously. If the problem of violence still persists, more extreme measures will be needed. These will consist of a combination of engineering, administrative, and work practice controls designed to eliminate risk (Awadalla & Roughton, 1998). These innovations tend to be costly, so agencies may try to avoid their use. However, it is essential for agencies to consider these engineering and administrative practice controls if all other means are failing.

Engineering controls remove hazards from the workplace or create physical barriers between the worker and the risk (Awadalla & Roughton, 1998). It has been suggested that, in high-risk agency settings, reception areas should be designed so that the receptionist and staff are protected by bulletproof safety glass. Metal detectors may also need to be placed at the agency to protect against the entry of guns or other dangerous contraband. These safety precautions will help to prevent dangerous people from being able to access people in the agency.

It should be assumed that some dangerous people will be able to enter the building even after protective devices have been installed. This would lead to other engineering controls that would be available when a potentially violent person is known to have entered the facility. The National Security Institute (NSI) suggests that alarm systems or panic buttons should be installed in registration areas, hallways, and offices (NSI, 1995). These systems should have a connection with the local police department in order to gain access for quick response. The panic buttons will alert other staff members that an emergency situation is at hand, but staff will need prior training in their use. Police officers should participate in this training.

Installation mechanisms, such as camera systems, will help the employees to obtain a complete view of their surroundings (U.S. Department of Labor: OSHA, 1996). Cameras should be installed at the reception area; in offices, to identify dangerous situations; and in the parking lot, to identify who is entering the facility. This will ensure that employees are aware of what is going on throughout the building and on the premises. Employees will need briefing on how to identify a dangerous situation and how to take action when such a situation has been identified.

Engineering controls may be installed, and it is essential that employees are aware of all the procedures that are set up with each control. "Administrative work practice controls . . . affect the way tasks are performed and must be understood and followed by managers, supervisors, and workers" (NSI, 1995). Establishing proper work practices is not a matter of simply writing a procedure. Proper work practices also require training, monitoring, and feedback. All equipment needs to be properly maintained for its effectiveness at all times.

Employees will need briefing on how to enter and exit secure areas. There must be a strict procedure on how to handle a situation when someone threatens harm to the agency. Security guards may be needed. They should be provided with training, by the institution, in principles of human behavior and control of violent persons (NSI, 1995).

It is clear that safety measures will prevent workplace violence; yet, if employees are not properly trained, safety measures will not be useful. Engineering controls help clinics to identify risk and take action when employees are in danger. It is essential that these same measures be considered when an agency is at high risk for workplace violence.

Policy to Address Workplace Violence

The common definition of workplace violence is: violence that arises out of disputes or adverse interpersonal relations between employees and employers in and around their place of employment. To better study and understand workplace violence, it is necessary to categorize it as OSHA has done. According to OSHA, there are three categories of workplace violence:

- Type I, Stranger Violence—Stranger versus employee, as in an armed robbery, accounts for 60% of all workplace homicides.
- Type II, Client Violence—Client versus employee is best exemplified by a social worker's being attacked by a client. This type of violence accounts for 30% of all workplace homicides.
- Type III, Employee Violence—Employee versus employee is best described by a situation wherein an employee attacks a supervisor. This accounts for 10% of all workplace homicides.

Keep in mind that the term *employees* may also refer to temporary help and to subcontractors who spend a significant amount of their workday in a particular workplace. The Type III category also includes domestic violence.

Although there is no OSHA regulation that deals specifically with workplace violence, the Occupational Safety and Health Act of 1970 (Jansson, 1993) mandates that all employers have a general duty to provide their employees with a workplace that is free from recognized hazards that are likely to cause death or serious physical harm. An employer can be found in violation of the general duty clause if it can be shown that a hazard existed or was foreseeable, and was likely to cause death or serious physical harm. In addition, one must have had or should have had knowledge of the hazard because it was present and recognizable by people on the premises, communications within the industry, or common sense.

According to Speer (1999), most workplace violence occurs only after earlier circumstances and behaviors have pointed to possible violence. Far from being a "random" occurrence, workplace violence is an event that, with proper training, employers can learn to predict and forestall. Employers may recognize their moral obligation to provide a safe workplace, but too many fail to take responsible steps to prevent and properly manage workplace violence. Enormous legal liability is attached to workplace violence, under several occupational health and safety statutes and numerous common-law claims.

In 1996, recognizing that violence in the workplace is a major contributor to employee injuries, OSHA issued voluntary guidelines addressing workplace violence in health care venues, social service workplaces, and nighttime retail establishments. These workplace violence guidelines suggested approaches for addressing the problem. OSHA identifies the four main elements of a recommended violence prevention program as: (a) management commitment and employee involvement, (b) worksite analysis, (c) hazard prevention and control, and (d) safety and health training (U.S. Department of Labor: OSHA, 1996).

IMPLICATIONS FOR SOCIAL WORK AGENCIES

Social work ethics absolutely prohibit retaliation against anyone who has asserted a claim of workplace discrimination or violence, and/or a violation of agency policy. Every instance of unlawful retaliation should be reported, in writing, to a supervisor, or the Director of Human Resources, or any other supervisor who is available. This should be done regardless of whether you or someone else has been subjected to retaliatory action.

Social work agencies should have a "zero tolerance" for discrimination, harassment, violence, and/or subsequent acts of retaliation. Any agency employee who retaliates against (a) anyone who has submitted a report of discrimination or of violation of agency policy or (b) anyone who cooperates in any investigation, will be disciplined up to and including discharge from employment.

If an applicant is invited into the next phase of the hiring process—a personal interview—the interviewer must be savvy enough to utilize the face-to-face interview to filter out difficult candidates. Mantell and Albrecht (1994) notes several questions that can be used by an interviewer to indicate potentially violence-prone individuals. The most notable question is: "When have you felt that you have been treated unfairly in your life?" Research reveals that an employee's perception of unjust treatment has been noted in nearly every case involving some type of violence on the job. Techniques such as behavior interviews, stress interviews, and target interviews have added to employers' ability to "red flag" questionable behavior. The Theory of Interview Techniques spans from assessment of an employee's goals to determining a candidate's basic qualifications, and to evaluating specific personality traits that may predispose individuals toward violence in the workplace (Chartrand, 1997b).

Thorough background checks should be the rule, not the exception, when considering a candidate for hire. Drug testing, reference checks, employment records, driving records, credit histories, academic records, and credit checks (all within the scope of the law) are encouraged as standard for employers' investigation. Employers should also test for psychological fitness using tools such as the MMPI. To predict a qualified and good fit with a company, management should evaluate every available resource. Careful hiring procedures that require thorough attention to details can reduce workplace violence.

THE SETTING AND THE INTERNAL
CHARACTERISTICS OF ORGANIZATIONS

The literature suggests that organizational and/or company factors may lead to increased violence in the workplace (Baron & Neuman, 1998). These variables are numerous and may include: treatment of employees by supervisors, environmental factors in the work setting, lack of employee support systems, stress having to do with the ways in which employees are dismissed (as in the case of downsizing), unfair treatment, and ostracism of personnel by fellow employees (Baron & Neuman, 1998). In a study of workplace harassment, 32% of the respondents indicated that they had observed others being "shouted at loudly or . . . exposed to insulting comments, insinuating glances, negative gestures, undue criticism, and unfairly damaging performance evaluations" (Baron & Neuman, 1998). The research suggests that these types of behaviors are potentially damaging to organizations and increase the likelihood of aggressive retaliation by employees. Obstructionism is especially relevant in work settings where an immediate superior has the power to minimize his or her employees and, as a result, a passive aggression is formed in the face of injustice.

DEBRIEFING IN THE AFTERMATH OF TRAUMA

A traumatic incident that occurs in a workplace can have an enormous impact on employees' emotional and physical functioning and can affect their productivity. "The event so overloads and overwhelms an individual that the psyche's normal coping mechanisms can't handle it. For the survivors, the workplace is no longer safe, but has become threatening" (Bensimon, 1994, p. 33). It is important for employers to know how to deal with the aftermath of a tragedy or crisis. To ease their grief and frustration, employees should have an outlet that is constructive and is supported by their employers.

Critical Incident Stress Debriefing (CISD) is one way to help employees process through their grief together in the workplace environment. CISD minimizes the negative effects of workplace violence by helping employees cope with stress reactions, grief, loss, and other trauma associated with the event (Plaggemars, 2000).

The Mitchell Model of CISD, a model for debriefing emergency responders, has been widely adapted and extended to applications with disaster and crime, and to survivors of trauma (Keim, 1999). The model has two main elements: (a) Informal Short Defusings and (b) Formal Debriefings. Informal Short Defusings take place within 1 to 4 hours of a traumatic incident. They have two purposes. The first purpose is to stabilize personnel involved in the incident and allow them reentry into the environment. This would be effective for emergency personnel who may be going in and out of a traumatic scene with only short breaks in between. The second purpose of defusing is to help those involved to return home after the incident (Spitzer & Burke, 1993).

Formal Debriefings are structured 3-hour sessions that are usually conducted within 24 to 72 hours following a traumatic incident. The phases of debriefing include the following:

1. Familiarizing participants with the process.
2. Having attendees share their involvement in the event and explain what their roles were.
3. Sharing personal thoughts.
4. Sharing emotional reactions.
5. Having facilitators assist attendees in developing an awareness that everyone is affected by the event differently—everyone behaves differently and has different physical, cognitive, and emotional reactions.
6. Reviewing the characteristics of stress and having the facilitators offer suggestions for stress reduction.
7. Giving participants information about the grief process, and contrasting suicide with the normal physiological responses to stress.
8. Summarizing the events that have taken place during the debriefing, and providing referrals for those who feel they need further assistance in coping with the traumatic event (Spitzer & Burke, 1993).

Debriefings, following a crisis, offer several benefits. They help to stabilize the workplace; improve productivity and retention of staff affected by the incident; reduce workers' compensation stress claims and hasten returns to work; help to lower the long-term incidence of generalized anxiety, panic attacks, and substance abuse among survivors; and decrease the likelihood of litigation (Buck, 1995). Critical Incident Stress Debriefing (CISD) has been utilized after such tragedies as the Oklahoma City bombing and the Columbine High School shootings.

Facilitators of CISD are trained to help employees who have been affected by a traumatic event. The CISD team can be comprised of people from within the organization, or an outside team can be used. Using an outside team in the event of a workplace crisis is beneficial because members of the home CISD team may have been affected by the event. "Since a crisis or disaster can strike at any time, every organization should be prepared to deal with the emotional aftermath of such incidents. To this end, risk managers can help ensure that the company has a debriefing organization it can contact when an emergency occurs" (Buck, 1995). It would be beneficial for companies to know about this procedure and become familiar with a CISD team in their area so they can be prepared when a tragedy occurs in or around their workplace.

CONCLUSION

Violence is a presence in today's workplace. Because of the severity and increase of workplace violence, primary, secondary, and tertiary interventions are needed. This chapter has discussed characteristics of potentially violent employees, assessment procedures, and multiple interventions such as employee education about workplace violence and provision of appropriate hardware. Security expansion, employee counseling and training, and crisis response teams are among the secondary interventions that were discussed. Tertiary interventions included engineering controls, alarm or panic buttons, bulletproof safety glass, and metal detectors. All of these interventions are important to maintaining a peaceful and violence-free work environment. Education in anger reduction and practitioner safety is necessary. Most important, the interventions discussed herein will provide a safe workplace for employees and will protect them from violence.

REFERENCES

Albrecht, S. (1996). *Crisis management for corporate self defense.* Los Angeles: Amacon.

Albrecht, S. (1997). *Fear and violence on the job.* Charlotte: Carolina Academic Press.

Aquino, K., Grover, S. L., Bradfield, N., & Allen, D. G. (1999). The effects of negative affectivity, hierarchical status, and self determination on workplace victimization. *Academy of Management Journal, 42*(3), 260–282.

Arthur, D. (1994). *An employers guide to policies and practices: Workplace testing.* New York: American Management Association.

Awadalla, C. A., & Roughton, J. E. (1998). Workplace violence prevention: The new safety focus. *Professional Safety, 43*(12), 31–35.

Baron, R. A., & Neuman, J. H. (1998). Workplace aggression is the iceberg beneath the tip of workplace violence: Evidence of its forms, frequency and targets. *Public Administration Quarterly, 21*(4), 446–464.

Barrett, K. E., Riggar, T. F., & Flowers, C. R. (1997a). Violence in the workplace: Examining the risk. *Journal of Rehabilitation Administration, 21*(2), 95–114.

Barrett, K. E., Riggar, T. F., & Flowers, C. R. (1997b). Violence in the workplace: Preparing for the age of rage. *Journal of Rehabilitation Administration, 21*(3), 171–188.

Bech, R., & Mak, M. (1995). Measurements of impulsivity and aggression. In E. Hollander & D. Stein (Eds.), *Impulsivity and aggression* (pp. 25–41). New York: Wiley.

Bensimon, H. F. (1994). Violence in the workplace. *Training and Development, 48*(1), 26–32.

Brockner, J., Tyler, T., & Cooper-Schneider, R. (1992). The influence of prior commitment to an institution on reactions to perceived unfairness. *Administrative Science Quarterly, 37*(2), 241–261.

Buck, W. T. (1995). Coping with crisis. *Risk Management, 42*(10), 58–62.

Chartrand, S. (1997a, September 9). Little attention given to workplace violence. *The New York Times,* p. C1.

Chartrand, S. (1997b, December 14). Employers devise new strategies to test job applicants. *The New York Times,* p. Cl.

Cole, L. J., Grubb, P. L., Sauter, S. L., Swanson, N. G., & Lawless, P. (1997). Psychosocial correlates of harassment, threats and fear of violence in the workplace. *Scandinavian Journal of Work, Environment and Health, 23,* 450–457.

Davis, D. A. (1997). *Threats pending fuses burning: Managing workplace violence.* Palo Alto, CA: Davies-Black.

Diamond, M. A. (1997). Administrative assault: A contemporary psychoanalytic view of violence and aggression in the workplace. *American Review of Public Administration, 27*(3), 228–250.

Duncan, T. S. (1995). Death in the office: Workplace homicides. In *The FBI Law Enforcement Bulletin* (reprint) [Online]. Available from: www.svn.net/mikekell.biovc .html

Fein, R. A., Vossekuil, B., & Holden, G. A. (1995). Threat assessment: An approach to prevent targeted violence. In *National Criminal Justice Reference Service* [Online]. Available from: www.ncjrs.org/txtfiles/threat.txt

Flannery, R. B. (1995). *Violence in the workplace.* New York: Crossroad.

Greenberg, L., & Barling, J. (1999). Predicting employee aggression against coworkers, subordinates and supervisors: The roles of person behaviors and perceived workplace factors. *Journal of Organizational Behavior, 20,* 897–913.

Grimme, S., & Grimme, D. (2000). *Violence in the workplace: The realities and the options* [Online]. Available from: www.ghrtraining.com/violenceworkplace.htm

Guardian Security Services. (1999). *Violence in the workplace* [Online]. Available from: www.stayout.com/violence.html

Illinois State Police. (2000). *Violence in the workplace: What is violence in the workplace?* [Online]. Available from: www.state.il.us/isp/viowplc/vwppl.html

Jansson, B. S. (1993). *The reluctant welfare state.* Pacific Grove, CA: Brooks/Cole.

Keim, J. (1999). Workplace violence and trauma: A 21st century rehabilitation issue. *Journal of Rehabilitation, 65*(1), 16–22.

Kenway, J., Fitzclarence, L., & Hasluck, L. (2000). Toxic shock: Understanding violence against young males in the workplace. *Journal of Men's Studies, 8* (2).

Kinney, J. A. (1995). *Violence at work: How to make your company safer for employees and customers.* Englewood Cliffs, NJ: Prentice Hall.

Leather, P., Beale, D., Lawrence, C., Brady, C., & Cox, T. (1999). Violence and work: Introduction and overview. In P. Leather, C. Brady, C. Lawrence, D. Beale, & T. Cox (Eds.), *Work related violence: Assessment and intervention* (pp. 3–18). New York: Routledge.

Lenius, P. (1999). Work place violence is a growing concern! *Contractor, 46*(10), 7–9.

Lion, J. R. (1999). The clinician's role in assessing workplace violence. *Psychiatric Clinics of North America, 22*(1), 101–108.

Maiuro, R. D., Vitaliano, P. P., & Cahn, T. S. (1987). A brief measure for the assessment of anger and aggression. *Journal of Interpersonal Violence, 2*(2), 166–178.

Mantell, M., & Albrecht, S. (1994). *Ticking bombs: Defusing violence in the workplace.* Burr Ridge, IL: Irwin.

Marino, S. (1997). Beware of Harry. *Industry Week, 246*(21), 38–40.

Mattman, J. W. (2000). *Preventing violence in the workplace* [Online]. Available from: www.noworkviolence.com/articles/preventing_violence.htm

Mehrabian, A. (1990). *The risk of eruptive violence scale* [Online]. Available from: www.kaaj.com/psvch/scales/vio.html

Miller, L. (1999). Workplace violence: Prevention, response and recovery. *Psychotherapy, 36*(2), 160–169.

Moore, L. R. (1997). Preventing homicide and acts of violence in the workplace. *Professional Safety, 42*(7), 20–23.

Morey, L. C. (1999). Personality Assessment Survey. In M. Maruish (Ed.), *The use of psychological testing for treatment planning and outcome assessment* (pp. 1083–1121). Hillsdale, NJ: Erlbaum.

National Credit Information Network. (1998). *The hiring experiences and the processes involved* [Online]. Available from: www.wdia.com/preempmenu.html

National Safe workplace Institute. (1994). *The cost of workplace violence to American business* [Online]. Available from: www.noworkviolence.com/articles/cost_of_workplace_violence.htm

National Security Institute. (1995). *Guidelines for workplace violence prevention programs* [Online]. Available from: www.nsi.org/Lebary/work/violence.htm

Neuman, J. R., & Baron, R. A. (1998). Workplace violence and workplace aggression: Evidence concerning specific forms, potential causes, and preferred targets. *Journal of Management, 24*(3), 391–425.

Nowack, K. (1997). *Personality inventories: The next generation. Performance in Practice.* American Society of Training and Development.

Osipow, S. H., & Davis, A. S. (1988). The relationship of coping resources to occupational stress and strain. *Journal of Vocational Behavior, 32*(1), 1–15.

Paul, R. J., & Townsend, J. B. (1998). Violence in the workplace: A review with recommendations. *Employee Responsibilities and Rights Journal, 11*(1), 1–14.

Plaggemars, D. (2000). EAPs and critical stress debriefing: A look ahead. *Employee Assistance Quarterly, 16*(1), 77–95.

Plutchik, R., & van Pragg, H. M. (1990). A self-report measure of violence risk. *Comprehensive Psychiatry, 31*(5), 450–456.

Resnick, P. J., & Kausch, O. (1995). Violence in the workplace: Role of the consultant. *Consulting Psychology Journal: Practice and Research, 47*(4), 213–222.

Reynolds, P. (1999). *Dealing with crime and aggression at work: A handbook for organizational action.* London, England: McGraw-Hill.

Smith, B. (1994). Cease fire! Preventing workplace violence. *Human Resource Focus, 71*(2), 25–26.

Speer, R. A. (1999). *What employers need to know about workplace violence* [Online]. Available from: www.workplacclaw.com/toknow.htm

Spielberger, C. D., Sydeman, S. J., Owen, A. E., & Marsh, B. J. (1999). Measuring anxiety and anger with the State-Trait Anxiety Inventory (STAI) and the State-Trait Anger Expression Inventory (STAXI). In M. Maruish (Ed.), *The use of psychological testing for treatment planning and outcome assessment* (pp. 993–1021). Hillsdale, NJ: Erlbaum.

Spitzer, W. J., & Burke, L. (1993). A critical incident stress debriefing program for hospital based health care personnel. *Health and Social Work, 18*(2), 149–161.

U.S. Department of Labor: Occupational Safety and Health Administration (OSHA). (1996). *Elements of a workplace violence prevention program* [Online]. Available from: www.oshaslc.gov/workplaceviolence/workplaceviolence.partII.html

U.S. Department of Labor: Occupational Safety and Health Administration (OSHA). (1999). *Workplace violence summary sheet* [Online]. Available from: www.osha.gov/oshinfo/priorities.violence.html

U.S. Office of Personnel Management. (1998). *Dealing with workplace violence: A guide for agency planners* [Online]. Available from: www.opm.gov/workplac

Vagg, P. R., & Spielberger, C. D. (1998). Occupational stress: Measuring job pressure and organizational support in the workplace. *Journal of Occupational Health Psychology, 3*(4), 294–305.

Yarborough, M. (1994). Securing the American workplace. *Human Resource Focus, 71*(9), 29–33.

Chapter 17

WORKPLACE VIOLENCE: PREVENTION AND INTERVENTION, THEORY AND PRACTICE

JUDITH A. WATERS, ROBERT I. LYNN, AND KEITH J. MORGAN

INTRODUCTION

On September 11, 2001, at 8:48 A.M., Eastern Daylight Savings Time, an estimated 25,000 people were either already at work or on their way to work (it was Election Day and some people stopped to vote) in the Twin Towers of the World Trade Center in New York City (Waters, 2002). Another 25,000 employees were at work in the Pentagon. It was a normal, sunny Tuesday morning in late summer. Secretaries, stockbrokers, bankers, building service workers, clerks, receptionists, security personnel, researchers, New York City and Port Authority employees, shopkeepers, restaurant managers and crews, military officers and civilian staff, as well as myriad other workers were busy at their desks or at their usual early morning tasks. Without waning, the terrorist attacks began. The first airliner crashed into Tower I of the World Trade Center, an icon of global financial power. Only a few minutes later, a second airliner struck Tower II, thus completely dispelling any thoughts that the first crash was an accident not premeditated murder. Three thousand eight hundred and twenty-two people are now considered missing and presumed dead. As of November 11, 2001, only 528 bodies have actually been identified, yielding a total of 4,346 fatalities in New York. The third crash targeted the Pentagon, an icon of American military prowess, where 125 people perished.

Earlier the same morning, several airline pilots and flight attendants, and hundreds of passengers, many of whom were flying for business, began to play their roles in a scenario that will stand out in recorded history for generations.

As far as we know at the present time, four airliners were involved. More than 300 passengers and crew as well as the terrorists are now dead. One of the hijacked planes was forced away from its supposed primary target of the White House or the Capitol by brave passengers who thwarted the plans of the terrorists. This plane crashed into a field in western Pennsylvania. In a macabre twist, many of the passengers were not only allowed, but were actually encouraged to use their cellular phones by the terrorists, thus giving us a permanent record of these events.

On that same morning, uncounted numbers of firefighters, police officers, and emergency medical teams were either on duty in the New York Metropolitan area and in the counties surrounding the Pentagon, or at home prepared to respond at a moment's notice to any emergency. When these first responders bid farewell to their families, left their homes, and reported to work, no one had a clue as to the devastation that day would bring. Close to 400 firefighters, police officers, and emergency service technicians were killed. The only "crime" that anyone committed that day was to go to work. (The data for this section were supplied by Stephanie Becker of The Today Show, The Office of the Mayor of New York City, The New York/New Jersey Port Authority, and Fox News.)

In the aftermath of the events of September 11, 2001, another threat has affected the workplace. Our legislators, the media, hospital staff, and post office workers have been exposed to anthrax, an often-deadly viral weapon in biological warfare. In the process of targeting government officials and television reporters in their offices, post office workers were put at risk for just doing their jobs and handling the mail. While only a few died, the fear drove people away from their jobs, and a hospital and several post offices were closed. The fear hangs menacingly over everyone's head like the proverbial sword of Damocles.

The terrorists must have considered the potential for widespread economic damage when they planned this mission. It was no accident that these sites were selected. Not only would the people working for the firms housed in the World Trade Center be affected, but the support businesses in surrounding areas would be forced to close, some airlines would face bankruptcy, and travel agencies, airport transportation, and the suppliers of food to the airlines, to name just a few employers, would suffer in the ripple effect from the attacks. Fear of future terrorism has affected everyone in the country, if not, the world (Johnson, 2001). The consequences of the events of September 11 include financing increased security efforts that can drain resources from other important company goals.

Many theorists have excluded terrorist activities from the study of workplace violence. However, that is no longer possible; these targets were clearly chosen due to work-related criteria. Our world has changed.

Workplace violence, excluding terrorist activities, accounts for a sizeable number of injuries and deaths in the United States every year. Many of them are preventable.

According to the Bureau of Labor Statistics, homicides were the second leading cause of death for employees between 1992 and 1996 (cited in Warchol, 1998). Of course, not all assaults result in death. However, even employees who are not physically harmed in any way may experience the consequences of a traumatic event, in the form of sleep disorders and other psychological symptoms (American Psychiatric Association, 2000). In 1999, the American Medical Association published an article about the impact that a terrorist's bombing of the Federal Building in Oklahoma City had on the survivors. The researchers (North et al., 1999) examined the rates of such psychiatric outcomes as posttraumatic stress disorder (PTSD), diagnostic comorbidity, functional impairment, and predictors of post-disaster psychopathology. The results of extensive interviews conducted six months after the bombing indicated that 45% of the 182 survivors studied suffered at least one of the post-disaster psychiatric disorders, and 34.3% had PTSD. Of those diagnosed with PTSD, 76% reported that they experienced the symptoms on the day of the bombing. Almost all of the survivors continue to suffer distressing intrusive reexperience and hyperarousal symptoms.

Some researchers feel that terrorist activities should not be included under the category of workplace violence. However, many events that target federal or other government facilities are specifically selected because of the large number of employees that are gathered in one place, and because the perpetrators want revenge against the government. Crisis teams must be prepared to address the needs of these employees.

At the turn of the twentieth century, the term *workplace violence* conjured up images of bloodied factory workers or coal miners on strike against the owners. The category included the violence associated with armed robberies and with the jobs of law enforcement professionals, such as police officers' response to a "break-in and entry." Now, *workplace violence* is also applied to instances of domestic violence carried out in a corporate office or a retail store, sexual harassment, multiple murders, the suicide of a perpetrator in a workplace situation, and terrorist activities. The term even includes lethal attacks on students, staff, and teachers in school buildings set in areas of the United States that were once thought of as safe and even peaceful. This chapter covers the broad range of cases that are classified as "workplace violence," examines the differences in definition, and explores the bases for the growing prevalence of incidents. Viable prevention strategies, threat assessment and management, counseling issues, the creation of crisis management teams, and the use of Roberts' crisis intervention model as a set of guidelines for addressing the consequences of workplace violence situations are discussed. Also, Roberts' model is placed in the context of another model that delineates the relationships among predisposing factors and responses to stressful life events.

Roberts' (2000) series of stages is best understood as a method of preventing transient stress responses from deteriorating into symptoms of pathology. If we place an individual in a global field that takes into account such important predisposing factors as state of premorbid physical health, repertoire of previous coping strategies, psychological status, including personality type and values, and level of education and skills, and we couple these factors with social and community supports, the result is the individual's level of hardiness or resilience (i.e., the ability to handle stressful events effectively) (Waters, 2002). Prevention programs are designed to enhance a person's hardiness factor and to reduce actual threats in the milieu. Changing perceptions is not sufficient. Next, we will examine the nature of a stressful life event: the severity of the event, its duration, and the potential outcome (positive as in recovery, or negative as in terminal illnesses). Whether the transient stress response leads to growth and the development of a self-protective, productive lifestyle—a return to the status quo—or descends into physical and/or psychological pathology (e.g., posttraumatic stress disorder, PTSD) also depends on the immediacy of the crisis intervention and the skill of the counselor in addressing the problems presented. For severe pathological responses, crisis intervention will be replaced by long-term treatment (see Figure 17.1).

In utilizing Roberts' crisis intervention model for workplace violence, certain modifications should be considered. Many situations in the category of workplace violence are actually emergencies requiring a series of specified steps that must be taken immediately, regardless of the emotional state of the victim or witnesses. Medical aspects have the first priority, along with law enforcement procedures to prevent further deaths or injuries. The police are also mandated to gather data from the victims and from any witnesses who can describe the assailants. "Securing the scene," however, will go a long way toward reestablishing everyone's equilibrium. In the immediate aftermath of the event, the crisis management team can begin its tasks of triage (assessing lethality) and establishing rapport with those involved. In a large-scale event such as the World Trade Center and Pentagon bombings, the number of people affected can be staggering. The pressures of addressing the needs of the victims and witnesses can even lead to stress reactions in the "first responders." The rest of Roberts' stages (e.g., assessing previous coping strategies, and developing evaluation plans) can be played out in subsequent

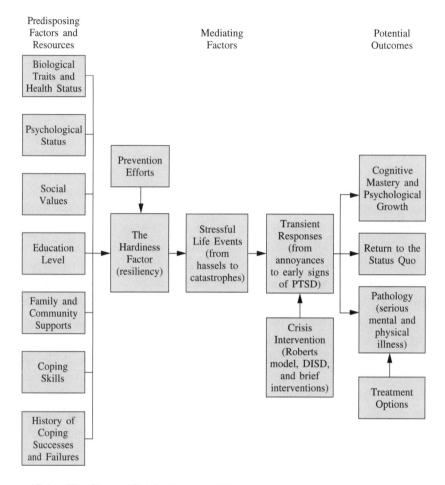

Figure 17.1   The Stress/Crisis/Trauma Model
Source: Based on the work of Waters, 2002; Dohrenwend & Dohrenwend, 1974.

contact with Employee Assistance Program counselors, crisis management teams, hospital mental health staff, or private practitioners. The more serious the event, the greater the need for effective case management, long-term follow-up, and referral. Interventions must also be directed at families and coworkers.

Post Workplace Violence Symptoms

Among the symptoms experienced by survivors of workplace violence are fears about returning to the site, feelings of incompetence and guilt, and a sense of powerlessness. In situations where there might have been unused opportunities to reduce the harm, the sense of incompetence, guilt, and powerlessness is magnified and may be further augmented by actual criticism or fear of criticism by supervisors, coworkers, family members of the victims, and the media.

Many employees working at facilities similar to the ones depicted on television and other media coverage of workplace violence (e.g., postal workers), fear that they too will become the future targets of their coworkers (Neuman & Baron, 1998). Since their situations may, in fact, be almost identical (i.e., organizations that have recently undergone "downsizing"), such fears may be grounded in reality. Everyone has heard of workers who have been "terminated" and who have returned to retaliate against the company. Thus, although employees at other sites are not actual victims, they may also suffer from stress, fear, and a vicarious and often recurring anxiety about the safety of the workplace.

Definitions of Workplace Violence

According to the National Institute on Occupational Safety and Health (cited in OSHA, 1996), workplace violence is any physical assault, threatening behavior, or verbal abuse that occurs in the work setting. It includes but is not limited to beatings, stabbing, suicide, shootings, rape, near suicides, psychological traumas such as threats, obscene phone calls, an intimidating presence, and harassment of any nature, such as being followed, sworn at, shouted at, or stalked.

The law enforcement community defines workplace violence as the commission of proscribed criminal acts or coercive behavior that occur in the work setting. It includes but is not limited to homicides, forcible sex offenses, kidnapping, assault, robbery, menacing, reckless endangerment, harassment, and disorderly conduct. The aggressor may use berating language or physical or verbal threats, or may damage personal property. "The workplace" is described as "any location, either permanent or temporary, where an employee performs any work-related duty. This includes, but is not limited to, the buildings and surrounding perimeters, including parking lots, field locations, clients' homes, and traveling to and from work assignments" (OSHA, 1996, p. 6). The violence may be committed by strangers (e.g., robbers), customers, clients, coworkers, patients (in the case of emergency room or nursing home incidents), and/or people who have a personal relationship with the worker.

According to the Occupational Safety and Health Administration (OSHA, 1996), "employers have a legal duty and moral obligation to provide a safe workplace . . . to prevent loss of life and injuries and to limit financial losses and potential liabilities" (p. 7). All acts of violence and threatening incidents, including verbal and nonverbal threats (e.g., gestures), should be treated seriously by management and investigated. When justified, perpetrators should be subject to appropriate consequences up to and including dismissal for cause. Although many incidents of workplace violence appear unpredictable (Waters, 2002) some events can be forecast and perhaps even avoided. For example, since data indicate that late-night establishments (e.g., convenience stores and gasoline stations) have long been the targets of violence, special precautions should be taken to improve their safety and security. Simply knowing that such strategies have been implemented should serve to reduce the anxiety of both clerks and customers.

The term "victim," whether applied to men or to women, suggests that the person (1) has been wrongfully harmed by a perpetrator and (2) is passively, centrally, and forever damaged by violence (Koss et al., 1994). The term "survivor of violence" is sometimes preferred. However, in many cases, "victim" is correct because the target of the violent act has not survived. The difference in terminology reflects a desire to avoid the implications of *victim blaming,* which, throughout the research literature, depicts victims as passive. The goal of counseling is to assist individuals in taking responsibility for making changes in their lifestyle, but attributing blame to the person often results in damaging consequences and potential delays in the healing process for the survivors of violence.

Workplace Violence Incidents

The following cases represent the nature and scope of workplace violence:

Case Examples

John

The headlines read "Attack in Airport Outrages Workers" (Frank, 1999, July 24, p. 1). In a case that had yet to be tried when this chapter was written, it was reported that a "violent outburst by an airline passenger . . . hospitalized a Continental Airlines employee with life-threatening injuries" (p. 1). The incident triggered protests by airline workers, who were already concerned by a phenomenon that has been labeled "air rage." In some situations, pilots have been forced to make emergency landings and "press charges against passengers who assault flight attendants, brawl with other passengers or threaten the crew" (p. 4). Sixteen percent of the airline incidents are attributed to conflicts over seat assignments, and 10% result from the prohibition against smoking. Estimates vary, but a recent study, commissioned during a Congressional subcommittee hearing on disruptive passengers, contended that drunkenness was the major factor in a quarter of the cases.

Case Examples *(Continued)*

Mark O. Barton

According to a *New York Times* article (Sack, 1999, July 30), at about 2:50 P.M. on a workday, Mr. Barton entered the Momentum Securities office in Atlanta, Georgia, and, without apparent warning or provocation, opened fire on the traders and customers. He killed four people in that office and then crossed the street and entered another brokerage firm, All-Tech Investment Group. There he killed five people. Previous to this chilling incident, Mr. Barton had worked as a "day trader," a high-risk, high-stress occupation, in both offices. Law enforcement officials found that Mr. Barton's second wife and his own two children by a previous marriage (Matthew, 12, and Elizabeth Mychelle, 7) had been murdered just prior to his rampage on Thursday (his wife on Tuesday, and his children on Wednesday). Although, in a letter that he left in the apartment where the three bodies were found, Mr. Barton admitted to the killings of his current family, he continued to deny the murder of his first wife and her mother in 1993. In addition to the 12 people he killed, Barton wounded another 12, 7 of whom were in critical condition at the time of this article. Mr. Barton committed suicide before he could be questioned.

"L"

In March 1991, an electronics manufacturing firm located in San Diego terminated several employees, including "L," who was a technician (Barrier, 1995). L continued to visit the company during the next 3 months, while he was seeking help in finding a new job. According to reports, he seemed to have maintained a "cordial relationship with his former employer" (p. 18). However, on a morning in June of the same year, L came to the facility and checked to see whether three of the company's executives were present. Later on the same day, he returned to the plant with a shotgun and ammunition. He also brought two radio-controlled pipe bombs and used them to start small fires in the building and to destroy the switchboard so that the receptionist was unable to call the police for help. He then went upstairs to the executive offices, where he killed one of the vice presidents and a regional sales manager who attempted to help the vice president. He was able to exit the premises and ride away on his bicycle, in full view of a crowd of stunned and horrified employees.

David Burke

Mr. Burke was a former employee of Pacific Southwest Airlines. In 1987, although he no longer possessed the badge that he needed to be able to board a

(continued)

Case Examples *(Continued)*

plane, he was passed through by airline security personnel because they recognized him. During the flight, he shot his former supervisors, who were on board, and the pilots of the plane. The plane crashed, killing everyone on board—passengers and crew alike (Duncan, 1995).

Patrick Sherrill

On August 20, 1986, Mr. Sherrill, a man with a history of problems at work, entered the post office where he worked in Edmond, Oklahoma. Before he committed suicide, he took the lives of 14 other postal workers (Duncan, 1995).

Robert Farley

Mr. Farley persisted in pursuing an unreciprocated relationship with a female coworker. Eventually, his behavior led to his being fired in 1986. Two years later, on the very day that he was summoned to a hearing for violating a restraining order requested by the same woman, he returned to his former workplace in "Silicon Valley." He brought a veritable arsenal with him, including a shotgun, a rifle, two handguns, bandoliers of extra ammunition, and gasoline. When he finally surrendered, he had killed 7 people and wounded 4 more, including his imagined girlfriend (Duncan, 1995).

Paul Calden

The last words that three former coworkers of Paul Calden would ever hear were "This is what you get for firing me." Mr. Calden, who had lost his job 9 months prior to committing the homicides, came back to his workplace (an insurance company in Tampa, Florida), entered the cafeteria, and opened fire. Five people were wounded and three of them died. Mr. Calden left the scene of the crime in a rental car and committed suicide in a park where he used to play as a child. According to an article in the *FBI Law Enforcement Bulletin* (Duncan, 1995), in some ways, Calden is considered the classic violence-prone former employee. The important point is that the category of crime that he committed is increasing and now constitutes a serious threat to the workplace (p. 20).

Francesia La Rose

In a case that attracted media attention, Francesia La Rose told Patrick Thomas (a man she had been dating) that she did not wish to continue their relationship.

Case Examples *(Continued)*

He refused to accept her decision and began a campaign of stalking her. Ms. La Rose reported that he kidnapped her, raped her, and actually threatened her life (*La Rose v. State Mutual Life Assurance Co.,* 1994). Eventually, Thomas called a supervisor at Ms. La Rose's office and demanded that she be fired. When the supervisor refused, Thomas informed the supervisor that if La Rose was not fired, he would come to the office and kill her. The very next day, he carried out his threat. He came to her fourth-floor office and shot her in the back. Although the building security team had previously been informed of Thomas's potential for harming La Rose, they could not identify him. *They had lost his photograph.* The supervisor did not warn La Rose, or call the police or inform security. Consequently, Thomas was able to enter the building unchallenged. No other precautions had been taken. La Rose's family (her parents and daughter) instituted a suit against State Mutual Life Assurance Co., alleging that it had not lived up to its responsibility to protect her adequately. The case went to the Supreme Court where Ms. La Rose's parents and child won their suit.

The following cases were reported in *Time* magazine (Toufexus, 1994):

Case Examples

A Fed Ex pilot took a claw hammer and attacked three others in the cockpit of the plane. He was already awaiting a disciplinary hearing for lying.

A purchasing manager in a suburban Chicago firm stabbed his boss to death. The reason given in the police report was that they couldn't agree on the paperwork!

A technician who quit his job because he ostensibly had trouble working for a woman, returned to his workplace with a 9mm Glock semiautomatic pistol. By the end of his rampage, he had killed two people, wounded two, and committed suicide by shooting himself in the head.

For the most part, our workplaces are considered safe and we can expect them to be safe havens, not hazardous to our health. The federal government requires that employers provide healthy, hazard-free environments—a mandate that includes not only protection from toxic substances but also protection from harassment by other employees and security from outside intruders. The previously cited incidents of violence in the workplace become particularly dramatic when examined in the context of presumed safety. These events become even more disturbing because they often appear indiscriminate and unpredictable. For example, prior to a recent incident of a shooting that wounded two employees and three children (one critically) in a Los Angeles Jewish Community Center, the perpetrator had killed a mailman born in the Philippines simply as a "target of opportunity" (Berthelsen, 1999). The mailman was murdered, according to the perpetrator, because he was "not white" and was an employee of the United States Government (p. 22). The man was in the wrong place at the wrong time.

In any number of situations, there is a tendency to try and blame victims for their own fate. There must be a reason why we, as cognitive processors, engage in such behaviors. If we cannot explain violent acts and then predict who will be a target (based on some observable variables), we will be forced to acknowledge that this is a capricious world that we cannot manage. Anyone can be a victim. That concept is very threatening. According to Windau and Toscano (1993) "Virtually no one is without risk of being killed on the job, although this risk varies by occupation" (p. 58). Just think of the number of world leaders such as John F. Kennedy, who have been attacked or killed "on the job" despite sophisticated intelligence and security systems. The essential problem is that people can easily commit crimes if they are also willing to be identified and to die for their impulses. To reduce our own personal fears, we need to establish effective perpetrator, site, and victim profiles. We need to dissect the worksite and, unfortunately, build walls and gates around it. We need metal detectors in our schools and hospitals. And, as B. F. Skinner once suggested, we may even need to add tranquilizers to the water system! Or perhaps, rather than treating the symptoms or building more walls, it would be better to see instances of workplace violence as indicators of underlying fractures in the cement that holds society together. If we wait, however, for those cracks to be identified and eventually repaired, we will lose too many of the primary and secondary victims of workplace violence. Consequently, security measures will remain necessary. In fact, we sometimes protect our industrial secrets better than we protect our employees!

The Nature and Scope of Workplace Violence

Baron and Neuman (1996) have divided workplace violence events into three levels. On the lowest level are demonstrations of hostility, such as verbal assaults and facial expressions. The verbal assaults include insults, use of profanity, threats, and "the silent treatment"—ostracism. The next level, labeled "Obstructionism," is typified by actions designed to interfere with another person's job performance or with an organization's ability to achieve its goals. The behaviors in this category include passive-aggressive acts (e.g., work slow-downs, withholding resources) and covert tactics that are difficult to prove and thus minimize the perpetrator's danger for discovery. Such acts include failure to return phone calls, absenteeism, deliberate lateness for meeting deadlines, other delaying tactics, and nonviolent sabotage. The third or highest level ranges from nonfatal physical acts and sexual assault to actual violence that severely injures or kills victims. Overt aggression toward an organization includes destruction of property or goods, damage to equipment (computer "viruses"), and theft that is not motivated by personal gain.

According to Bray (1995), workplace violence should not be equated with workplace abuse, which is a broader category. Workplace abuse incorporates acts such as sexual harassment and emotional abuse, which, although not violent, have the potential for escalating into acts of violence.

Neuman and Baron (1998) suggest that the only proper method for studying situations of workplace violence is to eliminate those events (e.g., terrorist acts and domestic violence) that have their antecedents outside of the site of the incident. For the purposes of research, such a distinction has some validity. However, for practical purposes, organizational decision makers and threat management teams must develop effective prevention strategies, security measures, and response programs that address the potential harm that can result when domestic violence spills over into the workplace. Corporations cannot ignore *any* source of violence. The La Rose case, although categorized as domestic violence, had serious legal and moral implications for corporate security organizations that do not provide adequate protection for employees who are in immediate danger.

In their analysis of workplace violence, Neuman and Baron argue that the focus should be on the underlying motivation for the crime rather than on the location of the event. It is our contention, however, that the location is critical. Various sites are chosen because they provide an opportunity for the perpetrator to do public damage to an individual—often, just because that individual (e.g., his wife or girlfriend) is gainfully employed. In some cases, the site represents the organization (e.g., the Pentagon).

Estimates of the prevalence of workplace violence differ. According to the Northwestern National Life Insurance Company (cited in Shoop, 1993), "more than 2 million people were attacked, 6 million threatened, and 16 million harassed in U.S. workplaces in a single year" (p. 76). More than a third of the perpetrators are customers and clients, over 40% are current and former employees, and only about 16% are strangers.

There are two major classes of workplace homicide victims: domestic partners and supervisors (usually women). A woman may be able to change her place of residence, but it is usually more difficult for her to change her job.

Thus, she is relatively easy to locate. Even if she is able to get a new position, she is probably most experienced in only one occupation—a fact that enables the perpetrator to track her to a new place of employment. Supervisors may not even be fully aware that an employee or former employee is planning a hostile act against them.

The employees who are most likely to be the victims of workplace homicide (38% of all cases) are frequently employed by local, state, or federal government offices. The federal government is the single largest employer in the United States, but it still employs only 15% of the workforce. Thus, it is clear that federal employees constitute a disproportionate number of victims. Post offices have the dubious distinction of having the highest number of victims. Government-run factories are second highest. The common factor may be the number of male employees in both of those categories. The average number of deaths in incidents such as attacks at post offices (including the offenders' suicides) is 2.5. Thirty-six percent of the assailants killed themselves.

It is possible that our analyses of workplace violence underestimate the prevalence of work-related attacks due to under-reporting (Warchol, 1998). For example, fewer than 50% of the nonfatal, but nevertheless violent workplace crimes are reported to the police. There are gender differences with respect to reporting as well. Male survivors (47%) are more likely than female survivors (38%) to report the incident to the police. Robbery is more frequently reported (73%) than rape (25%). Injured survivors (60%) are more likely to make a police report than those who were uninjured (42%). A significant proportion of the events involved someone close to the victim (e.g., a spouse, an ex-spouse, or a boyfriend or girlfriend) (Hellwege, 1995; Reichert, 1998). In a survey designed to assess the incidence of various forms of workplace violence and the consequences of those events, Warchol found that the most frequent explanations given for not reporting a workplace crime to the police were: (1) The victims (29%) had reported it to another official (e.g., a supervisor or a member of the company's security staff) and (2) The victim (19%) did not consider the circumstances serious enough to warrant a report. With respect to the first reason, reporting an event to a supervisor alone may lead to a "cover-up" and under-reporting of serious problems.

OSHA (1998) has mandated that "a fatality or a catastrophe that results in hospitalization of 3 or more employees must be reported to OSHA within 8 hours" (p. 5). This ruling applies to incidents of workplace violence as well as accidents and covers all establishments. The categories the ruling omits, however, are very important. The ruling leaves out less destructive acts that may be precursors to more dangerous situations and it omits stress responses that may appear months after the original event.

The primary target of workplace violence may be a single individual, a group, or the entire institution. Even if the original target is only one person, the "body count" may go much higher. In an effort to kill one person, a single assailant may shoot anyone and everyone who gets in his or her way. Although we referred earlier to the history of union-related strikes that involved many people, contemporary workplace crimes committed by nonstrangers are almost always the product of one perpetrator working alone (Duncan, 1995). However, with continued "downsizing," the pattern of the single perpetrator could always change. So far, there is little evidence that collaborative efforts, sabotage, and terrorist activities are the exception.

Workplace murder has grown to be the leading killer of working women (it has accounted for 35% of their fatal work-related injuries) and the second leading cause of death for men (OSHA, 1998a). The problem is most acute in what is termed the service sector: retail establishments, taxis, limousine services, and law enforcement (e.g., police and security personnel). Among the factors that contribute to the statistics are: being involved in the exchange of money with the public, working either alone or in small numbers, working late at night or early in the morning (e.g., fast-food outlets or convenience stores), working in known high-crime areas, guarding valuable property, and working in facilities such as community settings. (In a Jewish Community Center in Los Angeles, a lone gunman shot an office worker, a teenage counselor/assistant, and three small children.) Fifty-one percent of all workers injured on the job in the New York metropolitan area died of their wounds (OSHA, 1996).

With respect to nonfatal injuries, 22,396 workers were reported hurt in 1992 (Toscano & Weber, 1995); 56% of them were women. The most frequent violent acts were hitting, kicking, and beating. The primary perpetrator was a health-care patient (45%) and the primary targets were nurses' aides (30%). The sites with the most frequent incidents were nursing homes (27%). A survey of 1,400 nurse managers and administrators indicated that one-fourth had witnessed assaults with deadly weapons (AJNNEWSLINE, 1994). Eighty percent stated that emergency room personnel had been "hit, kicked, bitten, and otherwise attacked without weapons" (p. 62). Unfortunately, it was also reported that many security staff have had no real training and are incapable of protecting staff. Moreover, the reporting of violent incidents to the police is actively discouraged by administrators. In general, fewer than half of all nonfatal incidents are reported to the police (Reichert, 1998).

Men and women who work in government buildings experience more assaults than those who work in the private sector. Women who work in state facilities are eight times more likely to be injured than women working for private organizations. Those working for local governments are 5.5 times more likely to be attacked than women in the private sector.

Workplace violence, including threats and actual attacks, cost companies more than $4 billion in lost work, legal fees, and settlements in 1992 (Anfuso,

1994). According to the National Safe Workplace Institute (cited in Anfuso, 1994), a single incident can cost as much as $250,000.

We cannot isolate workplace violence from the violence that we face in other places, such as our homes, our communities, and our schools. A survey conducted by the Society for Human Resources Management (Smith, 1994) reported that personal conflicts account for 38% of workplace violence. Other statistics are: family and marital problems, 15%; alcohol and drug abuse involvement, 10%; nonspecific stress, 7.5%; firings and layoffs, 7%; and violent criminal past history, 2%.

Although domestic violence accounted for only 15% of the total number of workplace violence cases, that percentage translates into 13,000 acts against women at their work sites (Reynolds, 1997). Reynolds reports that 94% of corporate security and safety directors consider the spillage of domestic conflicts into the workplace to be a potentially explosive situation.

A National Institute of Occupational Safety and Health/Centers for Disease Control and Prevention (NIOSH/CDC) study, conducted by the National Safe Workplace Institute (Cordes, 1993), states that 97.5% of the perpetrators in cases of workplace violence are men; 36.1 years is the average age; 81% use firearms; 23.8% commit suicide following the event; and 16.1% have histories of mental health problems. It is also probable that the perpetrator served in the military, owns a weapon, and externalizes the blame for his own disappointments or losses. He may have a sense of entitlement and a felt need for retribution. Attackers are most likely to be supervisors or clients; harassers tend to be supervisors or coworkers. Victims of attack are twice as likely as victims of harassment to report the event (Shoop, 1993, p. 73). Most perpetrators are repeat offenders.

Very frequently, the assailants come to the site very well prepared (Duncan, 1995). They carry extra firearms and ammunition. Because they have a list of intended victims, these acts are clearly premeditated, not results of "temporary insanity."

One of the particularly disturbing characteristics of lone workplace assailants is that they rarely attempt to conceal their identities. These cases are similar to domestic violence incidents because, in both situations, the perpetrator usually lacks an immediate profit motive (although financial losses to the target are a consideration). Assaults on persons, sabotage, and vandalism are classic acts of revenge in which the perpetrator seeks to victimize the target at the same time he or she gratifies personal emotional needs. Perpetrators may feel justified in redressing their grievances. They project the causes for their personal losses onto other people and absolve themselves of any responsibility for the situation. They provide themselves with plausible excuses or rationalizations for events that led to the violence.

Among the personal determinants of violence are childhood backgrounds in which violence was an acceptable or preferred method of solving problems. Other factors include: low tolerance for frustration; lack of impulse control; inadequate communication, negotiating, and conflict resolution skills; and certain personality types that encompass at least some of these factors (e.g., Type A, Type B, and Type T).

Type A people tend to be impatient and irritable. They prefer to work alone. When they must work with others, they want to control the situation. Type B people tend to be more relaxed (than Type A people) about work, the need for marks of achievement, and recognition. Type A people lose their temper more frequently and demonstrate more of a tendency toward aggression than Type B people. Type T individuals are risk takers, both intellectually and physically (but not necessarily toward the same person or at the same time). Failure, as a result of being a high risk taker, can result in frustration, anger, and a desire to maintain one's own sense of self-esteem by blaming and punishing others. Mark O. Barton, who killed 12 people in Atlanta, Georgia, in the summer of 1999, was a "day trader," an extremely high-risk financial occupation. One of our concerns as professionals in this field is that many Type B people now find themselves working for Type A organizations or supervisors.

Another personality category is the "self monitor"—a person who is socially sensitive and is capable of altering his or her words and behaviors to give a favorable impression to others. High self monitors will be more willing to negotiate in order to resolve a conflict. Low self monitors may find themselves in escalating confrontations.

People with a "hostile attributional bias" have a tendency to appraise the behavior of others as being aggressive *even* when there is no hostile intent. Such perceptions can generate a negative halo effect. When the person conjures up unpleasant thoughts which, in turn, lead to anger and, eventually, to aggression.

The more people feel that their entitlements are being threatened and that they are not being treated fairly, the more they will attempt to rebalance the situation by seeking some sort of redress for their grievances. Should they fail at negotiations, thoughts of revenge will begin to occupy their mind. If not constrained by a threat of punishment or a fear of retaliation from the targeted organization or individual(s), they come closer to overt acts of aggression. If they believe that the conflict with or the provocation by others is intentional, they will feel compelled to respond, in order to defend their honor. Employees who are not treated with respect will eventually find a way to retaliate, even if the opportunity is only a work slowdown.

According to McMurry (1995), there are warning signs that are clear indicators of future violence. For example, *domestic batterers* very often have a history of violent acts, engage in stalking behavior, and make threats. (Remember the La Rose case.) In cases of domestic violence, the behavior may spread from the home or neighborhood to the workplace because the perpetrator feels a need to control all aspects of the victim's life. In fact, the job itself is a source of strain because it contributes to the target's financial independence and, in some instances, financial superiority. With respect to *disgruntled or former employees,* there may be early symptoms of depression, signs of paranoia, and threatening behaviors. *Dissatisfied customers or clients* may have engaged in stalking behavior prior to the overt violent act. Individuals in all these categories may have a history of psychiatric disorders and/or may have recently purchased weapons.

When a corporation reduces its workforce, individual employees may feel that they have been singled out for termination. With the assistance of outplacement firms and a generally favorable economy for skilled workers, those who have lost their jobs, with or without the benefit of "golden parachutes," may find themselves quickly reemployed with enhanced salary packages and fringe benefits. The key to the situation, with respect to downsizing, is the number of viable opportunities that exist in the job market.

Perpetrator Profiles

Kelleher (1997) has developed a profile of characteristics that indicate whether one is dealing with a potentially lethal employee. (Remember: Not all vulnerable or disgruntled employees engage in violence.) These traits include the standard demographics of sex (male), race (white), and age (30 to 60 years). Among the behavioral warning signs are the following: one or more triggering events within one year prior to the crime; vocalization or acting out of intentions before the crime; "strange, threatening or uncomfortable behaviors" observed by other employees; a history of violent behavior; alcohol or drug dependence; severe or chronic depression; pathological projection of blame onto others; "chronic or severely elevated frustration levels"; "preoccupation with weapons, paramilitary or publicized incidents of violence in the workplace" (p. 25). In the case of an individual homicide target (which may result in the murder of others at the immediate site), the perpetrator may exhibit "evidence of a romantic obsession" or "evidence of a severe delusional disorder that results in obsession with another individual" (p. 25). Kelleher has also delineated some indicators that call for immediate intervention with the employee. For example, if the employee begins to avoid the workplace or is guilty of unwarranted absences or lateness; if he or she seems very dependent on the supervisor; if his or her productivity and/or job performance declines noticeably; if relationships with coworkers appear strained; if there is a "significant increase in errors, mistakes, or safety violations"; and if there are indications of substance abuse (usually alcohol) (p. 23), it is the supervisor's responsibility to refer the individual for counseling by the Employee Assistance Program staff. Typically, the individual will display multiple signs (more than one or two) of these indicators.

With respect to a diagnosis, the individual may exhibit most of the symptoms of Antisocial Personality Disorder. (He or she may more commonly be labeled a sociopath.) The symptoms include: disregard for the safety, rights, and well-being of others; noncompliance with "laws, regulations, and social norms"; lack of impulse control; irritable and aggressive behavior; and "consistent irresponsibility" whether at home or at work (Kelleher, 1997, p. 21).

According to Blinder (1999), psychiatrists have already accumulated sufficient data to develop a profile of employees who may commit "lethal acts of revenge" (p. 6). He has delineated the traits that indicate a potential for extreme violence. For example, he postulates that "homicide-prone workers are profoundly narcissistic, exhibiting an overwhelming sense of entitlement and a predilection for deprecating others" (p. 6). Blinder suggests that such individuals perceive themselves as superior to others, who thus have no right to criticize them. He also describes homicide-prone individuals as self-styled "victims of injustice" (p. 6). They are also controlling, demanding, and relatively unresponsive to counseling or the use of reason. (This last trait is particularly disturbing.) In addition, they make their colleagues anxious, and they engage in the use of threatening remarks. They attribute their own mistakes to other people and they "harbor persistent and inappropriate anger" (p. 6). They also exhibit an interest in violent events depicted in the media. Blinder suggests that individuals with these traits should be handled very carefully when they are fired. The human resources staff should behave in "in a matter-of-fact way, with regret, and courtesy" (p. 6). It is critical to minimize the person's sense of humiliation. The company should also provide a liberal severance package that includes medical benefits. We also suggest offering outplacement services.

Although not all perpetrators fit the psychological profile suggested, Caudron (1998) postulates that "workers who commit acts of violence possess a lot of anger and connect this unfocused rage to management through the people they know and have had contact with . . ." (p. 1). We find it interesting to note that the perpetrators in some workplace violence situations are so intent on retribution for what they consider to be an unjust act that they do not appear to fear either identification or potential punishment. Indeed, they appear to welcome the limelight. Thus, such an individual is not constrained by the normal rules of human behavior that would deter other potential criminals. In following this pattern of behavior, they are similar to perpetrators in cases of domestic violence and to individuals who commit suicide following serious acts of violence. For many people, serious precipitating factors contribute to their rage. These issues may be: lost wages or failure to receive raises; lost career opportunities; changes in work schedule; disciplinary actions, including termination for cause; "downsizing"; workloads that they cannot handle; and harassment by managers that is intended to force an employee to quit. In some cases, human resources personnel become the "hatchet people" or the "enforcers," in the eyes of the employees. Caudron suggests that these personnel should take special precautions to avoid violence—for example, conducting termination interviews with another staff member present, and removing all dangerous (sharp, heavy) objects from the surface of the desk.

Not all cases of workplace violence need end in death. The next true case involves the utilization of Roberts' model to defuse a threat that could have escalated into an event with serious consequences but, with proper handling, was defused:

Case Example

Sam

Sam, a computer programmer, was a short-term employee; he had worked only eight months at a Fortune 500 company. The "learning curve" was considered to be rather steep for his position but, in general, Sam seemed to be well suited for the assignment. However, from the beginning, Sam kept to himself. His coworkers considered him to be a loner. He never ate lunch with the work group or socialized in any way. His supervisor was particularly concerned because, in moving the team forward, it would be necessary for Sam to collaborate very closely with his coworkers. Sam's supervisor had begun to realize that Sam's isolation could eventually develop into a potential performance problem. Initially, Sam was simply regarded as a "new hire" who needed time to adjust to the position, but it soon became apparent that, despite efforts to reach out to him, Sam was exhibiting antisocial behavior.

On the morning of the incident in question, the group was engaged in a very intense meeting to discuss impending deadlines for some highly visible corporate projects. Sam attended the meeting. However, he seemed extraordinarily agitated by the intensity of the discussion. He got up abruptly at one point, left the room, and returned 30 minutes later.

At the conclusion of the meeting, Sam's supervisor distributed individual and group assignments. Sam was asked to collaborate with a small team of coworkers on a project that would require long hours and weekend work to meet an imminent

Case Example (*Continued*)

deadline. At the conclusion of the meeting, Sam followed his supervisor to his office, where the actual confrontation occurred.

The event took place on a cold Friday afternoon in December. "Dr. X," Director of the Employee Assistance Programs for the company, received a frantic call from another employee. She reported that her supervisor had been trapped in his office by a coworker who was preventing the supervisor from leaving. Dr. X's immediate concern was for the safety of the supervisor. He also wanted to contain the incident and protect other employees. Thus, before responding to the situation, Dr. X phoned the security department and asked that appropriate personnel be sent to meet him at the office where the incident was in progress.

Dr. X's first step upon arrival was to assess the lethality of the situation. He then asked the security officers to cordon off the area, to minimize "secondary victimization." To establish rapport with Sam, Dr. X began to speak quietly to the 27-year-old computer programmer, who was still menacing his supervisor, "John." In Dr. X's estimation, Sam's posture and demeanor clearly resembled that of a snake staring at its prey, coiled, and ready to strike. Eventually, however, Dr. X was able to persuade Sam to permit John to leave the small office where he was cornered, and to allow Dr. X to enter in John's place. Dr. X asked Sam to sit at one end of a small conference table while Dr. X sat safely at the other end. Before he entered the room, Dr. X had instructed security personnel to summon the local police and an ambulance. Continuing to follow the guidelines of Roberts' model, Dr. X began to deal with Sam's perceptions and feelings, keeping in mind that Sam was both a client and an alleged perpetrator. To Dr. X, an experienced counselor, Sam's cognitive and affective processes seemed irrational.

Having assessed the situation carefully, Dr. X decided that Sam needed to be examined by a crisis team at the psychiatric unit of a local hospital. Given that evaluation, Dr. X asked the local police to join him in the room with Sam, and to provide backup as he informed Sam that hospitalization was the only alternative. When the police officers entered the room, Sam became highly agitated, flailed his arms wildly, cursed loudly, and threatened both Dr. X and the police. It took the strength of three trained police officers to restrain Sam and help him to calm down.

At this stage of the crisis intervention process, Sam would speak only to Dr. X. This response was clearly a result of an early step in the model: the establishment of rapport. Sam finally agreed to go to the hospital, but only if Dr. X would accompany him in the ambulance. Dr. X and a police officer then traveled with Sam to the hospital. A psychiatric assessment in the hospital revealed that Sam was in a psychotic state and exhibited hypomania. Hospitalization was immediate.

(*continued*)

Case Example *(Continued)*

Dr. X returned to his office and began to assess the impact of the incident on the supervisor, John, his family, and the coworkers. A debriefing process was necessary as soon as possible, to minimize trauma to both the primary and secondary victims. In planning the intervention, Dr. X took several factors into account. Not everyone reacts the same way, regardless of the event. However, some events are of such magnitude that they will be experienced as traumatic by almost everyone exposed to them. Other events will affect only a few people. Most will return to the status quo quickly, but a few will develop short and even long-term symptoms. The survivor's personal history and characteristics may predispose him or her to trauma reactions even when the threat doesn't seem to affect the rest of the workforce negatively.

In addressing the needs of John, John's family, and his coworkers, it was necessary to ask the following questions:

- How have they coped with stressful events in the past—adaptively or maladaptively?
- What kinds of trauma/crisis have they experienced previously?
- Who comprises their support systems?

It should come as no surprise that Dr. X found that John, was highly traumatized by the event. John's wife, also in a state of crisis, was fearful of John's returning to the workplace. Furthermore, she believed that Sam would discover their home address and threaten them outside the office.

John needed individual counseling to normalize his feelings, put the past event in perspective, and help him to explore the reality of his current situation. John's wife was suffering the effects of what is labeled "secondary victimization": persons close to the victim may exhibit signs and suffer symptoms similar to those of the victim. This was the case for John's wife. She also needed individual counseling.

Group sessions were held for all of the employees who worked on the same floor as Sam. Coworkers received formal debriefing from Dr. X, and this helped to normalize and stabilize the workplace. To accommodate the approximately 90 people who worked on this floor, three formal sessions were held during the morning immediately following the incident.

The impact of this incident on potential victims was clearly minimized by the immediate response of Dr. X, who, fortunately, was on site. John, the primary victim, was able to return to work within two weeks following the counseling sessions; he was given assurance that Sam would not return. John's wife also needed follow-up counseling, but the process resulted in a positive outcome for her as well.

For six weeks following the incident, coworkers continued to phone the EAP and request on-site individual counseling, which they received. This pattern underscores the value of having the EAP located at the workplace.

Case Example *(Continued)*

Sam was successfully treated and was released from the hospital with a positive prognosis. Following counseling, Sam decided to resign from his job and accept a new position with another company which required less work-related pressure.

Dr. X met with the in-house emergency response team to ensure that they were not suffering from secondary victimization. Besides providing the appropriate referrals, Dr. X anticipated the possibility of some recurring symptoms. He therefore reminded everyone of his "open-door" policy at the EAP office.

The following case was nonfatal but resulted in some injuries to the survivor:

Case Example

Ronald and Janet

Ronald met Janet when they both worked at an accounting firm. Mutual attraction led to their dating within six weeks of Ronald's joining the firm in the autumn of 1997. After several dates, Janet grew very apprehensive about Ronald's sudden temper outbursts, jealous fits, persistent telephone calls, and visits to her apartment at all hours of the night. Finally, Janet decided to stop dating Ronald, and met him at a local coffee house to break off the relationship. When he learned of her decision, Ronald quietly rose from the table and, before walking away, whispered into Janet's ear, "You're not getting rid of me that easily." A few days later, Ronald attacked Janet with a screwdriver in the parking garage of their office. A few men saw the attack, captured Ronald, and waited until the police arrived. Ronald was sentenced to a prison term. Janet luckily suffered only minor physical injuries that required two stitches. Her emotional response, however, was more serious.

The Course of Crisis Intervention and Therapy over Several Months

The literature on stress and human resources issues addresses the psychological trauma and ensuing therapeutic strategies for survivors of workplace violence (Bensimon, 1997). Immediate action, for example, best serves the emotional well-being of the victim, other employees, and the entire organization (Ceniceros, 1999; Jones, 1998). It appears that crisis intervention strategies coupled with therapeutic strategies that are contingent upon the trauma prove most effective. Work with survivors like Janet, for example, should incorporate issues of posttraumatic stress disorder (PTSD) and theories of abused women (Walker, 1994) within a specific crisis intervention model (Roberts, 2000), while also recognizing the contextual importance of the event's having occurred in a workplace environment (Brady, 1999).

Immediately following the attack and Ronald's arrest, Janet experienced a range of varied traumatic symptoms. As the police officers, paramedics, security personnel, and crisis counselors approached Janet, they were cognizant of her emotional state. Brady (1999) suggests that targets such as Janet will experience physical pain, shaking, crying, anger, and embarrassment—all symptoms that are easy to recognize. In addition, they may feel shock, disbelief, or confusion regarding the attack. Koss and colleagues (1994) delineate how the aftermath of a traumatic event may cloud victims' judgment. Thus, it is critical that the police, crisis workers, or peers establish rapport and provide an atmosphere of safety and trust, while defining the presenting problem (Roberts, 1990). The crisis workers must also understand that victims may not be coherent enough to accept any assurances or provide adequate information easily.

Crisis workers, peers, and police must also encourage victims to express their feelings, both immediately and in the days following the event. Among these emotions and symptoms, they can expect to feel resentment, depression, humiliation, and to have poor concentration as well as sleep difficulties (Brady, 1999). They are also likely to feel powerless, anxious, and vulnerable (Walker, 1994). In addition to assisting victims with their feelings, Jones (1998) underscores the need to hold a crisis debriefing with all employees within the first 72 hours following such an incident. Though not intended as a group therapy session, this procedure should reduce the feelings of anxiety and vulnerability in all employees. The safety of their world has been shattered by the violent attack on a coworker (Brady, 1999).

The debriefing of the employees occurs over a series of stages. In the first or "introductory" stage, the specific procedure is outlined to the staff (Brady, 1999). The element of confidentiality is strongly emphasized. The second or "fact" phase enables each employee who witnessed the event, or who personally knows the victim, to describe how the attack has impacted his or her life. The third phase, a "thought" phase, allows for an exploration of thoughts and feelings regarding the attack. The fourth or "symptom" phase encourages employees to discuss their physical and emotional responses to the attack. The fifth or "preparation" stage then focuses on the overall reactions from the group while detailing the longer-term effects they may expect to experience during the coming weeks and months. The debriefing concludes with a "future planning" stage that addresses the elements of coping and support required for all employees, including the victim, if they are to return to a normal work environment.

Brady (1999) cautions that the victim may dismiss both the severity of the event and its emotional toll. Unfortunately, this invites vulnerability to longer-term difficulties such as post-traumatic stress disorder (PTSD), feelings of burnout, lack of confidence, and situation-specific anxiety. There is also a danger of suicide. The processing of the intense affect occurs primarily within the first days and weeks following the traumatic event. Even with immediate counseling, Janet's sense of trust and security was shattered; she was angry and distrusting of others, including her coworkers and the mental health professionals (Walker, 1994). A successful mental health professional, working with someone like Janet, must demonstrate credibility, expertise, and patience in handling women's abuse issues so that the client can feel comfortable in the therapeutic sessions. In cases that mirror the sexual and physical assault on Janet, a female counselor would probably be a better choice than a man. However, not all practicing counselors agree. Many think that hiring a supportive male counselor can actually help the victim to readjust to a world in which men and women can work together.

Research suggests that post-traumatic stress disorder (PTSD) is the likely diagnosis following an attack such as the one on Janet (Koss & Harvey, 1991; Walker, 1991; 1994). The most recent version of *the Diagnostic and Statistical Manual of the American Psychiatric Association* (2000) indicates that the criteria for PTSD involve several patterns of behavior. The first pattern is a persistent reexperiencing of the trauma in at least one of the following ways: recurrent remembrances of the event, which cause distress; recurrent distressing dreams about the trauma; acting or feeling as if the event were actually reoccurring; and physical reactions to cues that trigger remembrances of the event (such as reentering the room where it occurred).

Individuals diagnosed as having PTSD avoid the cues associated with their trauma and attempt to flatten their own affect regarding the event in at least three of the following seven areas:

1. Avoidance of thoughts or emotions related to the traumatic event.
2. Avoidance of activities, places, or people (e.g., coworkers) associated with the event.
3. Inability to remember the basic elements of the event.
4. Decreased enjoyment or participation in what were once significant activities (e.g., hobbies or work).
5. Feelings of isolation from others.
6. A newly restricted range of emotions (i.e., the person can no longer express or feel love or joy).
7. A feeling of a shortened lifespan or an imminent end to a once endless future.

Another PTSD pattern involves a persistent increase in arousal in at least two of the following ways: Difficulty in sleeping, erratic angry outbursts, difficulty in concentrating, hypervigilance, and easily becoming frightened.

Within the three domains described above, symptoms must last for at least one month, and the disturbances must significantly alter or impair typical life functioning (American Psychiatric Association, 2000).

A vulnerable survivor of trauma, such as Janet, very often responds poorly to treatment immediately following the traumatic event (Black, 1982). Janet's prognosis for rebounding from the trauma and progressing through Roberts' (2000) stages successfully hinges upon her ability to request assistance. The act of seeking help is contingent upon adjustment style and personality type, according to McMahon, Schram, and Davidson (1993), who state that certain personality types (e.g., ambivalent-detached or dependent) exhibit higher levels of depression under very stressful situations than other personality types. Choca, Shanley, and Van Denburg (1992) underscore the fact that regardless of whether Janet exhibited symptoms of any psychological disorders prior to the event, the likelihood of her displaying Axis II symptoms intensifies following the event, either as a function of an actual premorbid condition or as a result of the intense affect produced by the attack.

Roberts (2000) stresses the understanding of former and current coping styles as a key to therapeutic efficacy. Hyer, Brandsma, and Boyd (1997) suggest that PTSD-diagnosed clients, such as Janet, cope with trauma according to their personality styles. For example, avoidant-personality types would likely cope with trauma by avoiding stress, whereas dependent-personality types cope by holding themselves responsible and avoiding any form of confrontation or detailed problem solving. Although various personality assessment measures have limitations when assessing PTSD (Choca & Van Denburg, 1997; Duckworth & Anderson, 1995), an identification of personality type would help the counselor to understand Janet's coping style, and, in turn, lead to a more effective course of treatment.

Roberts (2000) also emphasizes the importance of developing solutions and restoring cognitive functioning in the client. Once personality style is established, the next question centers on the relative efficacy of long- or short-term therapeutic work with a client like Janet. McCann and Pearlman (1990) recommend a set of guidelines in assessing the length of treatment. Short-term work (no more than six months) requires the following: conscious memories of the trauma; an ability to access those memories without too much psychological distress; an ego intact enough to allow the client to participate in the introspective process of therapy; an ability to meet all psychological needs; and minimal disruptions in the client's cognitive schemata. Conversely, long-term work (more than six months) seems to be indicated if the following elements exist: traumatic memories that appear fragmented and out of conscious awareness; severe disruptions of ego resources; an inability to meet central psychological needs; disrupted or skewed cognitive schemata; and a self-protective resistance to the change required for psychological healing and growth. Regardless of the duration of treatment, work with Janet, or with any of her coworkers who were traumatized by the attack, should utilize a supportive approach, especially when the traumatic memories seem intrusive and anxiety-producing. The counselor needs to establish a safe environment before discussing the traumatic event with the client. A counselor who is initiating PTSD-oriented therapy requires an understanding of the client's personality style, previous coping strategies, and current state of psychological distress, in order to restore the cognitive and emotional functions disrupted by the attack.

In the months following the incident, the organization should provide outlets for the other employees to discuss any emotional concerns or fears. Jones (1998) recommends utilizing the tragedy as a mechanism to initiate educational workshops regarding workplace stress, workplace violence, or sexual harassment. In addition, holding meetings in which employees can discuss their feelings allows the entire employee staff to deal effectively with the attack's occurrence in their workplace. Williams (1997) argues that workplace violence is a new phenomenon, but we contend that workplace attacks and the psychological trauma that follows these events mirror other tragedies, such as domestic violence or physical/sexual abuse, and can benefit from the utilization of strategies designed for other situations.

Determinants of Actual Workplace Aggression

Cordes (1993) attributes the prevalence of workplace violence to the following factors: the ready availability of guns, the glamorization of violence by the media, and the impact, on the average worker, of recent sweeping economic changes (p. 933).

Mantell (1994) suggests reasons for the rise in workplace violence: workers are paranoid and frustrated, and employers are careless, punitive, and autocratic. He contends that violence is the ultimate manifestation of stress. Determinants of work aggression include perceived unfair treatment, negative reactions to workforce reduction, and conflicts arising from workforce diversity and misunderstandings. In the last category are the perceptions, real or unfounded, that women and members of minority groups are stealing jobs from the dominant white male majority. Constant corporate competition and conflict, many times supported by the corporate culture, can escalate to violence. The breaking of norms established in the workplace (e.g., rate busting) can lead to ostracism and then to physical retaliation by angry coworkers. Organizational change, such as restructuring and/or mergers, leads to an elevated level of stress. Environmental factors may also irritate employees: extremes in temperature and humidity, poor lighting and air quality, high noise levels, poorly maintained equipment, and "speed-up" procedures on the assembly line, in an effort to reduce expenses.

Police Responses to Workplace Violence

It is important to remember that many of these events constitute serious crimes and must be addressed by law enforcement personnel. Their responsibilities include securing the scene from further violence, and investigating the crime by interviewing victims and witnesses as quickly as possible. Police officers actually need specific training in crisis intervention techniques because they are frequently the first "psychologists" on the scene. They must collect information while almost simultaneously meeting the emotional needs of victims and witnesses. Consequently, the priorities of police officers frequently conflict. What they need to do with respect to security and crime-scene investigation may interfere with the guidelines of effective crisis intervention. For the police, safety and security must always be the highest priorities. How these "first responders" deal with the trauma will influence the outcomes for everyone involved, including the first responders themselves. Police officers, emergency workers, and crisis management teams are all vulnerable to the impact of the stress associated with their job descriptions. The strain of their profession exacts a high toll in terms of stress-related disorders such as cardiac problems and alcoholism (Waters, Irons, & Finkle, 1982). In recent years, specialized teams (e.g., rape crisis teams) have been established to address the problems associated with sex crimes. However, the team may not always be available. Therefore, the police must be prepared to deal with victims, witnesses, and alleged perpetrators.

Organization Post-Incident Strategies

No individual can deal with all the needs of victims and witnesses at one time. We suggest that each organization should establish a trauma response team. The team's basic duties are to:

- Address the medical needs of the injured promptly.
- Report the incident to the police. A call to 911 will activate both the medical and law enforcement processes.
- Notify other relevant authorities (as required by law).

- Inform the appropriate members of the management team if they are not already aware of the event. (A communication plan should already be in place.)
- Arrange for appropriate debriefing and treatment for victims, witnesses, and other concerned individuals (e.g., family members).

In situations that are beyond the scope of most corporate EAPs (e.g., the World Trade Center and Pentagon bombings), critical incident stress management teams are called upon to provide a range of services designed to address the specific condition of each individual involved. The teams are also trained to address organizational needs.

RESPONSES TO MAJOR WORKPLACE DISASTERS

In less than one hour following the first terrorist attack on the World Trade Center's Twin Towers on September 11, 2001, the Red Cross national headquarters disaster mental health services staff notified the American Psychological Association (APA) Disaster Response Network (DRN) to activate their system (Daw, 2001). DRN members in New York City immediately reported to the Red Cross Manhattan headquarters. A disaster response center was quickly opened to provide services to the three most vulnerable groups: The families and coworkers of the missing and known dead and the rescue workers. APA's Office of Public Affairs provided experts on terrorism and trauma response to discuss the psychological aspects of the terrorist attacks in the media. The American Red Cross Disaster Services updated and distributed its guidelines (1991, 2001) to its centers.

During that first day, Red Cross Disaster Operations Centers were opened at the Pentagon and Dulles Airport outside of Washington DC, Logan Airport in Boston, and in San Francisco, Los Angeles, and Western Pennsylvania. DRN volunteers staffed all the centers. By the evening of September 11, licensed psychologists, social workers, and professional counselors had been contacted by their various professional organizations and asked to play their appropriate roles (e.g., training, debriefing, and counseling) in the disaster response efforts. Wednesday, September 12, found the response programs fully activated. APA had completed its "Coping with Terrorism" booklet and distributed information on the practitioner listservs. By Friday, a group of disaster specialists had been recruited to assist the federal government in addressing the events of the week. The American Psychological Association and the National Association of Social Workers have dedicated whole issues of their publications to describing first-hand observations, theoretical analyses, and recommendations concerning the continuing contributions that mental health service providers can make toward reducing the costs of exposure to catastrophes such as the events of September 11, 2001.

The mental health responses to the terrorist acts of September 11 were not without their critics (Herbert et al., 2001; Goode, 2001). There is a concern on the part of some trauma experts that even professionals who have not been exposed to the proper training may be too intrusive for many clients and can actually inflict more harm than good. It will take time to conduct the type of postevent research that can address this question. The danger of not responding to a person in need of counseling and referral should also be considered (North et al., 1999). Such events also place psychologists, social workers, and counselors at risk for developing acute stress responses (APA, 2000). As Johnson (2001) points out, this national tragedy, including the threat of bioterrorism, has affected even citizens in seemingly safe parts of America ("the fields of Iowa," p. 5). Thus, mental health professionals must be prepared to face fear in our clients, in the children, in our colleagues, and in ourselves.

The Corporate Response

The organization, under the legal doctrine of *respondeat superior,* may be held liable for the actions of its agents if those agents knew, or should have known, that a person was at risk for committing violence against others.

In *Ticking Bombs,* Mantell (1994) writes that even the best companies—those that have taken every possible security precaution—may still have psychotic employees who become triggered by events that are actually unrelated to their jobs. Barrier (1995) has already pointed out that no business can protect itself fully against its customers and employees. A more realistic approach is the development of policies and strategies to reduce potential harm. The human resources staff are expected to be careful in their hiring practices, but their efforts may prove fruitless with employees who have been with the company for years and have only developed problems later in their careers. A known record of violence, however, especially when combined with a history of alcohol and drug abuse, should raise warning flags.

When corporate Employee Assistance Programs address substance abuse, problems with personal finances, and marital and family difficulties by offering workshops, counseling sessions, and long-term referrals for the most serious situations, they can reduce the prevalence of workplace violence. By establishing a corporate culture that clearly demonstrates appreciation of all the employees and treats them with respect, a company will further reduce its vulnerability. No company can guarantee job security, but by using careful administrative practices, it can increase the workers' sense of security. On the other hand, paying enormous bonuses to corporate executives who earn their keep by reducing the workforce will only increase hostility. Reports of executives' high salaries feed the anger of lower-level employees.

In the United States, companies spend more than $22 billion each year on security—a higher amount than is spent on this country's police departments. To be fair, much of that expenditure is justified because companies also need to protect industrial secrets or safeguard hazardous work sites.

Corporate Responses to Domestic Violence

In 1995, several companies, including the Polaroid Corporation, Liz Claiborne, Inc., and Marshall's, Inc., joined together to establish the National Workplace Resource Center on Domestic Violence, in order to develop an effective model for employees who have been the targets of violence (Meier, 1996). The multidimensional program incorporates, among other components, counseling, relocation to new areas for women at high risk for further abuse, and enforcement of protective orders as well as increased security for women who have been stalked. Following a suggestion that grew out of a Congressional conference sponsored by Senator Joseph R. Biden, Jr., the Center advises placing notices, in companies' ladies' rooms, that list the telephone numbers of the local shelter and/or counseling services for abused women. Senior management at Liz Claiborne felt that conducting seminars on the topic of domestic violence was not a sufficient response, so they distributed brochures by putting them in each employee's mailbox.

Not many corporations have taken such an active and positive stance. Too many organizations have actually interfered with employees who wanted to testify in court, which reinforced many employees' feeling that retaliation for reporting or prosecuting a case was a possibility.

Prevention Programs: Large-Scale Organizations

Under government rulings, every employer is obligated to develop and implement workplace violence-prevention programs that balance safety, confidentiality, and the guidelines of federal disability legislation. Polaroid has established a model program (Solomon, 1998). Similar programs should publish a clearly articulated company workplace violence policy statement. They should also establish threat assessment teams that promptly evaluate potential hazards so that they can be controlled. Training and education constitute other important components of an effective prevention program. Employees must also be encouraged to report relevant incidents, which the team then investigates and evaluates.

Clear and accurate record keeping is essential, particularly when there is a possibility of future litigation. Any workplace violence policy must be based on a "zero tolerance" philosophy and must be applied fairly, without a hint of bias. The hazard assessment process should utilize anonymous questionnaires to identify the potential for violent incidents and the need for improved security. The survey should be updated every two years.

In large facilities, the corporation should require identification badges for all employees, sign-in and sign-out books, and an escort for visitors (e.g., vendors and clients). Procedures for dealing with emergencies or hostage situations should also be in place. The guidelines should include rules for when to call in-house security and/or local law enforcement agencies (e.g., assault incidents). It is also suggested that companies provide assistance and referrals for employees who are targets of domestic violence. The educational component should involve training that improves employees' vigilance to avoid muggings, robberies, rapes, and other assaults. Advice on self-protection in hotels is frequently given to women who travel for the company. One example: Make sure the hotel room is near the elevators and not at the end of a series of long halls. Such training programs should be given during working hours and use terminology that is easily understood by all employees. Managers and supervisors require additional training so that they are capable of recognizing potentially harmful situations. Everyone in the company should be aware of the procedures for getting prompt medical attention, whether the injury is an accident or the outcome of an incident of workplace violence.

Information on how to establish Threat Assessment Teams and sample procedures and questionnaires are available from the Occupational Safety and Health Administration (OSHA) of the U.S. Department of Labor.

Several relatively simple strategies can be utilized to reduce risk and to increase confidence in the workplace (OSHA, 1998b, p. 7):

1. Increase visibility and maintain adequate lighting. Operationally, that means: clear any obstructions, such as shrubbery, that block employees' view of the street. Parking areas should be well lit.

2. Use fences.

3. Use drop safes to limit the accessibility to cash. Require the use of credit cards, and establish a "no change" policy.

4. Install surveillance equipment.

5. Use door detectors to inform employees that someone is entering the facility.

6. Control the entrance of visitors via door buzzers.

7. Install silent and personal alarms that can alert the police or management to a threat.

8. Install physical barriers, such as bullet-resistant glass enclosures.

9. Increase staffing levels at night.

10. Keep doors, especially rear entrances, locked when not in use.

11. Develop safety procedures and policies for offsite responsibilities (e.g., pizza deliveries).

It has been suggested that emergency rooms and nursing homes address their risk by adding panic buttons, using locked entries, employing video cameras and direct lines to the police, and using full-time security, protective glass, and metal detectors (AJNNEWSLINE, 1994). Taking such precautions lessens the chronic anxiety felt by many nursing and medical staff members.

Downsizing Counseling Guidelines

The role of the outplacement counselor or EAP staff member in counseling an employee who has been or is about to be terminated is to defuse the potential for violence. Following is a list of strategies (adapted from Smith, 1994) that should be incorporated into the sessions, depending on the response of the employee:

- Anger: The louder the employee talks, the softer must be the counselor's approach. It is important that the counselor not escalate the situation or lose his or her own temper when challenged.

- Denial: When the employee indicates nonacceptance of the facts, it is the role of the outplacement counselor to help the individual realize that there is life after the company and getting one's resources organized is important.

- Depression: For the outplacement counselor, signs of depression, talk of suicide, and insomnia are all serious warning signals. The individual should be referred to the EAP counselor, who, in turn, may refer him or her for medical treatment or even hospitalization.

- Hysteria: It is difficult to assess what is an overreaction to being fired, especially if the employee has serious family pressures. However, when the employee exhibits symptoms of hysteria, the EAP should be called. Under no circumstances should an employee be permitted to leave the facility before he or she is stabilized.

Human resources and outplacement staff must take precautions themselves because employees may see them as agents of management and therefore responsible for their predicaments. Clear warning signals of impending violence include: verbal threats (both overt and subtle), threatening acts, major habit changes, open expressions of unusual and bizarre thoughts, a fixation with weapons, romantic obsessions, symptoms of depression, and signs of chemical dependency. Employees who constantly file what may appear to be unreasonable grievances or lawsuits are also high-risk (Toufexus, 1994).

CONCLUSION

Given the pressures of today's economy and some managerial practices, negative predisposing factors in the perpetrators, issues of domestic violence and terrorism, and the obvious accessibility of the workplace, we must engage in prevention activities that reduce potential harm, develop effective security procedures, and attempt to identify and defuse the anger and sense of entitlement that all too many perpetrators feel. With respect to early childhood influences (an issue we have not discussed here), we must attempt to replace aggressive tendencies with patience, and teach negotiating skills. On a more adult level, cultural norms of violence must be addressed realistically. However, while such strategies are being developed, we need to train our counselors and first responders in the techniques of threat assessment and crisis management.

REFERENCES

AJNNEWSLINE. (1994, December). ED nurses enlisting legislatures against rising workplace violence. *American Journal of Nursing, 62,* 65.

American Psychiatric Association. (2000). *Diagnostic and statistical manual of mental disorders: DSM-IV-TR.* Washington, DC: Author.

American Red Cross Disaster Services. (1999, 2001). *Coping with disaster: Emotional health issues for victims.* Author.

Anfuso, D. (1994, October). Workplace violence. *Personnel Journal,* 66–77.

Baron, R. A., & Neuman,J. H. (1996). Workplace violence and workplace aggression: Evidence on their relative frequency and potential causes. *Aggressive Behavior, 22,* 161–173.

Barrier, M. (1995, February). The enemy within. *Nation's Business, 83*(2), 18–24.

Barstow, D. (1999, July 30). In an office building, scenes of chaos, blood, and death. *New York Times,* A1, A14.

Bensimon, H. F. (1997, September). What to do about anger in the workplace. *Training and Development,* 28–32.

Berthelsen, C. (1999, August 15). Hundreds remember slain letter carrier. *New York Times, 22.*

Black, D. (1982). Children and disaster. *British Medical Journal, 285,* 989–990.

Blinder, M. (1999, September 15). Timely profile of a workplace menace: What to look out for. *Bottom Line: Personal,* 6.

Brady, C. (1999). Surviving the incident. In P. Leather, C. Brady, C. Lawrence, D. Beale, & T. Cox (Eds.), *Work-related violence: Assessment and intervention* (pp. 52–68). London: Routledge.

Bray, C. (1995, Spring). Defining workplace abuse. *Affilia, 10*(1), 87–91.

Caudron, S. (1998, August). Target: HR. *Workforce, 77*(8), 44.

Ceniceros, R. (1999, April 19). Response to workplace violence is called key. *Business Insurance,* 24–25.

Choca, J. P., & Van Denburg, E. (1997). *Interpretive guide to the Millon Clinical Multiaxial Inventory* (2nd ed.). Washington, DC: American Psychological Association.

Choca, J. P., Shanley, L., & Van Denburg, E. (1992). *Interpretive guide to the Millon Clinical Multiaxial Inventory.* Washington, DC: American Psychological Association.

Cordes, R. (1993, November). Causes of workplace violence examined. *Trial,* 93.

Daw, J. (2001). APA's Disaster Response Network: Help on the scene. *APA Monitor on Psychology, 32*(10), 14–15.

Duckworth, J. C., & Anderson, W. P. (1995). *MMPI & MMPI-2: Interpretation manual for counselors and clinicians* (4th ed.). Bristol, PA: Accelerated Development.

Duncan, T. S. (1995, April). Death in the office: Workplace homicides. *FBI Law Enforcement Bulletin,* 20–25.

Frank, A. (1999, July 24). Attack in airport outrages workers. *The Star Ledger, 1,* 4.

Goode, E. (2001, September 16). Some therapists fear services could backfire. *New York Times,* L21.

Herbert, J., et al. (2001). Primum non nocere. [Letter to the editors]. *APA Monitor on Psychology, 32*(10), 4.

Hellwege, J. (1995, May). Claims for domestic violence in the workplace may be on the rise. *Trial,* 94.

Hyer, L., Brandsma, J., & Boyd, S. (1997). The MCMIs and posttraumatic stress disorder. In T. Millon (Ed.), *The Millon inventories: Clinical and personality assessment* (pp. 191–216). New York: Guilford Press.

Johnson, N. G. (2001). We, the people. *APA Monitor on Psychology, 32*(10), 5.

Jones, M. P. (1998). When personal catastrophe hits the workplace. *Behavioral Health Management, 18,* 29–30.

Kelleher, M. D. (1997). *Profiling the lethal employee: Case studies of violence in the workplace.* Westport, CT: Praeger.

Koss, M. P., Goodman, L. A., Browne, A., Fitzgerald, L. F., Puryear-Keita, G., & Russo, N. F. (1994). *No safe haven: Male violence against women at home, at work, and in the community.* Washington, DC: American Psychological Association.

Koss, M. P., & Harvey, M. R. (1991). *The rape victim: Clinical and community interventions* (2nd ed.). Newbury Park, CA: Sage.

La Rose v. Mutual Life Assurance Co., No. 9322684 (Tex., Harris County 214th Jud. Dist. Ct. December 5, 1994).

Mantell, M. R. (1994, January/February). Ticking bombs. *Psychology Today, 20–21.*

McCann, I. L., & Pearlman, L. A. (1990). *Psychological trauma and the adult survivor: Theory, therapy, and transformation.* New York: Brunner/Mazel.

McMahon, F., Schram, L., & Davidson, R. (1993). Negative life events, social support, and depression in three personality types. *Journal of Personality Disorders, 7,* 241–254.

McMurry, K. (1995, December). Workplace violence: Can it be prevented? *Trial, 31*(12), 10–12.

Meier, B. (1996, March 10). When abuse follows women to work: Some companies respond to violence. *New York Times,* F11.

Neuman, J. H., & Baron, R. A. (1998, May–June). Workplace violence and workplace aggression: Evidence concerning specific forms and preferred targets. *Journal of Management, 24*(3), 391–411.

North, C. S., Nixon, S. J., Shariat, S., Mallonee, S., McMillen, J. C., Spitznagel, E. L., & Smith, E. M. (1999). Psychiatric disorders among survivors of the Oklahoma City bombing. *Journal of the American Medical Association, 99,* 755–762.

Occupational Safety and Health Administration (OSHA). (1996). *Workplace violence awareness and prevention.* Washington, DC: U.S. Department of Labor.

Occupational Safety and Health Administration (OSHA). (1998a). *Guidelines for preventing workplace violence for healthcare and social service workers.* Washington, DC: U.S. Department of Labor.

Occupational Safety and Health Administration (OSHA). (1998b). *Recommendations for workplace violence prevention in late-night retail establishments.* Washington, DC: U.S. Department of Labor.

Reichert, J. L. (1998, October). Government releases latest figures on workplace violence. *Trial, 34*(10), 103.

Reynolds, L. (1997, November). Fighting domestic violence in the workplace. *HR Focus,* p. 8.

Roberts, A. R. (2000). An overview of crisis theory and crisis intervention. In A. R. Roberts (Ed.), *Crisis intervention handbook: Assessment, treatment, and research* (pp. 3–30). New York: Oxford University Press.

Sack, K. (1999, July 30). Gunman in Atlanta slays 9, then himself. *New York Times,* A1.

Shoop, J. G. (1993, December). Workplace violence affects millions, survey finds. *Trial,* 76–77.

Smith, B. (1994, February). Cease fire! Preventing workplace violence. *HR Focus, 1,* 6, 7.

Solomon, C. M. (1998, February). Picture this: Polaroid addresses family to combat workplace violence. *Workplace,* 83–86.

Toscano, G., & Weber, W. (1995). Violence in the workplace. *Compensation and Working Conditions, 47*(4), 1–7.

Toufexus, A. (1994, April). Workers who fight firing with fire. *Times,* 35–37.

Walker, L. E. A. (1991). Posttraumatic stress disorder in women: Diagnosis and treatment of battered woman syndrome. *Psychotherapy, 28,* 21–29.

Walker, L. E. A. (1994). *Abused women and survivor therapy.* Washington, DC: American Psychological Association.

Warchol, G. (1998, July). *Workplace violence, 1992–1996. Bureau of Justice Statistics Special Report: National Crime Victimization Survey.* Washington, DC: U.S. Department of Justice, Office of Justice Programs.

Waters, J. (2002). Moving forward from September 11th. A stress/crisis/trauma model. *Brief Therapy and Crisis Intervention, 2*(1).

Waters, J., Irons, N., & Finkle, E. (1982). The police stress inventory: A comparison of events affecting officers and supervisors in rural and urban areas. *Police Stress, 5*(1), 18–25.

Williams, H. A. H. (1997). 10 steps to a safer workplace. *HR Focus, 74,* 9–11.

Windau, J., & Toscano, G. (1993). *Murder Inc. Homicide in the American workplace.* Washington, DC: U.S. Department of Labor, Bureau of Labor Statistics.

Chapter 18

DOMESTIC VIOLENCE IN THE WORKPLACE

PATRICIA BROWNELL and ALBERT R. ROBERTS

CURRENT TRENDS AND ISSUES

> - A teacher's aide was stalked into her workplace by a boyfriend with whom she had been attempting to break off a relationship. The boyfriend tried to drag her into an elevator that would take them to the roof. He intended to throw her off. The police were called and prevented this, but the director of the center, fearing harm to the children and other staff, refused to allow the aide to continue working at the school.
>
> - An insurance executive was badly beaten by her husband, who blackened her eye and cut her face so that she required stitches. She requested release time to relocate herself and her two children, recuperate from her medical injuries, and obtain a court order of protection. Her superior advised her that her accounts were suffering from her absences and lateness, her appearance was disturbing to clients, and she would have to be terminated.

Domestic violence is becoming recognized as a serious public epidemic that disproportionately affects women (Rymer, 1996). The U.S. Department of Labor has issued guidelines for workplace safety that recognize the impact of domestic violence on the workplace (U.S. Department of Labor, 1996b).

According to Dr. Nancy Isaac of the Harvard School of Public Health, the corporate sector has begun to recognize and address the issue of domestic violence in the workplace (Solomon, 1995; Walsteadt, 1995). In the public and not-for-profit work sectors, less has been done to implement policies intended to ensure the protection of victims and improve work performance.

Domestic violence is one manifestation of general violence in the workplace. Homicide is a leading cause of death in the workplace, and women are more likely to be victimized by someone they know than are men (Warchol, 1998).

The National Institute of Occupational Safety and Health (NIOSH), a government research group, has urged employers to prevent homicides at work, calling them a serious health hazard. The Occupational Safety and Health Administration (OSHA) has issued regulations that stop short of *requiring* employers to protect employees from the threat of violence, which ranks with other hazards such as lead exposure and insecure scaffolding (U.S. Department of Labor, 1996b).

One key issue regarding policies on workplace safety standards is how to stimulate employer participation in ensuring protection, in the workplace, for victims of domestic violence, their coworkers, and their clients. Recently, welfare reform legislation has drawn into the workplace large numbers of women whose primary reason for seeking public assistance was to flee domestic violence situations (Brownell, 1998; Tolman & Raphael, 2000).

A second key issue is how to protect workers who are subjected to domestic violence in the home from being victimized again through punitive workplace policies that penalize them if they need time off to seek medical care, counseling, and court orders of protection. The impact of domestic violence on the workplace goes beyond the experience of violence in the workplace (Brownell, 1996).

Domestic violence occurs most frequently in the home. However, it can and does spill out into the streets and the workplace. Domestic violence can affect the workplace in two ways:

1. When it occurs in the home, it can result in absenteeism, lost productivity at the workplace for the victims and the batterers, and high health care costs.

2. It has been associated with increased alcoholism and drug abuse among victims.

Domestic violence can also occur in the workplace, when an "intimate" batterer stalks the victim and gains entry into the workplace (Silverstein, 1994). This event can cause danger to coworkers and others, lowered staff morale, fear among employees, and liability concerns for employers. Repercussions for the victim can include lost work (and pay), negative work evaluations, and, possibly, loss of employment.

Increasing numbers of women are working to support households and are achieving positions of prominence. For various reasons, they may experience greater vulnerability to workplace attacks that can place them, their coworkers, and their clients at risk (Raphael, 1995). According to O'Regan (1995), one of the key issues affecting women's ability to leave an abusive relationship is financial independence. A job often becomes essential, to break the cycle of violence. However, when a woman escapes a battering relationship, the one place her batterer can find her is at her job (Pereira, 1995).

In the case example involving a teacher's aide, the domestic violence incident illustrates how disruptive and dangerous domestic violence can be. The case example of the insurance executive demonstrates that domestic violence incidents can have an impact on the workplace even when they do not occur there. Both cases exemplify how victims of domestic violence in the workplace can be penalized by employment policies that do not support domestic violence victims (Johnson, 1996).

According to the National Organization of Women (NOW), abusive husbands and partners harass 74% of employed battered women at work and cause 56% of them to be late for work at least 5 times a month, 28% to leave early at least 5 days a month, and 54% to miss at least 3 full days of work a month (NOW, 2001). Not only does this affect the victims' employment status—an estimated 20% reported losing their jobs and becoming dependent on welfare—but it has an adverse affect on employers as well.

Domestic violence reportedly costs employers $3–$5 billion annually as a result of worker absenteeism, higher health care premiums, and lower productivity. The impact on coworkers of domestic violence victims can be high as well. Witnessing violence, including domestic violence, in the workplace can be traumatic to coworkers, even if they have not been injured or threatened by the batterer (Everly, Lating, & Mitchell, 2000). Post-traumatic stress disorder, one outcome of a reaction to witnessing or experiencing a traumatic event, can result in absenteeism and lowered productivity among coworkers of domestic violence victims.

According to Warchol (1998), the National Crime Victimization Survey on Workplace Violence conducted between 1992 and 1996, intimates (current and former spouses and significant others) were identified by the victims as the perpetrators of about 1% of workplace violent crime. Women were more likely than men to be victimized by someone they knew, and men were more likely than women to commit workplace violence (Warchol, 1998).

Employers are increasingly aware of the cost of domestic violence to business. When human resources professionals were polled by *Personnel Journal* (April 1995), 74% stated that they believed domestic violence was a workplace issue. A survey of business leaders found that 57% of corporate executives believe domestic violence is a significant social problem, one-third stated that it has a negative impact on profits, and 40% knew of employees and other people who were affected by domestic violence (Starch, 1994). In another survey, 44% stated that it increases health care costs (Soler, 1999).

Unions are responding to domestic violence as an issue related to family life, public health, and the community (Family Violence Prevention Fund, 2001a). According to the U.S. Department of Labor's National Institute of Occupational Safety and Health (NIOSH), husbands and boyfriends commit, each year, about 13,000 acts of violence against female partners in the workplace, and domestic violence is a leading cause of homicide for women at work (U.S. Department of Labor, 1996a).

Women who receive public benefits under the Aid to Families with Dependent Children (AFDC) program for themselves and their families have been identified as targets of male partner abuse when they have entered training or employment programs that bridge the transition from welfare to work (Raphael, 1995). The Personal Responsibility and Work Opportunity Reconciliation Act of 1996 (P. L. 104–193), Title I, legislated a 5-year lifetime limit for Temporary Assistance to Needy Families (TANF) benefits. As a result, male partners' efforts to sabotage work and training efforts for TANF heads of households could ultimately affect women's ability to live with their children in the community, if they are not able to achieve or sustain gainful employment (Lloyd, 1997). The federal TANF program does not continue benefits past a maximum 5-year lifetime limit for most TANF households.

IDENTIFICATION AND CLASSIFICATION

Domestic violence can be defined as a pattern of physical (including sexual) and psychological assaults, threats, and controlling behavior, including financial coercion and economic control by one intimate partner or significant other against another (Family Violence Prevention Fund, 2001b). Victims of domestic violence are predominantly, but not exclusively, women. The Commonwealth Fund (1999) reported that nearly one-third of women in the United States reported being abused by a partner at some point in their lives.

Indicators of Abuse

Victims of domestic violence in the home may not choose to discuss the abuse in the workplace. However, if the abuse is identified and addressed in the workplace, professional counseling may assist a victim in resolving the abusive situation before it escalates further. Signs of possible abuse include:

- *Visible physical injuries:* bruises, cuts, burns, bite marks, fractures (especially around the face);

- *Stress-related illnesses:* chronic headaches and backache, gastrointestinal disorders, sleep disorders, chronic tiredness, anxiety conditions such as panic attacks;
- *Alcohol or other drug addictions:* evidence of efforts to self-medicate anxiety or chronic pain;
- *Depression:* expression of suicidal thoughts or foreboding and/or discussion of suicide attempts;
- *Absenteeism:* chronic absences or lateness;
- *Changes in job performance:* difficulty in concentrating, repeated mistakes, changes in work pace.

(New York State Office for the Prevention of Domestic Violence, 2001a)

Indicators of abuse on the job are also important to identify. Escalation could result in workplace violence. Signs and symptoms may include:

- *Unusual or excessive phone calls:* if calls are from a family member or significant other and elicit a strong emotional reaction;
- *Disruptive personal visits to the workplace:* from employee's spouse or significant other, or a former partner;
- *Threats of a personal nature:* phoned into coworkers or supervisors by unknown callers or someone known to an employee.

The signs and symptoms of abuse identified above may not signal that domestic violence is occurring or is about to occur; however, they suggest that a supervisor or professional at the workplace needs to explore the situation. There are two primary ways of doing so: (a) educate managers, supervisors, coworkers, and employees about domestic violence—how to identify it and what to do about it; and (b) establish procedures that allow victims or coworkers to report the possibility of domestic abuse to supervisors, managers, or professionals on staff who can investigate reports or intervene in a confidential manner.

Educating staff about domestic violence can inform and sensitize individuals about abusers' tactics. Victims and coworkers may not be aware that certain acts or patterns of behavior on the part of partners or significant others are considered domestic violence and could escalate into more dangerous behavior.

Some abusive behaviors include:

- *Emotional and psychological control:* name-calling; becoming extremely jealous or overprotective; humiliating or embarrassing the victim, especially in the presence of others; preventing or terminating friendships or isolating the victim from others, including family members.

- *Economic control:* denying access to bank accounts, credit cards, or means of transportation; controlling all finances and insisting on complete accountability of all money spent; attempting to sabotage work or school; and/or limiting access to health care or health insurance.
- *Threats:* verbally expressing an intention to harm family members and/or pets; displaying weapons; exhibiting loss of temper; threatening to call in false reports to authorities.
- *Acts of violence:* harming family members and/or pets; destroying personal property; forcing unwanted engagement in sexual acts.

When educational programs on domestic violence are designed and implemented in the workplace, they should include assurances that domestic violence can affect anyone; that all information divulged by or about staff is confidential; and that support and assistance will be provided to victimized employees (U.S. Office of Personnel Management, 1999). Protocols and procedures should be developed as part of any educational program in the workplace. If there is an employee assistance program (EAP) staffed by professionals, the EAP can take the lead in designing and implementing this program (Andragna, 1991).

EFFECTIVE PREVENTION PROGRAMS

Workplace programs that address domestic violence can take the form of prevention, protection, and/or intervention. Examples of prevention strategies include: employee education programs (such as brown-bag lunchtime seminars); poster campaigns and other initiatives intended to alert employees to the nature of domestic violence and what can be done to prevent it. Primary prevention often includes consciousness-raising facts and other information designed to prevent interpersonal violence in the home and to avoid its spilling over into the workplace.

Protective strategies may include: security protocols that ensure a safe and well-lit workplace; measures that enable the security department to become aware of orders of protection and initiate surveillance measures; and procedures that instruct managers and supervisors to grant leave time, without penalty, to employees who must go to court to seek safe shelter for themselves and their families.

A number of model protocols and programs have been developed for implementation in the workplace. They include protocols and programs developed by state and federal government agencies, the private sector, and unions (Family Violence Prevention Fund, 2001c; New York State Office for the Prevention of Domestic Violence, 2001b, c).

In 1996, the U.S. Department of Labor issued model guidelines for preventing workplace violence in health care and social service settings through the Occupational Safety and Health Administration (OSHA) (U.S. Department of Labor, 1996b). These guidelines (OSHA 31148-1996) targeted health and social service settings because statistics demonstrated that workers in these settings were at risk of experiencing workplace violence. While not intended specifically to address domestic violence in the workplace, the guidelines recognize that the workforce in these settings is predominately female. As noted, women are more likely then men to be victims of violent crime in the workplace by "intimates."

The U.S. Office of Personnel Management (OPM) published a manual entitled *Responding to Domestic Violence: Where Federal Employees Can Find Help.* This manual provides a format for instructions on internal policies and procedures in federal workplace locations and lists resources within the work location and in the community. Included are instructions on how to: work supportively with victims of domestic violence; identify signs and symptoms of abuse; interview victims; and track references and Web sites (U.S. Office of Personnel Management, 1999).

Local police domestic violence units, in collaboration with city agencies, have developed manuals on domestic violence in the workplace. The Montgomery County Police Domestic Violence Unit, in collaboration with the Baltimore City Commission on Women, in Baltimore, Maryland, developed a policy-and-procedures manual for the workplace: *A Partnership to End Domestic.* The manual is intended to assist businesses in developing their own internal policies, procedures, and training for addressing domestic violence in the workplace (Montgomery County Police Department, 1996).

Polaroid, Liz Claiborne, and Aetna Insurance Company are among the corporate leaders that are promoting policies and programs to address domestic violence in the workplace. At Polaroid, a comprehensive program was developed, including written protocols for management and workers. Polaroid's policy ensures that employees are provided with security and protection in the workplace, not revictimization through dismissal (Hardeman, 1995). Polaroid also stresses education of supervisors, and its CEO supports shelters for victims of domestic violence in the community (Hardeman, 1995).

Liz Claiborne promotes safety for domestic violence victims in the workplace by initiating some high-profile fund-raising events, and making domestic violence a funding priority for its corporate foundation (Ettinger, 1995). Special clothing sales are advertised as fund-raisers for domestic violence prevention and treatment programs, and proceeds are given out as grants to not-for-profit agencies (Ettinger, 1995).

Aetna Insurance Company actively engages in programs that have an impact on the insurance industry, such as health care reform and domestic violence (Moskey, 1995). Aetna assures its workers who are victims of domestic violence that they will not suffer reprisals if they come forward. Aetna has also strengthened security in its offices and has implemented security measures such as providing guards with copies of orders of protection and with pictures of batterers who may seek out their victims in the workplace.

Unions are also proactive in addressing domestic violence in the workplace. The American Federation of State, County and Municipal Employees (AFSCME) promotes the inclusion of domestic violence in the workplace as part of its agenda (Family Violence Prevention Fund, 2001c). In a publication entitled *Domestic Violence: What Unions Can Do,* edited by Norton, Moskey, and Bernstein (2001), instructions for unions include training of union members and stewards/delegates on issues related to domestic violence, including the importance of confidentiality for the victim. It also outlines what should be included in workplace and personal safety plans for members; provides a sample union resolution to address domestic violence in the workplace; and offers a sample of the language on domestic violence that should be negotiated into contracts with employers.

The model contract language identifies domestic violence as a human rights issue. Included are: a demand for workplace training and protocols on domestic violence, as well as policies on leave time, transfers and work schedules, workplace safety, health insurance, and discipline. The discipline policies allow a domestic violence victim to be exempt from discipline for time and leave issues, and ensure a referral to an employee assistance program and a legal assistance program. The policies also support disciplinary action against an employee—including a union member—who engages in domestic violence against another union member in the workplace (Norton et al., 2001).

Some unions, notably District Council 37, the New York City municipal employees' union, offer a model legal and social work program for members. The Municipal Employees Legal Services (MELS) Plan provides comprehensive counseling and legal services to victims of domestic violence who are members of the municipal labor force. Since 1981, MELS has offered legal and social work services to union members experiencing spouse and partner abuse. Related services include safety arrangements, housing relocation, family and job counseling, and emergency childcare arrangements (Norton et al., 2001).

State and local coalitions are active in promoting awareness of the dangers of domestic violence in the workplace (Minnesota Center Against Domestic Violence and Abuse [MCADVA], 2001; *Safe@Work* Coalition, 1999). MCADVA identifies and publicizes local and national government agencies and corporations that have initiated model practices and programs to address domestic violence in the workplace. The *Safe@Work* Coalition, with leadership from the office of the New York City Public Advocate, urges governments and businesses to strengthen domestic violence prevention and intervention efforts in the workplace.

EMPIRICALLY BASED INTERVENTIONS

Intervention strategies and initiatives can include short-term counseling and crisis intervention for affected employees, as well as for coworkers and others who may have experienced trauma when they witnessed systematic threats to or attacks on coworkers by domestic partners. Counseling may be provided in the workplace by social workers and other helping professionals employed by employee assistance programs, or through referrals to clinics or professionals in private practice (Andragna, 1991).

Short-term crisis intervention models, as described by Roberts (1996), can be effective in addressing the impact of employees' experiencing and/or witnessing workplace harassment and violence, and the associated costs in lost productivity and lowered staff morale. The seven-stage crisis intervention model developed by Roberts (Brownell, 1996) can assist domestic violence victims in the workplace through early identification of crisis precipitants, problem solving, and crisis resolution.

The stages of Roberts' crisis intervention model include:

1. Assessing lethality, which is critical to any domestic violence situation;
2. Establishing rapport with the victim;
3. Encouraging the victim to discuss feelings and symptoms;
4. Dealing with the emotions that emerge, in a nonjudgmental and reassuring way;
5. Exploring options with the victim;
6. Developing a plan of action;
7. Implementing the plan (Roberts, 1996).

Both the victim and the employer should be engaged in the victim's ensuring safety through security precautions; approval for time and leave, if necessary to obtain an order of protection and relocate; and, possibly, transfer to a more secure work setting.

CASE MANAGEMENT AND THE
STRENGTHS PERSPECTIVE

In addition to its role in short-term crisis intervention, a case management approach may be considered as an intervention strategy for addressing the impact of domestic violence in the workplace. Crisis intervention, short-term counseling, and advocacy have been the preferred methods of professional work with domestic violence victims (Dziegielewski & Swartz, 1997; Roberts, 1996), but a case management approach may be useful in assisting victims to formulate and implement a complex safety plan. The case management perspective emerged from notions of the importance of informal and formal support systems (Enos & Southern, 1996).

Stages of case management have been defined as advocacy, intake, assessment, classification, referral, intervention, and evaluation. These stages could apply to work with a domestic violence victim or a perpetrator (Enos & Southern, 1996). Case management is often associated with professional work with elderly, developmentally disabled, and ill clients, but it also can be a useful technique when working with victims of domestic violence.

Empowerment of domestic violence victims is an important concept, however. The movement of a victim to the role of a survivor means increasingly taking charge of decision making and responsibility for one's life and believing in one's ability to do so effectively. The role of a case manager in relation to a domestic violence victim is strongly associated with the strengths perspective. It is also relevant to work with domestic violence victims in the workplace. Maintaining employment is often an essential criterion for victims who wish to remain free from an abusive situation.

Advocacy can apply to systems and to legislative changes. The Violence Against Women's Act (VAWA) (1994, 2000) included protections for women in the workplace who are also victims of domestic violence. This important legislation was supported by coalitions of professional advocates and domestic violence survivors. Other important legislative changes have been achieved through advocacy by women concerned about domestic violence in the workplace (New York State Office for the Prevention of Domestic Violence, 2001d). Examples of state and federal laws related to domestic violence in the workplace include:

- *New York State Labor Law, Section 593(1):* This amendment to the labor law ensures that domestic violence victims who voluntarily leave employment because of domestic abuse are eligible for unemployment benefits.

- *New York State Penal Law, Section 215.14:* Chapter 331 of the Laws of 1996 requires employers, if given prior-day notice, to approve time off for victims or witnesses to pursue legal action related to domestic violence, and makes it a crime for employers to penalize employees who choose to exercise this right.

- *New York State Insurance Law 2612:* Chapter 174 of the Laws of 1996 prohibits insurance companies and health maintenance organizations from discriminating against domestic violence victims by defining domestic violence as a preexisting condition.

- *Occupational Safety and Health Laws:* State and federal laws require employers to maintain a safe work environment, and the federal Occupational Safety and Health Act (OSHA) includes a "general duty" clause that requires employers to provide a safe and secure work environment.

- *State and federal laws pertaining to firearms:* Under federal law, it is a crime for anyone to possess a gun while an order of protection is in effect. It should be noted that it is unlawful for anyone convicted of a domestic violence offense to possess firearms. Law enforcement and military personnel are not exempted from this amendment to the Gun Control Act.

FUTURE RESEARCH

More research on the impact of domestic violence on the workplace is needed in all sectors: private, not-for-profit, and public. According to Lloyd (1997), information is lacking on the effects of abuse on female workforce participation. This is especially critical as we move toward the reauthorization of the welfare reform legislation, which faces a sunset in 2002 (Tolman & Raphael, 2000).

Outcome evaluation research is also needed to determine the effectiveness of model programs implemented through government, business, and unions to ensure the safety of domestic violence victims in the workplace. Research is also needed to determine whether—and how many—employers are actually providing programs and services to address domestic violence in the workplace. Short-term crisis intervention models, such as the one developed by Roberts (1996), can be effective in addressing the impact of domestic violence on victims and coworkers, as well as the associated costs to the employer in lost productivity and lowered worker morale. To achieve such benefits, however, an employer must ensure that workers have access to such services.

Research should also determine whether recent legislation intended to protect the rights of domestic violence victims is effective. This review should apply to

the language of the legislation, as well as the extent to which it is being implemented effectively and as intended.

REFERENCES

Andragna, M. (1991, November/December). Wife abuse: An overview for the eap.
EAP Digest, 29–39.

Brownell, P. (1996). Domestic violence in the workplace: An emergent issue. *Crisis Intervention, 3,* 129–141.

Brownell, P. (1998). Women, welfare, work, and domestic violence. In A. R. Roberts
(Ed.), *Battered women and their families: Intervention strategies and treatment
programs* (2nd ed., pp. 291–309). New York: Spring.

Commonwealth Fund. (1999, May). *Health concerns across a woman's lifespan: 1998
survey of women's health.*

Dziegielewski, S. F., & Swartz, M. (1997). Social work's role with the domestic violence: Women and the criminal justice system. In A. R. Roberts (Ed.), *Social work
in juvenile and criminal justice settings* (2nd ed., pp. 421–437). Springfield, IL:
Charles C Thomas.

Enos, R., & Southern, S. (1996). *Correctional case management.* Cincinnati, OH:
Anderson.

Ettinger, R. (1995, October 19). *Domestic violence in the workplace.* Presented at the
conference sponsored by the New York City Human Resources Administration.

Everly, G. S., Lating, J. M., & Mitchell, J. T. (2000). Innovations in group crisis intervention. In A. R. Roberts (Ed.), *Crisis intervention handbook: Assessment, treatment and research* (pp. 77–97). New York: Oxford University Press.

Family Violence Prevention Fund. (2001a). *Policies and programs for your workplace.*
Available from: http://endabuse.org/programs

Family Violence Prevention Fund. (2001b). *Workplace impact: fact sheet.* [Online].
Available from: http://endabuse.org/programs

Family Violence Prevention Fund. (2001c). *Working to end domestic violence: American
workplaces respond to an epidemic.* [Online]. Available from: http://endabuse.org/
programs

Hardeman, J. (1995, October 19). *Domestic violence in the workplace.* Presented at the
conference sponsored by the New York City Human Resources Administration.

Johnson, H. (1996). Domestic violence is a serious problem for professional women.
In A. E. Sadler (Ed.), *Domestic violence* (pp. 123–131). San Diego, CA: Green-
haven Press.

Lloyd, S. (1997). *Domestic violence and women's employment.* Evanston, IL: Institute
for Policy Research, Northwestern University. [Online]. Available from: http://
northwestern.edu/IPR/publications/nupr/nuprv03n1/lloyd.html

Minnesota Center Against Violence and Abuse. (2001). *Interrupting the cycle of violence: Addressing domestic violence through the workplace.* Report produced

by the Ramsey County Initiative for violence-free families and communities. Minneapolis: University of Minnesota School of Social Work. [Online]. Available from: http://www.mincava.umn.edu/reports/interrup.asp

Montgomery County Police Domestic Violence Unit. (1996). A partnership to end domestic violence. In *Domestic violence in the workplace: A policy and procedures manual for the workplace.* Baltimore: Baltimore City Commission for Women.

Moskey, S. (1995, October 19). *Domestic violence in the workplace.* Presented at the conference sponsored by the New York City Human Resources Administration.

National Organization of Women (NOW). (2001). *Fact sheet on domestic violence.* New York: Now Legal and Educational Defense Fund. [Online]. Available from http://nownyc.org/factsheets/fsdomestic2.htm

New York State Office for the Prevention of Domestic Violence. (2001a). *Desk reference for recognizing and responding to domestic violence in the workplace.* Albany, NY. [Online]. Available from: http://opdv.state.ny.us/workplace/deskref.html

New York State Office for the Prevention of Domestic Violence. (2001b). *Employers: model domestic violence policy for counties.* Albany, NY. [Online]. Available from: http://www.opdv.state.ny.us/coordination/model_policy/employer.html

New York State Office for the Prevention of Domestic Violence. (2001c). *Model domestic violence and employee awareness and assistance policy for private businesses.* Albany, NY. [Online]. Available from: http://www.opdv.state.ny.us /workplace/privatepolicy/policy.html

New York State Office for the Prevention of Domestic Violence. (2001d). *State and federal laws related to domestic violence in the workplace.* Albany, NY. [Online]. Available from: http://www.opdv.state.ny.us/workplace/laws.html

Norton, D., Moskey, S. T., & Bernstein, E. (Eds.). (2001). *The workplace responds to domestic violence: A resource guide for employers, unions, and advocates.* Family Violence Prevention Fund. [Online]. Available from: http://www.afscme.org /wrlplace/domvio.htm

O'Regan, M. (1995, October 19). *Domestic Violence in the Workplace.* Presented at the conference sponsored by the New York City Human Resources Administration.

Pereira, J. (1995, March 2). Employers confront domestic violence. *Wall Street Journal,* B1.

Raphael, J. (1995). *Domestic violence: Telling the untold welfare to work story.* Chicago: Taylor Institute.

Roberts, A. R. (1996). Epidemiology and definitions of acute crisis in American society. In A. R. Roberts (Ed.), *Crisis management and brief treatment: Theory, technique and applications* (pp. 16–33). Chicago: Nelson-Hall.

Rymer, R. (1996, January). Murder in the workplace. *Self Magazine,* 108–131.

Safe @ Work Coalition. (1999). Press release. Available from: http://www.safeatwork .org

Silverstein, S. (1994, August 8). Stalked by violence on the job. *Los Angeles Times,* A1.

Soler, E. (1999). *Media briefing paper: Working to end domestic violence: American workplaces repond to an epidemic.* Family violence Prevention Fund. [Online]. Available from: http://fvpf.org/workplace/media.html

Solomon, C. M. (1995, April). Talking frankly about domestic violence. *Personnel Journal,* 62.

Starch, R. (1994). *Worldwide study for Liz Claiborne, Inc.*

Tolman, R. M., & Raphael, J. (2000). A review of research on welfare and domestic violence (Welfare and domestic violence review). *Journal of Social Issues.*

U.S. Department of Labor. (1996a). *Facts on working women: Domestic violence: A workplace issue.* Washington, DC: U.S. Department of Labor, Women's Bureau, No. 96-3.

U.S. Department of Labor. (1996b). *Guidelines for preventing workplace violence for health care and social service workers—OSHA 3148-1996.* Washington, DC: U.S. Department of Labor.

U.S. Office of Personnel Management. (1999). *Responding to domestic violence: Where federal employees can find help.* Washington, DC: U.S. Office of Personnel Management. [Online]. Available from: http://www.opm.gov/ehs\workplac\html\domestic.html

Walsteadt, J. (1995, September 8). Seminar for Executive Women International 48th annual meeting and conference.

Warchol, G. (1998). *Workplace violence, 1992–1996* (National Crime Victimization Survey). Washington, DC: U.S. Department of Justice, Bureau of Justice Statistics.

Author Index

Subject Index

A

Abuse:
  child, 21–22
  economic, 72
  emotional, 72
  indicators, 72, 417–419
  physical, 3, 72, 204–205
  sexual, 72, 204–205
Abuse Behavior Inventory (ABI),
  157–159
Abusive behaviors:
  acts of violence, 419
  economic control, 419
  emotional/psychological control,
    418–419
  threats, 419
Academic performance (school violence),
  339–340
Adolescent(s). *See* Youth/adolescent(s)
Adolescent Anger Control: Cognitive-
  Behavioral Techniques, 182, 183,
  277
Adolescent Antisocial Behavior Checklist
  (AABC), 154
Adolescent Violence Survey (AVS),
  154–155
Adults:
  measures for perpetrators of child
    abuse, 162–164
  measures for victims of abuse,
    160–162

measures for violent behavior in,
  156–164
Advocacy, 423
African American(s), 67–105, 142, 182,
  332–333, 338–341
  academic performance, 339
  accountability, 89
  children/adolescents (school violence),
    332–333
  chronology of problems facing violent
    African American men, 78–80
  circle ritual, 95–96
  communities, policy interventions,
    142
  Dealing with Anger: A Violence
    Prevention Program for African
    American Youth, 182
  deficit perspective, 89
  domestic violence in families, 67–105
  early exposure to violence as risk
    factor, 81–82
  early intervention programs, 338–339
  exposure to abuse, 340–341
  feminist theory, 76
  group approach, African American
    male perpetrators of domestic
    violence, 83–86
  heavy drinking and drug use as risk
    factor, 82
  historical perspective on violence and,
    67–71
  indicators of domestic abuse, 72